Accounting Information Systems

Twelfth Edition

International Student Version

Mark G. Simkin, Ph.D.
Professor
Department of Accounting and Information Systems
University of Nevada

Jacob M. Rose, Ph.D.
Professor
Department of Accounting and Finance
University of New Hampshire

Carolyn Strand Norman, Ph.D., CPA
Professor
Department of Accounting
Virginia Commonwealth University

WILEY

JOHN WILEY & SONS, INC.

In memory of my father, Edward R. Simkin
(Mark G. Simkin)

Chase your big dreams!
(Jacob M. Rose)

Thank you to my students—you're the best!
(Carolyn S. Norman)

ABOUT THE AUTHORS

Mark G. Simkin received his A.B. degree from Brandeis University and his MBA and Ph.D. degrees from the Graduate School of Business at the University of California, Berkeley. Before assuming his present position of professor in the Department of Accounting and Information Systems, University of Nevada, Professor Simkin taught in the Department of Decision Sciences at the University of Hawaii. He has also taught at California State University, Hayward, and the Japan America Institute of Decision Sciences, Honolulu; worked as a research analyst at the Institute of Business and Economic Research at the University of California, Berkeley; programmed computers at IBM's Industrial Development—Finance Headquarters in White Plains, New York; and acted as a computer consultant to business companies in California, Hawaii, and Nevada. Dr. Simkin is the author of more than 100 articles that have been published in such journals as *Decision Sciences, JASA, The Journal of Accountancy, Communications of the ACM, Interfaces, The Review of Business and Economic Research, Decision Sciences Journal of Innovative Education, Information Systems Control Journal,* and the *Journal of Bank Research.*

Jacob M. Rose received his B.B.A degree, M.S. degree in accounting and Ph.D. in accounting from Texas A&M University and he passed the CPA exam in the state of Texas. Dr. Rose holds the position of professor at the University of New Hampshire, where he is the director of the Master of Science in Accounting Program. He previously taught at Southern Illinois University, Montana State University, the University of Tennessee, Bryant University, and the University of Oklahoma, and he was an auditor with Deloitte and Touche, LLP. Professor Rose has been recognized as the top instructor in accounting at multiple universities, and he has developed several accounting systems courses at the graduate and undergraduate levels. He is also a prolific researcher, publishing in journals such as *The Accounting Review; Accounting, Organizations and Society; Behavioral Research in Accounting; Journal of Information Systems; International Journal of Accounting Information Systems; Journal of Management Studies*; and *Accounting Horizons.* Professor Rose has been recognized as the top business researcher at three universities, and he received the Notable Contribution to the Information Systems Literature Award, which is the highest research award given by the Information Systems Section of the American Accounting Association.

Carolyn Strand Norman received her B.S. and M.S.I.A. degrees from Purdue University and her Ph.D. from Texas A&M University. Dr. Norman is a Certified Public Accountant (licensed in Virginia) and also a retired Lieutenant Colonel from the United States Air Force. At the Pentagon, she developed compensation and entitlements legislation, working frequently with House and Senate staffers. Prior to assuming her current position, Dr. Norman taught at Seattle Pacific University where she coauthored the book, *XBRL Essentials* with Charles Hoffman, and was selected as Scholar of the Year for the School of Business and Economics. Dr. Norman has published more than 50 articles in journals such as *The Accounting Review; Accounting, Organizations and Society; Behavioral Research in Accounting; Journal of Accounting and Public Policy; Journal of Information Systems; Advances in Accounting Behavioral Research; Issues in Accounting Education;* and *Journal of Accounting Education.* She is currently the Interim Chair of the Accounting Department at Virginia Commonwealth University.

PREFACE

Information technologies affect every aspect of accounting, and as technologies advance, so does our accounting profession! For example, accountants no longer spend much of their day footing ledgers and making hand calculations. Today, accountants use the many helpful functions in spreadsheet software and update or change calculations instantly. And increasingly, the Internet continues to change the way accountants work.

Because most accounting systems are computerized, accountants must understand software and information systems to turn data into financial information and develop and evaluate internal controls. Business and auditing failures continue to force the profession to emphasize internal controls and to rethink the state of assurance services. As a result, the subject of accounting information systems (AIS) continues to be a vital component of the accounting profession.

The purpose of this book is to help students understand basic AIS concepts. Exactly what comprises these AIS concepts is subject to some interpretation, and is certainly changing over time, but most accounting professionals believe that it is the knowledge that accountants need for understanding and using information technologies and for knowing how an accounting information system gathers and transforms data into useful decision-making information. In this edition of our textbook, we include the core concepts of Accounting Information Systems indicated by chapter in the table below. The book is flexible enough that instructors may choose to cover the chapters in any order.

**ACCOUNTING INFORMATION SYSTEMS
COURSE CONTENT AREA COVERAGE**

AIS Applications	7, 8, 15
Auditing	12
Database Concepts	3, 4, 5
Internal Control	9, 10, 11
Management of Information Systems	1, 2, 13
Management Use of Information	1, 6, 7, 8, 14, 15
Systems Development Work	13
Technology of Information Systems	All chapters
Use of Systems Technology	All chapters

About This Book

The content of AIS courses continues to vary widely from school to school. Some schools use their AIS courses to teach accounting students how to use computers. In other colleges and universities, the course focuses on business processes and data modeling. Yet other courses emphasize transaction processing and accounting as a communication system and have little to do with the technical aspects of how underlying accounting data are processed or stored.

Given the variety of objectives for an AIS course and the different ways that instructors teach it, we developed a textbook that attempts to cover the core concepts of AIS. In writing the text, we assumed that students have completed basic courses in financial and managerial accounting and have a basic knowledge of computer hardware and software concepts. The text is designed for a one-semester course in AIS and may be used at the community college, baccalaureate, or graduate level.

Our hope is that individual instructors will use this book as a foundation for an AIS course, building around it to meet their individual course objectives. Thus, we expect that many instructors will supplement this textbook with other books, cases, software, or readings. The arrangement of the chapters permits *flexibility* in the instructor's subject matter coverage. Certain chapters may be omitted if students have covered specific topics in prior courses.

In the first chapter, we lay the basic foundation for the remainder of the text and set the stage for students to think about the pervasiveness of technology that is common to organizations and the impact technology has on the accounting profession. This chapter also includes a section on careers in AIS that is designed to introduce students to the career paths that combine accounting with the study of information systems. Students taking the AIS course may or may not have had an earlier course in information technology. Chapter 2 allows those who did not have such a course to learn about the latest technologies and emphasizes their use in accounting. For students who have had earlier courses in computers and/or information systems, this chapter serves as a review but might also contain new technologies that students have not studied in other courses.

Chapter 3 begins our coverage by discussing database concepts in general, describing how to design database tables and relationships, and discussing how databases promote efficient storage of the data needed to support business decisions. This chapter also responds to increasing instructor interest in teaching the REA approach to data modeling. Chapter 4 describes how to use the latest version of Microsoft *Access* to create databases and extract data from databases. Chapter 5 continues the discussion of how to use Microsoft *Access* to develop database forms and reports. Chapters 4 and 5 are more "how to" than the other chapters in the book, and they allow the instructor to guide students with hands-on experience in using software to implement the database concepts they have learned.

Chapter 6 describes the various tools that accountants can use to document an AIS for their own and others' understanding of information flows. Business processes and software solutions for improving those processes are gaining in importance in today's businesses. Chapters 7 and 8 discuss several core business processes and highlight a number of Business Process Management (BPM) solutions that are currently available in the marketplace. Instructors who focus on transaction cycles in their AIS courses may choose to use supplemental pedagogical tools, such as software and practice sets, to cover this material in more depth.

Although the subject of internal control appears repeatedly throughout the book, we examine this subject in depth in Chapters 9 and 10. These two chapters introduce students to internal controls that are necessary at each level of the organization. Chapter 11 focuses on computer crime, ethics, and privacy to help students understand the need for internal controls.

Chapter 12 introduces the topic of auditing in an IT environment. Information technology auditing is an increasingly important field and represents a great career opportunity for students who understand both accounting and IT. Recognizing that some students in AIS courses may have completed courses in management information systems (MIS) and thus are already familiar with systems development topics, the emphasis in Chapter 13 is on the accountant's role in designing, developing, implementing, and maintaining a system. Although we integrated Internet technology throughout this book, its influence on accounting information systems is so great that we devoted a special chapter to it. Chapter 14 provides a basic overview of Internet concepts, discusses financial reporting on the Internet including an expanded section on XBRL, explores the accounting components of e-business, and covers the issues of privacy and security. Finally, in Chapter 15, we discuss accounting and enterprise software, and the chapter provides advice related to AIS selection.

Special Features

This edition of our book uses a large number of special features to enhance the coverage of chapter material as well as to help students understand chapter concepts. This edition includes many new real-world Cases-in-Point, which are woven into the text material and illustrate a particular concept or procedure. Each chapter also includes a more detailed real-world case as an end-of-chapter *AIS-at-Work* feature.

Each chapter ends with a summary and a list of key terms. To help students understand the material in each chapter, this edition includes three types of end-of-chapter exercises: discussion questions, problems, and cases. This wide variety of review material enables students to examine many different aspects of each chapter's subject matter and also enables instructors to vary the exercises they use each semester.

There are two major supplements to this textbook. One is an instructor's manual containing suggested answers to the end-of-chapter discussion questions, problems, and cases. There is also a test bank of true-false, multiple-choice, and matching-type questions. The test bank includes short-answer problems and fill-in-the-blank questions so that instructors have a wide variety of choices.

What's New in the Twelfth Edition

This edition of our book includes a number of changes from prior editions. These include

- A new coauthor with an international reputation in the AIS community!

- All new database chapters. Material related to the design of databases and database theory is all presented in the first database chapter, rather than spread throughout three chapters. The following two chapters describe how to apply the theoretical concepts using Access 2010. The new approach allows instructors to easily select a desired emphasis: theory, application, or both. New database diagramming methods simplify the design process for students.

- Expanded coverage of topics that are increasingly important to accounting systems, including cloud computing, data mining, sustainability accounting, forensic accounting COBIT version 5, COSO's 2010 Report on Enterprise Risk Management, enterprise controls, and internal auditing of IT.

- The discussion of internal controls in Chapter 10 and auditing of IT in Chapter 12 are reorganized to reflect new PCAOB standards.

- An expanded section in Chapter 1 on career paths for accountants interested in forensic accounting.

- Many new *Case-in-Points* that identify examples of the discussion in the textbook. These examples illustrate the topic to give students a better grasp of the material.

- Chapter reorganization, with database chapters moved closer to the front, as requested by our adopters. Instructors still have the flexibility to integrate the database concepts and database development anywhere in their course.
- An updated glossary of AIS terms at the end of the book.
- New *AIS at Work* features at the end of many chapters to help students better understand the impact of systems in a wide variety of contexts.
- A number of new problems and cases at the end of chapters so that instructors have more choices of comprehensive assignments for students.

ACKNOWLEDGMENTS

We wish to thank the many people who helped us during the writing, editing, and production of our textbook. Our families and friends are first on our list of acknowledgments. We are grateful to them for their patience and understanding as we were writing this book. Next, we thank those instructors who read earlier drafts of this edition of our textbook and provided suggestions to improve the final version.

In addition, we are indebted to the many adopters of our book who frequently provide us with feedback. We sincerely appreciate Paula Funkhouser who helped us with our supplementary materials on this and several previous editions. Finally, we thank all of our many students who have given us feedback when we've used the book. We do listen!

Mark G. Simkin
Jacob M. Rose
Carolyn S. Norman

CONTENTS

Chapter 1

Accounting Information Systems and the Accountant

INTRODUCTION

The study of **accounting information systems (AISs)** is, in large part, the study of the application of **information technology (IT)** to accounting systems. This chapter describes the ways that IT affects financial accounting, managerial accounting, auditing, and taxation. We begin by answering the question "what are accounting information systems" and then look at some new developments in the field. Following this, we will examine some traditional roles of AISs in organizations.

Why should you study AISs? There are many reasons, which we will review briefly in this chapter, but one of the most important is the special career opportunities that will enable you to combine your study of accounting subjects with your interest in computer systems. In today's job market, accounting employers expect new hires to be computer literate. In addition, a large number of specialized and highly compensated employment opportunities are only available to those students who possess an integrated understanding of accounting and IT and can bring that understanding to bear on complicated business decisions. The last part of this chapter describes a number of special career opportunities for those with an interest in AISs.

WHAT ARE ACCOUNTING INFORMATION SYSTEMS?

What do the following have in common: (1) a shoebox filled with a lawyer's expense receipts, (2) the monthly payroll spreadsheet in the computer of an auto-repair shop, (3) the *Peachtree* accounting system for a small chain of dry-cleaning stores, and (4) the enterprise resource planning (ERP) system of a large manufacturer? The answer is that they are all examples of AISs. How can such a wide range of accounting applications each qualify as an AIS? The answer is that this is the essence of what AISs are—collections of raw and stored data (that together typically serve as inputs), processing methods (usually called "procedures"), and information (outputs) that serve useful accounting purposes. Do such systems have to be computerized? The first example—the shoebox—suggests that they do not. Can they be complicated? The last example—an ERP system—illustrates one that is.

Accounting Information Systems—A Definition

Accounting information systems (AISs) stand at the crossroads of two disciplines: accounting and information systems. Thus, the study of AISs is often viewed as the study of computerized accounting systems. But because we cannot define an AIS by its size, it is better to define it by what it *does*. This latter approach leads us to the following definition that we will use as a model in this book:

*Definition: An **accounting information system** is a collection of data and processing procedures that creates needed information for its users.*

Let us examine in greater detail what this definition really means. For our discussion, we'll examine each of the words in the term "accounting information systems" separately.

Accounting. You probably have a pretty good understanding of accounting subjects because you have already taken one or more courses in the area. Thus, you know that the accounting field includes financial accounting, managerial accounting, and taxation. AISs are used in all these areas—for example, to perform tasks in such areas as payroll, accounts receivable, accounts payable, inventory, and budgeting. In addition, AISs help accountants to maintain general ledger information, create spreadsheets for strategic planning, and distribute financial reports. Indeed, it is difficult to think of an accounting task that is not integrated, in some way, with an AIS.

The challenge for accountants is to determine how best to provide the information required to support business and government processes. For example, in making a decision to buy office equipment, an office manager may require information about the sources of such equipment, the costs of alternate choices, and the purchasing terms for each choice. Where can the manager obtain this information? That's the job of the AIS.

AISs don't just support accounting and finance business processes. They often create information that is useful to nonaccountants—for example, individuals working in marketing, production, or human relations. Figure 1-1 provides some examples. For this information to be effective, the individuals working in these subsystems must help the developers of an AIS identify what information they need for their planning, decision making, and control functions. These examples illustrate why an AIS course is useful not only for accounting majors but also for many nonaccounting majors.

Information (versus Data). Although the terms **data** and **information** are often used interchangeably, it is useful to distinguish between them. *Data* (the plural of *datum*) are raw facts about events that have little organization or meaning—for example, a set of raw scores on a class examination. To be useful or meaningful, most data must be processed into useful *information*—for example, by sorting, manipulating, aggregating, or classifying them. An example might be computing of the class average from the raw scores of a class examination.

Application	Examples of AIS Information
Supply chain management	Demand trends, inventory levels and warehouse management, supplier relationship management.
Finance	Cash and asset management, multicompany and multicurrency management, credit card transaction summaries.
Marketing	Sales management, sales forecasts and summaries, customer relationship management.
Human resources	Workforce planning tools and employee management, benefits management, payroll summaries and management.
Production	Inventory summaries, product cost analysis, materials requirement planning.

FIGURE 1-1 Examples of useful information an AIS can generate for various business functions.

Do raw data *have* to be processed in order to be meaningful? The answer is "not at all." Imagine, for example, that *you* take a test in a class. Which is more important to you—the average score for the class as a whole (a processed value) or *your* score (a raw data value)? Similarly, suppose you own shares of stock in a particular company. Which of these values would be *least* important to you: (1) the *average* price of a stock that was traded during a given day (a processed value), (2) the price *you* paid for the shares of stock (an unprocessed value), or (3) the *last* price trade of the day (another unprocessed value)?

Raw data are also important because they mark the starting point of an **audit trail**—that is, the path that data follow as they flow through an AIS. In a payroll system, for example, an input clerk enters the data for a new employee and the AIS keeps track of the wages due that person each pay period. An auditor can verify the existence of employees and whether each employee received the correct amount of money.

Case-in-Point 1.1 A former payroll manager at the Brooklyn Museum pleaded guilty to embezzling $620,000 by writing paychecks to "ghost employees." Dwight Newton, 40, admitted committing wire fraud by adding workers to the payroll who did not exist and then wiring their wages directly into a joint bank account that he shared with his wife. Under a plea agreement, Newton must repay the museum the stolen funds. He was ordered to forfeit $77,000 immediately, sell his Barbados timeshare, and liquidate his pension with the museum.[1]

Despite the potential usefulness of some unprocessed data, most end users need financial totals, summary statistics, or exception values—that is, processed data—for decision-making purposes. Figure 1-2 illustrates a model for this—a three-stage process in which (1) raw and/or stored data serve as the primary inputs, (2) processing tasks process the data, and (3) meaningful information is the primary output. Modern AISs, of course, harness IT to perform the necessary tasks in each step of the process. For example, a catalog retailer might use some Web pages on the Internet to gather customer purchase data, then use central file servers and disk storage to process and store the purchase transactions, and finally employ other Web pages and printed outputs to confirm and distribute information *about* the order to the appropriate parties.

Although computers are wonderfully efficient and useful tools, they also create problems. One is their ability to output vast amounts of information quickly. Too much information, and especially too much trivial information, can overwhelm its users, possibly causing relevant information to be lost or overlooked. This situation is known as **information overload**. It is up to the accounting profession to determine the nature and timing of the outputs created and distributed by an AIS to its end users.

Another problem with computerized data processing is that computers do not *automatically* catch the simple input errors that humans do. For example, if *you* were performing payroll processing, you would probably know that a value of "−40" hours

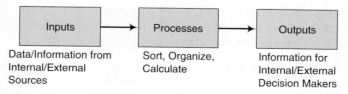

FIGURE 1-2 An information system's components. Data or information is input, processed, and output as information for planning, decision-making, and control purposes.

---

[1] http://www.payroll-fraud.com/rc009.html

for the number of hours worked was probably a mistake—the value should be ''40.'' A computer can be programmed to look for (and reject) bad input, but it is difficult to anticipate all possible problems.

Yet a third problem created by computers is that they make audit trails more difficult to follow. This is because the path that data follow through computerized systems is electronic, not recorded on paper. However, a well-designed AIS can still document its audit trail with listings of transactions and account balances both before and after the transactions update the accounts. A major focus of this book is on developing effective internal control systems for companies, of which audit trails are important elements. Chapters 9, 10, and 12 discuss these topics in detail.

In addition to collecting and distributing large amounts of data and information, modern AISs must also organize and store data for future uses. In a payroll application, for example, the system must maintain running totals for the earnings, tax withholdings, and retirement contributions of each employee in order to prepare end-of-year tax forms. These data organization and storage tasks are major challenges, and one of the reasons why this book contains three chapters on the subject (see Chapters 3, 4, and 5).

Besides deciding *what* data to store, businesses must also determine the best way to *integrate* the stored data for end users. An older approach to this problem was to maintain independently the data for each of its traditional organization functions—for example, finance, marketing, human resources, and production. A problem with this approach is that, even if all the applications are maintained internally by the same IT department, there will be separate data-gathering and reporting responsibilities within each subsystem, and each application may store its data independently of the others. This often leads to a duplication of data-collecting and processing efforts, as well as conflicting data values when specific information (e.g., a customer's address) is changed in one application but not another.

Organizations today recognize the need to integrate the data associated with their functions into large, seamless data warehouses. This integration allows internal managers and possibly external parties to obtain the information needed for planning, decision making, and control, whether or not that information is for marketing, accounting, or some other functional area in the organization. To accomplish this task, many companies are now using large (and expensive) **enterprise resource planning (ERP) system** software packages to integrate their information subsystems into one application. An example of such a software product is *SAP ERP*, which combines accounting, manufacturing, and human resource subsystems into an enterprise-wide information system—that is, a system that focuses on the *business processes* of the organization as a whole. We discuss these systems in more depth in Chapter 15.

SAP, SAS Institute, IBM, and Oracle have recognized the need for integrated information and therefore developed business intelligence software to meet this need. The latest innovation is **predictive analytics**, which these software developers are adding into their main software suites. Predictive analytics includes a variety of methodologies that managers might use to analyze current and past data to help predict future events. In March 2010, IBM opened a predictive analytics lab in China, which is the latest in an estimated $12 billion commitment to build out IBM's analytics portfolio.[2]

Case-in-Point 1.2   Accountants and other managers are using predictive analytics, a technique that takes advantage of data stored in data warehouses, to create systems that allow them to use their data to improve performance. FedEx uses these tools to determine how customers will react to proposed price changes or changes in service. The police force in

---

[2] http://itmanagement.earthweb.com/features/article.php/3872536/Business-Intelligence-Software-and-Predictive-Analytics.html

Richmond, Virginia, uses predictive analysis tools and a database of police calls and crime incident data to predict where and when crimes are most likely. Their system even includes information about weather and local events.[3]

Systems. Within the accounting profession, the term "systems" usually refers to "computer systems." As you probably know, IT advances are changing the way we do just about everything. Just a few years ago, the authors never imagined that people could someday purchase a book from a "virtual bookstore" on the Internet using a wireless laptop, while sipping on a latte in a Starbucks. The explosion in electronic connectivity and commerce is just one of the many ways that IT influences how people now access information or how firms conduct business. Today, IT is a vital part of what accountants must know to be employable.

Returning to our definition, you probably noticed that we did *not* use the term "computer," although we did use the term "processing procedures." You already know the reason for this—not all AISs are computerized, or even need to be. But most of the ones in businesses today are automated ones and thus the term "processing procedures" could be replaced by the term "computerized processing" for most modern AISs.

In summary, it is convenient to conceptualize an AIS as a set of components that collect accounting data, store it for future uses, and process it for end users. This abstract model of data inputs, storage, processing, and outputs applies to almost all the traditional accounting cycles with which you are familiar—for example, the payroll, revenue, and expenditure cycles—and is thus a useful way of conceptualizing an AIS. Again, we stress that many of the "end users" of the information of an AIS are not accountants, but include customers, investors, suppliers, financial analysts, and government agencies.

Accounting Information Systems and Their Role in Organizations

Information technology (IT) refers to the hardware, software, and related system components that organizations use to create computerized information systems. IT has been a major force in our current society and now influences our lives in many personal ways—for example, when we use digital cameras to take pictures, access the Internet to make a purchase or learn about something, or e-mail friends and family. It is perhaps less clear that computer technology has also had profound influences on commerce. In this **information age**, for example, fewer workers actually make products while more of them produce, analyze, manipulate, and distribute information *about* business activities. These individuals are often called **knowledge workers**. Companies find that their success or failure often depends upon the uses or misuses of the information that knowledge workers manage.

Case-in-Point 1.3 According to a 2010 report from InfoTrends, mobile knowledge workers make up more than 60 percent of the total workforce in Brazil, Germany, India, and Japan. This number is even higher in the United States—over 70 percent of the total workforce. Current projections suggest that these numbers are expected to grow through 2014.[4]

The information age has important implications for accounting because that is what accountants are—knowledge workers. In fact, accountants have always been in the "information business" because their role has been, in part, to communicate accurate and relevant financial information to parties interested in how their organizations are performing. The information age also includes the increasing importance and growth of **e-business**,

[3] Whiting, R. 2006. Predict the future—or try, anyway. *Information Week* (May): 38–43.
[4] http://www.infotrends.com/public/Content/Press/2011/01.20.2011a.html

conducting business over the Internet or dedicated proprietary networks and **e-commerce** (a subset of e-business), which refers mostly to buying and selling on the Internet.

In many ways, accounting is itself an information system—that is, a communicative process that collects, stores, processes, and distributes information to those who need it. For instance, corporate accountants develop financial statements for external parties and create other reports (such as *accounts receivable aging analyses*) for internal managers. But users of accounting information sometimes criticize AISs for only capturing and reporting *financial* transactions. They claim that financial statements often ignore some of the most important activities that influence business entities. For example, the financial reports of a professional basketball team would not include information about hiring a new star because this would not result in journal entries in the franchise's double-entry accounting system.

Today, however, AISs are concerned with nonfinancial as well as financial data and information. Thus, our definition of an AIS as an enterprise-wide system views accounting as an organization's primary producer and distributor of many different types of information. The definition also considers the AIS as *process focused.* This matches the contemporary perspective that accounting systems are not only financial systems.

WHAT'S NEW IN ACCOUNTING INFORMATION SYSTEMS?

The last few years have witnessed some of the most startling changes in the uses and applications of AISs, causing us to reassess our understanding and use of accounting data. Below are a few examples.

Cloud Computing—Impact for Accountants

In Chapter 2 we identify the basics of cloud computing, but in this section we want to discuss why this technology is important to accountants and then describe some of the current issues surrounding cloud computing as it relates to accounting professionals. According to Ron Gill, **cloud computing** is a way of using business applications over the Internet—such as the way you use the Internet for your bank transactions. Think of cloud computing as a way to increase IT capacity or add capabilities without investing in new infrastructure, training new people, or licensing new software. Mostly, we're talking about a subscription-based or pay-per-use service that makes IT's existing capabilities scalable whenever the need exists. Estimates suggest that the fast-growing cloud computing industry will reach $42 billion by 2012.[5]

Cloud computing resources may be categorized as data storage, infrastructure and platform, or application software (i.e., business applications such as purchases, HR, sales, etc.). If a firm would like to take advantage of cloud computing, it would most likely need to subscribe to all three of these categories from the service provider. For example, business applications depend on company data that is stored in the database, and data storage depends on the appropriate infrastructure.[6]

Experts identify a number of important benefits of using the cloud, as depicted in Figure 1-3. One is the ability to only pay for the applications that you use. Of course,

---

[5] Rashty, J. and J. O'Shaughnessy. 2010. Revenue recognition for cloud-based computing arrangements. *The CPA Journal* 80(11): 32–35.

[6] Du, H. and Y. Cong. 2010. Cloud computing, accounting, auditing, and beyond. *The CPA Journal* 80(10): 66–70.

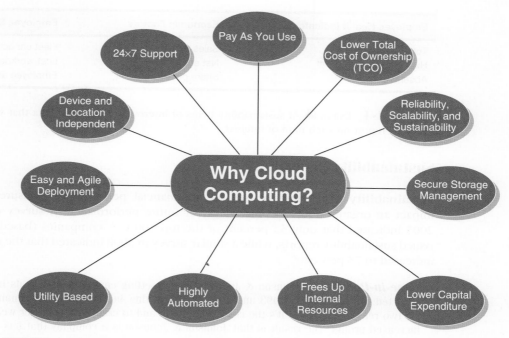

FIGURE 1-3 Examples of the reasons cloud computing is becoming popular. Source: N-Axis Software Technologies.

this sort of flexibility also suggests that a firm has the ability to quickly modify the scale of its IT capability. Another benefit is that an organization may not have to purchase or operate expensive hardware and software—providers own and operate the equipment and software, much as a taxi company owns and operates its own fleet of vehicles. Also, cloud computing providers offer only one (current) version of an application, so individual firms no longer have to deal with expensive, time-consuming upgrades for software.

Case-in-Point 1.4 For years, millions of people who attended the 10-day Taste of Chicago Festival carried around a 28-page brochure to find the various foods and music offerings. In 2009, the city posted this information online—a cloud technology from Microsoft that now delivers the same information right to the festival-goers' smartphones.[7]

Accountants always talk about cost-benefit trade-offs. We just identified several possible benefits surrounding this new technology, so it is appropriate to mention that there are also costs and/or concerns. The first potential concern is reliability of the Internet since this is the medium for delivering all cloud services. Other issues include (1) data security measures that the provider offers, such as appropriate internal controls, (2) the quality of service that the provider gives the firm (i.e., careful crafting of the service contract is similar to that of any outsourcing contract, which includes vigilant monitoring of services for quality purposes), and (3) the reliability of the service provider, such as ongoing concern issues. Accordingly, management accountants, internal auditors, and external auditors will need to evaluate the different risks that a firm may face if it decides to "use the cloud."

---

[7] Barkin, R. 2011. The cloud comes down to earth. Retrieved from http://americancityandcounty.com/technology/cloud-computing-201101/

Employee Health Indicators	Economic Factors	Employee Safety Factors
Tobacco use	Sales revenue	Fleet car accidents
High cholesterol	Net earnings	Lost workdays
Absenteeism	Share price	Employee accidents

FIGURE 1-4 Examples of sustainability items of interest to a firm and data that would be collected to report on each item of interest.

Sustainability Reporting

Sustainability reporting focuses on nonfinancial performance measures that might impact an organization's income, value, or future performance. A survey conducted in 2005 indicated that only 32 percent of the top 100 U.S. companies (based on revenue) issued sustainability reports, while a similar survey in 2008 indicated that the reporting rate increased to 73 percent.[8]

> *Case-in-Point 1.5* Johnson & Johnson began setting environmental goals in 1990, and reported to the public in 1993 and 1996. In 1998, they began annual sustainability reports for two reasons: because it's the right thing to do and to create shareholder wealth through increased profits. The result is that Johnson & Johnson is a company that has experienced continued and sustained growth.[9]

You might be asking yourself why this is an AIS issue if the information is "nonfinancial" in nature. As you will discover in Chapter 15, enterprise-wide systems are widely used to collect qualitative as well as quantitative information for decision making within organizations. In fact, management control systems are the backbone of sustainability reports. That is, organizations need to establish well-defined sustainability strategies that identify achievable and measurable goals.[10] Figure 1-4 identifies examples of sustainability items of interest to firms and some of the data that would be collected to report on each item of interest.

Suspicious Activity Reporting

A number of **suspicious activity reporting (SAR)** laws now require accountants to report questionable financial transactions to the U.S. Treasury Department. Examples of such transactions are ones suggestive of money laundering, bribes, or wire transfers to terrorist organizations. Federal statutes that mandate SARs include sections of the Annunzio-Wylie Anti-Money Laundering Act (1992), amendments to the Bank Secrecy Act of 1996, and several sections of the USA PATRIOT Act (2001). Institutions affected by these laws include (1) banks, (2) money service businesses such as currency traders, (3) broker dealers, (4) casinos and card clubs, (5) commodity traders, (6) insurance companies, and (7) mutual funds. Over the years, such filings have enabled the federal government to investigate a wide number of criminal activities, gather evidence, and in some cases, repatriate funds

---

[8] Borkowski, S., M. Welsh, and K. Wentzel. 2010. Johnson & Johnson: A model for sustainability reporting. *Strategic Finance* 92(3): 29–37.

[9] Borkowski, S., M. Welsh, and K. Wentzel. 2010. Johnson & Johnson: A model for sustainability reporting. *Strategic Finance* 92(3): 29–37.

[10] Busco, C., M. Frigo, E. Leone, and A. Riccaboni. 2010. Cleaning up. *Strategic Finance* 92(1): 29–37.

sent overseas. Testimony to the importance of suspicious activity reporting is the growth of SAR filings—from about 62,000 reports in 1996 to over 1.6 million reports in 2008.

Case-in-Point 1.6 A cooperating witness indicated that a pharmaceutical network was selling controlled drugs through affiliated Web sites to customers without authorized prescriptions. To evade U.S. laws, the owners located their headquarters in Central America and their Web servers in the Middle East. A federal investigation and a SAR filed by a financial institution involved in the matter documented almost $5 million in suspicious wire transfers. The result was indictments against 18 individuals and the repatriation of over $9 million from overseas accounts as part of the forfeiture proceedings.[11]

Suspicious activity reporting impacts AISs in several ways. Because so much of the information within AISs is financial, these systems are often used to launder money or fund criminal activities. A corollary to this fact is that AISs document financial activities in the course of daily transaction processing, and therefore become important sources of SAR evidence and subsequent legal action. Finally, SAR can act as a deterrent to criminal or terrorist activities—and therefore an important control for AISs.

Figure 1-5 contains a classification of SAR reports for 10 years of filings from banks and other depository institutions—one of the most important sources of these filings. In this figure, note the importance of money laundering and check fraud.

Rank	Suspicious Activity Type	Filings (Overall)	Percentage (Overall)%
1	BSA/Structuring/Money Laundering	1,503,003	48.28
2	Check Fraud	333,862	10.72
3	Other	270,152	8.68
4	Counterfeit Check	155,141	4.98
5	Credit Card Fraud	154,506	4.96
6	Mortgage Loan Fraud	113,071	3.63
7	Check Kiting	101,107	3.25
8	Identity Theft	69,325	2.23
9	False Statement	67,902	2.18
10	Defalcation/Embezzlement	63,392	2.04
11	Unknown/Blank	63,069	2.03
12	Consumer Loan Fraud	53,588	1.72
13	Misuse of Position or Self Dealing	30,899	0.99
14	Wire Transfer Fraud	29,574	0.95
15	Mysterious Disappearance	26,465	0.85
16	Debit Card Fraud	17,480	0.56
17	Commercial Loan Fraud	16,524	0.53
18	Counterfeit Instrument (Other)	13,542	0.43
19	Computer Intrusions	12,307	0.40
20	Counterfeit Credit/Debit Card	12,177	0.39
21	Terrorist Financing	3,178	0.10
22	Bribery/Gratuity	2,932	0.09
	Total:	3,113,196	100.00

FIGURE 1-5 A classification of suspicious activity report filings using Form TD F 90-22.47 from depository institutions, April 1, 1996 to December 31, 2006. Source: Web site of the U.S. Treasury Department (2008).

---

[11] http://www.fincen.gov/law_enforcement/ss/html/Issue14-story5.html

Forensic Accounting, Governmental Accountants, and Terrorism

Forensic accounting has become a popular course at many universities over the past decade and some universities now have a number of specialized courses that are included in a fraud examination track or a forensic accounting track so that students may specialize in this area of accounting.[12] In general, a forensic accountant combines the skills of investigation, accounting, and auditing to find and collect pieces of information that collectively provide evidence that criminal activity is in progress or has happened. British Prime Minister Gordon Brown claims that financial information and forensic accounting has become one of the most powerful investigative and intelligence tools available in the fight against crime and terrorism.[13]

Terrorists need money to carry out their criminal activity, and as a result, forensic accountants have become increasingly important in the fight against such activities because forensic accountants use technology for data mining. For example, a program that is well known to auditors is Audit Command Language (ACL), which is a popular data extraction software tool that can be used to spot anomalies and trends in data.

One example of the use of AISs for this purpose is banking systems that trace the flow of funds across international borders. Other examples include (1) identifying and denying financial aid to terrorist groups and their sympathizers; (2) tracing arms and chemical orders to their final destinations, thereby identifying the ultimate—perhaps unauthorized—purchasers; (3) using spreadsheets to help plan for catastrophic events; (4) using security measures to control cyber terrorism; and (5) installing new internal controls to help detect money laundering and illegal fund transfers.

But where do terrorists get the money to finance their activities? Generally speaking, they rely on the following sources for funding: state sponsors, individual contributions, corporate contributions, not-for-profit organizations, government programs, and illegal sources—and here is where government accountants can play an important part in the fight against terrorism. Apparently, terrorists choose to live unpretentiously, they exploit weaknesses in government assistance programs, and are skillful at concealing their activities.[14] Similar to forensic accountants, governmental accountants can use data-extraction software to spot anomalies, suspicious activity, or red flags that might suggest illegal transactions.

Corporate Scandals and Accounting

Although corporate frauds and scandals are hardly new, the latest set of them has set records for their magnitude and scope. Of particular note are the Enron scandal and the case against Bernard Madoff. The Enron scandal is important because of the amount of money and jobs that were lost and also because so much of it appears to be directly related to the adroit manipulation of accounting records. Although the details of these manipulations are complex, the results were to understate the liabilities of the company as well as to inflate its earnings and net worth. The opinion of most experts today is that the mechanics of these adjustments might not have been illegal, but the intent to defraud was clear and therefore criminal.

---

[12] Examples include Georgia Southern University, West Virginia University, and North Carolina State University.
[13] Nelson, D. 2011. The role of forensic accounting in terrorism. Retrieved from http://www.ehow.com/pring/facts_5895389_role-forensic-accounting-terrorism.html
[14] Brooks, R., R. Riley, and J. Thomas. 2005. Detecting and preventing the financing of terrorist activities. *The Journal of Government Financial Management* 54(1): 12–18.

Accounting rules allow for some flexibility in financial reporting. Unfortunately, some financial officers have exploited this flexibility to enhance earnings reports or present rosier forecasts than reality might dictate—that is, they "cooked the books." Examples are Scott Sullivan, former Chief Financial Officer at WorldCom, Inc., Mark H. Swartz, former Chief Financial Officer at Tyco International, Inc., and Andrew Fastow, former Chief Financial Officer at Enron. While some accountants have been guilty of criminal and unethical behavior, others have emerged from the scandals as heroes. These include Sherron Watkins, who tried to tell Ken Lay that the numbers at Enron just didn't add up, and Cynthia Cooper, an internal auditor at WorldCom, who blew the whistle on the falsified accounting transactions ordered by her boss, Scott Sullivan.

As the credit crunch worked its way through the economy in 2008, a number of financial institutions either collapsed or narrowly avoided doing so and accounting was in the news once again. In March 2009, Bernard Madoff pleaded guilty to 11 federal felonies and admitted that he turned his wealth management business into a **Ponzi scheme** that defrauded investors of billions of dollars. Named for Charles Ponzi, this is a pyramid fraud in which new investment funds are used to pay returns to current investors. The fraud relies on new money continuously entering the system so that investors believe their money is actually earning returns. The problem is that when new money stops flowing, the pyramid collapses.

ACCOUNTING AND IT

IT is pervasive and impacts every area of accounting. Instantaneous access is available to the Internet via mobile communication devices such as cell phones, iPads, smart phones, and so on, which enable activities to take place anytime and anywhere. For example, managerial accountants can complete important work tasks while traveling in the field, auditors can communicate with each other from remote job sites (auditing the same client), staff accountants can text message one another from alternate locations, and tax experts can download current information on tax rulings.

Figure 1-6 provides an overview of the major areas within the field of accounting that are impacted by IT. This section of the chapter considers the influence of IT on each of them.

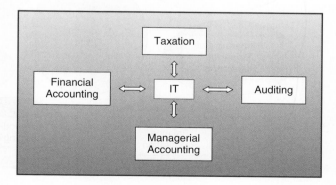

FIGURE 1-6   Overview of the major areas of accounting that are impacted by information technology.

Financial Accounting

The major objective of **financial accounting information systems** is to provide relevant information to individuals and groups *outside* an organization's boundaries—for example, investors, federal and state tax agencies, and creditors. Accountants achieve these informational objectives by preparing such financial statements as income statements, balance sheets, and cash flow statements. Of course, many managers *within* a company can also use financial reports for planning, decision making, and control activities. For example, a manager in charge of a particular division could use such profitability information to make decisions about future investments or to control expenses.

Figure 1-7 depicts an organization's financial accounting cycle, which begins with analyzing and journalizing transactions (e.g., captured at the point of sale) and ends with its periodic financial statements. Accounting clerks, store cashiers, or even the customers themselves input relevant data into the system, which stores these data for later use. In financial AISs, the processing function also includes posting these entries to general and subsidiary ledger accounts and preparing a trial balance from the general ledger account balances.

Nonfinancial Data.   The basic inputs to, and outputs from, traditional financial accounting systems are usually expressed in monetary units. This can be a problem if the AIS ignores nonmonetary information that is also important to users. For example, an investor might like to know what the prospects are for the future sales of a company, but many financial AISs do not record such information as unfulfilled customer sales because such sales are not recognizable financial events—even though they are important ones. This is the basic premise behind **REA accounting**—the idea of also storing important nonfinancial information about *resources, events*, and *agents* in databases precisely because they are

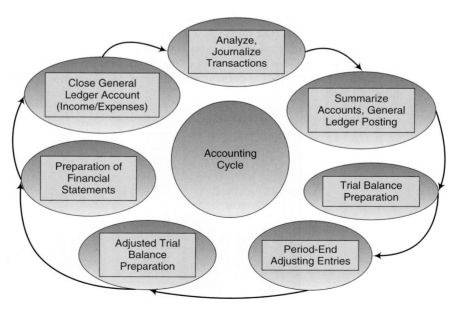

FIGURE 1-7   The accounting cycle. Source: http://bookkeeping-financial-accounting-resources .com/images/accountingcycle.jpg.

relevant to the decision-making processes of their users. We discuss the REA framework in greater detail in Chapter 6.

Inadequacies in financial performance measures have encouraged companies to consider nonfinancial measures when evaluating performance. Some of the advantages include: (1) a closer link to long-term organizational strategies; (2) drivers of success in many industries that are intangible assets (such as intellectual capital and customer loyalty), rather than the assets allowed on balance sheets; (3) such measures that can be better indicators of future financial performance; and (4) investments in customer satisfaction that can improve subsequent economic performance by increasing revenues and loyalty of existing customers, attracting new customers, and reducing transaction costs.[15]

Several professional associations now formally recognize that nonfinancial performance measures enhance the value of purely financial information. For example, in 1994, a special committee of the American Institute of Certified Public Accountants (AICPA) recommended several ways that businesses could improve the information they were providing to external parties by including management analysis data, forward-looking information such as opportunities and risks, information about management and shareholders, and background information about the reporting entity. Similarly, in 2002, the American Accounting Association (AAA) Financial Accounting Standards Committee recommended that the Securities and Exchange Commission (SEC) and the Financial Accounting Standards Board (FASB) encourage companies to voluntarily disclose more nonfinancial performance measures.

Real-Time Reporting. Another impact of IT on financial accounting concerns the timing of inputs, processing, and outputs. Financial statements are periodic and most large companies traditionally issue them quarterly, with a comprehensive report produced annually. With advances in IT that allow transactions to be captured immediately, accountants and even the AIS itself can produce financial statements almost in real time. Of course, some of the adjustments that accountants must make to the records are not done minute by minute, but a business can certainly track sales and many of its expenses continuously. This is especially useful to the retailing executives, many of whom now use dashboards. We discuss dashboards in more depth in Chapter 15 and also show an example of a sales dashboard (Figure 15-8).

Interactive Data and Extensible Business Reporting Language. A problem that accountants, investors, auditors, and other financial managers have often faced is that data used in one application are not easily transferable to another. This means that accountants may spend hours preparing spreadsheets and reports that require them to enter the same data in different formats over and over. **Interactive data** are data that can be reused and carried seamlessly among a variety of applications or reports. Consider, for example, a data item such as total assets. This number might need to be formatted and even calculated several different ways for reports such as filings with the SEC, banks, performance reports, and so on. With interactive data, the data are captured once and applied wherever needed.

Interactive data require a language for standardization that "tags" the data at its most basic level. As an example, for total assets, this would be at the detail level for each asset. **Extensible business reporting language (XBRL)** is emerging as the language of choice for this purpose. As of 2010, the SEC requires public companies to file their financial

---

[15] http://nikhils-nick18.blogspot.com/2010/06/non-financial-performance-measures-what.html

reports in XBRL format. In addition, many companies, software programs, and industries are beginning to incorporate XBRL for creating, transforming, and communicating financial information. We discuss XBRL in more detail in Chapter 14 and you can learn about its status at http://www.xbrl.org.

Case-in-Point 1.7 The Federal Deposit Insurance Corporation (FDIC) insures bank deposits over a specific amount. FDIC wanted to create an Internet-based Central Data Repository that stored all the call (quarterly) data they received from more than 7,000 banks. They convinced their software vendors to incorporate XBRL language to standardize the data. The tagged data the FDIC receives from banks now has improved accuracy and can be published and made available to users much more quickly than before.[16]

Managerial Accounting

The principal objective of managerial accounting is to provide relevant information to organizational managers—that is, users who are internal to a company or government agency. Cost accounting and budgeting are two typical parts of a company's managerial accounting system. Let us examine each of them in turn.

Cost Accounting. Due to globalization, decentralization, deregulation, and other factors, companies are facing increased competition. The result is that companies must be more efficient and must do a better job of controlling costs. The **cost accounting** part of managerial accounting specifically assists management in measuring and controlling the costs associated with an organization's various acquisition, processing, distribution, and selling activities. In the broadest sense, these tasks focus on the *value added* by an organization to its goods or services, and this concept remains constant whether the organization is a manufacturer, bank, hospital, or police department.

Take health care for an example. Although much controversy surrounded the health care legislation that was signed into law in 2010, there is one fact that most agree upon—that the health care industry is a very large portion of the U.S. economy and that it is growing rapidly as the baby boomer generation reaches retirement age. These facts, coupled with increased regulatory demands on health care providers and hospitals, suggest the need for sophisticated accounting systems to maintain critical data, as well as the need for up-to-date reports for decision making.

Case-in-Point 1.8 Survey data from more than 100 hospital CFOs suggest five major themes regarding the evolution of financial practices in health care. Two of those themes are (1) a greater focus on internal controls, supported by information and management systems, and (2) an increased reliance on business analysis (i.e., requirement to develop and measure business performance).[17]

Activity-Based Costing. One example of an AIS in the area of cost accounting is an **activity-based costing (ABC) system**. Traditionally, cost accountants assigned overhead (i.e., indirect production costs) on the basis of direct labor hours because the number of labor hours was usually directly related to the volume of production. The problem with this traditional system is that, over time, increasing automation has caused manufacturers

---

[16] http://www.xbrl.org/us/us/FFIEC%20White%20Paper%2002Feb2006.pdf
[17] Langabeer, J., J. DellliFraine, and J. Helton. 2010. Mixing finance and medicine. *Strategic Finance* 92(6): 27–34.

to use less and less direct labor. Thus, managers became frustrated using this one method of assigning overhead costs when a clear relationship between labor and these overhead expenses no longer seemed to exist. Instead, managers in a variety of manufacturing and service industries now identify specific activities involved in a manufacturing or service task, and then assign overhead costs based on the resources directly consumed by each activity.

Although activity-based costing techniques have been available for several decades, they are more common now that computerized systems can track costs. Moreover, these systems can move an organization in new strategic directions, allowing corporate executives to examine fundamental business processes and enabling them to reengineer the way they do business. ABC systems can also play an essential strategic role in building and maintaining a successful e-commerce business because they can answer questions about production costs and help managers allocate resources more effectively.

Case-in-Point 1.9   Chrysler, an American car manufacturer, claims that it has saved hundreds of millions of dollars since introducing activity-based costing in the early 1990s. ABC showed that the true cost of certain parts that Chrysler made was 30 times what had originally been estimated, a discovery that persuaded the company to outsource the manufacture of many of those parts.[18]

Corporate Performance Measurement and Business Intelligence.   Another example of an AIS used in the area of cost accounting is in corporate performance measurement (CPM). In a **responsibility accounting system**, for example, managers trace unfavorable performance to the department or individuals that caused the inefficiencies. Under a responsibility accounting system, each subsystem within an organization is only accountable for those items over which it has control. Thus, when a particular cost expenditure exceeds its standard cost, managers can take immediate corrective action.

In addition to the traditional financial measures, cost accountants also collect a variety of nonfinancial performance measures to evaluate such things as customer satisfaction, product quality, business innovation, and branding effectiveness. The **balanced scorecard** measures business performance in four categories: (1) financial performance, (2) customer knowledge, (3) internal business processes, and (4) learning and growth. A company may choose to rank these categories to align with their strategic values. For example, a company may stress "customer knowledge" because customer satisfaction is important to its market position and planned sales growth.

Balanced scorecards and corporate performance measurement are not new ideas. But with the Internet, integrated systems, and other advanced technologies, balanced scorecards and other approaches to CPM are becoming increasingly valuable **business intelligence** tools. Businesses use **key performance indicators (KPIs)** to measure and evaluate activities in each quadrant of the balanced scorecard. For instance, a financial KPI might be return on investment. In the customer area, a company might track the number of new customers per month.

Also new is the use of **dashboards** (Figure 1-8) to monitor key performance metrics. Dashboards usually appear in color, so that red, for example, might indicate a failure to meet the goal. Another indicator might be up and down arrows to show how a key activity performs for a certain time period. Dashboards are especially useful to managers who appreciate the presentation of important performance data in easy-to-understand graphic formats.

---

[18] http://www.economist.com/node/13933812

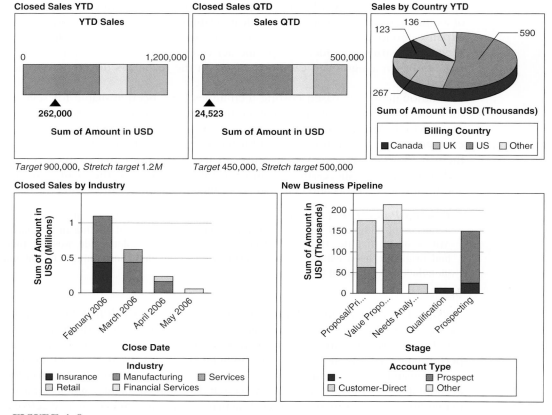

FIGURE 1-8 An example of an executive dashboard.

> ***Case-in-Point 1.10*** Accounting and advisory firms often work with organizations to select appropriate software to serve their information and IT needs. Most dashboards can be adapted for use at the highest level of the firm—even at the board of directors' level—or at any level below. Four of the industry leaders that offer software that can design a dashboard are IBM (Cognos), Actuate (PerformanceSoft), SAP (Business Objects/Pilot Software), and iDashboard.[19]

Budgeting. A budget is a financial projection for the future and is thus a valuable managerial planning aid. Companies develop both short- and long-range budget projections. Short-range budget projections disclose detailed financial plans for a 12-month period, whereas long-range budgets are less-detailed financial projections for five or more years into the future. Management accountants are normally responsible for an organization's budget.

A good budgetary system is also a useful *managerial control* mechanism. Because managers use budgets to predict future financial expectations, they can compare the causes of significant variations between *actual* and *budgeted* results during any budget period. Through timely performance reports that compare actual operating results with prescribed norms, managers are able to identify and investigate significant variations. While negative variations are normally cause for concern, favorable budget variations are not always good

---

[19] Ballou, B., D. Heitger, and L. Donnell. 2010. Creating effective dashboards. *Strategic Finance* 91(9): 27–32.

news either. For example, managers might find cheaper inputs and have a positive variation from the standard cost, but such savings might cause quality problems with the finished product. Regardless of whether variations are positive or negative, managers can use the information for better decision making.

Auditing

The traditional role of auditing has been to evaluate the accuracy and completeness of a corporation's financial statements. In recent years, however, the individuals working in CPA firms would probably argue that they are actually in the assurance business—that is, the business of providing third-party testimony that a client complies with a given statute, law, or similar requirement. Historically, the growth of such assurance services can be traced to a conference of the AICPA in 1993, which created a Special Committee on Assurance Services to identify and formalize some other areas (besides financial audits) in which accountants could provide assurance services. Figure 1-9 describes the first six areas identified by the committee.

Today, there are several additional areas in which auditors can perform assurance work, many involving AISs. One example is to vouch for a client's compliance with the new HIPAA laws—for example, the privacy requirements of the Health Insurance Portability and Accountability Act. Another example is **CPA Trust Services**, a set of professional service areas built around a set of common principles and criteria related to the risks and opportunities presented by IT environments. Trust services include online privacy evaluations, security audits, tests of the integrity of information processing systems, verification of the availability of IT services, and tests of systems confidentiality.

Despite the rise in ancillary assurance services, auditors mainly focus on traditional financial auditing tasks. As noted earlier, computerized AISs have made these tasks more challenging. For example, automated data processing also creates a need for auditors to

---

Risk Assessment

Provide assurance that an organization's set of business risks is comprehensive and manageable.

Business Performance Measurement

Provide assurance that an organization's performance measures beyond the traditional measures in financial statements are relevant and reasonable for helping the organization to achieve its goals and objectives.

Information Systems Reliability

Provide assurance that an organization's information system has been designed to provide reliable information for decision making.

Electronic Commerce

Provide assurance that organizations doing business on the Internet can be trusted to provide the goods and services they promise, and that there is a measure of security provided to customers.

Health Care Performance Measurement

Provide assurance to health care recipients about the effectiveness of health care offered by a variety of health care providers.

Eldercare Plus

Provide assurance that various caregivers offering services to the elderly are offering appropriate and high-quality services.

FIGURE 1-9 Assurance services identified by the American Institute of Certified Public Accountants Special Committee on Assurance Services.

evaluate the risks associated with such automation. Chapter 12 discusses the audit of computerized AISs and the ways in which auditors use IT to perform their jobs.

In addition to the auditing and assurance businesses mentioned above, many CPA firms also perform management consulting tasks—such as helping clients acquire, install, and use new information systems. The AIS at Work feature at the end of this chapter describes one such consulting area. However, the corporate accounting scandals mentioned earlier have led members of the SEC and the U.S. Congress to question whether a CPA firm can conduct an independent audit of the same systems it recently assisted a client in installing and using—a concern intensified when audit staff at Arthur Andersen LLP apparently deliberately destroyed auditing papers for the Enron corporation that many believe would have confirmed doubts. Thus, the Sarbanes-Oxley Act of 2002 (SOX) expressly forbids such potential conflicts of interest by disallowing CPA firms from simultaneously acting as a "management consultant" and the "independent auditor" for the same firm.

Despite this requirement, however, there are still many areas in which CPA firms provide consulting services to clients. Examples include business valuations, litigation support, systems implementation, personal financial planning, estate planning, strategic planning, health care planning, financing arrangements, and forensic (fraud) investigations.

Taxation

Although some individuals still complete their income tax returns manually, many now use computer programs such as TurboTax for this task. Such tax preparation software is an example of an AIS that enables its users to create and store copies of trial tax returns, examine the consequences of alternative tax strategies, print specific portions of a return, and electronically transmit complete copies of a state or federal tax return to the appropriate government agency.

IT can also help tax professionals research challenging tax questions—for example, by providing access to electronic tax libraries online, and more up-to-date tax information than traditional paper-based libraries. Also, tax professionals may subscribe to an online tax service by paying a fee for the right to access databases of tax information stored at centralized computer locations. Online services can provide tax researchers with databases of federal and state tax laws, tax court rulings, court decisions, and technical advice.

CAREERS IN ACCOUNTING INFORMATION SYSTEMS

Our introductory remarks to this chapter suggest a variety of reasons why you should study AISs. Of them, perhaps the most interesting to students is the employment opportunities available to those who understand both accounting and information systems.

Traditional Accounting Career Opportunities

Certainly, a number of traditional accounting jobs are available to those who choose to study accounting as well as AISs. After all, what accounting system is not also an AIS? Because technology now plays such a strong role in accounting, managerial accounting, auditing, and taxation, AIS majors enjoy the advantage of understanding both traditional accounting concepts and information systems concepts. Recognizing the importance to accountants of knowledge about information systems, the AICPA developed a new designation: **Certified**

Information Technology Professional (CITP), which accountants can earn if they have business experience and if they pass an examination.

Systems Consulting

A consultant is an outside expert who helps an organization solve problems or provides technical expertise on an issue. **Systems consultants** provide help with issues concerning information systems—for example, by helping an organization design a new information system, select computer hardware or software, or reengineering business processes (so that they operate more effectively).

One of the most important assets a consultant brings to his or her job is an objective view of the client organization and its processes and goals. AIS students who are skilled in both accounting and information systems make particularly competent systems consultants because they understand how data flow through accounting systems as well as how business processes function. Systems consultants can help a variety of organizations, including professional service organizations, private corporations, and government agencies. This broad work experience, combined with technical knowledge about hardware and software, can be a valuable asset to CPA clients. Because it is likely that a newly designed system will include accounting-related information, a consultant who understands accounting is particularly helpful. Many systems consultants work for large professional service organizations, such as Accenture or Cap Gemini Ernst & Young. Others may work for specialized organizations that focus on the custom design of AISs.

Consulting careers for students of AISs also include jobs as **value-added resellers (VARs)**. Software vendors license VARs to sell a particular software package and provide consulting services to companies, such as help with their software installation, training, and customization. A VAR may set up a small one-person consulting business or may work with other VARs and consultants to provide alternative software solutions to clients.

> *Case-in-Point 1.11* Martin and Associates is a regional consulting firm in the Midwest, started by Kevin Martin in 1983. Kevin, a CPA, left a job with a large accounting firm to open an accounting business that helps companies implement AISs. Today the company describes itself as a "firm dedicated to delivering accounting, ERP, and CRM solutions to our clients and alliances." The staff at Martin and Associates are professionals with CPA and IT experience—many have dual degrees or double majors.[20]

Certified Fraud Examiner

As we discussed earlier in this chapter, forensic accounting is becoming a sought after area for accountants to study and develop their skills. At the same time, due to increased concerns about terrorism and corporate fraud, these specialized accountants are in high demand. An accountant can acquire the **Certified Fraud Examiner (CFE)** certification by meeting the qualifications of the Association of Certified Fraud Examiners (ACFE). To become a Certified Fraud Examiner, an individual must first meet the following qualifications: have a bachelor's degree, at least two years of professional experience in a field either directly or indirectly related to the detection or deterrence of fraud, be of high moral character, and agree to abide by the Bylaws and Code of Professional Ethics of the ACFE. If these are met, then the individual may apply for the CFE examination.

---

[20] http://www.martinandassociates.com

Information Technology Auditing and Security

Information technology (IT) auditors concern themselves with analyzing the risks associated with computerized information systems. These individuals often work closely with financial auditors to assess the risks associated with automated AISs—a position in high demand because so many systems are now computerized. Information systems auditors also help financial auditors decide how much time to devote to auditing each segment of a company's business. This assessment may lead to the conclusion that the controls within some portions of a client's information systems are reliable and that less time need be spent on it—or the opposite.

IT auditors are involved in a number of activities apart from assessing risk for financial audit purposes. Many of these auditors work for professional service organizations, such as Ernst & Young, Deloitte & Touche, PricewaterhouseCoopers, or KPMG. Figure 1-10 identifies a partial listing of the types of services offered by Ernst & Young.

IT auditors might be CPAs or be licensed as **Certified Information Systems Auditors (CISAs)**—a certification given to professional information systems auditors by the **Information Systems Audit and Control Association (ISACA)**. To become a CISA, you must take an examination and obtain specialized work experience. Many CISAs have accounting and information systems backgrounds, although formal accounting education is not required for certification. IT auditors are in more demand than ever today, in part because of the Sarbanes-Oxley legislation, specifically Section 404, which requires documenting and evaluating IT controls.

Case-in-Point 1.12 While efficiencies in compliance with requirements of the Sarbanes-Oxley Act of 2002 will help in the future, the number of hours necessary to document and evaluate internal controls, including IT controls, means more work for those with IT audit skills. According to 2004 and 2005 surveys by the Controllers' Leadership Roundtable research, audit fee increases for the Big Four, in compliance with Section 404, ranged from 78 percent for Deloitte & Touche to 134 percent for PricewaterhouseCoopers.[21]

Sometimes the best way to assess the risks associated with a computerized system is to try to breach the system, which is referred to as **penetration testing**. These tests are usually conducted within a systems security audit in which the organization attempts to determine the level of vulnerability of their information systems and the impact such

---

Assurance Services
- Financial statement attestation
- Internal control reporting
- Assess procedures and controls concerning privacy and confidentiality, performance measurement, systems reliability, outsourced process controls, information security

Business Risk Services

Fraud Investigation and Dispute Services

Technology and Security Risk Services

Specialty Advisory Services

FIGURE 1-10 A sample of the many types of services offered by Ernst & Young LLP, one of the largest international professional service organizations.

---

[21] Goff, J. 2005. Fractured fraternity. *CFO Magazine* (September): 1–3.

weaknesses might have on the viability of the organization. If any security issues are discovered, the organization will typically work swiftly to correct the problems or at least mitigate the impact they might have on the company.

AIS AT WORK
Consulting Work for CPAs

Businesses and government entities have always been concerned about disaster recovery or continuity planning. However, the events of September 11, 2001, and Hurricane Katrina made everyone even more aware of the necessity of preparing for a disaster. Auditors can help. Continuity planning is an internal control specifically designed to ensure that operations, including IT functions, can continue in the event of a natural or man-made disaster. IT and Internet technologies are vulnerable to man-made attacks, such as viruses and worms. The absence of a continuity plan is a reportable condition under Statement on Auditing Standards No. 60, *Communication of Internal Control Related Matters Noted in an Audit*.

A CPA can help a business to draw up a business continuity plan. As noted in a recent article in *New Accountant*, some Fortune 500 companies will pay $40,000 or more for such a disaster recovery planning engagement.[22] These plans include sections on backup and recovery procedures for all IT, off-site locations for data storage, and information about hot (fully equipped for immediate use) or cold (leased facilities that do not include hardware and software) sites available for use should physical facilities become inaccessible or damaged. The plans also include contact information for the management recovery team. Copies of the plan, of course, must be stored off-site. Ideally, each member of the management recovery team has at least one copy at home or in another easily accessible location off-site.

A disaster recovery plan is of no use if it is not tested regularly. Such testing is vital to learn where there may be weaknesses. As an example, during an early Internet worm crisis, many managers found that they were actually storing information regarding who to contact in an emergency on their computers! Naturally, when the computers went down so did this vital information. Full-blown testing of a disaster recovery plan is expensive and time consuming. Sometimes it is difficult for managers to understand the importance of it since they can't see a direct link to enhancing their income. However, the auditor may need to make the case.

SUMMARY

✓ Computerized information systems collect, process, store, transform, and distribute financial and nonfinancial information for planning, decision making, and control purposes.

✓ Data are raw facts; information refers to data that are meaningful and useful.

✓ Accountants and other managers are using predictive analytics, a technique that takes advantage of data stored in data warehouses to improve performance.

---

[22] Reed, R., and D. Pence. 2006. Enhancing consulting revenues with disaster recovery planning. *New Accountant* 714: 13–14.

✓ IT refers to the hardware, software, and related system components that organizations use to create computerized information systems.

✓ Cloud computing is a way of using business applications over the Internet.

✓ The basic concept of sustainability reporting is that a company focuses on nonfinancial performance measures that might impact its income, value, or future performance.

✓ By law, the accountants in many specific financial institutions must now file suspicious activity reports that document potential instances of fraud, money laundering, or money transfers to terrorist organizations.

✓ A forensic accountant combines the skills of investigation, accounting, and auditing to find and collect pieces of information that collectively provide evidence that criminal activity is in progress or has happened.

✓ Some of the recent corporate scandals involved manipulation of accounting data, which led to the passage of legislation to protect investors.

✓ IT affects virtually every aspect of accounting, including financial and managerial accounting, auditing, and taxation.

✓ Financial accounting information is becoming increasingly relevant and important as advances in IT allow for creation of new reporting systems.

✓ Managerial accounting is impacted by IT in the following areas: balanced scorecards, business intelligence, dashboards, and other key performance indicators.

✓ Auditors perform many types of assurance services, in addition to financial statement attestation.

✓ The availability of tax software and extensive tax databases influences both tax preparation and tax planning.

✓ There are many reasons to study AISs, and one of the most important is the availability of many exciting career opportunities.

KEY TERMS YOU SHOULD KNOW

accounting information systems (AIS)
activity-based costing (ABC) systems
audit trail
balanced scorecard
business intelligence
Certified Fraud Examiner (CFE)
Certified Information Systems Auditors (CISAs)
Certified Information Technology Professional (CITP)
cloud computing
cost accounting
CPA Trust Services
dashboards
data
e-business
e-commerce
enterprise resource planning (ERP) system
extensible business reporting language (XBRL)
financial accounting information systems
forensic accounting

information
information age
information overload
Information Systems Audit and Control Association (ISACA)
information technology (IT)
information technology (IT) auditors
interactive data
key performance indicators (KPIs)
knowledge workers
penetration testing
Ponzi scheme
predictive analytics
REA accounting
responsibility accounting system
suspicious activity reporting (SAR)
sustainability reporting
systems consultants
value-added resellers (VARs)

DISCUSSION QUESTIONS

1-1. Take a survey of the students in your class to find out what jobs their parents hold. How many are employed in manufacturing? How many are employed in service industries? How many could be classified as knowledge workers?

1-2. Hiring an employee and taking a sales order are business activities but are not accounting transactions requiring journal entries. Make a list of some other business activities that would not be captured as journal entries in a traditional AIS. Do you think managers or investors would be interested in knowing about these activities? Why or why not?

1-3. Advances in IT are likely to have a continuing impact on financial accounting. What are some changes you think will occur in the way financial information is gathered, processed, and communicated as a result of increasingly sophisticated IT?

1-4. XBRL is emerging as the language that will be used to create interactive data that financial managers can use in communication. How do you think the use of interactive data might enhance the value of a company's financial statements?

1-5. Discuss suspicious activity reporting. For example, do you think that such reporting should be a legal requirement, or should it be just an ethical matter? Do you think that the majority of SAR activity is illegal, or are these mostly false alarms?

1-6. Managerial accounting is impacted by IT in many ways, including enhancing CPM. How do you think a university might be able to use a scorecard or dashboard approach to operate more effectively?

1-7. Look again at the list of assurance services shown in Figure 1-9. Can you think of other assurance services that CPAs could offer which would take advantage of their AIS expertise?

1-8. Interview a sample of auditors from professional service firms in your area. Ask them whether they plan to offer any of the assurance services suggested by the AICPA. Also, find out if they offer services other than financial auditing and taxation. Discuss your findings in class.

1-9. This chapter described several career opportunities available to students who combine a study of accounting with course work in AISs, information systems, and/or computer science. Can you think of other jobs where these skill sets would be desirable?

1-10. This chapter stressed the importance of IT for understanding how AISs operate. But is this the only skill valued by employers? How important do you think analytical thinking skills or writing skills are? Discuss.

PROBLEMS

1-11. What words were used to form each of the following acronyms? (Hint: each of them can be found in the chapter.)

a. AAA	**i.** CPM	**q.** PATRIOT Act
b. ABC	**j.** ERP	**r.** REA
c. AICPA	**k.** FASB	**s.** SAR
d. AIS	**l.** HIPAA	**t.** SEC
e. CFO	**m.** ISACA	**u.** SOX
f. CISA	**n.** IT	**v.** VARs
g. CITP	**o.** KPI	**w.** XBRL
h. CPA	**p.** OSC	

1-12. The accounting profession publishes many journals such as the *Journal of Accountancy, Internal Auditor, Strategic Finance,* and *Management Accounting.* Choose three or four issues from each of these journals and count the number of articles that are related to IT. In addition, make a list of the specific technology discussed in each article (where possible). When you are finished, decide whether you believe IT is influencing the field of accounting.

1-13. Nehru Gupta is the controller at the Acme Shoe Company, a large manufacturing company located in Franklin, Pennsylvania. Acme has many divisions, and the performance of each division has typically been evaluated using a return on investment (ROI) formula. The return on investment is calculated by dividing profit by the book value of total assets.

In a meeting yesterday with Bob Burn, the company president, Nehru warned that this return on investment measure might not be accurately reflecting how well the divisions are doing. Nehru is concerned that by using profits and the book value of assets, division managers might be engaging in some short-term finagling to show the highest possible return. Bob concurred and asked what other numbers they could use to evaluate division performance.

Nehru said, "I'm not sure, Bob. Net income isn't a good number for evaluation purposes. Since we allocate a lot of overhead costs to the divisions on what some managers consider an arbitrary basis, net income won't work as a performance measure in place of return on investment." Bob told Nehru to give some thought to this problem and report back to him.

Requirements

1. Explain what managers can do in the short run to maximize return on investment as calculated at Acme. What other accounting measures could Acme use to evaluate the performance of its divisional managers?

2. Describe other instances in which accounting numbers might lead to dysfunctional behavior in an organization.

3. Search the Internet and find at least one company that offers an information system (or software) that might help Nehru evaluate his company's performance.

1-14. In a recent article in the *New York Times,* Jeff Zucker—CEO of NBC-Universal—described the digital age as "trading analog dollars for digital pennies."[23] Discuss this comment from the viewpoint of each of the following:

a. A music company executive   **b.** A consumer   **c.** A TV executive

1-15. What is new in the field of AISs today? Select one new trend that was not mentioned in the chapter, but that you feel is important. Write a short report describing your findings. Be sure to provide reasons why you feel that your choice of topic is important, and therefore of interest to others in your class.

1-16. The participants of such recreational activities as hang gliding, soaring, hiking, rock collecting, or skydiving often create local "birds-of-a-feather" (affinity) organizations. Two examples are the Chicago sky divers (http://www.chicagoskydivers.com) or the soaring club of western Canada (http://www.canadianrockiessoaring.com). Many of these clubs collect dues from members to pay for the printing and mailing costs of monthly newsletters. Some of them maintain only minimal accounting information on manual pages or, at best, in spreadsheets.

a. What financial information are such clubs likely to collect and maintain?

b. Assuming that the club keeps manual accounting records, would you consider such systems accounting information systems? Why or why not?

c. Assume that the club treasurer of one such organization is in charge of all financial matters, including collecting and depositing member dues, paying vendor invoices, and preparing

---

[23] Arango, T. 2008. Digital sales exceed CDs at Atlantic. *New York Times* (November 26): p. B7.

yearly reports. Do you think that assigning only one person to this job is a good idea? Why or why not?

d. What benefits would you guess might come from computerizing some or all of the club's financial information, even if there are less than 100 members? For example, do you think that such computerization is likely to be cost effective?

1-17. Many companies now provide a wealth of information about themselves on their Web sites. But how much of this information is useful for investment purposes? To help you answer this question, imagine that you have $10,000, which you *must* invest in the common stock of a publicly held company.

a. Select a company as specified by your instructor and access its online financial reports. Is the information contained in the reports complete? If not, why not? Is the information contained in these reports sufficient for you to decide whether or not to invest in the company? If not, why not?

b. Now select an online brokerage Web site such as E*Trade and look up the information of that same company. Does the information provided by the brokerage firm differ from that of the company itself? If so, how? Again, answer the question: Is the information contained in these reports sufficiently detailed and complete for you to decide whether to invest in it? If not, why not?

c. Access the Web site of an investment rating service such as Value Line. How does the information on this third site differ from that of the other two? Again, answer the question: "Is the information contained on the site sufficiently detailed and complete for you to decide whether to invest in the stock? If not, why not?"

d. What do these comparisons tell you about the difference between "data" and "information"?

1-18. The Web site of FinCen—the Financial Crimes Enforcement Center Network (a department of the U.S. Treasury)—maintains a Web site at http://www.fincen.gov. On the left side of its home page, you will find links to information for various types of companies including banks, casinos, money service businesses, insurance companies, security and futures traders, and dealers in precious metals and jewelry—that is, the companies mandated by various federal laws to file SARs. Select three of these types of companies, and for each type, use the information provided on these secondary pages to list at least two types of financial transactions or activities that should be considered "suspicious."

CASE STUDIES

The Annual Report

The annual report is considered by some to be the single most important printed document that companies produce. In recent years, annual reports have become large documents. They now include such sections as letters to the stockholders, descriptions of the business, operating highlights, financial review, management discussion and analysis, segment reporting, and inflation data as well as the basic financial statements. The expansion has been due in part to a general increase in the degree of sophistication and complexity in accounting standards and disclosure requirements for financial reporting.

The expansion also reflects the change in the composition and level of sophistication of users. Current users include not only stockholders but also financial and securities analysts, potential investors, lending institutions, stockbrokers, customers, employees, and (whether the reporting company likes it or not) competitors. Thus, a report that was originally designed as a device for communicating basic financial information now attempts to meet the diverse needs of an expanding audience.

Users hold conflicting views on the value of annual reports. Some argue that annual reports fail to provide enough information, whereas others believe that disclosures in annual reports have expanded to the point where they create information overload. The future of most companies depends on acceptance by the investing public and by their customers; therefore, companies should take this opportunity to communicate well-defined corporate strategies.

Requirements

1. The goal of preparing an annual report is to communicate information from a company to its targeted users. (a) Identify and discuss the basic factors of communication that must be considered in the presentation of this information. (b) Discuss the communication problems a company faces in preparing the annual report that result from the diversity of the users being addressed.

2. Select two types of information found in an annual report, other than the financial statements and accompanying footnotes, and describe how they are useful to the users of annual reports.

3. Discuss at least two advantages and two disadvantages of stating well-defined corporate strategies in the annual report.

4. Evaluate the effectiveness of annual reports in fulfilling the information needs of the following current and potential users: (a) shareholders, (b) creditors, (c) employees, (d) customers, (e) financial analysts.

5. Annual reports are public and accessible to anyone, including competitors. Discuss how this affects decisions about what information should be provided in annual reports.

6. Find the annual report for a company that includes sustainability reporting. What information does the company disclose? Do you think such information is helpful to investors?

Performance Management Company

Neil Rogers is the controller for Performance Management Company (PMC), a manufacturing company with headquarters in San Antonio, Texas. PMC has seven concrete product plants located throughout the Southwest region of the United States. The company recently switched to a decentralized organizational structure. In the past, the company did not try to measure profitability at each plant. Rather, all revenues and expenses were consolidated to produce just one income statement.

Under the new organizational structure, each plant is headed by a general manager, who has complete responsibility for operating the plant. Neil asked one of his accountants, Scott McDermott, to organize a small group to be in charge of performance analysis. This group is to prepare monthly reports on performance for each of the seven plants. These reports consist of budgeted and actual income statements. Written explanations and appraisals are to accompany variances. Each member of Scott's group has been assigned to one specific plant and is encouraged to interact with management and staff in that plant to become familiar with operations.

After a few months, Neil began receiving complaints from the general managers at several of the plants. The managers complained that the reports were slowing down operations and they felt as though someone was constantly looking over their shoulders to see if they were operating in line with the budget. They pointed out that the performance analysis staff is trying to do their job (i.e., explanation of variances). The most vocal plant manager claimed that "those accountants can't explain the variances—they don't know anything about the industry!"

The president of PMC, Ross Stewart, also complained about the new system for performance evaluation reporting. He claimed that he was unable to wade through the seven detailed income statements, variances, and narrative explanations of all variances each month. As he put it, "I don't have time for this and I think much of the information I am receiving is useless!"

Requirements

1. Do you think it is a good idea to have a special staff in charge of performance evaluation and analysis?

2. In a decentralized organization such as this one, what would seem to be the best approach to performance evaluation?

3. What information would you include in a performance evaluation report for Mr. Stewart?

Chapter 2

Information Technology and AISs

INTRODUCTION

In automated accounting systems, information technology (IT) serves as a platform on which other system components rely. The purpose of this chapter is to discuss IT subjects in detail—especially as they relate to AISs. Because most students in AIS courses have already taken a survey computer class, the discussions here are brief. This chapter may nonetheless serve as a review of computer hardware and software concepts or as a study of how IT helps organizations accomplish strategic accounting goals.

It is helpful to view an accounting information system as a set of five interacting components: (1) hardware, (2) software, (3) data, (4) people, and (5) procedures. Computer hardware is probably the most tangible element in this set, but "hardware" is only one piece of the pie—and not necessarily the most important piece. For example, most organizations spend more money on people (in wages and salaries) than on computer hardware and software combined. Similarly, computer hardware must work together with the other system components to accomplish data processing tasks. Without computer software, for example, the hardware would stand idle. Without data to process, both the hardware and the software would be useless. Without procedures, accounting data could not be gathered accurately or distributed properly. And finally, without people, it is doubtful that the rest of the system could operate for long or be of much use.

What all this means is that "information technology" is a fuzzy term that includes more than computer hardware. In this chapter, we concentrate on computer hardware (in the next three sections of the chapter) and software (in the final section). But you should remember that these items must interact with all the other system components to create successful AISs.

Case-in-Point 2.1 CPA Crossings is a small consulting company in Rochester, Minnesota, that provides IT services to both CPA firms and the organizations they serve. In helping companies install document management systems, general partner John Higgins notes that such matters as (1) defining work flow policies and procedures and (2) understanding the difference between document management systems and electronic documents themselves are the keys to successful implementations—not "technology."[1]

THE IMPORTANCE OF INFORMATION TECHNOLOGY TO ACCOUNTANTS

Although it may be tempting to dismiss "information technology" as more important to computer people than accountants, this would be a mistake. In fact, most of the references

---

[1] Higgins, J. 2006. Street talk: Reader views. *Accounting Technology* 22(3): 7.

at the end of this chapter make it clear that "IT" and "accounting systems" are intimately related. Here are six reasons why IT is important to accountants.

Six Reasons

One reason for IT's importance is that information technology must be compatible with, and support, the other components of an AIS. For example, to automate the accounting system of a dry-cleaning business, the owners will have to consider what tasks they'll want their system to accomplish, identify what software package or packages can perform these tasks, and perhaps evaluate several different computer hardware configurations that might support these packages. These concerns are the subject of "systems analysis"—the topic covered in Chapter 13.

A second reason why information technology is important is because accounting professionals often help clients make hardware and software purchases. For example, large expenditures on computer systems must be cost-justified—a task usually performed with accounting expertise and assistance. For this reason, many consulting firms now specialize in, or have departments for, management advisory services to perform these consulting tasks. Understanding IT is critical to these efforts.

A third reason why information technology is important to accountants is because auditors must evaluate computerized systems. Today, it is no longer possible for auditors to treat a computer as a "black box" and audit around it. Rather, auditors must audit through or with a computer. This means that auditors must understand automation and automated controls and also be able to identify a computerized system's strengths and weaknesses. We discuss these matters in Chapter 12.

A fourth reason why IT is important to accountants is because they are often asked to evaluate the efficiency (e.g., costliness and timeliness) and effectiveness (usually strategic value) of an existing system. This is a daunting task, requiring a familiarity with the strengths and weaknesses of the current system, as well as an understanding of what alternate technologies might work better.

A fifth reason why information technology is important to accountants is because IT profoundly affects the way they work today and will work in the future. This includes new ways of gathering and recording information; new types of systems that accountants will use (both to perform personal tasks and to communicate their work to others); new types of hardware, software, and computer networks upon which these systems will run; and even new ways to audit these systems.

Case-in-Point 2.2 Target is a retailer with 1,755 stores in the United States (in 2011) and over $60 billion in retail sales. Many of its suppliers claim that the chain's sophisticated technology is "the best in the business," enabling managers to make fast, accurate decisions on its many merchandising operations. Attention to detail is also important, including color coding department areas within the store and automating operations at checkout stands. Says Target president Kenneth Woodrow, "If people have to wait in line, it means we don't respect their time."[2]

A final reason why information technology is important to accountants is because understanding how IT affects accounting systems is vital to passing most accounting certification examinations. For example, sections of both the CPA and CMA examinations contain questions about information technology.

---

[2] Frederick, J. 2008. Target adheres to core strategy in midst of tough economy. *Drug Store News* 30(5): 130.

The Top Ten Information Technologies

Annually, the AICPA conducts a voluntary annual survey of its members to identify the "top 10 information system technologies" affecting the study and practice of accounting. Figure 2-1 provides the set for 2010. For the sixth year in a row, "information security" tops the list, although the general topic of "security" involves almost all the other items in the list as well.

Because of their importance, we discuss many of the items in Figure 2-1 in various chapters of the text itself. For example, Chapters 9, 10, 11, 12, and 14 discuss the topic of information security (item 1 on the list). Similarly, we discuss backup solutions and disaster recovery in Chapter 3, small business software in Chapter 15, and mobile computing in Chapter 1.

INPUT, PROCESSING, AND OUTPUT DEVICES

Figure 2-2 suggests that the hardware of a computer system includes the computer itself—for example, a microcomputer—as well as the keyboards, printers, hard disks, and similar devices that help the computer perform input and output tasks. These devices are commonly called **peripheral equipment** because they typically surround the computer and help it process data.

One way to classify peripheral equipment is by the tasks they perform. Thus, *input equipment* (such as computer mice and keyboards) enable users to enter data into a computer system, *output equipment* (such as monitors and printers) enable users to see processed results, *secondary storage devices* (such as hard disks) enable users to store data for future reference, and *communications equipment* (such as internal networking cards) enable users to transmit data over data networks. Like any other system, these distinct pieces of computer equipment must work together to accomplish data processing tasks.

Most accounting transactions are processed in a three-phase operation called the **input-processing-output cycle**. For convenience, we shall look at technologies that assist AISs in each of these areas in this order.

Input Devices

The starting point of the input-processing-output cycle—especially when processing accounting data—is input. Thus, even where the amount of data is small, most AISs require input methods and procedures that ensure complete, accurate, timely, and cost-effective ways of gathering and inputting accounting data. Usually, there are several ways of capturing accounting data, so system designers must pick those input procedures and devices that best meet these system objectives.

Source Documents and Data Transcription.
The starting point for collecting accounting data in many AISs is a **source document**. Manual examples include time cards, packing slips, survey forms, employee application forms, patient intake forms, purchase invoices, sales invoices, cash disbursement vouchers, and travel reimbursement forms. Computerized examples include airline reservation screens, bank deposit screens, and Web-based customer-order forms.

Source documents are important to AISs because (1) they are human readable and (2) they can be completed by the user. Source documents are also important because

Rank	Item	Explanation
1	Information Security	The ability to protect the components of an AIS from such threats as viruses, password intrusions, and physical harm.
2	Securing and controlling information distribution	Protecting and securing the transmission and distribution of digital data—for example, using encryption.
3	Backup solutions, disaster planning, and business continuity	The ability to continue business operations in the event that a disaster such as an earthquake occurs.
4	Secure electronic collaboration	The need to secure electronic transmissions for both clients and collaborating employees.
5	Paperless technology	The ability of employees to communicate and produce digital documents.
6	Laptop security	The need to secure laptops from theft, the data they transmit (from being compromised) and the information they store if the device itself is lost or stolen
7	Small business software	The importance of new Microsoft Office, Google Apps, and similar software for office productivity.
8	Mobile computing	An employee or contractor's ability to work anywhere and communicate with the office at any time.
9	Tax software and electronic filing	A tax filer or preparer's ability to create and/or file a tax return electronically.
10	Server virtualization and consolidation	The ability of a large single server to do the work of serveral smaller ones.

FIGURE 2-1 The AICPA's Top 10 Information Technologies for 2010. Source: AICP.org.

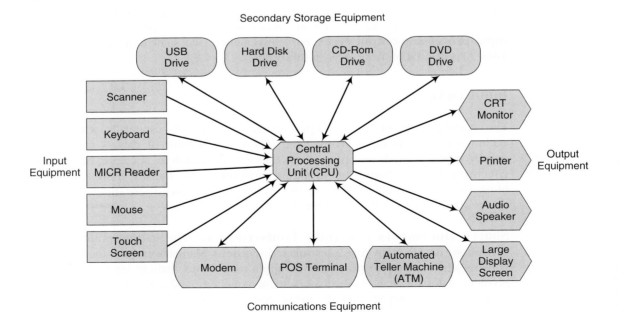

FIGURE 2-2 A central processing unit and examples of peripheral equipment.

they provide evidence of a transaction's authenticity (e.g., a signed cash disbursement voucher authorizes a cash disbursement), are the starting point of an audit trail, and (in emergencies) can serve as backup in the event that the computer files created from them are damaged or destroyed.

The greatest disadvantage of manually prepared source documents is that they are not machine readable. Thus, in order to process source-document data electronically, the data must first be transcribed into machine-readable media. This **data transcription** is mostly an inefficient, labor-intensive, time-consuming, costly, and nonproductive process that has the potential to bottleneck data at the transcription site, embed errors in the transcribed data, and provide opportunities for fraud, embezzlement, or sabotage. Is it any wonder, then, that most AISs capture data that are already in machine-readable formats? The paragraphs that follow describe some devices that overcome these problems.

POS Devices.   Because most of the information required by retailers can be captured at the point at which a sale is made, retail businesses now commonly use automated **point-of-sale (POS) devices** to gather and record pertinent data electronically at that time. One example is the "smart cash registers" that connect to off-site computers. Another example is the **bar code readers** that interpret the *universal product code (UPC)* commonly printed on supermarket and variety store items (Figure 2-3). Non-UPC bar codes are used extensively in transportation and inventory applications to track shipments (e.g., Federal Express), by warehouse employees to log received merchandise, by universities to identify equipment, by the U.S. Post Office to route mail, and by publishers to identify books using ISBN numbers (see the bar code on the back of this book for an example).

POS systems allow retailers to centralize price information in online computers, avoid the task of affixing price stickers to individual items on retail store shelves, and update prices easily when required. With such systems, for example, the sales data obtained at the checkout counter of a convenience store can be transmitted directly to a computer where they can be verified for accuracy, reasonableness, and completeness and also stored for later uses—for example, preparing sales reports. Figure 2-4 lists other advantages of POS data collection systems, which are actually growing in use despite the maturity of the technology.

Magnetic Ink Character Recognition.   The banking industry pioneered the development of magnetically encoded paper, commonly called **magnetic ink character recognition (MICR)**. You are probably familiar with MICR characters—the odd-looking numbers printed on the bottom of your checks (Figure 2-5). This type font has been standardized for the entire country by the American National Standards Institute (ANSI). Thus, a check you write anywhere in the United States or Canada is machine readable by any bank.

FIGURE 2-3   An example of the universal product code (UPC), which is often preprinted on the labels of retail products for merchandise identification and computerized checkout.

1. Clerical errors, such as a salesperson's incorrect reading of a price tag, are detectable, and even potentially correctable, automatically.

2. Such standard procedures as the computation of a sales tax, the multiplication of prices times quantities sold, or the calculation of a discount can be performed using the register-terminal as a calculator.

3. Processing errors caused by illegible sales slips can be reduced.

4. Credit checks and answers to questions about customers' account balances are routinely handled by using the cash register as an inquiry terminal.

5. The inventory-disbursements data required for inventory control are collected as a natural part of the sales transaction.

6. A breakdown listing by the computer of sales by type of inventory item, dollar volume, sales clerk, or store location is possible because the data required for such reports are collected automatically with the sales transaction and may be stored for such use.

7. Sales and inventory personnel levels can be reduced because the manual data processing functions required of such personnel have largely been eliminated.

FIGURE 2-4   Advantages of POS systems.

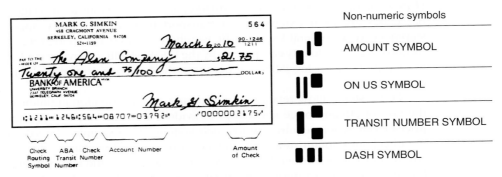

FIGURE 2-5   The MICR symbols of the American Banking Association (ABA).

One advantage of MICR coding is that it is both machine readable and human readable. Another advantage is that MICR coding is quite flexible: documents of varying sizes, thicknesses, or widths may be used. The chief disadvantage of MICR is that the magnetic strength (called the "magnetic flux") of the characters diminishes over time. This makes MICR documents unreliable when they must be input repeatedly.

Optical Character Recognition.   **Optical character recognition (OCR)** uses optical, rather than magnetic, readers to interpret the data found on source documents. Typical OCR devices use light-sensing mechanisms and laser technology to perform the character-recognition function required to interpret recorded data. **Mark-sense media** (such as the type used in computerized exams) use simple rectangles or ovals as "characters" that you blacken with a pencil. More sophisticated versions of OCR can read complete character sets of numbers and letters (Figure 2-6a) and are therefore more versatile as input.

Accounting uses of OCR include the billing statements of public utility companies, credit card issuers, and insurance companies, mortgage payment coupons, telephone bills, subscription renewal forms, and airline tickets. Most of these forms are **turnaround documents**—that is, documents that are initially prepared by a company, then sent to individuals, and finally returned to the organization for further data processing. Like MICR

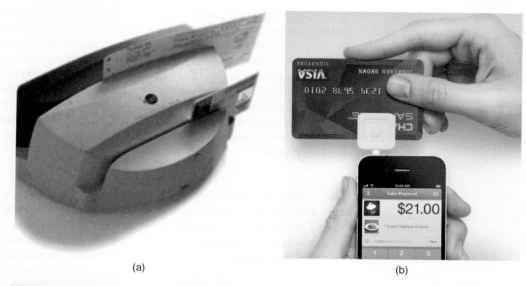

(a)   (b)

FIGURE 2-6   Some common computer input devices. (a) This versatile optical character reader from Scan Corporation can read OCR characters, bar codes, and magnetic stripes. (b) This credit card reader from Squareup™ allows small business owners such as electricians or limousine drivers to use their cell phones for customer credit card payments. Source: ADATA Technology (USA) Co., Ltd.

encoding, the chief advantage of OCR is a source document that is both human readable and machine readable.

Plastic Cards with Magnetic Strips.   Many plastic cards have a magnetic strip attached to one side of them that can store permanent information and therefore provide input data when required. Typically, the "mag strip" stores information about the user—for example, a checking account number, credit card number, room number, or security clearance code. In the United States, the magnetic strip on these cards has been divided into distinct physical areas, and by agreement, each major industry using these cards has its own assigned space. Thus, the International Airline Transport Association (IATA), the American Banking Association (ABA), and the savings and loan industry each encode information pertinent to their individual needs on such plastic cards without fear that, by accident, these cards will be misused in another application.

AISs use mag-strip cards to capture data at the time these cards are used (Figure 2-6b). For example, credit cards can include passwords that ATM machines can examine every time someone uses the card. This also facilitates data gathering because reliable electronic equipment reads the strip, thus eliminating human error.

Case-in-Point 2.3   In the United States, many gambling casinos issue mag-strip "club cards" to their customers, who use them as internal credit cards for playing slot machines, poker machines, and so forth. These cards free customers from the task of cashing checks or getting change. But these same cards also enable casinos to gather data on player activities—information that managers can subsequently use to make better decisions about extending credit limits or providing complimentary meals and hotel rooms.[3]

Microcomputer Input Devices.   Many specialized devices now help users input data into their microcomputers. *Keyboards* are perhaps the most common input device.

---

[3] From the authors.

Computer mice, touch pads, joy sticks, and similar devices enable users to control a screen cursor, create graphic images, reposition screen objects, or select items from display menus. *Touch screens* enable users to make menu choices simply by touching a display screen with a finger or stick. *Web cams* provide live video input to a computer. *Computer pens* or *styluses* permit users to enter data on video screens and are especially popular with signature screens at store checkout counters or **personal data assistant (PDA) devices** such as Blackberries. These PDAs enable their users to make phone calls as well as maintain personal data such as address books, appointment calendars, and check registers. Newer models also incorporate wireless technology that provides access to the Internet—a practical feature for e-mail users.

Digital Cameras. Although many people only use digital cameras in recreational settings, accountants also use them for documenting (1) inventories of large assets such as trucks, cranes, and buildings, (2) damage to vehicles or offices due to accidents, vandalism, or natural disasters for insurance purposes, and (3) new or existing employees for identification and security purposes. Like many cell phones, newer digital cameras can upload pictures directly to the Internet—an advantage, for example, when instant documentation is useful. As suggested by the following Case-in-Point, the benefits of digital photographs must be weighed against their potential social costs.

Case-in-Point 2.4 Red-light cameras automate the process of ticketing motorists who drive through red traffic lights (Figure 2-7). Such cameras enable municipalities to enforce driving laws at important traffic intersections and often substantially increase revenues from traffic violations. Proponents of red-light cameras argue that red-light cameras reduce accidents and that the funds they generate can be used to pay for other important police work. Critics counter that the cameras are *only* revenue generators and that they pose an important threat to an individual's right to privacy.[4]

FIGURE 2-7 An example of a red-light camera. Source: istockphoto.

---

[4] http://www.thenewspaper.com/news/18/1886.asp

Biometric Scanners. Many accounting applications must verify that a user has legitimate access to a system—for example, can view corporate personnel files. Authentication systems based on *what you know* require you to input codes, account numbers, passwords, or similar values. These are low-security systems because users can easily forget, lose, or guess such information, making these systems vulnerable to attack and misuse. Systems based on *what you have* require physical keys, magnetic cards, or similar physical media—but suffer many of the same problems as password-based authenticating systems.

Biometric scanners authenticate users based on *who they are. Behavioral systems* recognize signatures, voices, or keystroke dynamics. *Physiological systems* recognize fingerprints, irises, retinas, faces, and even ears. Most of these devices connect directly to computer USB ports or are integrated in computer keyboards, mice, or Web cams. The two most common biometric systems use fingerprint or iris scanners to authenticate users (Figure 2-8). While most fingerprints have similar features, for example, experts have yet to discover pairs with the same minute details since 1892 when records were kept. Iris scans record vein patterns in the colored portion of the eye and are even more accurate than fingerprints because of the wider variability in vein patterns and the fact that even the right and left eye of the same person are not identical.

Biometric authentication begins with *enrollment*—the process of creating digital templates for legitimate users. Template files are small, requiring about 256 bytes for a fingerprint and 512 bytes for an iris scan. To authenticate a user, the scanner takes a new sample from the individual and compares it to known templates. Unlike passwords, the new samples will not perfectly match the template. The *hamming distance* measures how close the two match.

Case-in-Point 2.5 The AICPA now requires the fingerprints of all candidates wishing to take the CPA exam. The system, maintained by Prometric, matches each candidate's fingerprint with other personal identification in order to increase the security and integrity of the exams—over 60,000 test sections each year.[5]

(a) fingerprint scanner   (b) iris scanner

FIGURE 2-8 (a) An inexpensive USB fingerprint scanner. Source: Courtesy of BioEnable. (b) An inexpensive iris scanner. Source: Courtesy of LG Electronics.

---

[5] Anonymous. 2008. CPA exam now requires fingerprints. *Practical Accountant* 4(6): 7.

Central Processing Units

Once data have been captured (and perhaps transcribed into machine-readable formats), they usually must be processed to be valuable to decision makers. These processing tasks are performed by the **central processing unit (CPU)** of a computer system (Figure 2-9). In the computer industry, the terms *computer* and *CPU* are often used interchangeably.

Computing power starts with the most limited microcomputers (aka "personal computers" or "PCs") and increases in capabilities such as speed, multiuser support, and peripheral equipment with **minicomputers**, **mainframe computers**, and **supercomputers**. A growing segment of the microcomputer market is the portable systems—that is, netbook computers, laptop computers, and the even more compact PDAs and cell phones.

Steve Jobs, president of Apple Computer Corporation, describes computing today as the "post PC era." Electronic readers and **computer tablets** such as the Kindle and iPad devices are a new category of portable computing systems that fit neatly into this vision. Although many people now buy these devices for personal uses, commercial applications are emerging. We provide one example in the following Case-in-Point, and another example in the AIS-in-Action feature at the end of this chapter.

Case-in-Point 2.6 Michael Klein is the president of OpenAir, an airline charter company in Gaithersburg, Maryland, and an avid iPad user. He is one of many airline pilots who now take these devices on flights instead of the bulky manuals and charts once required by the Federal Aviation Administration. The FAA approved the devices in early 2011, and airlines hope to save millions of dollars in reduced paper costs with them. "It's better than paper," says Klein. "It does everything for you."[6]

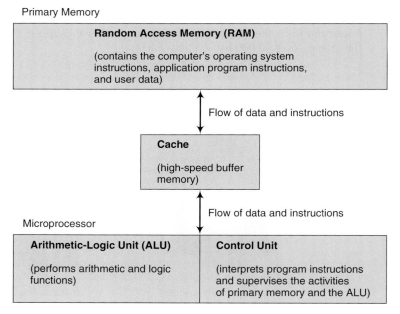

FIGURE 2-9 A schematic of a central processing unit. In some computers, the "Level 2" (high-speed buffer) cache is part of the microprocessor unit.

---

[6] Levin, A. 2011. iPads give flight to paperless airplanes. *USA Today* (March 18): 1.

The accounting systems of the smallest businesses—for example, a bicycle repair shop—can often be implemented entirely on a desktop microcomputer. In contrast, the inventory control systems of the nation's largest vendors—for example, Walmart—require multiuser systems that may employ several centralized mainframes working in tandem.

One of the biggest challenges facing businesses today is identifying the right combination of computing technologies—that is, computers of various sizes, networks, and related software—that best meet their IT needs. Dollar for dollar, organizations usually get the most processing power and the cheapest software with microcomputers, which helps explain why modern organizations buy so many of them. Reasons to retain older mainframe systems include (1) the need to support multiuser processing capabilities that work best on such systems; (2) the advantages of centralized processing—for example, simplified control over hardware, software, and user accesses to databases; and (3) the huge costs that organizations typically incur when replacing these **legacy systems**.

Primary Memory.   Figure 2-9 indicates that the two main components of a CPU are its primary memory and its microprocessor, with *cache*, or buffer, memory serving as the interface between these components. The purpose of **primary memory** is to store data and program instructions temporarily for immediate processing and execution. In microcomputers, this primary or *random access memory (RAM)* consists of individual *bytes,* each capable of storing a single character of data—for example, a letter or punctuation mark. RAM capacities are typically measured in *gigabytes* (billions of bytes). Most accounting software require minimum amounts of primary memory to operate properly, so "RAM size" is often a key concern when matching computer hardware to software requirements for smaller AIS applications.

Microprocessors.   Computers cannot manipulate data or execute instructions directly in primary memory. Rather, these tasks are performed by the CPU's **microprocessor**. Examples include Intel Corporation's Core i5 and i7 chips. The *arithmetic-logic unit (ALU)* portion of these microprocessor chips performs arithmetic tasks (such as addition and multiplication), as well as logic tasks (such as comparisons). In contrast, the *control unit* of the processor supervises the actual data processing—for example, transferring data from primary memory to the ALU, performing the required task (e.g., adding two numbers together), and transferring the answer back to primary memory. Multicore processors such as Intel's quad-core models integrate more than one processor on the same chip, thus potentially improving processing speeds beyond those of single-core chips.

Computers, Processor Speeds, and AISs.   Computer processing speeds are typically measured in megahertz (MHz or millions of computer clock cycles per second) or MIPS (millions of instructions per second). However, the most important thing to know about processor speeds is that they are rarely important in accounting applications. This is because the input-processing-output cycle characteristic of most accounting tasks requires input and output operations as well as processing procedures in order to perform specific tasks. An example is a payroll application, which must input, process, and output the data from each time card. The speeds of the input/output (I/O) operations involved in this application are orders of magnitude slower than the internal speeds of the processor(s), thus explaining why most computers are **I/O bound**, not process bound computers. What this means to accounting applications is that designers must typically look elsewhere for ways to speed computer *throughput*—that is, the time it takes to process business transactions such as payroll time cards—for example, by employing faster data transmission.

Output Devices

Accounting data are meaningless if they cannot be output in forms that are useful and convenient to end users. Printed, **hard-copy output** is one possibility, but video or **soft-copy output** on monitor screens, audio output, and file output to secondary storage devices such as hard disks are other possibilities that we explore here. Outputs are especially important to AISs because their outputs are usually the basis of managerial decision making and therefore the goal of the entire system.

Printers.   The hope for a *paperless office* has yet to be realized, and most AISs still produce many types of printed outputs—for example, transaction summaries, financial statements, exception reports, spreadsheet-based budget reports, word processing documents, and graphs. Many printers now also perform the functions of fax machines, copiers, and scanners, enabling these devices to serve as input devices, transmission devices, and standalone copying devices.

Printers fall into three general categories: (1) dot matrix, (2) ink jet, and (3) laser. **Dot-matrix printers** are impact printers that employ tiny wires in a print head to strike an inked ribbon and create tiny dots on a print page. These printers are popular with small-business users because they are inexpensive and can print multipart (''carbon'') paper—an important feature commonly used in commercial cash registers to print multiple copies of credit card receipts.

Ink-jet printers create characters by distributing tiny bubbles or dots of ink onto pages. The print resolutions of these printers (commonly measured in *dots per inch* or *dpi*) tend to be higher than dot-matrix printers, while printing speeds (commonly measured in *pages per minute* or *ppm*) tend to be lower than laser printers. But most ink-jet printers can print in color—a capability lacking in many dot-matrix and laser printers—enabling them to print graphics and colored pictures as well as text documents.

Laser printers create printed output in much the same way as duplicating machines. The costs of laser printers are higher than dot-matrix or ink-jet printers, but print quality is usually superior and output speeds are much faster. Laser printers are often the printer of choice for commercial users because of this speed advantage. Many laser printers can now also print in color. Additionally, many of the newer printers can be connected wirelessly to local area networks, allowing their owners to print documents from both local and remote locations.

Video Output.   Because hard-copy outputs clutter offices with paper and take time to print, many AISs use fast, *soft-copy* video screen displays instead. Computer monitors are perhaps the most common type of video output, but the airport display screens showing arrivals and departures, stadium scoreboards, highway billboards, and the signage of many private stores are also forms of computerized video outputs.

The monitors of most netbook, laptop, and desktop computers use flat-panel, *liquid crystal display (LCD)* or *plasma screens* to create video outputs in the same way that televisions do. The **picture elements (pixels)** in both types of screens are tiny, discrete dots of color that are arranged in a matrix. Super video graphics adapter (SVGA) refers to a pixel matrix of about 1,200 (in width) by 800 pixels (in height). High definition displays such as found in HDTVs typically use 1,280 pixels by 720 pixels. However, the exact dimensions are not standardized and vary with the manufacturer.

Multimedia.   **Multimedia** combines video, text, graphics, animation, and sound to produce multidimensional output. By definition, multimedia presentations also require advanced processor chips, sound cards, and fast video cards to work properly. One accounting use of multimedia is storing the pictures of employees in personnel files. Another is recording verbal interviews with audit clients. A third is preparing instructional disks for tax accountants. Accounting uses of multimedia are likely to grow as the cost of producing multimedia applications becomes cheaper and new applications are found for this stimulating form of output. Multimedia applications are now also common on the Internet.

SECONDARY STORAGE DEVICES

Primary memory is **volatile memory**, meaning memory that loses its contents when electrical power is lost. In contrast, AISs must store data on permanent media that maintain their accuracy and integrity, yet permit these systems to access and modify information quickly and easily. This is the purpose of **secondary storage** (also called *mass storage* or *auxiliary storage*). Like primary memory, the basic unit of secondary storage is a *byte*, and secondary storage capacities are measured in *kilobytes* (1,024 bytes), *megabytes* (1,024 kilobytes), *gigabytes* (1,024 megabytes), or *terabytes* (1,024 gigabytes).

In this section, we examine several types of secondary storage: magnetic (hard) disks, CD-ROMs, DVD disks, Blu-Ray discs, and USB flash disks. Common to all these media is the concept of a computer record. Like manual systems, computerized AISs must maintain information about payroll activities, warehouse inventories, and accounts receivable data in permanent files. In each such file, a **computer record** is a collection of information about one file entity—for example, one employee on a payroll file (Figure 2-10).

Magnetic (Hard) Disks

A **magnetic (hard) disk** (Figure 2-11) consists of one or more spinning platters, each surface of which has an iron oxide coating that can be magnetized to record information. The smallest hard disks use only a single, double-sided platter, whereas larger-capacity hard disks use multiple platters. The disk system can access (or write) records from any portion of the platter by moving its read/write heads in toward the center of the disk platters or outward to their outer edges. To avoid contamination from dust or smoke particles, most hard disks are permanently sealed in their boxes.

To further guard against disk failures as well as increase storage capacities, manufacturers now also offer **redundant arrays of inexpensive disks (RAIDs)**—see Figure 2-12. In effect, these are stacks of hard disks, each similar to the disk system shown in Figure 2-11. RAIDs are also commonly used for archiving functions—and therefore critical to AISs in the event of an unforeseen disaster.

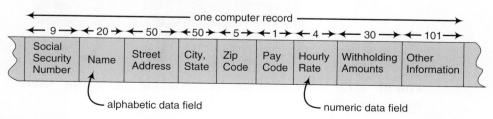

FIGURE 2-10 The format for the computer record of an employee on a payroll file.

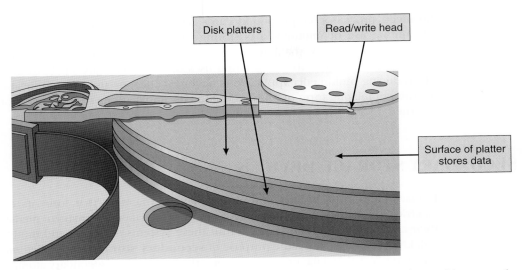

FIGURE 2-11 A schematic of a multiplatter hard disk. The read/write head assembly moves the read/write heads inward (toward the central spindle) or outward as needed, allowing the system to access the data on any portion of any platter.

One advantage of magnetic disk media is their large storage capacities—now commonly measured in *gigabytes* for microcomputers and *terabytes* for commercial AISs. Another advantage is their fast data transfer rates, which now can exceed 100 million characters per second. Finally, perhaps their most important advantage is the ability to directly access any specific record without sequential searching—a capability made possible by the fact that disk records are assigned individual disk addresses (that act like post office box addresses). This accessing capability is useful for online applications such as airline reservations or bank account inquiries, when users require immediate access to specific records, and explains why magnetic disks are also called *direct access storage devices (DASDs)*.

FIGURE 2-12 A redundant array of inexpensive disks (RAID). Source: http://www.orbitmicro.com.

CD-ROMs, DVDs, and Blu-Ray Discs

Three types of secondary storage devices currently popular with microcomputer users are CD-ROMS, DVDs, and Blu-ray discs. All three media store data digitally and read disk information optically.

CD-ROMs. The term **CD-ROM** is an acronym for "compact disk-read only memory." The name is appropriate because CD-ROMs are the same size and appearance as audio CDs. CD-ROMs contain microscopic pits that are etched along a spiraling track in their substrate surfaces. Laser beams interpret the presence or absence of a pit as the "one" or "zero" of binary codes.

CD-ROMs come in three types. The oldest, prerecorded versions are similar to those on which music or software is distributed. Newer "CD-R" media are blank CD-ROMs that can be recorded (only once) with inexpensive CD encoding devices. These are **worm (write-once, read-many) media**. Finally, the newest "CD-RW" media are rewritable, allowing AISs to use them as low-capacity hard disks.

One advantage of CD-ROMs is the fact that they are a removable medium with storage capacities in excess of 650 megabytes per disk—the equivalent of 300,000 pages of text! This makes CD-ROMs ideal for storing large amounts of accounting data or reference materials. Because CD-ROMs are read with laser beams, data transfer rates are also very fast and wear and tear is minimal, even with continuous usage. Finally, the worm characteristic of CD-ROMs and CD-Rs make them useful for archiving files securely (i.e., storing files on a medium that cannot be changed). But CD-ROMs suffer from at least one drawback—the fact that worm media cannot be updated (because new information cannot be written on them once they have been encoded).

DVDs. A digital video disk or **DVD** closely resembles a CD-ROM in that it too is a five inch plastic disk that uses a laser to encode microscopic pits in its substrate surface. But the pits on a DVD are much smaller and encoded much closer together than those on a CD-ROM. Also, a DVD can have as many as two layers on each of its two sides (compared to the single-layered, single-sided CD-ROM). The end result is a medium that can hold as much as 17 gigabytes of data—over 25 times the capacity of a standard CD-ROM disk. The two greatest advantages of DVDs are therefore (1) a storage medium that can archive large amounts of data and (2) a single, light-weight, reliable, easily transportable medium. Newer DVDs are writeable and even rewriteable.

Blu-Ray Discs. **Blu-ray disc** writers encode the same-size disk medium as CDs and DVDs, but the disks can store more information on them—up to 25 gigabytes of data. The disks first became commercially available in 2006, and their name comes from the blue color of the shorter wavelength laser beams used to encode and read the disks. BD-Rs are read-only media that can be written only once, while BD-REs can be erased and re-recorded multiple times.

At present, most Blu-ray discs in the United States and Canada are used for movies and video games, mainly because their standard format enables easy recording in high definition and also inhibits illegal copying better than DVD formats. But accounting applications are growing—especially their use as a backup medium for large databases.

FIGURE 2-13 This USB flash drive from AData corporation plugs into a standard USB connector on a microcomputer. Despite its small size, it stores one gigabyte of data. Source: ADATA Technology (USA) Co., Ltd.

Flash Memory

Flash memory is solid-state memory that comes in various forms. Examples include the flash drives that use the USB ports of microcomputers (Figure 2-13), the PCMCIA memory cards used with laptops, the memory sticks used in digital cameras, the memory cards used with video games, and the RAM of newer microcomputers. The term "solid state" means that there are no moving parts (unlike the hard disk in Figure 2-11)—everything is electronic rather than mechanical.

USB drives can store gigabytes of data in an erasable format. Because data transfer rates are high and the devices themselves compact, they are particularly useful to accountants for creating backups of important files and transporting them off-site. Costs are low—under $20 for smaller capacity USB drives.

Image Processing and Record Management Systems

The life cycle of business documents begins with their creation, continues with their storage and use, and ends with their destruction. Two important tools that can help managers with such tasks are image processing systems and record management systems.

Image Processing. **Image processing** allows users to store graphic images in digital formats on secondary storage media (e.g., the images taken by digital cameras). Thus, image processing systems are able to capture almost any type of document electronically, including photographs, flowcharts, drawings, and pages containing hand-written signatures. Commercial users of image processing include (1) insurance companies that use image processing to store claims forms and accident reports, (2) banks that use image processing to store check images, (3) hospitals that use image processing to store medical diagnostic scans, and (4) the internal revenue service that uses image processing to capture and store tax return data.

Image processing offers several advantages. One is the fast speeds at which images can be captured—a benefit of special importance to high-volume users such as banks. Another advantage is the reduced amount of physical storage space required (compared to paper storage). A third advantage is the convenience of storing images in computer records, which can then be sorted, classified, retrieved, or otherwise manipulated as needs require. A final advantage is the ability to store images in central files, thus making copies available to many users at once, even at the same time. (This last advantage is an important benefit to government agencies and medical offices, where personnel no longer have to ask "who's got the file?" This is the topic of the AIS at Work at the end of Chapter 8.)

Record Management Systems. Simple record management systems enable businesses to systematically capture and store documents. More modern **electronic document and record management systems (EDRMs)** extend such capabilities by helping organizations manage the workflow of electronic documents during document development, provide collaborative tools that enable several users to work on the same document, and allow organizations to create and store multiple versions of documents.

It is easy to understand why business and government organizations use EDRM tools. For legal reasons, for example, businesses may need to retain both current and old policy manuals, contracts, or employment records. Similarly, it is convenient to automate the termination of documents when contracts expire, employees quit, or new policies replace old ones.

DATA COMMUNICATIONS AND NETWORKS

Data communications refers to transmitting data to and from different locations. Many accounting applications use data communications in normal business operations. For example, banking systems enable individual offices to transmit deposit and withdrawal information to centralized computer locations, airline reservation systems enable passengers to book flights from remote locations, and stock brokerage systems enable brokers to transmit buy and sell orders for their customers. Accountants must understand data communication concepts because so many AISs use them and also because so many clients acquire AISs that depend on them. In addition, auditors must sometimes audit the capabilities of a network—for example, evaluate its ability to transmit information accurately and to safeguard the integrity of the data during such transmissions.

Communication Channels and Protocols

A *communication channel* is the physical path that data take in data transmissions. Examples include (1) the twisted-pair wires of telephone lines, (2) coaxial cables, (3) optical fibers, (4) microwaves, and (5) radio (satellite) waves. Local area networking applications (discussed shortly) typically use the first three of these, while Internet applications often use all five of them.

To transmit data over these communications channels, the digital pulses of the sending computer must be translated into the sound patterns, light pulses, or radio waves of the communications channel. Over voice-grade telephone lines, this translation is performed by a **modem** (an acronym for "modulator-demodulator"). The transmission rates are commonly measured in *bits per second (bps)*.

Integrated services digital network (ISDN) is an international data communications standard that transmits data, voice message, or images at a standard rate of 128k bps over the Internet. A similar data transmission service is a **digital subscriber line (DSL)**, which supports data communications rates up to 9 megabits per second. Finally, large data communications installations using fiber optic cables and similar wide-band channels can currently transmit data up to 266 million bps. Future optic fiber transmission rates will transmit data at speeds up to 2.2 billion bps—speeds high enough to transmit motion-picture images in real time.

In all data communications applications, the sending and receiving stations must use a compatible transmission format. A **data communications protocol** refers to the settings that provide this format. Two common protocols are *TCP (transmission control protocol)*, which networks commonly use for e-mails, and *HTTP (hypertext transmission protocol)*, which networks commonly use for Web pages.

Local and Wide Area Networks

One important use of data communications is in **local area networks (LANs)**. Figure 2-14 shows that a LAN consists of microcomputers, printers, terminals, and similar devices that are connected together for communications purposes. Most LANs use **file servers** to store centralized software and data files and also to coordinate data transmissions among the other LAN devices and users. Most local area networks occupy a single building, although LANs covering several buildings are also common. In the past, installers hardwired LAN devices together. Today, many LANs are wireless—a convenience to users, who no longer need to worry about where to place computer equipment in their offices, but an added security hazard to network administrators.

LANs provide several users access to common hardware, software, and computer files, as well as to each other. The following are some advantages of LANs:

1. **Facilitating communications.** The number one reason why businesses install LANs today is to support e-mail.
2. **Sharing computer equipment.** For example, a LAN can provide users access to the same printers or Internet servers.
3. **Sharing computer files.** LANs enable several users to input or output data to or from the same accounting files.
4. **Saving software costs.** It is often cheaper to buy a single software package for a local area network than to buy individual packages for each of several workstations.
5. **Enabling unlike computer equipment to communicate with one another.** Not all computers use the same operating system or application software. LANs enable different computers using different software to communicate with one another.

Wide area networks (WANs) are computer networks spanning regional, national, or even global areas. For example, a WAN enables a national manufacturing company to

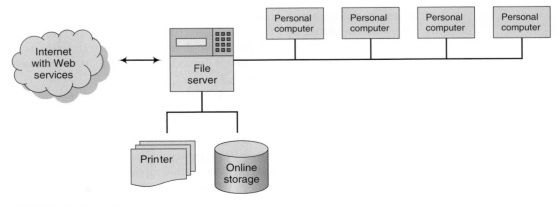

FIGURE 2-14 A local area network with representative devices.

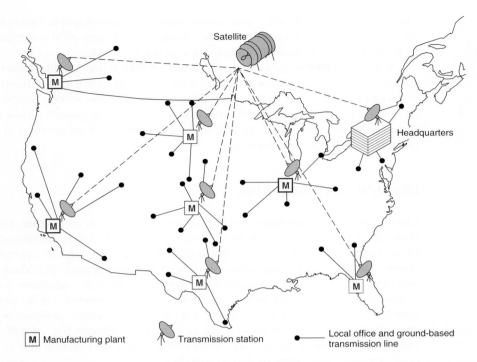

FIGURE 2-15   A wide area network that a large organization might use to connect regional users and computers.

connect several manufacturing, distribution, and regional centers to national headquarters, and therefore to each other, for communications purposes (Figure 2-15). WANs typically use a multitude of communication channels for this purpose, including leased phone lines, microwave transmitters, and perhaps even satellite transmissions. Rather than developing and maintaining their own WANs, many organizations employ public carriers, the Internet, or third-party network vendors to transmit data electronically.

Case-in-Point 2.7   IGT is the world's largest slot machine manufacturer, but nearly half its profits derive from its Megabucks® system—a wide-area network of progressive slot machines located on the floors of participating casinos in various states of the United States. In Nevada, the company links the machines together over private communications lines, enabling the company to both monitor its slot machines and display the growing jackpots in real time as customers play. (You can view the current jackpot in your home state by first selecting http://www.igt.com/play-igt.aspx and then selecting your state in the drop-down box.) To date, Megabucks has created more than 1,000 millionaires and paid more than $3.8 billion in major jackpots. Only one lucky player has won the Megabucks jackpot twice—once for $4.6 million in 1989 and again for $21.1 million in 2005 (when he was 92).[7]

AISs use WANs to gather financial data from remote sites, distribute accounting information to and from headquarters, and support e-mail communications among users. WANs are therefore typically complex, multifaceted systems that serve many users for many purposes. For example, the wide area networks of large *Internet service providers (ISPs)* such as America Online allow subscribers to access centralized databases through local phone lines. Similarly, regional supermarket chains use WANs to gather inventory data,

---

[7] For more information about IGT's Megabucks systems, go to http://www.igt.com.

cash receipts data, and sales information from the many stores in their chains. WANs can also be dedicated to specific tasks. For example, most bank ATM machines are connected to WANs for the purpose of centralizing account information.

Many WANs are organized in a hierarchy, in which the individual microcomputers of a specific branch office are connected to a file server on a local area network, the file servers of several LANs are connected to a regional computer, and several regional computers are connected to a corporate mainframe. This hierarchical approach allows a large company to gather, store, and distribute financial and nonfinancial information at the appropriate geographic level of the company.

Client/Server Computing

Client/server computing is an alternative technology to mainframe and/or hierarchical networks. Depending on the type of client/server system, data processing can be performed by any computer on the network. The software application, such as a spreadsheet program, resides on the client computer—typically, a microcomputer. The database and related software are stored on networked file servers. Although mainframe systems normally centralize everything (including the control of the system), client/server applications distribute data and software among the server and client computers of the system. As a result, client/server computing is a way to achieve the overall objective of an **enterprise network**. In so doing, more computing power resides in user desktops, yet all organizational computers are linked together.

Components of Client/Server Systems. Figure 2-16 shows that a client/server system may be viewed as a set of three interacting components: (1) a presentation component, (2) an application-logic component, and (3) a data-management component. The *presentation component* of a client/server system is the user's view of the system—that is, what the user sees onscreen. This view may resemble the familiar screens of the user's home computer or may differ considerably from them. Simple client/server systems that focus on this presentation task are called *distributed presentation systems*. Most Internet applications illustrate this category.

The *application-logic component* of a client/server system refers to the processing logic of a specific application—for example, the logic involved in preparing payroll checks. Thus, client/server computing differs from simple ''host/terminal computing'' in the user's

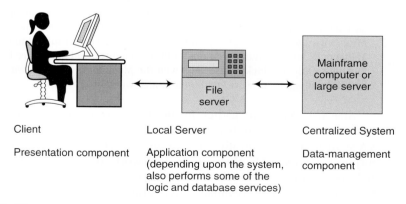

Client   Local Server   Centralized System

Presentation component   Application component (depending upon the system, also performs some of the logic and database services)   Data-management component

FIGURE 2-16 Components of a client/server system.

new ability to (1) query or manipulate the warehoused data on the server, (2) ask what-if questions of the server's data, (3) process a transaction that may affect data stored on both client and server computers, or (4) alter data stored elsewhere on the network. Some systems enable users to write their own data queries (that ask for specific information from the server database) and also to store such queries on local files for later uses.

The processing tasks involved in each application are typically shared unequally between the client computer and the server, with the division of labor depending on the particular application. For example, in a payroll application, the client's contribution may be limited to validating the data entered into the system, while in a word processing application, the client computer might perform nearly all the processing tasks required.

Finally, the *data-management component* of a client/server system refers to its databases and data-storage systems. Some applications rely on a centralized mainframe for this task. More typically, however, multiple copies of the databases reside on large, regional file servers, thereby speeding user access to the data they contain. These systems are also the most complex and therefore pose the greatest challenges to accountants for control and audit tasks.

Advantages and Disadvantages. The advantages of client/server computing include the flexibility of distributing hardware, software, data, and processing capabilities throughout a computer network. A further advantage can be reduced telecommunications costs—an advantage that enabled Avis Rent-a-Car to save a half minute on each of its 23 million annual customer calls, and therefore $1 million. A third advantage is the ability to install *thin-client systems*, which use inexpensive or diskless microcomputers, instead of more expensive models, to save money on system acquisition and maintenance costs. The managers of Mr. Gatti's, a Texas chain of 300 pizza restaurants, for example, estimate that it will save about 45 percent on its maintenance costs using such a system.

One disadvantage of a large client/server system is that it must maintain multiple copies of the same databases, which it then stores on its various regional servers. This makes backup and recovery procedures more difficult because multiple copies of the same file (or several parts of a single file) now exist on several different computers. This multiple-copy problem also causes difficulties in data synchronization (i.e., the need to update all copies of the same file when a change is made to any one of them).

Changing from one version of an application program to another is also more difficult in client/server systems because the system usually requires consistency in these programs across all servers. User access and security are also more difficult because access privileges may vary widely among employees or applications. Finally, the need for user training is often greater in client/server systems because employees must not only know how to use the data and application programs required by their jobs but must also understand the system software that enables them to access these databases and programs from local work stations.

Wireless Data Communications

A recent survey by Intuit revealed that over 70 percent of the small businesses in the United States have mobile employees, and by all accounts, that number is growing. The term **wireless communications**, also called **Wi-Fi** (for "wireless fidelity"), means transmitting voice-grade signals or digital data over wireless communication channels. Wi-Fi creates a wireless Ethernet network using access hubs and receiver cards in PCs, cell phones, and PDAs, thereby turning cell phones and similar wireless devices into cordless, multifunction "Web appliances."

Wireless devices have become important tools for business professionals, helping accountants in particular stay in touch with fellow employees, clients, and corporate networks. Early e-mailing uses of wireless communications have now been joined by job-dependent financial functions such as recording sales orders, entering time and billing information, and—as suggested by the following Case-in-Point—even preparing the payroll.

Case-in-Point 2.8 It wasn't until the middle of his son's little league game that Eddie Elizando realized he hadn't prepared the payroll for the employees at his small CPA company. Mr. Elizando was nowhere near his corporate office, but this wasn't a problem. Using his new iPhone, Mr. Elizando called his payroll service, entered data by clicking through the appropriate payroll program, and accomplished the task remotely between innings of the game. An added bonus: one of Mr. Elizando's employees was his wife, who still wanted to be paid![8]

The two key dimensions of Wi-Fi applications are "connectivity" and "mobility." The connectivity advantage means the ability to connect to the Internet, LAN, or WAN without physical wires or cables. To accomplish this, Wi-Fi devices use **wireless application protocol (WAP)**, a set of communication standards and *wireless markup language* (a subset of XML optimized for the small display screens typical of wireless, Internet-enabled appliances). Two important types of wireless communications are RFID applications and NFC communications.

RFID. **Radio frequency identification (RFID)** enables businesses to identify pallets and even individual items without unpacking them from shipping crates. *Passive RFID tags* have no power source (and therefore cannot wear out) but can nonetheless "answer" inquiries from energized sources. *Active RFID tags* are actually chips with antennas, have their own power source, enjoy ranges of more than 100 meters, and are generally more reliable than passive tags.

Perhaps the most noticeable use of RFID tags is as user identifiers in transportation systems (Figure 2-17). For example, the subway systems of New York City, Moscow, and Hong Kong use them, as do some of the toll roads and parking lots in the states of New York, New Jersey, Pennsylvania, Massachusetts, Georgia, Florida, and Illinois. Similar systems may be found in Paris, the Philippines, Israel, Australia, Chile, and Portugal. To toll-road travelers, RFID systems represent a convenient way of paying user fees and

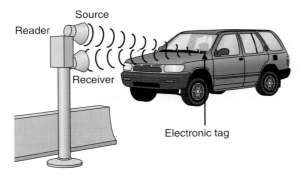

FIGURE 2-17 Reading an RFID tag at a toll booth.

---

[8] Defelice, A. 2007. Working in a wireless world. *Accounting Technology* 23(10): 30–34.

reducing wait times in tollbooth lines. To their operators, these systems are a convenient way of gathering accounting data and updating customer accounts.

> **Case-in-Point 2.9** Recent RFID applications include employee ID badges, library books, credit cards, and even tire-tread sensors. Similarly, many retailers now require their suppliers to include tags that identify merchandise. Walmart and Target are two of a growing list of large retailers that now require their major suppliers to include RFID tags in the cases and pallets sent to their various distribution centers. The tags are superior to bar codes, which require a line of sight for reading, must appear on the outside of cartons, and can be lost or defaced. Bank of America and Wells Fargo are two of the largest RFID users, with each tagging over 100,000 corporate assets. If your car has a keyless ignition system, you're also using RFID technology.[9]

NFC. **Near field communication (NFC)** enables mobile devices such as cell phones, PDAs, and laptop computers to communicate with similar devices containing NFC chips (Figure 2-18). With NFC devices, for example, you can make travel reservations on your PC, download airline tickets to your mobile phone or PDA, and check in at a departure gate kiosk with a swipe of your mobile device—all with no paper or printing.

In effect, NFC represents RFID communications for the masses. But the operating range of NFC devices is limited to 20 centimeters or about 8 inches—a limitation that helps avoid unintentional uses. The transit systems in China, Singapore, and Japan now use NFC systems, as do Visa International's credit card system and chip-enabled posters of the Atlanta Hawk's basketball team.

NFC technology is a joint product development of Sony, Philips, and Nokia. Three possible communication modes are (1) *active* (bidirectional), (2) *passive* (one way), and (3) *transponder* (batteryless and therefore powered only by an external communication source). Current NFC-standardized communication speeds are between 106 k and 424 kbps—considerably less than the 1 to 7 Mbps speeds of Bluetooth or Wi-Fi data transmissions. But passive NFC chips cost as little as 20 cents and are currently considerably cheaper than these alternate communication devices.

Cloud Computing

As noted in Chapter 1, the term *cloud computing* refers to a range of computing services on the Internet—for example, access to computer software programs, backup and recovery file services, and even Web page development and hosting. The term gets its name from the

FIGURE 2-18 Near field communication devices.

---

[9] Desjardins, D. 2005. Implementation easier as No. 2. *DSN Retailing Today* 44(7): 34.

common use of a cloud symbol to represent the Internet itself—refer back to Figure 2-14. Most commercial applications of cloud computing are types of outsourcing—that is, situations in which one organization hires another to perform a vital service. An accounting application is the use of tax preparation software, which the customer accesses over the Internet from the vendor for a fee—an example of "**software as a service**" **(SAAS)**. Many cloud service vendors have familiar names, including Amazon, Google, Yahoo, IBM, Intel, Sun Microsystems, and Microsoft. The first cloud computing conference took place in May 2008 and attracted over 1,000 attendees. Chapters 1 and 14 discuss clouding computing in more detail.

COMPUTER SOFTWARE

As noted in the introduction to this chapter, it is impossible to discuss information technology without also recognizing the importance of **computer software**. Computer hardware serves as a base, or platform, upon which two types of computer software typically reside: (1) operating systems and (2) application software. This chapter concludes by briefly discussing each of these types of software.

It is difficult to overstate the importance of software to AISs. Both in industry and in private homes, computer software performs tasks such as computing spreadsheets, paying corporate bills, routing parcels on conveyor belts, answering telephones, or reserving airline seats. Automated AISs depend on software to function properly. But this dependency also presents important challenges to accountants. For example, every system that influences cash accounts or affects other corporate resources must also contain automated controls to ensure the reliability, completeness, and authenticity of computer inputs, processing, and outputs. Similarly, all AIS software must initially be designed, acquired, and installed by someone. These facts help explain why accountants are often such an integral part of the teams that shop for, test, and audit such systems.

Operating Systems

An **operating system (OS)** is a set of software programs that helps a computer, file server, or network run itself and also the application programs designed for it. Examples of operating systems for microcomputers include MacOS, Windows 7, and Linux. Operating systems for larger computers include UNIX, Windows.Net server, and OS2. Some of these operating systems are designed as single-user operating systems (e.g., Windows 7), while others are designed as multiuser operating systems for LANs (e.g., Microsoft Windows Server and Novell Netware). Operating systems for very small systems such as PDAs and cell phones include Android, Windows Mobile, Blackberry, Bluetooth, Palm OS, and Symbian OS. Most of these operating systems combine many convenient software tools in one package and use **graphical user interfaces (GUIs)** with menus, icons, and other graphics elements (instead of instruction commands) to identify system components and launch processing applications (apps).

On computers of any size, the operating system is typically the first piece of software loaded (booted) into primary memory when the computer powers up. System tasks for single-user OSs include testing critical components on boot-up, allocating primary memory among competing applications (i.e., managing the multitasking demands of several Windows sessions), managing system files (such as directory files), maintaining system security, and (in larger computers) gathering system performance statistics. The system tasks for multiuser OSs are even more complicated than for single-user systems because more users are involved and more coordination of system resources is required. These multiuser OSs maintain job queues of programs awaiting execution, create and check password files, allocate primary memory to several online users, apportion computer time in time-sharing (**multiprocessing**) environments, and accumulate charges for resource usage.

Application (end-user) programs are designed to work with ("run under") a particular operating system. An operating system helps run application programs by coordinating those programs' input and output tasks, by managing the pieces of an application program that is too large to fit entirely in RAM, and by monitoring their execution.

The **utility programs** that come with operating systems help users perform tasks such as copying files, converting files from one format to another, compressing files, performing system diagnostics, and building disk directories. Another task is to manage **virtual storage**—that is, disk memory that a computer system uses to augment its limited primary memory. Finally, today's operating systems also run **antivirus software**. As explained more fully in Chapter 11, a **virus** is a destructive program that, when active, damages or destroys computer files or programs. Today's operating systems include antivirus software routines that guard against the virus programs a user might accidentally introduce into his or her computer system from external sources. However, because new viruses continue to appear, users should update this software at least monthly.

Application Software

The term **application software** refers to computer programs that help end users such as accountants perform the tasks specific to their jobs or relevant to their personal needs. One category of application software is the **personal productivity software** familiar to most accountants—for example, word processing software (for creating documents and reports), spreadsheet software (for creating worksheets of rows and columns and also for graphing the data), database software (for creating files and databases of personal information), and personal finance software (for paying bills, creating personal budgets, and maintaining investment portfolio data).

Another category of application software is the personal productivity software designed for commercial uses. Examples include *project management software* (for coordinating and tracking the events, resources, and costs of large projects such as construction projects or office moves), *computer-aided design (CAD) software* (for designing consumer products, fashion clothing, automobiles, or machinery), and *presentation graphics software* (for creating slides and other presentations).

A third category of application software is the accounting software that performs familiar tasks such as preparing payrolls, maintaining accounts receivable files, executing accounts payable tasks, controlling inventory, and producing financial statements. Often, developers integrate these tasks in complete accounting packages. Because of the particular relevance of such software to AISs, Chapter 9 discusses such packages in greater detail.

Yet a fourth type of application software is *communications software* that allows separate computers to transmit data to one another. Microcomputer examples include communications packages (for simple data transmissions between computers), Web browsers (for accessing and displaying graphics information on the Internet), backend software (that enables Web servers to communicate with large, commercial databases of customer and product information), and e-mail software (for creating, transmitting, reading, and deleting e-mail messages).

Finally, a fifth type of application software is the relatively new **enterprise resource management (ERP) software** that enables businesses and government agencies to transmit and manipulate financial data on an organization-wide basis. An example is SAP. These systems are particularly important to electronic commerce (e-commerce) applications—for example, because a simple sale over the Internet simultaneously affects accounts receivable, inventory, and marketing subsystems.

Programming Languages

To develop application software, developers must write detailed instructions in **programming languages** that computers can understand and execute. FORTRAN, COBOL, and RPG are examples of older programming languages that developers used to create minicomputer and mainframe AISs (i.e., the older but still viable legacy systems). Newer computer languages include C++ (favored for its ability to manipulate data at the bit level), Visual Basic (favored for creating Windows-like user interfaces), HTML (an editing language favored for creating Web pages), and Java (favored for its ability to run on many different types of computers).

Most of the newer programming languages are **object-oriented programming languages**, meaning that they encourage programmers to develop code in reusable modules called *objects*, which are easier to develop, debug, and modify. Both Visual Basic and C++ are **event-driven programming languages**—that is, programming languages where code responds to events such as a user clicking on a menu item with a mouse.

Figure 2-19 illustrates how developers create application programs using these programming languages. The process begins when computer programmers write instructions in a *source* programming language such as Visual Basic. In a second step, the developers translate this *source code* into the machine language (*object code*) that a computer understands. Yet another computer program called a **compiler** performs this translation in a second step called a *compilation.* The output from the compilation is the object code, which a computer can then load and execute. When end users buy application software packages, they buy compiled computer programs in machine language that are ready to execute on their specific computers.

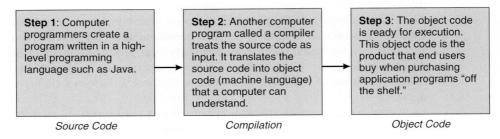

FIGURE 2-19 How computer programmers create application software.

AIS AT WORK
Using iPads at the Mercedes-Benz Car Dealership[10]

Customers at a Mercedes-Benz dealership are now likely to talk to salespeople armed with iPads when they want to finance or lease their new cars or when they bring their older cars back at lease end. Why an iPad? Simple: The iPads let dealership employees stay close to the customer on the sales floor when discussing promotional incentives, financing terms, or leasing arrangements.

Once a pilot program but now corporate policy, iPad applications utilize Apple's Safari Web browser and customized MB Financial Advantage programs to allow employees to complete loan applications or the paperwork for end-of-lease turn-ins on the spot—not in some back office. MB considers the iPad a better option than a smart phone application because the system displays more information on a single screen and both a salesperson and a customer can see the screen at the same time. This makes lease-end check-ins as simple as returning a rental car, for example, and the system can e-mail the customer a copy of the completed form.

Because customers buying cars like to close deals on the spot, perhaps the biggest problem Mercedes had to solve was obtaining customer signatures on completed electronic loan forms. As suggested by the accompanying picture, MB solved this problem in a particularly innovative way—by allowing customers to sign with their finger!

SUMMARY

✓ It is useful to view an AIS as a collection of hardware, software, data, people, and procedures that work together to accomplish processing tasks.

✓ Information technology will become even more important to accountants as AISs continue to incorporate technological advances and also as this technology becomes more important to them when performing their daily professional tasks.

---

[10] Murphy, C. 2010. 7 Tips for using the iPad in business. *InformationWeek* (November 1): 26.

✓ To achieve their objectives, computerized AISs must input, process, store, and output information and, often, utilize data communications.

✓ The starting point for most AIS data processing is either an electronic or a manual source document. Electronic data eliminate many errors that are introduced by human input. POS devices, MICR readers, OCR readers, and magnetic strip readers enable AISs to capture data that are already in machine-readable formats.

✓ Biometric scanners help AISs limit access to legitimate users. Two of the most reliable types of scanners read fingerprints or irises.

✓ The central processing unit (CPU) performs the data-manipulating tasks of the computer system. In order of increasing power, these units are micro- or personal computers, minicomputers, mainframe computers, and supercomputers. Newer systems include smart phones and computer tablets.

✓ All CPUs have primary memories and microprocessors. Most AISs are I/O bound, not process bound.

✓ Two major output devices are printers and video monitors. Three important types of printers are dot-matrix printers, ink-jet printers, and laser printers. Laser printers are often the most preferred because they are the fastest, have the highest print resolutions, and can now also print in color.

✓ Secondary storage devices enable AISs to store and archive data on permanent media. Magnetic disks, CD-ROMs, DVDs, and flash memories are the most common secondary storage devices.

✓ Image processing allows users to capture and store visual graphs, charts, and pictures in digital formats on such media.

✓ Data communications enable AISs to transmit data over local and wide area networks. Many AISs now use LANs or WANs for e-mail, sharing computer resources, saving software costs, gathering input data, or distributing outputs. Wi-Fi technology such as RFID and NFC applications significantly increases our ability to access information accurately as well as communicate efficiently with others.

✓ Cloud computing refers to the use of service providers over the Internet. Applications include access to computer software programs, backup and recovery file services, and Web page development and hosting.

✓ The software of an AIS performs the specific data processing tasks required. Operating systems enable computers to run themselves and also to execute the application programs designed for them.

✓ Application software enables end users to perform work-related tasks. Categories of such software include personal productivity software, integrated accounting packages, and communication packages. Programming languages enable IT professionals to translate processing logic into instructions that computers can execute.

KEY TERMS YOU SHOULD KNOW

antivirus software

application software

bar code reader

biometric scanner

Blu-ray disc

CD-ROM

central processing unit (CPU)

client/server computing

compiler

computer record

computer software

computer tablet

data communications

data communications protocol

data transcription

digital subscriber line (DSL)

dot-matrix printer

DVD

electronic document and record management
  systems (EDRMs)

enterprise network
enterprise resource management (ERP)
   software
event-driven programming languages
file servers
flash memory
graphical user interfaces (GUIs)
hard-copy output
I/O bound
image processing
ink-jet printers
input-processing-output cycle
integrated services digital network (ISDN)
laser printers
legacy systems
local area networks (LANs)
magnetic (hard) disk
magnetic ink character recognition (MICR)
mainframe computers
mark-sense media
microprocessor
minicomputers
modem (modulator-demodulator)
multimedia
multiprocessing
near field communication (NFC)
object-oriented programming languages

operating system (OS)
optical character recognition (OCR)
peripheral equipment
personal data assistant (PDA) devices
personal productivity software
picture elements (pixels)
point-of-sale (POS) devices
primary memory
programming languages
radio frequency identification (RFID)
redundant arrays of inexpensive disks (RAIDs)
secondary storage
soft-copy output
software as a service (SAAS)
source document
supercomputers
turnaround documents
utility programs
virtual storage
virus
volatile memory
Wi-Fi
wide area networks (WANs)
wireless application protocol (WAP)
wireless communications
worm (write-once, read-many) media

DISCUSSION QUESTIONS

2-1. Why is it important to view an AIS as a combination of hardware, software, people, data, and procedures?

2-2. Why is information technology important to accountants?

2-3. Why do most AISs try to avoid data transcription?

2-4. Name several types of computer input devices and explain in general terms how each one functions.

2-5. How do you feel about red-light cameras? Should cities be allowed to use them? Why or why not?

2-6. Identify the three sections of a CPU, and describe the functions of each component. How are microprocessor speeds measured? Why are such speeds rarely important to AISs?

2-7. Identify several types of printers. What are the advantages and disadvantages of each type?

2-8. What is the function of secondary storage? Describe three types of secondary storage media, and describe the advantages and disadvantages of each type.

2-9. What is image processing? How is image processing used in AISs?

2-10. What are data communication protocols? Why are they important?

2-11. What are local area networks? What advantages do LANs offer accounting applications?

2-12. What is client/server computing? How does it differ from host/mainframe computing? What are some of the advantages and disadvantages of client/server systems?

2-13. What are the names of some current cloud computing vendors other than those discussed in the text? Do you think that all firms should use cloud vendors, or are there some reasons why they should be avoided?

2-14. What are windowing operating systems, multitasking operating systems, and graphical user interfaces? Why are they useful to AISs?

2-15. Name some general classes of application software. What tasks do each of your software classes perform?

2-16. What are computer programming languages? Name some specific languages and describe briefly an advantage of each.

PROBLEMS

2-17. Which of the following are input equipment, output equipment, CPU components, secondary storage devices, or data communications related?

a. ALU	**f.** POS device	**j.** OCR reader
b. CD-ROM	**g.** MICR reader	**k.** magnetic (hard) disk
c. keyboard	**h.** laser printer	**l.** ATM
d. modem	**i.** flash memory	**m.** primary memory
e. dot-matrix printer		

2-18. All of the following are acronyms discussed in this chapter. What words were used to form each one and what does each term mean?

a. POS	**i.** OS	**p.** WAN
b. CPU	**j.** MHz	**q.** RFID
c. OCR	**k.** pixel	**r.** WAP
d. MICR	**l.** CD-ROM	**s.** Wi-Fi
e. ATM	**m.** worm	**t.** ppm
f. RAM	**n.** modem	**u.** dpi
g. ALU	**o.** LAN	**v.** NFC
h. MIPS		

2-19. Which of the following holds the most data?

a. One DVD disk

b. One hard disk (capacity: 160 gigabytes)

c. Ten CD-ROMs

2-20. An advertisement for a desktop microcomputer says that it includes a 500-gigabyte hard drive. Exactly how many bytes is this? (Hint: see the discussions on secondary storage.)

2-21. Brian Fry Products manufactures a variety of machine tools and parts used primarily in industrial tasks. To control production, the company requires the information listed below. Design an efficient record format for Brian Fry Products.

a. Order number (4 digits)

b. Part number to be manufactured (5 digits)

c. Part description (10 characters)

d. Manufacturing department (3 digits)

e. Number of pieces started (always less than 10,000)

f. Number of pieces finished

g. Machine number (2 digits)

h. Date work started

i. Hour work started (use 24-hour system)

j. Date work completed

k. Hour work completed

l. Work standard per hour (3 digits)

m. Worker number (5 digits)

n. Foreman number (5 digits)

2-22. Go to the AICPA Web site at http://www.aicpa.org. What are the top 10 information technologies for the current year? How do these items compare with the list in Figure 2-1? Is it common for new items to appear, or do you think this list is "stable" from year to year?

2-23. Your state has recently decided to install an RFID system for its toll roads. The current plan is to sell nonrefundable transponders for $20 and allow users to deposit up to $1,000 in their accounts. To assist the IT personnel, the system's planners want to develop a list of possible accounting transactions and system responses. Using your skills from earlier accounting classes, what debit and credit entries would you make for each of the following activities? (Feel free to develop your own accounts for this problem.)

a. A user buys a new transponder for $20.

b. A user adds $100 to his account.

c. A user discovers that a data entry clerk charges his credit card $1,000 instead of $100 when adding $100 to his account.

d. An individual leaves the state, turns in his transponder, and wants a cash refund for the $25.75 remaining in his account.

e. A good Samaritan turns in a transponder that he finds on the side of the road. There is a $10 reward for this act, taken from the owner's account.

2-24. Select a type of computer hardware that interests you and write a one-page report on three possible choices of it. Examples include monitors, USB drives, external hard drives, or even new laptops. Your report should include a table similar to the one shown here that includes: (1) embedded pictures of your choices, (2) major specifications (e.g., storage capacities, pixel sizes, and data transfer rates), (3) the suggested retail price of each item, (4) the likely "street price" of the item, and (5) the name of the vendor that sells the item at the street price.

The major deliverable is a one-page report that includes (1) the table identified above, (2) an explanation of why you chose to examine the hardware you did, and (3) an indication of which particular item you would buy of your three choices.

Mickey Mouse USB	Octopus USB	Jack knife USB
spec	spec	spec
spec	spec	spec

Source: ADATA Technology (USA) Co., Ltd.

CASE STUDIES

Pucinelli Supermarkets (Validating Input Data)

Pucinneli Supermarkets is similar to most other grocery store chains that use the 12-digit UPC code on packages to check out customers. For a variety of reasons, it is important that the computer systems using these codes validate them for accuracy and completeness. To perform this task, UPCs automatically include a "check digit" that can also be computed from the other digits in the code. Using the bar code shown in Figure 2-3 as an example, the system works as follows:

1. The UPC includes all numbers in the bar code, and therefore is 064200115896 for the example here. The length is 12 digits as required.
2. The check digit is the last digit in the code—a "6" for this example.
3. Starting on the left, add the digits up to, but not including, the check digit in the odd-numbered positions (i.e., the numbers in the first, third, fifth, etc., position) together. Multiply this sum by three.
4. Add the digits up to, but not including, the check digit in the even-numbered positions (i.e., the second, fourth, sixth numbers, etc.).
5. Add the values found in steps 3 and 4.
6. Examine the last digit of the sum. If it is 0, the computed check digit is also 0. If the last digit of the result is not zero, subtract this digit from 10. The answer is the computed check digit and must equal the last number in the UPC code.

UPC code:	064200115896
Length test:	**Ok**
Check digit is:	**6**
Sum of odd digits	19
Sum of even digits	17
Odd digits ×3	57
Sum	74
Last digit	4
Computed check digit	6
Conclusion	Valid number

To illustrate, suppose the UPC barcode is 064200115896 as shown. The steps for this example are

1. The length is 12 as required.
2. The last value is "6" so this is the check digit.
3. Add the odd-position digits: $0 + 4 + 0 + 1 + 5 + 9 = 19$. Multiply this sum by 3: $19 \times 3 = 57$.
4. Add the even-position digits: $6 + 2 + 0 + 1 + 8 = 17$.
5. We add these two values together. The sum is $57 + 17 = 74$.
6. The last digit in this sum is "4," the check digit is not 0, and we therefore subtract 4 from 10 to get "6." The computed value of "6" found in step 5 matches the check digit "6" in step 2, and we therefore conclude that this UPC code is valid.

Requirements

Develop a spreadsheet to perform the tests described here and test your model with the following UPC codes. (1) 639277240453, (2) 040000234548, (3) 034000087884, (4) 048109352495, and (5) one UPC value of your own choosing (drawn from something you own or see). For each number, indicate whether the UPC number is valid or invalid. Include a print out of all your work, plus a copy of the formulas for at least one of your tests. Hints: (1) You should enter your initial UPC code as "text"—not a number. (2) You can use Excel's LEN function to perform the desired length test and Excel's IF function to test whether the entered value passes it. (3) You should use Excel's MID function to parse each digit for these computations. (4) You can use Excel's IF test again to reach the conclusion (e.g., "valid number").

Savage Motors (Software Training)

Savage Motors sells and leases commercial automobiles, vans, and trucks to customers in southern California. Most of the company's administrative staff work in the main office. The company has been in business for 35 years, but only in the last 10 years has the company begun to recognize the benefits of computer training for its employees.

The company president, Arline Savage, is thinking about hiring a training company to give on-site classes. To pursue this option, the company would set up a temporary "computer laboratory" in one of the meeting rooms, and the trainers would spend all day teaching one or more particular types of software. You have been hired as a consultant to recommend what type of training would best meet the firm's needs.

You begin your task by surveying the three primary corporate departments: sales, operations, and accounting. You find that most employees use their personal computers for only five types of software: (1) word processing, (2) spreadsheets, (3) database, (4) presentations, and (5) accounting. The accompanying table shows your estimates of the total number of hours per week used by each department on each type of software.

Department (number of employees)	Word Processing	Spreadsheet	Database	Presentation	Accounting
Sales (112)	1,150	750	900	500	700
Operations (82)	320	2,450	650	100	500
Accounting (55)	750	3,600	820	250	2,500

Requirements

1. Create a spreadsheet illustrating each department's average use of each application per employee, rounding all averages to one decimal point. For example, the average hours of word processing for the sales department is $1,150/112 = 10.3$ hours.

2. Suppose there were only enough training funds for each department to train employees on only one type of application. What training would you recommend for each department?

3. What is the average number of hours of use of each application for all the employees in the company? What training would you recommend if funds were limited to only training one type of application for the entire company?

4. Using spreadsheet tools, create graphs that illustrate your findings in parts 1 and 2. Do you think that your graphs or your numbers better "tell your story"?

5. What alternatives are there to on-site training? Suggest at least two alternatives and discuss which of your three possibilities you prefer.

Morrigan Department Stores (The Ethics of Forced Software Upgrading)

Morrigan Department Stores is a chain of department stores in Australia, New Zealand, Canada, and the United States that sells clothing, shoes, and similar consumer items in a retail setting. The top managers and their staff members meet once a year at the national meeting. This year's meeting took place in Hawaii—a geographical midpoint for them—and several accounting managers participated in a round-table discussion that went as follows:

Roberta Gardner (United States): One of our biggest problems in our Auckland office is the high cost and seemingly constant need to upgrade our hardware and software. Every time our government changes the tax laws, of course, we must acquire software that reflects those changes. But why do we need new hardware too? All this discussion of "64-bit machines" is a mystery to me, but the IT department says the hardware in the old machines quickly become outdated.

Donalda Shadbolt (New Zealand): I'll say! If you ask me, all these upgrades are costly, time consuming, and even counter-productive. I do a lot of work on spreadsheets, for example, and constantly ask myself: "Why do I have to spend hours relearning how to format a simple column of numbers in the newest version of Excel?" It takes time and effort, it's frustrating, and in the end, I've spent hours relearning skills that I already know how to do in the older version.

Linda Vivianne (Canada): I know what you mean, but the newer hardware is faster, cheaper, and more capable than the old machines. Hard drives have moving parts in them, for example, and they eventually wear out. The newer software runs under the newer operating systems, which are also more competent and have more built-in security such as antivirus software.

Ed Ghymn (Australia): I agree with you, Linda, but I think a lot of these new capabilities are more hype than real. If the security software was competent, we wouldn't need all those patches and upgrades in the first place. And why must we upgrade so often, just to get newer capabilities that most of us don't even need?

Alex McLeod (Australia): I don't think anyone can stop the march of progress. I think the real problem is not the upgrades to new software, but the fact that our company expects us to learn it without proper training. Personally, I don't buy my boss's argument that "you're a professional and should learn it on your own."

Linda Vivianne (Canada): I'm also beginning to realize just what advantages there are in outsourcing some of our accounting applications to cloud service providers. That won't solve all our problems because we all still need word processing and spreadsheet capabilities, but at least we can let cloud providers deal with the software upgrades for our accounting software. Given how dispersed we are, that might also make it easier for us to consolidate our financial statements at year's end too.

Requirements

1. Do you think that Roberta Gardner's description of "64-bit machines" is accurate? Why or why not? Explain your reasons in detail, drawing upon additional Internet discussions to help you answer this question.

2. Summarize some of the arguments *against* upgrading hardware and software at the Morrigan Department Stores. It is ok to mention additional, reasonable arguments that are not included in the case.

3. Summarize the arguments *for* upgrading hardware and software at the Morrigan Department Stores. Again, it is ok to mention additional, reasonable arguments that are not included in the case.

4. Do you agree with Ed Ghymn's argument that many upgrades are "more hype than real"? Why or why not?

5. Many software vendors such as Microsoft, Adobe, and Apple ship software packages with both known and unknown defects in them. Do you feel that it is ethical for them to do so? Why or why not?

6. Do you agree or disagree with the argument made in this case that many hardware and/or software upgrades are unnecessary? Why or why not?

7. Do you agree with Alex McLeod's statement that a company should formally train its employees every time it upgrades its software? If not, do you agree with his boss that professionals should learn to use at least some software upgrades on their own? Explain your answer in detail.

8. Do you think it was necessary for the participants to physically meet at one location? Couldn't they simply hold a virtual meeting over the Internet? Explain your answer in detail.

Chapter 3

Data Modeling

INTRODUCTION

Civilizations have collected and organized accounting data for at least 6,000 years. The ancient Babylonians, for example, stored clay tablets in their temples that recorded information such as inventory, payroll records, and real estate transactions. Modern AISs use computers rather than clay tablets, but many of the same basic requirements remain—the systematic recording of data, convenient and useful organization of data, ability to create useful reports from data, and easy access to required information. This chapter examines how to *design* a database that is efficient and effective, while the next two chapters examine how to *build* and *use* a database. We begin by describing some database concepts and then discuss database design and data modeling techniques in more depth.

AN OVERVIEW OF DATABASES

Many requirements from the ancient Babylonian days remain today. Even the most basic AIS needs to systematically record accounting data and organize accounting records in logical ways. Most often, these objectives are achieved by storing accounting data in a database. For this reason, it is essential for accountants to understand the basic principles of database-driven systems.

What Is a Database?

A **database** is a large collection of organized data that can be accessed by multiple users and used by many different computer applications. In many large firms, massive databases store all of the data used by almost every function in the organization. Data in databases are manipulated by specialized software packages called **database management systems (DBMSs)**. Databases are used to store the data that comprise nearly all accounting systems, such as inventory systems, general ledger systems, and production scheduling systems. Most accounting systems involve complex combinations of data stored in databases, processing software, and hardware that interact with one another to support specific storage and retrieval tasks. Most accounting databases are **relational databases**, which are groups of related, two-dimensional tables.

Technically, not every collection of data is a database. For example, time-card data from a weekly payroll system or budget data might be stored in single computer files, such as Excel files, that are generally too simplistic to be called databases. Most commercial databases are very large and complex collections of proprietary data that developers carefully design and protect and that form the core of accounting information systems.

Significance of Databases

It is difficult to overstate the importance of computerized databases to AISs. Nearly every accounting system that influences financial reports involves the extensive use of databases. For example, accounts receivable applications require vast amounts of information about customers' accounts, accounts payable applications require information about suppliers, and payroll applications require information about employees. In many publicly traded firms, the databases needed to support accounting systems cost hundreds of millions of dollars to design and maintain, and firms rely on these databases to make key business decisions and conduct their day-to-day operations. The extensive use of databases in accounting systems makes it important to understand issues that databases can raise for companies and accounting professionals. These issues include:

- *Critical information.* The information stored in an organization's databases is sometimes its most important and valuable asset. Equifax, for example, is one of the nation's largest credit bureaus, maintaining credit information about millions of Americans. Its credit files *are* its business.

- *Volume.* Many firms' databases are truly enormous. For example, Sprint keeps records on over 50 million customers and inserts about 70,000 records to its database every second. Amazon.com has a database with more than 40 terabytes of data, and YouTube visitors watch more than 100 million video clips from its database every day. Designing, using, and maintaining databases of such great size requires substantial resources.

- *Distribution.* The databases of some organizations are centralized (i.e., data is stored in a single location). Many other databases, however, are distributed (i.e., duplicated in local or regional computers as processing needs dictate). Distributing data can make it difficult to (1) ensure data accuracy, consistency, completeness, and (2) secure information from unauthorized access.

- *Privacy.* Databases often contain sensitive information—for example, employee pay rates or customer credit card numbers. This information must be protected from those unauthorized to access it. The internal control procedures that protect databases from unwarranted access are often considered the most critical controls in an organization.

  > *Case-in-Point 3.1* Heartland Payment Systems processes credit card transactions for many different credit and debit card companies. In 2009, hackers illegally accessed hundreds of millions of Heartland Payment Systems' credit card transactions in what has been called the largest breach of credit card data in history. Heartland was required to pay substantial fines and settlement fees.[1]

- *Irreplaceable data.* The information contained in most accounting databases is unique to the organization that created it and is typically priceless. Many organizations would fail shortly after losing the information contained in their accounting databases. For this reason, the security of databases is critical to the organization.

- *Need for accuracy.* The data stored in databases must be complete, comprehensive, and accurate. The consequences of inaccurate data can be substantial. It is easy to imagine severe consequences of very small data errors. Consider a physician removing an incorrect limb during surgery because of one attribute in a database table (e.g., left versus right limb).

---

[1] http://abcnews.go.com/Technology/Media/10-top-data-breaches-decade/story?id=10905634

Case-in-Point 3.2   Studies of large medical databases indicate that as many as 60 percent of patient records in these databases contain errors, which makes it nearly impossible to accurately identify trends in medical care or the effectiveness of various treatment options.[2]

- *Internet uses.* As you might imagine, databases are critical components of both internal and external corporate Web systems. Databases store information related to product information for online catalog sales, e-mails, product registration data, employment opportunities, stock prices, and so on. Internet applications often store customer-entered data such as online product orders, credit card numbers, subscription information, airline reservations, and university-student registration data.

Storing Data in Databases

To be useful, the data in an organization's databases must be stored efficiently and organized systematically. In order to understand how databases store information, it is important to first understand three database concepts: (1) the data hierarchy, (2) record structures, and (3) database keys.

The Data Hierarchy.   Storing accounting data in databases involves organizing the data into a logical structure. In ascending order, this **data hierarchy** is

$$\text{data field} \rightarrow \text{record} \rightarrow \text{file} \rightarrow \text{database}$$

The first level in the data hierarchy is a **data field**, which is information that describes a person, event, or thing in the database. In a payroll file, for example, data fields would include employee names, employee identification numbers, and pay rates for the employees. Other names for a data field are *attribute, column,* or simply, *field.*

At the second level, data fields combine to form a complete record. A database **record** (also called a *tuple*) stores all of the information about one entity (i.e., person, event, or thing). For example, all of the information about one inventory part in an inventory file, one employee in a payroll file, or one customer in a customer file. At this point, it may be helpful to liken the structure of a database to the data in a spreadsheet. Imagine that customer data is stored in a spreadsheet such that each row represents a customer and each column represents the various pieces of information that are stored for each customer. Each column in this spreadsheet defines an individual data field, and each row defines a separate record.

At the third level of the data hierarchy, a set of common records forms a file, or using database and Microsoft Access terminology, a *table.* Thus, a file or table contains a set of related records—for example, a set of customer records or inventory records. **Master files** typically store permanent information—for example, part numbers, part descriptions, and location codes for the individual records in an inventory parts master file. **Transaction files** typically store transient information—for example, inventory disbursements and replenishments for a specific period.

Finally, at the highest level, several tables create a complete database (i.e., a collection of tables that contain all of the information needed for an accounting application). In an inventory application, for example, the database might contain a part-number master table, a supplier table, a price table, an order transaction table, and so forth, as well as several other tables that would help end users organize, access, or process inventory information efficiently.

---

[2] Gallivan, S., and C. Pagel. 2008. Modelling of errors in databases. *Health Care Management Science* 11(1): 35–40.

Social Security number	Last name	First name	Dept. code	Pay rate	Date of hire	Over-time OK?	Other info.
575-64-5589	Smythe	Teri	A	12.85	10-15-2001	yes	....

FIGURE 3-1 Examples of data fields in an employee record.

Record Structures. The specific data fields in each record of a database table are part of what is called the **record structure**. In many accounting applications, this structure is fixed, meaning that each record contains the same number, same type, and same-size data fields as every other record in the file. This would likely be the case for the employee record illustrated in Figure 3-1. In other applications, the number of data fields in each record might vary, or the size of a given data field in each record might vary. For example, in a file of customer complaints, the memo field in each record might vary in length to accommodate different-size descriptions of customer problems.

Database Keys. The **primary key** is the data field in each record that uniquely distinguishes one record from another in a database table. Primary keys are required for every record in a database and they are unique. For the employee record in Figure 3-1, the primary key would be the employee's Social Security number. End users and computer programs use primary keys to find a specific record—for example, the record for a particular employee, inventory item, or customer account. It is also possible for a record to have a primary key that consists of more than one data field.

Some accounting records contain data fields called **foreign keys** that enable them to reference one or more records in other tables. The foreign key in one table always matches the primary key of the related table. For example, in addition to the employee table in Figure 3-1, a firm might have a department table with the data fields shown in Figure 3-2. The primary key for the department table is the department code (e.g., "A," "B," and so forth). With this arrangement, the department code field in the employee record of Figure 3-1 would be a foreign key that the database system could use to reference the appropriate department record from the department table. These foreign keys enable a database system to combine the information from both tables to produce a report such as the one in Figure 3-3.

Note that each line of this report contains information from the records in two tables: the employee records in Figure 3-1 and the department records in Figure 3-2.

Additional Database Issues

Small database systems such as the types used by very small businesses or sole proprietorships tend to be fairly straightforward and manageable. However, large, multi-user databases pose special challenges for their designers and users because of their complexity. Here, we describe some database design concerns that are of special importance to accounting applications.

Department code (primary key)	Manager	Number of employees	Location	Secretary phone	Other info.
A	B. Wright	45	Bldg. 23	x8734	...

FIGURE 3-2 A sample record from a department file.

Employee Roster Friday, July 28, 20XX Last Name	First Name	Dept.	Manager	Location	Secretary Phone
Garadis	Sue	B	Garadis	Bldg. 23	ext. 9330
Gold	Karen	A	Wright	Bldg. 23	ext. 8734
Hale	Lois	C	Hale	Bldg. 24	ext. 8655
Smythe	Teri	A	Wright	Bldg. 23	ext. 8734
Wright	Barbara	A	Wright	Bldg. 23	ext. 8734

FIGURE 3-3 A formatted report that uses data from two tables.

Administration. Without an overall supervisor, a large commercial database is somewhat like a rudderless ship—that is, an entity without cohesion or direction. Similarly, it does not make sense to permit database designers to work unsupervised or to develop large databases without also creating accountability for subsequent changes. A **database administrator** supervises the design, development, and installation of a large database system, and is also the person responsible for maintaining, securing, and changing the database. As a result of the administrator's many duties and powers, it is essential that the administrator be both skilled and trustworthy.

Case-in-Point 3.3 A database administrator at Certegy Check Services used his knowledge of the firm's database to steal personal records from over 8 million customers. In another case, a database administrator for an oil and gas production firm created secret users in a database system that allowed him to access the system after he stopped working for the firm. When the firm terminated his contract, he sabotaged the firm's systems, which could have resulted in a serious environmental disaster. These cases highlight the powers of the database administrator and the critical importance of hiring highly qualified and trustworthy employees for this position.[3]

Documentation. Databases undergo changes throughout their design, development, and use. This makes documentation critical. Descriptions of database structures, contents, security features, E-R diagrams (discussed later in this chapter), and password policies are examples of important documentation materials. The **data dictionary** is a critical component of database documentation that describes the data fields in each database record. A data dictionary is basically a data file about the data itself.

Figure 3-4 identifies information that a data dictionary might contain (listed under the Entry column) and an example of such information for a Social Security number data field (listed under the Example column). In this figure, the data dictionary indicates that the Social Security number data field must be nine characters, is a *text* data field (rather than a *number* data field because it is not manipulated mathematically), has no default value, and so forth. Entries in the data dictionary describe each data field in each record of each table (file) of an AIS database. When developers add a new data field to the record structure of an existing table, they also add the appropriate information about the new field to the data dictionary.

---

[3] http://www.computerworld.com/s/article/9129933/IT_contractor_indicted_for_sabotaging_offshore_rig_management_system_

Item	Entry	Example
1	Field name	Social Security number
2	Field size	9 characters
3	Type of data field	text
4	Default value	none
5	Required?	yes
6	Validation rule(s)	all digits must be numeric characters
7	Range	none
8	Source document	employee application form
9	Programs used to modify it	payroll X2.1
10	Individuals allowed access	payroll personnel
11	Individuals not allowed access	non-payroll personnel

FIGURE 3-4 Examples of information that might be stored in a data dictionary for the Social Security number data field of a payroll database.

Data dictionaries contain **metadata**, or data *about* data, and have a variety of uses. One use is as a documentation aid for those who develop, correct, or enhance either the database or the computer programs that access it. As suggested in items 10 and 11 of Figure 3-4, an organization can also use a data dictionary for security purposes—for example, to indicate which users can or cannot access sensitive data fields in a database.

Accountants can also make good use of a data dictionary. A data dictionary can help establish an audit trail because it identifies the input sources of data items, the potential computer programs that use or modify particular data items, and the management reports that use the data. When accountants help design a new computer system, a data dictionary can help them trace data paths in the new system. Finally, a data dictionary can serve as a useful aid when investigating or documenting internal control procedures.

Data Integrity. IT professionals estimate that it costs about 10 times as much to correct information that is already in a database than it does to enter it correctly initially. Even simple errors in databases can lead to costly mistakes, bad decisions, or disasters (think about air traffic controllers, for example). For these reasons, the software used to create databases should include edit tests that protect databases from erroneous data entries. These **data integrity controls** are designed by database developers and are customized for different applications. Examples include tests for data completeness, conformance to the data type specified for the data field, valid code tests (e.g., a state code such as CA), and reasonableness tests (e.g., regular payroll hours worked must be between 0 and 40). We will further discuss these issues in Chapter 10.

Processing Accuracy and Completeness. Within the context of database systems, *transaction processing* refers to the sequence of steps that a database system uses to accomplish a specific processing task. AISs need **transaction controls** to ensure that the database system performs each transaction accurately and completely.

To illustrate, imagine an inventory application with two types of inventory records: raw materials records and work-in-process records. An inventory manager wishes to subtract 200 units from a particular raw materials record and add the same number of units to a corresponding work-in-process record. Now suppose that the database system executes the first part of this transaction (i.e., subtracts 200 units from the raw materials record) and then stops operating for some reason. This is a problem because the transaction has not been executed completely and the balance-on-hand field in the current work-in-process record is incorrect. To overcome this problem, databases should process a transaction either entirely or not at all. Database systems maintain an auditable log of transactions to help achieve this goal. When a specific transaction only partially executes, the system is able to recover by verifying that a problem has occurred, reversing whatever entries were made, and starting anew. In accounting applications, the ability to audit any particular transaction to ensure processing accuracy and completeness is critical.

Concurrency.   In multi-user systems, it is possible for more than one user to access the same database at the same time. Without **concurrency controls**, it is possible for two or more users to access the same *record* from the same table at the same time. This creates problems. To illustrate, suppose that User A and User B access the same inventory record at the same time. The initial balance-on-hand field for this record is 500 units. When User A accesses this record, the system transfers the entire record to A's work area. User A wants to add 100 units to the balance-on-hand field. The result is a new balance of 600 units. User A completes this transaction, the system writes the new record back to the disk, and the new balance on hand in this record is now 600 units.

When User B accesses this same record at the same time, the system also transfers the same initial record to B's work area. User B wants to decrease the balance on hand by 200 units. The result is a balance of 300 units because this user also starts with an initial balance on hand of 500 units. Assuming that B completes this transaction after A is done, the system updates to reflect the transaction completed by B. The end result is an inventory record with a balance on hand of 300 units, not the correct value of 400 (= 500 + 100 − 200). To guard against this problem, database systems include locking mechanisms that do not allow multiple users to access the same record at the same time. Rather, databases require that one user's transaction is completed before the next user can make further changes to the database.

Backup and Security.   As noted earlier, the information in many accounting databases is critical to the day-to-day operations of a company and is typically irreplaceable. Databases must be protected. A key security feature of any database, therefore, is a set of backup procedures that enable the organization to re-create its data if the original copies are lost or damaged.

Case-in-Point 3.4   New Zealand experienced a massive earthquake in 2010 that destroyed a number of businesses and their data centers. Shortly after the quake, a partner from Ernst & Young stated that businesses with recovery plans were much better able to survive than businesses without a plan. Many businesses struggled to even survive after the earthquake, but according to Ian Forrester, director of a large business continuity provider, "companies who had a detailed plan in place had a lot less stress and were able to continue work so customers didn't notice the interruption, even where offices and premises had been destroyed."

In addition to backup security, an organization must also protect databases from unauthorized access. A system should have the ability to assign, maintain, and require employees to use passwords and guard against unwarranted intrusions. Similarly, database systems can use encryption techniques to scramble data into unintelligible formats, thereby protecting data even if an unauthorized user obtains access to the company's database. This is especially important when database information resides on laptops, which can easily be lost or stolen.

Case-in-Point 3.5 The Government Accountability Office (GAO) recently announced that IRS computers and data are at risk because visitors and low-level users of systems can take advantage of weak access controls and lack of encryption to gain access to secured federal data. The IRS plans to correct these deficiencies by 2013.[4]

A final database security feature involves the use of **view controls** that limit each user's access to information on a need-to-know basis. For example, a defense contractor will limit its employees' access to many files that contain sensitive information. We cover intrusion detection systems and controls in Chapter 10.

STEPS IN DEVELOPING A DATABASE USING THE RESOURCES, EVENTS, AND AGENTS MODEL

At a state department of social services, the director wants to know how many inquiries were made for a certain type of medical assistance last month. At the headquarters of a department store chain, a vice president wants to know how many credit customers made partial payments on their accounts last week. At a local university bookstore, a manager wants to know how many book orders went unfilled last year.

In each case above, a decision maker needs information. AISs must gather pertinent data and store the information in formats that enable managers to obtain timely answers to important questions. The challenges involved in creating large, useful databases include determining what data to collect and how to gather, record, organize, and store the data in ways that satisfy multiple objectives. Key goals include (1) identifying the reports desired by users of the system; (2) finding hardware and software solutions that can adequately perform the data-gathering, storage, and reporting tasks involved; (3) keeping the databases from becoming too large, complex, and unwieldy; (4) protecting the privacy of sensitive information; and (5) avoiding data redundancy, which means storing the same data repeatedly in different tables. To accomplish these and other goals, databases must be carefully designed to serve their intended uses.

When a company wants to create a database, it often hires a database consultant to help design a database that meets the organization's needs. Based on the information obtained from managers and end users, the expert employs a process called **data modeling** to design the database. This can be the most challenging step in the process of creating a database because the designer must collect a considerable amount of information through investigation and interviews and must then determine the needs of all stakeholders as accurately and completely as possible. This process is both an art and a science.

Although there are a number of different models that may be used to design a database, the **REA model** has been demonstrated to be very effective for designing databases to be used in accounting systems. REA is an acronym for resources (R), events (E), and agents (A). The basic assumption of this model is that business events affect firm resources and involve agents (i.e., people) who participate in the event. Many describe the REA model as event driven, meaning that it focuses on the important business events that managers must understand to make their decisions. Use of the REA model involves the following steps: (1) identify business and economic events, (2) identify entities, (3) identify relationships among entities, (4) create entity-relationship diagrams, (5) identify the attributes of data entities, and (6) create database tables and records. The following discussions describe each of these steps in detail, using the sales process as an example.

---

[4] http://www.govinfosecurity.com/articles.php?art_id=3095

Step 1—Identify Business and Economic Events

Chapters 7 and 8 will discuss key business processes in accounting systems and describe the events involved in these processes. There are two main types of events: economic events and business events. **Economic events** typically affect an organization's financial statements. An example of an economic event is a sale on account. This event increases an entity's accounts receivable (balance sheet) and increases a sales revenue account (income statement).

Critics of traditional financial accounting systems have stated that debit/credit systems often ignore organizational activities and events that are important to managers, investors, and creditors. **Business events** do not affect financial statements but can affect important aspects of an organization. One example of such an event is the discovery that a construction project will likely cost far more than was budgeted. While there is no journal entry for the event, this would certainly be important information that managers need to know. Other examples of business events include hiring a new CEO or making a valuable discovery during research and development. Again, these events do not require journal entries, but the information will affect critical decisions made by the firm.

When creating a database using an REA approach, a system designer will try to record all events that are relevant for management decision making in the database, whether they are business or economic events. By including both types of events in the database, users can access and obtain important information about both business and economic activities.

Step 2—Identify Entities

Databases contain data about objects of interest called **entities**. Database entities include business and economic events plus information about *who* and *what* were involved in those activities. **Agents** are the *who* associated with events. Agents are classified as either internal or external. Internal agents work within the firm for which a database is designed (e.g., salespeople), while external agents are outside of the firm (e.g., customers). Most events involve both internal and external agents. For example, both a salesperson and a customer participate in a merchandise sale. The sale is made to a customer by a salesperson.

Events use, change, transfer, or generate **resources**. For example, a merchandise sale will transfer an inventory resource to a customer and generate a cash resource for the firm. Resources represent things of economic value. Common examples of resources are cash, raw materials, and inventory.

The REA model helps designers identify database entities because each resource, event, and agent represents an entity in a relational database. Figure 3-5 provides several examples of each type of entity. You may notice that Figure 3-5 does not list accounts receivable

Resources	Events	Agents
Cash	Sales	Customer (external)
Equipment	Purchase	Employee (internal)
Inventory	Receive goods	Manager (internal)
Plant facilities	Hire an employee	Vendor (external)

FIGURE 3-5 Examples of resource, event, and agent entities.

as a resource. This is because the REA model does not recognize receivables or payables as resources. Rather, receivables and payables represent *claims* to resources rather than resources themselves. Similarly, the REA model does not treat billing as a business or economic event because creating a paper bill replicates information about an economic event such as a sale. Similarly, a paper bill produced in a billing process is not a resource, as it does not have economic value. The bill represents a claim to cash, which is an economic resource.

Step 3—Identify Relationships Among Entities

Entities are related to other entities. For instance, a sale involves the exchange of merchandise inventory to a customer. The relationship between a sale and inventory or between a sale and a customer is called a *direct relationship*. Inventory and customer also share a relationship, but it is an *indirect relationship*. The REA model helps database designers define the relationships between entities. In the REA model, events typically have direct relationships with resources and agents, and also with other events. The links between resources and agents are *through* events. The relationships between entities ultimately determine the ability to create reports from the data. Reports can logically combine data from any entities that are linked, either directly or indirectly.

Data modelers need to know about entity relationships in order to create links between database tables. Without these links, database users cannot access data from more than one table at a time. Before we can determine the best way to link database tables, we must first understand the nature of the relationships among entities. We describe relationships in terms of **cardinalities**. Cardinality describes how entities are related, and we often abbreviate the description of the cardinality between two entities as either *one-to-one (1:1), one-to-many (1:N),* or *many-to-many (N:N)*. This terminology refers to the maximum number of one entity that can occur given its relationship to another entity.

We examine the relationships between two entities in two directions, and each direction of the relationship can yield a different maximum cardinality. For example, consider the relationship between a customer entity and a sale entity. The customer–sale relationship has a one-to-many cardinality. For a given customer, there can be many sale events (i.e., a single customer can be involved in many sales transactions over time). Thus, the sale has a maximum of many in this relationship. Examining this pair of entities from the other direction, we see that one sale involves just one customer. Thus, the maximum number of customers for a single sale is one, and we define the customer–sale relationship as one-to-many. Figure 3-6 depicts this relationship graphically, where | represents a maximum of 1, and > represents a maximum of many.

Cardinalities also have minimums. Considering the same example as above, one customer can be involved in many sales transactions, but some customers may not have been involved in any sales because they have never purchased anything from the firm. As a result, we say that the minimum number of sales for a customer is 0, which is indicated with a °. Reading this relationship in the other direction, we need to determine the minimum number of customers for a sale. Given that a sale cannot be made unless there

FIGURE 3-6 Maximum cardinality example.

FIGURE 3-7 Maximum and minimum cardinality example.

FIGURE 3-8 Cardinality example.

is a customer, the minimum number of customers is 1. Figure 3-7 depicts the relationship with both minimum and maximum cardinalities.

To read this relationship, we start on one side of the relationship and assume that the initial entity is singular. Then, we read the minimum and maximum cardinalities of the related entity. We would read the cardinalities described above as (1) one sale is made to a minimum of one customer and a maximum of one customer and (2) one customer has a minimum of zero sales and a maximum of many sales.

Cardinalities are sometimes difficult to grasp at first, but they become easier to understand with practice. So let's try another one. What does the cardinality notation in Figure 3-8 tell us?

Part of the answer is that each type of inventory item (e.g., blue jeans) can be sold many times, but some inventory items (e.g., new brands that have not yet been marketed) have never been sold. Also note that cardinalities are not fixed across organizations but vary according to the rules or controls of a specific enterprise. For example, if the item being sold was unique and could be sold only one time, then the maximum cardinality for the item entity would change to 1, rather than many. The other half of this relationship indicates that each sale must be for at least one inventory item and may be for many inventory items. For example, you would have to actually sell something in order to have a sale, and you could be selling a white shirt plus some jeans and a jacket as part of the same sale.

There are a three other points we want to make about cardinalities. First, you will often find that events involve single agents but that agents are involved in events many times. As a result, agent–event relationships are often one-to-many relationships. Second, in the case of a sequence of events, you will typically notice that the first event must occur before the next event can occur. Thus, the minimum cardinality for the first event will be 1. This would be the case between a Sale and a subsequent Cash Receipt (see Figure 3-9). The Cash Receipt cannot occur unless there was first a sale. From the other direction, the cardinality says that a sale relates to a minimum of zero cash receipts (because some customers will not pay) and a maximum of many cash receipts (because some customers

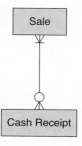

FIGURE 3-9 Cardinality example for business events.

may pay in installments). Again, plainly stated, this means that you cannot have a cash receipt without a sale, and you could receive several cash receipts for a sale. Finally, examination of cardinalities can also be helpful in understanding an organization and can tell us something about the controls for a given business event. Notice that Figure 3-9 tells us, for example, that this firm allows installment payments. Otherwise, the maximum cardinality for the cash receipts would be 1.

Step 4—Create Entity-Relationship Diagrams

Database designers use a graphical documentation technique called the **entity-relationship (E-R) diagram** to depict entities and their relationships. We have already introduced you to the basic elements of E-R diagrams in the preceding figures related to cardinalities. The diagram consists of three items: rectangles, connecting lines, and cardinality notations. Rectangles represent entities and connecting lines depict relationships. E-R diagrams depict all of the entities and the relationships graphically. In addition, the diagrams are arranged as events that occur in temporal sequence when using the REA modeling approach. Therefore, a reader can quickly see the main business events and the order in which events occur. In addition, the resources are arranged on the left and people appear on the right (i.e., the diagram is ordered from left to right as resources, events, and agents). Recall that each event will be related to at least one resource, internal agent, and external agent. Figure 3-10 provides an example of an E-R diagram for a simple sales process.

Step 5—Identify Attributes of Entities

Eventually, the entities that the database designer identifies become tables in a database. In other words, a database contains a table for every entity in the E-R diagram. The tables consist of records, each containing data fields that describe the entity's **attributes**. Figure 3-11 shows four database tables for our merchandise sale example: (1) an event (Customer Order), (2) a resource (Inventory), (3) an external agent (Customer), and (4) an internal agent (Salesperson).

Entities have characteristics or **attributes** that describe them. The data within a table are based on the attributes of the entity. For example, a salesperson is an agent entity. The

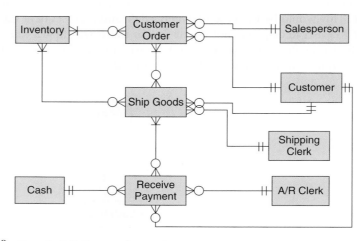

FIGURE 3-10   Sample E-R diagram for a sale process.

Customer Order Table (Event)

Order #	Employee #	Customer #	Date	Comments
1003	M24SP	B104	01/03/2011	
1004	R63SP	P202	01/03/2011	Ship ASAP
1005	M24SP	S200	01/03/2011	
1006	W11SP	C100	01/03/2011	

Inventory Table (Resource)

Item #	Description	Unit Cost	Sales Price	Beg QOH
1400	Goodie Bar	$0.20	$0.40	13025
1500	Almond Delight	$0.25	$0.45	5010
1600	Gummy Lions	$0.60	$0.95	20109
1700	Pecan Bar	$0.70	$1.09	4508
1800	Milky Bars	$0.18	$0.30	2207

Customer Table (Agent)

Customer #	Name	Address	City	State	Zip Code	Credit Limit
A101	Amanda Wills	22 Yellow Ln.	Charlotte	NC	79803	$20,000.00
B104	Boris Bailey	321 Church St.	Oxford	OH	45056	5,000.00
C100	Carly Riccardi	1899 Green St.	Dayton	OH	43299	10,000.00
P202	Peggy Martin	1260 Main St.	Columbus	OH	43320	10,000.00
S200	Bill Safer	860 Broad St.	Fairfax	VA	22030	5,000.00

Salesperson Table (Agent)

Employee #	Name	Address	City	State	Zip Code	Dept ID	Date Hired
A06SP	Sally Anderson	3026 Skye Ln.	Columbus	OH	43213	247	1/31/1989
M24SP	Randy Merit	262 Main St.	Bexley	OH	43209	182	7/2/1999
R63SP	Barry Rogers	80 N. Long St.	Gahanna	OH	43215	247	1/16/2001
R73SP	Jim Rudolph	64 Lantern Ave.	Columbus	OH	43213	76	8/15/2000
W11SP	John Walker	1028 Fields Ln.	Lancaster	OH	43307	182	9/1/1992

FIGURE 3-11 Four sample tables in a relational database.

attributes are the data fields *describing* each salesperson. What data should you collect about a salesperson? First, it is necessary to include an attribute that uniquely identifies each salesperson within the Salesperson table. This is the primary key that we discussed earlier. The salesperson's identification number, which could be the employee's Social Security number, is a good choice for the primary key. Other attributes to include in the table might be last name, middle name, first name, phone number, address, e-mail, date of birth, date hired, department assignment, salary, and so on. You do not want to include attributes that the system can calculate or that require manual updates. For example, you would not want to include an attribute for the number of years that the employee has worked for the organization, because you would need to update the attribute every year. Rather than store the number of years, it is better to include an attribute for the date hired and a formula that calculates the current number of years of service based on the current date.

It is not always easy to decide what attributes to include for an entity. There are, however, two guidelines you can use. First, the attributes should describe one entity and that entity only. For example, if you have an inventory table, you would not include information about the vendor in this table. You can reference the vendor, but the name, address, and other information about the vendor belongs in a separate Vendor table. Second, you should only include entities that are singular. In other words, do not create attributes that are lists of data. An example of such a list would be an attribute for all of the children's names for an employee. The database would not be able to store this attribute because there could be many names, but there is only space for one child's name in the database table. We will discuss how to deal with such problems in this chapter's section on normalization.

Step 6—Convert E-R Diagrams into Database Tables

Each entity in the E-R diagram becomes a table in the completed database. However, a database is likely to contain more tables than the total number of entities in the E-R diagram. This can occur because linking tables together sometimes requires the creation of additional tables. In databases, tables are linked using foreign keys as previously described. For example, in Figure 3-11, the Customer # in the Customer Order table is a foreign key that references the primary key of a particular customer in the Customer table. The relationship between the primary key and foreign key enables the database software to link the two tables together. If you wanted to create a customer order report that shows the *name of the customer* associated with each order, the links allow the creation of this report.

Creating links between tables is simple when the relationship between the entities is one-to-one or one-to-many. In one-to-one relationships, the foreign key can be in either table. If entities occur in sequence, the foreign key will usually be in the second event. In one-to-many relationships, the foreign key will be on the many side of the relationship. Looking at the sample E-R diagram for a sales process in Figure 3-10, for example, we see that the cardinality between a Salesperson and Customer Order is one-to-many. To create a foreign key, we would use the primary key from the Salesperson table as the foreign key in the customer order table. Looking at Figure 3-11, this is the case. The primary key for the Salesperson table, Employee #, appears in the Customer Order table as an attribute. This is the link between the two tables.

Linking tables with foreign keys becomes problematic when there is a many-to-many relationship between two entities. New **relationship tables** are necessary when you have many-to-many relationships. The reason for this is that, without relationship tables, there would be fields in a database table that could contain many possible values. For example, there is a many-to-many relationship between Sale and Inventory in Figure 3-10. If we placed the inventory item number in the Sale table as a foreign key, it would not be possible to input the value for the inventory item number, because there can be many items related to a single sale. Similarly, an item can be sold many times, making it impossible to input a single sale number for a given item. Figure 3-12 shows the relationship table that is necessary to join the Sales and Inventory Item entities.

How many tables, including relationship tables, will we have for a complete database of the Sales process described in Figure 3-10? Looking at the diagram, we see that there are nine entities, which will require nine tables. There are also three many-to-many relationships: (1) Inventory and Customer Orders, (2) Inventory and Sales, and (3) Sales and Receive Payment. Therefore, we would have 12 tables in the finished database: nine tables for entities and three additional ''joining'' tables.

Figure 3-13 lists all the database tables and their attributes for our sales process example. Because data modeling is a creative process, there are other possible sets of database tables and other attributes that you might include in a database for a sales process. Figure 3-13 is one example.

Sale #	Item #	Quantity
1003	1400	230
1004	1400	430
1005	1600	180
1005	1800	200
1005	1900	360
1006	1400	80
1006	1800	100

FIGURE 3-12   A relationship table joining the Customer Order and Inventory tables.

Inventory Table

Item#, Description, Unit Cost, Sales Price, Beginning Quantity on Hand, Beginning Quantity on Hand Date

Cash Table

Account#, Account Type, Bank, Beginning Balance, Beginning Balance Date

Customer Order Table

Order#, [Employee#], [Customer#], Date, Comments

Sales Table

Sale#, [Employee#], [Customer#], Ship Date, [Order#]

Receive Payment Table

Cash Receipt#, Amount Received, Date, [Employee#], [Account#]

Employee Table

Employee#, First Name, Middle Name, Last Name, Address, City, State, Zip Code, [Department#], [Job Classification Code], Date of Birth, Date Hired, Last Date of Review

Customer Table

Customer#, Company Name, Address[1], City, State, Zip Code, Contact Person, Credit Limit

Inventory/Order Relationship Table

Order#, Item#[2], Quantity

Inventory/Sale Relationship Table

Sale#, Item#, Quantity

Sale/Receive Payment Relationship Table

Sale#, Cash Receipt#

Order/Sale Relationship Table

Order#, Sale#

[1]May use multiple addresses for different departments or for shipping versus billing.
[2]Relationship tables require two fields together to represent a primary key. Either field alone would not be unique to a record.

FIGURE 3-13   A schematic of database tables for the sales process. (*Note:* Underlining signifies a primary key and brackets denote foreign keys.)

NORMALIZATION

Normalization is a methodology for ensuring that attributes are stored in the most appropriate tables and that the design of the database promotes accurate and nonredundant storage of data. The process of normalization can result in the creation of new tables to include in the database. There are multiple levels of normalization. We shall examine the first three levels—first normal form, second normal form, and third normal form—as these three normal forms address the vast majority of problems when designing database tables.

First Normal Form

A database is in **first normal form (1 NF)** if all of a single record's attributes (data fields) are singular. That is, each attribute has only one value. Figure 3-14 shows a set of university parking ticket data with repeating groups in its rightmost four columns. (Real parking tickets will contain many more data fields than shown here, but we will keep things simple to focus on normalization tasks.) Databases cannot store more than one value in the same data field (i.e., column) of the same record, so we must do something to overcome this limitation.

A solution to this problem is to use a separate record to store the information for each parking ticket. Figure 3-15 illustrates the results. For this file, the ticket number serves as the primary key. There are no repeating groups for any one column, and there is no longer a violation of the first normal form.

Although we now have corrected the problem associated with nonsingular attributes, several problems remain. One difficulty is a large amount of *data redundancy* (i.e., the fact that much of the information in this table is repetitive). Another problem is that we have created an *insertion anomaly,* which is a situation where desired data cannot be entered into the database. In particular, the current version of this database reveals that it only

Social Security Number	Last Name	First Name	Phone Number	License Plate State	Number	Ticket Number	Date	Code	Fine
123-45-6789	Curry	Dorothy	(916)358-4448	CA	123 MCD	10151	10/15/10	A	$10
						10152	10/16/10	B	$20
						10121	11/12/10	B	$20
134-56-7783	Mason	Richard	(916)563-7865	CA	253 DAL	10231	10/23/10	C	$50
						12051	12/5/10	A	$10

FIGURE 3-14   A set of unnormalized parking ticket data.

Ticket Number	Social Security Number	Last Name	First Name	Phone Number	State	License Plate Number	Date	Code	Fine
10151	123-45-6789	Curry	Dorothy	(916)358-4448	CA	123 MCD	10/15/2010	A	$10
10152	123-45-6789	Curry	Dorothy	(916)358-4448	CA	123 MCD	10/16/2010	B	$20
10121	123-45-6789	Curry	Dorothy	(916)358-4448	CA	123 MCD	11/12/2010	B	$20
10231	134-56-7783	Mason	Richard	(916)663-7865	CA	253 DAL	10/23/2010	C	$50
12051	134-56-7783	Mason	Richard	(916)663-7865	CA	253 DAL	12/5/2010	A	$10

FIGURE 3-15   The data from Figure 3-14 in first normal form.

stores information about students with parking tickets. Students with registered cars but no parking tickets will have no records in this file—a difficulty if school administrators also want to use this file for car registration purposes. A third problem is a *deletion anomaly,* which occurs when more data is deleted than is desired by the database user. When we delete records after students pay their tickets, we will no longer have car registration records on file for anyone who has paid all of his or her tickets.

Second Normal Form

To solve the problems described above, we now consider **second normal form (2 NF)**. A database is in second normal form if it is in first normal form and all the attributes in each record depend entirely on the record's primary key. To satisfy this requirement for our student parking ticket example, let us split our student information into two files—a *Car Registration File* and a *Ticket File*—as shown in Figure 3-16. This approach results in a more efficient design and also eliminates much of the first file's data redundancy. Notice that the solution to both the insertion and deletion anomalies is the same—make more tables.

In our new Car Registration table, what should serve as the primary key? At first glance, you might guess "Social Security number." If students are able to register only one car, then this choice might be satisfactory. If students can register more than one car, then it makes more sense to use the license plate number as the primary key. Remember: the primary key must uniquely identify a record, and this would not be possible if one person (with one Social Security number) had two records in this table.

What about a primary key for our new Ticket table? In this table, the ticket number serves this purpose, while the student's license plate number serves as the foreign key. The foreign key enables a database to link appropriate records together—for example, to trace

---

Car Registration File

Social Security Number	Last Name	First Name	Phone Number	(primary key) License Plate State	Number
123-45-6789	Curry	Dorothy	(916)358-4448	CA	123 MCD
134-56-7783	Mason	Richard	(916)563-7865	CA	253 DAL
.	.	.	.	.	.
.	.	.	.	.	.

Ticket File

(primary key) Ticket Number	State	(foreign key) License Plate Number	Date	Code	Fine
10151	CA	123 MCD	10/15/10	A	$10
10152	CA	123 MCD	10/16/10	B	$20
10231	CA	253 DAL	10/23/10	C	$50
10121	CA	123 MCD	11/12/10	B	$20
12051	CA	253 DAL	12/5/10	A	$10
.	.	.	.	.	.
.	.	.	.	.	.

FIGURE 3-16 The data of Figure 3-15 in second normal form.

a particular parking ticket to the car's registered owner. It also enables database users to answer such questions as "Does a particular student have any outstanding parking tickets?"

Third Normal Form

Although we are making headway in our database design, our goal is to create a database that is in **third normal form (3NF)**. A database is in third normal form if it is in second normal form and contains no **transitive dependencies**. This means that the same record does not contain any data fields where data field A determines data field B. The Ticket table in Figure 3-16 suffers from this problem because the ticket code data field (e.g., a code of A) determines the amount of the fine (e.g., $10).

One way to solve this problem is to store the data for parking fines in a new Parking Violations Code table as shown in Figure 3-17. This enables us to eliminate the redundant information (the fine data field) in the Ticket table of Figure 3-16 and streamline our data. Figure 3-17 illustrates the results. The ticket codes (A, B, and so forth) in the Ticket table serve as a foreign key that links the information in the Ticket table to an entry in the Parking Violations Code table. We now have a database in third normal form.

Car Registration File

| | | | | (primary key) | |
Social Security Number	Last Name	First Name	Phone Number	License Plate State	Number
123-45-6789	Curry	Dorothy	(916)358-4448	CA	123 MCD
134-56-7783	Mason	Richard	(916)563-7865	CA	253 DAL
.	.	.	.	.	.
.	.	.	.	.	.
.	.	.	.	.	.

Ticket File

(primary key) Ticket Number	(foreign key) License Plate State	Number	Date	(foreign key) Code
10151	CA	123 MCD	10/15/10	A
10152	CA	123 MCD	10/16/10	B
10231	CA	253 DAL	10/23/10	C
10121	CA	123 MCD	11/12/10	B
12051	CA	253 DAL	12/5/10	A
.	.	.	.	.
.	.	.	.	.

Parking Violations Code File

(primary key) Code	Fine	Explanation
A	$10	meter expired
B	$20	parking in no-parking zone
C	$50	no parking sticker
.	.	.
.	.	.

FIGURE 3-17 The data of Figure 3-16 in third normal form.

Large databases tend to become very complicated, with multiple tables that are linked together with foreign keys. The database in Figure 3-17, for example, is more complex than our original file in Figure 3-14, but it is also more efficient. For example, this database design will allow its users to (1) store the car registration information of all students, even if they do not have any parking tickets, (2) alter a student's name, phone number, or license plate by altering only one record in the Car Registration file—not several of them, as would be required using the file in Figure 3-14, and (3) easily change the fine amount for a parking ticket. Finally, this database design allows us to eliminate redundant information and therefore makes file storage more efficient.

AIS AT WORK
New Databases for the Green Economy[5]

Databases are used to track firms' financial performance throughout the world. Modern database systems store all of the data needed to produce financial statements and create the nonfinancial reports needed for strategic decision making. A new form of database system and related software applications are rapidly entering the market.

As firms and governments have become more aware of the risks associated with climate change, carbon emissions are beginning to be considered liabilities that should be reported on the balance sheet or at least disclosed. Keeping track of carbon, therefore, is becoming a priority. Firms are adopting new technology called Enterprise Carbon and Energy Management (ECEM) systems to integrate with their existing business databases. These new systems are designed to collect the data necessary to improve efficiency and reduce energy consumption, develop carbon reduction plans, improve relations with shareholders and the public, and comply with new regulations. Another goal for these systems is to reduce the risks associated with climate change. The concerns related to climate change risks have grown so rapidly that the Securities and Exchange Commission (SEC) now requires publicly traded companies to assess climate change risks and estimate potential effects on financial results. Database technology will be essential for organizing the vast amounts of data needed to conduct such risk assessments.

According to Forrester research surveys, ECEM systems are being adopted at an astonishing rate. During a period of just six months in 2010, the number of companies who had adopted this technology nearly doubled. It may soon be commonplace for accounting databases to include complex climate predictions and emissions data.

SUMMARY

✓ Almost every AIS uses databases to store accounting data.

✓ Primary keys and foreign keys enable database systems to identify database records uniquely as well as link records to one another.

✓ Large, multi-user accounting databases pose several concerns for accounting professionals. These include the administration and supervision of database development and maintenance; the need for documentation; the importance of data integrity, data processing accuracy, data completeness;

---

[5] http://www.greenbiz.com/blog/2010/10/21/five-reasons-why-carbon-management-software-next-big-thing

database security and backup; and the need for concurrency controls to safeguard data when two users wish to access the same record.

✓ The REA model is a methodology that enables database designers to model databases by focusing on resources, events, and agents.

✓ Using E-R diagrams, the REA model graphically depicts the entities needed for a database and the types of relationships between them. The ultimate goal is to determine what data to store and how to organize the data.

✓ Databases must be designed carefully. The process of normalization enables designers to minimize data redundancy, eliminate insertion and deletion anomalies, and remove transitive dependencies. The goal is to develop a database that is at least in third normal form.

KEY TERMS YOU SHOULD KNOW

agent	foreign keys
attributes	master files
business event	metadata
cardinalities	normalization
concurrency controls	primary key
data dictionary	REA model
data field	record
data hierarchy	record structure
data integrity controls	relational databases
data modeling	relationship table
database	resources
database administrator	second normal form (2NF)
database management system (DBMS)	third normal form (3NF)
economic event	transaction controls
entity	transaction file
entity-relationship (E-R) diagram	transitive dependencies
first normal form (1NF)	view controls

DISCUSSION QUESTIONS

3-1. Why are databases important for accounting information systems? Describe some concerns and explain why each one is important.

3-2. What is the hierarchy of data in databases? Provide an example for a particular accounting application.

3-3. What are primary keys in accounting databases and what purpose do they serve?

3-4. Name some specific accounting files and a potential primary key for each one.

3-5. Describe each of the following database issues that are relevant to accounting systems, and give an example of each: (1) data integrity, (2) transaction accuracy and completeness, (3) concurrency processing, and (4) security.

3-6. What is the REA model? How does REA differ from more traditional accounting views of data collection and storage? Hint: would a traditional accounting database store data about personnel matters?

3-7. What are database cardinalities? Give some examples of cardinalities for an accounting application other than sales.

3-8. What is an entity-relationship diagram? What can you determine about an organization from examining an E-R diagram?

3-9. Suppose that a data modeler creates a database that includes a Sales table and a Salesperson table. Would you be likely to need a relationship table to link these two entities? Why or why not?

3-10. What is the process of normalization? What levels are there, and why do database developers seek to normalize data?

PROBLEMS

3-11. An internal auditor should have a sound understanding of basic data processing concepts such as data organization and storage in order to adequately evaluate systems and make use of retrieval software.

  a. Define the following terms as used in a data processing environment (all are nouns): (1) field, (2) record, and (3) file.

  b. Define a database. List two advantages and two disadvantages of a database system.

  (CIA adapted.)

3-12. What attributes (i.e., table columns) would you be likely to include in a Cash table? In a Cash Receipts table?

3-13. Describe the meaning of each of the entity-relationship diagrams shown in Figure 3-18.

3-14. Draw an entity-relationship diagram for the following: Sales of inventory are made to customers by salespeople. After the sale, cash is received by cashiers.

3-15. Draw an entity-relationship diagram for the following: An accounting firm holds recruiting events for college students. At these events, recruiters are seeking students with particular skills.

3-16. Give some examples of attributes you would include in a Customer table. Would you use one data field or two for the customer name? Why?

3-17. Design tables to store the following attributes (make sure that all tables are in third normal form): customer name, customer address, customer phone, and names of customers' children.

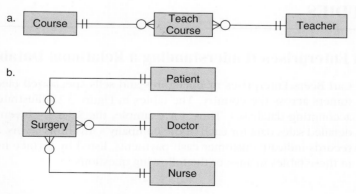

FIGURE 3-18 Entity-relationship diagrams for Problem 3-13.

3-18. Design tables to store the following attributes (make sure that all tables are in third normal form): student name, student phone number, classes taken by student, student address, class number, class time, class room, and student's grade for each class.

3-19. Bonadio Electrical Supplies distributes electrical components to the construction industry. The company began as a local supplier 15 years ago and has grown rapidly to become a major competitor in the north central United States. As the business grew and the variety of components to be stocked expanded, Bonadio acquired a computer and implemented an inventory control system. Other applications such as accounts receivable, accounts payable, payroll, and sales analysis were gradually computerized as each function expanded. Because of its operational importance, the inventory system has been upgraded to an online system, while all the other applications are operating in batch mode. Over the years, the company has developed or acquired more than 100 application programs and maintains hundreds of files.

Bonadio faces stiff competition from local suppliers throughout its marketing area. At a management meeting, the sales manager complained about the difficulty in obtaining immediate and current information to respond to customer inquiries. Other managers stated that they also had difficulty obtaining timely data from the system. As a result, the controller engaged a consulting firm to explore the situation. The consultant recommended installing a DBMS, and the company complied, employing Jack Gibbons as the database administrator.

At a recent management meeting, Gibbons presented an overview of the DBMS. Gibbons explained that the database approach assumes an organizational, data-oriented viewpoint as it recognizes that a centralized database represents a vital resource. Instead of being assigned to applications, information is more appropriately used and managed for the entire organization. The operating system physically moves data to and from disk storage, while the DBMS is the software program that controls the data definition library that specifies the data structures and characteristics. As a result, both the roles of the application programs and query software, and the tasks of the application programmers and users are simplified. Under the database approach, the data are available to all users within security guidelines.

a. Explain the basic difference between a file-oriented system and a database management system.

b. Describe at least three advantages and at least three disadvantages of the database management system.

c. Describe the duties and responsibilities of Jack Gibbons, the database administrator.

(CMA Adapted.)

CASE STUDIES

Carl Beers Enterprises (Understanding a Relational Database)

Carl Beers Enterprises manufactures and sells specialized electronic components to customers across the country. The tables in Figure 3-19 illustrate some of the records in its accounting databases. Thus, for example, the Sales by Inventory Number records show detailed sales data for each of the company's inventory items, and the Customer Payments records indicate customer cash payments, listed by invoice number. Use the information in these tables to answer the following questions.

Sales by Inventory Number

Item Number	Invoice Number	Quantity	Price Each
I-1	V-1	1	2,000
	V-3	1	2,000
	V-6	3	1,575
I-2	V-5	2	3,000
	V-6	10	3,500
I-3	V-3	6	1,000
I-4	V-1	2	600
	V-5	2	300
I-5	V-3	2	4,000
	V-7	3	3,000
I-6	V-2	2	5,000
	V-4	2	5,000
	V-5	2	5,000
	V-7	2	7,000

Sales by Invoice Number

Invoice Number	Amount	Customer Number	Date	Salesperson Number
V-1	7,200	C-1	July 1	S-12
V-2	10,000	C-2	July 12	S-10
V-3	16,000	C-5	July 22	S-10
V-4	10,000	C-2	July 26	S-10
V-5	16,600	C-5	July 31	S-10
V-6	35,000	C-3	Aug 1	S-10
V-7	23,000	C-4	Aug 2	S-11

Sales by Salesperson

Salesperson Number	Quarterly Sales	Commission Rate
S-10	?	.10
S-11	?	.10
S-12	?	.12
S-78	0	.08

Customer Payments

Invoice Number	Remittance Advice Number	Amount
V-1	R-3	7,200
V-2	R-1	1,666
V-2	R-5	1,666
V-3	R-4	16,000
V-4	R-2	10,000
V-5	R-4	16,600

Customer Data

Customer Number	Customer Name	Accounts Receivable Amount	Sales-person
C-1	Dunn, Inc.	?	S-12
C-2	J. P. Carpenter	?	S-10
C-3	Mabadera Corp.	?	S-10
C-4	Ghymn and Sons	?	S-99
C-5	D. Lund, Inc.	?	S-10

FIGURE 3-19 Sample of some of the records in the Carl Beers Enterprises accounting databases.

Requirements

1. The Sales by Inventory Number records are listed by inventory item number. How is this useful? Why might this information also be useful if it were listed by invoice number instead of inventory number?

2. In the Sales by Invoice Number, invoice V-3 shows a sales amount of $16,000. What was the name of the customer that made this purchase? What specific inventory items did this customer purchase? How much did this customer pay for each item?

3. Customers can choose among one of three payment options: (1) 5 percent discount if immediate cash payment, (2) 2 percent discount off list amount if total invoice paid by the fifteenth day of the month following purchase, or (3) deferred payment plan, using six monthly payments. Which option does J. P. Carpenter appear to be using for invoice V-2?

4. Using just the information provided, what are the quarterly sales amounts for salespeople S-10, S-11, and S-12?

5. Assume that customers C-1 through C-5 began this quarter with net accounts receivable balances of zero. What are their balances now?

Souder, Oles, and Franek LLP (Data Modeling with REA)

Souder, Oles, and Franek LLP is an international consulting firm headquartered in Chicago, Illinois. The E-R diagram in Figure 3-20 shows a simplified version of the company's process for purchasing and paying for equipment and supplies.

Requirements

1. Insert appropriate cardinalities for the relationships in the E-R diagram developed with the REA data modeling approach.

2. Describe the database table attributes for this model. You will need a table for each entity, as well as one or more relationship tables. Identify first the table name, then indicate the primary key by underlining it. Show any foreign keys by framing them in brackets (e.g., [Vendor #]). Include at least three fields in each table. Below is an example for the Vendor table and the Order Goods table:

   Vendor #: Name, Street Address 1, Street Address 2, City, State, Zip Code, Phone Number, E-mail, Fax, Contact, Comments.
   Order #: Date, [Vendor #], [Employee #], Shipping Instructions, Comments.

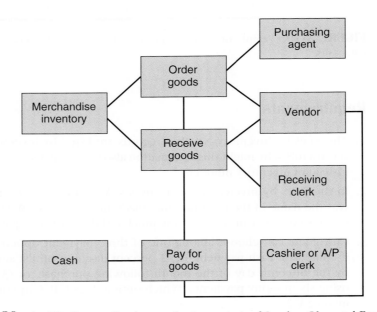

FIGURE 3-20   An E-R diagram for the purchasing system of Souder, Oles, and Franek LLP.

Swan's Supplies (Normalizing Data)

Swan's Supplies is a wholesaler of sporting goods equipment for retailers in a local metropolitan area. The company buys sporting goods equipment direct from manufacturers and then resells them to individual retail stores in the regional area. The raw data in Figure 3-21 illustrate some of the information required for the company's purchase order system. As you can see, this information is characteristic of accounting purchase order systems but is not well organized. In fact, because of the repeating groups in the rightmost columns, it cannot even be stored in a database system.

Requirements

Store this data in a spreadsheet to make it easy to manipulate. Then perform each of the following tasks in turn:

1. Reorganize the data in first normal form and print your spreadsheet. Why is your data in first normal form?
2. Reorganize the data from part 1 into second normal form and print your spreadsheet. Why is your data in second normal form?
3. Reorganize the data from part 2 into third normal form and print your spreadsheet. Why is your data in third normal form?

Purchase Order Number	Date	Customer Number	Customer Name	Customer Phone Number	Item Number	Item Description	Unit Cost	Unit	Quantity Ordered
12345	01/03/2011	123-8209	Charles Dresser, Inc.	(752)433-8733	X32655	Baseballs	$33.69	dozen	20
					X34598	Footballs	53.45	dozen	10
					Z34523	Bball Hoops	34.95	each	20
12346	01/03/2011	123-6733	Patrice Schmidt's Sports	(673)784-4451	X98673	Softballs	35.89	dozen	10
					X34598	Footballs	53.45	dozen	5
					X67453	Soccer balls	45.36	dozen	10

FIGURE 3-21 Some purchasing data for Swan's Supplies.

Chapter 4

Organizing and Manipulating the Data in Databases

INTRODUCTION

In theory, system developers should first design databases, using the techniques described in Chapter 3, and then construct them later. In practice, organizations create many commercial databases from collections of preexisting manual files, nonintegrated computerized files, personal or informal files, or the databases of acquired companies. Thus, the key databases of a company are often in a state of continuous evolution, reevaluation, and revision.

The previous chapter introduced the concept of databases and discussed data modeling—the process of designing database tables. This chapter focuses on ways to use databases in AISs and the actual construction of a functioning database in Microsoft Access. We begin with a discussion of the software used to create databases (i.e., database management systems) and then describe how to implement Access database tables in practice. Next, we discuss how to retrieve data from a database. Finally, we examine a few special types of databases and current advances in database technology.

CREATING DATABASE TABLES IN MICROSOFT ACCESS

After you have normalized your database tables, you are ready to actually create database tables and input records. Typically, these tasks are completed with a database management system.

Database Management Systems

A database management system (DBMS) is a software system that enables users to create database records, delete records, query (i.e., select subsets of records for viewing or analysis), alter database information, and reorganize records as needed. This section of the chapter explains how to perform some of these tasks in greater detail.

A DBMS is not a database. Rather, a DBMS is a separate computer program that enables users to create, modify, and utilize a database of information efficiently, thus allowing businesses to separate their database system operations from their accounting system applications. This enables organizations to change record structures, queries, and report formats without also having to reprogram the accounting software that accesses these database items. It also enables businesses to upgrade either system independently of other systems.

Examples of microcomputer DBMS packages include Microsoft Access, Alpha 5, dQuery, Filemaker Pro, and Lotus Approach. Examples of DBMSs that run on client/server systems or mainframes include ADABAS, Microsoft SQL Server, DB2, Oracle, MySQL, Sybase, Ingrus, and Supra. Most microcomputer DBMSs are single-user systems, whereas others (for larger applications) are multi-user systems. Each system is limited in how many concurrent users it can support, the maximum number of transactions per hour it can process, and so forth. Also, not every accounting package can interface with every database, so managers should make sure that any new accounting software they acquire can also work with their existing databases, and vice versa.

> **Case-in-Point 4.1** Annual global spending on database management systems is approximately $30 billion, and the major database providers (e.g., MySQL, Oracle, and IBM DB2) are some of the largest software companies in the world.[1]

An Introduction to Microsoft Access

Microsoft Access is a popular database that many businesses and individuals use for small database applications. The procedures for creating tables and entering records in several alternative database systems are similar to those used in Access. This chapter assumes the use of Access 2010.

After launching Access 2010, click on the "Blank database" icon in the top portion of the screen in Figure 4-1, and you will launch the option to open a new blank database. A panel will appear on the right side of your screen asking you to name your database. The default name is "Database1.accdb." You should rename your database to something more meaningful—for example, "Payroll Database" (blanks are permitted in Access database names).

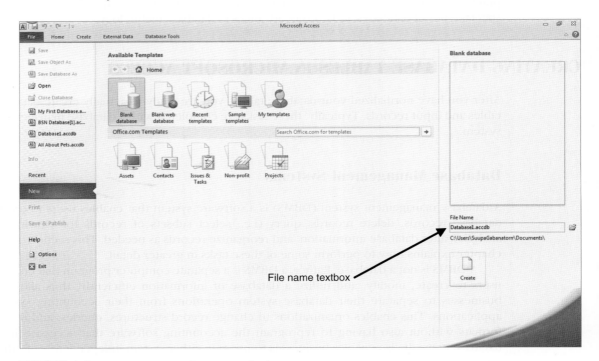

FIGURE 4-1 Opening screen for Access database program.

---

[1] http://www.marketresearchanalyst.com

Your next task is to decide where to store the database. To do this, look to the right of the File Name textbox (where you named your database from the previous step) and find the file folder with an arrow icon. Clicking on this icon will display a Microsoft "Save As" dialog box (not shown) that enables you to select where to store your database. After you have done this, click on the "Create" button in the lower-right portion of Figure 4-1.

Creating Database Tables

As you already know, database tables store data about specific entities—for example, customers, vendors, or employees. To illustrate how to create tables in Access, let's create a table of employee payroll records similar to the one we previously described in Figure 3-1.

Defining a Record Format.
The ribbon across the top in Figure 4-2 shows seven tabs: File, Home, Create, External Data, Database Tools, Fields, and Table. The figure also shows two important components. First, Access assumes that your next job is to create a table of records and accordingly supplies the default name "Table1" in the left portion of the screen in Figure 4-2. Second, the system assumes that each record will have at least one data field with default name "ID."

Before you enter data in your new database, you must first define the record structure for your table. *It is much easier to spend time developing this format prior to entering data than to spend hours changing it later.* Figure 4-3 displays the form for developing the record fields and field properties for the tables in your database. To get to this screen, right click on the table name "Table1" from Figure 4-2 and select "Design View" from the set of choices. You will be asked to name and save the table. You should include the conventional *tbl* prefix in any name you create for a table. Thus, we will use the name "tblPayroll MasterFile" for our table name. The screen in Figure 4-3 will appear, and it is a template for creating the data fields of your records.

To define a record format, begin typing the name of the first data field you wish to create—for example, the term "SocSecNum"—in the upper-left portion of the screen in Figure 4-3. When you do, the following three columns will appear in that area of the screen: (1) Field Name (which is required), (2) Data Type (also required), and (3) Description (optional). Let's look at each of these items separately.

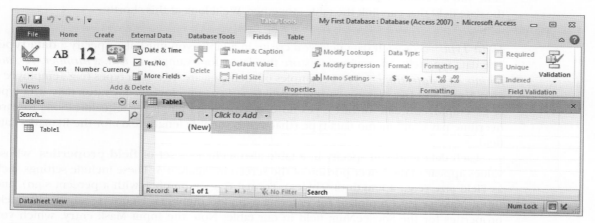

FIGURE 4-2   Opening screen for creating a table in Access.

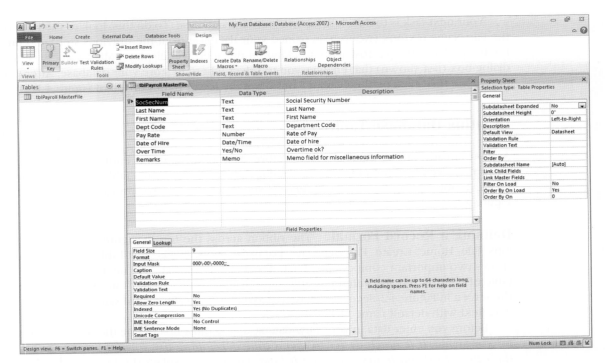

FIGURE 4-3 Payroll MasterFile table displaying field name, data type, description, and field properties for SocSecNum.

Field Name.   Field names are the names you assign to the data fields in your record. As illustrated in Figure 4-3, you can embed blanks in field names and capitalize selected letters in names as desired. Two general rules to follow when naming data fields are (1) use mnemonic names (that help you remember their use such as "Zip code") and (2) do not use excessively long names (which become cumbersome to use).

Although it isn't obvious from Figure 4-3, you can use the same field name in each of two tables—the field names in tables are completely independent of one another. In fact, using the same field names for the same data—for example, "Vendor #"—in both a Vendor table and a Vendor Invoices table often makes sense because this makes it easy to identify the data field that can link the tables together. We'll look at this shortly.

Data Type.   For each data field you create in a table, you must also specify a **data type**. The data type tells Access how to store the data—for example, as *text*, a *number, yes/no, memo*, or a *date/time*. Several examples of such data are: text data types (e.g., employee's First Name and Last Name); currency data type (e.g., employee's pay rate); date data type (e.g., employee's date of hire); yes/no data type (e.g., employee's qualifications to earn overtime pay); and memo data type (that stores variable length text) for the Remarks data field.

Each data field you specify in a table also includes a set of **field properties**, whose values appear in the lower portion of the screen in Figure 4-3. These include settings such as Field Size (e.g., a length of 9 bytes), Format (e.g., a number with a percent sign), and Input Mask (e.g., a template for entering a phone number). Figure 4-3 shows the field properties for the SocSecNum field in our table. Note the Input Mask entry, which you can select from a drop-down set of items if you click on this property. You might also be curious why we defined this as a text field rather than a number field. The reason is because this data value is not really a number that we can mathematically manipulate, but rather a code. Thus, we create it as a text field and limit its Field Size property to nine characters (see the bottom portion of Figure 4-3).

Finally, if you use a number data type, you must also select the type of number you wish to use—for example, *integer, long integer, single* (a small decimal value), or *double* (a large decimal value). These choices are important when using numeric data fields to link tables together—the fields must match exactly for the link to work.

Description.   The last item that you can create for each data field in a table is its description. This is an optional field that you can ignore when defining record structures. However, as you can see from the figure, data field descriptors help document the table itself and can also describe exception conditions or contain special notes.

Identifying a Primary Key.

Recall that a primary key is the data field in each record that uniquely identifies the record. After you have defined the data fields in your table, you should designate a primary key. For our payroll file example, we will use the employee's Social Security number (SocSecNum) as the primary key. One way to designate this field as the primary key is to click on the name of this field and then select "Primary Key" icon (🔑) from the banner at the top of the screen. An alternate way is to right click on the field with your mouse and select "primary key" from the set of choices in the drop-down list. The end result in either case will be the same—a little key icon appearing in the first column opposite the data field you selected, as illustrated in Figure 4-3. Note that relationship tables require a two-part primary key.

Saving a Table.

You can save your current work at any time by clicking on the Save icon in the menu at the top of your screen. If you attempt to close your table at this point (by clicking on the X in the upper-right portion of the screen), Access will prompt you to save the table.

Creating Relationships

After creating your tables, it is important to know how to create relationships between the tables. As you've seen from earlier discussions, these relationships link tables together. They also enable users to create multitable reports, such as the one in Figure 3-3. To illustrate how to create relationships in Access, assume that you have created a department table with records similar to the one in Figure 3-2. Figure 4-4 illustrates the record structure for this table, which we named "tblDepartments." The Department Code is the primary key for this table.

You now have two tables—"tblDepartments" and "tblPayroll MasterFile." They are related in a one-to-many relationship because each department has many employees, but each employee belongs to only one department. The department code is common to both tables, although its name differs slightly from one table to another. (We purposely used different names to demonstrate the fact that the names do not have to match exactly to link tables.) This field will act as the foreign key in the Payroll MasterFile table. To create a relationship between the two tables, follow these steps:

- *Step 1—Select tables.* Select "Relationships" from the "Database Tools" tab. From the tables listed on the left of your screen, right click on the table you wish to link (tblPayroll

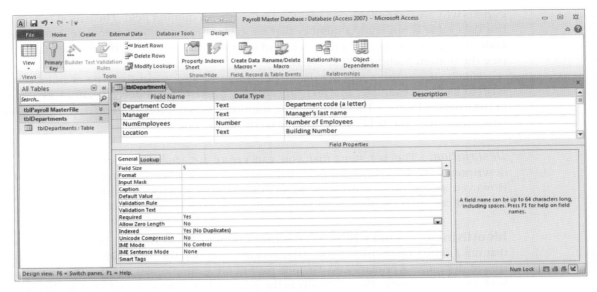

FIGURE 4-4 Departments table with properties for the department code.

Master File: Table), drag it into the Relationships window, and release the mouse. Now do the same with the tblDepartments: Table. You should now see boxes for the two tables in the Relationships window of Figure 4-5, but there will not be a line drawn between the two tables. That's our next task.

- *Step 2—Link the tables.* To link the two tables together, drag and drop the Department Code name from either table to the similar name in the other table. When you do, you should also see the Edit Relationships dialog window of Figure 4-5. This window enables you to enforce **referential integrity**. Check this box. In the context of this example, referential integrity is a control that prohibits users from creating employee records with references to nonexistent departments. (It does not affect your ability to create a department with no employees, however.)

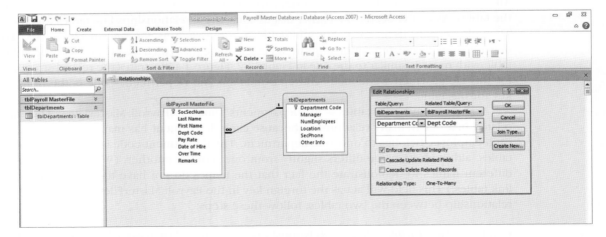

FIGURE 4-5 Linking tables and enforcing referential integrity of table relationships.

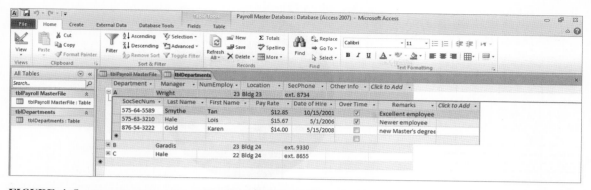

FIGURE 4-6   Showing subordinate data for multitable relationships.

If you follow these steps successfully, you should end up with a Relationships window with linked tables as shown in Figure 4-5. What you've done is link the tables together, using the Department Code as a foreign key. One dramatic way to see this linkage is to open the Departments table in run view (Figure 4-6). Note that there are now plus marks to the left of each department, indicating linked records. If you click on one of these plus marks with your mouse, you'll be able to see these records, as illustrated in Figure 4-6. Although it isn't obvious, the relationship you've created for your two tables will also enable you to create multitable reports. We'll explain how to do that in Chapter 5.

The databases that we have constructed are simple, text-based databases (i.e., they include data that can be organized and categorized according to the values stored in text or numeric data fields). It is important to recognize that databases can handle a wide variety of data formats. Databases store text, hypertext links, graphics, video, sound, and so on. For example, real estate brokers store pictures and narrated tours of listed properties, police departments store mug shots and voiceprints of prisoners, and publishing houses enhance the descriptions of everything from cookbooks to encyclopedias. Your employer could use a database to store your picture in an employee file (Figure 4-7), or even your current location (Figure 4-8).

FIGURE 4-7   The employee records of this security database contain both text data and the picture of each employee.

FIGURE 4-8 A database system with geotagging capability can record a user's precise location. Source: iStockphoto.

Case-in-Point 4.2 The U.S. Air Force recently warned that using social media sites such as Facebook could reveal servicemen's and women's position to enemies and threaten national security. Many sites have a feature called geotagging, which stores a user's global position within the site's database. Photographs taken with certain cell phones can also store geotags within the properties of the picture files. Location-based sites and files can reveal the precise locations of users. Indeed, many firms use geotagging capabilities to track raw materials and inventory.[2]

ENTERING DATA IN DATABASE TABLES

Creating Records

After specifying the names, data types, sizes, descriptions, and primary key for the data fields in our table, you can create individual records for it. To do so, you must switch to *datasheet* (or run) *view*. An easy way to do this is to close the design view of this table and then select the Datasheet view from the View menu in the upper-left portion of the Access screen in Figure 4-3.

After making these choices, you should see a screen similar to Figure 4-9. This is a table in datasheet view, and you are now free to input the data for individual records. Begin by entering data in the row with the asterisk (∗) and use the tab key to transition from data field to data field. Every time you complete the data entry for a new record, Access will save the record in the appropriate table automatically.

If you make a mistake while entering data, you can use your backspace key or delete key to correct it just as you would when correcting text in a word processor. Also, if you wish, you can delete an entire record by clicking on the first column to select an entire row (record) and then hitting the delete key. Because Access saves changes immediately, it will first remind you (via a small dialog box) that such a change will be permanent. If you indicate that this is your intent, Access will proceed to delete the record.

---

[2] http://www.informationweek.com/news/government/mobile/showArticle.jhtml?articleID=228300144

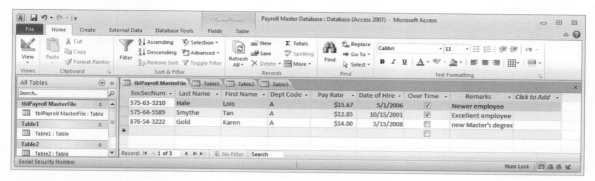

FIGURE 4-9 Dataview sheet for Payroll MasterFile table.

Ensuring Valid and Accurate Data Entry

The **data definition language (DDL)** of a DBMS enables its users to define the record structure of any particular database table tab (i.e., the individual fields that each record will contain). Thus, DDL is the language that DBMSs use to create the data dictionaries that we described in Chapter 3. Well-conceived record structures can serve as controls over the accuracy of critical accounting data. For example, strong data definitions could prevent errors such as typing "4" instead of "40" for hours worked, "NU" instead of "NY" for the state code in a mailing address, or "UPC" instead of "UPS" for the shipper code. Although it is impossible to guard against every possible type of error, database designers can use the following tools found in typical DBMSs to catch many of them.

Proper Data Types for Fields. Using Microsoft Access, one input control is inherent in the data type that you assign to a particular data field. For example, if you create a data field as a number data type, Access will reject all character inputs that are not numbers. Similarly, if you declare a data field as a date data type, Access will reject all input values (including alphabetic letters or punctuation marks) that cannot be part of a date. This is why it is often better to use data types *other than text* for data fields.

Input Masks. **Input masks** limit users to particular types of data in specific formats—for example, "123-45-6789" for a Social Security number, "(123)456-7890" for a telephone number, or "8/9/10" for a date. Although system designers use special symbols for the mask, the DBMS interprets these symbols as input requirements and acts accordingly. At data-entry time, the user will see the formatted part of the mask—for example, "___-__-____" for a Social Security number. Input masks help users input data correctly in databases by indicating a general input format, thereby reducing data-entry errors. Such masks also enable the system to reject incompatible data—for example, a letter mistakenly input in a numeric field.

Default Values. A third control over the accuracy of data entry is to specify a **default value** for the data fields of new records. For example, a payroll program could include the number "40" in the hours-worked data field for all employees who typically work 40 hours each week. Again, default values help guard against input errors as well as speed data entry.

Drop-Down Lists. You have likely seen combo boxes on Web pages that contain drop-down lists of choices. Database systems such as Access 2010 enable you to use

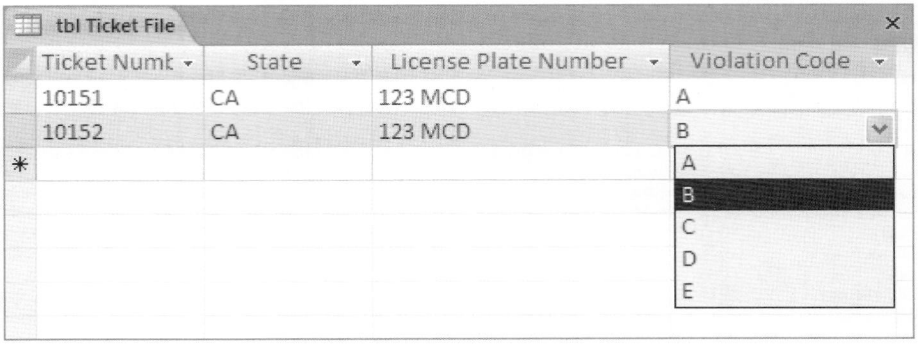

FIGURE 4-10   An example of a combo box at run time for the violation code of the Ticket File table.

similar boxes for your tables or forms (Figure 4-10). Although such boxes are convenient alternatives to typing data manually, they also control input errors because they limit user entries to valid inputs. In Access, another advantage of using a combo box is that you can store the choices for it as the values of a separate table, adding to the flexibility of the database itself.

Validation Rules.   One of the most versatile data-entry controls is the ability to create custom validation tests using a **validation rule**. Using Microsoft Access, for example, you create such rules as a record-structure property of a data field. Figure 4-11 illustrates an example for the "Fine Amount" data field of the Parking Violations Code table from Chapter 3, Figure 3-17. This (numeric) data field shows the amount of money that a person must pay for a particular parking violation. In Figure 4-11, the expression *Between 1 And 100* that appears in the properties window on the left side specifies the acceptable range of values. The error message in the message box on the right displays the "Validation Text" that you specify in this field's properties window. This is what will appear in a message box when a user attempts to enter a value (such as "200") that falls outside the allowable range.

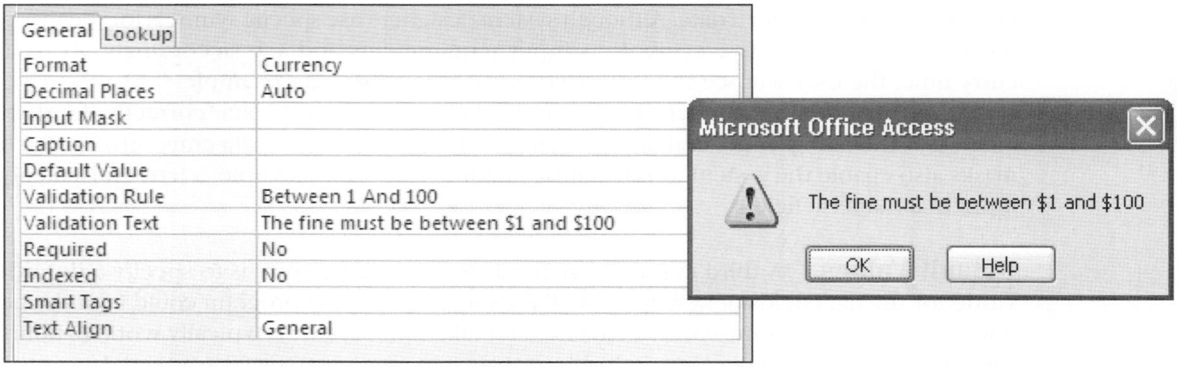

FIGURE 4-11   (Left) The properties window for the fine amount data field of the Parking Violations table. (Right) The error message that a user would see if he or she attempts to enter a value for this field that falls outside the specified range.

Validation rules can be simple, such as the one in Figure 4-11, or much more complex. For example, Access also enables you to use mathematical computations, predefined functions, and logical operators to create more complex validation rules. An example is *Between 1 And 100 AND Not 77,* which means that the entry value must fall in the specified range and cannot be "77." Another example is *Between [fldStartDate] and [fldEndDate],* which means that the date entered must be between an employee's hire date and his or her termination date.

Case-in-Point 4.3 Validation rules can accomplish more than just reducing data-entry errors. Pacific Timesheet makes employees' human resource data and related validation rules transparent to employees requesting time off. By making the validation rules transparent, employees are less likely to request time off when they fail to meet the requirements for the request. The system discourages requests for time off that will be denied, saving the valuable time of human resource personnel and helping employees understand why their requests are declined.[3]

Referential Integrity.   A final data-entry control is to enforce referential integrity in relational database tables. This feature controls certain inconsistencies among the records in relational tables. Consider, for example, the possibility of *deleting* a Parking Violations Code record from the third database table in Figure 3-17 (e.g., deleting the record for Code A—meter expired). We can't allow such a deletion because this would disrupt all of the *references* to that record in the Ticket table. For the same reason, we can't allow new records in the Ticket table to reference nonexistent codes in the Parking Violations Code table—for example, a ticket with Code Z (if such a code didn't exist). This would be a parking ticket for a nonexistent violation.

Database management systems make it easy to enforce referential integrity. In Access, for example, you simply check a box in the Edit Relationships dialog window at the time that you create the relationship—see Figure 4-12. This enforcement performs two

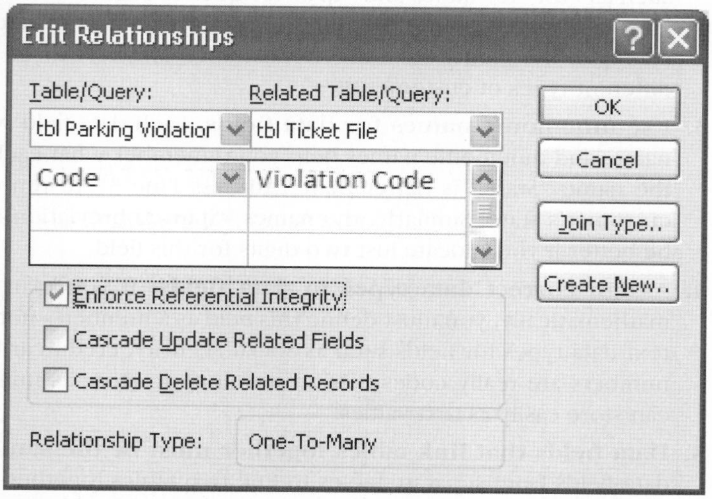

FIGURE 4-12   This dialog box appears when you first create a relationship in Microsoft Access. Clicking the check box to Enforce Referential Integrity does just that.

---

[3] http://www.newswiretoday.com/news/81080/

vital functions. First, it does not allow record deletions in the *one* table of a one-to-many relationship. Second, it does not allow a user to create a new record in the *many* table of a one-to-many relationship that references a nonexistent record on the *one* side. Case 4–23 illustrates these concepts in more detail.

In Figure 4-12, note that the Edit Relationships window in Access provides two additional boxes that you might check: one that allows Cascade Update Related Fields and one that allows Cascade Delete Related Records. These options enable you to override the referential integrity rules just described (although Access will warn you first). If you chose the first of these options, for example, you could delete a record in the Parking Violations Code file, and Access would also delete the reference to that record in the records of the Ticket file. (This would not be desirable here; however, it would leave you with tickets in the Tickets file with no violation code in them.) The second option allows you to delete a record from the one side of a one-to-many relationship, even if there are matching records on the many side. For example, if you delete a record in the Car Registration table, Access will then delete all the ticket records associated with that record (car) in the Ticket File table.

Tips for Creating Database Tables and Records

The preceding discussions described how to create tables and records in a database. There are many things that can go wrong when performing these tasks. Here are some guidelines to help you avoid them.

1. **Design first; create tables and records last.** Some people don't have time to do things right—only time to do things over. Don't be one of them. A careful definition of database entities and their relationships can prevent many problems later.

2. **Name tables systematically and use conventional tbl prefixes.** Even small databases contain many tables, queries, forms, and reports. Using conventional prefixes such as "tbl" for tables and "qry" for queries enables database designers to distinguish among them. You may also find it useful to name related tables systematically—for example, use names such as "tblCustomer_MasterFile" or "tblCustomer_Returns" for different types of customer files.

3. **Use mnemonic names for data fields.** Each data field within a record must have a name, and mnemonic names help you remember what each field means. For example, the name "State" is better than "Address Line 3" to represent the data field for the customer's state. Similarly, the names "State Abbreviation" or "State Code" may even be better if you allocate just two digits for this field.

4. **Assign correct data types to data fields.** If you plan to manipulate a data field mathematically, you must define this field as a number—not a text field. You should use text data types for fields such as Social Security, credit card, or phone numbers. These numbers are really codes that are too long to store as numbers, but ones that Access can store easily as text values.

5. **Data fields that link tables together must be the same data type.** If you use the data fields from separate tables to link two tables together, these fields *must* be of the exact same data type. Thus, you cannot link tables together if the foreign key in one table is a text field and the other is a date field. As noted earlier, when using "number" data fields, the *type* of number must also match—for example, each data field must be a long integer. Violating this rule is one of the most common errors novices make when creating database tables and relationships in Access.

6. **Limit the size of data fields to reasonable lengths.** Access assigns a default size of "255" characters to text fields. If, for example, you designate a state code of only two digits, you should change the default size to two digits. This will limit users to entering no more than two digits. A similar guideline applies to Social Security numbers, telephone numbers, product numbers, and similar values of predetermined, fixed length.

7. **Use input masks.** As explained earlier, an input mask is a template that outlines the expected values for a data field. An example of a phone number input mask is (999)000-0000, which limits the values in a phone number field to 10 numeric digits. Input masks help ensure accurate data input and help reduce mistakes.

EXTRACTING DATA FROM DATABASES: DATA MANIPULATION LANGUAGES

The totality of the information in a database and the relationships between its tables are called the database **schema**. Thus, the schema is a map or plan of the entire database. Using the previous student parking example, the schema would be all the information that a university might store about car registrations and parking tickets.

Any particular user or application program will normally be interested in (or might be limited to) only a subset of the information in the database. This limited access is a **subschema**, or *view*. For example, one subschema for our parking database might be the information required by the university registrar—for example, the student's name, Social Security number, and outstanding parking tickets. Subschemas are important design elements of a database because they dictate what data each user needs, and also because they protect sensitive data from unauthorized access.

The terms schema and subschema describe a simple idea—the distinction between the design of a database on one hand and the uses of a database on the other. The goal is to design a database schema that is flexible enough to create all of the subschemas required by users. The following sections describe several ways to create subschemas.

Creating Select Queries

The purchasing agent of a manufacturing company needs to know what inventory balances are below their reorder points. A payroll manager wants to know which employees are eligible to receive year-end bonuses. A tax assessor is interested in those areas of the city that have experienced the most real estate appreciation.

What these individuals have in common is the need for specific information from one or more database tables. **Queries** allow database developers to create customized subschemas. For example, using the student car registration database, you might want to (1) look up something about a specific student (e.g., the license plate number of his or her car), (2) change the information in a specific record (e.g., update a student's phone number), (3) delete a record (e.g., because the person sells his or her car), or (4) list file information selectively (e.g., prepare a list of all students with California license plates). A **dynaset** is a dynamic subset of a database that you create with such queries, and the purpose of a **data manipulation language (DML)** is to help you create such dynasets.

Case-in-Point 4.4   Internal auditors are charged with evaluating internal controls, operational efficiency, business risks, and other critical factors for success. The volume of data that internal auditors examine has expanded rapidly over the past decade, and internal auditors are developing new tools and testing procedures to detect risks and operational inefficiencies in complex environments. Conducting database queries is now a valuable and important skill for internal auditors. One example of modern application of queries by internal auditors involves employee phone records. Firms can analyze the phone calls made by their employees in order to reduce telecommunications costs and ensure compliance with policies related to telecommunications. Queries of long-distance call records allow internal auditors to detect misuse of phone services.[4]

One-Table Select Queries.   A **select query** creates a dynaset of database information based on two types of user-specified criteria: (1) criteria that determine which records to include and (2) criteria that determine which data fields to include *from* those records. Figure 4-13 illustrates a simple select query that displays particular information from a single table using Microsoft Access. This example asks the system to display the last name, first name, phone number, state licensed, and license plate number for all cars with California license plates.

You can create several types of queries with Access 2010. One is a simple *filter query* that references only one table. Another combines the information from several tables. A third type is an action query. We look at each of these queries next.

Single Criterion.   To create a simple filter query, first click the Create tab on the main menu bar. In the Create menu, click "Query Design." Access will display a small dialog box that allows you to select the table(s) on which to base your query. To create the query in Figure 4-13, we need only the tbl Car Registrations File. The bottom portion of Figure 4-13 shows the layout in which to enter your data fields and the selection criteria for them.

Your next task is to select the data fields in each record you wish to display. One way to do this is to click on the first (left-most) cell in the Field row in the lower portion of the Query panel. An arrow will appear in this cell. Click on this arrow and a drop-down list of available data fields will appear. Select the field from this list that you wish to display in the

---

tbl Car Registration ...
*
🔑 Social Security Numb
Last Name
First Name
Phone Number
State Licensed
Number License Plat

Field:	[Last Name]	[First Name]	[Phone Number]	[State Licensed]	[Number License Plate
Table:	tbl Car Registration F	tbl Car Registration F	tbl Car Registration F	tbl Car Registration F	tbl Car Registration F
Sort:					
Show:	☑	☑	☑	☑	☑
Criteria:				="CA"	
or:					

FIGURE 4-13   A simple query to select all car registrations with CA (California) license plates.

---

[4] Watson, M., and K. Dow. 2010. Auditing operational compliance: The case of employee long distance piracy. *Issues in Accounting Education* 25(3): 513–526.

current column (we selected Last Name in the figure). Continue across the panel until you have selected all the fields you need. Alternate methods of selecting data fields for queries in Access 2010 are (1) double-clicking on the desired field name in the table list of the upper panel or (2) dragging the field name to the column.

Next, you must specify the selection criteria for the query. For example, to display only those records with California licenses enter "=CA" in the criteria box under "State Licensed." You will see CA is now enclosed with quotation marks, which Access automatically adds for you. Basic comparison operators are also available for setting criteria—that is, = (equals), < (less than), > (greater than), > = (greater than or equal to), < = (less than or equal to), and <> (not equal to).

You are now ready to run the filter. To do this, click the exclamation point with the word "Run" on the left portion of the main menu. The results of your query will appear as shown in Figure 4-14. You can toggle back and forth between design and run modes by clicking on the View option in the Results section of the left side of the main menu.

After you have created a query, most DBMSs enable you to save it in a separate file for later use, thus eliminating the need to rewrite it. This allows end users to run pre-made queries that are created by designers and database experts. The letters "qry" are the standard naming prefix for queries. Thus, as you can see in Figure 4-14, we named our query "qryCalifornia License Plates."

Multiple Criteria.   It is also possible to specify multiple criteria in a query. For example, suppose you wanted a list of all car registrants whose cars had California license plates *and* whose last names were "Curry." To create such a query in Access, simply type the name "Curry" in the "Last Name" column and in the *same* Criteria row as the "CA." Access interprets criteria appearing in the same row as an "and" operation. The results will be all those records with last name "Curry" *and* whose license plate state is "CA." Similarly, if you specify three criteria in the same row, then Access will find database records in the table satisfying all three requirements.

Sometimes, you might want to search for records that satisfy alternate requirements—for example, car registrants whose cars have California license plates *or* whose last names are "Curry." To create such a query in Access, use multiple lines at the bottom of the Query dialog box in Figure 4-13. The result of this query will be all records that satisfy *either* requirement. (The system will also include records satisfying both requirements.)

Last Name	First Name	Phone Number	State Licensed	Number License Plate
Curry	Dorothy	(916) 358-4448	CA	123MCD
Jones	Roberta	(987) 654-2132	CA	876JJH
Kerr	Stephen	(916) 764-3211	CA	498SEK
Mason	Richard	(916) 563-7865	CA	253DAL
Tajiri	Colleen	(916) 543-2211	CA	897ABC

Home   Create   External Data   Database Tools

Relationships   qryCalifornia License Plates

FIGURE 4-14   The result of the query in Figure 4-13.

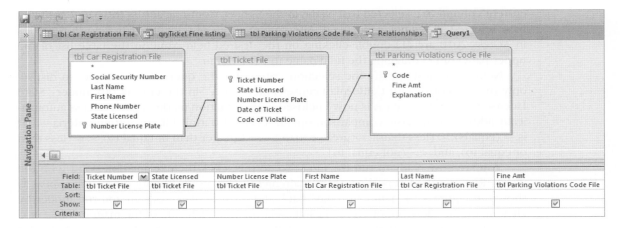

FIGURE 4-15 A multiple-table query.

Multitable Select Queries.

Many accounting applications require information that must be drawn from more than one database table. For example, suppose you wanted to create a report similar to the following:

Ticket Number	License Plate	Registered Car Owner	Listed Phone Number	Amount of Ticket
10151	CA 123 MCD	Dorothy Curry	(916) 358–4448	$10.00
10152	CA 123 MCD	Dorothy Curry	(916) 358–4448	$20.00
10231	CA 253 DAL	Richard Mason	(916) 563–7865	$50.00

Notice that the information in this report comes from three different tables: the ticket number and license plate number come from the Tickets table, the registered car owner's name and phone number come from the Car Registrations table, and the amount of each ticket comes from the Parking Violations Code table. To create such a report, you must first join the tables using the Relationships window as we described earlier in the chapter.

Your next step is to construct the query. Follow the steps outlined above for creating simple queries, being careful to select the data fields shown in Figure 4-15. The results should be similar to those shown in Figure 4-16.

Ticket Numb ▾	State Licens ▾	License Plat ▾	First Name ▾	Last Name ▾	Fine Amt ▾
10151	CA	123 MCD	Dorothy	Curry	$10.00
10152	CA	123 MCD	Dorothy	Curry	$20.00
10231	CA	253 DAL	Richard	Mason	$50.00
10121	CA	123 MCD	Dorothy	Curry	$20.00

FIGURE 4-16 The results of the multiple-table query in Figure 4-15.

The tasks performed by a query such as the one shown in Figure 4-15 are nontrivial. To appreciate this, imagine that you had to create the report described above manually. Assume that there were over 100,000 parking tickets and millions of car registration records in the database. Sorting and organizing the records would take weeks. A computerized DBMS can accomplish this task and print the results almost instantly—an amazing accomplishment if you think about it!

Creating Action Queries

Although most queries simply extract information from database tables, some accounting tasks require users to update or delete multiple records in a single operation. Microsoft Access supports the **action queries** listed below. You can create any of these queries by selecting the appropriate choice from the options that appear at the top of the screen after clicking on the Design tab while in the Query Tools menu (Figure 4-17).

- *Delete queries.* Enables you to delete table records selectively. Examples include the ability to delete employees who have left the organization, students who drop out of school or graduate from school, or inventory products no longer sold by the company.
- *Append queries.* Enables you to append records from one table to the end of another table. Accounting examples include the ability to add the payroll records for the current period to a year-to-date table or to consolidate the employees from two departments into a single table.
- *Update queries.* Enables you to alter selected table records systematically. Accounting examples include the ability to raise all suggested retail prices of a particular product line by 10 percent, lower the salaries of all those employees with a low performance rating by 5 percent, or add a fixed handling charge to all customer purchases over a set limit.
- *Make-table queries.* Enables you to create a new table from the records that you select in an existing table. For example, a university might want to create a separate table of all graduating seniors. Auditors might use this query is to create a separate table of all records that have been deleted in order to maintain an audit trail.

Some other queries available in the Access Query Wizard are:

- *Simple query Wizard.* Does the same thing as described previously under One-Table Select Queries.
- *Crosstab queries.* Enables you to perform a statistical analysis of the data in a table and provide the cross-tabulation results in a row-and-column format similar to a pivot table in Excel. For example, a crosstab query might show the average invoice amount for each vendor in a Vendor table or the average credit purchase amount for each customer living in a specified zip code.

FIGURE 4-17 The Query Wizard screen of options available in Access.

- *Find-duplicates queries.* Enables you to find those records with duplicate entries in a specified field. Many common auditing tasks require such queries—for example, finding duplicate customer orders, finding employees with the same Social Security or employee number, or searching for different vendor records with the same address. Note that a simple select query might enable you to find *one example* of such duplicates. A find-duplicates query enables you to find *all duplicates* with a single query.

- *Find-unmatched queries.* Enables you to find the records in one table with no matching record in another table. For example, such queries enable auditors to identify those weekly payroll records with no matching master employee records or to identify vendor invoices with no matching supplier record.

Guidelines for Creating Queries

The preceding discussions described various kinds of select queries and action queries. Here are some guidelines to help you create error-free queries using Microsoft Access:

1. *Spell accurately and be sensitive to capitalization.* The criteria for Access select queries are case sensitive. For example, you will not get matches if you specify California licenses as "Cal" or "Ca" in a criteria line if the entries in the underlying database table are "CA."

2. *Specify AND and OR operations correctly.* If you want a query to satisfy two conditions simultaneously (i.e., perform an AND operation), enter the criteria on the *same line* of your query. If you want a query to satisfy *either* of two conditions (i.e., perform an OR operation), place them on successive criteria lines.

3. *Tables must be joined properly.* If you wish to construct a multitable query, the tables should first be joined properly in the Access Relationships window.

4. *Name queries systematically.* Query names should begin with the standard "qry" prefix. It also helps to assign mnemonic query names—for example, "qryCustomers _in_California" or "qryGraduating_Seniors."

5. *Choose data fields selectively.* Double-clicking on the asterisk (∗) in the data field list of a table (e.g., the first symbol in each of the three table lists in Figure 4-15) enables you to include *all* the data fields from that table in your query. Because most commercial database tables have many data fields, using this option can result in a large number of data fields (i.e., columns in the lower portion of your query).

Structured Query Language

In addition to using a DML in a DBMS, you can also access selected information from a database using a *data query language.* The American National Standards Institute (ANSI) has adopted standards for one such query language: **structured query language (SQL)**. This language is important because most relational databases such as Access support it. Figure 4-18 shows how you could construct the request for records with California license plates using SQL.

SQL is a useful tool for auditors because understanding SQL allows an auditor to retrieve data from many database systems, both small and large. In most contemporary business environments, an auditor can no longer retrieve data from paper reports. Instead, data must be acquired from the computerized accounting information system. SQL allows a user to

```
SELECT (LastName, FirstName, PhoneNumber, LicPlateState, LicPlateNo)
FROM CarRegistrationFile
WHERE LicPlateState = CA;
```

FIGURE 4-18   An example of SQL instructions for the example of Figure 4-13. These instructions will list the last name, first name, phone number, license plate state, and license plate number of all cars with license plate state code "CA."

specify the table and fields that the user wants to retrieve, using commands such as FROM, SELECT, and WHERE. FROM identifies the table source and SELECT chooses the data fields to include in the query. The WHERE command can specify criteria, such as selecting sales orders in excess of a specified dollar amount.

Sorting, Indexing, and Database Programming

In addition to accessing or listing records selectively, a DBMS also enables you to reorganize a table. One way to do this is by sorting records, which means physically rewriting records on a disk in the desired order. This is both time consuming and usually unnecessary. It is faster and easier to index your records (by setting the Indexed property to "Yes" in Figure 4-10), which simply creates a table of record keys and disk addresses that accomplishes the same purpose as sorting. Thus, when users specify "sort" in queries, Access does not physically reorder records but instead temporarily assembles the information in correct order for display purposes.

Finally, even the best DBMS software cannot anticipate every user's processing needs. For this reason, advanced DBMSs include programming tools that enable users to develop their own processing applications. Users commonly develop customized data-entry screens, which enable them to include better data descriptions and more detailed instructions for data-entry personnel on the input screens. Similarly, programming languages (such as VBA for Microsoft Access) enable users to create custom processing routines—for example, to create their own data-validation routines. This end-user programming is important because it enables users to perform their own data processing without the technical assistance of IT professionals.

Online Analytical Processing and Data Mining

Online Analytical Processing (OLAP).   **OLAP** involves using data-extraction tools to obtain complex information that describes *what* happened and also *why* it happened. Several software developers now market OLAP packages. Examples include *Integration Server* (Arbor Software), *Holos* (Seagate Technology), *PowerDimensions* (SyBase), *Plato* (Microsoft), and *WhiteLight* (WhiteLight Systems). Some of these tools work only with specific databases, while others interface with several of them. Most allow end users to perform their own database analyses, including data mining (discussed shortly) and creating **pivot tables**, which are two-dimensional statistical summaries of database information (and similar to the pivot tables in *Microsoft Excel*).

Data Mining.   Closely connected to OLAP is the concept of **data mining**, which means using a set of data analyses and statistical tools to detect relationships, patterns, or trends among stored data. For example, data mining tools might enable an auditor to find falsified invoices or overstated revenues. Data mining can help advertisers to cross-sell products or offer tie-in promotions, help retailers decide product placements in their stores (e.g., placing snacks near the frozen pizza section), and help sales managers increase customer satisfaction. Because data mining tools can sift through massive amounts of corporate data to detect patterns, they can be particularly effective tools for firms seeking to better understand their customers or their cost drivers.

A wide variety of software tools now provide data mining capabilities, and many data mining tools are included in OLAP software, database software, and artificial intelligence algorithms. In addition, users can purchase specific software packages for data mining tasks—for example, *Darwin* (Oracle), *Intelligent Miner* (IBM), *Enterprise Miner* (SAS), or *Clementine* (SPSS).

Although the most popular uses of data mining are related to sales and marketing, there are many accounting applications as well. One possibility is for auditors to use data mining to detect credit card anomalies or suspicious behavior. For example, fraudulent credit card transactions may follow a pattern, such as an increase in the total amount of purchases immediately following a credit card theft or products with special characteristics (such as ones that can easily be sold). Another application is for investors to use data mining tools to predict corporate bankruptcies. The use of data mining is also expanding in the audit profession.

> *Case-in-Point 4.5* Data mining can be employed to analyze the text in corporate e-mail and external communications. Recent psychology research demonstrates that employees' and executives' word choices can effectively detect lies and fraud. Future auditors are likely to employ advanced data mining techniques to analyze e-mails, corporate press releases, and minutes of board of director meetings.[5]

RECENT DATABASE ADVANCES AND DATA WAREHOUSES

Use of relational databases is widespread in business applications throughout the world. Recent technological advances are changing the way firms design and use these database systems. Two of the most critical advances are cloud computing and XML.

Cloud Computing

Cloud computing is a form of Internet-based computing. Instead of applications being stored on individual workstations, software is provided through the Internet, processing occurs on a Web of computers, and information is ultimately sent to the user's computer. Cloud computing allows companies to expand their IT capabilities without investing in significant hardware, software, or training. All that is necessary is a subscription to a service that offers the software and processing capabilities that the firm needs.

The use of cloud computing is expanding rapidly in small businesses and large corporations because of its low costs, scalability, and simplicity relative to creating in-house systems. Cloud services revenue was approximately $70 billion in 2010. Shifts toward cloud computing have major implications for modern database systems. New services called **Database-As-A-Service (DAAS)** are beginning to emerge. DAAS allows firms to outsource their databases to cloud service providers. For example, the databases behind consumer Web sites such as Amazon.com can be outsourced completely to

---

[5] Hunton, J., and J. Rose. 2010. 21st century auditing: Advancing decision support systems to achieve continuous auditing. *Accounting Horizons* 24(2): 297–312.

providers who also manage Internet sales systems and Web interfaces. Enterprise Resource Planning systems that contain all of the data for an entire organization can also be outsourced to cloud computing vendors. DAAS systems remove the need for firms to hire their own database administrators, design and maintain database systems, or purchase hardware. Thus, while the basic principles of databases will remain the same, the providers of database systems are changing. As databases move from within firms to "the cloud," new considerations for accountants will emerge. In particular, controls over confidential firm data will be critical in the new cloud environment. Imagine the difficulty involved in protecting firm data that is no longer maintained on private servers within the firm, but is instead being managed on the Web.

Another common example of cloud computing involves backup services—that is, creating duplicate copies of critical data for security purposes. Just as individual users can backup files on synchronized external hard disks, businesses can contract with such vendors as *Carbonite, Mozy*, and *SOS* to create similar backups over the Internet. These vendors can often perform the same backup tasks less expensively and more reliably, and of course, such contracts shift the security responsibility from the database owner to the Internet vendor. But such cloud computing also carries risks—in particular, the danger of relying upon an external party to protect sensitive data as well as properly maintaining the backups.

Case-in-Point 4.6   Those companies maintaining large databases have at least one thing in common: the need to protect their data against intrusion, theft, and corruption. This is one reason why experts predict that, in the next few years, most businesses and government agencies will abandon on-site data storage and maintain all their critical databases on the media of online backup and storage service providers.[6]

Data Warehouses

Where feasible, it often makes sense to pool the data from separate applications into a large, common body of information called a **data warehouse**. The data in a data warehouse are rarely current. Rather, they are typically "older information" that was initially collected for other reasons during the conduct of normal operations and daily activities of an organization. For example, in recording a sale, an AIS collects data about the customer, the product, the timing of the sale, and so on. Extended histories of this information can be helpful in predicting things such as future sales of new products. In order to analyze large volumes of historical data, the data must first be amassed in a central location—the data warehouse.

Case-in-Point 4.7   In 2010, researchers proposed a new application of data warehouses. By using data warehouses to accumulate large amounts of information about security breaches both within a firm and across firms, organizations will be able to predict future attacks on their information systems. Predicting attacks will allow organizations to develop more effective security procedures and better allocate resources to technologies for protecting firm data. These new data warehouses for security breaches will allow firms to detect patterns that would not be apparent in smaller data sets.[7]

---

[6] http://ezinearticles.com/?Professionals,-Big-Businesses-Rely-on-Online-Backup-Services&id=5421978
[7] Kim, P., and L. Steen, 2010. Can management predict information security threats utilizing a data warehouse? *Journal of Information Systems Applied Research* 3(15).

To be useful, the data in data warehouses should have the following characteristics: (1) free of errors, (2) defined uniformly, (3) span a longer time horizon than the company's transaction systems, and (4) optimized data relationships that allow users to answer complex questions—for example, queries requiring information from several diverse sources.

One advantage of a data warehouse is to make organizational information available on a corporate-wide basis. For example, the marketing representatives of a company can gain access to the company's production data and thereby be better able to inform customers about the future availability of desired, but as yet unmanufactured, products. This idea is also central to the concept of an **enterprise-wide database** or enterprise resource planning (ERP) system (i.e., large repositories of organizational data that come from, and are available to, a wide range of employees).

Case-in-Point 4.8 With more than 9 million customers, KeyBank is the thirteenth largest bank in the United States. To help market financial products, the bank created a million-dollar DB2 data warehouse that allows its managers to determine what investments its customers prefer (e.g., CDs or mutual funds) and how best to sell products (e.g., direct mail or Internet). Bank officials credit the data warehouse, the decision tools that mine it, and the ability of different departments to share data, for increasing customer contacts by 200 percent and a 100 percent return on the investment in 14 months.[8]

Building a data warehouse is a complex task. The developers must first decide what data to collect, how to standardize and scrub (clean) the data to ensure uniform accuracy and consistency, and how to deal with computer records that are often not normalized. One reason for these difficulties is that the data in data warehouses may come from numerous sources. As a result, the same data element can have two different representations or values—for example, an eight-digit numeric product code in the AIS and a six-digit alphabetic character code in a production application. Similarly, one corporate division might capture sales daily while another collects the same data weekly. The developers must determine data standards in both cases, reconcile any discrepancies, and account for missing fields and misspellings. Another challenge is to build the data warehouse in such a way that users can access it easily and find answers to complex questions. Finally, data warehouses must be extremely secure, as they contain enterprise-wide data that must be protected.

When corporate executives believe the rewards for building a data warehouse do not outweigh the costs, they can consider a **data mart**. Data marts are smaller than data warehouses, and they typically focus on just one application area—for example, marketing data. However, in most other ways, they are similar to data warehouses.

AIS AT WORK
Using Data Mining to Predict Financial Disasters[9]

Typically, we think about looking for patterns in numbers when talking about data mining. For example, a firm might want to learn which products generate the most profits during different seasons, or it may seek to better understand its customers' purchasing patterns. Data mining, however, can also be applied to text, such as stories in the popular

---

[8] http://www.key.com
[9] Cecchini, M., H. Aytug, G. Koehler, and P. Pathak. 2010. Making words work: Using financial text as a predictor of financial events. *Decision Support Systems* 50(1): 164–175.

press, corporate e-mail, and even the financial statements themselves. Auditors, regulators, financial analysts, and investors may soon have a wide array of data mining tools available for predicting firms' future performance.

The SEC requires all publicly traded firms to file electronically, which has created a huge volume of corporate filings that users can mine to discover patterns in data. A new data mining technique involves analyses of the Management Discussion and Analysis (MD&A) section of the 10-K form, which the SEC requires. The MD&A is a narrative where management describes the prior year's results and discusses future plans. The new data mining technique identifies firms that are likely to experience financial distress (such as bankruptcy) by studying the words in the MD&A section.

The main idea is to develop lists of keywords that are associated with firms that go bankrupt by examining the MD&A of all firms that go bankrupt during a period of time. Then, the system scans an individual firm's MD&A and determines whether there is a pattern of key words that is similar to those found for bankrupt firms. When the similarity is high, the likelihood of bankruptcy is also high. According to its developers, the system accurately distinguishes between firms that go bankrupt versus those that do not go bankrupt with 80 percent accuracy. Again, this prediction is based solely on the statements made by management in the MD&A, without any examination of actual financial data. If analyzing only management statements can help predict bankruptcy, then advanced data mining systems that simultaneously analyze financial data, media coverage, MD&A, e-mails, and so on may prove to have substantial predictive accuracy.

SUMMARY

- ✓ Database management systems (DBMSs) enable users to create their own databases using data definition languages (DDLs) and manipulate file data using data manipulation languages (DMLs).

- ✓ Designers can integrate a variety of data-validation techniques to help ensure data integrity. Examples include choosing data types carefully for data fields, using input masks, using default values, creating a wide variety of validation rules, and enforcing referential integrity.

- ✓ Microsoft Access is a popular database management system that small businesses can use to create complete accounting systems. The chapter illustrated the techniques you can use to create database tables and records with this software.

- ✓ An important use of databases is to extract selected information from it, and Access provides a number of tools for constructing select queries and action queries. These tools allow users to extract data from a single table or from multiple tables. Following the guidelines in this chapter can help you avoid errors when creating such queries.

- ✓ Two additional ways of extracting information from databases are using structured query language (SQL) and online analytical processing (OLAP) tools.

- ✓ Users can also manipulate database information by sorting, indexing, using data mining tools, or performing specialized tasks with end-user programming languages.

- ✓ Accountants are likely to need to extract data from a database or data warehouse at one time or another, using data manipulation languages such as queries, OLAP, or data mining tools.

- ✓ Cloud computing and data mining are changing the design and delivery of database management systems.

- ✓ Data warehouses typically combine the information from separate databases into large sets of cross-functional data repositories that can help businesses increase data-retrieval efficiency, output productivity, and long-term profitability.

KEY TERMS YOU SHOULD KNOW

action query	field properties
data definition language (DDL)	input masks
data manipulation language (DML)	online analytical processing (OLAP)
data mart	pivot tables
data mining	query
data type	referential integrity
data warehouse	schema
Database-As-A-Service (DAAS)	select query
default value	structured query language (SQL)
dynaset	subschema
enterprise-wide database	validation rule

DISCUSSION QUESTIONS

4-1. This chapter described how to create tables and records in Microsoft Access. What other database management systems are available? Use the Internet to learn more about these systems.

4-2. Identify the different data types available for creating data fields in Microsoft Access. Similarly, identify the different types of numbers (e.g., long integer) you can use if you define a field as a data type. (Hint: create a data field in a throwaway database table, assign it a number data type, and examine the possibilities for the Field Size property.)

4-3. Create a Salesperson table and a Customer Order table using the data in Figure 3-11. Create records for each table using the data provided. Add one more Salesperson record with your own name and an employee number of your choosing. Also add at least one customer order with your number as the salesperson. Finally, create a relationship for the two tables. Create hard-copy documentation of your work.

4-4. What are database management systems? Are they the same as databases? Why are DBMSs classified as software and not hardware?

4-5. What are data definition languages (DDLs)? How are they related to DBMSs?

4-6. Why do database developers link tables together? How is this done using Access?

4-7. What is data validation? Why is it important? Give some examples of how to validate data inputs using Access.

4-8. What are data manipulation languages? How are these languages related to database management systems? How are these languages related to databases?

4-9. What is SQL? How is SQL like an Access query? How is it different?

4-10. What is online analytical processing? How is OLAP related to databases? What is a pivot table and how are pivot tables and OLAP related?

4-11. What is the difference between *sorting records* and *indexing records* in a database?

4-12. What is data mining? How is data mining useful to profit-seeking companies? What are some accounting uses of data mining?

4-13. What is cloud computing? How will it influence accounting systems?

4-14. What are data warehouses? How are they like databases? How do they differ from databases?

4-15. Why would a company be interested in creating a data warehouse? Why would a company *not* be interested in creating a data warehouse?

PROBLEMS

4-16. The Query Corporation employs the individuals listed in Figure 4-19. Use Access or another DBMS required by your instructor to create a database of this information and then perform the following queries.

    a. List all employees in Department 5. Print this list.

    b. List all employees with first name Brenda. Print this list.

    c. List all those employees with pay rates over $6.50. Print this list.

    d. List all those employees eligible for overtime (T = yes; F = no). Print this list.

4-17. Use the Web to find current examples of data warehousing software. Why do companies create data warehouses and what are some accounting uses of such warehouses?

4-18. Use the Web to find current examples of online analytical processing (OLAP). Why do companies use OLAP? What is the connection between OLAP and databases?

4-19. The information in Figure 4-20 is for the employees of the Marcia Felix Corporation. Use a DBMS software package to create a database for it.

    a. What record structure did you design? Identify the names, widths, and other characteristics of each field in a typical record.

    b. Sort these employees by department. Print this list.

    c. Sort these employees by test score. Print this list.

    d. Sort these employees by department and alphabetically by last name within department.

    e. What is the average pay rate for these employees?

    f. What is the average pay rate for females? What is the average for males?

    g. What females scored over 70 on their examinations? What males scored over 50?

Record Number	Last Name	First Name	Social Security Number	Dept	Pay Rate	Over-time
1	ADCOX	NORMAN	901795336	1	6.50	Yes
2	KOZAR	LINDA	412935350	1	6.50	Yes
3	MCLEAN	KAY	405751308	1	7.50	No
4	CUNNINGHAM	TOM	919782417	3	7.50	Yes
5	DANIELS	PATRICIA	517351609	3	5.50	Yes
6	MCGUIRE	ANNE	201891647	3	5.50	Yes
7	REEDER	BRENDA	619294493	3	5.50	Yes
8	BLOOM	BRENDA	513321592	4	6.25	Yes
9	DAVIS	DENISE	517351608	4	5.50	Yes
10	DUFFY	LESLIE	314532409	4	8.50	No
11	HARPER	LINDA	615824130	4	5.75	Yes
12	MORGAN	MEREDITH	704563903	4	6.25	Yes
13	WELSH	KAREN	216253428	4	8.25	No
14	CHAPIN	GEORGE	203767263	5	7.50	Yes
15	FINN	JOHN	715386721	5	6.25	Yes
16	HALPIN	MARSHA	913541871	5	6.50	Yes
17	LAURIN	PHILIP	514484631	5	6.50	Yes
18	MIAGLIO	PEGGY	414224972	5	6.25	Yes
19	TURNER	BRENDA	713589164	5	8.50	No
20	ZORICH	MILDRED	504455827	5	6.50	Yes

FIGURE 4-19 Employees of the Query Corporation.

Personnel File
Date: October 10, 20xx

	Employee Number	Score on Aptitude Test	Department ID	Current Pay Rate	Sex
BAKER, JEFFREY L.	1692	73	A	$7.50	M
BARRETT, RAYMOND G.	3444	53	B	7.45	M
BLISS, DONALD W.	6713	55	D	6.80	M
BOWERS, PAUL D.	2084	42	B	5.90	M
BUCHANAN, CINDY	3735	41	E	7.80	F
CHEUNG, WAI KONG	8183	55	C	7.80	F
CONRAD, MARK E.	8317	58	D	9.60	M
DAILY, REBECCA E.	2336	45	D	8.90	F
DRISCOLL, DAVID M.	5210	47	D	7.70	M
ERICKSON, KURT N.	2217	53	B	8.50	M
FRANTZ, HEIDI L.	6390	55	A	6.90	F
GARROW, SCOTT D.	8753	61	A	7.40	M
HARDENBROOK, LISA A.	7427	40	C	6.70	F
JACKSON, GREG W.	4091	67	D	8.90	M
LANGLEY, JERRY W.	3262	86	E	9.40	M
LUBINSKI, TRAVIS M.	3865	37	D	7.50	M
LYNCH, SHERENE D.	7857	66	D	8.90	F
MARKHAM, KYLE R.	6766	62	A	7.90	M
MCGUIRE, TANA B.	4052	55	A	9.20	F
MONACH, SHERI L.	8082	48	B	9.10	F
MOORE, MICHAEL S.	2431	67	E	8.50	M
NELSON, JOHN R.	5873	46	B	7.40	M
PAPEZ, PETER M.	7799	41	E	8.30	M
PETTINARI, DARIN M.	1222	56	B	8.40	M

FIGURE 4-20 Employee data for the Marcia Felix Corporation.

CASE STUDIES

BSN Bicycles I (Creating a Database from Scratch with Microsoft Access)

Bill Barnes and Tom Freeman opened their BSN bicycle shop in 2005. Not counting Jake—a friend who helps out occasionally at the store—Bill and Tom are the only employees. The shop occupies a small commercial space that was once a restaurant. The former kitchen now stores spare parts and provides space for bicycles repairs while the former dining area in the front is now the retail sales area. The corporate office is just a desk and file cabinet in the back corner of the retail area.

Bill and Tom are more friends and bicycling enthusiasts than businessmen. They've pretty much sunk their life savings into the shop and are anxious that it succeed. In the first year of operations, they worked hard to convert the space into its present condition, which includes an old-timey sign above the door with their name ''BSN Bicycles.''

With all the other work that had to be done the first year, marketing efforts have been limited to chatting with friends, distributing flyers at bicycle races and similar sporting events, and placing a few advertisements in the local newspaper. Similarly, the owners haven't paid much attention to accounting tasks. Who has time with all the other things that had to get done? But at least two things are now clear to the owners: (1) some of their loyal customers prefer to buy items on credit, and (2) all of their suppliers want to be paid on time.

Right now, BSN's customer credit system is a box of 3 × 5 cards. Each handwritten card contains customer information on the front and invoice information on the back (Figure 4-21). When a customer pays an invoice, one of the owners simply crosses off the invoice information on the card. The supplier accounts system is similar, except that the vendor box of 3 × 5 cards is green, whereas the customer box is gray.

Jake is a part-time student at the local community college. He recently completed a course on microcomputer applications that included a segment on Microsoft Access. He doesn't know very much about database theory, but thinks that converting the shop's current accounting systems to a DBMS might be a good idea. He thinks, for example, that BSN needs a Customer table and a Vendor (supplier) table. He also thinks that BSN will need an Inventory table to keep track of inventory, but that even more tables might be required. Can you help them?

Requirements

1. Identify the resources, events, and agents for BSN's accounting systems. Draw one or more E-R diagrams that illustrate the relationships between these items.

2. Identify the tables that you would need to create a working database for the company's receivables, payables, and inventory.

3. Using Access or another DBMS required by your instructor, create at least three records for each of the tables you identified in part 2. Hints: (1) Use the information on the front of the 3 × 5 card in Figure 4-21 for the customer record structure. (2) The data fields for the Vendors table should include the vendor ID, vendor name and address information,

(a) The front of a 3x5 BSN customer card.

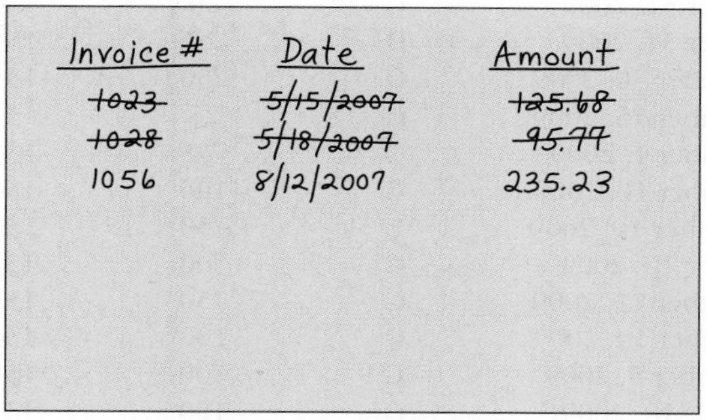

(b) The back of a 3x5 BSN customer card.

FIGURE 4-21   A customer record for the BSN company.

phone number, fax number, and contact person. (3) The data fields for the Inventory table should include item number, item description, units (e.g., dozen, each, etc.), unit cost, unit retail sales price, and quantity on hand.

4. Create relationships for your various tables.

5. Document your work by printing hard copies of each table in data sheet view and each relationship.

Furry Friends Foundation I (Creating a New Database from Scratch)

The Furry Friends Foundation is a nonprofit organization that finds homes for abandoned animals that are suitable for adoption. FFF began operations with a bequest from a wealthy gentleman who lived his life taking care of stray animals and wanted to be sure that such animals were looked after once he was gone. Although the amount the foundation started with was sufficient to set up an office and begin operations, it depends on continuing donations to run daily operations.

FFF has been keeping their records on 4 × 6 cards. Over the years, the foundation has had requests for year-end statements that document their donations to the Foundation for tax purposes. (Usually, donations are given with a particular type of animal in mind—for example, "for dogs.")

Now that the number of contributors exceeds 500, the president has decided to develop a database to handle the foundation's accounting and reporting needs. The following is a sample of some of the records at FFF.

FFF Contributor File

Contributor ID	Last Name	First Name	Street Address	City	State	Zip	Phone
13456	Smythe	Jonathan	1845 Backpack Lane	Franktown	NV	55655	(501)666-1234
13480	Lawrence	Marie	9190 Teepee Road	Doolittle	NV	54984	(501)767-1114
13484	Funky	Robert	5815 Pearly Gate Lane	Happiness	NV	53887	(501)995-7654

FFF Donation File

Donation Date	Animal Code	Amount	Contributor ID
September 30, 2009	C	25	13456
September 20, 2009	D	125	13456
October 15, 2009	C	25	13456
October 15, 2009	D	10	13456
October 31, 2009	C	20	13456
October 31, 2009	D	20	13456
November 30, 2009	D	250	13456
November 15, 2009	C	25	13456
December 1, 2009	O	70	13456
December 10, 2009	C	100	13480
September 10, 2009	C	250	13480
October 10, 2009	C	500	13480
November 11, 2009	C	150	13480
December 14, 2009	D	100	13484
September 5, 2009	C	100	13484
October 10, 2009	O	100	13484
November 8, 2009	O	100	13484
December 15, 2009	D	50	13484

FFF Animal Code Table

Contribution for	Code
Dogs	D
Cats	C
Hamster	H
Guinea Pig	G
Rabbit	R
Other	O

Requirements

1. Using Access or a similar relational database, create the tables needed to set up a database for contributors, contributions, and whether the contributions are to be used for dogs, cats, hamsters, guinea pigs, rabbits, or nonspecified.

2. What did you use for the primary record key of the FFF donation file table? Why did you use it?

3. Using Access or similar software as required by your instructor, add yourself as a contributor.

4. Create relationships for the tables.

5. Document your work by printing hard copies of each table in datasheet view and the relationships report that shows how they are related.

BSN Bicycles II (Creating Queries in Access)

Business has been growing at BSN Bicycles, and the store owners have been using their Access database to store information about their customers. Now that the store is a little more established, the owners are thinking more about how best to attract more customers to their store. One idea is to see where their current customers live. The owners also want a complete list of their credit customers.

Requirements

1. If you have not already done so, create a database for BSN and the Customer table described in the BSN Bicycles I case. Be sure to create at least 10 customer records for the company, including one with your name. Several of the customers should also live in the state of Virginia (VA) and several customers should have zip code "12345." The Virginia customers and the customers with zip code 12345 do not have to be the same.

2. If you have not already done so, create several invoices for your customers.

3. Create a query that selects all customers living in Virginia. Print your results.

4. Create a query that selects all customers living in zip code 12345. Print your results.

5. Create a query that selects all customers living in Virginia who also have zip code 12345.

6. Create a query that selects all credit customers. (Hint: use the word "Yes" for the criteria in this query.)

Furry Friends Foundation II (Creating Queries for Databases)

Recall from the Furry Friends Foundation I case that the Furry Friends Foundation is a nonprofit organization that finds homes for abandoned animals. The foundation has recently computerized some of its operations by storing its accounting data in a relational database. One reason for this was to enable it to more easily answer questions about donations. This portion of the case provides some examples of such questions and gives you practice creating database queries to answer them.

Requirements

1. If you have not already done so, create the tables and relationships described in the Furry Friends Foundation I case.

2. Using Access or similar software as required by your instructor, create three donations for yourself. You should be donating to dogs in one contribution, cats in the second contribution, and unspecified in the third contribution.

3. Create a query that selects all customers donating to cats. Print your results.

4. Create a query that selects all contributors who donated over $50. Print your results.

5. Create a query that selects all contributors who donated over $100 to dogs. Print your results.

Chapter 5

Database Forms and Reports

INTRODUCTION

The previous chapters illustrated how to design a database with several tables and also how to construct queries to select information from these tables. Two more important database tools are forms and reports. The first section of this chapter discusses how to create forms and also how to use forms for input and output tasks. The second section of this chapter discusses how to create reports. Both sections illustrate these tasks using Microsoft Access, but the skills discussed here are also applicable to other database software such as FoxPro or Oracle.

FORMS

Figure 5-1 illustrates an example of a database **form**—that is, a custom-designed screen for entering records or displaying existing records. As you can see in Figure 5-1, a form has three major sections: (1) a heading section, which appears at the top of the form; (2) a detail section, which usually occupies the majority of the form and typically displays the record information; and (3) a navigation bar, which always appears at the bottom of the form.

Although there is no requirement to use a form for entering data into a database table, there are several reasons why using a form is better than using a **datasheet screen** such as the one in Figure 5-2 for this task. One advantage of forms is that a datasheet displays many

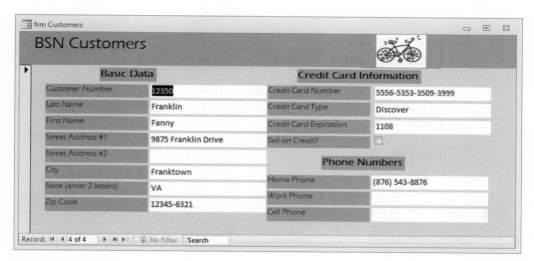

FIGURE 5-1   An example of a database form at run time.

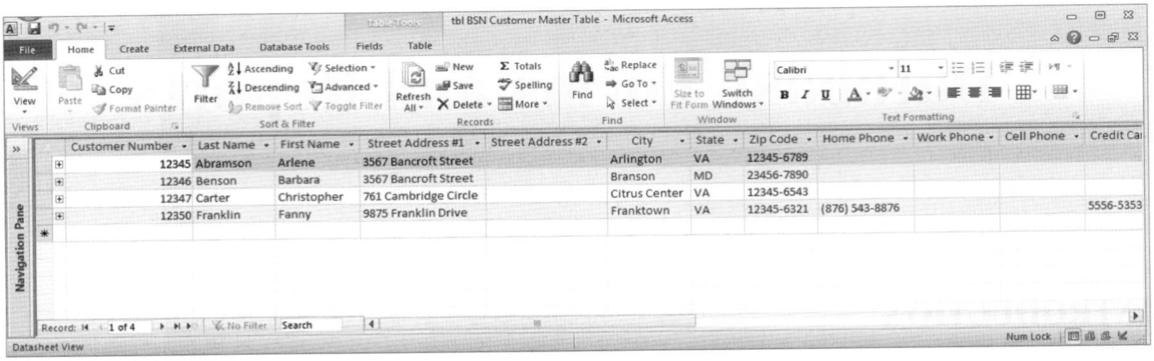

FIGURE 5-2 A portion of the Customers table (in datasheet view) from the BSN Database.

records at once, making it possible to accidentally type over existing information instead of creating a new record. Another advantage is that a form can display all the data-entry textboxes for an entire record in one screen, whereas a datasheet typically requires users to keep tabbing to the right to enter data for off-screen items (Figure 5-2).

A third advantage of forms is that you can customize them. Figure 5-1 illustrates several examples of such customization, including (1) custom header information (e.g., the label with the words "BSN Customers") at the top of a form, (2) text, logos, artwork, and (as shown) pictures for graphic interest, (3) more complete names (instead of the default database names) to identify each field in the database table (e.g., "Customer Number" instead of "CustNo"), (4) the ability to group similar fields together in the form (e.g., the phone numbers), (5) the ability to add explanations or special instructions in the form to help users understand how to enter data (e.g., see the label for the State field), and (6) customized tab ordering that governs the order in which textboxes become active on the form.

Taken together, the various advantages of forms make them better for controlling and validating data input than datasheet screens. That is, forms help prevent data-entry errors, which is a critical component of the reliability of data and essential to strong internal control (which we discuss in more detail in Chapter 10).

Creating Simple Forms

To create a custom form for a database table in Access, you can design a form from scratch by selecting *Blank Form* from the Form menu in Figure 5-3, but it is often easier to use the **Form Wizard** for this.

If you click on the Form Wizard icon, you will see dialog boxes similar to the ones in Figure 5-4. Follow these steps to create a form in Access:

FIGURE 5-3 Create menu showing the Form Wizard in Access 2010.

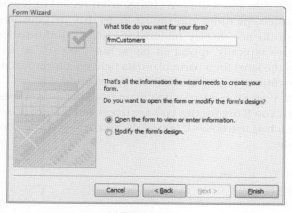

(a) First screen.

(b) Second screen.

(c) Third screen.

FIGURE 5-4 The three dialog boxes in the Form Wizard.

Step 1—Enter the appropriate settings in the Form Wizard dialog boxes. In the drop-down option on the left side of Figure 5-4a, select the table you want your form to reference (e.g., *tbl BSN Customer Master Table*). You will also need to select the fields you want to display *on* the form. Clicking on the button with the >> symbol selects all the fields from your table in your form—a typical choice. You can also click on individual field names with your mouse and then click on the > button to select data fields one by one.

Use the second dialog box in Figure 5-4b to select a layout for your form—typically *Columnar* because this setting enables you to include all the data fields on one form. Finally, in the third dialog box of the Form Wizard (Figure 5-4c), you will need to create a name for your form. As with many other database objects, you should use the conventional prefix for a form name—*frm*—and then create a name that helps you remember the form's application.[1] In Figure 5-4c, for example, we have named the form *frmCustomers*. At this point, you can click on the Finish button in the last dialog box and you're done. The Form

---

[1] In Chapters 4 and 5 we have recommended prefixing all files with tbl, frm, and rpt. Microsoft Access 2010 also includes icons on the left side of each file name that indicate the file type.

Wizard will then create the form with the settings you've indicated and list the completed form among those available for use in the main menu for forms.

Step 2—Customize the form. If you open your form in design view, you will see something like the one in Figure 5-5. This figure helps make clear that a form has two modes—run mode, which looks similar to Figure 5-1, and design mode, which looks similar to Figure 5-5. In fact, the form in Figure 5-5 was the starting point for the completed form in Figure 5-1. This screen contains form objects such as labels and textboxes that you can delete (by first clicking on the object and then hitting the delete key on your keyboard), reposition (by clicking on and dragging them with your mouse), or customize in many other ways.

The objects such as textboxes and labels that appear on a form are examples of **form controls**. When customizing a form, it is important to distinguish between bound controls and unbound controls. **Bound controls** are textboxes, drop-down boxes, and similar controls that depend on the underlying data and therefore change from record to record. In contrast, **unbound controls** are labels, pictures, and similar items that are consistent from record to record in a form and do not display underlying database information. On Access forms, labels and textboxes typically appear in pairs, but they are, in fact, separate objects. Thus, you can delete the label for a particular data field on a form and the accompanying (bound) textbox will continue to display database information.

You can add additional controls to your form by selecting them from the Form Design Tools (Figure 5-6a). Typical objects that you'll use for this task are labels and picture boxes, but you can also add bound controls such as textboxes if you wish. You can view the Tools only when your form is in design mode.

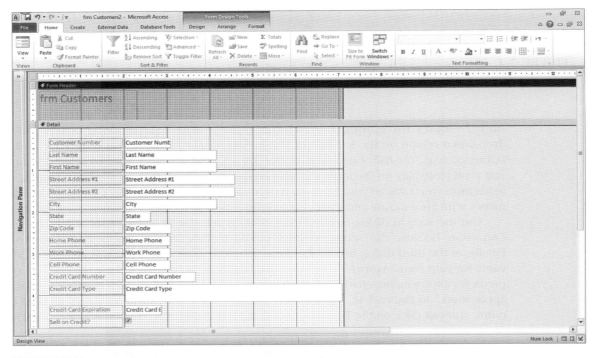

FIGURE 5-5 The starting format for the form in Figure 5-1.

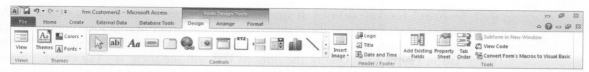

(a) Selected controls in Design Tools.

Property Sheet

Selection type: Text Box

Work Phone

Format	Data	Event	Other	All

Control Source	Work Phone
Text Format	Plain Text
Input Mask	!\(999") "000\-0000;;_
Default Value	
Validation Rule	
Validation Text	
Filter Lookup	Database Default
Enabled	Yes
Locked	No
Smart Tags	

(b) An example of a Properties window. Note the "Control Source" and "Input Mask" settings for this particular control—a textbox that displays a work phone number.

FIGURE 5-6   An example of (a) the Forms Controls window and (b) a Properties window.

To add a control to your form, left click on the control in the Toolbox and then use your mouse to draw the selected object on your form. For example, in Figure 5-1, you can see additional labels (e.g., the heading "BSN Customers" in the header portion of the form or the label "Phone Numbers" in the detail portion of the form) and also a picture of a bicycle (which we created with an Image object from the Toolbox). The size of the object depends on how large you drew it when you first created it, but you can resize any control on your form using the dots, or **sizing handles**, which appear on the border of your control when you click on it in the form.

Finally, to customize a control on a form, use the object's **Property Sheet window** (Figure 5-6b) to make individual settings for control objects. In effect, each form object has separate settings and its own Property Sheet window. To view the Property Sheet for a particular control, right click on an object in your form and select "Properties" from the drop-down list of choices that appears. This window allows you to change a wide range of settings—for example, the font size, font weight, or boldness of the text in labels. Of particular importance is the **Control Source property** of an object, which you will find among the settings in the Data tab portion of the Property Sheet window and which links the control to an underlying data field. Bound controls have a Control Source setting, whereas unbound objects do not.

Step 3—Refine your design.   You can toggle back and forth between run mode and design mode by clicking on the *Form* and *Design* options. Form (i.e., Run) mode allows you to see how your form looks at run time and reveals what further work you need to perform to complete your form's design. In design mode, you can select multiple form objects at once (by depressing the control key and clicking on several objects successively) and then use the formatting options from the Format menu (on the main menu bar) to resize, align, and consistently space objects on your form.

Step 4—Reset the tab order.   If you rearrange objects in your form in design mode, there is a good chance you will also want to reset the **tab order** of your form controls—that is, the order in which each control becomes active in run mode. To do so, click on the Design tab in Figure 5-6a. One of the options you will see there is "Tab Order." If you click on this choice, Access will provide a small dialog window that enables you to reset this order. Here, you can create a custom order for the objects in your form or, more simply, click on the "Auto Order" button at the bottom of this window to have Access automatically reset the tab order. The new, auto-order sequence makes form controls become active sequentially from top to bottom and from left to right.

Using Forms for Input and Output Tasks

As noted earlier, database forms provide a convenient tool for entering data into database tables and displaying data from database tables. Both tasks require use of the navigation bar at the bottom of the form—that is, the portion of the screen that looks like this:

You can use this navigation bar for both the input and output tasks explained below.

Displaying Information.   The number in the middle of the navigation bar (e.g., "2") indicates which record currently displays in your form. Clicking on the ⏮ symbol causes Access to display the first record in the underlying database table, while clicking on the ⏭ symbol displays the last record in the table. Clicking on the ◄ symbol displays the *previous record* (the record just before the current one), while clicking on the ► symbol displays the *next record* (record just after the current one). You can also access the previous record or next record using the page up or page down keys on your keyboard.

Forms also enable you to *change* the information already in a database table. For example, if a customer moves to a new address or changes his or her phone number, you would want to alter this information in the appropriate table. It is a simple matter to enter the new information for the appropriate record using a form for this task. Changing data in a form causes Access to automatically update the information in the underlying table.

Using Forms to Create New Records.   If you wish to add a new record, you can use a form for this task as well. First, click on the ►∗ button in the navigation bar. The system will then display the first available empty record (i.e., the one at the end of the underlying table) and allow you to enter the information for a new table entity—for example, the data for a new customer.

A useful feature in Access is that any data field that you include in a form automatically inherits all properties that you set for that field in the underlying table. This means that the same edit tests and data restrictions apply to the field for data entry, whether you enter the data in datasheet view or in form view. For example, if you create an input mask for a phone number that looks like this: (999)000-0000, Access will display the mask for this data field when you start entering data in your form at run time. Similarly, if you restrict a certain field to Integer data (e.g., a zip code), the system will not allow you to enter alphabetic text for that field. Finally, if you create a range test in your form (e.g., limit input to values between "0" and "40" hours), Access will not allow you to enter a value of "50" for that field in your form. Thus, properties at the table level are powerful internal controls because they are also active in the forms used to update data or create new records.

Case-in-Point 5.1 Database forms are all around you. For example, when you make a purchase on a Web site such as Amazon.com, you are interacting with a database form. The choices you select from menus and drop-down boxes are used to enter data into databases and query database tables.

Printing Forms. You can print a form just as easily as you print any other Microsoft document—that is, by using the "Print" option from the File tab.

Subforms—Showing Data from Multiple Tables

A **subform** is a form within a form that displays data related to the information in the main form. Figure 5-7 is an example—the original customer form from Figure 5-1 with a new subform showing an invoice for a particular customer. This explains why there are two navigation bars in the figure—the initial one at the bottom of Figure 5-1 and a new one in the subform of Figure 5-7. If you advance through the records of the customer table using the lower navigation bar, you will see the information for each customer in the main form. Conversely, if you advance through the records of the subform, you will see the invoices for a particular customer—if they exist.

Creating Subforms. Subforms display subordinate information related to the information in the main form. This reflects the one-to-many relationship of the underlying data. In Figure 5-7, for example, each customer might have several invoices, but each invoice is related to only one customer. To create a subform such as the one in Figure 5-7 requires that *customers* and *invoices* have a one-to-many relationship. To create a form with a subform in Access, your first task is to make sure that the data in the two tables are related via the Relationships window and verify that the relationship is one-to-many.

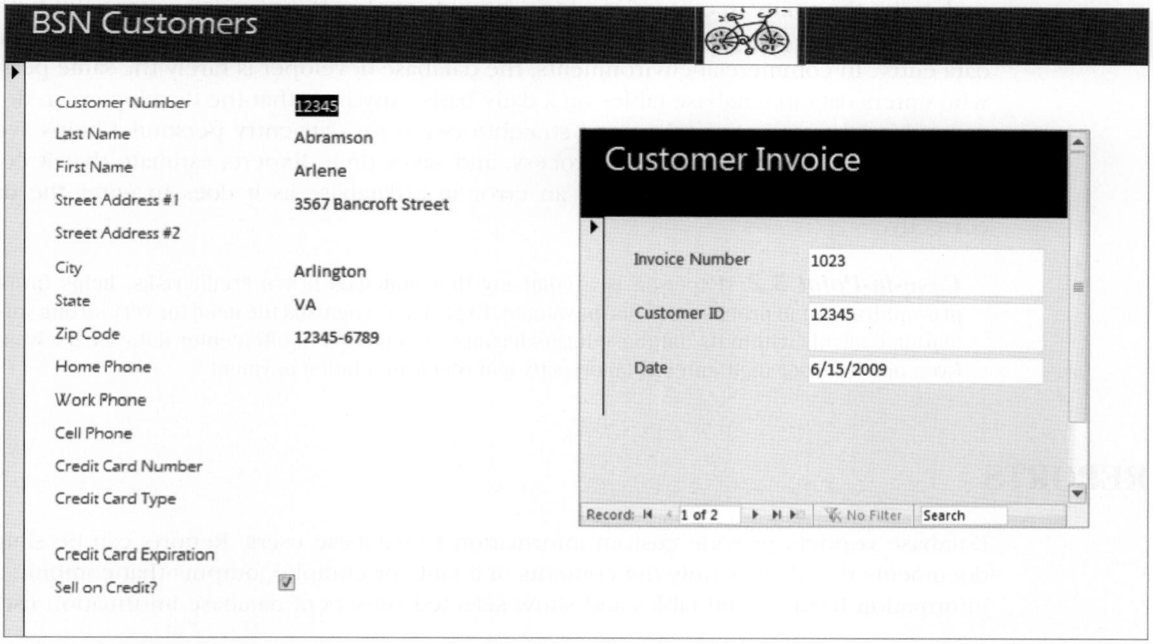

FIGURE 5-7 A form with a subform.

In Access, there are two principal methods for creating a form with a subform. One approach is to identify the subform at the time you use the Form Wizard. First, you would use the dialog box in Figure 5-4a to select the data for the main form as explained above. But before continuing to the next form, you would also click on the drop-down menu in this dialog box and select a second table from the list. If a one-to-many relationship exists between the two tables, the Form Wizard will recognize your wish to create a subform within your main form and will create one for you.

A second way to create a subform is to add one to an existing form *after* you've created the main form. To duplicate our form with a subform, open the form in Figure 5-1 in design view and use your mouse to extend the size of the details section of the form (to make room for the subform). Then, click on the Subform icon in the Toolbox shown in Figure 5-6a and use your mouse to draw a rectangle in the detail section of your form. This procedure causes Access to launch the Subform Wizard, which will ask you for settings similar to those shown in Figure 5-4—for example, ''which table do you want to use for the subform,'' ''how do you want the data to appear in the subform,'' and so forth.

In design mode, your resulting form and subform will not look exactly like the one in Figure 5-7. For example, you will probably have to resize the outer dimensions of the subform to fit the data and perhaps reword the text in the label at the top of the subform. With a little bit of work, however, you should be able to design the forms to look like Figure 5-7. If you need to resize the column widths of your subform, however, you can do that at run time rather than at design time—a helpful advantage because you can see live data at run time.

Concluding Remarks About Forms

Database forms enable you to add records to a database table, modify the data in existing records of a table, or simply view the data in a table. Although forms are not needed for such tasks, the ability to customize a form, provide explanations for data-entry fields within forms, and create convenient tab orderings are especially useful features for ensuring valid data entry. In commercial environments, the database developer is rarely the same person who enters data in database tables on a daily basis. Anything that the developer can do to make this job more convenient and straightforward for data-entry personnel helps avoid errors, streamlines the data-entry process, and saves time. Experts estimate that it costs about 10 times as much to *correct* an error in a database as it does to enter the data correctly.

> *Case-in-Point 5.2* Experian is a company that manages firm's credit risks, helps firms prevent fraud, and processes firms' payments. Experian recognizes the need for very strong validation controls within its database forms because its customers often enter data themselves. Even one letter or digit entered incorrectly can result in a failed payment.[2]

REPORTS

Database **reports** provide custom information to database users. Reports can be simple documents that display only the contents of a table or complex outputs that combine the information from several tables and show selected subsets of database information useful

---

[2] http://www.experian.com

for decision making. If you're using Access to print something on paper, the chances are high that you are using a report to perform this task. This means that many items that you might not consider a "report" are treated as one by Access—for example, an invoice for a particular customer or a document that shows the name and address of a vendor.

Case-in-Point 5.3   The National Motor Vehicle Title Information System requires all insurance companies and salvage yards to forward the VIN numbers of vehicles that have been totaled to a national database. The reports from this database will enable consumers to obtain information such as a car's odometer reading or theft report, as well as the reason for its condition—for example, a flood.[3]

Unlike forms, reports are strictly outputs and do not allow users to input data into databases. The next sections of the chapter explains how to create simple reports, how to create reports containing calculated fields, how to create reports based on queries instead of tables, and how to create reports containing grouped data.

Creating Simple Reports

Figure 5-8 illustrates the print preview of a simple report—a listing of selected information about the customers in BSN's Customers table. The first step in creating such reports is *not* to use your database system at all, but rather to decide what information to include in the report and how best to display that information in a printed document. We stress again that spending a few minutes designing the general format of a report (even if on the back of an old envelope) may save you hours of redesign work later.

A typical report has seven major components: (1) report heading, (2) page header, (3) group header, (4) detail lines or body, (5) group footer, (6) page footer, and (7) report footer. Figure 5-9 describes these items in greater detail. Perhaps the most important is the Detail Lines section, which is similar to the detail section of a form. The detail section displays information from the records of database tables. After you have a general idea of

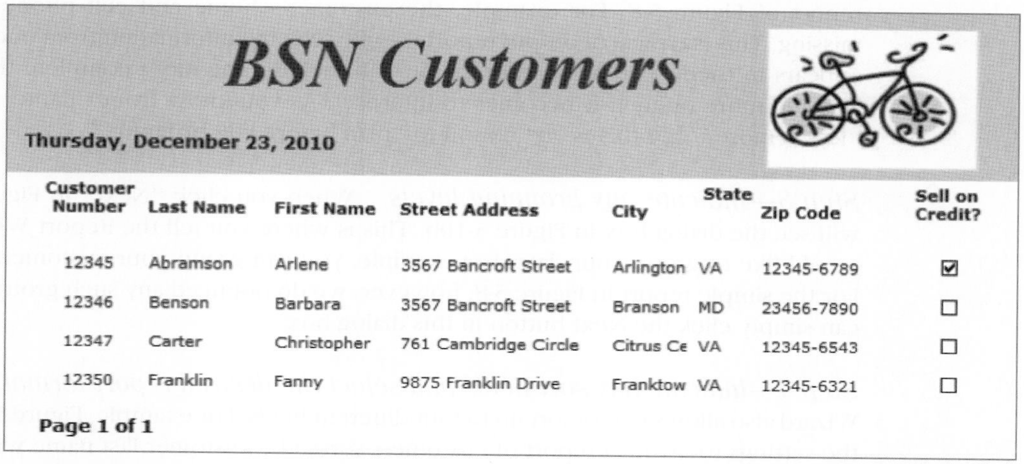

BSN Customers

Thursday, December 23, 2010

Customer Number	Last Name	First Name	Street Address	City	State	Zip Code	Sell on Credit?
12345	Abramson	Arlene	3567 Bancroft Street	Arlington	VA	12345-6789	☑
12346	Benson	Barbara	3567 Bancroft Street	Branson	MD	23456-7890	☐
12347	Carter	Christopher	761 Cambridge Circle	Citrus Ce	VA	12345-6543	☐
12350	Franklin	Fanny	9875 Franklin Drive	Franktow	VA	12345-6321	☐

Page 1 of 1

FIGURE 5-8   A print preview of a portion of a simple Access report.

---

[3] http://www.kiplinger.com/magazine/archives/2009/01/used_car_blacklist.html

Component	Where It Appears	Typical Content
Report header	First page of the report	Company name and address, date prepared or relevant time period, company logo
Page header	Top of each page	Identification of each data field below it
Group header	Beginning of each group of records	Identification of a new group of data
Detail lines	Body of the report	The individual data fields of, and computed data fields from, underlying database tables
Group footer	End of each group	Control totals or other statistics such as maximums, minimums, or averages for the group
Page footer	Bottom of each page	Page number, report number
Report footer	Last page of the report	End-of-report identifier, grand totals

FIGURE 5-9   The components of a database report.

the format for your report, you can develop the report itself using these components. An easy way to do so is by using the Report Wizard in Access, following these steps:

Step 1—Launch the Report Wizard.   To launch the **Report Wizard**, select the Create option from the main menu and then select "Report Wizard" (see again Figure 5-3). The first dialog box you will see is the one in Figure 5-10a.

Step 2—Select the underlying data source and desired fields.   You can base a report on a table, as we will do in this case, or on a query (which could integrate the data from several tables). To create the report in Figure 5-8, however, we will need only the Customers table. Thus, to replicate our work, select *tbl BSN Customer Master Table* from the drop-down list in Figure 5-10a and then select the appropriate fields using the data field selector buttons (> and >>) as needed.

Notice that not all the information in the Customers table appears in the Customer report of Figure 5-8. For example, the customer's home and cell phone numbers are missing. This is typical of output reports—only selected information from underlying tables appears in them. The more information you include, the more complete the report, but also the more difficult it becomes to interpret. As you know from Chapter 1, sometimes "less is more," and this is one reason to "plan before you program."

Step 3—Indicate any grouping levels.   When you click "Next" in Figure 5-10a, you will see the dialog box in Figure 5-10b. This is where you tell the Report Wizard how you would like to group your data. For example, you can group your customers by zip code. For the simple report in Figure 5-8, however, we do not need any such groupings, and you can simply click the Next button in this dialog box.

Step 4—Indicate any sort fields and select the desired report format.   The Report Wizard also allows you to sort up to four different fields. For example, Figure 5-10c indicates the settings to create a report of customers sorted by customer last name within zip code. After you have selected the sort fields, click Next in the dialog box. The fourth screen in the Report Wizard appears (Figure 5-10d) and allows you to select a particular report layout. For line-by-line listings—the typical choice in simple reports—select "Tabular." You can also choose between "Portrait" or "Landscape" print options here.

Step 5—Name the report. After clicking Next in the dialog box shown in Figure 5-10d, you will see the dialog box in Figure 5-10e. Here, you have the opportunity to name your report. The standard prefix for a report is *rpt,* which is the reason we've named our report *rptCustomers_by_ZipCode.*

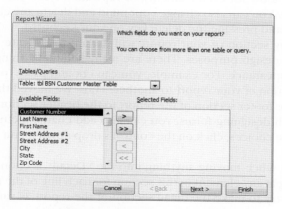

(a) The first screen in the Report Wizard.

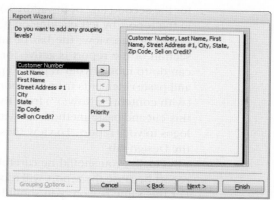

(b) The second screen in the Report Wizard.

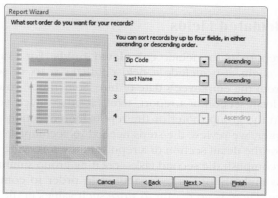

(c) The third screen in the Report Wizard.

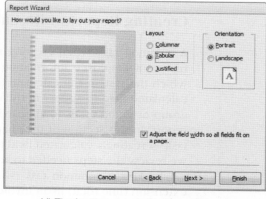

(d) The fourth screen in the Report Wizard.

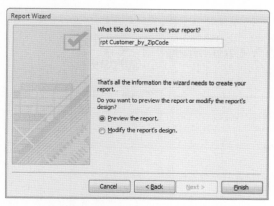

(e) The fifth screen in the Report Wizard.

FIGURE 5-10 The dialog boxes of the Report Wizard.

Step 6—Modify the design of the report as desired. When you finish with the Report Wizard, you may need to modify the report design still further. If you open your new report in design view, you will see a screen similar to the one in Figure 5-11. This interactive screen enables you to modify the height or width of labels or textboxes (using their sizing handles); change the font size and font characteristics (e.g., italic, bold) of headings (using the Properties window for each element); or reposition items (as we did for the second line of the address). You can also change your mind and delete any element in the report by left clicking on it and pressing the delete key on your keyboard.

In design view, the bar of any section of your report will darken to indicate which section of the report is active for design purposes. There are many additional things you can do to modify your report's appearance. For example, you can cut and paste (or copy and paste) elements from one portion of your report to another. Thus, we moved the date (with content "=Now()") from the footer section of the report to the header section using this cut-and-paste method. As with designing forms, you can also add charts, pictures, or logos to your report. To view these choices, click on the control's drop-down menu within the Design tab.

Finally, you should be careful when moving anything into the "Detail" section of the report because the report will repeat any element in this section for each line of the report. For this same reason, you should try to make the detail section of the report as simple as possible—it will save room on lengthy reports.

Creating Reports with Calculated Fields

A common task when creating reports is to include **calculated fields**. For example, a report of employee information might also include a field entitled "years of service," which the system can calculate from the employee's date of hire. Sometimes, you want a calculated field to appear in the detail section of a report, while at other times, you want group or grand totals to appear in the group footer or the report footer sections of your report. In this section of the chapter, we review the steps needed to accomplish the first task—creating a calculated field for the detail section of a report. In the following section, we review the steps needed to accomplish the second task—creating group summaries.

In AISs, a common task is to multiply prices by quantities in order to compute an extension (line total) in an invoice. There is no reason to *store* such values in the records

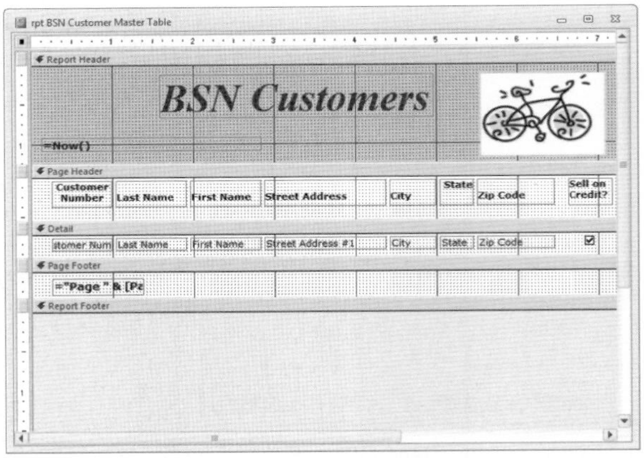

FIGURE 5-11   An Access report at design time.

rptCustomer_Invoices

BSN Invoice Extensions
Tuesday, June 30, 2009

Invoice #	Item Number	Item Description	Quantity	Unit Price	Extension
1023					
	G123-786	Hot Rider Gloves --Men's Medium	1	$24.95	$24.95
	G453-324	Mogul Tire Pump Model 3G	2	$34.95	$69.90
	S123	Basic Bicycle Tune UP	1	$39.95	$39.95
	S124	Repair Flat Tire	1	$19.95	$19.95
				Invoice Total:	$154.75

Invoice #	Item Number	Item Description	Quantity	Unit Price	Extension
1024					
	S123	Basic Bicycle Tune UP	1	$39.95	$39.95
				Invoice Total:	$39.95

Invoice #	Item Number	Item Description	Quantity	Unit Price	Extension
1025					
	S125	Replace Shifter	1	$49.95	$49.95
	S127	Replace Seat	1	$15.95	$15.95
	G124-464	Hot-RiderGloves--Woman's Medi	1	$24.95	$24.95
				Invoice Total:	$90.85

FIGURE 5-12   The print preview of a report that contains a calculated field (in the last column of the report).

of a relational database because we can *compute* such values whenever we need them. This is why we only stored prices and quantities in the Customer_Invoice_Details table. However, when we print customer invoice information on a report, we need to show such computations.

It is usually easiest to create calculated fields using queries rather than tables for the underlying data. To illustrate, suppose we wanted to create the report shown in Figure 5-12—a report that shows invoice extensions for all current invoices for BSN. To create such a report, follow these steps:

Step 1—Create the query with a calculated field.   Figure 5-13 shows the query for our report. To create this query, we begin by selecting the tables needed to calculate invoice totals. One such table is the Customer_Invoice_Details table. The records in this table contain the item number and the quantity ordered but not the name of the item purchased or its price. For this information, we need the Products_And_Services table.

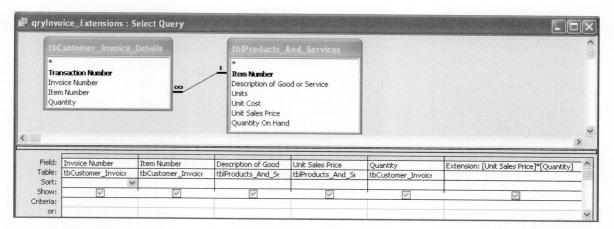

FIGURE 5-13   A query with a calculated field.

Figure 5-13 is the design view for our query. We have selected the two tables we need for our task and also the desired fields—that is, the item number, the description of the good or service (both taken from the tblProducts_And_Services table), and the quantity (taken from the tblCustomer_Invoice_Details table). For convenience, it is a good idea to select these items in the order in which you want them to appear in your final invoice, but this isn't required.

To create the calculated field, select the first available column in the query design screen and type the *name* of your calculated field. We chose the name "Extension," but this choice is arbitrary. You can also choose a name with more than one word (e.g., "Extension Calculation"), but be careful *not* to choose a term with the same name as an existing data field.

Type a colon following your calculated field name and then input the formula for your calculated field. Use an asterisk for a multiplication sign and a forward slash (/) for a division sign. Also, be careful to spell the field names in your formulas exactly as they appear in your underlying database tables. (If you misspell a field name, Access will not indicate that you've made an error, but instead will assume you're creating a parameter query and ask you for the data at run time.) Finally, place square brackets around your field names to indicate that you are referencing existing data fields.

When you have completed your query, you can test it by clicking on the Run button (the exclamation point icon) in the main menu. If things work properly, you will see something like the screen in Figure 5-14. Note that although the data in Figure 5-14 is from a query, the screen in Figure 5-14 is interactive. Thus, for example, if you change the item number of a given line, Access will look up the new product description and the new price, change the new extension, and display everything as quickly as you can enter the new item number on the screen.

Step 2—Create the report based on your query. It now remains to create the report. Using the steps outlined above, you can use the Report Wizard to create the final report in Figure 5-12. Base your report on the query you created in Step 1 above and select all available fields.

The second screen of the Report Wizard will ask you if you wish to group your data (refer back to Figure 5-10b). Access will recognize that you have a one-to-many relationship between "invoice numbers" and "invoice details" and should show you this possibility by default. If it does not, however, select this option so that your invoice details for the

qryInvoice_Extensions				
Item Numbe ▾	Item Description ▾	Unit Price ▾	Quantity ▾	Ext ▾
G124-464	Hot-RiderGloves--Woman's Medi	$24.95	1	$24.95
S127	Replace Seat	$15.95	1	$15.95
S125	Replace Shifter	$49.95	1	$49.95
S124	Repair Flat Tire	$19.95	1	$19.95
S123	Basic Bicycle Tune UP	$39.95	1	$39.95
G453-324	Mogul Tire Pump Model 3G	$34.95	2	$69.90
G123-786	Hot Rider Gloves --Men's Medium	$24.95	1	$24.95
S123	Basic Bicycle Tune UP	$39.95	1	$39.95
*				

FIGURE 5-14   Partial results for the query in Figure 5-13 at run time.

same invoice will be grouped together. Then continue with the remainder of the Report Wizard questions. Be sure to name your report something appropriate—for example, rptInvoice_Details. When you finish answering questions in the Report Wizard, you should then reformat your report as needed. The results should look similar to Figure 5-12.

Creating Reports with Grouped Data

The report in Figure 5-12 contains useful data, but obviously lacks some critical information. What is the name of the customer associated with each invoice? What is his or her address? What is the total for each invoice? A manager would likely want this information to appear in an invoice report. Finally, it might be useful to organize the report by customer last name rather than by invoice number.

A **control break** is the technical term for the point at which a group changes from one type to the next in a report. Examples of control breaks include a change in zip code for the addresses in customer listings, a change in the department number for a listing of employees, and a change in a service classification for the yellow pages of a phone book. Control breaks are often the points at which managers want to see subtotals, maximums, minimums, averages, or similar subgroup summaries.

To create control breaks for the report in Figure 5-12, we need to modify its design to include group totals for each invoice. Figure 5-15 illustrates the format for the final report, which includes new information and provides totals for each invoice. To create it, we will follow the steps outlined above for creating reports with calculated fields—that is, (1) create a query to generate the desired information, (2) use the Report Wizard to create an initial report based on this query, and (3) reformat our report as needed to achieve the desired end product. Here are the detailed steps:

Step 1—Create the underlying query.   Our first task is to create the underlying query for this report. Figure 5-16 shows a portion of this query during its design.

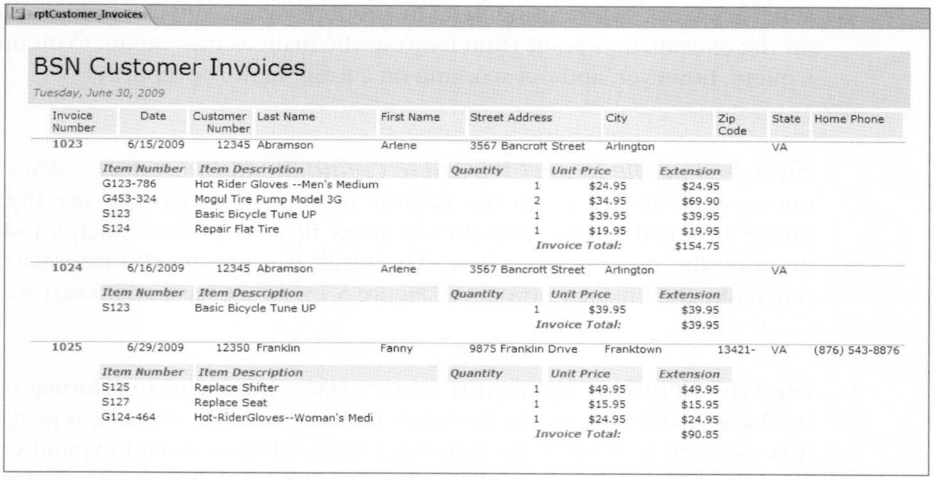

FIGURE 5-15   The invoice report of Figure 5-12, expanded to include customer information and invoice totals.

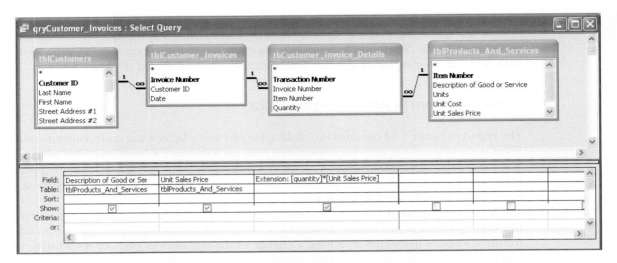

FIGURE 5-16 Part of the query used to create the report illustrated in Figure 5-15.

The upper portion of the query screen in Figure 5-16 identifies the four tables required to build the query. If you study the information contained in the final report of Figure 5-15, you will realize *why* we needed four tables for this task. We needed the *Customers* table to provide the name and address information for each customer. We needed the *Invoice* table to provide the customer number for each invoice. We needed the *Customer Invoice Details* table to provide the item number and the order quantity for each detail line of an invoice. We needed the *Products and Services* table to provide the item description and sales price per unit for each item purchased. Finally, we had to create a calculated field—the extension of quantities times prices for each detail line—as described in the previous section of this chapter.

When queries become as complex as this one, it is a good idea to run them and make sure they work before using them in a report. Again, you can perform this task by clicking on the exclamation point (Run icon) in the main Access menu. (You must be working on a query, however, and not working on a form, table, or report.)

Step 2—Use the Report Wizard to create the initial report.   After creating our initial query, we will then go to the Reports portion of Access and use the Report Wizard to create an initial report. You already know how to perform such a task, and we will not describe the process again here. The result is a report whose format will not look very much like the finished product in Figure 5-15, so we have additional work to do!

Step 3—Reformat the report as desired.   It remains to reformat our report. Because we have also reviewed the activities for this step, we will not repeat them here. Again, it is useful to remember the following items: (1) you should expand the size of unbound labels so that their entire text shows, (2) you can delete any control you don't need, (3) you can move both bound and unbound controls from one part of a report to another, and (4) the Format menu enables you to resize, align, and reposition objects consistently on your report.

Concluding Remarks About Reports

This section of the chapter illustrated how to create reports in Access, including reports that contain calculated fields and reports that calculate subtotals for grouped data. Reports are the desired end product of complex database systems. That is, managers need to convert vast amounts of data into useful information for decision making. This is the function of reports—they turn data into information. It is also important to remember at this point that reports cannot be created unless all of the needed data has been collected and appropriately organized. For this reason, database designers must speak with managers and other end users to determine what reports they need *before* designing the database.

AIS AT WORK
Mother Lode Bicycles[4]

Although the BSN Bicycle company is fictitious, Mother Lode Bicycles in Sparks, Nevada, is not. Founded in 1996 by two friends—Dave McDonald and Mark Kennedy—the 2,400-square-foot shop sells road and mountain bikes to local customers as well as to out-of-towners visiting the area. Bike prices range from $200 to $5,000. Sales of bikes, clothing, and biking accessories are 90 percent of the store's income; repairs make up the rest.

In many ways, running a bike shop is similar to running any small business. One partner manages the inventory, stocks the store shelves, and deals with the marketing and advertising parts of the business. The other partner deals with employees, supervises repairs, and interacts with customers. Their biggest problems are (1) making enough money to cover the overhead (especially during the months after Christmas and prior to spring cycling) and (2) the fact that the store must stay open seven days a week.

For accounting tasks, the store's owners rely on QuickBooks™ from Intuit and the bookkeeping expertise of Mark's wife. With the exception of employees, the store does not sell items on credit so there are no receivables. Mark personally supervises payables, taking advantage of cash discounts where possible and negotiating longer payment schedules with suppliers during the slower selling seasons of the year.

Most of the shop's inventory consists of items that sit on shelves and racks in the retail portion of the store, with just a few parts and unassembled bikes stored in the back room—a combination storeroom-warehouse-office-dining room. Inventory control is also a combination of elements, including visual inspection, working with sales representatives to keep merchandise levels up, and the expertise of the owners for ordering or not ordering items for the slower or busier season to follow. Mark is considering acquiring a point-of-sale system with a backend database, which he thinks will help the company become better aware of its best sellers as well as keep closer tabs on stock on hand.

SUMMARY

✓ Databases use forms to input data into, and to view data from, the records in tables.

✓ If you use forms to create new records, the data fields in the customized forms automatically inherit the same properties, attributes, and input restrictions that were created for them in the design of the table.

---

[4] From the authors.

✓ The navigation bar at the bottom of a form enables you to view the first, last, next, and previous record in the underlying table.

✓ You can use subforms to display "many" records related to the record in the main form in a one-to-many relationship—for example, the outstanding invoices for a specific customer.

✓ You typically design and develop reports to create hard-copy outputs. In Access, reports are based either directly on tables or on queries that reference tables.

✓ A typical report has seven major components: (1) report heading, (2) page headings, (3) group headings, (4) detail or body, (5) group footer, (6) page footer, and (7) report footer.

✓ You should name forms and reports systematically. The standard prefix for a form is *frm*, and the standard prefix for a report is *rpt*.

✓ Most databases do not store calculated fields such as invoice line extensions (prices times quantities). Instead, we calculate these fields with queries.

✓ Many reports contain data with grouped data—for example, a set of lines for a given invoice or a set of invoices for a given customer. It is also possible to require a report to show control totals, averages, maximum, or minimum values for each group. In Access, you can create such figures using the Report Wizard and its grouping options.

KEY TERMS YOU SHOULD KNOW

bound control	Property Sheet window
calculated field	report
control break	Report Wizard
Control Source property	sizing handles
datasheet screen	subform
form	tab order
form controls	unbound control
Form Wizard	

DISCUSSION QUESTIONS

5-1. What are some of the advantages and disadvantages of database forms?

5-2. Would you rather use a form or a datasheet for entering data into a database table? Why?

5-3. To create a form, would you rather use the Form Wizard in Access or create the form from scratch? Why?

5-4. What is a subform? Why do forms have subforms? How do you create subforms in Access?

5-5. Why do database developers customize forms? Why isn't it sufficient to use the form as initially created by the Form Wizard?

5-6. What is the purpose of a database report? What information do such reports contain?

5-7. The chapter suggested that it is important to design the format of a report before creating the report itself. Do you agree with this suggestion? Why or why not?

5-8. Do you think that we will still use hard-copy reports in the future, or will they be replaced with soft-copy ones? Defend your answer.

5-9. Would you rather use the Report Wizard to create the format of a report or design one yourself from scratch? Why?

5-10. What is a calculated field in a report? Provide some examples. Why do reports contain calculated fields?

5-11. Why don't databases store calculated fields as normal fields in database tables? Do you think they should?

5-12. Why are calculated fields created with database queries? Why not create them directly with reports?

PROBLEMS

5-13. A form's navigation bar has five symbols on it. Identify each one and indicate its use.

5-14. A database report has seven major sections in it.

    a. Identify each one and provide a short explanation of each section.

    b. Identify a report that might be generated in a database application and indicate what data might be found in each section of the report for your example.

5-15. Provide a short explanation of the difference between each of the following sets of terms:

    a. Bound control versus unbound control

    b. Design mode versus run mode

    c. ◄ Symbol versus ► symbol on a form's navigation bar

    d. Form versus subform

    e. Normal data field versus calculated data field

    f. Page header versus page footer

    g. Report header versus report footer

    h. A report based on a table versus a report based on a query

5-16. Using the Customers table in the BSN database that accompanies this book and following the directions in this chapter, create the form in Figure 5-1. Make sure that you reformat the default positions of the various textboxes as shown in the figure.

    a. Add a label in the heading portion of your form that contains the term "Prepared by:" and add your name. Print a single copy of your completed form.

    b. Use the navigation bar at the bottom of your form. What is the first record? What is the last record?

    c. Add a new record to this form with your name as the customer. Print a copy of this form.

    d. Close your form, go to the Tables portion of the database, and open the Customers table in datasheet view (see Figure 5-2). Verify that your new record is there. Now, add a second record with your name again. Are you surprised that you can do this?

5-17. If you have not done so already, use the Customers table in the BSN database that accompanies this book and the directions in this chapter to create the form in Figure 5-1. Make sure that you reformat the default positions of the various textboxes as shown in the figure. Now add a subform to your form so that it looks like Figure 5-7. To do this, open your initial form in design view, select the subform tool from the Toolbox Controls, and add a subform. Answer the questions for the Subform Wizard to select the Invoices table. When you have completed these tasks, also do the following:

    a. Use the navigation bar of the main form to go to the last record in the Customers table. Print the form for this record.

    b. Use the navigation bar of the main form to find a record with invoices. Then use the navigation bar of the subform to select a particular invoice. Which one did you select? Print this form.

5-18. Using the Customers table in the BSN database that accompanies this book and following the directions in this chapter, create the report in Figure 5-8. Note that you will have to reformat and perhaps reposition several labels and add both labels and a graphic in the header portion of the report.

    a. Add a label in the heading portion of your report that contains the term "Prepared by:" and add your name. Print a single copy of your completed report.

    b. Who is the first customer in your report? Who is the last customer in your report?

5-19. Use the Customers table in the BSN database that accompanies this book and the Report Wizard to create the report in Figure 5-15. Note that you will have to reformat and perhaps reposition several labels and add both labels and a graphic in the header portion of the report. Note that you will first have to create the underlying query for this report. Use Figures 5-12 through 5-19 as guides for this task. Print the final report.

CASE STUDIES

A Form for BSN Suppliers (Creating a Simple Form in Access)

The BSN Company requires a form with which to view its existing suppliers conveniently and also to create records for new suppliers. Figure 5-17 contains a suggested format for this form.

Requirements

1. Using the Vendors table in the BSN database that accompanies this book, create the initial form using the Form Wizard. Note that you will have to reposition some of the data fields in the form, add the term "Abbrev." to the label for the State field, and add the following items in the heading of the form: (1) a label with text "BSN Vendors," (2) a label with your name, and (3) a graphic (which can be different from the one shown in the figure).

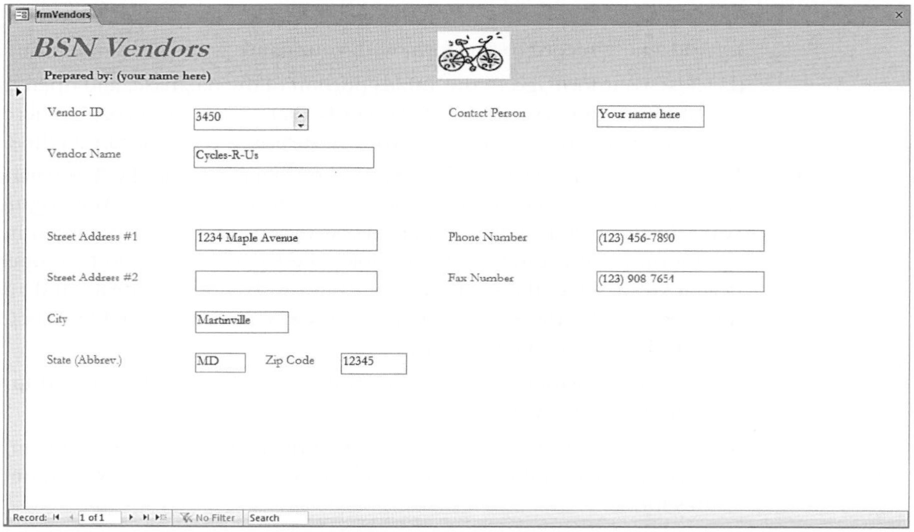

FIGURE 5-17 A form for entering and viewing vendor information in the BSN database.

2. Run your completed form to make sure it works. What is the first record that shows in your form? What is the last record?

3. While in run mode, tab through the individual data fields of any particular record and note that you do *not* tab through the data fields column by column. Return to design view and adjust the tab order by selecting View/Tab Order from the main menu and make the necessary adjustments. What is the correct Tab Order, and how did you make these adjustments?

4. Go back to run mode for your form and click on the ▶∗ symbol to add the information in Figure 5-17 to the Vendors table. Note that you should use your own name as the Contact Person for this vendor.

5. Print just this form to document your work, following the steps in the text for this task.

6. Now that you have used your new form, what additional improvements would you make to further streamline data-entry tasks?

A Form and Subform for BSN Suppliers (Creating Forms with Subforms in Access)

Create the form in Figure 5-17 and then add a subform to it that shows purchase orders for each vendor. Figure 5-18 provides a suggested format. To accomplish this task, follow these steps: (1) start with the Vendor form in design mode, (2) click on the subform control in the Toolbox, and (3) follow the steps in the Subform Wizard to complete your work.

Requirements

1. Run your new form to make sure it works properly and then print a copy of your new form to document your work. Make sure your name is in the header portion of the form.

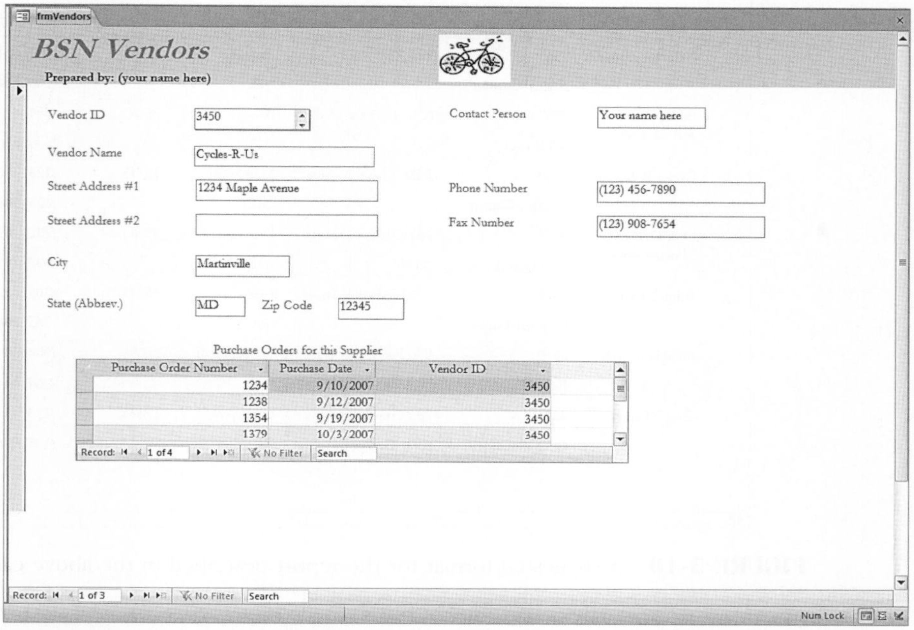

FIGURE 5-18 A suggested format for the form and subform.

2. Select a vendor for which there are outstanding purchase orders. Click on the ▶ symbol in the navigation bar of the main form. What happens?

3. Click on the ▶ symbol in navigation bar of the subform. What happens?

4. Create a new purchase order for your current vendor using your new subform. Do you think it makes sense to be able to create a new purchase order that has no detail lines? Why or why not?

A Listing of BSN Suppliers (Creating Simple Reports in Access)

The BSN Company would like a hard-copy report of all the current vendors in its database. Figure 5-19 provides a suggested format for the report. Note that your report header should include the company title, the current date, your name, and a graphic. Also note that the detail section contains multiple lines. Create a similar report for homework.

Requirements

1. Print the complete report.
2. Who is the first supplier and who is the last supplier?

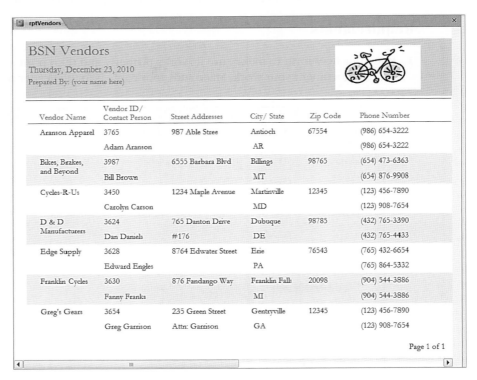

FIGURE 5-19 A suggested format for the report described in the above case.

Chapter 6

Documenting Accounting Information Systems

INTRODUCTION

The previous three chapters introduced you to the importance of databases to accounting information systems and described how to design, build, and use databases. In these chapters you also learned how to create E-R diagrams, which are essential forms of documentation. This chapter describes other critical documentation methods that developers use to design and describe accounting systems.

Documentation explains how AISs operate and is therefore a vital part of any accounting system. For example, documentation describes the tasks for recording accounting data, the procedures that users must perform to operate computer applications, the processing steps that AISs follow, and the logical and physical flows of accounting data through systems. This chapter explains in greater detail why accountants need to understand documentation and describes tools for diagramming complex systems.

Accountants can use many different types of logic charts to trace the flow of accounting data through an AIS. For example, document flowcharts describe the physical flow of order forms, requisition slips, and similar documents through an AIS. These flowcharts pictorially represent data paths in compact formats and save pages of narrative description. System flowcharts are similar to document flowcharts, except that system flowcharts usually focus on the electronic flows of data in computerized AISs. Other examples of documentation include process maps, data flow diagrams (DFDs), program flowcharts, and decision tables. This chapter describes these documentation aids, as well as some computerized tools for creating them.

Today, many end users develop computer applications for themselves. This end-user programming is very helpful to managers, who consequently do not require IT professionals to develop simple word processing, spreadsheet, or database applications. But end-user programming can also be a problem because many employees do not know how to document their work properly or simply don't do so. The final section of this chapter examines the topic of end-user programming and documentation in greater detail.

WHY DOCUMENTATION IS IMPORTANT

Accountants do not need to have the ability to program complex systems, but it is important for them to understand the documentation that describes how processing takes place. **Documentation** includes the flowcharts, narratives, and other written communications that describe the inputs, processing, and outputs of an AIS. Documentation also describes the logical flow of data within a computer system and the procedures that employees must follow to accomplish application tasks. Here are nine reasons why documentation is important to AISs.

Case-in-Point 6.1   A recent survey of practitioners found that system documentation has become increasingly important as organizations seek to better understand their own business processes and also comply with legislation that requires this understanding, such as the Sarbanes-Oxley Act.[1]

1. *Depicting how the system works.* Observing large AISs in action is an impractical way to learn about them, even if they are completely manual. In computerized systems, it is impossible to understand systems without thorough documentation because the processing is electronic and therefore invisible. Examination of written descriptions and diagrams of the inputs, processing steps, and outputs is an efficient method for understanding key components of systems. This is one purpose of documentation—to help explain how an AIS operates. Documentation helps employees understand how a system works, assists accountants in designing controls for it, demonstrates to managers that it will meet their information needs, and assists auditors in understanding the systems that they test and evaluate.

    The Internet contains many examples of flowcharts or logic diagrams that help individuals understand unfamiliar tasks or processes. For example, some universities use them to show students what classes to take and when they should take them to complete their majors in a timely manner. The University of Washington has flowcharts that show how to obtain grants and other types of funding. The University of Illinois at Urbana-Champaign uses elaborate diagrams to depict what happens when a faculty member's employment terminates. Figure 6-1 is a logic diagram from the University of Arizona Web site that shows employees how to file a claim for reimbursement. If the employee would like additional information for any step in the process, a click of the mouse on the appropriate flowchart symbol reveals additional information. The charts are intended to simplify long narratives describing how to file reimbursements.

2. *Training users.* Documentation also includes user guides, manuals, and similar operating instructions that help people learn how an AIS operates. Whether distributed manually in

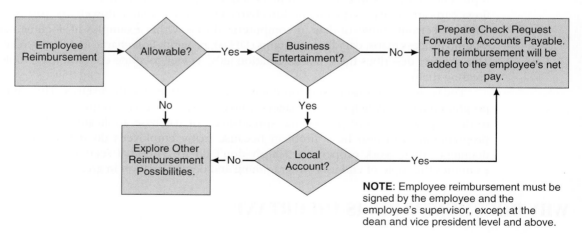

FIGURE 6-1   Example of a flowchart used at the University of Arizona to help employees file a reimbursement claim. For additional information, individuals simply click on the appropriate symbol.

---

[1] Bradford, M., S. Richtermeyer, and D. Roberts. 2007. System diagramming techniques: An analysis of methods used in accounting education and practice. *Journal of Information Systems* 21(1): 173–212.

hard-copy format or electronically in help files or "get-started tours" of microcomputer applications, these documentation aids help train users to operate AIS hardware and software, solve operational problems, and perform their jobs better.

3. *Designing new systems.* Documentation helps system designers develop new systems in much the same way that blueprints help architects design buildings. We have seen how to create blueprints for databases with E-R diagrams. Professional IT personnel commonly hold structured walkthroughs in which they review system documentation to ensure the integrity and completeness of their designs and to identify design flaws. Well-written documentation and related graphical systems-design methodologies play key roles in reducing systems failures and decreasing the time spent correcting emergency errors. Conversely, poorly designed systems often lead to large-scale errors and expensive write-offs.

4. *Controlling system development and maintenance costs.* Personal computer applications typically employ prewritten, off-the-shelf software that is relatively reliable and inexpensive. In contrast, custom-developed business systems can cost millions of dollars and can be less reliable. Good documentation helps system designers develop **object-oriented software**, which is software that contains modular, reusable code. This object-orientation helps programmers avoid writing duplicate programs and facilitates changes when programs must be modified later. If you have ever replaced a specialized part in your car, you have some idea of how frustrating, time consuming, and expensive nonstandardization can be, and therefore how useful object-oriented programming might be to business organizations.

5. *Standardizing communications with others.* The usefulness of narrative descriptions can vary significantly, and a reader can interpret such descriptions differently from what the writer intended. Documentation aids such as E-R diagrams, system flowcharts, and data flow diagrams are more standardized tools, and they are more likely to be interpreted the same way by all parties viewing them. Thus, documentation tools are important because they help describe an existing or proposed system in a common language and help users communicate with one another about these systems.

6. *Auditing AISs.* Documentation helps depict audit trails. When investigating an AIS, for example, the auditors typically focus on internal controls. In such circumstances, documentation helps auditors determine the strengths and weaknesses of a system's controls and therefore the scope and complexity of the audit. Similarly, auditors will want to trace sample outputs to the original transactions that created them (e.g., tracing inventory assets back to original purchases). System documentation helps auditors perform these tasks.

7. *Documenting business processes.* Understanding business processes can lead to better systems and better decisions. Documentation helps managers better understand how their businesses operate, what controls are involved or missing from critical organizational activities, and how to improve core business activities.

8. *Complying with the Sarbanes-Oxley Act.* Section 404 of the Sarbanes-Oxley Act of 2002 (SOX) requires publicly traded companies to identify the major sources of business risks, document their internal control procedures, and hire external auditors to evaluate the validity and effectiveness of such procedures. Documentation is therefore crucial for analyzing the risks of errors, frauds, omissions, and problems with important business processes, as well as helping auditors evaluate the controls used to mitigate such risks—that is, some of the major tasks required by SOX.

Almost everyone acknowledges that the costs of complying with SOX are enormous, and many also believe that SOX gave documentation a new life. To save money, many companies now use software packages to help them automate SOX documentation tasks. We describe some examples of such software in a later section of this chapter. While Auditing Standard No. 5 (AS5) has reduced some of the documentation burdens created by SOX, documentation requirements for internal controls and risk assessments remain much more substantial than during periods prior to the enactment of SOX.

9. *Establishing accountability.* Manual signatures on business and government documents allow employees and government agents to execute their responsibilities, create audit trails, and establish accountability for their actions. An example is a **signed checklist** that outlines the month-end journal entries an accountant must perform. Such checklists verify that an accountant performed these tasks, that a reviewer approved them, and that both individuals are accountable for the accuracy of the work. Similar comments apply to the checklists for preparing financial statements, tax returns, auditing papers, budgets, and similar accounting documents. Including such checklists with the statements themselves documents the work that the employees performed as well as the procedures and controls involved in the work. Signed approvals (e.g., manager-approved purchase requests) create similar levels of accountability for large expenditures.

> **Case-in-Point 6.2** Quality documentation, clear evidence of proper authorization, and the establishment of accountability can yield benefits in addition to improved systems design and better internal control. During recent and challenging economic times, layoffs are at a record high. As a result, wrongful termination lawsuits are also on the rise. Lawyers suggest that an employer's best defense in these lawsuits is clear documentation of employee duties and the procedures that they should follow. When managers fail to clearly document business processes and employees' responsibilities and actions related to the business, employers have difficulties defending their termination or promotion decisions.[2]

PRIMARY DOCUMENTATION METHODS

Despite the many reasons that documentation is important, most organizations find that they document less than they should. One explanation for this deficiency is that organizations often create or implement large AISs under tight deadlines. In such cases, the urgency to develop *a system that works* overrides the need for *a system that is well documented.* Another reason is that most IT professionals prefer creating systems more than documenting them. Thus, many developers actively resist it, arguing that they will "get around to it later" or that documenting is a job for nonexistent assistants.

Insufficient and deficient documentation costs organizations time and money, and good documentation can be as important as the software it describes. We next describe the methods that are available to document AISs. Chapter 3 described E-R diagrams. Four other common documentation methods are data flow diagrams, document flowcharts, system flowcharts, and process diagrams.

---

[2] http://www.theledger.com/article/20090427/COLUMNISTS/904275005

Data Flow Diagrams

System designers primarily use **data flow diagrams (DFDs)** in the development process—for example, as a tool for analyzing an existing system or as a planning aid for creating a new system. Because documented data flows are important for understanding an AIS, many of the remaining chapters of this book use DFDs to illustrate the flow of data in the AISs under discussion.

Different types of diagrams give different views of systems, which is why reviewers may need multiple diagrams to fully comprehend a system. For example, an E-R diagram indicates the resources, events, and agents about which the business collects data and stores in a database. A DFD describes the sources of data stored in a database and the ultimate destinations of these data.

Data Flow Diagram Symbols.

Figure 6-2 illustrates the four basic symbols used in DFDs. A rectangle or square represents an external data source or data destination—for example, a customer. To show this, a DFD would include the word "customer" inside a data source or destination symbol. In Figure 6-2, the term *external entity* (an entity outside the system under study) does not necessarily mean that it is an entity external to the company. Thus, for example, a "customer" might be another division of the same company under study.

Data flow lines are lines with arrows that indicate the direction that data flow in the system. For this reason, every data source symbol will have one or more data flow lines leading away from it, and every data destination symbol will have one or more data flow lines leading into it. For clarity, you should label each data flow line to indicate exactly what data are flowing along it.

A circle or bubble in a DFD indicates a system entity or process that changes or transforms data. (Some authors prefer to use squares with rounded corners for this symbol.) In physical DFDs (discussed shortly), the label inside a bubble typically contains the title of the person performing a task—for example, "cashier." In logical DFDs (also discussed shortly), the label inside the bubble describes a transformation process—for example, "process cash receipts."

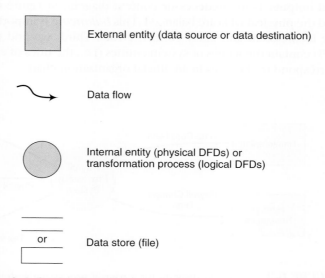

FIGURE 6-2   Symbols for data flow diagrams.

Finally, DFDs use a set of parallel lines or an open rectangle to represent a store or repository of data. This is usually a file or database table. If data are permanently stored, a data store symbol is mandatory. If data are collected over time and stored in some temporary place, you are not required to use a file symbol for this (although experts recommend including one for clarity).

Context Diagrams.   We typically draw DFDs in levels that show increasing amounts of detail. Designers first prepare a high-level DFD called a **context diagram** to provide an overview of a system. Figure 6-3 is an example of a context diagram for payroll processing.

The DFD in Figure 6-3 shows the inputs and outputs of the application (payroll processing) as well as the data sources and destinations external to the application. Thus, this context diagram uses rectangles to identify Timekeeping and Human Resources as external entities, despite the fact that these departments are internal to the company. This is because these entities are external to the payroll processing system under study. The data flow lines connecting these entities to and from the system (e.g., time card data) are system interfaces.

Physical Data Flow Diagrams.   A context diagram shows very little detail. For this reason, system designers usually elaborate on the elements in context DFDs by decomposing them into successively more detailed levels. These subsequent DFDs show more specifics, such as processing details or the inputs and outputs associated with each processing step.

The first level of detail is commonly called a **physical data flow diagram**. Figure 6-4 is an example for our payroll illustration. The circles in the physical DFD of Figure 6-4 identify the data-entry clerk who enters payroll information into the computer, the payroll cashier who distributes paychecks to employees, and the tax accountant who sends tax information to the Internal Revenue Service.

Figure 6-4 illustrates several important characteristics of physical DFDs. First, we observe that each circle contains a number as well as a title. Including a number in each circle makes it easier to reference it later. This also assists designers in the decomposition tasks discussed shortly. Second, we notice that a physical DFD includes the same inputs and outputs as its predecessor context diagram in Figure 6-3—that is, the context DFD and the physical DFD are balanced. This *balancing* is important because unbalanced DFDs are inconsistent and likely contain errors. Third, we find that all circles in the physical DFD contain the names of system entities (i.e., the titles of employees). These titles should correspond to the titles in an official organization chart.

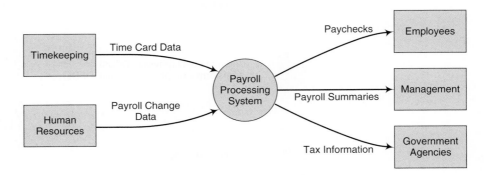

FIGURE 6-3   A context diagram for a payroll processing system.

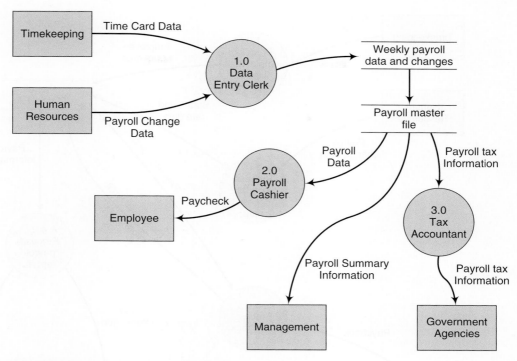

FIGURE 6-4 A physical data flow diagram.

Finally, we see that a physical DFD lists the job title of only one typical employee in an entity symbol, despite the fact that several employees may perform the same task—for example, several data-entry clerks or payroll cashiers. This last characteristic also applies when several employees perform the same task at different locations—for example, a company has several payroll cashiers who distribute paychecks at each of its manufacturing facilities. Representing types of employees, rather than individual employees, keeps DFDs simple and makes them easier to interpret.

Logical Data Flow Diagrams.   A physical DFD illustrates the internal and external entities that participate in a process but does not give the reader a good idea of what these participants do. For this task, we need **logical data flow diagrams**.

Figure 6-5 is a logical DFD for the payroll illustration in Figure 6-4. In Figure 6-5, note that each circle no longer contains the name of a system entity, but instead contains a verb that indicates a task the system performs. For example, instead of a single circle with the title "Data-Entry Clerk," as in Figure 6-4, the logical DFD in Figure 6-5 shows two circles with the titles "Process employee hours worked" and "Process payroll change data"—because these are separate data processing tasks that clerks perform.

From the standpoint of good system design and control, describing system processes is important because understanding how a system performs tasks can be more important than knowing what tasks the system performs. For example, all payroll systems prepare paychecks, but not all payroll systems do this exactly the same way. The differences may require different hardware, software, procedures, or controls. Logical DFDs help designers decide what system resources to acquire, what activities employees must perform to run these systems, and how to protect and control these systems after they are installed.

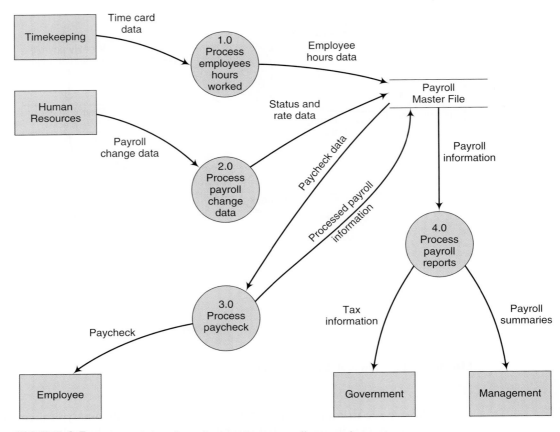

FIGURE 6-5 A logical data flow diagram for a payroll processing system.

Figure 6-5 is called a **level 0 data flow diagram** because it shows only in broad terms what tasks a system performs. Most systems are more complex than this and therefore require more detail to describe them completely. The task of creating such detail is called **decomposition**, which becomes necessary because DFD designers try to limit each level diagram to between five and seven processing symbols (circles).

Figure 6-6 shows an example of a **level 1 data flow diagram**—an "explosion" of symbol 3.0 (in Figure 6-5) with the caption "process paycheck." Here, we see that "process paycheck" entails computing gross pay, payroll deductions, and net pay. If necessary, you can also show ancillary computer files at this level.

To fully document the system, you would continue to perform these decomposition tasks in additional DFDs. For example, you might decompose the procedure "compute payroll deductions" in circle 3.2 of Figure 6-6 into several additional processes in lower-level DFDs—for example, create separate DFDs for "compute medical deductions," "compute savings plan deductions," "compute tax deductions," and so forth. In this way, a set of DFDs become linked together in a hierarchy.

Guidelines for Drawing Data Flow Diagrams

Creating DFDs is as much art as science. The following rules can help you make them easier to interpret and assist you in avoiding simple errors.

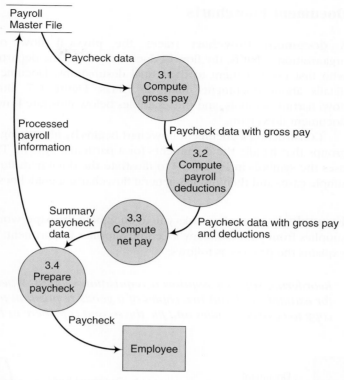

FIGURE 6-6   An exploded view of the "process paycheck" bubble of Figure 6-5.

1. Avoid detail in high-level DFDs (i.e., in levels 0 and 1). Where appropriate, combine activities that are performed at the same place or same time or that are logically related.

2. As a general rule, each logical DFD should contain between five and seven processing circles (or bubbles). This guideline helps you simplify the diagrams and avoid showing too much detail in high-level DFDs.

3. Different data flows should have different names to avoid confusion related to the data produced and used by different processes.

4. Unless they are outside the system or used for archiving, all data stores should have data flows both into and out of them. Thus, an internal file symbol that lacks both of these data flow lines typically involves a diagramming error.

5. Even if a file is temporary, it is usually desirable to include it in a DFD.

6. Classify most of the final recipients of system information as external entities.

7. Classify all personnel or departments that process the data of the current system as internal entities.

8. Display only normal processing routines in high-level DFDs. Avoid showing error routines or similar exception tasks.

9. Where several system entities perform the same task, show only one to represent them all. This rule also applies when system personnel perform the same task at different locations of the organization—for example, at different plants.

Document Flowcharts

A **document flowchart** traces the physical flow of documents through an organization—that is, the flow of documents from the departments, groups, or individuals who first created them to their final destinations. Document flowcharts provide more details about documents than do DFDs. Figure 6-7 illustrates common document flowcharting symbols, and the examples below illustrate how to use them to create basic document flowcharts.

Constructing a document flowchart begins by identifying the different departments or groups that handle the documents for a particular system. The flowchart developer then uses the symbols in Figure 6-7 to illustrate the document flows. Let us first examine two simple cases and then discuss general flowcharting guidelines.

Example 1. Your boss asks you to document the paperwork involved in acquiring office supplies from your company's Central Supplies Department. Your administrative assistant explains the process as follows:

Reordering supplies requires a requisition request. When I need more stationery, for example, I fill out two copies of a goods requisition form (GRF). I send the first copy to central supplies and file the second copy here in the office.

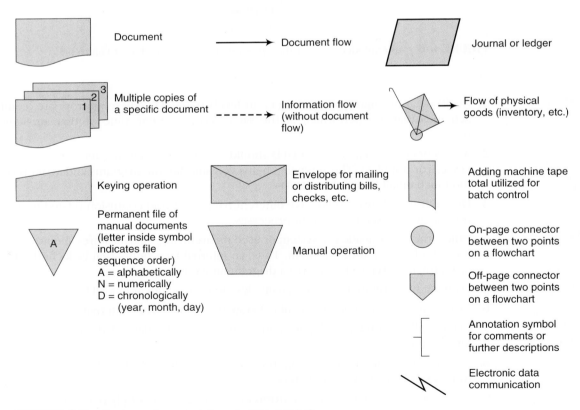

FIGURE 6-7 Common document flowcharting symbols.

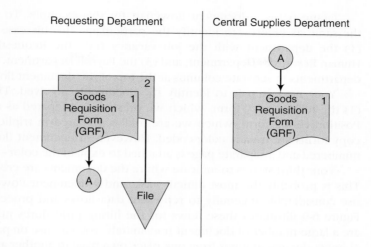

FIGURE 6-8 A simple document flowchart.

There are two departments involved in this example—your department (which we will call the Requesting Department) and the Central Supplies Department. Thus, you should begin by naming these departments in the headings on your document flowchart (Figure 6-8). Next, you draw two copies of the GRF under the heading for the Requesting Department because this is the department that creates this form. You number these copies 1 and 2 to indicate two copies.

Finally, you indicate where each document goes: copy 1 to the Central Supplies Department and copy 2 to a file in the Requesting Department. A document's first appearance should be in the department that creates it. A solid line or the on-page connectors shown here indicate its physical transmittal from one place to another. You then redraw the transmitted document to indicate its arrival at the department that receives it. Figure 6-8 illustrates the completed flowchart for this narrative.

Example 2. Now consider a slightly more complex example—the task of hiring a new employee at your company. The process begins when a department develops a vacancy. The Human Resources (HR) director explains the process as follows:

> *The department that develops a vacancy must first complete a job vacancy form, which it forwards to my department. We then advertise for the position and, with the help of the requesting department, interview applicants. When the vacancy is filled, the HR Department prepares a position hiring form (PHF) in triplicate. We file the first copy in a manual file, which is organized by employee Social Security number. We staple the third copy to the job vacancy form and return it to the Requesting Department, where clerks file it alphabetically by employee last name.*
>
> *The HR Department forwards the second copy of the PHF to the Payroll Department. The Payroll Department uses the form as an authorization document to create a payroll record for the new employee. Thus, the information on the form is keyed directly into the company's computer system using an online terminal located in the payroll office. This copy of the PHF is then filed numerically for reference and also as evidence that the form has been processed.*

Figure 6-9 is a document flowchart for this example. To draw it, your first step is the same as before—to identify the participants. In this case there are three of them: (1) the department with the job vacancy (i.e., the Requesting Department), (2) the Human Resources Department, and (3) the Payroll Department. You identify each of these departments in separate columns at the top of the document flowchart.

Your next step is to identify the documents involved. There are two major ones: (1) the Job Vacancy form, which we presume is prepared as a single copy, and (2) the Position Hiring form, which we are told is prepared in triplicate. In practice, multiple-copy forms are usually color-coded. However, in document flowcharts, these are simply numbered and a separate page is attached to explain the color–number equivalencies.

Your third step is to indicate where the documents are created, processed, and used. This is probably the most difficult task, and a document flowchart designer must often use considerable ingenuity to represent data flows and processing activities accurately. Figure 6-9 illustrates these flows for the hiring procedures just described. Where there are a large number of document transmittals, you can use on-page connectors (circles) to connect document flows from one place on a page to another and avoid complicated flow lines. Thus, Figure 6-9 uses several on-page connectors (with letters A, B, and C) to avoid cluttering the chart. You should use a unique identifier in each connector (such as a letter) for identification purposes. You can also use off-page connectors (to connect data flows to other pages) if necessary.

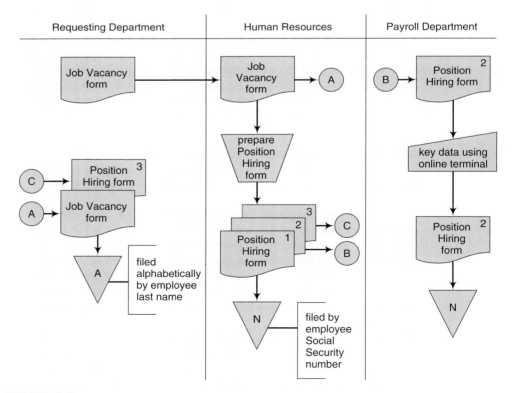

FIGURE 6-9 A document flowchart illustrating the flow of documents involved in the hiring of a new employee.

When constructing document flowcharts, some analysts also include the movement of physical goods—for example, moving inventory from a receiving department to an inventory storeroom. Document flowcharts typically use hand-truck symbols for this task. Some document flowcharts also illustrate information flows that do not involve documents (for example, a sales clerk telephoning to check a customer's account balance before approving a credit sale). Thus, the term "document" broadly includes all types of organizational communications and data flows. It is also important to recognize that document flowcharting symbols are not standardized across all firms.

Guidelines for Drawing Document Flowcharts

You can use the following guidelines to simplify the process of creating document flowcharts.

1. Identify all the departments that create or receive the documents involved in the system. Use vertical lines to create "swim lanes" to separate each department from the others.

2. Carefully classify the documents and activities of each department, and draw them under their corresponding department headings.

3. Identify each copy of an accounting document with a number. If multiple-copy documents are color-coded, use a table to identify the number–color associations.

4. Account for the distribution of each copy of a document. In general, it is better to over-document a complicated process than to under-document.

5. Use on-page and off-page connectors to avoid diagrams with lines that cross one another.

6. Each pair of connectors (a *from* and a *to* connector in each pair) should use the same letter or number.

7. Use annotations if necessary to explain activities or symbols that may be unclear. These are little notes to the reader that help clarify your documentation.

8. If the sequence of records in a file is important, include the letter "A" for alphabetical, "N" for numeric, or "C" for chronological in the file symbol. As indicated in guideline 7, you can also include a note in the flowchart.

9. Many flowcharts in practice use acronyms (e.g., GRF or PHF in the preceding examples). To avoid confusion, use full names (possibly with acronyms in parentheses) or create a table of equivalents to ensure accuracy in identifying documents.

10. Consider using automated flowcharting tools. See the section of this chapter on CASE tools for more information.

Case-in-Point 6.3 Some accountants disagree about the usefulness of document flowcharts relative to other documenting tools, but one manuscript reviewer of this book wrote: "Flowcharting is one of the most essential skills, in my opinion, for a student to learn in a systems course. During my tenure at a CPA firm, I had the opportunity to document several accounting information systems, and document flowcharting was the key skill. When word got around the office that I was a good flowcharter, I got placed on more important clients, furthering my career."

System Flowcharts

Whereas document flowcharts focus on tangible documents, **system flowcharts** concentrate on the computerized data flows of AISs. Thus, a system flowchart typically depicts the electronic flow of data and processing steps in an AIS. Figure 6-10 illustrates some common system flowcharting symbols. Most of these symbols are industry conventions that have been standardized by the National Bureau of Standards (Standard $\times 3.5$), although additional symbols are now necessary to represent newer data transmission technologies—for example, wireless data flows.

Some system flowcharts are general in nature and provide only an overview of the system. These are *high-level system flowcharts*. Figure 6-11 is an example. The inputs and

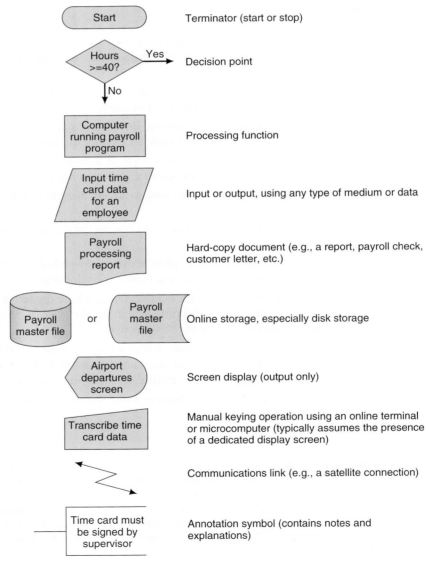

FIGURE 6-10   Some common system and programming flowcharting symbols.

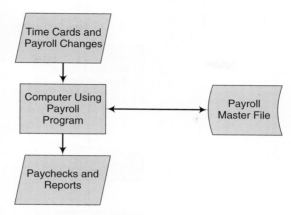

FIGURE 6-11 A high-level system flowchart for payroll processing.

outputs of the system are specified by the general input and output symbol, a parallelogram. In more detailed system flowcharts, the specific form of these inputs and outputs would be indicated—for example, by magnetic disk symbols.

Figure 6-11 refers to only one process—processing payroll. A more detailed system flowchart would describe all the processes performed by the payroll program and the specific inputs and outputs of each process. At the lowest, most detailed level of such documentation are program flowcharts that describe the processing logic of each application program. We will examine program flowcharts later in this chapter.

Like document flowcharts, the process of drawing system flowcharts is probably best understood by studying an illustration. Figure 6-12 is a system flowchart for the following example.

The Sarah Stanton Company is a magazine distributor that maintains a file of magazine subscribers for creating monthly mailing labels. Magazine subscribers mail change-of-address forms or new-subscription forms directly to the company, where input personnel key the information into the system through online terminals. The computer system temporarily stores this information as a file of address change or new-subscription requests. Clerical staff key these data into computer files continuously, so we may characterize it as "daily processing."

Once a week, the system uses the information in the daily processing file to update the subscriber master file. At this time, new subscriber names and addresses are added to the file, and the addresses of existing subscribers who have moved are changed. The system also prepares a Master File Maintenance Processing Report to indicate what additions and modifications were made to the file. Once a month, the company prepares postal labels for the magazine's mailing. The subscriber master file serves as the chief input for this computer program. The two major outputs are the labels themselves and a Mailing Labels Processing Report that documents this run and indicates any problems.

The system flowchart in Figure 6-12 documents the flow of data through the company's computerized system. Thus, it identifies sources of data, the places where data are temporarily stored, and the outputs on which processed data appear. In Figure 6-12, for example, the system flowchart begins with the subscriber request forms and documents

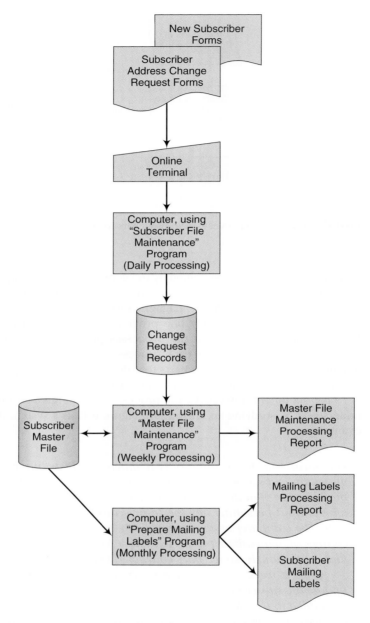

FIGURE 6-12 A system flowchart illustrating the computer steps involved in maintaining a subscriber master file and creating monthly mailing labels.

the flow of data on these forms through the keying phase, master-file-maintenance phase, and finally, the monthly mailing phase.

Indirectly, system flowcharts also indicate processing cycles (daily, weekly, or monthly), hardware needs (e.g., disk drives and printers), areas of weak or missing application controls, and potential bottlenecks in processing (e.g., manual data entry). In Figure 6-12, we can also identify the major files of the system (a temporary log file of change-request records and a subscriber master file) and the major reports of the system.

Finally, note that each processing phase of a system flowchart usually involves preparing one or more control reports. These reports provide processing-control information (e.g., counts of transactions processed) for control purposes and exceptions information (e.g., the identity of unprocessed transactions) that helps employees correct the errors detected by the system.

Guidelines for Drawing System Flowcharts

System flowcharts depict an electronic **job stream** of data through the various processing phases of an AIS and therefore also illustrate audit trails. Each time the records of a file are sorted or updated, for example, a system flowchart should show this in a separate processing step. Recognizing the usefulness of system flowcharts, both the American Institute of Certified Public Accountants (AICPA) and the Institute of Management Accountants (IMA) consistently include test questions in their professional examinations that require a working knowledge of system flowcharts.

Although no strict rules govern exactly how to organize a system flowchart, the following list provides some guidelines.

1. System flowcharts should read from top to bottom and from left to right. In drawing or reading such flowcharts, you should begin in the upper-left corner.

2. Because system flowcharting symbols are standardized, you should use these symbols when drawing your flowcharts—do not make up your own.

3. A processing symbol should always be found between an input symbol and an output symbol. This is called the **sandwich rule**.

4. Use on-page and off-page connectors to avoid crossed lines and cluttered flowcharts.

5. Sketch a flowchart before designing the final draft. Graphical documentation software tools (discussed shortly) make this job easier.

6. Add descriptions and comments in flowcharts to clarify processing elements. You can place these inside the processing symbols themselves, include them in annotation symbols attached to process or file symbols, or add them as separate notes in your systems documentation.

Process Maps

A *business process* is a natural group of business activities that create value for an organization. **Process maps** document business processes in easy-to-follow diagrams. Did you understand the logic diagram in Figure 6-1 at the beginning of the chapter? It's an example of a process map. Studies suggest that process maps are among the easiest to draw and are also among the easiest for novices to follow.

In businesses, a major process is usually the sales or order fulfillment process. A process map for this process (Figure 6-13) shows activities such as customers placing orders, warehouse personnel picking goods, and clerks shipping goods. Managers can create similar maps that show just about any other process—for example, how an organization processes time cards for a payroll application, how a business responds to customer returns, or how a manager deals with defective merchandise.

Case-in-Point 6.4 Increased competition and tighter profit margins have forced companies to look for places where they might be able to save money. One large accounting firm has

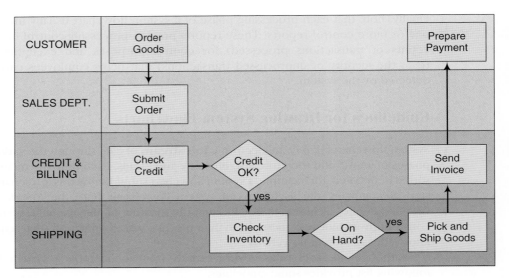

FIGURE 6-13   A process map for the order fulfillment process (created with Microsoft Word).

used process mapping software to assist clients in evaluating and redesigning their business processes. For example, the firm's business reengineering practice helped a financial services company cut its costs and become more efficient. The company was able to cut in half the time it took to approve a loan—and it needed 40 percent fewer staff to do it.

Internal and external auditors can use process maps to help them learn how a department or division operates, document what they have learned, and identify internal control weaknesses or problems in existing operations. An additional benefit is to use such maps as training aids. Consultants frequently use process maps to help them study business processes and redesign them for greater productivity. Accountants and managers can also use this tool to help them describe current processes to others.

Like most other types of documentation, you can draw process maps in multilevel versions called *hierarchical process maps* that show successively finer levels of detail. Such maps are especially popular on the Web because viewers can click on individual symbols to see more information for any given process or decision. Figure 6-14, for example, illustrates a second-level process map for checking credit that might link to the ''Check Credit'' box in Figure 6-13.

Guidelines for Drawing Process Maps

Process maps vary considerably across firms, and the symbols found in Web versions are remarkably inconsistent. Nonetheless, it is possible to use the flowchart symbols that you already know to create process maps, including (1) a rectangle (to represent a process), (2) a diamond (to represent decisions), (3) an oval (to depict the starting and ending points for a process), (4) an off-page connector, and (5) a document symbol. Creating a good process map requires a blend of art, science, and craftsmanship, all of which mostly comes with practice. Here are some guidelines to use when drawing process maps.

1. Identify and define the process of interest. The goal is to stay focused on the scope of the process you are trying to map.

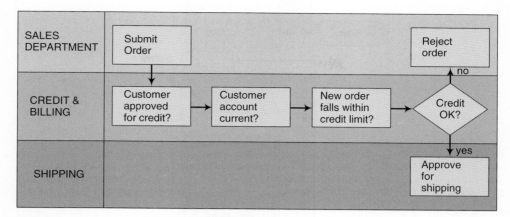

FIGURE 6-14   A second-level process map for the credit approval process of Figure 6-13.

2. Understand the purpose of each process map. Is it to identify bottlenecks? Discover redundancies?

3. Meet with employees to get their ideas, suggestions, and comments. Don't hesitate to ask challenging or probing questions.

4. Remember that processes have inputs, outputs, and enablers. An example input is an invoice; an output could be a payment check for a supplier, and an enabler helps a process achieve results. In AISs, information technology is a common enabler.

5. Show key decision points. A process map will not be an effective analytical tool without decision points (the intellectual or mental steps in a process).

6. Pay attention to the level of detail you capture. Did you capture enough detail to truly represent the process and explain it to others?

7. Avoid mapping the *should-be* or *could-be*. Map the process that is in place.

8. Practice, practice, practice.

OTHER DOCUMENTATION TOOLS

There are many other tools for documenting AISs besides data flow diagrams, document flowcharts, system flowcharts, and process maps. Two of them are (1) program flowcharts and (2) decision tables. Because these tools are used mostly by consultants and IT professionals rather than accountants, we will describe them only briefly. Accountants should have some familiarity with these tools, however, because they may see them—for example, when reviewing the design for a revised accounting system.

Program Flowcharts

Because large computer programs today involve millions of instructions, they require careful planning and the coordinated work of hundreds of systems analysts and programmers. Typically, organizations use **structured programming** techniques to create these large programs in a hierarchical fashion, that is, from the top down. This means that the developers design the main routines first and then design subroutines for subsidiary processing as major processing tasks become clear.

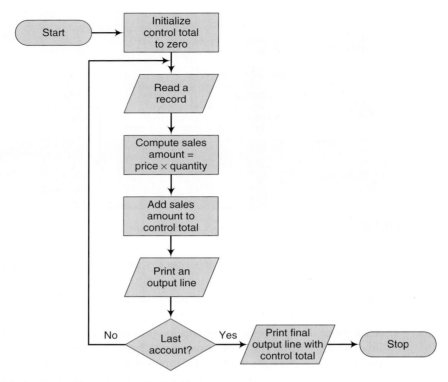

FIGURE 6-15   A program flowchart for a sales application.

To help them plan the logic for each processing routine, IT professionals often create **program flowcharts** (Figure 6-15) that outline the processing logic of computer programs as well as the order in which processing steps take place. After designing such program flowcharts, the developers typically present them to colleagues in a structured walkthrough or formal review of the logic. This process helps the reviewers assess the soundness of the logic, detect and correct design flaws, and make improvements. On approval, the program flowcharts become blueprints for writing the instructions of a computer program as well as documenting the program itself.

Program flowcharts use many of the same symbols as system flowcharts (refer back to Figure 6-10). A few specialized symbols for program flowcharts are the diamond symbol (which indicates a decision point in the processing logic) and the oval symbol (which indicates a starting or stopping point).

Like system flowcharts and data flow diagrams, program flowcharts can be designed at different levels of detail. The highest-level program flowchart is sometimes called a macro program flowchart, which provides an overview of the data processing logic. A lower-level program flowchart would indicate the detailed programming logic necessary to carry out a processing task. Figure 6-15 is a detailed (lower-level) program flowchart for a sales report application.

Decision Tables

When a computer program involves a large number of conditions and subsequent courses of action, its program flowchart tends to be large and complex. A **decision table** (Figure 6-16)

			Rules			
			1	2	3	4
	Conditions					
Condition stub	Account balance less than $5		Y	N	N	N	Condition entries
	Account balance less than $1,000		*	Y	*	N	
	Account 1 year old or less		*	*	Y	N	
	Actions						
Action stub	Pay no interest		X				Action entries
	Pay 5 percent interest			X	X		
	Pay 5.5 percent interest					X	

FIGURE 6-16 This is a decision table to help a credit union decide how much interest to pay each account. An asterisk (*) means that the condition does not affect the course of action.

is a table of conditions and processing tasks that indicates what action to take for each possibility. Sometimes, decision tables are used as an alternative to program flowcharts. More commonly, they are used in conjunction with these flowcharts. To illustrate a decision table, consider the following scenario:

A credit union pays interest to its depositors at the rate of 5 percent per year. Accounts of less than $5 are not paid interest. Accounts of $1,000 or more that have been with the credit union for more than one year get paid the normal 5 percent, plus a bonus of 0.5 percent.

Figure 6-16 presents a decision table for the credit union that shows how much interest to pay each account. Note that the decision table consists of four parts: (1) the condition stub outlines the potential conditions of the application, (2) the action stub outlines the available actions that can be taken, (3) the condition entries depict the possible combinations of conditions likely to occur, and (4) the action entries outline the action to be taken for each combination of conditions.

The rules at the top of the decision table set forth the combination of conditions that may occur and the action entries show what to do for each condition. For the illustration at hand, three conditions affect the data processing of each account: (1) an account balance less than $5, (2) an account balance less than $1,000, and (3) an account one year old or less. As defined, each of these conditions can now be answered "yes" or "no." Figure 6-16 is a decision table for the illustration at hand, in which Y stands for "yes" and N stands for "no." The combination of Y's and N's in each column of the table illustrates each possible condition the system might encounter. Using X's, the decision table also shows what course of action should be taken for each condition (i.e., how much interest should be paid to each account).

The major advantage of decision tables is that they summarize the processing tasks for a large number of conditions in a compact, easily understood format. This increases system understanding, resulting in fewer omissions of important processing possibilities. Decision tables also serve as useful documentation aids when new data processing conditions arise or when changes in organizational policy result in new actions for existing conditions. This advantage is particularly important to AISs because of organizational concern for accuracy and completeness in processing financial data.

One drawback of decision tables is that they do not show the order in which a program tests data conditions or takes processing actions, as do program flowcharts. This is a major deficiency because the order in which accounting data are tested or processed is often as important as the tests or processes themselves. A second drawback is that decision tables require an understanding of documentation techniques beyond flowcharting. Finally, decision tables require extra work to prepare, and this work may not always be cost-effective.

Software Tools for Graphical Documentation and SOX Compliance

Accountants, consultants, and system developers can use a variety of software tools to create **graphical documentation** of existing or proposed AISs. The simplest tools include presentation software, such as Microsoft PowerPoint, as well as word processing and spreadsheet software such as Microsoft Word and Excel. The advantages of using such tools closely parallel those of using word processing software instead of typewriters (e.g., easily revised documents, advanced formatting capabilities and coloring options, and a variety of reproduction capabilities). For example, the authors used Microsoft Word to create the process maps in Figures 6-13 and 6-14.

Microsoft Word, Excel, and PowerPoint.
Using the ''AutoShapes'' option in the Drawing Toolbar of Microsoft Word, Excel, or PowerPoint, you can reproduce most of the graphics symbols and logic diagrams in this chapter. (The connectors in Excel are different from, as well as better than, simple lines because they adjust automatically when you reposition symbols in your charts.) Two additional advantages of using Excel to create graphical documentation are the ability to create large drawings (that exceed the margins of word processing documents) and the option to embed computed values in flowcharting symbols. Problem 6–21 at the end of the chapter describes how to use Excel to create such graphical documentation.

CASE Tools.
The capabilities of specialized graphical documentation software exceed those of word processing or spreadsheet packages. These **CASE (computer-assisted software engineering) tools** automate such documentation tasks as drawing or modifying flowcharts, drawing graphics and screen designs, developing reports, and even generating code from documentation. Thus, CASE tools are to flowcharts what word processors are to text documents. Figure 6-17 is an example of a CASE package being used to draw a data flow diagram.

Most CASE products run on personal computers. Examples include *iGrafx* (Micrografx, Inc.), *allCLEAR* (Proquis, Inc.), *SmartDraw* (SmartDraw LLC.), and *Visio* (Microsoft Corp.). These products are especially popular with auditors and consultants who use them to document AISs using the techniques discussed above, as well as to analyze the results. Graphical documentation software enables its users to create a wide array of outputs, including data flow diagrams, entity-relationship diagrams (described in Chapter 3), system flowcharts, program flowcharts, process maps, and even computer network designs.

Front-end CASE tools focus on the early (front-end) tasks of systems design—for example, requirements-design activities. *Backend CASE tools* automate the detailed design tasks required in the later stages of a project—for example, developing detailed program

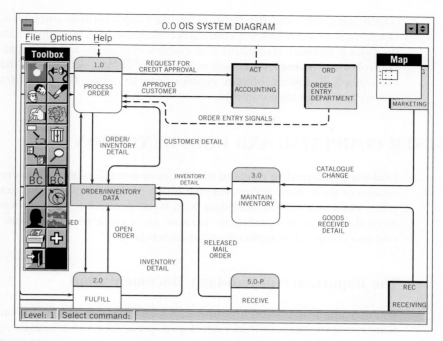

FIGURE 6-17 This CASE tool is a software program called Excelerator™, which is used here to create a data flow diagram. The toolbox on the left contains symbols that the user can select for his or her diagram.

flowcharts. Integrated CASE (I-CASE) packages enable users to perform both types of tasks and can even generate computer code directly from logic diagrams. As a result, these tools support **rapid application development (RAD)** and help organizations reduce development costs.

Graphical documentation software tools enable their users to generate documentation quickly and consistently, as well as to automate modifications to this documentation later as changes are required. They include templates and models that allow users to document almost any business and system environment. But these packages only create what they are told to create. Like word processors, they lack imagination and creativity, and they also require training to use them effectively.

SOX and AS5 Compliance. Many businesses now use specialized software packages to automate the tasks required by Section 404 of the Sarbanes-Oxley Act of 2002 and standards of the Public Company Accounting Oversight Board (PCAOB). Since the adoption of Auditing Standard No. 5 (AS5) by the PCAOB, companies are placing more emphasis on entity-level controls (such as the tone at the top, management override of internal controls, and the overall control environment) than in prior years. Just as word processing software makes document revisions easier, these ''compliance software packages'' enable businesses to reduce the time and costs required to satisfy legal requirements.

Symantec Control Compliance Suite (Symantec Corporation), for example, auto-mates processes required by SOX that are intended to reduce IT risks. *OpenPages FCM*

(OpenPages, Inc.) and *BizRights* (Approva Corp.) provide somewhat similar capabilities. OpenPages FCM includes a compliance database and workflow management tools and provides a software dashboard that enables executives to verify that specific managerial controls are now in place as well as to identify control deficiencies that might affect financial reports. BizRights software enables firms to reduce the risk of fraud by continuously testing and monitoring controls.

END-USER COMPUTING AND DOCUMENTATION

End-user computing refers to the ability of non-IT employees to create computer applications of their own. Today, we take much of this computing for granted—for example, when employees manipulate data with word processing, spreadsheet, database management systems, or tax packages—because all of these programs were developed to allow end users to develop applications for themselves.

The Importance of End-User Documentation

End-user applications often perform mission-critical functions for busy organizations. In many cases, the outputs of user-developed spreadsheets and database applications find their way into financial systems and ultimately influence an organization's financial statements. Thus, end users should document their applications for many of the same reasons that professionals must document applications. Managers, auditors, and other system users need to understand how user-developed systems work in order to prevent errors created by these systems. In addition, if an employee leaves an organization, other employees need to be able to use these applications and interpret their outputs.

Unfortunately, documentation of end-user applications is often overlooked or is performed so poorly that it might as well be overlooked. Such oversight can be costly. For example, time is wasted when other employees must alter the system but lack the basic documentation to accomplish this task. Thus, even if the developer is the only one in the office who uses a particular application, managers should insist that he or she document it.

> **Case-in-Point 6.5** The Institute of Internal Auditors (IIA) released a white paper in 2010 that guides internal auditor's evaluations of end-user applications. Because nearly all organizations use employee-developed software such as spreadsheets, the IIA observes that such software may pose threats to organizations (including honest mistakes, noncompliance with regulations, and fraud). As a result, the IIA states that it is critical to evaluate and document these systems.[3]

The specific items that should be used to document any particular end-user application will, of course, vary with the application. For example, businesses often find it convenient to use systematic file names to identify word processing documents and to embed these

---

[3] The Institute of Internal Auditors. 2010. *Global Technology Audit Guide (GTAG) 14: Auditing User-Development Applications*. The Institute of Internal Auditors. Altamonte Springs, Florida.

1. Name of the developer.
2. Name of the file where the application is stored.
3. Name of the directories and subdirectories where the application is stored.
4. Date the application was first developed.
5. Date the application was last modified, and the name of the person who modified it.
6. Date the application was last run.
7. Name and phone number of person to call in case of problems.
8. Sources of external data used by the system.
9. Important assumptions made in the application.
10. Important parameters that must be modified in order to change assumptions or answer "what-if" questions.
11. Range names used in the application and their locations in the spreadsheet.

FIGURE 6-18   Examples of information to include when documenting spreadsheets.

file names within the reports to help others find them later. Figure 6-18 provides some ideas for documenting spreadsheet applications.

Policies for End-User Computing and Documentation

To avoid the creation of redundant or ineffective systems and poor documentation of systems developed by employees, businesses should establish and follow the guidelines outlined here to control end-user applications development:

1. *Formally evaluate large projects.* Employees should be allowed to create a large application only after it has withstood the scrutiny of a formal review of its costs and benefits. When projects are large, higher-level management should be involved in the go-ahead decision.

2. *Adopt formal end-user development policies.* Employees usually do not develop poor applications because they wish to do so but because no organizational policies exist that restrict them from doing so. Policy guidelines should include procedures for testing software, examining internal controls, and periodically auditing systems.

3. *Formalize documentation standards.* At this point in the chapter, the importance of formal documentation should be self-evident. What may be less obvious is the need to create procedures for ensuring that employees meet these documentation standards.

4. *Limit the number of employees authorized to create end-user applications.* This restricts applications development to those employees in whom management has confidence, or perhaps who have taken formal development classes.

5. *Audit new and existing systems.* The more critical an end-user system is to the functioning of a department or division, the more important it is for organizations to require formal audits of such systems for compliance with the guidelines outlined previously.

AIS AT WORK
Better System Documentation Helps Protect
Minnesota's Environment[4]

The Minnesota Pollution Control Agency is charged with protecting Minnesota's environment. The agency recently realized that it has collected vast amounts of data for nearly 40 years, but it still does not have reliable methods for assessing many of its functions and their effectiveness. To enhance the agency's effectiveness, the CIO decided that the agency needs detailed business process mapping and documentation. The purpose of the new documentation is to help the agency better understand their existing business processes and identify the current bottlenecks.

The agency undertook four main steps in its documentation efforts. First, they identified the critical business processes and defined these processes. Next, the agency gathered information about the processes by interviewing key personnel and performing walk-throughs of processes. Third, processes were graphically mapped using the forms of documentation described in this chapter. Finally, experts within the agency analyzed the existing processes in order to identify opportunities for improvement.

While the business process modeling task is still ongoing, some of the initial benefits of the new documentation are a reduction in the percentage of backlogged permits from 40 percent to 9 percent, streamlined reporting processes to the federal government, and better understanding of the key risks involved in business processes.

SUMMARY

- ✓ Nine reasons to document an AIS are (1) to explain how the system works, (2) to train others, (3) to help developers design new systems, (4) to control system development and maintenance costs, (5) to standardize communications among system designers, (6) to provide information to auditors, (7) to document a business's processes, (8) to help a company comply with the Sarbanes-Oxley Act of 2002 and AS5, and (9) to establish employee accountability for specific tasks or procedures.

- ✓ Data flow diagrams provide both a physical and a logical view of a system, but concentrate more on the flow and transformation of data than on the physical devices or timing of inputs, processing, or outputs.

- ✓ A document flowchart describes the physical flow of documents through an AIS, for example, by providing an overview of where documents are created, sent, reviewed, and stored, and what activities they trigger.

- ✓ A system flowchart describes the electronic flow of data through an AIS, indicates what processing steps and files are used and when, and provides an overview of the entire system.

- ✓ Process maps also describe the flow of information through an organization, use only a few symbols, and (to many) are among the easiest to draw and understand.

- ✓ Two additional documentation tools are program flowcharts and decision tables. Accountants do not need to be programmers to evaluate or design an accounting information system, but they should understand in general terms how these tools work.

---

[4] http://www.theusdaily.com/articles/viewarticle.jsp?id=1264630&type=TechnologyComm

✓ A variety of software tools exist for documenting AISs. These include standard personal productivity tools such as word processing and spreadsheet software, specialized CASE tools, and software packages designed to help companies comply with SOX and AS5.

✓ End-user computing is important because it is used extensively and also because such applications often contribute significantly to the efficiency of specific departments or divisions. But many employees do not document their applications very well, and this often costs time and money.

KEY TERMS YOU SHOULD KNOW

CASE (computer-assisted software engineering) tools	level 0 data flow diagram
context diagram	level 1 data flow diagram
data flow diagrams (DFDs)	logical data flow diagrams
decision table	object-oriented software
decomposition	physical data flow diagram
document flowchart	process maps
documentation	rapid application development (RAD)
end-user computing	sandwich rule
graphical documentation	signed checklist
job stream	structured programming
	system flowcharts

DISCUSSION QUESTIONS

6-1. Why is documentation important to accounting information systems? Why should accountants be interested in AIS documentation?

6-2. Distinguish between document flowcharts, system flowcharts, data flow diagrams, and program flowcharts. How are they similar? How are they different?

6-3. What are document flowcharts? How does a document flowchart assist each of the following individuals: (1) a systems analyst, (2) a systems designer, (3) a computer programmer, (4) an auditor, and (5) a data security expert?

6-4. Flowcharting is both an art and a science. Guidelines can be used to make better flowcharts. What are these guidelines for document, system, and data flow diagram flowcharts?

6-5. What are the four symbols used in data flow diagrams? What does each mean?

6-6. Why are data flow diagrams developed in a hierarchy? What are the names of some levels in the hierarchy?

6-7. Look at the process map in Figure 6-5. Trace the steps in the order fulfillment process. Do you think this figure is more helpful than a narrative would be in understanding the flow of events in the process?

6-8. What is the purpose of a decision table? How might decision tables be useful to accountants?

6-9. What are CASE tools? How are they used? How do CASE tools create documentation for AISs? If you were a systems analyst, would you use a CASE tool?

6-10. What is end-user computing? Why is documentation important to end-user computing? What guidelines should companies develop to control end-user computing?

PROBLEMS

6-11. To view the flowchart shapes in Microsoft Excel, select the following options from the main menu: Insert\Shapes. There should be approximately 28 of them (using Excel 2010). If you allow your mouse to hover over a specific symbol, its title and meaning will appear in a tool-tip box. Finally, if you click on a specific symbol, your mouse icon will change to a cross-hair and you will be able to draw this symbol on your spreadsheet. Create a list with items similar to the one below that contains all the symbols in your version of Excel.

Predefined Process

6-12. Draw a document flowchart to depict each of the following situations.

    a. An individual from the marketing department of a wholesale company prepares five copies of a sales invoice, and each copy is sent to a different department.

    b. The individual invoices from credit sales must temporarily be stored until they can be matched against customer payments at a later date.

    c. A batch control tape is prepared along with a set of transactions to ensure completeness of the data.

    d. The source document data found on employee application forms are used as input to create new employee records on a computer master file.

    e. Delinquent credit customers are sent as many as four different inquiry letters before their accounts are turned over to a collection agency.

    f. Physical goods are shipped back to the supplier if they are found to be damaged upon arrival at the receiving warehouse.

    g. The data found on employee time cards are keyed onto a hard disk before they are processed by a computer.

    h. The data found on employee time cards are first keyed onto a floppy diskette before they are entered into a computer job stream for processing.

    i. A document flowchart is becoming difficult to understand because too many lines cross one another. (Describe a solution.)

    j. Three people, all in different departments, look at the same document before it is eventually filed in a fourth department.

    k. Certain data from a source document are copied into a ledger before the document itself is filed in another department.

6-13. Develop a document flowchart for the following information flow. The individual stores in the Mark Goodwin convenience chain prepare two copies of a goods requisition form (GRF) when they need to order merchandise from the central warehouse. After these forms are completed, one copy is filed in the store's records and the other copy is sent to the central warehouse. The warehouse staff gets the order and files its copy of the GRF form in its records. When the warehouse needs to restock an item, three copies of a purchase order form (POF) are filled out. One copy is stored in the warehouse files, one copy goes to the vendor, and the third copy goes to the accounts payable department.

6-14. The Garcia-Lanoue Company produces industrial goods. The company receives purchase orders from its customers and ships goods accordingly. Assuming that the following conditions apply, develop a document flowchart for this company:

    a. The company receives two copies of every purchase order from its customers.

b. On receipt of the purchase orders, the company ships the goods ordered. One copy of the purchase order is returned to the customer with the order, and the other copy goes into the company's purchase order file.

c. The company prepares three copies of a shipping bill. One copy stays in the company's shipping file, and the other two are sent to the customer.

6-15. The data-entry department of the Ron Mitchell Manufacturing Company is responsible for converting all of the company's shipping and receiving information to computer records. Because accuracy in this conversion is essential, the firm employs a strict verification process. Prepare a document flowchart for the following information flow:

a. The shipping department sends a copy of all shipping orders to the data-entry department.

b. A data-entry operator keys the information from a shipping order onto a diskette.

c. A supervisor checks every record with the original shipping order. If no errors are detected, the diskette is sent to the computer operations staff and the original shipping order is filed.

6-16. Amanda M is a regional manufacturer and wholesaler of high-quality chocolate candies. The company's sales and collection process is as follows. Amanda M makes use of an enterprise-wide information system with electronic data interchange (EDI) capability. No paper documents are exchanged in the sales and collection process. The company receives sales orders from customers electronically. On receipt of a sales order, shipping department personnel prepare goods for shipment and input shipping data into the information system. The system sends an electronic shipping notice and invoice to the customer at the time of shipment. Terms are net 30. When payment is due, the customer makes an electronic funds transfer for the amount owed. The customer's information system sends remittance (payment) data to Amanda M. Amanda M's information system updates accounts receivable information at that time.

Draw a context diagram and a level 0 logical data flow diagram for Amanda M's sales and collection process.

6-17. The order-writing department at the Winston Beauchamp Company is managed by Alan Most. The department keeps two types of computer files: (1) a customer file of authorized credit customers and (2) a product file of items currently sold by the company. Both of these files are direct-access files stored on magnetic disks. Customer orders are handwritten on order forms with the Winston Beauchamp name at the top of the form, and item lines for quantity, item number, and total amount desired for each product ordered by the customer.

When customer orders are received, Alan Most directs someone to input the information at one of the department's computer terminals. After the information has been input, the computer program immediately adds the information to a computerized "order" file and prepares five copies of the customer order. The first copy is sent back to Alan's department; the others are sent elsewhere. Design a system flowchart that documents the accounting data processing described here. Also, draw a data flow diagram showing a logical view of the system.

6-18. The LeVitre and Swezey Credit Union maintains separate bank accounts for each of its 20,000 customers. Three major files are the customer master file, the transaction file of deposits and withdrawal information, and a monthly statement file that shows a customer's transaction history for the previous month. The following lists the bank's most important activities during a representative month:

a. Customers make deposits and withdrawals.

b. Employers make automatic deposits on behalf of selected employees.

c. The bank updates its master file daily using the transaction file.

d. The bank creates monthly statements for its customers, using both the customer master file and the transactions file.

e. Bank personnel answer customer questions concerning their deposits, withdrawals, or account balances.

f. The bank issues checks to pay its rent, utility bills, payroll, and phone bills.

Draw a data flow diagram that graphically describes these activities.

6-19. The Jeffrey Getelman Publishing Company maintains an online database of subscriber records, which it uses for preparing magazine labels, billing renewals, and so forth. New subscription orders and subscription renewals are keyed into a computer file from terminals. The entry data are checked for accuracy and written on a master file. A similar process is performed for change-of-address requests. Processing summaries from both runs provide listings of master file changes.

Once a month, just prior to mailing, the company prepares mailing labels for its production department to affix to magazines. At the same time, notices to new and renewal subscribers are prepared. These notices acknowledge receipt of payment and are mailed to the subscribers. The company systems analyst, Bob McQuivey, prepared the system flowchart in Figure 6-19 shortly before he left the company. As you can see, the flowchart is incomplete. Finish the flowchart by labeling each flowcharting symbol. Don't forget to label the processing runs marked computer.

6-20. The Bridget Joyce Company is an office products distributor that must decide what to do with delinquent credit-sales accounts. Mr. Bob Smith, the credit manager, divides accounts into the following categories: (1) accounts not past due, (2) accounts 30 days or less past due, (3) accounts 31 to 60 days past due, (4) accounts 61 to 90 days past due, and (5) accounts more than 90 days past due. For simplicity, assume that all transactions for each account fall neatly into the same category.

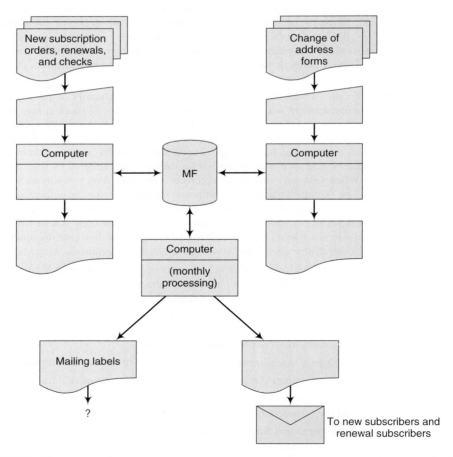

FIGURE 6-19 System flowchart for processing the subscription orders and changes for the Jeffrey Getelman Company.

Mr. Smith decides what to do about these customer accounts based on the history of the account in general and also the activity during the account's delinquency period. Sometimes, for example, the customer will not communicate at all. At other times, however, the customer will either write to state that a check is forthcoming or make a partial payment. Mr. Smith tends to be most understanding of customers who make partial payments because he considers such payments acts of good faith. Mr. Smith is less understanding of those customers who only promise to pay or who simply ignore follow-up bills from the company.

Mr. Smith has four potential actions to take in cases of credit delinquency. First, he can simply wait (i.e., do nothing). Second, he can send an initial letter to the customer, inquiring about the problem in bill payment and requesting written notification of a payment schedule if payment has not already been made. Third, he can send a follow-up letter indicating that a collection agency will be given the account if immediate payment is not forthcoming. Fourth, he can turn the account over to a collection agency. Of course, Mr. Smith prefers to use one of the first three actions rather than turn the account over to a collection agency because his company receives only half of any future payments when the collection agency becomes involved.

a. Create a decision table for the Bridget Joyce Company and provide a set of reasonable decision rules for Mr. Smith to follow. For now, ignore the influence of a customer's credit history.

b. Expand the decision table analysis you have prepared in question "a" to include the credit history of the customer accounts. You are free to make any assumptions you wish about how this history might be evaluated by Mr. Smith.

6-21. Follow the directions in Problem 6-11 to access Excel's drawing tools and then re-create the two program flowcharts shown in Figure 6-20. Draw each flowchart on a separate work sheet. Rename the first sheet "Main" and the second sheet "Sub." To embed text inside a symbol,

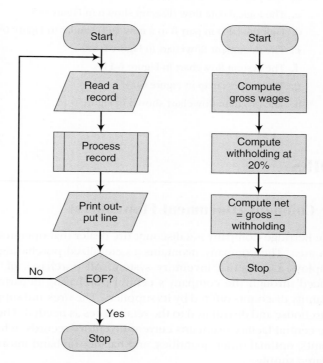

FIGURE 6-20 Draw the flowchart on the left on one Excel sheet and the flowchart on the right on a second sheet.

right click on that symbol with your mouse and then choose "Edit Text" from the drop-down menu that appears. To center text inside a symbol, highlight the text and then click on the centering icon in the main toolbar.

Create the words "Yes" and "No" that appear in this flowchart using Text Box selection from the Insert menu. To eliminate the black (default) borders around these words, right click on a Text Box and select Format Shape. Select the line color option and choose "No line" from the "Line Color" options on the right. Finally, you can fine-tune the position of any object by clicking on its border, holding the left button, and dragging the text box.

Linking Flowcharts

After drawing these two flowcharts, we want to link them together. In this case, we want the user to click on the "Process Record" symbol in the main flowchart and then be able to view the second spreadsheet you've created on the alternate sheet. To create this link, right click on the "Process Record" symbol and then select Hyperlink from the main menu.

When the Hyperlink dialog box appears, first select "Place in this Document" from the choices on the left side of the box and then click on the name of the sheet in which you've drawn the second flowchart ("Sub") in the lower box on the right. If you wish, you can also select a particular cell for linking in the top box—a handy feature if you've drawn your flowchart in a lower portion of the Sub sheet. That's it! Now, when you move your mouse over the "Process Record" symbol in the "Main" sheet, your mouse icon should turn into a hand, indicating that clicking on this symbol links you to the supporting document's sheet.

Using Excel software and the skills described above, re-create the documents from the list below or the ones required by your instructor:

    a. The context diagram in Figure 6-3.

    b. The physical DFD in Figure 6-4.

    c. The logical data flow diagram shown in Figure 6-5.

    d. Link the DFD in part b to a new DFD similar to Figure 6-6.

    e. The document flowchart in Figure 6-8.

    f. The system flowchart in Figure 6-11.

    g. The process map in Figure 6-13.

    h. The program flowchart shown in Figure 6-15.

CASE STUDIES

The Berridge Company (Document Flowcharts)

The Berridge Company is a discount tire dealer that operates 25 retail stores in a metropolitan area. The company maintains a centralized purchasing and warehousing facility and employs a perpetual inventory system. All purchases of tires and related supplies are placed through the company's central purchasing department to take advantage of the quantity discounts offered by its suppliers. The tires and supplies are received at the central warehouse and distributed to the retail stores as needed. The perpetual inventory system at the central facility maintains current inventory records, which include designated reorder points, optimal order quantities, and balance-on-hand information for each type of tire or related supply.

The participants involved in Berridge's inventory system include (1) retail stores, (2) the inventory control department, (3) the warehouse, (4) the purchasing department, (5) accounts payable, and (6) outside vendors. The inventory control department is responsible for maintenance of the perpetual inventory records for each item carried in inventory. The warehouse department maintains the physical inventory of all items carried by the company's retail stores.

All deliveries of tires and related supplies from vendors are received by receiving clerks in the warehouse department, and all distributions to retail stores are filled by shipping clerks in this department. The purchasing department places every order for items needed by the company. The accounts payable department maintains the subsidiary ledger with vendors and other creditors. All payments are processed by this department. The documents used by these various departments are as follows:

Retail Store Requisition (Form RSR). The retail stores submit this document to the central warehouse whenever tires or supplies are needed at the stores. The shipping clerks in the warehouse department fill the orders from inventory and have them delivered to the stores. Three copies of the document are prepared, two of which are sent to the warehouse, and the third copy is filed for reference.

Purchase Requisition (Form PR). An inventory control clerk in the inventory control department prepares this document when the quantity on hand for an item falls below the designated reorder point. Two copies of the document are prepared. One copy is forwarded to the purchasing department and the other is filed.

Purchase Order (Form PO). The purchasing department prepares this document based on information found in the purchase requisition. Five copies of the purchase order are prepared. The disposition of these copies is as follows: copy 1 to vendor, copy 2 to accounts payable department, copy 3 to inventory control department, copy 4 to warehouse, and copy 5 filed for reference.

Receiving Report (Form RR). The warehouse department prepares this document when ordered items are received from vendors. A receiving clerk completes the document by indicating the vendor's name, the date the shipment is received, and the quantity of each item received. Four copies of the report are prepared. Copy 1 is sent to the accounts payable department, copy 2 to the purchasing department, and copy 3 to the inventory control department; copy 4 is retained by the warehouse department, compared with the purchase order form in its files, and filed together with this purchase order form for future reference.

Invoices. Invoices received from vendors are bills for payment. The vendor prepares several copies of each invoice, but only two copies are of concern to the Berridge Company: the copy that is received by the company's accounts payable department and the copy that is retained by the vendor for reference. The accounts payable department compares the vendor invoice with its file copy of the original purchase order and its file copy of the warehouse receiving report. On the basis of this information, adjustments to the bill amount on the invoice are made (e.g., for damaged goods, for trade discounts, or for cash discounts), a check is prepared, and the payment is mailed to the vendor.

Requirements

1. Draw a document flowchart for the Berridge Company using the symbols in Figure 6-7.

2. Could the company eliminate one or more copies of its RSR form? Use your flowchart to explain why or why not.

3. Do you think that the company creates too many copies of its purchase orders? Why or why not?

Classic Photography Inc. (Systems Flowcharts)

Jenny Smith owns Classic Photography Inc., a company that restores photos for its clients and creates electronic images from the restored photos. The company also frames restored photos and creates sophisticated custom artworks. Artworks include materials such as glass and frames that are purchased from local suppliers. In addition to supplies for displays, the company purchases office supplies and packaging materials from several vendors.

Classic Photography uses an off-the-shelf accounting software package to prepare internal documents and reports. As employees note a need for supplies and materials, they send an e-mail to Jenny, who acts as the office manager and company accountant. Either Jenny or her assistant Donna enters order information into the accounting system and creates a purchase order that is faxed to the supplier. Jenny or Donna may also call the supplier if there is something special about the product ordered.

When ordered materials and supplies arrive, either Jenny or Donna checks the goods received against a copy of the purchase order and enters the new inventory into the computer system. Jenny pays bills twice each month, on the first and the fifteenth. She checks the computer system for invoices outstanding and verifies that the goods have been received. She then enters any information needed to produce printed checks from the accounting system. Classic Photography mails checks and printed remittance advices (portions of the vendor bill to be returned) to suppliers.

Requirements

1. Create a systems flowchart for the purchase and payment processes.

2. Comment on the value, if any, that having a systems flowchart describing this process would have to Jenny.

The Dinteman Company (Document Analysis)

The Dinteman Company is an industrial machinery and equipment manufacturer with several production departments. The company employs automated and heavy equipment in its production departments. Consequently, Dinteman has a large repair and maintenance department (R&M department) for servicing this equipment.

The operating efficiency of the R&M department has deteriorated over the past two years. For example, repair and maintenance costs seem to be climbing more rapidly than other department costs. The assistant controller has reviewed the operations of the R&M department and has concluded that the administrative procedures used since the early days of the department are outmoded due in part to the growth of the company. In the opinion of the assistant controller, the two major causes for the deterioration are an antiquated scheduling system for repair and maintenance work and the actual cost to distribute the R&M department's costs to the production departments. The actual costs of the R&M department are allocated monthly to the production departments on the basis of the number of service calls made during each month.

The assistant controller has proposed that a formal work order system be implemented for the R&M department. With the new system, the production departments will submit a service request to the R&M department for the repairs and/or maintenance to be completed, including a suggested time for having the work done. The supervisor of the R&M department will prepare a cost estimate on the service request for the work required (labor and materials) and estimate the amount of time for completing the work on the service request. The R&M supervisor will return the request to the production department that initiated the request. Once the production department approves the work by returning a copy of the service request, the R&M supervisor will prepare a repair and maintenance work order and schedule the job. This work order provides the repair worker with the details of the work to be done and is used to record the actual repair and maintenance hours worked and the materials and supplies used.

Production departments will be charged for actual labor hours worked at a predetermined standard rate for the type of work required. The parts and supplies used will be charged to the production departments at cost. The assistant controller believes that only two documents will be required in this new system—a Repair/Maintenance Service Request initiated by the production departments and a Repair/Maintenance Work Order initiated by the R&M department.

Requirements

1. For the Repair/Maintenance Work Order document
   a. Identify the data items of importance to the repair and maintenance department and the production department that should be incorporated into the work order.
   b. Indicate how many copies of the work order would be required and explain how each copy would be distributed.
2. Prepare a document flowchart to show how the Repair/Maintenance Service Request and the Repair/Maintenance Work Order should be coordinated and used among the departments of Dinteman Company to request and complete the repair and maintenance work, to provide the basis for charging the production departments for the cost of the completed work, and to evaluate the performance of the repair and maintenance department. Provide explanations in the flowchart as appropriate.
   (CMA Adapted.)

Chapter 7

Accounting Information Systems and Business Processes: Part I

INTRODUCTION

In this chapter and the following chapter, we introduce the fundamentals of business processes and then focus on several core business processes that are common to many businesses. We begin with a brief refresher of the basics of financial accounting. Although you may be wondering why we talk about the bookkeeping process in this textbook, these concepts are actually at the heart of an AIS. That is, fundamental elements of accounting are embedded in modern accounting information systems, and they are the basis for a company's annual financial statements. These fundamental elements include journals, ledgers, accounts, trial balances, and financial statements. We discuss these concepts from the perspective of simple paper journals and records because this simplifies the discussion of the key business processes. It is important to recognize, however, that business processes in firms with large database-driven AISs will often not involve paper source documents or traditionally formatted journals or ledgers.

The nature and types of business processes vary, depending on the information needs of a specific organization. Nevertheless, a number of business processes are common to most organizations. In this chapter, we examine business transactions related to the sales process (sales and cash collection) and the purchasing process (expenditures for materials and supplies and cash payment).

Businesses are under tremendous pressure to cut costs, reduce capital expenditures, and become as efficient as possible at their core competencies. As a result, companies search globally to achieve efficiencies—it's called *business without boundaries*. In the final portion of this chapter, we give examples of business processes that are commonly outsourced or offshored. We then examine some business process management solutions that are available to improve business processes regardless of their location.

BUSINESS PROCESS FUNDAMENTALS

An accounting cycle can begin in a number of different ways. For instance, accounting personnel can create a transaction from a source document, or a customer may order products online. Regardless of how the process starts, at the end of the process we issue annual financial reports and close the temporary accounts in preparation for a new cycle.

Overview of the Financial Accounting Cycle

An AIS records each transaction or business event affecting an organization's financial condition in journals or ledgers.

Journals.   Accounting personnel record transactions in a journal. Of course, this is rarely an actual paper journal anymore—it's more likely an electronic entry in an accounting information system. In many cases, these entries are made directly into database tables. The journal is a chronological record of business events by account. A journal may be a special journal or a general journal. Special journals capture a specific type of transaction. They are usually reserved for transactions occurring frequently within an organization. In a computerized system, special journals may take the form of special modules with their own files. For example, an accounting clerk would likely record a credit sale in an accounts receivable module. In more automated systems, entries into the accounting system may be entirely electronic, such as through scanning a bar code.

Companies can set up a special journal for virtually any type of transaction. Common ones are sales journals, purchase journals, cash receipts journals, and cash disbursements journals. If you think about it, almost all accounting transactions a business organization records fall into one of these categories. Special journals include entries for all but a few types of transactions and adjusting journal entries, such as for depreciation. The general journal records these entries.

Ledgers.   Journal entries show all aspects of a particular transaction. Each entry shows debit and credit amounts, the transaction date, the affected accounts, and a brief description of the event. Once an AIS records a journal entry, it next posts the entry in the general ledger. Within an AIS, a general ledger is a collection of detailed monetary information about an organization's various assets, liabilities, owners' equity, revenues, and expenses. The general ledger includes a separate account (often called a *T account* because of its shape) for each type of monetary item in an organization. While journal entries record all aspects of business transactions, an AIS separately posts the monetary amounts in each account to the various accounts in the general ledger. A company's chart of accounts provides the organizational structure for the general ledger. The chart of accounts makes use of a block coding structure (discussed later in this chapter).

Trial Balances and Financial Statements.   Once an AIS records journal entries and posts them to the general ledger, it can create a trial balance. The trial balance is a listing of all accounts and their debit and credit balances. After debit and credit dollar amounts in this trial balance are equal, an accountant will record any necessary adjusting journal entries. Adjusting entries include journal entries for depreciation and other unrecorded expenses, prepaid expenses, unearned revenues, and unrecorded revenue. Once the debit and credit amounts in this adjusted trial balance are equal, an AIS is ready to produce financial statements.

Financial statements are the primary output of a financial accounting system. These financial statements include an income statement, balance sheet, statement of owners' equity, and cash flow statement. The accounting cycle does not end when an AIS generates financial statements. The computerized system must close temporary accounts, such as revenue and expense accounts, so that a new cycle can begin. This is necessary because users are interested in income information for a specific period of time. Because balance sheet accounts show financial performance at a specific point in time, they are permanent and need not be closed. Thus, an AIS will carry these amounts forward to the next accounting cycle. Figure 1-7 shows an illustration of the accounting cycle and Figure 7-1 summarizes the steps in the accounting cycle.

Coding Systems

Accounting information systems depend on codes to record, classify, store, and retrieve financial data. Although it is possible in a manual system to use simple alphabetic

1. Record transaction in a journal.
2. Post journal entries to a ledger.
3. Prepare an unadjusted trial balance.
4. Record and post adjusting journal entries.
5. Prepare an adjusted trial balance.
6. Prepare financial statements.
7. Record and post closing journal entries.
8. Prepare a post-closing trial balance.

FIGURE 7-1   A summary of the steps in the accounting cycle.

descriptions when preparing journal entries, computerized systems use **numeric codes** (codes that use numbers only) or **alphanumeric codes** (codes that use numbers and letters) to record accounting transactions systematically. For example, a manual journal entry might include a debit to the "Direct Materials Inventory" account. In a computerized system, the debit might be to account "12345." Alphanumeric codes are important in computerized systems, as they help to ensure uniformity and consistency. Suppose that a clerk entered a debit to "Direct Materials Inventory" one time and another time entered the debit to "Dir. Materials Inventory." A computer would set up a new account the second time, rather than recognizing the intended account.

Types of Codes.   AISs typically use several types of codes: (1) mnemonic codes, (2) sequence codes, (3) block codes, and (4) group codes. **Mnemonic codes** help the user remember what they represent. The product codes S, M, L, and XL are examples of mnemonic codes describing apparel sizes. As the name implies, a **sequence code** is simply a sequential set of numbers used to identify customer accounts, employee payroll checks, customer sales invoices, and so forth. **Block codes** are sequential codes in which specific blocks of numbers are reserved for particular uses. In a typical application, the lead digit, or two lead digits, in the sequence code acts as the block designator and subsequent digits are identifiers. AISs use block codes to create a chart of accounts (Figure 7-2). Combining two or more subcodes creates a **group code**, which is often used as product codes in sales catalogs.

Design Considerations in Coding.   There are a number of important factors to consider when designing an accounting code. First, it must serve some useful purpose. For example, if a product code in a manufacturing firm is part of a responsibility accounting system, at least one portion of the code must contain a production department code. Second, it must be consistent. Using Social Security numbers as employee identifiers is a good example of this design consideration. Third, managers must plan for future expansion (e.g., the creation of extra accounts).

COLLECTING AND REPORTING ACCOUNTING INFORMATION

As you might imagine, most of the accounting data collected by an organization ultimately appear on some type of internal and/or external report. Thus, the design of an effective AIS usually begins with the outputs (reports) that users will expect from the system. Although this might seem counterintuitive, we discuss the reasons for this in Chapter 13.

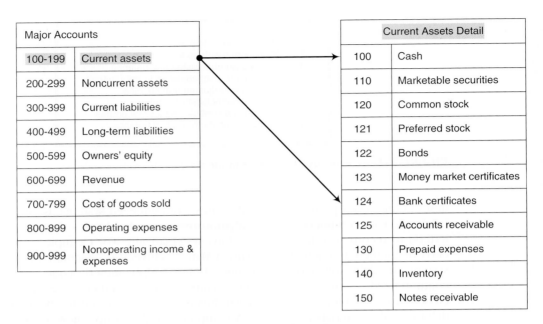

FIGURE 7-2   A block code used for a company's chart of accounts.

Among the outputs of an AIS are: (1) reports to management, (2) reports to investors and creditors, (3) files that retain transaction data, and (4) files that retain current data about accounts (e.g., inventory records). Perhaps the most important of these outputs are the reports to management because these reports aid decision-making activities. As you might imagine, the formats of these various reports might be very different. These reports might be hard-copy (paper) reports, soft-copy (screen) reports, e-copy (CD and other electronic media) reports, or audio outputs. If a manager queries a database system, the monitor shows the requested data and the system produces a hard-copy report only upon demand. Graphics enhance reports in any form. Many reports today appear on company Web sites. While Web page design is beyond the scope of this book, it is important to recognize that the rules for preparing good reports apply to Web page reports as well as hard-copy and other multimedia reports.

Designing Reports

Users need many different types of accounting reports—some might be every hour and others not as often. An AIS might issue some reports only when a particular event occurs. For example, an AIS might issue an inventory reorder report only when the inventory for a certain product drops below a specified level. Such an event would probably result in an **exception report**, which is a list of exceptional conditions. As another example, suppose that a purchase order has an authorization signature but contains some inaccurate or missing information. In this case, the AIS would generate an exception report. The report would include a table that identifies the error, or errors, and would suggest a possible solution to fix the error. After correcting the error, the purchase order would require a new authorization signature. This signature would clear the exception from the report.

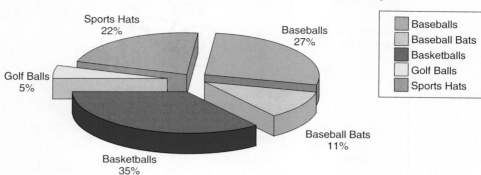

FIGURE 7-3   A pie chart showing the percentage of sales from various product lines.

Characteristics of Good Reports.   Good output reports share similar characteristics regardless of their type, such as (1) useful, (2) convenient format, (3) easy to identify, and (4) consistent. For example, summary reports should contain financial totals, comparative reports should list related numbers (e.g., budget versus actual figures) in adjacent columns, and descriptive reports (e.g., marketing reports) should present results systematically. Sometimes the most convenient format is graphical, such as a pie chart (Figure 7-3). Other graphical formats include bar charts and trend lines.

Identification and Consistency.   Good managerial reports always contain fundamental identification, including headings (company name, organizational division or department, etc.), page numbers, and dates. For example, a report loses its information value if you do not know the time period it covers. Balance sheets and similar reports should show the date as of a specific point in time. Reports such as lists of current employees, customers, and vendors should also indicate a specific date. Income statements and similar reports should show a span of dates for the reporting period (e.g., for the month ended January 31, 2012).

AIS reports should be consistent: (1) over time, (2) across departmental or divisional levels, and (3) with general accounting practice. Consistency over time allows managers to compare information from different time periods. For example, a manager might want to compare a sales report for June with a similar report for the month of May of the same year. This manager might also look at sales for June of prior years to evaluate whether performance is improving or deteriorating. Similarly, reports should be consistent across departmental levels so that supervisors may compare departmental performance. Finally, report formats should be consistent with general accounting practice so that managers and investors can understand and use these reports.

From Source Documents to Output Reports

Companies use a variety of source documents to collect data for the AIS. The chief concerns in the data collection process are accuracy, timeliness, and cost-effectiveness. An example of a source document is the *purchase order* in Figure 7-4. This source document represents a purchase order (number 36551) generated from the BSN Bicycles' database system to purchase goods from the Lu Company, a sporting goods distributor. In a paper-based environment, employees typically prepare several copies of a purchase order for

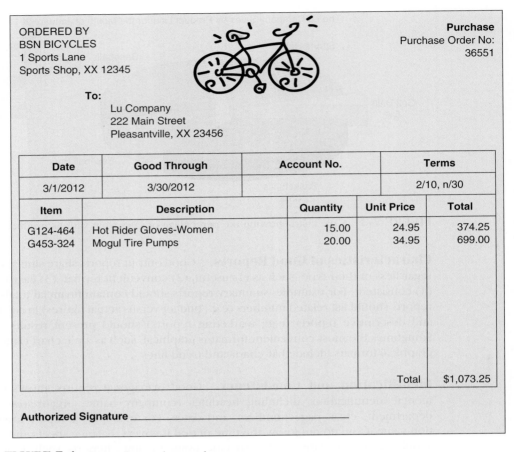

ORDERED BY
BSN BICYCLES
1 Sports Lane
Sports Shop, XX 12345

Purchase
Purchase Order No:
36551

To:

Lu Company
222 Main Street
Pleasantville, XX 23456

Date	Good Through	Account No.	Terms
3/1/2012	3/30/2012		2/10, n/30

Item	Description	Quantity	Unit Price	Total
G124-464	Hot Rider Gloves-Women	15.00	24.95	374.25
G453-324	Mogul Tire Pumps	20.00	34.95	699.00
			Total	$1,073.25

Authorized Signature _____

FIGURE 7-4 A sample purchase order.

internal use (these may be hard copies or computer images). For instance, the purchasing department keeps one copy to document the order and to serve as a reference for future inquiries. Accounting and receiving departments also receive copies. Purchase orders are normally sequentially numbered for easy reference at a later date.

Based on this purchase order, the Lu Company ships merchandise and sends a sales invoice to BSN Bicycles. Figure 7-5 illustrates the *sales invoice* document. The sales invoice duplicates much of the information on the original purchase order. New information includes the shipping address, a reference to the purchase order number, the shipping date, due date, the sales invoice number, and the customer identification number. The Lu Company might produce as many as six copies of the sales invoice. Two (or more) copies are the bill for the customer. The shipping department keeps a third copy to record that it filled the order. A fourth copy goes to the accounting department for processing accounts receivable. The sales department retains a fifth copy for future reference. Finally, the inventory department receives a sixth copy to update its records related to the specific inventory items sold.

Source documents of the types illustrated here help manage the flow of accounting data in several ways. First, they dictate the kinds of data to be collected and help ensure consistency and accuracy in recording data. Second, they encourage the completeness of accounting data because these source documents clearly enumerate the information

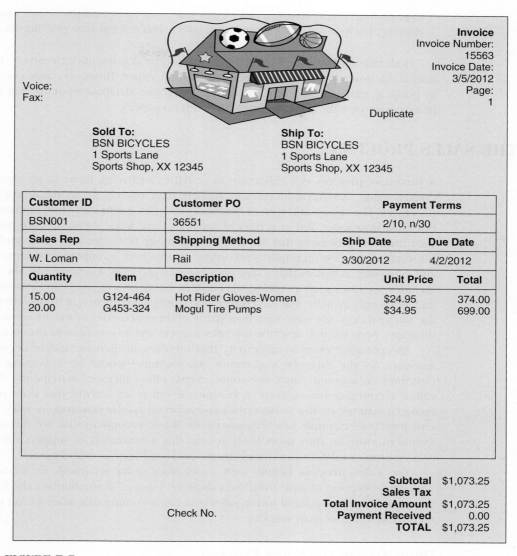

FIGURE 7-5 A sample sales invoice.

required. Third, they serve as distributors of information for individuals or departments. Finally, source documents help to establish the authenticity of accounting data. This is useful for purposes such as establishing an audit trail, testing for authorization of cash disbursement checks or inventory disbursements, and establishing accountability for the collection or distribution of money. Many source documents are actually database- or Internet-based forms that are used to input data electronically. Reducing the use of paper forms can create significant efficiencies.

Case-in-Point 7.1 Woerner Turf is a company that produces turf grass and sod for landscaping. The company recently implemented a new software package by Microsoft Great Plains Business Solutions that consolidated its sales order screen. It eliminated or condensed data-entry fields to create a single screen. It is not uncommon for a sales person to enter orders as often as 50 to 100 times each day. The new design, which is similar to the paper form used previously, reduces order entry time from three minutes to one. This increased efficiency allows sales staff to spend more time selling and less time entering data.[1]

Both manual and computerized AISs use source documents extensively. In many AISs, source documents are still written or printed on paper. However, large companies (such as publicly traded firms) rely heavily on integrated database systems that handle many transactions virtually (i.e., electronically with no paper).

THE SALES PROCESS

A **business process** is a collection of activities and work flows in an organization that creates value. An AIS collects and reports data related to an organization's business processes. The nature and type of business processes might vary from industry to industry, but most businesses and government agencies have some common core processes. Two core business processes that are common to many businesses are *sales* and *purchasing.* Information processing requires recording, maintaining, grouping, and reporting business and economic activities that make up a business process. For example, the sales process includes activities such as taking sales orders, filling orders, managing customer inquiries, and receiving payment. The AIS collects and stores data for each of these activities as part of the sales process. We have seen how many of these activities or events are depicted in E-R diagrams. Now we will describe the sales process and its component events in more detail.

An economic event is an activity that involves an increase and/or decrease in dollar amounts on the financial statements. An example would be collecting cash from a customer on account. Since economic events affect financial statements, they are often called accounting transactions. A business event is an activity that does not affect the financial statements but is nevertheless important to the business. A sales order from a customer is an example of a business event. While accountants do not record all business events in journals, they most likely record this information to support decision making (e.g., customer relationship management, discussed later in this chapter).

The **sales process** begins with a customer order for goods or services and ends with the collection of cash from the customer. Figure 7-6 summarizes the AIS objectives, inputs, and outputs related to the sales process, assuming that sales are on credit and for merchandise rather than services.

Objectives of the Sales Process

Revenues result from an organization's sale of goods or services. They may also result from donations or gifts, as in the case of many not-for-profit organizations. An organization that generates revenues but fails to collect these revenues regularly may find it cannot pay its bills. Many people unfamiliar with accounting make the incorrect assumption that companies with positive incomes cannot go out of business. The reality is that bankruptcy results from inadequate cash flow, not from insufficient income. A primary objective in processing revenues is to achieve timely and efficient cash collection.

To process sales in a timely manner, an organization must be able to track all revenues that customers owe the firm. Once the AIS recognizes these revenues, the system needs to monitor the resulting cash inflows. A good AIS matches each revenue with a valid transaction. Maintaining customer records is an important function of the AIS for the

---

[1] http://www.greatplains.com/solutions

The Sales Process

Objectives

Tracking sales of goods and/or services to customers
Filling customer orders
Maintaining customer records
Billing for goods and services
Collecting payment for goods and services
Forecasting sales and cash receipts

Inputs (Source documents)

- Sales order
- Sales invoice
- Remittance advice
- Shipping notice
- Debit/credit memoranda

Outputs (Reports)

- Financial statement information
- Customer billing statement
- Aging report
- Bad debt report
- Cash receipts forecast
- Customer listing
- Sales analysis reports

FIGURE 7-6 Objectives, inputs, and outputs associated with processing revenue transactions.

revenue process. This includes validating a customer's bill-paying ability and payment history, assigning credit limits and ratings to customers, and tracking all customers' outstanding invoices. Processing revenues includes filling customers' orders, and this requires an interface with the inventory control function. The AIS should bill customers only for products shipped. The sales process must also allow for certain exceptions—for example, sales returns.

Forecasting is another objective of the AIS to help management in its planning function. The AIS must analyze sales orders, sales terms, payment histories, and other data. For example, sales orders are a good indicator of future revenues, and the terms of sale provide information about likely dates of collection on accounts.

Events in the Sales Process. Figure 7-7 illustrates an AIS for the sales process in a systems flowchart. This view assumes an online sales order. Notice that e-mails and electronic images replace many of the paper documents. The flowchart also assumes that the AIS uses a centralized database that integrates all data files (discussed in Chapters 3, 4, and 5). The following fictitious example describes the sales process shown in Figure 7-7.

Example. Hiroshi Ajas needs to purchase books for his classes this semester. He decides to buy the books online from Textbooks.com. In verifying the order, Textbooks.com's AIS also verifies Hiroshi's credit card and checks its inventory to make sure the books are available. The company then sends Hiroshi an e-mail confirmation, verifying the transaction. Textbooks.com's AIS notifies its warehouse via e-mail to pack and ship the books. The warehouse processes the shipment information and creates a packing slip. Warehouse personnel then package the packing slip with the books and send them to Hiroshi. The day that Textbooks.com ships the books, it also charges Hiroshi's credit card.

The major events in Textbooks.com's sales process are the sales order, the shipment of goods, and the customer payment. The company will record information about each of these events. This information allows them to produce a variety of reports—such as book sales by regions of the country. The next two sections describe the information inputs and outputs of the sales process.

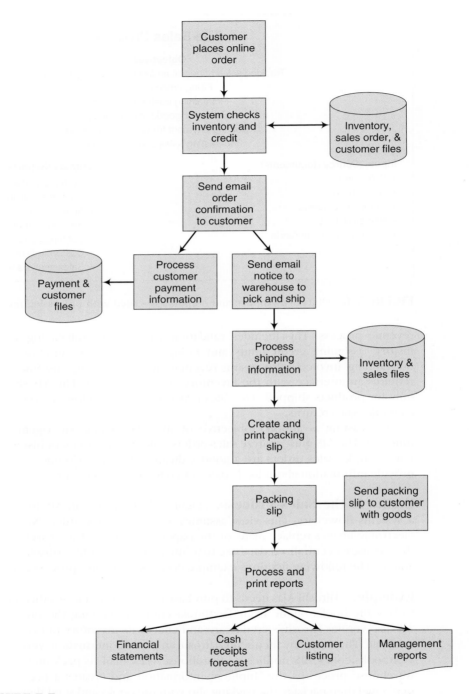

FIGURE 7-7 High-level systems flowchart of the sales process in an online environment.

Inputs to the Sales Process

Figure 7-8 shows a data flow diagram of the sales process, which identifies the data inputs and information outputs of the process. As noted in the example, an AIS typically creates a *sales order* at the time a customer contracts goods or services. In this example, an accounts receivable clerk uses this sales order to prepare a sales invoice or the customer might generate one herself using the Web page of an online retailer. The *sales invoice* reflects the product or products purchased, the price, and the terms of payment. When the customer makes a payment, a *remittance advice* may accompany the payment. When you pay your Visa or MasterCard bill, for example, the portion of the bill you return with your check is a remittance advice.

In addition to sales orders, sales invoices, checks, and remittance advices, *shipping notices* are another input to sales processing. When the warehouse releases goods for shipment, the warehouse clerk prepares a shipping notice. A copy of this notice may serve as a *packing slip* and would be included in the package with the goods. A copy of this document is also sent to the accounts receivable department and is used as a prompt for the department to bill the customer.

Debit/credit memoranda are source documents affecting both the sales and purchasing processes. An organization issues these memoranda to denote the return of damaged goods or discrepancies in the amount owed. For example, let's assume that Hiroshi's package with the textbooks arrived, but two of the books were damaged and two were the wrong textbooks. Hiroshi would return the four books (worth $400) to Textbooks.com. However, Hiroshi must wait until the company receives the books and processes the return before he will be issued a *credit* to his account (credit card) for the $400.

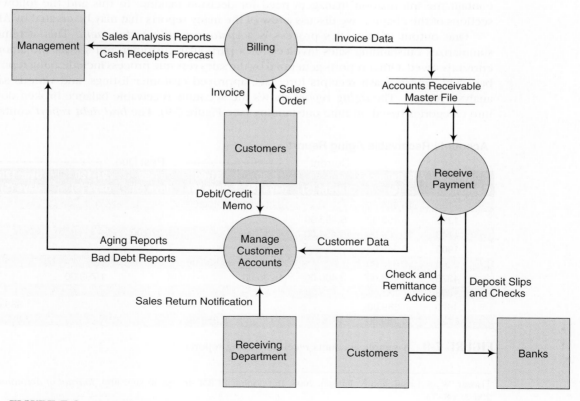

FIGURE 7-8   Data flow diagram of the sales process.

If a company finds that it has charged a customer too little for goods sold, the company would issue a *debit memorandum.* This debit memorandum signifies a debit to the customer's account receivable with the company to reflect the amount not charged originally. The customer now owes more to the company.

Business organizations use the data they collect about their customers and sales transactions to improve customer satisfaction and increase profitability. As a result, firms are purchasing or developing **customer relationship management (CRM)** software to gather, maintain, and use customer data to provide better customer service and enhance customer loyalty. However, think broadly here about potential uses of CRM software. For example, many universities are now purchasing CRM solutions to help them better manage their current and potential customers (i.e., students). These software packages help various schools and colleges within a university manage course enrollments, communications, invoice and payment processing, and perhaps most importantly, to stay connected with graduates who will potentially become donors.

Case-in-Point 7.2 Even public accounting firms benefit from CRM systems. CPA firms now collect detailed data about their clients and client's industries. Understanding clients makes it less likely that clients will be lost to competitor firms. CPA firms also store data about potential clients in order to identify new prospects and market opportunities.[2]

Outputs of the Sales Process

Processing sales transactions creates several outputs. An AIS uses some of these outputs to produce external accounting reports (such as financial statements) as well as internal reports (such as management reports). Management reports can be in any format and contain the information managers need for decision making. In this and the following sections of the chapter, we discuss a few of the many reports that may be created by AISs.

One output of the sales process is a *customer billing statement.* This statement summarizes outstanding sales invoices for a particular customer and shows the amount currently owed. Other reports generated by the sales revenue process include aging reports, bad debt reports, cash receipts forecasts, approved customer listings, and various sales analysis reports. The *aging report* shows the accounts receivable balance broken down into categories based on time outstanding (see Figure 7-9). The *bad debt report* contains

Accounts Receivable Aging Report

		Current	Past Due				
Customer #	A/R Balance ($)	Current ($)	0-30 days ($)	31-60 days ($)	61-90 days ($)	91-120 days ($)	over 120 days ($)
1106	15,460.00		10,000.00	5,460.00			
1352	6,453.00	6,453.00					
1743	18,684.00	13,454.00			5,230.00		
1903	2,349.00						
2258	6,530.00			6,530.00			
4378	5,434.00	2,400.00	1,235.00			1,799.00	
4553	173.00	173.00					
4623	389.00						389.00
5121	4,189.00			2,356.00			1,833.00

FIGURE 7-9 A sample accounts receivable aging report.

---

[2] Lassar, W., S. Lassar, and N. Rauseo. 2008. Developing a CRM strategy in your firm. *Journal of Accountancy* 206(2): 68-73.

information about collection follow-up procedures for overdue customer accounts. In the event that a customer's account is uncollectible, the account is written off to an allowance account for bad debts. A detailed listing of the allowance account may be another output of the sales process.

All of the data gathered from source documents in processing sales transactions serve as inputs to a *cash receipts forecast.* Data such as sales amounts, terms of sale, prior payment experience for selected customers, and information from aging analysis reports and cash collection reports are all inputs to this forecast.

We previously indicated that maintaining customer records is an important function of the AIS in the sales process. The billing or accounts receivable function should approve new customers, both to ensure that the customers exist and to assess their bill-paying ability. This may require obtaining a credit report from a reputable credit agency. The billing function assigns each new customer a credit limit based on credit history. From time to time, the AIS produces an *approved customer listing* report. This report is likely to show customer ID numbers (for uniquely identifying each customer), contact name(s), shipping and billing addresses, credit limits, and billing terms.

If an AIS captures (or converts) appropriate sales data electronically, it can also produce various *sales analysis reports.* These include sales classified by product line, type of sale (cash, credit, or debit card), or sales region. However, the sales process can produce effective sales analysis reports only if the AIS captures appropriate sales data. Again, customer relationship management solutions help managers take advantage of this data to maximize revenue and to provide better customer service.

THE PURCHASING PROCESS

The **purchasing process** begins with a request (or an order) for goods or services and ends with payments to the vendor. Figure 7-10 shows the objectives, inputs, and outputs associated with purchasing events. Our discussion assumes that credit purchases are for

---

The Purchasing Process

Objectives
Tracking purchases of goods and/or services from vendors
Tracking amounts owed
Maintaining vendor records
Controlling inventory
Making timely and accurate vendor payments
Forecasting purchases and cash outflows

Inputs (Source documents)
- Purchase requisition
- Purchase order
- Vendor listing
- Receiving report
- Bill of lading
- Packing slip
- Debit/credit memoranda

Outputs (Reports)
- Financial statement information
- Vendor checks
- Check register
- Discrepancy reports
- Cash requirements forecast
- Sales analysis reports

FIGURE 7-10   Objectives, inputs, and outputs associated with the purchasing process.

goods (i.e., inventory) rather than for services. But in general, purchases may be for either goods or services and for cash or on credit.

Objectives of the Purchasing Process

Credit transactions create accounts payable. Accounts payable processing closely resembles accounts receivable processing; it is the flip side of the picture. With accounts receivable, companies keep track of amounts owed *to* them from their customers. An accounts payable application tracks the amounts owed *by* a company to vendors. The objective of accounts payable processing is to pay vendors at the optimal time. Companies want to take advantage of cash discounts offered and also avoid finance charges for late payments.

Maintaining vendor records is as important to the purchasing process as maintaining customer records is for the sales process. The purchasing department is responsible for maintaining a *list of authorized vendors.* This entails ensuring the authenticity of vendors as well as finding reputable vendors who offer quality goods and services at reasonable prices. Vendor shipping policies, billing policies, discount terms, and reliability are also important variables in the approval process. Businesses today are strengthening their relationships with their vendors or suppliers, recognizing that they are partners in a **supply chain**. One of the most successful supply chain management partnerships is that of Walmart and Procter & Gamble.

> **Case-in-Point 7.3** There is a long-standing supply chain partnership between Procter & Gamble (P&G) and Walmart. When P&G's products run low at Walmart distribution centers, Walmart's information system sends an automatic alert to P&G to ship more inventory. In some cases, the system communicates at the individual store level, which allows P&G to monitor the shelves through real-time satellite link-ups. Both firms are recognized as leaders in supply chain management.[3]

The purchase of goods affects *inventory control.* The objective of inventory control is to ensure that an AIS records all goods purchased for, and dispensed from, inventory. The inventory control component of the purchasing process interfaces with production departments, the purchasing department, the vendor, and the receiving department.

A final objective of the purchasing process is forecasting cash outflows. The addition of outstanding purchase requisitions, purchase invoices, and receiving reports provides an estimate of future cash requirements. With the forecast of cash receipts produced by the sales process, this estimate allows an organization to prepare a cash budget.

Events in the Purchasing Process. Figure 7-11 shows a systems flowchart that describes the purchasing process. As with the sales process, the flowchart assumes a centralized database and a mix of paper documents and electronic images. The following fictitious example describes the purchasing process shown in Figure 7-11.

Example. Sandra Michaels is an employee at Textbooks.com who needs to purchase a new computer. She pulls up the purchase requisition form from the company's intranet and fills in the appropriate information. She then sends the completed form to her supervisor for approval, who approves the request and clicks the "Submit" button to forward Sandra's request electronically to the purchasing department. A purchasing agent creates an electronic purchase order based on the information Sandra provided. The agent consults the vendor file to locate an authorized vendor for the requested computer. The

---

[3] http://www.gartner.com/DisplayDocument?doc_cd=213740

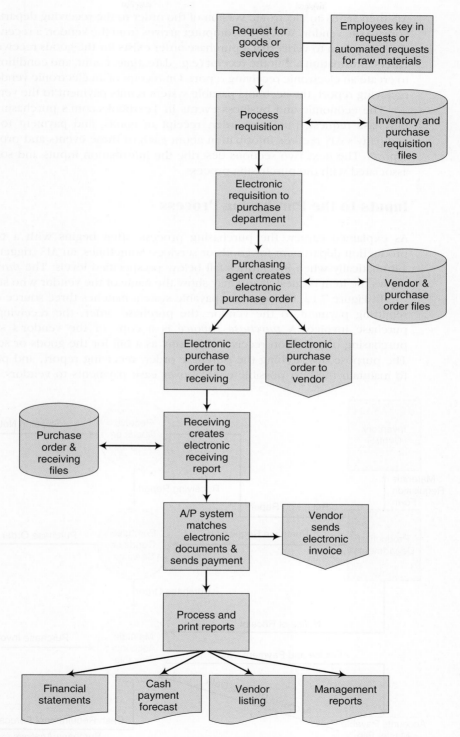

FIGURE 7-11   High-level systems flowchart of the purchasing process in an online environment.

AIS then sends an electronic version of the order to the receiving department and another copy to the vendor. When the computer arrives from the vendor, a receiving clerk consults the AIS system to verify that a purchase order exists for the goods received. The clerk then enters information about the receipt (e.g., date, time, count, and condition of merchandise) to create an electronic receiving report. On receipt of an electronic vendor invoice and the receiving report, the accounts payable system remits payment to the vendor.

The economic and business events in Textbooks.com's purchasing process are the purchase request, purchase order, receipt of goods, and payment to the vendor. The company's AIS records information about each of these events and produces a variety of reports. The next two sections describe the information inputs and some of the reports associated with the purchasing process

Inputs to the Purchasing Process

As explained earlier, the purchasing process often begins with a requisition from a production department for goods or services. Sometimes, an AIS triggers purchase orders automatically when inventories fall below prespecified levels. The *purchase requisition* shows the item requested and may show the name of the vendor who supplies it.

In Figure 7-12, the accounts payable system matches three source documents before remitting payment to the vendor: the purchase order, the receiving report, and the purchase invoice. A *purchase invoice* is a copy of the vendor's sales invoice. The purchasing organization receives this copy as a bill for the goods or services purchased. The purpose of matching the purchase order, receiving report, and purchase invoice is to maintain the best possible control over cash payments to vendors. For example, the

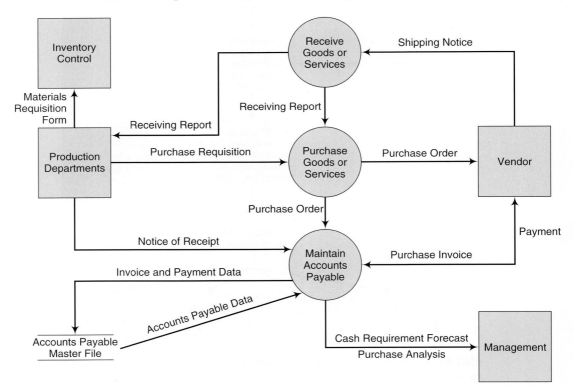

FIGURE 7-12 Data flow diagram of the purchasing process.

absence of one of these documents could signify a duplicate payment. A computerized AIS can search more efficiently for duplicate payments than a manual system. For example, auditors can instruct an AIS to print a list of duplicate invoice numbers, vendor checks for like dollar amounts, and similar control information.

The purchase requisition initiates the purchase order. Besides the information on the requisition, the purchase order includes vendor information and payment terms (Figure 7-4). The purchasing department typically prepares several copies (or images) of the purchase order. In a paper-based system, the purchasing clerk sends one copy of the purchase order to the receiving department to serve as a receiving report or, preferably, to prompt the receiving department to issue a separate receiving report. This copy of the purchase order is specially coded (or color-coded) to distinguish it from other copies of the purchase order if there is no separate receiving report. The receiving department copy might leave out the quantities ordered that are identified in the purchase order. This is done for control purposes, so that workers receiving the goods must do their own counts, rather than simply approving the amounts shown on the purchase order.

Another source document, a bill of lading, accompanies the goods sent. The freight carrier gives the supplier a bill of lading as a receipt, which means the carrier assumes responsibility for the goods. It may contain information about the date shipped, the point of delivery for freight payment (either shipping point or destination), the carrier, the route, and the mode of shipment. The customer may receive a copy of the shipping notice with the purchase invoice. This is important to the accounts payable subsystem, since accounts payable accruals include a liability for goods shipped free on board (FOB) from the shipping point. Goods shipped this way have left the vendor, but the customer has not yet received them. Another source document, the packing slip, is sometimes included in the merchandise package. This document indicates the specific quantities and items in the shipment and any goods that are on back order. The next time you order goods through a catalog or over the Internet, look for a packing slip, such as the one shown in Figure 7-13, in the container with your merchandise.

Outputs of the Purchasing Process

Typical outputs of the purchasing process are vendor checks and accompanying check register, discrepancy reports, and a cash requirements forecast. The check register lists all checks issued for a particular period. Accounts payable typically processes *checks* in batches and produces the *check register* as a by-product of this processing step. **Discrepancy reports** are necessary to note any differences between quantities or amounts on the purchase order, the receiving report, and the purchase invoice.

The purpose of a discrepancy report is to ensure that no one authorizes a vendor check until the appropriate manager properly reconciles any differences. For example, assume that a receiving report indicates the receipt of 12 units of product, whereas the purchase order shows that a company ordered 20 units and the purchase invoice bills the company for these 20 units. The accounts payable function records the liability for 20 units and notes the situation on a discrepancy report for management. This report would trigger an investigation. For example, it is possible that the vendor made two shipments of merchandise and one shipment has yet to be received. If this is the case, receipt of the second shipment clears this discrepancy from the next report. However, if this is not the case, it is important for management to determine the cause of the discrepancy as soon as possible.

The purchasing process produces a *cash requirements forecast* in the same manner that the sales process produces a cash receipts forecast. By looking at source documents

BlueBooks

http://www.bluebooks.com
orders@bluebooks.com

BlueBooks.com
1100 Industrial Drive, #44
Mountaintown, IL 55005
USA

Toll–Free: (800) 555-5555
Voice: +1 (305) 655-6890
FAX: +1 (305) 655-1245

Bill Jones
100 Lakeview Drive
Summerville, MI 02187

Your order of July 26, 2011 (Order ID 678-134568-9504123)

Qty	Item	Description	Format	Our Price	Total
In This Shipment					
1	Betty Crocker Cookbook: 1500 Recipes for the Way You Cook Today, 11th Edition	Betty Crocker	Hardcover	$29.99	$29.99
1	Weight Watches In 20 Minutes	Weight Watchers	Hardcover	$29.95	$29.95
			Subtotal:		$59.94
			Shipping & Handling:		5.67
			Order Total:		65.61
			Paid:		65.61
			Balance Due:		0.00

This shipment completes your order.

You can always check the status of your orders from the "Your Account" link on our homepage.

FIGURE 7-13 A sample packing slip.

196

such as outstanding purchase orders, unbilled receiving reports, and vendor invoices, an AIS can predict future cash payments and their dates. Naturally, this forecast is easier to make with a computerized system than with a manual system.

Information Technology (IT) Used in the Sales and Purchasing Processes.

Much of the input and output related to business processes is now electronic, and that includes the sales and purchasing processes. For instance, inputs (sales order or purchase requests) can be voice inputs, touch-tone telephone signals, bar codes, video signals, magnetic ink characters (as on checks), scanned images, or key strokes from a computer. Salespeople in the field typically use laptop computers, handheld devices, portable bar code scanners, or other types of input devices to enter data. With wireless capability, they can enter information in real time.

Case-in-Point 7.4 If you have moved lately, you probably watched a moving company representative walk through your home with a bar code scanner and a sheet of paper with various bar codes for different pieces of furniture and other items in your home. After the walk through, the representative can quickly download the information to a laptop, print out an estimate of the cost of your move, and discuss the estimate with you—all in the same visit!

Automated data-entry technology helps companies reduce costs and provide better customer service. For example, bar code scanners that are commonly used in most retail stores gather essential inventory data (and help to avoid human error) for the retailer, and they also help expedite the check-out process for customers. In addition, some retailers are using biometric technology that offers customers convenience and faster checkouts, and offers retailers savings in transaction costs. Here's how biometric payment works: to set up an account, customers scan their fingerprint at an in-store kiosk, enter their phone number, and then submit checking and credit card account information. To make a purchase, they place their finger on a scanner at the register, enter their phone number, and choose how they want to pay (credit, debit, or checking).[4]

Case-in-Point 7.5 In 1916, Clarence Saunders (a very innovative businessman in Memphis, TN) opened the first Piggly Wiggly® grocery store—the very first self-service grocery store. Saunders recently decided to be innovative again and started a pilot program to test the use of biometric payments. Within three months of starting the pilot program at four Piggly Wiggly grocery stores, 15 percent of its customers who normally did not pay by cash enrolled in the Pay By Touch system. Those users increased their store visits by 15 percent, which translates into an additional 7,350 transactions a year. Not only did they come more often, those shoppers also spent 12 percent more on groceries.[5]

IT supports the purchasing process in a variety of ways. For example, an organization might determine that some inventory items can be reordered automatically and electronically when the company reaches a predetermined minimum quantity of those inventory items. An automatic reorder can be generated by the computer system, sent electronically to the vendor, and the vendor can be paid electronically by using EDI. We discuss this aspect of e-Commerce more in depth in Chapter 14. After purchases arrive, our next concern is inventory management. To effectively manage inventory, we might use different technologies. Below, we describe two cases where organizations decided to use **RFID tags** (a computer chip with a tiny antenna) to manage inventory. The first

---

[4] http://money.cnn.com/2006/01/24/magazines/fortune/pluggedin_fortune_biometrics
[5] http://www.pigglywiggly.com/cgi-bin/customize?aboutus.html and http://money.cnn.com/2006/01/24/magazines/fortune/pluggedin_fortune_biometrics

is the Boeing Company, and the second is ConocoPhillips. In both cases, the vendors of the manufactured goods place the RFID tags on the items. The interesting point about RFID tags is that they can contain a complete history of the individual part, and then the purchaser can add or delete information to or from the tag as the part proceeds through the supply chain.

Case-in-Point 7.6 The Boeing Co. uses RFID tags to track between 1,700 and 2,000 mission-critical parts on each of its 747 jetliners, but that's really not very many when you consider that each of these jetliners has about 6 million parts. The parts that are tagged with RFID are those that are either very expensive or frequently require maintenance and replacement. Information stored on the RFID tag helps trace parts and reduces cycle time to solve service problems. For example, before RFID, if one of the three computers in the cockpit of a 747 needed to be replaced, a mechanic would have to get on his back with a flashlight and a mirror to search for a serial number. Now, the mechanic can walk into a cockpit with an RFID reader and locate the faulty computer with just a couple of clicks.[6]

Case-in-Point 7.7 ConocoPhillips uses RFID tags to track employees on offshore oil rigs. The tags allow the firm to identify the exact location of every employee in case of an emergency and to ensure that employees only enter areas where they have authorization to work.[7]

CURRENT TRENDS IN BUSINESS PROCESSES

Organizations frequently divide business processes into "core processes" and "other processes." In the past, managers and management accountants focused on cost management, while managers and internal auditors primarily focused on improving core processes. In all cases, the goal was typically to make these processes as efficient as possible. Now, organizations are critically examining their processes to determine which ones to keep and which ones to outsource. Results from a 2008 Accenture survey suggest that companies outsource for strategic advantages as much as for cost savings, as we highlight in the following Case-in-Point.

Case-in-Point 7.8 The senior executives who responded to a recent Accenture survey credit outsourcing with increasing their sense of control over business performance, and the most common control gains that they mentioned are

- Improved planning (47 percent)
- Greater reliability of business information (39 percent)
- A stronger grasp of business outcomes (37 percent)
- More effective implementation of ideas (33 percent)
- Increased revenue (32 percent)[8]

Business Processes Outsourcing (BPO)

Companies outsource business processes such as human resources, finance and accounting, customer services, learning services and training, and information technology. A recent

---

[6] http://epsfiles.intermec.com/eps_files/eps_cs/Boeing_cs_web.pdf
[7] http://www.rfidjournal.com/article/view/8000
[8] http://www.accenture.com/us-en/Pages/insight-outsourcing-control-travel-tourism-summary.aspx

survey estimated the global **business process outsourcing (BPO)** market for human resources services to be approximately $450 billion.

Case-in-Point 7.9   CNA is one of the largest insurance companies in the United States, providing services (core processes) such as risk management, information services, underwriting, and claims administration. Rather than develop training programs for their employees, CNA outsourced this business process to another company. Similarly, many universities outsource a number of operations they used to perform themselves—for example, landscaping, food services, or janitorial services—so that they can focus on core functions more directly related to educating students.

Today's combination of networked enterprises and globalization has given rise to a business model called **business without boundaries**. Companies no longer have all of their employees in one location, working on various business processes such as HR, accounting, production, and others. Employees may be located anywhere in the world, and they are. The result is a new dimension to outsourcing called **offshoring**—moving jobs offshore—to countries such as India, China, Canada, Mexico, or Malaysia.

Of course, not all outsourced business processes are accomplished by employees in foreign countries. Many of these processes are still accomplished by businesses in the United States. Nevertheless, all business processes are under a great deal of scrutiny by managers and management accountants as companies become more strategically oriented toward revenue generation and more vigilant about managing costs.

The important point for accountants is that, at some point, you will most likely be on a team of professionals in your organization that will study the costs and benefits of either keeping a business process in-house or outsourcing the function. If the team decides that the organization should keep the process, then the next task might be to decide what business process management (BPM) software the company should use to automate that process. Software companies are developing a wide variety of business process solutions to help managers integrate their existing data and applications into efficient and effective business systems. If the decision is to outsource the process, then accountants will most certainly be involved in analyzing the many costs and benefits/concerns associated with the decision.

Business Process Management Software

Business Process Management (BPM) software packages help companies collect corporate knowledge, data, and business rules into a business system to improve core business processes. Think of BPM as a combination of software tools and management practices that enable entities to accomplish business processes more efficiently. As a result, managers have timely access to performance data related to clients, projects, financials, and people to improve company performance—and these benefits are available even to smaller businesses, as the following Case-in-Point describes.

Case-in-Point 7.10   The Sleeter Group is a nationwide community of experts who provide QuickBooks consulting services to small business owners—and they also announce their Annual Award List of "Awesome Add-ons for QuickBooks." For 2011, this list includes ViewMyPaycheck (a cloud where employees can access paychecks), SmartVault V3 (a document management system), ShipGear (for integrating accounting and shipping), and a number of other very innovative BPM solutions![9]

---

[9] http://www.sleeter.com/awesomeaddons

AIS AT WORK
Economic Downturn Promotes Onshoring[10]

For the past decade, we read one story after another of yet another company that had outsourced or offshored a business process to another firm. Most troubling to Americans were the business processes and the many jobs associated with those functions that were moved to other countries, especially India, China, and the Philippines. Management of these firms claimed that such business decisions were necessary for their companies to remain competitive and to generate value for shareholders. Recent downturns in the economy, an increased labor pool, and decreased real estate prices may have changed the equation, however.

Many experts suggest that offshoring has now reached a plateau. Companies are beginning to reconsider earlier decisions to offshore—and are bringing jobs back to the United States or choosing not to offshore new jobs. One such company, DESA Heating Products (DHP) of Bowling Green, Kentucky, announced in 2008 that the company would move their manufacturing production from China back to Bowling Green. Although DHP had outsourced hundreds of manufacturing jobs to China, management decided to reverse that decision and bring those jobs back to its Kentucky factory. The rationale for this decision focuses on two factors: quality and cost. And when you think about it, these are both critical factors for a company's success because today's customers demand the best quality products at the lowest price.

The Governor of Kentucky claimed that DHP's decision to bring their production back to the United States is a strong indicator of evolving outsourcing trends in the global economy. So what exactly are these trends? A recent report from a global consulting firm contains a number of clues: transportation costs, wage inflation, currency fluctuations, and quality issues.

Perhaps DHP's experience with offshoring can help us understand the Governor's claim. First, Chinese workers are now demanding higher wages for their labor, which means that Chinese workers are no longer an economical solution to labor costs in the United States (19 percent increase in China compared to 3 percent in the United States since 2003). Second, significant fluctuations in oil prices cause great difficulty in budgeting the costs of transportation of goods produced in China—especially for the large, heavy products that DHP produces.

Third, Kentucky's central location in the United States means that DHP is only one day's drive from 70 percent of the population in the United States. That translates to products in the hands of DHP's customers in 12 hours instead of the six to eight weeks to ship from China. And finally, DHP expects to save money in warranty repairs and replacement costs—manufacturing costs that tripled on the products made in China.

 ## SUMMARY

✓ The fundamentals of any business process include journals, ledgers, accounts, trial balances, and financial statements.

✓ When planning a new AIS, developers usually start by designing the outputs from the system.

---

[10] http://www.networkworld.com/news/2007/081707-study-onshoring.html; http://www.bgchamber.com/media_room/blog/2008/07/desa-to-expand-bowling-green.php

✓ The fundamental instrument for collecting data in a typical AIS is the source document.

✓ Two business processes that are common to many business organizations are the sales process and the purchasing process.

✓ The sales process begins with a customer order and ends with the collection of cash from the customer.

✓ Important source documents associated with the sales process are sales orders, sales invoices, remittance advices, shipping notices, and customer checks.

✓ The primary outputs of the sales process are reports such as a cash receipts report, a bad debt report, and a customer listing report.

✓ For the purchasing process, the AIS is concerned with timely payment for purchased goods and services.

✓ Source documents common to the purchasing process include purchase requisitions, purchase orders, receiving reports, purchase invoices, and bills of lading.

✓ Although companies still outsource to better manage costs, they now outsource and offshore business processes for strategic advantages.

✓ Some of the business processes that are most likely to be outsourced or offshored are human resources, finance and accounting, customer services, learning services and training, and information technology.

KEY TERMS YOU SHOULD KNOW

alphanumeric code	group code
block code	mnemonic code
business process	numeric code
Business Process Management (BPM) software	offshoring
business process outsourcing (BPO)	purchasing process
business without boundaries	RFID tags
customer relationship management (CRM)	sales process
discrepancy reports	sequence code
exception report	supply chain

DISCUSSION QUESTIONS

7-1. As you might imagine, the chart of accounts for a manufacturing firm would be different from that of a service firm. Not surprisingly, service firms differ so much that software now exists for almost any type of firm that you could name. Think of yourself as an entrepreneur who is going to start up your own business. Now, go to Office Depot, Staples, or a similar office supply store (or search online) to find at least two different software packages that you might use for the type of firm you are going to start up. What does the Chart of Accounts include? Are both software packages the same? What are the differences between the packages?

7-2. What are the purposes of accounting codes? How are they used? Bring to class some examples of codes used by manufacturing firms, accounting firms, and merchandising firms.

7-3. What are some typical outputs of an AIS? Why do system analysts concentrate on managerial reports when they start to design an effective AIS? Why not start with the inputs to the system instead?

7-4. What are some criteria that systems designers should consider when developing managerial reports for an AIS? How do system designers know what to include on reports?

7-5. Visit a local business and collect some examples of source documents used in an AIS. For each source document you collect, discuss its purpose(s). Are different source documents required for manufacturing firms versus merchandising organizations? Are all the business source documents paper based?

7-6. This chapter discussed many inputs to an organization's sales process. What are the specific data items needed to add a new customer and record a sales order?

7-7. How does a data flow diagram for the sales process differ from a system flowchart describing that process?

7-8. How are the inputs and outputs of the purchasing process likely to be different for a restaurant versus an automobile manufacturer?

7-9. Explain the term *business without boundaries*. How is this changing the nature of organizations and who accomplishes various business processes?

7-10. What do we mean when we say companies are offshoring business processes?

7-11. Some businesses choose offshoring to solve the issue of expertise, especially for IT personnel. These companies claim they simply cannot find enough qualified employees in the United States to do certain technology jobs. Do you agree with this assessment? Why or why not?

7-12. Search the Web for unusual and interesting uses of RFID tags. Find at least two that are unusual and share those with your classmates.

7-13. Discuss the privacy issues created by the use of RFID tags. Do you support the use of RFID tags for personal ID, customer relationship management, and inventory tracking? Why or why not?

PROBLEMS

7-14. Listed below are several types of accounting data that might be coded. For each data item, recommend a type of code (mnemonic, sequence, block, or group) and support your choice.

  a. Employee identification number on a computer file

  b. Product number for a sales catalog

  c. Inventory number for the products of a wholesale drug company

  d. Inventory part number for a bicycle manufacturing company

  e. Identification numbers on the forms waiters and waitresses use to take orders

  f. Identification numbers on airline ticket stubs

  g. Automobile registration numbers

  h. Automobile engine block numbers

  i. Shirt sizes for men's shirts

  j. Color codes for house paint

  k. Identification numbers on payroll check forms

  l. Listener identification for a radio station

  m. Numbers on lottery tickets

  n. Identification numbers on a credit card

  o. Identification numbers on dollar bills

  p. Passwords used to gain access to a computer

  q. Zip codes

  r. A chart of accounts for a department store

s. A chart of accounts for a flooring subcontractor

t. Shoe sizes

u. Identification number on a student examination

v. Identification number on an insurance policy

7-15. Novelty Gadgets is a marketer of inexpensive toys and novelties that it sells to retail stores, specialty stores, and catalog companies. As an accountant working for the company, you have been asked to design a product code for the company. In analyzing this problem, you have discovered the following:

a. The company has three major product lines: (1) toys and games, (2) party and magic tricks, and (3) inexpensive gifts. There are major subproducts within each of these product lines, and the number of these categories is 25, 18, and 113, respectively.

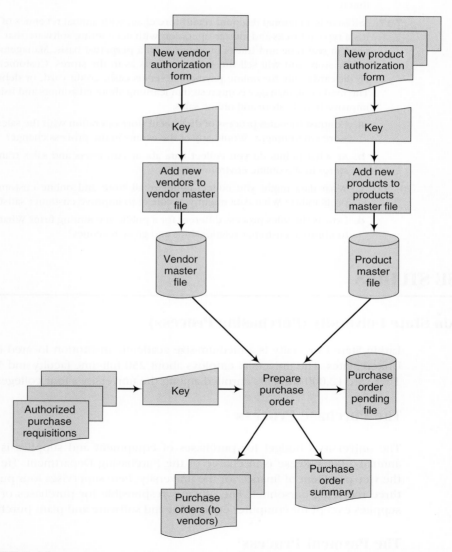

FIGURE 7-14   System flowchart illustrating the preparation of purchase orders for P. Miesing and Company.

    b. The company has divided its selling efforts into five geographic areas: (1) the United States, (2) the Far East, (3) Europe and Africa, (4) South America, and (5) International (a catchall area). Each major geographic area has several sales districts (never more than 99 per area). Between one and 20 salespeople are assigned to each district.

    c. As noted earlier, there are three major categories of customers, and certain customers can also purchase goods on credit. There are five different classes of credit customers, and each rating indicates the maximum amount of credit the customer can have. Design a group code that Novelty Gadgets could use to prepare sales analysis reports. Be sure to identify each digit or position in your code in terms of both use and meaning.

7-16. Figure 7-14 is a system flowchart for P. Miesing and Company's purchase order event. Prepare a narrative to accompany the flowchart describing this purchase order event. Include in your narrative the source documents involved, the computerized data processing that takes place, data inputs used to prepare purchase orders, and the outputs prepared from the processing function.

7-17. SSR-Save is a national discount retail store chain with annual revenues of more than $1 billion. It's a typical bricks-and-mortar operation with accounting software that records sales transactions in real time and tracks inventories on a perpetual basis. Management is considering an online store and will sell the same products as in the stores. Customers will be able to use credit cards only for online payments (versus cash, credit card, or debit card in the stores). The marketing manager is interested in learning about customers and using the information to improve both in-store and online sales.

    a. Contrast the sales process of their retail store operation with the sales process in an online store environment. Would any of the events in the process change?

    b. At what points do you collect data about customers and sales transactions in the retail store? In the online environment?

    c. What data might you collect about retail store and online customers to improve your profitability? What data might you collect to improve customer satisfaction?

    d. How is the sales process different for a public accounting firm? What data can they collect to improve customer relationships and grow revenues?

CASE STUDIES

Larkin State University (Purchasing Process)

Larkin State University is a medium-size academic institution located in the Southeastern United States. The university employs about 250 full-time faculty and 300 staff personnel. There are 12,000 students enrolled among the university's four colleges.

The Purchase Process

The university's budget for purchases of equipment and supplies is about $25 million annually. Peter Reese is in charge of the Purchasing Department. He reports directly to the vice president of finance for the university. Pete supervises four purchasing clerks and three receiving personnel. The office is responsible for purchases of all equipment and supplies except for computer equipment and software and plant purchases or additions.

The Payment Process

The various departments across campus manually fill out hard-copy purchase requisition forms when there is a need for equipment/supplies. Each department forwards these forms to the Purchasing Department. If the request is for computer equipment or software, the requisition is forwarded to the Department of Information Technology for action.

Purchase requisitions are assigned to one of the three purchasing clerks by department. For instance, one purchasing clerk makes purchases for all university departments beginning with the letters A through G (Accounting – Geology). Purchasing clerks check the requisition to make sure it is authorized and then consult the Approved Vendor Listing to find a supplier. The clerk may contact a supplier for pricing and product specification. Once this task is complete, the purchasing clerk enters the purchase requisition and vendor and price information into the computer system, which prints out a multiple-part purchase order. Clerks send copies of the purchase order to Central Receiving, to the vendor, and to the Accounts Payable Department. (The university considered using EDI for its purchases, but chose not to adopt it because of the large number of vendors used.)

When Central Receiving receives an order, a receiving clerk consults the Purchase Order file to make sure the correct product and quantity have been delivered. The clerk also checks the product for damage. Central receiving does not accept any overshipments. Receiving clerks forward accepted shipments to the adjacent warehouse for distribution to the appropriate department. Clerks file one copy of the Receiving Report, send one copy to the Purchasing Department, and forward a third copy to Accounts Payable.

George Vaughn is the Supervisor of Accounts Payable. Two accounting clerks report to him. He assigns invoices to them for payment based on vendor name. One clerk processes payments for vendors A through M, and the other clerk handles payments to all vendors with names beginning with letters N through Z. The clerks match each vendor invoice with a copy of the receiving report and purchase order before entering it into the computer for payment by due date. There are often discrepancies among the three documents. This requires frequent phone calls to the vendor, the Receiving Department, or Purchasing for resolution. As a result, the company frequently makes payments late and loses out on cash discounts.

Requirements

1. Identify the important business events that occur within Larkin's purchase/payment process.
2. What changes would you suggest to the current process to take advantage of information technology?

The Caribbean Club (Customer Relationship Management)

The Caribbean Club is one of Virgin Island's hottest night spots. It's a great place for locals to meet after work and relax with friends, it's a popular destination for tourists who stay on the island, and it's always on the list of fun entertainment choices for the crowds from the cruise ships that dock in the harbor.

The reason the club is so popular with such a variety of customers is because the founder of the club, Ross Stewart, always has such innovative and visionary ideas that delight the patrons. For example, every night of the week the club features different activities or shows, including beach volleyball, Caribbean shows with calypso singers, world-class musicians who play steel drums, and other island delights.

Since Ross was a former accountant and auditor with one of the largest public accounting firms in New Zealand, he is very accustomed to brainstorming sessions to generate ideas and surface concerns. He brought this practice with him to the Caribbean and holds brainstorming sessions with his "club associates" (which is what he calls all of the employees at the club) once every month to identify new and novel ideas to increase the popularity and profitability of the club.

As you might imagine, the patrons of a night club are there to relax and enjoy themselves. So, the associates thought it would be a great idea to somehow be able to recognize their regular patrons so that they wouldn't have to trouble them with a bill every time a server came to their table with another round of drinks. After all, if the Club wanted these people to "feel like they were at home with friends," the patrons shouldn't have to bother with trying to decide who owed what to pay the bill. What a nuisance!

So Ross and his associates came up with the idea to implant their regular customers with an implantable microchip. The idea was to make the chip fun—to give it an elite status so that their regular patrons would want to be implanted. To dramatize the elite status of the chip, Ross decided that the Club would have a special area where only those with chips, the VIPs, would be admitted. And of course, this area would have various exclusive services for these members. The chip would allow the VIPS to be recognized and to be able to pay for their food and drinks without any ID—they would simply pass by a reader and the Club would know who they are and their credit balance. Ross also wanted the information system supporting the chip to be a customer relationship management tool.

Requirements

1. What do you think of this idea? That is, what are the advantages and disadvantages of this idea for the Caribbean Club?

2. If you were Ross, what information would you want the CRM to collect? Search the Internet to see if you can find a CRM software package that seems appropriate for the Club. Why did you select this particular software?

3. What are the advantages and disadvantages for the patrons?

4. If you were a passenger on a cruise ship, or staying at a resort on the island, would you get the chip implanted? Why or why not?

Chapter 8

Accounting Information Systems and Business Processes: Part II

INTRODUCTION

In the previous chapter we identified two processes that are common to most organizations: the sales process and the purchasing process. This chapter continues the discussion of business processes by exploring three additional processes: resource management, production, and financing. The resource management process includes human resources and fixed assets. The production manufacturing cycle entails the conversion of raw materials (another resource) into finished goods available for sale. Finally, the financing process involves the ways that organizations fund their operations (i.e., through borrowing or by selling shares of ownership).

Many organizations, such as government agencies, have specialized information needs, apart from the typical AIS requirements for information about revenues, purchases, and resources. The second section of this chapter considers some unique accounting information needs of organizations.

Maximizing the efficiency of every business process is critical to business success in today's *business without boundaries* operating environment. Sometimes managers decide that a current business process isn't working and must be reengineered. This is usually the case, for example, when a firm decides to implement a new enterprise-wide IT system. As a result, they turn to business process reengineering, which is the topic of the final section of this chapter.

THE RESOURCE MANAGEMENT PROCESS

Two resources that managers must closely manage, and require appropriate data, are an organization's human resources and its fixed assets. Because the inputs, processing, and outputs for human resources and fixed assets are quite different, we examine them separately (Figure 8-1).

Human Resource Management

The "economic meltdown" in the fall of 2008 has been one of the most challenging times for resource managers as they try to deal with cash flow problems, bankruptcies, plant closings, and layoffs. An organization's **human resource (HR) management** activity includes the personnel function, which is responsible for hiring or laying off employees. HR must properly maintain the personnel and payroll records for employees, as well as handle the many actions associated with employee terminations. Nevertheless, the primary

---

Human Resource Management Process

Objectives

Hiring, training, and employing workers
Maintaining employee earnings records
Complying with regulatory reporting requirements
Reporting on payroll deductions
Making timely and accurate payments to employees
Providing an interface for personnel and payroll activities

Inputs (Source documents)
- Personnel action forms
- Time sheets
- Payroll deduction authorizations
- Tax withholding forms

Outputs (Reports)
- Financial statement information
- Employee listings
- Paychecks
- Check registers
- Deduction reports
- Tax (regulatory) reports
- Payroll summaries

FIGURE 8-1   Objectives, inputs, and outputs for the human resource management process.

objective of the personnel function is to hire, train, and employ appropriately qualified people to do an organization's work.

In the past, HR professionals used technology to handle administrative tasks such as time clocking and payroll. However, many business process management (BPM) software packages are now available to automate the core processes that normally occur in an HR office. For example, HR departments are increasingly turning to technology to help with such diverse responsibilities as recruitment, oversight of legal and regulatory compliance, benefits administration, training, performance evaluation, and safeguarding confidential employee information.

Case-in-Point 8.1   Merix, a global supplier of advanced technology and printed circuit boards, focuses on the financial performance of its recruiting process. Using a cost-per-hire calculation, Merix determines whether its recruiting process is functioning at peak efficiency. Goals for this measure are set to assure that HR is financially responsive to the organization and is an efficient support service. Further, tracking this measure allows Merix to more effectively budget human resources expenditures for the coming year based on projections of staffing needs.[1]

Although the main purpose of **payroll processing information systems** is to pay employees for their work, such systems also maintain employee earnings records (a payroll history), comply with various government tax and reporting requirements, report on various deduction categories (e.g., pension funds and group insurance), and interact with other personnel functions. Figures 8-2 and 8-3 show sample system flowcharts for the personnel function and for the payroll function.

Inputs to Human Resource Management Processing.   The source documents used in payroll processing are personnel action forms, time sheets, payroll deduction authorizations, and tax-withholding forms. The personnel department sends *personnel*

---

[1] http://www.merix.com

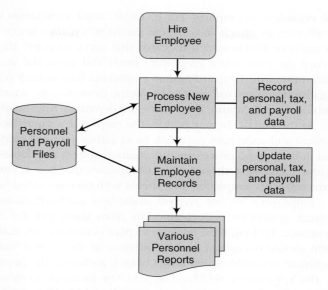

FIGURE 8-2   Systems flowchart of the AIS for the personnel function.

action forms to payroll that document the hiring of new employees or changes in employee status. For example, payroll receives a personnel action form when an employee receives a salary increase. This document is very important for control purposes. For example, auditors will detect an employee who increases his or her own salary when they fail to find a personnel action form authorizing the increase.

Many companies use *time sheets* to track the hours that employees work. The source of information for these time sheets varies widely with the level of technology that

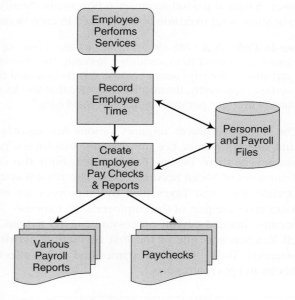

FIGURE 8-3   Systems flowchart of the AIS for the payroll function.

the organization employs. For example, some companies use a time clock that requires employees to punch in (on time cards) when they arrive for work. Others use picture ID cards or RFID-enabled ID cards that serve to verify the identity of an employee and record the time when employees enter and leave the workplace or a specific location within the firm. To guard against employees having their friends punch in for them, some organizations now use various biometric devices (e.g., fingerprints or iris scans) to identify employees and capture their entry and departure from workplaces.

At the end of the pay period, the employee's supervisor verifies the number of hours worked and authorizes payment. Next, either a payroll clerk or an internal control embedded in the payroll processing information system checks for the appropriate authorization before processing these hours. Companies that use a job cost information system can cross-reference employee time sheets with time recorded on individual jobs.

Employees fill out *payroll deduction authorizations* that direct the payroll processing system to deduct amounts from gross pay for items such as health and life insurance, parking fees, retirement plan contributions, and union dues. An authorization form should document each deduction. In the United States, every employee must also complete tax-withholding forms, which authorize the payroll system to reduce gross pay by the appropriate withholding tax. The information system uses each employee's W-4 withholding form to calculate the correct withholding for federal income taxes.

Outputs of Human Resource Management Processing. The outputs of human resource management processing include employee listings, check registers, paychecks, deduction reports, tax reports, and payroll summaries. As you might imagine, the processing of paychecks should include very strict internal control procedures (covered in Chapters 9 and 10). *Employee listings* show current employees and may contain addresses and other demographic information. *Check registers* accompany each printing of paychecks and list gross pay, deductions, and net pay. Payroll clerks use the check register information to make journal entries for salary and payroll-tax expenses. *Deduction reports* can contain summaries of deductions for all employees in a department, a division, or company wide. Finally, the payroll function issues various *payroll summaries* that help managers analyze expenses. A typical payroll summary report might classify payroll expenses by department or job or show total overtime hours worked in each department.

> **Case-in-Point 8.2** The city of Reno, Nevada, is one of many cities in the United States seeking ways to lower its expenditures. Recently, the issue of overtime pay for firemen came to the attention of the city council because reports indicated that there were excessive amounts of overtime. Apparently, the number of firemen that the city could hire was limited, but not the amount of overtime pay these individuals could earn.[2]

The U.S. government requires various *tax reports* for income tax, Social Security tax, and unemployment tax information. Employees pay some taxes in their entirety, but employers share others. For instance, both the employee and the employer pay equal amounts of Social Security taxes. The payroll system allocates shared taxes to the appropriate accounts. Taxes paid by employees are allocated to payroll expense, but employer taxes are part of the employer's tax expense.

Because manual payroll processing can be tedious, repetitive, and error-prone, the payroll function was one of the first accounting activities to be computerized in many organizations. Today, many companies find it cost-effective to outsource the process for paychecks and payroll reports.

---

[2] From the authors.

Case-in-Point 8.3   Automatic Data Processing, Inc., or ADP, is the world's largest payroll service provider. More than 500,000 companies in 15 countries outsource their payroll processing and, in some cases, their human resource administration to ADP. The company has been in business for over 50 years and pays more than one in six private sector employees in the United States.[3]

Fixed Asset Management

Even small organizations generally own many fixed assets, which management must track as they are purchased and used. The objective of the **fixed asset management (FAM)** function is to manage the purchase, maintenance, valuation, and disposal of an organization's fixed assets (also called "long-term assets" because they last more than one year).

In thinking about how complex it might be to track fixed assets, imagine the endless number of fixed assets that are owned by a large, publicly traded firm such as Boeing (which has about $23 billion in fixed assets on its balance sheet). A firm must record each fixed asset on its books when it purchases the asset. In addition, the firm must maintain depreciation schedules for its fixed assets. Many large firms will calculate depreciation using five or more different depreciation methods because of different calculation requirements for financial statements prepared according to Generally Accepted Accounting Principles (GAAP), federal income tax reporting, Alternative Minimum Tax (AMT), state tax reporting, and so forth. Employees often move fixed assets around within an organization, and although an AIS should keep track of all asset locations, this can be quite difficult in practice. Bar codes affixed to physical assets make this job easier.

Because fixed assets often require repairs, an AIS should also track repair costs and distinguish between revenue expenditures and capital expenditures. Revenue expenditures are ordinary repair expenses, whereas capital expenditures add to the value of assets. Finally, the AIS calculates the amount of gain or loss upon disposal of individual fixed assets. By comparing the amount received for the asset with the asset's book value, the AIS can compute a gain or loss. Fortunately, software companies offer a variety of solutions to help managers and automate these processes.

Case-in-Point 8.4   BNA Software offers a fixed assets system for small and midsize firms that handles inventory reporting, management, regulatory compliance, estate planning, and even auditing of the inventory account. The software also allows for tracking of mobile inventory and integrates with ERP packages.[4]

Increasingly, organizations are adopting **enterprise asset management (EAM) systems** to automate the management of a broad spectrum of assets. For example, Green Bay Packaging, Inc. is using an EAM solution to streamline purchasing, reduce inventory, and trim machine downtime and maintenance costs. Because of reduced overall operating expenses, the company expects the software to pay for itself in six months. Avantis makes a global EAM solution that focuses on maintenance, inventory, procurement, and invoicing efficiencies. Finally, the U.S. government purchased a $1.9 million EAM system to integrate data and coordinate logistics for the 5,000-plus major rebuilding projects underway in Iraq.

Inputs to Fixed Asset Management Processing.   Fixed asset processing begins with a request for a fixed asset purchase. The individual making the request enters the appropriate information on a purchase requisition form (typically an e-form). *Fixed asset*

---

[3] http://www.adp.com/corporate/adp_corpoverview_main.html
[4] http://www.cpatechnologyadvisor.com

requests usually require approval by one or more managers, especially where purchases require substantial investments. Other documents associated with fixed asset purchases are receiving reports, supplier invoices, and repair and maintenance records. The receiving department either scans in the information electronically to the AIS or fills out a *receiving report* on receipt of a fixed asset. The asset's supplier sends an *invoice* when it ships the asset. Sometimes a company builds a fixed asset, for example, a warehouse, rather than acquiring it from an outside vendor. Here, processing fixed assets requires a *work order* detailing the costs of construction.

Those responsible for a particular fixed asset should complete a *fixed asset change form* when transferring fixed assets from one location to another. The fixed asset change form also records the sale, trade, or retirement of fixed assets. Fixed asset management requires maintaining repair and maintenance records for each asset individually or for categories of fixed assets. The department performing this service should record these activities on a *repair and maintenance form.* This form notifies the AIS to update expense or asset accounts. Figure 8-4 is a systems flowchart that shows fixed asset acquisition, maintenance, and disposition.

Outputs of Fixed Asset Management Processing.   One output of the fixed asset processing system is a listing of all fixed assets acquired during a particular period. A *fixed asset register* lists the identification number of all fixed assets held by a company and each asset's location. The *depreciation register* shows depreciation expense and accumulated depreciation for each fixed asset. *Repair and maintenance reports* show the current period's repair and maintenance expenses, as well as each fixed asset's repair and maintenance history. Finally, a *report on retired assets* reflects the disposition of fixed

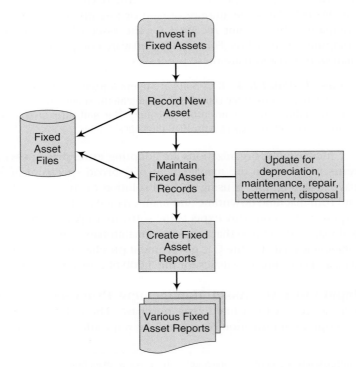

FIGURE 8-4   Systems flowchart of the AIS for the fixed asset management function.

Fixed Asset Management Process

<u>Objectives</u>

Tracking purchases of fixed assets
Recording fixed asset maintenance
Valuing fixed assets
Allocating fixed asset costs (recording depreciation)
Tracking disposal of fixed assets

Inputs (Source documents)
- Purchase requisition
- Receiving reports
- Supplier invoices
- Construction work orders
- Repair and maintenance records
- Fixed asset change forms

Outputs (Reports)
- Financial statement information
- Fixed asset register
- Depreciation register
- Repair and maintenance reports
- Retired asset report

FIGURE 8-5 Objectives, inputs, and outputs for the fixed asset management process.

assets during the current period. Figure 8-5 summarizes the objectives, inputs, and outputs of the fixed asset management process.

THE PRODUCTION PROCESS

The **production process** (sometimes called the conversion process) begins with a request for raw materials and ends with the transfer of finished goods to warehouses.

Objectives of the Production Process

The objective of a manufacturing organization's production process is to convert raw materials into finished goods as efficiently as possible. Today's production of goods and services often requires expensive factory machinery, such as computer-assisted design (CAD) technology or robotics (used in the manufacture of automobiles).

Accounting for the acquisition and use of production machinery is part of the fixed asset management process described in the previous section of this chapter. Another important objective of an AIS's production process is collecting cost accounting data for operational managers, who then can make informed decisions with respect to the products produced in their departments. Figure 8-6 identifies the objectives, inputs, and outputs associated with the production of goods and services.

Cost Accounting Subsystem. Because the cost of goods sold is likely to be the largest expense on a manufacturing firm's income statement, a critical part of the production process is an AIS's **cost accounting subsystem**. The cost accounting subsystem provides important control information (e.g., variance reports reflecting differences between actual and standard production costs) and varies with the size of the company and the types of product produced. As you might guess, a bakery producing baked goods would collect very different data in its AIS than that of an automobile manufacturer. Cost accounting subsystems for manufacturing organizations are commonly job costing, process costing, or activity-based costing systems.

Production Process

Objectives

Track purchases and sales of inventories
Monitor and control manufacturing costs
Control inventory
Control and coordinate the production process
Provide input for budgets

Inputs (Source documents)
- Materials requisition form
- Bill of materials
- Master production schedule
- Production order
- Job time cards

Outputs (Reports)
- Financial statement information
- Material price lists
- Periodic usage reports
- Inventory status reports
- Production cost reports
- Manufacturing status reports

FIGURE 8-6   Objectives, inputs, and outputs commonly associated with the production process.

A **job costing information system** keeps track of the specific costs for raw materials, labor, and overhead associated with each product or group of products, called a "job." This type of costing system is most appropriate for manufacturers of large-scale or custom products, such as home builders or book publishers. Manufacturers of homogeneous products (such as soft drinks or toothbrushes) that are produced on a regular and continuous basis use a **process costing information system**. In this system, it is not feasible or practical to keep track of costs for each item or group of items produced. Instead, process costing systems use averages to calculate the costs associated with goods in process and finished goods produced.

Activity-based costing (ABC) systems help managers describe processes, identify cost drivers of each process, and then determine the unit costs of products created in each process. By studying their business processes, managers are in a better position to recognize opportunities to improve those processes. Thus, activity-based costing gives managers a better understanding of their processes, an improved ability to allocate indirect costs to those processes, and a better understanding of the true cost of each product. The systems flowchart in Figure 8-7 shows a typical information flow for production in a manufacturing firm.

Just-in-Time (JIT) Inventory Systems.

Inventory control ensures that the production process handles inventory transactions appropriately so that the financial statements correctly state the value of the inventory and cost of goods sold. Carrying inventory has a number of costs associated with it, including storage, obsolescence, shrinkage, or reduction in sales value.

Toyota (of Japan) popularized the use of **just-in-time (JIT) inventory** systems. Some managers refer to a JIT system as a "make-to-order inventory system." This phrase indicates that the organization produces goods to fill an order rather than to fill inventory. The objective of a JIT system is to minimize inventories at all levels. Each stage in the production operation manufactures (or acquires) a part just in time for the next process to use it. While the best possible JIT system would maintain zero inventory balances, this is often not practical in real-world applications. Manufacturing organizations need some inventories to protect against interruptions in supply from manufacturers and fluctuations in demand for their finished goods that are beyond the manufacturer's control.

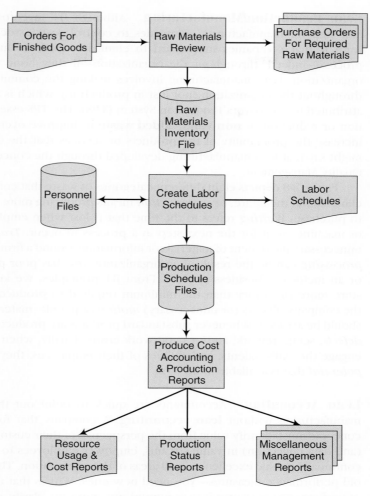

FIGURE 8-7 Systems flowchart of the AIS for the production process in a manufacturing organization.

A JIT system requires a reliable and high-quality AIS. If the AIS does not process transactions on a timely and accurate basis, manufacturing processes may lack the raw materials inventory necessary to maintain a constant work flow. Inefficient processing of transactions can also lead to shortages of finished goods that, in turn, translate into lost sales. This leads some organizations to be proactive and reengineer the process.

Case-in-Point 8.5 JIT is a great concept for a company that is intent on efficiently managing stock, but it makes life difficult for the accounts payable department, which is responsible for paying many JIT invoices. For example, Dell Computer Company found itself ordering certain parts as frequently as 12 times a day. The A/P department was inundated with paper invoices. GE Capital dispatched several of its Six Sigma analysts, known as *black belts*, to Dell to analyze its A/P process. The consultants mapped out the entire process (using documentation procedures similar to those described in Chapter 6) and then recommended that Dell change to an Internet-based electronic filing process. The move saves Dell over $2 million per year.[5]

---

[5] http://www.ge.com/sixsigma

Lean Production/Manufacturing. Although JIT inventory systems are an important step for manufacturing companies to control costs associated with inventory, the truth is that companies must learn to eliminate waste throughout the manufacturing process—indeed, throughout the organization—if they hope to become a world class organization. Lean manufacturing involves making the commitment to eliminate waste throughout the organization (not just in production), which is a philosophy that is often attributed to the Toyota Production System (TPS). The TPS essentially focuses on elimination or reduction of **non-value-added waste** to improve overall customer value and to increase the profitability of the products or services that the organization offers. So we might say that lean manufacturing developed through the concepts of JIT as well as Total Quality Management.

Figure 8-8 depicts eight different categories of waste that companies hope to reduce or eliminate. In the figure, *overproduction* means producing more than your customers want to purchase. *Waiting* refers to the time that is lost when employees, products, services, or machines wait for the next step in a process to occur. *Transportation* identifies the unnecessary movement of materials or information around a firm or organization. Excessive *processing* can be the result of an organization that has poor products, defective inputs, or an inefficient business process. From JIT principles, we know that it is wasteful to store more *inventory* than the minimum required to produce the goods or services of the company. Excess (or unnecessary) *motion* of people, materials, products, or anything should be avoided. Whenever substandard products are produced, companies end up with *defects*, scrap, rework, and/or paperwork errors. Finally, when organizations do not fully engage the skills, talents, and abilities of their employees, they lose some of the *human potential* that is available to the firm.

Lean Accounting. Accountants are quick to point out that you cannot have lean manufacturing without **lean accounting**. A company that follows lean manufacturing concepts must identify value from the perspective of their customers, organize production (and data collection) in value streams, empower employees to make decisions, and then continually pursue excellence in all areas of the organization. Thus, you can't use the same old performance measures—you need new ones. Why is that the case? Because the goal of performance measures is to communicate, motivate, clarify, and evaluate. Management accountants use performance measures to give managers information and feedback for decision making. Traditional performance measures typically support only top managers

---

Types of non-value-added waste

- Human potential
- Defects
- Motion
- Inventory
- Processing
- Transportation
- Waiting
- Overproduction

FIGURE 8-8 Categories of waste that are the focus of lean operations management. Source: Burton, T., and S. Boeder, *The lean extended enterprise: Moving beyond the four walls to value stream excellence* (2003), Boca Raton, FL: J. Ross Publishing.

as decision makers. Lean manufacturing requires that many leaders (i.e., employees other than high-level managers) be empowered as decision makers, which means they also need timely information to be effective.

While reengineering the traditional performance measures would be ideal, this is often not possible. However, management accountants, managers, and empowered team members can work together to identify critical data that the AIS must collect to support lean production. At a minimum, these data should include metrics that will help managers and team members make wise decisions regarding methods to reduce or eliminate waste that is identified in Figure 8-8 (overproduction, waiting, transportation, processing, inventory, motion, defects, and human potential).

Jan Brosnahan, the controller for Watlow Electric Manufacturing Co. (WEM), describes how her team adopted lean accounting, which means measuring and evaluating results by **value stream management** rather than by *traditional departments* (such as customer service, purchasing, etc.). For example, an order fulfillment value stream includes all metrics from the sales/order entry point, through manufacturing, all the way to after-sales support. Each value stream has a leader who is responsible for coaching and profitability of the specific metrics identified for that value stream. Standard costs, variances, and overhead allocations are not the drivers of decisions—rather, only directly incurred costs are used for decision making.

Lean accounting will have many implications throughout organizations of the future. On the basis of the many changes that WEM implemented in their company to support lean accounting, there are two areas that may need to be evaluated by management accountants—the collection of data in the AIS and the chart of accounts that the company uses. Fortunately, AISs that are built upon a relational database (see Chapters 3, 4, and 5) can be modified to support lean accounting. Regarding the chart of accounts (covered in Chapter 7), the accountants at each organization will need to work with managers and team leaders to determine the most appropriate coding system to use, based on the value streams that are identified.

Inputs to the Production Process

When a production manager needs raw materials, he or she issues a *materials requisition form* to acquire more material from a storeroom or warehouse where the raw materials are kept. If the level of inventory falls below a certain predetermined level, the inventory control clerk issues a purchase requisition to the purchasing department (probably an e-form, and this might be an automatic determination that is transmitted electronically to the vendor). Finished goods consist of a complex array of parts or subassemblies. For example, an armchair consists of four legs, a seat, two arms, and a back. The *bill of materials* shows the types and quantities of parts needed to make a single unit of product.

An important input to the production process is the *master production schedule*, which shows the quantities and the timing of goods needed to meet quantities required for anticipated sales. The marketing department's sales projections, combined with desired inventory levels, are inputs to the production order, which authorizes the manufacture of goods and dictates the production schedule. Tracking labor time is important to a job costing system because one employee may work on many jobs and one job might require the work of many employees. An input to a job costing system is the *job time card*. This card shows the distribution of labor costs to specific jobs or production orders. Each worker completes a job time card (usually daily or weekly), detailing the hours worked on specific operations and jobs.

Typically, large and medium-size firms use enterprise resource planning (ERP) systems to collect essential data about their production operations so that they can better manage these processes. ERPs are multimodule software packages backed by large databases that help a manufacturer effectively track, monitor, and manage product planning, parts purchasing, maintaining inventories, interacting with suppliers, providing customer service, and tracking orders. We discuss ERP software in more depth in Chapter 15.

In conjunction with ERPs, manufacturers have often replaced manual data entry with automated technologies such as bar code readers, radio frequency (RF) technology, RFIDs, handheld devices, GPS locators, and other advanced technologies. These input technologies can be used individually or combined in innovative ways to significantly reduce input errors (compared to human data entry) and support fast, accurate, real-time production and data collection.

Case-in-Point 8.6   Mail-order fulfillment of drug prescriptions is a booming business for the U.S. Veteran's Administration, CVS, Kaiser Permanente, and others. When mail-order prescription centers first started, a worker would stand next to a printer, wait for a label to be printed, wrap the label around the bottle, and put it in a box. The box traveled to the next worker who read the label, found the correct pill-counter station, held the bottle under the counter as the bottle filled, replaced the lid on the bottle and sent the prescription down the line for final packing. It took 20–30 people to complete the operation. Now, a computer system, using plastic transport carriers (called "pucks") with RFID tags in the base, automates this entire process. The prescription and the puck are linked in the system and travel along the conveyor automatically, eliminating the need for human intervention until the prescription is ready to be placed in the mailing envelope.[6]

Other technologies are being combined in innovative ways to improve management's ability to track and monitor production. For example, United Parcel Service (UPS) uses combinations of technology to manage the efficiency of their deliveries and control costs.

Case-in-Point 8.7   UPS deployed a new fleet tracking system in 2010. The system combines GPS technology, telematics, and Bluetooth technology to record data about trucks. The system analyzes information such as the number of times a truck is put into reverse, the number of minutes a truck idles, whether or not the driver wears a seatbelt, and over 200 other pieces of information. Using this information, UPS has already found methods for reducing fuel usage by over 1.4 million gallons per year.[7]

Outputs of the Production Process

Examples of output reports for the production process include materials price lists, periodic usage reports, inventory reconciliation reports, detailed inventory status reports, production cost reports, and manufacturing status reports. The *materials price list* shows the prices charged for raw materials. The purchasing department updates this list. Cost accountants use price lists to determine the standard costs needed to budget production costs. *Periodic usage reports* show how various production departments use raw materials.

---

[6] http://www.intermec.com/eprise/main/Intermec/Content/Technology/DataCapture/DataCapture?section=casestudies
[7] http://www.automotive-fleet.com/Article/Story/2010/07/GREEN-FLEET-Telematics-Sensor-Equipped-Trucks-Help-UPS-Control-Costs.aspx

Managers scrutinize these reports to detect waste by comparing raw material usage to output (finished goods) produced.

A company using a perpetual inventory system issues an inventory reconciliation report. When auditors take a physical inventory, the accounting subsystem compares the physical inventory results with book balances and notes discrepancies on this *inventory reconciliation report.* Another report important for inventory control purposes is the periodic detailed *inventory status report.* This report allows purchasing and production managers to monitor inventory levels.

Cost accountants use *production cost reports* to calculate budget variances. Some manufacturing organizations use standard costing systems that allow them to compare standard costs with actual costs and compute variances for materials, labor, and overhead. The production cost report details the actual costs for each production operation, each cost element, and/or each separate job. *Manufacturing status reports* provide managers with information about the status of various jobs. Because manufacturing a product usually requires coordination of many operations, it is important to report on production status regularly.

Of course, as more companies move to lean production and manufacturing methods, some of these production reports will be replaced with value stream management metrics that may be more useful for decision making.

THE FINANCING PROCESS

The **financing process** describes how a company acquires and uses financial resources such as cash, other liquid assets, and investments. Cash and liquid assets are an organization's working capital. The financing process interfaces with the revenue, purchasing, fixed asset, and human resource processes. Much of the capital available in an organization comes from sales revenue and is used to pay expenses and personnel and to buy fixed assets.

Besides obtaining financial resources through the sales of goods and services, most organizations also acquire funds by borrowing cash or selling ownership shares. The financing process includes managing these activities. Figure 8-9 is a data flow representation of the financing process.

Objectives of the Financing Process

The financing process has a number of objectives. These include managing cash effectively, minimizing the cost of capital, investing for maximum returns, and projecting cash flows. Effective cash management requires collecting cash as soon as possible and spending it carefully. To collect cash quickly, an organization's AIS can provide useful information about how quickly customers pay their bills. An AIS can also show trends in cash collections.

Organizations can use **lock-box systems** to reduce the float period during which checks clear the bank. A lock-box system is an effective cash management tool because banks typically require several days, and sometimes a full week, to provide an organization with credit for out-of-state checks. With a lock-box system, a company directs its customers to mail their checks on account to a lock-box in their home state. A local bank collects the checks in the lock-box, clears the checks, sends the customer payment data in an electronic format, and deposits the cash into the company's account. In this way, cash is available for use more quickly. Figure 8-10 identifies additional benefits that companies might realize by using a lock-box system.

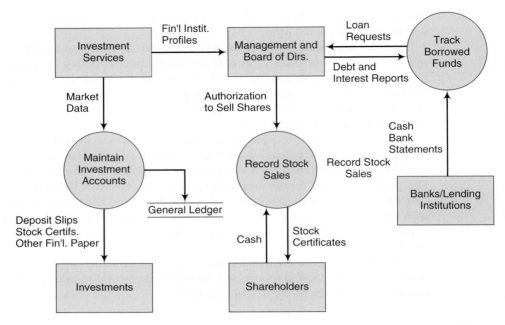

FIGURE 8-9 A data flow diagram of the financing process. This data flow diagram does not include cash management related to sales revenue, purchases, payroll, or fixed assets.

Electronic funds transfer (EFT), or electronic payment, is another cash management technique that is very common. Using EFT, business organizations eliminate paper documents and instead transfer funds electronically. Similarly, most companies today pay their employees electronically by directly depositing the funds to each employee's bank account directly rather than issuing a paper check.

Managing cash on the expenditure side means paying cash as bills come due and taking advantage of favorable cash discounts. While an organization wants to make sure there is cash available for timely payments to vendors and employees, it is also possible to have too much cash on hand. Idle cash is an unproductive asset, and short-term investments often earn less return than long-term investments. Effective cash management means cash balances are not unreasonably high and managers invest excess cash wisely. Managers in

---

Benefits of a Lock-Box System

- Better-managed large-volume deposit customers
- Capture market share with lock-box services
- Process any coupon payment format
- Reduce operating costs
- Increase efficiencies
- Cross-selling opportunities through daily access

- Online home page marketing capabilities
- Flexible implementation options
- Archive all check payment information online
- Research images for all lock-box transactions
- Capture greater share of wallet

FIGURE 8-10 Additional benefits firms may realize by using a lock-box system. Source: Web site for ImageWay® Payment Processing.

large companies monitor excess cash and invest it for very short time periods, sometimes less than a day.

Minimizing the cost of capital (i.e., the cost of obtaining financial resources) requires management to decide how much cash to borrow and how many shares of ownership (stock) to sell. Borrowed funds require interest payments. While businesses do not pay interest to shareholders, they do pay dividends. Financial managers frequently use **financial planning models** to help them select an optimal strategy for acquiring and investing financial resources. These models require an information system that can make complex calculations and consider alternative investment, borrowing, and equity (sales of stock) strategies.

A final objective of the financing process is to project cash flows. An output of the revenue process is a cash receipts forecast, and the purchasing and human resource processes contribute to a forecast of cash disbursements. The financing process makes use of these forecasts to invest excess funds and determine debt and equity strategies. The AIS for the financing process contributes to cash flow predictions through estimates of interest and dividend payments and receipts. Figure 8-11 summarizes the objectives, inputs, and outputs of this process.

Inputs to the Financing Process

Many inputs to the financing process originate outside an organization. Externally generated data or source documents might include remittance advices, deposit slips, checks, bank statements, stock market data, interest data, and data about financial institutions. Chapter 7 explained that a *remittance advice* accompanies a customer's payment on account. Banks provide *deposit slips* to document account deposits. For example, you receive a deposit slip when you make a cash deposit to your account through an automated teller machine and a credit slip when you purchase gasoline with your debit card.

Regardless of whether companies transfer funds electronically or receive/issue paper checks, accountants use the company's *bank statement* to reconcile any account discrepancies and as proof of payment. Accountants use bank statements to reconcile the cash account balance in the company's ledger against the cash balance in the bank account.

Financing Process

Objectives

Effective cash management
Cost of capital optimization
Earn maximum return on investments
Project cash flows

Inputs (Source documents)	Outputs (Reports)
• Remittance advices	• Financial statement information
• Deposit slips	• Cash budget
• Checks	• Investment reports
• Bank statements	• Debt and interest reports
• Stock market data	• Financial ratios
• Interest data	• Financial planning model reports
• Financial institution profiles	

FIGURE 8-11 Objectives, inputs, and outputs associated with the financing process.

Discrepancies between these two accounts arise from outstanding checks, deposits in transit, and various other transactions. Sometimes, of course, discrepancies are due to errors or even fraud. Because cash is a company's most liquid asset, AISs use control procedures to help protect against misappropriations.

Outputs of the Financing Process

Like all other business processes, the financing process provides general ledger information to help an AIS produce periodic financial statements. Examples include interest revenue and expense, dividend revenue and expense reports, and summaries of cash collections and disbursements. It also provides information about balances in debt, equity, and investment accounts. Besides providing general ledger information, the financing process of an AIS produces a *cash budget* showing projected cash flows.

The AIS for the financing process can produce a variety of reports about investments and borrowings. Investment reports may show changes in investments for a period, dividends paid, and interest earned. Reports on borrowings could show new debt and retired debt for a period. These reports should list the lending institutions, interest rates charged, and payments of principal and/or interest for the period.

Managers perform *ratio analyses* to manage an organization's capital effectively. Significant ratios, such as return on investment and debt to equity, help management make decisions regarding investment and borrowing strategies. A company's financial planning model calculates and reports these ratios. The planning model also prepares recommendations regarding the appropriate mix of debt versus equity financing, and short- versus long-range investments. Figure 8-12 is a sample systems flowchart for the financing process.

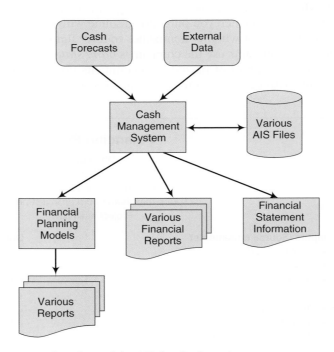

FIGURE 8-12 Systems flowchart of the AIS for the financing process.

BUSINESS PROCESSES IN SPECIAL INDUSTRIES

The term **vertical market** refers to markets or industries that are distinct in terms of the services they provide or the goods they produce. When you think about it, most organizations fit into a vertical market category. For example, an accounting firm is a professional service organization while a grocery store is in the retail industry. However, large conglomerates may operate in several different vertical markets—for instance, many large manufacturers have branched out to also provide professional and financial services. The same is true of retail firms. Consider, for example, Sears, Roebuck and Co. While still known primarily as a retailer, a large share of the company's profit comes from providing consumer credit.

Vertical markets with specialized AIS-related needs include professional services; not-for-profit, health care, retail, construction, government, banking, and financial services; and hospitality. This section describes a few of these types of organizations in terms of their unique characteristics and AIS needs.

Professional Service Organizations

Professional service organizations are business establishments providing a special service to customers such as accounting, legal services, engineering, consulting, and architectural services. Compared with organizations that provide tangible goods (such as automobile manufacturers), professional service organizations have several unique operating characteristics: (1) no merchandise inventory, (2) emphasis on professional employees, (3) difficulty in measuring the quantity and quality of output, and (4) small size. These are common characteristics, although not every organization in this industry segment has all of them. For instance, some accounting and consulting firms are relatively large. They have hundreds of partners and international offices in cities throughout the world.

Because professional service organizations do not maintain a product inventory, they do not need an AIS that tracks inventory levels. Instead, the primary accounting information needed by professional service organizations relates to time and billing for their professional staff. **Time and billing information systems** are similar to job order costing systems—they track hours and costs associated with each job (i.e., each client) and each employee (i.e., professional staff). There are two major outputs of the time and billing system: (1) the client bill and (2) the professional staff member's record of billable hours (hours actually spent working on client business).

Figure 8-13 shows an example of a software consulting firm's client bill. The client bill may detail the number of hours worked by every professional staff member and the rate charged by each. For example, an audit client might incur charges for audit staff, supervisors or seniors, managers, and partners. An AIS multiplies the hours worked by each staff member by his or her respective billing rate to compute the total charge. Time and billing systems can also show other charges on the bill or client invoice—for example, charges for overhead and detailed charges for phone, fax, mail, support staff, and copy costs.

Billable hours are important in a professional service organization. Law firms, for example, stress the importance of accumulating an accurate accounting of the number of billable hours. Nonbillable hours are hours spent on training, marketing, and general research. While these activities are important, they do not directly generate revenue for a law firm. A time and billing system can track each staff member's hours in many ways. The increments of time recorded vary by firm. Some professional service firms record

<u>Smith & Smith Partners</u>
8888 Newbury Rd.
Glenwood, NC 00301
Office: 634/344-9845
Fax: 634/344-5468

Mr. Bob Townsend
234 Bayberry St.
Rocktown, NC 12093

Invoice #:   2309
Invoice Date: July 26, 2011
Terms: Net 15 Days
Due Date: August 26, 2011
Customer #:   12088

FOR SERVICES RENDERED

Work Type	Date	Description	Employee	Time
Chargeable	3/17/11	Planning	MAS	0.60
No Charge	3/19/11	Issues/Resolves	SBC	0.25
Chargeable	3/20/11	Processing Error & Corrections	MAS	0.60
			Total Hours:	**1.20**
			Not Charged Hours:	**0.25**
			Chargeable Hours:	**1.20**
			Invoice Dollar Total:	**$200.00**

FIGURE 8-13   A sample client bill for a software consulting firm.

every 15 minutes spent working on a client job. Some law firms even record time in six-minute increments. Because time is literally money, it is important to keep records that are as detailed and accurate as possible.

Automation helps professional service organizations keep accurate records of billable hours. For example, phone systems can record the amount of time spent on calls to and from clients, and the phone system can enter values directly into the time and billing system. A copy machine in which users enter client numbers for each job is another tool that helps assign copy costs to client accounts. Finally, as professional staff members rely increasingly on their computers for their work, special computer programs can automatically record the time spent on each job as the staff member logs on to different programs with client-oriented passwords.

Not-for-Profit Organizations

Not-for-profit organizations provide services for the protection and betterment of society. Examples include public schools, museums, churches, and governmental agencies. Not-for-profit organizations differ from for-profit businesses in that they (1) are usually staffed by volunteers as well as professional employees, (2) do not emphasize maximizing net income, (3) are usually not as affected by market forces as are for-profit organizations, and (4) sometimes have a political emphasis.

As with other organizations in vertical markets, not-for-profit organizations have special accounting information needs that reflect their unique characteristics. For example, public schools (such as a university) must keep records of students' schedules, grades, health records, and so on. Religious organizations, on the other hand, must track members and account for donations. The federal government (certainly the largest not-for-profit organization) must value various unique assets that are not traded in a public market. How much, for instance, is the Lincoln Memorial or Interstate 95 worth, and how would you determine the annual depreciation for these assets?

In general, it is the lack of a profit goal that most influences the special AIS needs of not-for-profit organizations. Accounting standards, such as the Financial Accounting Standards Board's Statement No. 117, Financial Statements of Not-for-Profit Organizations, now require the financial statements to more closely resemble those of profit-seeking entities. However, the internal reporting systems of not-for-profit organizations focus on funds, rather than income. Fund accounting systems show the resources available for carrying out an organization's objectives. Funds may be restricted for special purposes (e.g., funds donated to a university for student scholarships) or available for general use. To reconcile the internal and external accounting systems, an AIS of a not-for-profit institution must be able to reconcile between these two different reporting structures.

Although the effectiveness of not-for-profit organizations cannot be evaluated using profit measures, some mechanism for performance evaluation is still desirable. A frequently used mechanism is a budgetary AIS. By comparing actual performance against planned activity, the managers in not-for-profit entities can determine how well they met their goals. Many not-for-profit entities (especially governmental organizations) employ formal long-range budgetary techniques. These budgets include projections of future activity that may serve as performance measures when compared with actual data. One difficulty often encountered in not-for-profit budgetary systems is the lack of a monetary measure of performance output. Consequently, managers must often use *process measures* (i.e., nonmonetary measures) to measure performance. In a police department, for example, the process measures might be number of arrests, number of homicides, or burglary rates. Public universities might use the number of students graduating each academic year or retention rates.

A good short-range budgetary planning and controlling system is typically more important to a not-for-profit entity than to a profit-oriented company. The reason is the fixed, rather than flexible, nature of these organizations' annual budgets. In a not-for-profit organization, budgetary revisions are difficult, if not impossible, to carry out once the budget year begins. For example, at publicly financed state universities, biannual state legislators approve annual operating budgets years in advance, which cannot be changed in off years. Thus, in those not-for-profit organizations subject to fixed or static budgets, good short-range planning is necessary to obtain accurate budget projections for the coming year.

Health Care Organizations

The dollars spent on health care have made this vertical market segment the target of much controversy and concern as the United States struggles to contain health care costs. As a result, health care reform remains a very important political issue. Interestingly, the AISs associated with health care are a large part of the controversy. Paperwork has been a

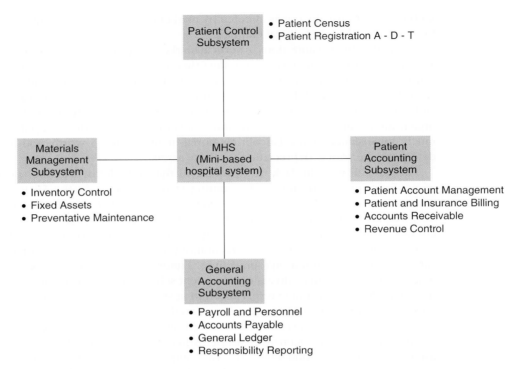

FIGURE 8-14   Mini-based hospital system.

bottleneck in delivering efficient health care, and it is also an important cost. Figure 8-14 shows examples of the many subsystems in a health care organization's AIS.

Health care entities share many characteristics with professional service organizations and not-for-profit institutions. Like these entities, health care organizations do not provide tangible goods to their customers (except for drugs). In addition, health care organizations also count professional staff as their most important asset resource. Some health care organizations are public and operate on a not-for-profit basis. Finally, output is exceptionally difficult to measure for this industry. For example, a patient may get well due to the quality of health care received, or the patient may simply get well due to his or her body's ability to overcome an illness. On the other hand, some patients die despite excellent health care and heroic measures.

The special accounting information needs of health care organizations primarily relate to **third-party billing**. Health care organizations usually do not bill their customers directly for services received. Rather, they bill insurance companies or government agencies who, in turn reimburse these service providers. Typically, bills to third-party payers (insurance companies) use standardized codes for both the medical diagnosis and the procedures performed by medical personnel. Although standardized codes promote efficiency in processing information, coding can still be difficult. For example, sometimes a diagnosis is hard to pinpoint, and medical personnel often do procedures for multiple purposes. Reimbursement from an insurance company depends on the codes used. In addition, one plan may cover a particular procedure, and another may not. Because doctors often have discretion in making a diagnosis or prescribing a procedure, the accounting staff needs to understand the nuances of the codes and general classifications. Errors in coding can be costly, and not just in terms of the processing costs associated with them. Errors can lead to a patient's inability to obtain coverage for charges and also potentially be viewed as fraud by insurance carriers.

Payment policies and filing forms may vary among third-party insurers. Government insurance (Medicare and Medicaid) presents another problem in terms of claim forms. These health care programs are state administered and each state has special filing requirements. The several hundred medical insurance carriers in the United States all use the same coding base. However, clerical personnel and AISs do not uniformly apply these codes. As previously mentioned, special AIS needs for the health care industry relate mostly to third-party billing, but other features of the industry also require special processing.

Health care AISs generally need to maintain patient information. Hospitals, doctors' offices, and nursing homes all need systems to efficiently schedule patients. Home health care services need to keep track of travel costs for employees. Information needs may be unique to very specific industry segments. Physical therapy offices, chiropractic practices, ophthalmologists, optometrists, and dental offices each have some very special information needs. For example, physical therapy offices are different from other medical offices in that a patient may spend an hour in therapy on many different kinds of equipment. An AIS might charge differently for 10 minutes spent in the whirlpool versus 10 minutes on exercise equipment. The following case describes one specialized health care software program.

Case-in-Point 8.8   Chiropractic software programs help chiropractors with many of their business processes. For example, Advantage Software includes scheduling, medical records management, accounting, insurance claims, and other features that are desirable for this industry. The software tracks patient histories, treatments, payments, appointments, and claims.[8]

BUSINESS PROCESS REENGINEERING

Business process reengineering (BPR) is about redesigning business processes that are no longer efficient or effective. BPR is a continuous process that involves the analysis of an existing process to find areas for improvement (Figure 8-15). As an example, consider an order process that begins with inquiries from a customer about the products available for sale and ends when the customer pays cash to complete a sale. In many organizations, several individuals handle the order process. Each person has responsibility for a particular function: a receptionist or secretary may handle inquiries, a salesperson follows up on product inquiries, warehouse personnel assume responsibility for filling the order, an accounts receivable clerk bills the customer, and so on. This division of responsibility can make it difficult for some organizations to fill customer orders quickly. The result: dissatisfied customers. Through BPR, inefficient processes such as the one described above are identified and then either improved or replaced with a new process.

Reengineering the order process may result in an integration of functional activities so that one specified individual handles customers from start to finish. This redesign means a customer knows who to talk to when an order is late and the customer is not passed

---

[8] http://www.advantagesoftware.com/chiropractic.html

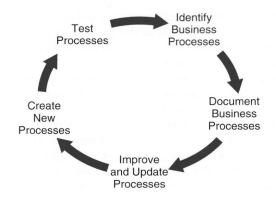

FIGURE 8-15 The business process reengineering cycle.

around from one person to another when problems occur. As we discussed earlier in this chapter, this might be an opportunity for the firm to evaluate the possibility of *value stream management*.

Case-in-Point 8.9 Approving an insurance application at Mutual Benefit Life previously included 30 steps performed by 19 people in five departments. Because paperwork moved among so many workers, an approval took from five to 25 days. When the insurance company reengineered its system, it abolished existing job descriptions and departmental boundaries. In their place, the company created the position of "case manager" and provided each manager with the authority to perform all application approval tasks. Because every case manager is in charge of the entire process associated with approving applications, files are not passed around. The results have been fewer errors, decreased costs, and a significantly reduced turnaround time for approval. A new application can now be processed in approximately four hours, with an average approval turnaround time of two to five days.

Why Reengineering Sometimes Fails

Despite the best efforts of managers, some BPR initiatives fail. There are several reasons for these failures, including unrealistic expectations, employee resistance, and lack of top management support. Some organizations that contract with consultants for BPR services expect significant improvements in their products and services and expect significantly lower costs. Successful BPR projects can result in increased profit and more satisfied customers, but often not to the extent envisioned. Employees frequently dread hearing the term "BPR" because it has become synonymous with "downsizing." It is often a challenge to get employees to embrace change, especially change that may make what they do more difficult or potentially unnecessary.

While employee resistance is often fatal to BPR efforts, management support can help overcome some of the obstacles. BPR needs champions in top management. Successful BPR efforts also need top managers who are good communicators and are willing to give employees both good and bad news. Managers who try to mask the downside of change are likely to run into difficulty. Finally, managers should consider the professional help of **change management consultants** to facilitate this complex process and overcome potential negative reactions.

AIS AT WORK
Reengineering Health Care Systems[9]

Imagine if you still went to the grocery store and the clerk at the register had to manually enter the price of every item you purchased. Imagine if airlines still used only paper tickets—the ones with the carbon paper on the back of each flight segment. Imagine . . . well, you get the point. But, isn't that still the way business is accomplished at many doctors' offices? At almost every visit, you're handed a clipboard with a form (or several forms) and must fill out the exact same information you did the last time you came for an appointment! Estimates suggest that fewer than 25 percent of all hospitals and health care providers in the United States use electronic medical records or digitized clinical systems. Even fewer physician practices use such technology.

The U.S. government plans to spend approximately $20 billion to support the expansion of medical record systems. The purpose is to give your doctors and the administrators of hospitals more information. Improving the collection, organization, accuracy, and accessibility of information should lead to improved health care and reduced costs. Imagine, for example, that your personal physician has prescribed a medication that cannot be taken with many other common medications because of dangerous interactions. If you are admitted to the emergency room as a result of an accident, high-quality medical records will prevent emergency room doctors from giving you medication that will interact with your current prescription. One study estimated that over 100,000 people in the United States die each year because of preventable medical errors that digital medical records can help eliminate. For example, if a particular drug is pulled off the market, a doctor could quickly and easily identify the patients who need to be notified. These are very tangible benefits that result from reengineering medical records!

SUMMARY

✓ This chapter discusses three additional business processes: resource management, production, and financing.

✓ The resource management process includes two areas of interest: human resource management and fixed asset management. Human resource management encompasses both the personnel activities in an organization and the payroll events.

✓ The production process includes the events related to converting raw materials into finished goods inventories.

✓ The concept of lean manufacturing is a commitment to eliminate waste throughout the organization (not just in production).

✓ A company that follows lean manufacturing concepts must identify value from the perspective of their customers, organize production (and data collection) in value streams, empower employees to make decisions, and then continually pursue excellence in all areas of the organization.

✓ To support lean manufacturing concepts, the firm must also adopt lean accounting concepts, which means measuring and evaluating results by value stream management rather than by traditional departments.

---

[9] MacKinnon, W., and M. Wasserman. 2009. Implementing electronic medical record systems. *IT Professional* 11(6): 50–53.

✓ The financing process overlaps all the other processes since it is concerned with the acquisition and use of funds needed for operations.

✓ The financing process also includes investing, borrowing, and stock-selling activities.

✓ Cash management is an important part of the financing process. Sound cash management requires companies to constantly monitor cash balances, investing any excess and covering temporary shortfalls with bank loans.

✓ There are many other business processes unique to specific industries. Each industry, or vertical market segment with specialized processes, has associated custom AIS needs.

✓ Current technology, combined with management scrutiny of business processes, provides opportunities to reengineer business processes in ways that help organizations achieve their objectives.

✓ Business process reengineering (BPR) is the practice of examining business processes and redesigning them from scratch.

✓ Many companies today are engaged in BPR as a way to improve customer service and satisfaction, increase profitability, and decrease costs.

KEY TERMS YOU SHOULD KNOW

business process reengineering (BPR)	lean accounting
change management consultants	lean production/manufacturing
cost accounting subsystems	lock-box systems
electronic funds transfer (EFT)	non-value-added waste
enterprise asset management (EAM) systems	payroll processing information system
financial planning model	process costing information systems
financing process	production process
fixed asset management (FAM)	third-party billing
human resource (HR) management	time and billing information systems
job costing information systems	value stream management
just-in-time (JIT) inventory	vertical markets

DISCUSSION QUESTIONS

8-1. The resource management process includes events associated with both personnel and payroll functions. Describe four data items that could be used by both functions. Describe two data items for each function that would not necessarily be needed by the other (e.g., spouse name for personnel but not payroll).

8-2. Why are accounting transactions associated with payroll processing so repetitive in nature? Why do some companies choose to have payroll processed by external service companies rather than do it themselves?

8-3. In this chapter, we discussed many data inputs to an organization's production process. What are the specific data items to input to a system when adding a new raw materials inventory item? What specific data items need to be input when a worker records time spent on the production line?

8-4. What nonfinancial information would be important for an AIS to capture about a manufacturing firm's production process?

8-5. What are the basic concepts of lean manufacturing? What concepts are the root of lean production and lean manufacturing?

8-6. Find an example of a firm that is using lean manufacturing concepts. Has the company realized any improvements? What are they?

8-7. Can you find an example of a firm that is using lean production concepts that are supported by lean accounting? How are they doing?

8-8. Are the inputs and outputs of a production process likely to be different for a home builder than for a cement company? How?

8-9. There are many vertical market industries with special accounting information needs apart from the industries discussed in this chapter. Identify three additional vertical market industries. What are the unique characteristics of these industries that affect their AISs?

8-10. Discuss specific steps you would take as a manager to ensure that a business process reengineering effort is successful.

PROBLEMS

8-11. Choose an industry described in this chapter and find out what vertical market accounting software is available for that industry. You may use resources such as the library, trade associations, interviews with organizations within the industry, or interviews with software consultants.

8-12. Literally thousands of business process management (BPM) solutions are available to help managers accomplish tasks in a more effective, efficient manner. Assume that you work in a payroll processing function and your supervisor asked you to select a BPM solution for your company. Which BPM software would you select and why? Identify the vendor, the name of the software package, and several of the features that you thought would be most beneficial to your company.

8-13. Now, assume that you work in the internal audit function at a company that is considering a software package to help automate the process of complying with the requirements of the Sarbanes-Oxley Act of 2002. Which BPM software would you select and why? Identify the vendor, the name of the software package, and several of the features that you thought would be most beneficial to your company.

8-14. Assume that you started your own law practice 10 years ago, specializing in estate planning, and you currently employ five attorneys, two legal assistants, one legal secretary, and a bookkeeper/receptionist. The firm has always used a manual accounting system, which includes procedures for time and billing. How could an automated time and billing system help your firm? Search the Internet for a specific technology to automatically capture a professional employee's time spent on a particular client engagement. What is the name of the software package and what are the primary features of this BPM software?

CASE STUDIES

Hammaker Manufacturing I (AIS for New Manufacturing Firm)

Dick Hammaker has been fascinated with Corvette cars, especially convertibles, since he was a teenager. Dick grew up in Michigan and worked part-time through his high school and college years at a car manufacturer, so he knew the business well. Not surprisingly, when he graduated from college he bought his first car, a used Corvette convertible, and became a member of the local Corvette Club of America.

As an accounting graduate, Hammaker was hired by one of the large automobile manufacturers in Michigan and was selected for the "fast-track" management training program. After five years, Hammaker decided to leave Michigan and start a specialty parts manufacturing company strictly for Corvettes. Before he even left Michigan, a potential customer contacted him—the repair shop was replacing the black convertible top on a 1967 Corvette that the owner was going to sell for $76,995!

Hammaker decided to locate his company, Hammaker Manufacturing Co. (HMC), in Northern Virginia since this is the site of the oldest Corvette Club of America. Dick knows he will need the appropriate technology to support his company, so he decided to focus on this aspect of his company prior to starting any production activities. His first action was to hire a CFO (Denise Charbonet) who could work with Lloyd Rowland (a software consultant) to determine the inputs and outputs needed for an AIS for the new company. Of particular concern is the data the AIS will need to collect regarding inventories. As Dick, Denise, and Lloyd know, inventory management will be a key factor for the success of HMC since Corvette cars are unique—parts are needed for cars from the 1960s!

Dick believes that an AIS will give him the data and information needed for good decision making—especially to manage inventory investments. HMC's customers are primarily Corvette specialty repair shops, and they typically demand parts only as needed, but exactly when needed. Inventory can be very costly for HMC if they must stockpile many specialty parts to be able to quickly meet customer orders.

Hammaker knows from his work experience in Michigan that there are a number of costs associated with holding inventories (warehousing, obsolescence, and insurance costs)—money that could be put to better use elsewhere. Dick knows that he will need to buy raw materials from suppliers and hold raw materials inventories plus make-to-stock parts, or customers will find other parts suppliers.

Denise and Lloyd meet to discuss the issues. They decide that they need to do two things. First, they need to determine what AIS software package would be best for the new company, one that is particularly focused on inventory control (or one with an inventory control module that would be well-suited for HMC). Second, they need to decide what data elements they need to capture about each inventory item to optimize inventory management and control. Denise notes that while some inventory descriptors are easy to determine, such as item number, description, and cost, others are more difficult. For instance, inventory on hand and inventory available for sale could be two different data items since some of the inventory on hand might be committed but not yet shipped.

Requirements

1. Explain how an AIS could help HMC optimize inventory management and control.
2. What data elements should HMC include in the new AIS to describe each inventory item?

Hammaker Manufacturing II (Business Process Reengineering or Outsourcing)

Implementation of a new AIS went smoothly, for the most part. It is 15 years later, and now HMC is interested in mapping a variety of their business processes to determine whether improvements can be made and whether business process reengineering should be considered. Hammaker asked Denise to work with the consulting firm analysts to determine the feasibility of these two options and also to consider the possibility of outsourcing. Denise does not know much about outsourcing and she is not sure which process (or processes) Dick might want to outsource.

Denise discovers that a number of developing countries have the capacity and the labor to make the parts that HMC is currently producing and at much cheaper prices. Further, Denise discovers that many companies are outsourcing and offshoring a number of processes that used to be accomplished by company employees. Denise makes a note to herself to check the number of employees in each of the following departments: HR, computer support, accounting, and janitorial services. She also decides to query the AIS to determine what performance measures are available to assess the efficiency and effectiveness of each of these departments. Denise places a call to Lloyd Rowland to discuss this issue with him.

HMC is not unionized, but Denise ponders the legal and social issues associated with outsourcing jobs, since many of the 365 employees at Hammaker Manufacturing have been with the company for well over a decade.

Requirements

1. Identify tools that would help Denise and Rowland map HMC's business processes. Which processes do you think they should work on first? Why those processes?

2. Identify at least six reasons why companies choose to outsource a business process. Which of these reasons might Dick use to make his decision to outsource or to attempt BPR?

3. Is producing automotive parts a "core" business process for HMC? Explain.

4. Do companies ever outsource "core" business processes? Search the Internet to see if you can find an example of a company or an industry that outsources core business processes. What are they? Why are they doing this?

5. What social or legal issues might Denise consider? Be specific and explain why these issues might be important to HMC.

6. What would you recommend if you were one of the analysts at the consulting firm? Explain.

Hammaker Manufacturing III (Lean Production/Lean Accounting)

HMC continues to be profitable. Although Denise and Lloyd Rowland mapped several business processes five years ago to determine whether HMC should work on process improvements or consider business process reengineering, they never really finished that effort nor did HMC decide whether to outsource any processes. Hammaker still thinks that HMC could be more efficient and more profitable, but he's not really sure how the company can achieve this next level of excellence.

About a year ago, Denise started reading books and trade journals on the topics of business strategy, lean production, and lean manufacturing. So when Dick approached her regarding his intent to improve the company, she began to share with him some of the insights she had gained over the past year on business strategy and how their current AIS might not be capturing the most useful metrics for optimal decision making. Denise mentioned that the next Lean Accounting Summit will be in September and suggested that she and her three financial analysts go to the four day conference to gain a better understanding of lean production and accounting concepts to determine how they might be able to better support HMC and Dick's goal of improving the company.

Requirements

1. If Dick decided to adopt the business strategy of lean production, what changes might he and his managers consider?

2. Explain how HMC might benefit from implementing lean production/manufacturing concepts.

3. Why would it be important for Denise and her financial analysts to attend the Lean Accounting Summit? What benefits would you expect them to acquire from this conference that would be useful at HMC?

Chapter 9

Introduction to Internal Control Systems

INTRODUCTION

Protecting the assets of an organization has always been an important responsibility of management. However, the incredible advancements in IT as well as the pervasive use of IT across organizations of all sizes have dramatically changed how managers establish and monitor internal controls. Indeed, the pervasiveness of IT also has a profound impact on internal and external auditors and how they assess the strength of the internal control environment. Protecting such assets requires organizations to develop and implement an effective internal control system—a system that can also perform other functions such as helping ensure reliable data processing and promoting operational efficiency in an organization.

This chapter and the next cover the topic of internal controls—that is, the controls established to protect the assets of an organization. This chapter defines internal control, corporate governance, and IT governance within organizations. We also identify the components of an internal control system, the importance of enterprise risk management as it relates to internal controls, as well as the different types of internal controls. Finally, we discuss methods used in organizations to evaluate controls and to determine which control procedures are cost-effective.

Internal Control Defined

Internal control describes the policies, plans, and procedures implemented by the management of an organization to protect its assets, to ensure accuracy and completeness of its financial information, and to meet its business objectives. Usually the people involved in this effort are the entity's board of directors, the management, and other key personnel in the firm. The reason this is important is that these individuals want reasonable assurance that the goals and objectives of the organization can be achieved (i.e., effectiveness and efficiency of operations, reliability of financial reporting, protection of assets, and compliance with applicable laws and regulations).[1] Figure 9-1 identifies key laws, professional guidance, and reports that focus on internal controls.

In 2001, the AICPA issued Statement on Auditing Standards **(SAS) No. 94**, "The Effect of Information Technology on the Auditor's Consideration of Internal Control in a Financial Statement Audit." This SAS cautions external auditors that the way firms use IT might impact any of the five internal control components, which we discuss later in this chapter. That is, auditors must realize that internal controls are both manual and automated, and therefore, auditors might need to adopt new testing strategies to obtain sufficient evidence that an organization's controls are effective. Because of the complexity of IT environments,

---

[1] http://www.coso.org

Date	Act/Report	Significant Provisions Pertaining to Internal Controls
1977	Foreign Corrupt Practices Act	• Requires publicly owned companies to implement internal control systems; Only applies to publicly owned corporations registered under Section 12 of the 1934 Securities and Exchange Act
1977	Treadway Commission Report	• Recommends development of common definition for internal control, guidance for judging effectiveness of internal control, methods to improve internal controls
1992	Committee of Sponsoring Organizations (COSO) Report	• Title: *Internal Control—Integrated Framework*; Defines internal control and describes its components; Presents criteria to evaluate internal control systems; Provides guidance for public reporting on internal controls; Offers materials to evaluate internal control system
1992	COBIT—Control Objectives for Business and IT	• A framework for IT management; Provides managers, auditors, and IT users a set of generally accepted measures, indicators, processes, best practices to maximize benefits of IT and develop appropriate IT governance and control
2001	SAS No. 94	• Guidance to auditors about information technology on internal controls; Describes benefits/risks of IT to internal controls and how IT affects the components of internal controls
2002	Sarbanes-Oxley Act, Section 404	• Requires publicly traded companies to issue "internal control report" that states management is responsible for establishing and maintaining adequate internal control structure; Management must annually assess effectiveness of internal controls; Independent auditor for firm must attest to/report on managements' assessment
2004	Committee of Sponsoring Organizations (COSO) Report	• Focuses on enterprise risk management; Includes five components of COSO 1992 Report; Adds three components: objective setting, event identification, risk response
2005	COBIT, Ver. 4.0	• Includes 34 high-level objectives that cover 215 control objectives categorized in four domains: Plan and Organize, Acquire and Implement, Deliver and Support, and Monitor and Evaluate
2006	SAS No. 112	• Establishes standards/provides guidance to auditors of nonpublic entities on communicating matters related to entity's internal control over financial reporting observed during a financial statement audit; auditor must have working knowledge of COSO framework
2007	COBIT, Ver. 4.1	• Better definitions of core concepts; Improved control objectives; Application controls reworked; Business and IT goals improved
2009	COSO Guidance on Monitoring	• Identifies three broad principles for monitoring: establish baseline, design and execute procedures, assess and report results
2010	Report on ERM (Commissioned by COSO)	• Survey of 460 senior executives: state of ERM relatively immature; noted dissatisfaction with oversight of ERM; limited processes for identifying and tracking risks; 2004 COSO Report used by most organizations

FIGURE 9-1 Background information on internal controls.

auditors will most likely need to use computer-assisted auditing techniques (CAATs) to test the automated controls in an organization. We discuss these techniques in depth in Chapter 12.

An important piece of legislation with respect to internal controls is the **Sarbanes-Oxley Act of 2002**. One key provision of this law is **Section 404**, which reaffirms that management is responsible for establishing and maintaining an adequate internal control structure. At the end of each fiscal year, corporate officers must attest to the effectiveness and completeness of the internal control structure, thus making them personally liable for this structure within the firm. We cover the Sarbanes-Oxley Act in more depth in Chapter 12.

Internal Control System

An **internal control system** consists of the various methods and measures designed into and implemented within an organization to achieve the following four objectives: (1) safeguard assets, (2) check the accuracy and reliability of accounting data, (3) promote operational efficiency, and (4) enforce prescribed managerial policies. An organization that achieves these four objectives is typically one with good **corporate governance**. This means managing an organization in a fair, transparent, and accountable manner to protect the interests of all the stakeholder groups.[2] The 1992 COSO Framework is widely used by managers to organize and evaluate their corporate governance structure. This framework was developed to improve the quality of financial reporting through business ethics, effective internal controls, and corporate governance.[3]

1992 COSO REPORT

The **1992 COSO Report** is important because it established a common definition of internal control for assessing control systems, as well as determined how to improve controls. According to the report, controls can serve many important purposes, and for this reason, many businesses look at internal control systems as a solution to a variety of potential problems (such as dealing with rapidly changing economic and competitive environments, as well as shifting customer demands and priorities). According to the COSO report, an internal control system should consist of these five components: (1) the control environment, (2) risk assessment, (3) control activities, (4) information and communication, and (5) monitoring. We discuss each one below.

Control Environment

The **control environment** establishes the "tone at the top" of a company and influences the control awareness of the company's employees. It is the foundation for all the other internal control components and provides discipline and structure. There are a number of factors that are included in the control environment. First, and usually the most important, is top management's oversight, integrity, and ethical principles that guide the organization. This includes the attention and direction provided by the board of directors, as well as top management's philosophy and operating style. Equally important are the policies and procedures that management develops to assign authority and responsibility across the organization, as well as the policies for developing its employees.

The management of most large and medium-size enterprises have separate internal audit departments, whose internal auditors are responsible for operational reviews within the organization. Small enterprises usually cannot afford their own internal audit departments, but they can hire outside consultants or ask managers to test compliance with operating policies. Regular reviews are important to organizations of all sizes to ensure that top management is fully informed regarding operational effectiveness and efficiency.

Case-in-Point 9.1 A commonly used source of information on reported cases of material weaknesses for publicly traded companies is Audit Analytics. One of the categories in this

---

[2] http://www.us.kpmg.com/microsite/Attachments/corp_govern_newstrat.pdf
[3] http://www.coso.org

database is "senior management, tone, or reliability." A recent study of this particular category shows that audit firms issued adverse internal control opinions to 93 public companies because of weaknesses in tone at the top.[4]

Risk Assessment

It is not possible or even desirable to install controls for every possible risk or threat. The purpose of **risk assessment** is to identify organizational risks, analyze their potential in terms of costs and likelihood of occurrence, and implement only those controls whose projected benefits outweigh their costs. A general rule is the more liquid an asset, the greater the risk of its misappropriation. To compensate for this increased risk, stronger controls are required. The COSO report recommends the use of a *cost-benefit analysis* (discussed and illustrated later in this chapter) to determine whether the cost to implement a specific control procedure is beneficial enough to spend the money.

Control Activities

These are the policies and procedures that the management of a company develops to help protect all of the different assets of the firm, based on a careful risk assessment. Control activities include a wide variety of activities throughout the firm and are typically a combination of manual and automated controls. Some examples of these activities are approvals, authorizations, verifications, reconciliations, reviews of operating performance, and segregation of duties. Through properly designed and implemented control activities, management will have more confidence that assets are being safeguarded and that the accounting data processed by the accounting system are reliable.

Information and Communication

Managers must inform employees about their roles and responsibilities pertaining to internal control. This might include giving them documents such as *policies and procedures manuals* (discussed later) or posting memoranda on the company's intranet. This could also include training sessions for entry-level personnel and then annual refresher training for continuing employees. Regardless of the method, all employees need to understand how important their work is, how it relates to the work of other employees in the firm, and how that relates to strong internal controls. It is equally important that management understand the importance of keeping good working relationships between all layers of management so that employees feel safe communicating any possible problems they may find. When this is the case, employees at all levels can actually enhance the effectiveness of good internal controls. Also, they will be much more likely to point out any problems they may detect, and corrective action can be initiated.

Case-in-Point 9.2 Whistle-blowing systems help employees feel safe communicating problems or suspected wrongdoing to management. However, some employees struggle with reporting problems because they are not sure how to report what they know or fear possible consequences of doing so. One solution to this problem is to outsource the whistle-blower

---

[4] Hermanson, D., D. Ivancevich, and S. Ivancevich. 2008. Tone at the top. *Internal Auditor* (November): 39–45.

system. A recent survey of Chief Audit Executives reports that 60 percent of the organizations in the survey had outsourced their reporting systems.[5]

Monitoring

The evaluation of internal controls should be an ongoing process. Managers at various levels in the organization must evaluate the design and operation of controls and then initiate corrective action when specific controls are not functioning properly. This could include daily observations and scrutiny, or management might prefer regularly scheduled evaluations. The scope and frequency of evaluations depend, to a large extent, on management's assessment of the risks the firm faces.

Status of 1992 COSO Report

In recognition of the increasingly complex business environment, COSO commissioned PwC to update the 1992 COSO Framework. The project is not intended to change how internal controls are designed, assessed, or managed. Instead, the intent of the update effort is to provide more comprehensive and relevant conceptual guidance and practical examples. For example, COSO said they need to refine certain concepts and guidance in the 1992 framework to reflect the evolution of the operating environment as well as the changed expectations of regulators and other stakeholders. COSO also intends to improve guidance on operations and compliance beyond financial reporting. The revised framework will most likely be published in 2012.[6]

UPDATES ON RISK ASSESSMENT

2004 Enterprise Risk Management Framework

COSO determined that additional guidance should be published to help organizations do a more comprehensive assessment of risk. The result was the 2004 COSO *Enterprise Risk Management—Integrated Framework*, which focuses on **enterprise risk management (ERM)** and builds upon the 1992 COSO *Internal Control—Integrated Framework* (ICIF). The ERM Framework (Figure 9-2) includes the five components of ICIF (control environment, risk assessment, control activities, information and communication, and monitoring) and adds three additional components: objective setting, event identification, and risk response.

Objective Setting.   ERM offers management a process for setting objectives for the firm—that is, the purposes or goals the firm hopes to achieve. ERM helps an organization determine if the objectives are aligned with the organizational strategy and that goals are consistent with the level of risk the organization is willing to take. An enterprise's objectives are viewed from four perspectives: (1) strategic: the high-level goals and the mission of the firm; (2) operations: the day-to-day efficiency, performance, and profitability of the firm; (3) reporting: the internal and external reporting of the firm; and (4) compliance: with laws and regulations.

---

[5] Baker, N. 2008. See no evil, hear no evil, speak no evil. *Internal Auditor* (April): 39–43.

[6] http://www.complianceweek.com/coso-commissions-update-for-internal-control-framework/article/192017/

RISK CUBE

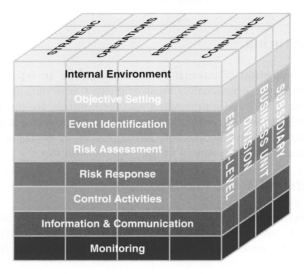

FIGURE 9-2 2004 COSO Enterprise Risk Management—Integrated Framework. Source: COSO Enterprise.

Event Identification and Risk Response.

Organizations must deal with a variety of uncertainties because many events are beyond management control. Examples include natural disasters, wars, unexpected actions of competitors, and changing conditions in the marketplace. However, it is critical for management to identify these external risks as quickly as possible and then consider internal and external factors regarding each event that might affect its strategy and achievement of objectives. Depending on the type or nature of events, management might be able to group some of them together and begin to detect trends that may help with risk assessment.

> *Case-in-Point 9.3* The responsibility of the Director of the Arkansas Department of Finance and Administration (DFA) is to ensure that state agencies operate uniformly and efficiently. To help the Director achieve these DFA objectives, each state agency is required to perform a risk assessment once every two years and to complete a "Risk Assessment and Control Activities Worksheet." This worksheet (Figure 9-3) helps department managers across the state to think about their operations through a risk assessment lens.[7]

The objective of risk assessment is to manage and control risk by identifing threats, analyzing the risks, and implementing cost-effective countermeasures to avoid, mitigate, or transfer the risks to a third party (through insurance programs or outsourcing). As they identify and categorize risks, managers will be in a better position to determine the probable effects on the organization. They can then formulate and evaluate possible response options for the organization. In developing options, managers need to consider the level of risk they are willing to assume, as well as the trade-offs between costs and benefits of each choice. A number of computerized risk assessment software tools already exist to help managers with this task.

---

[7] http://www.arkansas.gov/dfa/accounting/acc_ia_risk.html

Risk Assessment and Control Activities Worksheet

Department: _____

Activity: _____

Prepared By: _____

Date Prepared: _____

| Goals & Objectives | Risk Assessment | | | Actions to Manage Risks/ Control Activities |
| | Risks | Significance/Impact | Likelihood | |
(1)	(2)	(3)	(4)	(5)

1   List all operations, financial reporting and compliance objectives associated with the activity. Goals should be clearly defined, measurable and attainable.

2   List all identified risks to the achievement of each goal and objective. Consider both internal and external risk factors. For each goal and objective, several different risks can be identified.

3   For each risk, estimate the potential impact on operations, financial reporting or compliance with laws and regulations, assuming that the risk occurs. Consider both quantitative and qualitative costs. Use **Large**, **Moderate** or **Small**.

4   For each risk, assess the likelihood of the risk occurring. Use **probable**, **reasonably possible**, or **remote**. Alternatively use **High**, **Medium** of **Low**.

5   For each risk with large or moderate impact and probable (high) or reasonable (medium) likelihood of occurrence, list both the actions to mitigate the risk to an acceptable level and the control activities that help ensure that those actions are carried out properly and in a timely manner. If no action is present to manage the risk and/or no control activity is present, an action plan to address the risk and an associated timeline should be included.

FIGURE 9-3   An example of a risk assessment and control activities worksheet. Source: http://www.arkansas.gov/dfa/accounting/acc_ia_risk.html.

Case-in-Point 9.4 Managers need to ask themselves about the possible impact of certain risks—would it be minimal, significant, serious, or catastrophic? RiskPAC is an example of a business risk software system that organizations can use to detect and eliminate vulnerabilities in information systems and data security. CPACS, the company that developed RiskPAC, defines "risk assessment" as identification of the major risks and threats to which an organization's reputation, business processes, functions, and assets are exposed. RiskPAC helps organizations determine the possibility that a harmful incident will occur (very likely, possible, probable, or very unlikely).[8]

COSO's 2010 Report on ERM[9]

To better understand the use of, consideration of, or reliance on the COSO ERM Framework, COSO decided to commission North Carolina State University to conduct a survey in the summer of 2010. The survey, called the Enterprise Risk Management Initiative, targeted individuals who are involved in leading ERM related processes—or individuals who are knowledgeable about those efforts—within their organization. Responses were collected from 460 individuals who answered questions that addressed both risk management practices and perceptions about the strengths and weaknesses of COSO's ERM Framework. Several of the key findings are the following:

1. Most believe that the ERM Framework is theoretically sound and clearly describes key elements of a robust ERM process.
2. Almost 65 percent of respondents were fairly familiar or very familiar with COSO's ERM Framework.
3. In over half of the organizations, the Board of Directors had not formally assigned risk oversight responsibilities to one of its subcommittees.
4. The state of ERM appears to be relatively immature.

EXAMPLES OF CONTROL ACTIVITIES

Because each organization's accounting system is unique, there are no standardized control policies and procedures that will work for every company. This means that each organization designs and implements specific controls based on its particular needs. However, certain control activities are common to every organization's internal control system. The ones that we will examine here are (1) a good audit trail, (2) sound personnel policies and practices, (3) separation of duties, (4) physical protection of assets, (5) reviews of operating performance, and (6) timely performance reports. We describe each of these in more detail below.

Good Audit Trail

The basic inputs to an AIS are usually business transactions that it records and measures monetarily. A good audit trail enables auditors to follow the path of the data from the initial source documents (for instance, a sales invoice) to the final disposition of the data on a

---

[8] http://www.cpacsweb.com/riskpac.html (business continuity planning software products).
[9] http://www.coso.org/documents/COSOSurveyReportFULL-Web-R6FINALforWEBPOSTING111710.pdf

report. In addition, managers and auditors can trace data from transactions on reports (such as expenses on an income statement) back to the source documents. In both instances, an auditor can verify the accuracy of recorded business transactions. Without a good audit trail, errors and irregularities are more likely to happen and not be detected.

To establish its audit trail, a company needs a *policies and procedures manual* that includes the following items:

- A chart of accounts that describes the purpose of each general ledger account so that employees enter the debits and credits of accounting transactions in the correct accounts.

- A complete description of the types of source documents individuals must use to record accounting transactions. Also, include the correct procedures to prepare and approve the data for these documents.

- A comprehensive description of the authority and responsibility assigned to each individual—for example, the person who sets credit limits for customers.

Sound Personnel Policies and Procedures

Employees at every level of a company are a very important part of the company's system of internal control. This is becoming increasingly obvious as managers downsize and right-size their organizations to streamline operations and cut costs. Consequently, there are fewer employees, and these employees have more responsibility and oversight than in the past. The obvious result is that the opportunity for misappropriation is greater than before.

In addition, the capabilities of a company's employees directly affects the quality of the goods and services provided by the company. In general, competent and honest employees are more likely to help create value for an organization. Employees work with organizational assets (e.g., handling cash, producing products, acquiring and issuing inventory, and using equipment). Competent and honest employees, coupled with fair and equitable personnel policies, lead to efficient use of the company's assets. Most organizations post their personnel policies and procedures on their Web site so that they are easily accessible to all employees at any time.

Case-in-Point 9.5   Employees at the University of Arizona have ready access to a wealth of information regarding the university's personnel policies by searching the Human Resources Policy Manual (HRPM). The HRPM is available on the university Web site and includes policies on employment, benefits, compensation, employee relations, training and employee development, and additional university policies (e.g., conflict of interest, code of research ethics, and others).[10]

In general, little can be done to stop employees who are determined to embarrass, harm, or disrupt an organization. For example, several employees may conspire (*collude*) to embezzle cash receipts from customers. But, companies can encourage ethical behavior among employees in several ways. First, review the rules and the Code of Conduct. A number of organizations have too many "picky" rules that employees do not understand. To avoid this type of problem, managers should create rules that make a positive contribution to the productivity and effectiveness of a company and then explain the rationale for these rules to employees. Secondly, managers should always lead by example. Figure 9-4 identifies some examples of personnel policies that firms might adopt.

---

[10] http://www.hr.arizona.edu/09_rel/clsstaffmanual.php

1. Specific procedures for hiring and retaining competent employees.
2. Training programs that prepare employees to perform their organizational functions efficiently.
3. Good supervision of the employees as they are working at their jobs on a daily basis.
4. Fair and equitable guidelines for employees' salary increases and promotions.
5. Rotation of certain key employees in different jobs so that these employees become familiar with various phases of their organization's system.
6. Vacation requirement that all employees take the time off they have earned.
7. Insurance coverage on those employees who handle assets subject to theft (fidelity bond).
8. Regular reviews of employees' performances to evaluate whether they are carrying out their functions efficiently and effectively, with corrective action for those employees not performing up to company standards.

FIGURE 9-4 Examples of personnel policies that firms might adopt. Source: www.hr .arizona.edu.

All employees should be required to take their earned vacations (personnel policy 6 in Figure 9-4). This is important for two reasons. First, if employees are embezzling assets from an organization, they will not want to take a vacation—someone else will do their jobs, increasing the likelihood of detection. Second, required vacations help employees to rest, enabling them to return refreshed and ready to perform their job functions more efficiently.

For employees who handle assets susceptible to theft, such as a company's cash and inventory of merchandise, it is a good personnel policy (number 7 in Figure 9-4) to obtain some type of insurance coverage on them. Many organizations obtain **fidelity bond** coverage from an insurance company to reduce the risk of loss caused by employee theft of assets. The insurance company investigates the backgrounds of the employees that an organization wants to have bonded. When an insurance company issues one of these bonds, it assumes liability (up to a specified dollar amount) for the employee named in the bond.

Case-in-Point 9.6 Fidelity bonds are also called employee dishonesty bonds and are intended to cover your company when the unthinkable happens—you have a dishonest employee! For example, if you operate a home-cleaning service and have employees in other people's homes, an employee dishonesty bond will cover your company in case one of your employees steals from your customers.[11]

Separation of Duties

The purpose of **separation of duties** is to structure work assignments so that one employee's work serves as a check on another employee (or employees). When managers design and implement an effective internal control system, they must try to separate certain responsibilities. If possible, managers should assign the following three functions to different employees: authorizing transactions, recording transactions, and maintaining custody of assets.

---

[11] http://www.businessservicereviews.com/small-business-insurance-quotes/fidelity-bond-insurance/

Authorizing is the decision to approve transactions (e.g., a sales manager authorizing a credit sale to a customer). *Recording* includes functions such as preparing source documents, maintaining journals and ledgers, preparing reconciliations, and preparing performance reports. Finally, *custody of assets* can be either direct (such as handling cash or maintaining an inventory storeroom) or indirect, such as receiving customer checks through the mail or writing checks on a company's bank account. If two of these three functions are the responsibility of the same employee, problems can occur. We describe three real-world cases that demonstrate the importance of separating duties. Immediately following each case is a brief analysis of the problem.

Case-in-Point 9.7 The controller of a Philippine subsidiary confessed to embezzling more than $100,000 by taking advantage of currency conversions. The controller maintained two accounts—one in Philippine pesos to deposit funds collected locally and the other account in U.S. dollars so he could transfer funds from the Philippine account to the U.S. account. The auditor became suspicious when he noticed that each transfer was rounded to the nearest thousand in pesos and dollars. For example, one day the statements showed an $885,000 (pesos) transfer from the local currency account and a transfer of exactly $20,000 into the U.S. dollar account. Further investigation revealed that the controller was actually withdrawing cash from the peso account, keeping some of the money, and depositing only enough pesos in the U.S. currency account to show a transaction of exactly $20,000. Because the withdrawal and the deposit took place almost simultaneously, the U.S. controller never suspected any wrongdoing.[12]

Analysis. The control weakness here is that the controller had responsibility for both the *custody* of the cash (depositing the locally collected funds in pesos) and the *recording* of the transactions (the deposit of the funds in the local account and the transfer of funds to the U.S. account). Consequently, he had control of the money throughout the process and was able to manipulate cash transfers to embezzle small amounts of money each time and then falsify the transactions that were recorded in each of the bank accounts to conceal the embezzlement activity.

Case-in-Point 9.8 The utilities director of Newport Beach, California, was convicted of embezzling $1.2 million from the city of Newport Beach over an 11-year period. The utilities director forged invoices or easement documents that authorized payments—for example, to real or fictitious city property owners for the rights to put water lines through their land. Officials within the Finance Department gave him the checks for delivery to the property owners. The utilities director then forged signatures, endorsed the checks to himself, and deposited them in his own accounts.

Analysis. The control weakness here is that the utilities director had physical *custody* of checks for the transactions he previously *authorized.* Due to the lack of separation of duties, the director could authorize fictitious transactions and subsequently divert the related payments to his own accounts.

Case-in-Point 9.9 The executive assistant (EA) to the president of a home improvement company used a corporate credit card, gift checks, and an online payment account to embezzle $1.5 million in less than three years. The EA arranged hotel and airline reservations and coordinated activities for the sales team. She was also responsible for reviewing the corporate credit card bills and authorizing payment. The president gave her the authority to approve

---

[12] Jacka, J. 2001. Rounding up fraud. *Internal Auditor* (April): 65.

amounts up to $100,000. When the EA realized that no one ever asked to look at the charges on the corporate credit card bill, she began making personal purchases with the card.[13]

Analysis.   The control weakness here is that the EA was responsible for both *recording* the expenses and then *authorizing* payment of the bills. As a result, she quickly realized that she had nearly unlimited access to a variety of sources of funds from the company—and then found other ways to have the company pay for the things she wanted (i.e., gift checks and a PayPal account that she set up).

The *separation of duties* concept is very important in IT environments. However, the way this concept is applied in these environments is often different. In today's information systems, for example, a computer can be programmed to perform one or more of the previously mentioned functions (i.e., authorizing transactions, recording transactions, and maintaining custody of assets). Thus, the computer replaces employees in performing the function (or functions). For example, the pumps at many gas stations today are designed so that customers can insert their debit or credit cards to pay for their gas. Consequently, the computer performs all three functions: authorizes the transaction, maintains custody of the "cash" asset, and records the transaction (and produces a receipt if you want one).

Physical Protection of Assets

A vital control activity that should be part of every organization's internal control system is the physical protection of its assets. Beyond simple protection from the elements, the most common control is to establish accountability for the assets with custody documents. Three application areas for this are (1) inventory controls, (2) document controls, and (3) cash controls.

Inventory Controls.   To protect inventory, organizations keep it in a storage area accessible only to employees with custodial responsibility for the inventory asset. Similarly, when purchasing inventory from vendors, another procedure is to require that each shipment of inventory be delivered directly to the storage area. When the shipment arrives, employees prepare a *receiving report* source document. This report, as illustrated in Figure 9-5, provides documentation about each delivery, including the date received, vendor, shipper, and purchase order number. For every type of inventory item received, the receiving report shows the item number, the quantity received (based on a count), and a description.

The receiving report also includes space to identify the employee (or employees) who received, counted, and inspected the inventory items as well as space for remarks regarding the condition of the items received. By signing the receiving report, the inventory clerk (Roger Martin in Figure 9-5) formally establishes responsibility for the inventory items. Any authorized employee can request inventory items from the storage area (for instance, to replenish the shelves of the store) and is required to sign the inventory clerk's *issuance report,* which is another source document. The clerk is thereby relieved of further responsibility for these requisitioned inventory items.

Document Controls.   Certain organizational documents are themselves valuable and must therefore be protected. Examples include the corporate charter, major contracts with other companies, blank checks (the following Case-in-Point), and registration statements required by the Securities and Exchange Commission. For control purposes, many organizations keep such documents in fireproof safes or in rented storage vaults off-site.

---

[13] Sutphen, P. 2008. Stealing funds for a nest egg. *Internal Auditor* (August): 87–91.

Sarah's Sporting Goods Receiving Report		No. 7824
Vendor: Richards Supply Company		**Date Received:** March 14, 2012
Shipped via: UPS		**Purchase Order** **Number:** 4362

Item **Number**	**Quantity**	**Description**
7434	100	Spalding basketballs
7677	120	Spalding footballs
8326	300	Spalding baseballs
8687	600	Penn tennis balls

Remarks:
Container with footballs received with water damage on outside, but footballs appear to be okay.

Received by: Roger Martin	**Inspected by:** Roger Martin	**Delivered to:** Annie Taylor

FIGURE 9-5 Example of receiving report (items in boldface are preprinted).

Case-in-Point 9.10 The Finance Office in Inglewood, California, did not have adequate controls over important documents. As a result, a janitor who cleaned the Finance Office had access to blank checks that were left on someone's desk. The janitor took 34 blank checks, forged the names of city officials, and then cashed them for amounts ranging from $50,000 to $470,000.

Organizations that maintain physical control over blank checks may still be at risk of embezzlement by using a method known as a **demand draft**. If you write a check to your 12-year-old babysitter, she has all the information needed to clean out your account, since all she needs is your account number and bank routing number. Originally, demand drafts were used to purchase items over the phone (i.e., from telemarketers). Now, they're commonly used to pay monthly bills by having money debited automatically from an individual's checking account. Not surprisingly, due to the limited amount of information needed to make a demand draft, the potential for fraud is substantial. The irony of the demand draft system is that it may mean that paper checks are ultimately more risky to use than e-payments.

Case-in-Point 9.11 The Urban Age Institute, a nonprofit organization that focuses on planning new urban sustainability initiatives, received an e-mail from a would-be donor who asked for instructions on how to wire a $1,000 donation into the agency's account. Not thinking anything unusual about the request, the group sent its account numbers. The donor used this information to print $10,000 worth of checks, which the donor cashed and then used Western Union to wire the money to her new Internet boyfriend in Nigeria. The director at the Institute later discovered that the donor used the Institute's account number and bank routing number to obtain checks at Qchex.com. Fortunately, the Institute discovered the fraud and was able to close its checking account before money was withdrawn to cover the $10,000 in checks, which had already been deposited into the donor's Bank of America account.[14]

Cash Controls. Probably the most important physical safeguards are those for cash. This asset is the most susceptible to theft by employees and to human error when employees handle large amounts of it. In addition to fidelity bond coverage for employees who handle cash, companies should also (1) make the majority of cash disbursements for authorized expenditures by check rather than in cash and (2) deposit the daily cash receipts intact at the bank.

If a company has various small cash expenditures occurring during an accounting period, it is usually more efficient to pay cash for these expenditures than to write checks. For good operating efficiency, an organization should use a *petty cash fund* for small, miscellaneous expenditures. To exercise control over this fund, one employee, called the *petty cash custodian,* should have responsibility for handling petty cash transactions. This employee keeps the petty cash money in a locked box and is the only individual with access to the fund.

Cash Disbursements by Check. A good audit trail of cash disbursements is essential to avoid errors and irregularities in the handling of cash. Accordingly, most organizations use prenumbered checks to maintain accountability for both issued and unissued checks.

When paying for inventory purchases, there are two basic systems for processing vendor invoices: nonvoucher systems and voucher systems. Under a *nonvoucher system,* every approved invoice is posted to individual vendor records in the accounts payable file and then stored in an open-invoice file. When an employee writes a cash disbursement check to pay an invoice, he or she removes the invoice from the open-invoice file, marks it paid, and stores it in the paid-invoice file. Under a *voucher system,* the employee prepares a *disbursement voucher* that identifies the specific vendor, lists the outstanding invoices, specifies the general ledger accounts to be debited, and shows the net amount to pay the vendor after deducting any returns and allowances as well as any purchase discount. Figure 9-6 illustrates a disbursement voucher. Like the receiving report (Figure 9-5), we depict paper copies, but both of these processes are most likely electronic in today's organizations.

As Figure 9-6 discloses, the disbursement voucher summarizes the information contained within a set of vendor invoices. When the company receives an invoice from a vendor for the purchase of inventory, an employee compares it to the information contained in copies of the purchase order and receiving report to determine the accuracy and validity of the invoice. An employee should also check the vendor invoice for mathematical accuracy. When the organization purchases supplies or services that do not normally involve purchase order and receiving report source documents, the appropriate supervisor approves the invoice.

A voucher system has two advantages over a nonvoucher system: (1) it reduces the number of cash disbursement checks that are written, since several invoices to the same vendor can be included on one disbursement voucher, and (2) the disbursement voucher is an internally generated document. Thus, each voucher can be prenumbered to simplify the tracking of all payables, thereby contributing to an effective audit trail over cash disbursements.

---

[14] http://www.msnbc.msn.com/id/7914159/

Sarah's Sporting Goods Disbursement Voucher				No. 76742	

Date Entered: August 9, 2012

Debit Distribution

Prepared by: $\mathcal{S}M$

Vendor Number: 120

Remit to:
Valley Supply Company
3617 Bridge Road
Farmington, CT 06032

Account No.	Amount
27-330	$750.00
27-339	450.00
28-019	300.00
29-321	425.00

Vendor Invoice			Returns & Allowances	Purchase Discount	Net Remittance
Number	**Date**	**Amount**			
4632	6/28/2012	$1,250.00	$150.00	$22.00	$1,078.00
4636	7/10/2012	675.00	0.00	13.50	661.50
Voucher Totals:		$1,925.00	$150.00	$35.50	$1,739.50

FIGURE 9-6 Example of disbursement voucher (items in boldface are preprinted).

Cash Receipts Deposited Intact. It is equally important to safeguard cash receipts. As an effective control procedure, an organization should *deposit intact* each day's accumulation of cash receipts at a bank. In the typical retail organization, the total cash receipts for any specific working day come from two major sources: checks arriving by mail from credit-sales customers and currency and checks received from retail cash sales.

When cash receipts are deposited intact each day, employees cannot use any of these cash inflows to make cash disbursements. Organizations use a separate checking account for cash disbursements. When organizations "deposit intact" the cash receipts, they can easily trace the audit trail of cash inflows to the bank deposit slip and the monthly bank statement. On the other hand, if employees use some of the day's receipts for cash disbursements, the audit trail for cash becomes quite confusing, thereby increasing the risk of undetected errors and irregularities.

Reviews of Operating Performance

As a result of the Sarbanes-Oxley Act (SOX), the internal audit function of an organization typically reports directly to the Audit Committee of the Board of Directors. This makes the internal audit department independent of the other corporate subsystems and enhances objectivity when reviewing the operations of each subsystem. The internal audit staff makes periodic reviews called **operational audits** of each department or subsystem within its organization. These audits focus on evaluating the efficiency and effectiveness of operations within a particular department. On completion of such an audit, the internal auditors make recommendations to management for improving the department's operations.

In performing operational reviews, the internal auditors may find that certain controls are not operating properly. For example, the corporate policy manual might state that separate individuals should receive and record customer payments. But there is no guarantee that this is what actually happens. If practice is not according to policy, it is the internal auditor's job to identify such problems and inform management.

UPDATE ON MONITORING

Guidance on Monitoring Internal Control Systems

Since publishing the 1992 COSO Report, COSO observed that many organizations did not fully understand the benefits and potential of effective monitoring. As a result, organizations were not effectively using their monitoring results to support assessments of their internal control systems. Accordingly, in 2009, COSO published a more comprehensive report called Guidance on Monitoring Internal Control Systems (GMICS).[15] This guidance more carefully explains the monitoring component of the 1992 COSO Report.

The 2009 Report rests on two principles: (1) Ongoing and/or separate evaluations of internal controls help management determine whether the internal control system continues to function as expected over time. (2) Internal control deficiencies or weaknesses should be identified and communicated to the proper individuals in a timely fashion so that management can make corrections promptly. Thus, the GMICS suggests that these two principles can be achieved most effectively when monitoring is based on these three broad elements (Figure 9-7):

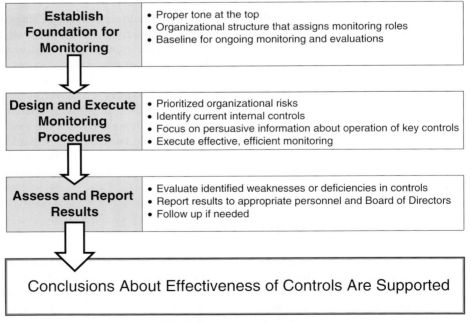

FIGURE 9-7 Overview of 2009 COSO Guidance on Monitoring. Source: COSO Enterprise.

---

[15] http://www.coso.org/documents/COSO_Guidance_On_Monitoring_Intro_online1_002.pdf

1. Establish a foundation for monitoring (e.g., determine the current baseline).
2. Design and execute monitoring procedures (e.g., collect persuasive information about risks that might affect organizational objectives and the key controls that are intended to mitigate such risks).
3. Assess and report the results of monitoring those key controls.

The following figure shows these broad elements in a graphical format, indicating that they are interconnected and can help the management of an organization to effectively monitor the control system and persuasively document that effectiveness.

Reviews of Operating Performance versus Monitoring

While "reviews" and "monitoring" might sound like the same thing, there is a subtle difference between them. Organizations rarely have enough time or internal auditors to audit every department or division every year. Consequently, some areas of the company may have an internal audit review only once every three to five years. So, an operational audit is a review of the operations of a department or a subunit of the organization and occurs on a regular basis, but not every year. One of the tasks during the operational audit is to test the internal controls that are in place.

On the other hand, effective monitoring within the context of the COSO Framework is both risk based and principles based and considers all five components of internal control. Monitoring is a high-level, comprehensive review of firm-wide objectives and risks. With such information, managers can identify critical controls to mitigate identified risks, and then develop appropriate tests of those controls to be persuasively convinced that the controls are operating as expected. And as we know, many different types of events can happen in one part of the world that suddenly (and unexpectedly) cause a risk for companies in other parts of the world.

2011 COBIT, VERSION 5[16]

ISACA is an audit and control association that issued the first version of **Control Objectives for Information and related Technology (COBIT)** in 1996. It released Version 5 of COBIT in 2011, which was driven by a major strategic effort to "tie together and reinforce all ISACA knowledge assets." The resulting version consolidates and integrates COBIT 4.1, Val IT 2.0, Risk IT frameworks, as well as the Business Model for Information Security (BMIS) and the IT Assurance Framework (ITAF).

ISACA created the COBIT framework to be business focused, process oriented, controls based, and measurement driven. If we examine the mission statement for COBIT, we can quickly understand why corporations commonly use this framework:

> *To research, develop, publicize and promote an authoritative, up-to-date international set of generally accepted information technology control objectives for day-to-day use by business managers, IT professionals and assurance professionals.*[17]

The COBIT framework takes into consideration an organization's business requirements, IT processes, and IT resources to support COSO requirements for the IT control

---

[16] http://www.isaca.org
[17] http://www.itgi.org

environment. This suggests that managers must *first* tend to the requirements outlined in the 1992 COSO Report and set up an internal control system that consists of these five components: (1) the control environment, (2) risk assessment, (3) control activities, (4) information and communication, and (5) monitoring. The next step managers should take is to work through the guidelines contained in the 2004 COSO Report (perhaps using a worksheet like the one in Figure 9-3 to set objectives, identify possible risk events, and consider appropriate risk responses the organization might need to take should an event occur).

Once the internal control system is in place (i.e., managers have worked through the 1992 and the 2004 COSO Frameworks), IT managers work with operational managers throughout the organization to determine how IT resources can best support the business processes. To achieve appropriate and effective governance of IT, senior managers of the organization will typically focus on five areas. First, managers need to focus on strategic alignment of IT operations with enterprise operations. Second, they must determine whether the organization is realizing the expected benefits (value) from IT investments. Third, managers should continually assess whether the level of IT investments is optimal. Fourth, senior management must determine their organization's risk appetite and plan accordingly. Finally, management must continuously measure and assess the performance of IT resources. Here again is an opportunity for managers to consider a "dashboard" to have access to key indicators of these five focus areas to support timely decision making.

Perhaps it was the Sarbanes-Oxley Act, and the many governance lapses prior to the enactment of this legislation, that prompted the IT Governance Institute (ITGI) to recognize a need for and to develop a framework for IT governance. This governance framework, called Val IT, is a formal statement of principles and processes for IT management. Val IT is tightly integrated with COBIT. While COBIT helps organizations understand if they are doing things right from an IT perspective, Val IT helps organizations understand if they are making the right investments and optimizing the returns from them. So, COBIT focuses on the execution of IT operations, and **Val IT** focuses on the investment decision. Figure 9-8

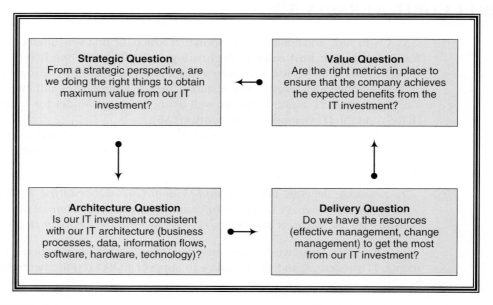

FIGURE 9-8 The integration of COBIT and Val IT. Source: Adapted from the ISACA Web site (http://www.isaca.org).

diagrams the integration of COBIT and Val IT, which is described in considerable depth in "The Val IT Framework 2.0 Extract."[18] In essence, this is also a model for continuous improvement for an organization's IT governance program.

To better understand the importance and value of COBIT and Val IT, there are three helpful publications that you can download for free at the ISACA Web site (http://www.isaca.org). These are (1) Val IT Framework 2.0, (2) Val IT Getting Started with Value Management, and (3) Val IT The Business Case.

TYPES OF CONTROLS

We can classify a company's control procedures into three major types: *preventive controls, detective controls,* and *corrective controls.* This section examines each of these types of control procedures in more detail.

Preventive Controls

Preventive controls are controls that management puts in place to prevent problems from occurring. For example, a company might install a firewall to prevent unauthorized access to the company's network, thereby safeguarding the disclosure, alteration, or destruction of sensitive information from external hackers. ERM (discussed earlier in this chapter) helps managers identify areas where preventive controls should be in place. Under the section called "Event Identification," we said that management must identify possible events that represent a problem to the firm and then identify appropriate safeguards for those problems.

James Cash calls this **scenario planning**, and it means that management identifies various scenarios that range from minor concerns to major disasters that could occur.[19] Management should include a number of informed individuals in these brainstorming sessions, such as the IS team, IT auditors, external auditors, and perhaps risk-management consultants. First, management documents each scenario. Then, it must establish preventive controls to minimize the likelihood of each problem they identify.

Detective Controls

Because preventive controls cannot stop every possible problem from occurring, organizations also need strong **detective controls** that alert managers when the preventive controls fail. As an example, assume that a company's information system prepares daily responsibility accounting performance reports for management that computes variations of actual production costs from standard production costs. If a significant variance occurs, a manager's report signals this problem, and the manager can initiate corrective action. Examples of *detective security controls* are log monitoring and review, system audits, file integrity checks, and motion detection.

Corrective Controls

Corrective controls are procedures a company uses to solve or correct a problem. Organizations can initiate corrective action only if corrective controls are in place. A

---

[18] http://www.isaca.org
[19] Cash, J. 1997. It's reasonable to prepare. *Information Week* 654 (October): 142.

company establishes corrective controls to remedy problems it discovers by the detective controls. An example of a corrective control procedure might be to change the company's procedures for creating backup copies of important business files. More than ever before, companies realize the importance of corrective controls, based on the incredible economic and physical impact of natural disasters over the past decade.

> *Case-in-Point 9.12*   The recent BP oil spill in the Gulf of Mexico, labeled as the worst oil disaster in U.S. history, focuses a spotlight on the impact of control failures and reinforces the responsibility of internal auditors to constantly monitor the internal control systems of an organization. While estimates vary regarding the total amount of oil that spilled into the Gulf, the fact remains that the clean-up efforts (corrective controls) are extensive and evolving.[20]

EVALUATING CONTROLS

Once controls are in place, it is a wise practice for management to evaluate them. We introduced several frameworks at the beginning of this chapter that companies might use to evaluate their internal controls, but regardless of *how* management chooses to evaluate their internal controls, it is clear that they *must* do this. On the basis of the requirements contained in SOX, the New York Stock Exchange (NYSE) adopted rules that require all companies listed on this exchange to maintain an internal audit function to provide management and the audit committee ongoing assessments of the company's risk management processes and system of internal control for financial reporting.

Requirements of the Sarbanes-Oxley Act

As previously discussed, the Sarbanes-Oxley Act of 2002 significantly changed the way internal auditors and management view internal controls within an organization. In particular, Section 404 contains very specific actions that the management of a publicly traded company must perform each year with respect to the system of internal controls within the organization. Specifically, the annual financial report of the company must include a report on the firm's internal controls. This report must include the following:

- A statement that management acknowledges its responsibility for establishing and maintaining an adequate internal control structure and procedures for financial reporting.
- An assessment, as of the end of the fiscal year, of the effectiveness of the internal control structure and procedures for financial reporting.
- An attestation by the company's auditor that the assessment made by the management is accurate.

A number of experts believe that some interesting synergies may have happened as a result of companies becoming SOX compliant. Recall that the purpose of SOX was to improve transparency and accountability in business processes and financial accounting. For this to happen, internal auditors and the management of companies had to study their processes very carefully. However, if these same firms already implemented an ERP system, then most likely they already have reengineered some of their business processes.

---

[20] Jackson, R. 2010. The state of control. *Internal Auditor* 67(5): 35–38.

During the evaluation of those processes, it is likely that the appropriate internal controls were considered and included, enabling SOX compliance. In addition, for management to comprehensively consider the requirements of SOX, they most likely used the Enterprise Risk Management framework in the 2004 COSO Report.

Cost-Benefit Analysis

Companies develop their own optimal internal control package by applying the cost-benefit concept. Under this concept, employees perform a cost-benefit analysis on each control procedure considered for implementation that compares the expected cost of designing, implementing, and operating each control to the control's expected benefits. Only those controls whose benefits are expected to be greater than, or at least equal to, the expected costs are implemented.

To illustrate a cost-benefit analysis, assume that the West End Boutique sells fashionable high-end ladies' clothing, jewelry, and other accessories. The owner is concerned about how much inventory customers have shoplifted during the last several months and is considering some additional controls to minimize this shoplifting problem. If no additional controls are implemented, the company's accountant estimates that the total annual loss to the boutique from shoplifting will be approximately $120,000. The company is considering two alternative control procedures to safeguard the company's inventory (Figure 9-9).

Based on the owner's goal of reducing shoplifting, alternative #1 (hiring six security guards) is the ideal control procedure to implement. Shoplifting should be practically zero, assuming that the guards are properly trained and perform their jobs in an effective manner. Even if shoplifting is completely eliminated, however, alternative #1 should not be implemented. Why not? It costs too much. The control's expected cost ($240,000 a year) is greater than the control's expected benefit ($120,000 a year, which is the approximate annual shoplifting loss that would be eliminated).

If the owner implements alternative #2 (hiring two security guards plus installing cameras and mirrors), the boutique's accountant estimates that the total annual loss from shoplifting could be reduced from $120,000 to $25,000. The net benefit is $95,000 (= $120,000−$25,000). Because the second alternative's expected benefit ($95,000 a year reduction of shoplifting) exceeds its expected cost ($80,000 a year), the boutique's owner should select alternative #2.

Alternative #1	Alternative #2
Hire six plain-clothed security guards to patrol the boutique. Based on the annual salaries that would have to be paid to the security guards, this control would cost West End Boutique an estimated $240,000 a year.	Hire two plain-clothed security guards who would patrol the aisles, and install several cameras and mirrors throughout the company's premises to permit managers to observe any shoplifters. The estimated annual cost of this control would be $80,000.

FIGURE 9-9   Internal control alternatives for West End Boutique.

The point of this cost-benefit analysis example is that in some situations, the design and implementation of an *ideal control procedure* may be impractical. We are using the term **ideal control** to mean a control procedure that reduces to practically zero the risk of an undetected error (such as debiting the wrong account for the purchase of office supplies) or irregularity (such as shoplifting). If a specific control's expected cost exceeds its expected benefit, as was true with the alternative #1 control procedure discussed above, the effect of implementing that control is a decrease in operating efficiency for the company. From a cost-benefit viewpoint, therefore, managers are sometimes forced to design and implement control procedures for specific areas of their company that are less than ideal. These managers must learn to live with the fact that, for example, some irregularities may occur in their organizational system, and these problems will not be detected by the internal control system.

Another approach to cost-benefit analysis attempts to quantify the risk factor associated with a specific area of a company. *Risk assessment,* as discussed earlier, is an important component of an internal control system. In general, the benefits of additional control procedures result from reducing potential losses. A measure of loss should include both the *exposure* (that is, the amount of potential loss associated with a control problem) and the *risk* (that is, the probability that the control problem will occur). An example of a loss measure is expected annual loss computed as follows:

$$\text{Expected annual loss} = \text{risk} \times \text{exposure per year}$$

The **expected loss** is based on estimates of risk and exposure. To determine the cost-effectiveness of a new control procedure, management estimates the expected loss both with and without the new procedure. After completing these calculations, the estimated benefit of the new control procedure is equal to the reduction in the estimated expected loss from implementing this procedure. Employees compare the estimated benefit to the incremental cost of the new control procedure. Whenever the estimated benefit exceeds this incremental cost, the company should implement the newly designed control procedure.

To demonstrate this method of cost-benefit analysis, assume that a company's payroll system prepares 12,000 checks biweekly. Data errors sometimes occur, which require reprocessing the entire payroll at a projected cost of $10,000. The company's management is considering the addition of a data validation control procedure that reduces the error rate from 15 percent to 1 percent. This validation control procedure is expected to cost $600 per pay period. Should the data validation control procedure be implemented? Figure 9-10 illustrates the analysis to answer this question.

Figure 9-10 indicates that the reprocessing cost expected (= expected loss) is $1,500 without the validation control procedure and $100 with the validation control procedure. Thus, implementing this control procedure provides an estimated reprocessing cost reduction of $1,400. Because the $1,400 estimated cost reduction is greater than the $600 estimated cost of the control, the company should implement the procedure: the net estimated benefit is $800.

A Risk Matrix

Cost-benefit analyses suffer from at least three problems. One is that not all cost considerations can be expressed easily in monetary terms and that *nonmonetary* (or *qualitative*) items are often as important in evaluating decision alternatives in a cost-benefit analysis. For

	Without Control Procedure	With Control Procedure	Net Expected Difference
Cost of payroll reprocessing	$10,000	$10,000	
Risk of data errors	15%	1%	
Reprocessing cost expected ($10,000 × risk)	$ 1,500	$ 100	$1,400
Cost of validation control procedure (an incremental cost)	$ 0	$ 600	$ (600)
Net estimated benefit from validation control procedure			$ 800

FIGURE 9-10 Cost-benefit analysis of payroll validation control procedure.

example, when an airport contemplates whether or not to install a control that might save lives, it might be difficult to quantify the benefits. Admittedly, this is an extreme example, but the point remains: often qualitative factors exist in a decision-making situation, which requires a degree of subjectivity in the cost-benefit analyses.

Another problem with cost-benefit analyses is that some managers are not comfortable with computations involving probabilities or averages. What does it mean, for example, to state that on average, 2.5 laptops are lost or stolen each year? Finally, a third problem with cost-benefit analyses is that it requires an evaluation of all possible risks and a case-by-case computation of possible safeguards. Typically, companies will run out of money for controls long before they run out of risks to mitigate.

A possible solution to this third problem is to develop a **risk matrix**, which is a tool especially useful for prioritizing large risks. As you can see in Figure 9-11, a risk matrix classifies each potential risk by mitigation cost and also by likelihood of occurrence. As a result, highly likely, costly events wind up in the upper-right corner of the matrix, while events with small likelihoods of occurrence or negligible costs wind up in the lower left corner. This helps managers see which events are most important (the upper-right ones), and therefore how to better prioritize the money spent on internal controls.

	Cost to Organization			
Likelihood of Occurrence	Negligible	Marginal	Critical	Catastrophic
Certain	Busy Street			
Likely		Hit by car		
Possible			Hit by piano	
Unlikely			Burst Dam	
Rare	Locust Swarm			Stampede

FIGURE 9-11 Example of a risk matrix.

AIS AT WORK
Using the Company Credit Card as a Nest Egg?[21]

Laura Jones, 22 years old, was very excited! She just got hired at a regional home improvement company as the executive assistant to the president. The company was eagerly planning an aggressive expansion of operations and was looking for ambitious and eager employees—willing to work hard as team players. To realize growth, the president knew the company had to be very active in the industry. Thus, the company sponsored booths at trade shows, attended industry conferences, and had morale-building events for its sales team in exciting places such as Hawaii.

Laura's responsibilities included making all the arrangements for these activities. She made hotel and airline reservations and coordinated activities for the sales team. She was also responsible for reviewing the corporate credit card bills and authorizing payments. The president gave her the authority to approve amounts up to $100,000. However, when Jones realized that no one ever asked to look at the charges on the corporate credit card bill, she began making personal purchases with the card. If total charges exceeded $100,000, she simply forged the president's signature on the approval form. When she learned that the accounts payable department accepted approvals from the president by e-mail, she would slip into his office when he was at a meeting or out of town, access his computer, and send herself an approval e-mail.

The temptation was so great that she began to find additional ways the company could pay for things she wanted. For example, she soon discovered that she could also purchase gift checks with the corporate credit card, and over a two year period she bought more than $150,000 in gift checks to buy items for herself, her family, and some friends.

When Laura had been with the firm for slightly less than three years, her scheme was discovered. An agent at the credit card company noticed some questionable transactions involving Jones and the corporate credit card. When the internal auditors investigated the transactions, they discovered that Jones had embezzled more than $1.5 million.

 ## SUMMARY

- ✓ An organization's internal control system has four objectives: (1) to safeguard assets, (2) to check the accuracy and reliability of accounting data, (3) to promote operational efficiency, and (4) to encourage adherence to prescribed managerial policies.

- ✓ It is management's responsibility to develop an internal control system.

- ✓ The control environment, risk assessment, control activities, information and communication, and monitoring are the five interrelated components that make up an internal control system.

- ✓ Six control activities to include in each organization's internal control system are: (1) a good audit trail, (2) sound personnel policies and practices, (3) separation of duties, (4) physical protection of assets, (5) internal reviews of controls by internal audit subsystem, and (6) timely performance reports.

---

[21] Sutphen, P. 2008. Stealing funds for a nest egg. *Internal Auditor* (August): 87–91.

✓ Within these six activities, specific control procedures should be designed and implemented for each company based on its particular control needs.

✓ There are three types of controls: preventive, detective, and corrective.

✓ To develop an optimal internal control package, management should perform a cost-benefit analysis on each potential control procedure or consider a risk matrix if there are qualitative considerations that cannot be ignored.

✓ A company should implement only those controls whose expected benefits exceed, or at least equal, their expected costs.

KEY TERMS YOU SHOULD KNOW

1992 COSO Report	internal control
control environment	internal control system
Control Objectives for Information and related Technology (COBIT)	operational audits
	preventive controls
corporate governance	risk assessment
corrective controls	risk matrix
demand draft	Sarbanes-Oxley Act of 2002
detective controls	(SAS) No. 94
enterprise risk management (ERM)	scenario planning
expected loss	Section 404
fidelity bond	separation of duties
ideal control	Val IT

DISCUSSION QUESTIONS

9-1. What are the primary provisions of the 1992 COSO Report? The 2004 COSO Report?

9-2. What are the primary provisions of COBIT?

9-3. Why are the COSO and COBIT frameworks so important?

9-4. Briefly discuss the interrelated components that should exist within an internal control system. In your opinion, which component is the most important and why?

9-5. Why are accountants so concerned about their organization having an efficient and effective internal control system?

9-6. Discuss what you consider to be the major differences between preventive, detective, and corrective control procedures. Give two examples of each type of control.

9-7. Why are competent employees important to an organization's internal control system?

9-8. How can separation of duties reduce the risk of undetected errors and irregularities?

9-9. Discuss some of the advantages to an organization from using a voucher system and prenumbered checks for its cash disbursement transactions.

9-10. What role does cost-benefit analysis play in an organization's internal control system?

9-11. Why is it important for managers to evaluate internal controls?

9-12. Why did COSO think it was so important to issue the 2009 Report on monitoring?

PROBLEMS

9-13. You have been hired by the management of Alden, Inc. to review its control procedures for the purchase, receipt, storage, and issuance of raw materials. You prepared the following comments, which describe Alden's procedures.

- Raw materials, which consist mainly of high-cost electronic components, are kept in a locked storeroom. Storeroom personnel include a supervisor and four clerks. All are well trained, competent, and adequately bonded. Raw materials are removed from the storeroom only upon written or oral authorization from one of the production foremen.

- There are no perpetual inventory records; hence, the storeroom clerks do not keep records of goods received or issued. To compensate for the lack of perpetual records, a physical inventory count is taken monthly by the storeroom clerks, who are well supervised. Appropriate procedures are followed in making the inventory count.

- After the physical count, the storeroom supervisor matches quantities counted against a predetermined reorder level. If the count for a given part is below the reorder level, the supervisor enters the part number on a materials requisition list and sends this list to the accounts payable clerk. The accounts payable clerk prepares a purchase order for a predetermined reorder quantity for each part and mails the purchase order to the vendor from whom the part was last purchased.

- When ordered materials arrive at Alden, they are received by the storeroom clerks. The clerks count the merchandise and see that the counts agree with the shipper's bill of lading. All vendors' bills of lading are initialed, dated, and filed in the storeroom to serve as receiving reports.

a. List the internal control weaknesses in Alden's procedures.

b. For each weakness that you identified, recommend an improvement(s).

9-14. Listed below are 12 internal control procedures or requirements for the expenditure cycle (purchasing, payroll, accounts payable, and cash disbursements) of a manufacturing enterprise. For each of the following, identify the error or misstatement that would be prevented or detected by its use.

a. Duties segregated between the cash payments and cash receipts functions.

b. Signature plates kept under lock and key.

c. The accounting department matches invoices to receiving reports or special authorizations before payment.

d. All checks mailed by someone other than the person preparing the payment voucher.

e. The accounting department matches invoices to copies of purchase orders.

f. Keep the blank stock of checks under lock and key.

g. Use imprest accounts for payroll.

h. Bank reconciliations performed by someone other than the one who writes checks and handles cash.

i. Use a check protector.

j. Periodically conduct surprise counts of cash funds.

k. Orders placed with approved vendors only.

l. All purchases made by the purchasing department.

9-15. Rogers, North, & Housour, LLC is a large, regional CPA firm. There are 74 employees at their Glen Allen, SC office. The administrative assistant at this office approached Mr. Rogers, one of the partners, to express her concerns about the inventory of miscellaneous supplies (e.g., pens, pencils, paper, floppy disks, and envelopes) that this office maintains for its clerical workers. The firm stores these supplies on shelves at the back of the office facility, easily accessible to all company employees.

The administrative assistant, Sandra Collins, is concerned about the poor internal control over these office supplies. She estimates that the firm loses about $350 per month because of theft of supplies by company employees. To reduce this monthly loss, Sandra recommends a separate room to store these supplies and that a company employee be given full-time responsibility for supervising the issuance of the supplies to those employees with a properly approved requisition. By implementing these controls, Sandra believes this change might reduce the loss of supplies from employee misappropriation to practically zero.

a. If you were Mr. Rogers, would you accept or reject Sandra's control recommendations? Explain why or why not.

b. Identify additional control procedures that the firm might implement to reduce the monthly loss from theft of office supplies.

9-16. Ron Mitchell is currently working his first day as a ticket seller and cashier at the First Run Movie Theater. When a customer walks up to the ticket booth, Ron collects the required admission charge and issues the movie patron a ticket. To be admitted into the theater, the customer then presents his or her ticket to the theater manager, who is stationed at the entrance. The manager tears the ticket in half, keeping one half for himself and giving the other half to the customer.

While Ron was sitting in the ticket booth waiting for additional customers, he had a brilliant idea for stealing some of the cash from ticket sales. He reasoned that if he merely pocketed some of the cash collections from the sale of tickets, no one would ever know. Because approximately 300 customers attend each performance, Ron believed that it would be difficult for the theater manager to keep a running count of the actual customers entering the theater. To further support his reasoning, Ron noticed that the manager often has lengthy conversations with patrons at the door and appears to make no attempt to count the actual number of people going into the movie house.

a. Will Ron Mitchell be able to steal cash receipts from the First Run Movie Theater with his method and not be caught? Explain.

b. If you believe he will be caught, explain how his stealing activity will be discovered.

9-17. The Palmer Company manufactures various types of clothing products for women. To accumulate the costs of manufacturing these products, the company's accountants have established a computerized cost accounting system. Every Monday morning, the prior week's production cost data are batched together and processed. One of the outputs of this processing function is a production cost report for management that compares actual production costs to standard production costs and computes variances from standard. Management focuses on the significant variances as the basis for analyzing production performance.

Errors sometimes occur in processing a week's production cost data. The cost of the reprocessing work on a week's production cost data is estimated to average about $12,000. The company's management is currently considering the addition of a data validation control procedure within its cost accounting system that is estimated to reduce the risk of the data errors from 16 percent to 2 percent, and this procedure is projected to cost $800 per week.

a. Using these data, perform a cost-benefit analysis of the data validation control procedure that the management is considering for its cost accounting system.

b. On the basis of your analysis, make a recommendation to the management regarding the data validation control procedure.

CASE STUDIES

Gayton Menswear (Risk Assessment and Control Procedures)

The Gayton Menswear company was founded by Fred Williams in 1986 and has grown steadily over the years. Fred now has 17 stores located throughout the central and northern parts of the state. Since Fred was an accounting major in college and worked for a large regional CPA firm for 13 years prior to opening his first store, he places a lot of value on internal controls. Further, he has always insisted on a state-of-the-art accounting system that connects all of his stores' financial transactions and reports.

Fred employs two internal auditors who monitor internal controls and also seek ways to improve operational effectiveness. As part of the monitoring process, the internal auditors take turns conducting periodic reviews of the accounting records. For instance, the company takes a physical inventory at all stores once each year, and an internal auditor oversees the process. Chris Domangue, the most senior internal auditor, just completed a review of the accounting records and discovered several items of concern. These were:

- Physical inventory counts varied from inventory book amounts by more than 5 percent at two of the stores. In both cases, physical inventory was lower.
- Two of the stores seem to have an unusually high amount of sales returns for cash.
- In 10 of the stores, gross profit has dropped significantly from the same time last year.
- At four of the stores, bank deposit slips did not match cash receipts.
- One of the stores had an unusual number of bounced checks. It appeared that the same employee was responsible for approving each of the bounced checks.
- In seven of the stores, the amount of petty cash on hand did not correspond to the amount in the petty cash account.

Requirements

1. For each of these concerns, identify a risk that may have created the problem.
2. Recommend an internal control procedure to prevent the problem in the future.

Emerson Department Store (Control Suggestions to Strengthen a Payroll System)

As a recently hired internal auditor for the Emerson Department Store (which has approximately 500 employees on its payroll), you are currently reviewing the store's procedures for preparing and distributing the weekly payroll. These procedures are as follows.

- Each Monday morning the managers of the various departments (e.g., the women's clothing department, the toy department, and the home appliances department) turn in their employees' time cards for the previous week to the accountant (Morris Smith).
- Morris then accumulates the total hours worked by each employee and submits this information to the store's computer center to process the weekly payroll.
- The computer center prepares a transaction tape of employees' hours worked and then processes this tape with the employees' payroll master tape file (containing information

such as each employee's Social Security number, exemptions claimed, hourly wage rate, year-to-date gross wages, FICA taxes withheld, and union dues deducted).

- The computer prints out a payroll register indicating each employee's gross wages, deductions, and net pay for the payroll period.
- The payroll register is then turned over to Morris, who, with help from the secretaries, places the correct amount of currency in each employee's pay envelope.
- The pay envelopes are provided to the department managers for distribution to their employees on Monday afternoon.

To date, you have been unsuccessful in persuading the store's management to use checks rather than currency for paying the employees. Most managers that you have talked with argue that the employees prefer to receive cash in their weekly pay envelopes so that they do not have to bother going to the bank to cash their checks.

Requirements

1. Assume that the store's management refuses to change its current system of paying the employees with cash. Identify some control procedures that could strengthen the store's current payroll preparation and distribution system.
2. Now assume that the store's management is willing to consider other options for paying employees. What alternatives would you suggest?

Chapter 10

Computer Controls for Organizations and Accounting Information Systems

INTRODUCTION

This chapter continues the discussion of internal controls from Chapter 9 by focusing on controls related to information technology. Control Objectives for Information and related Technology (COBIT) is a governance framework designed to help organizations control IT and maximize the value created by IT. COBIT provides a methodology for analyzing IT controls, but the process is lengthy and very complex—a detailed description of the many components of the COBIT framework is beyond the scope of a textbook chapter. In order to discuss IT controls in a more intuitive format, we organize this chapter according to three main classifications of IT-related controls, which are consistent with broad classifications in Auditing Standard No. 5 (AS5), COBIT, and COSO. Following AS5, we begin at the top level and work our way down to more specific controls at the application level. The three categories are: enterprise level controls, general controls, and application controls. Enterprise level controls affect the entire organization, including other IT controls. The next level includes general controls for IT, which are controls that involve the entire AIS and other IT-based systems. Finally, at the third level, application controls are designed to protect transaction processing (i.e., to ensure complete and accurate processing of data). These controls are typically programmed into specific modules and applications within the accounting information system.

ENTERPRISE LEVEL CONTROLS

Enterprise controls are those controls that affect the entire organization and influence the effectiveness of other controls. As we discussed in the previous chapter, management's philosophy, operating style, integrity, policies, and procedures are all important characteristics that influence the tone of a company, and these characteristics represent the highest level of enterprise controls. The tone set by management helps to establish the level of security and control consciousness in the organization, which is the basis for the control environment. Enterprise level controls are particularly important because they often have a pervasive impact on many other controls, such as IT general controls and application-level controls.

In 2007, the Public Company Accounting Oversight Board (PCAOB) released Auditing Standard No. 5, "An Audit of Internal Control over Financial Reporting that Is Integrated with an Audit of Financial Statements." This Standard introduces a framework describing entity-level controls at varying levels of precision (direct, monitoring, and indirect).[1] The

---

[1] http://pcaobus.org/Standards/Auditing/Pages/Auditing_Standard_5.aspx

external auditor must evaluate these controls, and management must ensure that these controls are in place and functioning. We identified a number of these controls in Chapter 9: management's ethical values, philosophy, assignment of authority and responsibility, and the effectiveness of the board of directors. Additional controls that are also very important include the following:

- Consistent policies and procedures, such as formal codes of conduct and fraud prevention policies. For example, a company may require all employees to periodically sign a formal code of conduct stipulating that computer resources are to be used only for appropriate business purposes and any acts of fraud or abuse will be prosecuted.
- Management's risk assessment process.
- Centralized processing and controls.
- Controls to monitor results of operations.
- Controls to monitor other controls, including activities of the internal audit function, the audit committee, and self-assessment programs.
- The period-end financial reporting process.
- Board-approved policies that address significant business control and risk management practices.

Risk Assessment and Security Policies

One level below the tone of the organization is the organization's **security policy**—a comprehensive plan that helps protect an enterprise from both internal and external threats. The policy is based on assessment of the risks faced by the firm. Figure 10-1 presents issues that organizations should consider when developing this policy.

Key Issues for Developing Security Policies

- Evaluate information assets and identify threats to these assets
- Assess both external and internal threats
- Perform a risk assessment
- Determine whether information assets are underprotected, overprotected or adequately protected
- Create a team for drafting the policy
- Obtain approval for the policy from the highest levels of the organization
- Create the specific security policies
- Implement the policies throughout the organization
- Develop policy compliance measures and enforce the policies
- Manage the policies

FIGURE 10-1   Issues that should be considered when developing a security policy.
Source: *Creating and Enforcing an Effective Information Security Policy*, ISACA Journal, Journal On-line © 2005 ISACA®. All rights reserved. Used by permission.

In developing its security policies, an organization should consider ISO/IEC 27002, the international information security standards that establish information security best practices. This Standard includes 12 primary sections: risk assessment, security policy, organization of security, asset management, human resources security, physical security, communications, access controls, acquisition and development, security incident management, business continuity management, and compliance. ISO certification is becoming an important consideration as more businesses maintain a Web presence. The first step to becoming certified under ISO/IEC 27002 is to comply with the Standard, and one way to measure and manage compliance is to use a risk analysis tool such as the COSO enterprise risk management (ERM) framework that we discussed in Chapter 9.

Integrated Security for the Organization

A current trend in security practice is to merge **physical security** and **logical security** across an organization. Physical security refers to any measures that an organization uses to protect its facilities, resources, or its proprietary data that are stored on physical media. Logical security uses technology to limit access to only authorized individuals to the organization's systems and information, such as password controls. Figure 10-2 identifies a number of examples of physical and logical security measures that firms commonly employ. The IT Governance Institute published a document that specifically addresses security, called *Information Security Governance: Guidance for Boards of Directors and Executive Management,* 2nd edition (2006).

Many firms now use an integrated approach to security by combining a number of logical and physical security technologies, including firewalls, intrusion detection systems, content filtering, vulnerability management, virus protection, and virtual private networks. An **integrated security** system, supported by a comprehensive security policy, can significantly reduce the risk of attack because it increases the costs and resources needed by an intruder. According to security experts, convergence (of physical and logical security) is the single most overlooked gap in enterprise-wide security—that is, the most insidious security risks are those that slip between physical and logical security systems. Figure 10-3 and the following example illustrate this.

Physical Security	Logical Security
• Facility monitoring (surveillance systems, cameras, guards, exterior lighting) • Access controls to facilities/data center/computers (biometrics, access cards) • Alarm systems (fire, burglar, water, humidity, power fluctuations) • Shred sensitive documents • Proper storage/disposal of hard drives and other electronic storage media • Secure storage of backup copies of data and master copies of critical software	• e-IDs and passwords • System authentication • Biometrics • Logs of logon attempts • Application-level firewalls • Anti-virus and anti-spyware software • Intrusion detection systems • Encryption for data in transit • Smart cards

FIGURE 10-2 Examples of physical security and logical security measures.

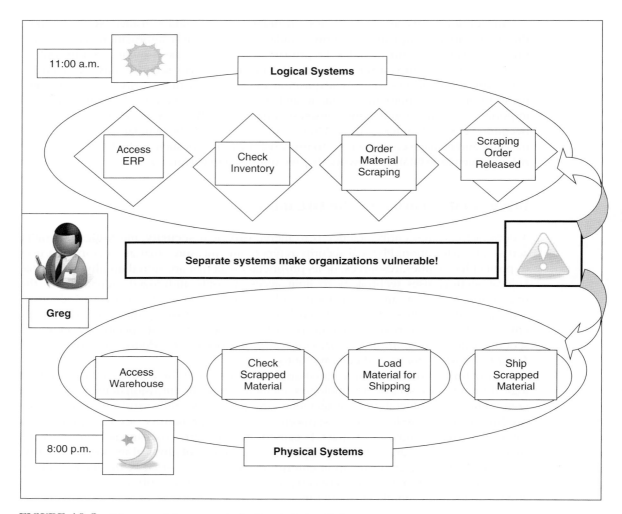

FIGURE 10-3 Diagram of the example in Case-in-Point 10.1.

Case-in-Point 10.1 Assume Greg Smith is authorized to scrap inventory. He also has an access badge for the warehouse where the scrapped inventory is located and can enter the warehouse after hours. Although independently these actions are not particularly interesting, when combined they create a wide variety of problems that could go unnoticed if the physical and logical security systems are not integrated—such as fraud, which could lead to misstated financial statements.

The U.S. government considers computer security a critical issue. The National Institute of Standards and Technology (NIST) issued guidelines on computer security controls for federal information systems. NIST believes that these security guidelines will play a key role in helping federal agencies effectively select and implement security controls and, by using a risk-based approach, do so in a cost-effective manner.[2] This document, which is

---

[2] http://csrc.nist.gov/groups/SMA/fisma/index.html

mandatory for most federal systems, influences controls for systems at all governmental levels. Security controls (management, operational, and technical safeguards) are critical to protect the confidentiality, integrity, and availability of a computer system and its information.

GENERAL CONTROLS FOR INFORMATION TECHNOLOGY

IT general controls protect the IT infrastructure, major components of the IT systems, and data. General controls primarily ensure that (1) access to programs and data is granted only to authorized users; (2) data and systems are protected from change, theft, or loss; and (3) development of and changes to computer programs are authorized, tested, and approved before their use. **IT general controls** affect the integrity of the entire information system. Accordingly, controls at this level are critical for reliance on the application controls that are programmed into specific components of the information system. For example, imagine that an AIS lacks control over access to financial statement records. If employees can access and change data in the financial statements at will, then the data in the financial statements will be unreliable. Even if there were thousands of application controls that ensured accurate processing of all financial data, the lack of adequate access controls to prevent unauthorized changes to the data make the financial data unreliable.

Access to Data, Hardware, and Software

Regulating who is permitted logical access to computers and files is a critical general control in terms of safeguarding sensitive organizational data and software. Remote terminals may be placed anywhere in the country and hooked up to a company's servers through Internet connections. As a result, it is difficult to safeguard logical computer access with direct physical surveillance of terminals. Most computer systems therefore use passwords to restrict access. Such codes vary in length and type of password information required, but all have the same intent: to limit logical access to the computer only to those individuals authorized to have it.

Organizations should encourage employees to create **strong passwords**. Each character that is added to a password increases the protection that it provides. Passwords should be eight or more characters in length; 14 characters or longer is ideal. For instance, a 15-character password composed only of random letters and numbers is about 33,000 times stronger than an eight-character password composed of characters from the entire keyboard.[3] An ideal password combines both length and different types of characters. The greater the variety of characters (letters, numbers, and symbols) that are included in a password, the harder it is to hack.

Passwords can be a problem because they can be lost, given away, or stolen. Thus, security can be increased significantly by using biometrics and/or integrated security measures. **Biometric identification** devices *identify* distinctive user physical characteristics such as voice patterns, fingerprints, facial patterns and features, retina prints, body odor, signature dynamics, and keyboarding methods (i.e., the way a user types certain groups of characters). When an individual wants to access a company's computer system, his or her biometric identifications are matched against those stored in the system. A match must occur for the individual to be given access to the computer system.

---

[3] http://www.microsoft.com/athome/security/privacy/password.mspx

Security for Wireless Technology.   As we mentioned in Chapter 1, an important change in today's business environment is the desire for instantly connecting with one another and rapidly exchanging ideas and data. Wireless fidelity (Wi-Fi) technology is based on radio wave transmissions, which makes the transmitted information vulnerable to interception. As a result, organizations that rely on wireless technology must understand the vulnerabilities that exist and explore the various methods of compensating for this risk.

Probably one of the largest users of wireless technology is the education sector. Worldwide, colleges and universities are installing wireless local area networks (WLANs) for a variety of reasons, including: a technologically savvy and highly mobile audience (students and faculty); older, often historic buildings (which cannot be wired); and innovative curricula that make use of wireless applications. Probably the most important control for wireless technology is installing a **virtual private network (VPN)**, which is a security appliance that runs behind a university's (or a company's) firewall and allows remote users to access entity resources by using wireless, handheld devices.

Case-in-Point 10.2   Texas A&M University's network infrastructure connects more than 340 buildings and 90,000 wired ports. The VPN network allows authorized users to access the University's network with whatever type of mobile device they choose (e.g., PDAs, laptops, and digital mobile phones).[4]

The risk of unauthorized access to data through electronic eavesdropping is minimized by using **data encryption**. It can be used to prevent a company's competitors from electronically monitoring confidential data transmissions. Encryption converts data into a scrambled format prior to their transmission and converts the data back into a meaningful form once transmission is complete. Figure 10-4 shows an example of using encryption keys to scramble accounting data and convert it back into readable form. The encrypted data can be read only by a person with a matching decryption key. Data encryption is relatively inexpensive, which makes it a very efficient control.^

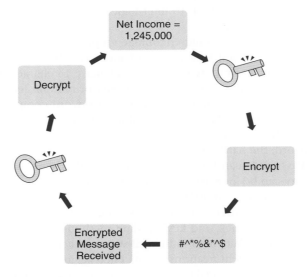

FIGURE 10-4   Data encryption.

[4] http://nis.tamu.edu/index.php

Case-in-Point 10.3 Check Point, a firm specializing in IT security, analyzed the use of smartphones by businesses in 2010. The firm found that 70 percent of respondents indicated that their companies' smartphones lacked any type of encryption. Further, nearly 90 percent of respondents indicated that they carried sensitive data on USB memory sticks that did not have encryption. The study indicates some serious shortfalls in current IT controls.[5]

Controls for Networks.

Desktop computers are often placed throughout the organization and linked to a centralized computer to form a *distributed data processing (DDP) system.* The basic objective of each remote computer is to meet the specific processing needs of the remote location and communicate summary results to the centralized (host) computer.

DDP systems are still viable in today's business organizations. Large volumes of data are regularly transmitted over long-distance telecommunications technologies. As with wireless technology, the routine use of systems such as DDP and client/server computing increases the potential control problems for companies. These problems include unauthorized access to the computer system and its data through **electronic eavesdropping** (which allows computer users to observe transmissions intended for someone else), hardware or software malfunctions causing computer network system failures, and errors in data transmission. Managers use data encryption to protect information. For example, many companies are encrypting all of their e-mail messages on local area networks (LANs) and wide area networks (WANs).

To reduce the risk of computer network system failures, companies design their network capacity to handle periods of peak transmission volume. Redundant components, such as servers, are used so that a system can switch to a backup unit in the event of hardware failure. A control procedure, such as a **checkpoint**, helps to recover from such a failure. Under a *checkpoint control procedure,* which is performed at periodic intervals during processing, a company's computer network system temporarily does not accept new transactions. Instead, it completes updating procedures for all partially processed transactions and then generates an exact copy of all data values and other information needed to restart the system. The system records the checkpoint data on a separate disk file and repeatedly executes this process several times per hour. Should a hardware failure occur, the system is restarted by reading the last checkpoint and then reprocessing only those transactions that have occurred since the checkpoint.

Two control procedures that reduce the risk of errors in data transmission are routing verification procedures and message acknowledgment procedures. **Routing verification procedures** help to ensure that no transactions or messages are routed to the wrong computer network system address. They work in the following manner: any transaction or message transmitted over a network should have a *header label* that identifies its destination. Before sending the transaction or message, the system should verify that the transaction or message destination is valid and is authorized to receive data. Finally, when the transaction or message is received, the system should verify that the identity of the receiving destination is consistent with the transaction's or message's destination code.

Message acknowledgment procedures are useful for preventing the loss of part or all of a transaction or message on a computer network system. For example, if messages contain a *trailer label,* the receiving destination (or unit) can check to verify that the complete message was received. Furthermore, if large messages or sets of transactions are transmitted in a batch, each message or transaction segment can be numbered sequentially. The receiving destination can then check whether all parts of the messages or transactions

---

[5] http://www.checkpoint.com/press/2010/GlobalEndpointSurvey.html

were received and were in the correct sequence. The receiving unit will signal the sending unit regarding the outcome of this evaluation. Should the receiving unit detect a data transmission error, the data will be retransmitted once the sending unit has been signaled about this error.

Controls for Personal Computers.   Developing control procedures for an organization's portable laptops and desktop PCs begins by taking an inventory of them throughout the organization. The various applications for which each PC is used should also be identified. This should be followed by classifying each PC according to the types of *risks* and *exposures* associated with its applications. To discourage outright theft of desktop PCs, many companies bolt them in place or attach monitors to desks with strong adhesives. A control procedure for laptops is to lock them in cabinets before employees leave at night. Additional control procedures for laptops are identified in Figure 10-5.

PCs are relatively inexpensive. Therefore, it may not be cost-effective for a company to go to elaborate lengths to protect them. What companies should do is use inexpensive, yet effective, control procedures for PCs. It should be noted that because of the compact nature of laptop PCs, theft of these assets has become a big problem for both corporate entities and government agencies.

Case-in-Point 10.4   Recently, an insurance company handled $1 billion in claims for stolen laptops in a single year. In a survey of major corporations and large government agencies conducted a few years ago by the Computer Security Institute and the FBI computer crime squad, 69 percent of the respondents acknowledged incidents of laptop theft. One hundred and fifty organizations cited a total of over $13 million in financial losses. The average annual price tag of losses per organization was $86,920.

Control Procedures for Laptops	
Control Procedure	**How to Use the Procedure**
Identify your laptop	• Which model? What configuration? What is the serial number? Are there any other unique identifiers? Without these details, law enforcement agencies, airlines, hotels, and so on, have little chance of retrieving your company's stolen laptop.
	• Keep a copy of all relevant information about your laptop in a safe place. Leave it in your desk at the office or at your home. Never tape the relevant information to the laptop or store the information electronically on the laptop's hard disk.
Use nonbreakable cables to attach laptops to stationary furniture	• For example, in a hotel room be sure to use a cable or other security device to attach the laptop to some stationary object such as a desk or some other piece of heavy furniture.
Load Antivirus software onto the hard disk	• Automatically perform an Antivirus scan whenever the laptop is turned on or whenever a diskette is inserted.
	• Have Antivirus scanning software check all changed or new files.
	• Keep Antivirus software current. Keep virus definitions current.
Back up laptop information	• Never keep backups in the laptop case.
	• While traveling, keep backup diskettes in a pocket or briefcase.
	• If possible, back up to your company's internal network via modem, when you are out of the office.
	• Back up frequently and test regularly to ensure data integrity.

FIGURE 10-5 Additional control procedures for laptops.

As laptops and tablet devices become more sophisticated, people are using them as primary PCs and are saving large amounts of critical data on portable drives. Three simple safeguards are (1) back up important laptop data often, (2) password protect them, and (3) encrypt sensitive files. Organizations can also install antitheft systems in laptops and portable devices—for example, software that uses the integrated Web cam to take a picture of whoever uses it next or GPS systems can track the equipment itself.

Case-in-Point 10.5 "Laptops hardly ever get backed up," laments Scott Gaidano, president of DriveSavers, "and because laptops are portable, they get into more adventures." Among the many disasters he has seen regarding laptop computers include the following: one fell into the Amazon River, one melted in a car fire, one was run over by a bus, and four were dumped in bathtubs. In each case, although the machine was trashed, the data were salvaged. And recently, the company has saved digital media that included everything from official photos of the President to images of athletes at the Sydney Olympics to cosmetic surgery photos.[6]

Protection of Systems and Data with Personnel Policies

An AIS depends heavily on people for creating the system, inputting data into the system, supervising data processing during computer operations, distributing processed data to authorized recipients, and using approved controls to ensure that these tasks are performed properly. General controls within IT environments that affect personnel include: separation of duties, use of computer accounts, and identifying suspicious behavior.

Separation of Duties. Within IT environments, separation of duties should be designed and implemented by requiring *separate* accounting and IT subsystems or departments and also by *separate* responsibilities within the IT environment.

Separate Accounting and Information Processing from Other Subsystems. An organization's accounting and information processing subsystems are support functions for the other organizational subsystems and should be independent, or separate, from the subsystems that use data (accumulated by the accounting function and processed by the information processing subsystem) and perform the various operational activities. To achieve this separation, the functional design identified in Figure 10-6 should exist within organizations.

Methods to Separate Accounting and Other Systems

1. User subsystems initiate and authorize all systems changes and transactions.
2. Asset custody resides with designated operational subsystems.
3. Corrections for errors detected in processing data are entered on an error log, referred back to the specific user subsystem for correction, and subsequently followed up on by the *data control group* (discussed shortly).
4. Changes to existing systems as well as all new systems require a formal written authorization from the user subsystem.

FIGURE 10-6 Functional design to separate accounting and information processing subsystems from other subsystems.

---

[6] http://www.photoshopsupport.com/photoshop-blog/06/08/scott-gaidano-drivesavers.html

Separate Responsibilities Within IT Environment. Highly integrated AISs often combine procedures that used to be performed by separate individuals. Consequently, an individual who has unlimited access to the computer, its programs, and live data also has the opportunity to execute and, subsequently, conceal a fraud. To reduce this risk, a company should design and implement effective *separation of duties* control procedures. Figure 10-7 describes several functions within a company's IT environment, where it is essential to divide the *authority* and *responsibility* for the functions.

The design and implementation of effective separation-of-duties control procedures make it difficult for any one employee to commit a successful fraudulent activity. However, detecting fraud is even more challenging when two or more individuals *collude* to override separation-of-duties control procedures. A recent survey by the Association of Certified

Function	Explanation of Function/Division
Systems analysis function	• Analyze information, process needs, design/modify application programs. • The person performing this function should not perform other related functions. For example, do not allow a programmer for a bank to use actual data to test her program for processing loan payments (she could conceivably erase her own car loan balance).
Data control function	• Use a data control group; maintain registers of computer access codes; help acquire new accounting software (or upgrades); coordinate security controls with specific computer personnel (e.g., database administrator); reconcile input/output; distribute output to authorized users. • Should be independent of computer operations. This function inhibits unauthorized access to computer facility and contributes to more efficient data processing operations.
Programming function	• Require formal authorizations for program changes; submit written description of changes to a supervising manager for approval; test changes to programs prior to implementation.
Computer operations function	• Rotate computer operators among jobs to avoid any single operator always overseeing the same application. • Do not give computer operators access to program documentation or logic. • Two operators in the computer room during processing of data; maintain a processing log and periodically review for evidence of irregularities. • Without these control procedures a computer operator could alter a program (e.g., to increase his salary).
Transaction authorization function	• For each batch of input data, user subsystems submit signed form to verify input data are authorized and proper batch control totals are compiled. • Data control group personnel verify signatures and batch control totals before processing data. • These procedures help prevent errors (e.g., a payroll clerk cannot submit unauthorized form to increase pay rate).
AIS library function	• Maintain custody of files, databases, and computer programs in separate storage area called the AIS library. • Limit access to files, databases, and programs for usage purposes to authorized operators at scheduled times or with user authorization; maintain records of all usage. • The librarian does not have computer access privileges.

FIGURE 10-7 Divide certain authority and responsibility functions within an IT environment.

Fraud Examiners (ACFE) reports that over 36 percent of all fraud cases are committed by two or more individuals who work together to embezzle organizational assets. The median loss in these cases is $500,000, compared to a median loss of $115,000 in fraud cases that involve only one person.[7]

> *Case-in-Point 10.6*   The former D.C. tax manager, Harriette Walters, was able to embezzle more than $48 million over two decades largely because the culture in the finance office in the District of Columbia was one of apathy and silence. Walters and 10 accomplices, who did not work for the city, pleaded guilty to creating and laundering bogus tax refund checks. The embezzlement scheme is the largest involving a city or state government.[8]

Use of Computer Accounts.   Most computer networks maintain a system of separate computer accounts. Each user has an account, and each account has a unique password. When the user logs onto the computer, the system checks the password against a master list of accounts. Only users with current passwords can access computer resources. Some organizations also use account numbers to allocate computer charges to departments. This control procedure is important to protect scarce computer resources from unauthorized use.

While passwords have been the most used security method to grant users access, IT administrators have a variety of problems with them. Individuals paste their passwords on their monitors, share them with others, or choose simple passwords that are relatively easy for a hacker to guess. As a result, many firms now use biometric identification instead, as discussed earlier.

Identifying Suspicious Behavior.   The 2008 ACFE survey notes that employees who are defrauding their organizations often display certain behaviors (**red flags**) that can alert co-workers and supervisors to trouble. Examples include lavish spending or becoming very irritable or secretive. In particular, the survey results indicate that in over 38 percent of the cases of fraud, the fraudsters were living beyond their means, 34 percent had financial difficulties, 20 percent had ''wheeler-dealer'' attitudes, 19 percent were unwilling to share duties (control issues), and 17 percent had family problems or were in the middle of a divorce. Sadly, the survey results indicate that the highest percentage of fraud involved employees in the accounting department (29 percent of all cases reported by survey participants).

While it might be difficult for co-workers or supervisors to know intimate details of co-workers' personal lives, some of these behaviors may be observed without directly confronting the suspicious co-worker. The threats to an organization by its own employees should never be underestimated. To add emphasis to the need to be alert, PWC's Global State of Information Security Study estimated that people inside organizations were the culprits in 69 percent of database breaches, and new technologies (e.g., ERPs, B2B processes, and mobile devices) make organizational data even more vulnerable to potential misappropriation.[9] Accordingly, it is essential for organizations to safeguard computer files in an AIS from both intentional and unintentional errors. Figure 10-8 describes several reasons for these safeguards.

---

[7] http://www.acfe.com/documents/2008-rttn.pdf

[8] Nakamura, D., and H. Harris. 2008. Report on embezzlement blames ''culture of apathy and silence.'' *Washington Post* (December 16): B04.

[9] Roth, J., and D. Espersen. 2008. The insider threat. *Internal Auditor* (April): 71–73.

Reasons for Safeguarding Files

1. The computer files are not human-readable. Controls must be installed to ensure that these files *can* be read when necessary.

2. The typical computer file contains a vast amount of data. In general, it is not possible to reconstruct such files from the memories of employees.

3. The data contained on computer files are in a very compact format. The destruction of as little as one inch of recording medium means the loss of thousands of characters of data.

4. The data stored on computer files are permanent only to the extent that tiny bits have been recorded on the recording tracks. Power disruptions, power surges, and even accidentally dropping a disk pack, for example, may cause damage.

5. The data stored on computer files may be confidential. Information such as advertising plans, competitive bidding plans, payroll figures, and innovative software programs must be protected from unwarranted use.

6. The reconstruction of file data is costly no matter how extensive a company's recovery procedures. It is usually more cost-effective to protect against file abuse than to depend on backup procedures for file protection.

7. File information itself should be considered an asset of a company. As such, it deserves the same protection accorded other organizational assets.

FIGURE 10-8   Reasons for safeguarding computer files from both accidental and intentional errors.

Protection of Systems and Data with Technology and Facilities

In addition to protecting systems and data by controlling personnel, organizations must adequately plan for the protection of hardware and software resources and design software to protect data assets.

File Security Controls.   The purpose of file security controls is to protect computer files from either accidental or intentional abuse. For example, this requires control procedures to make sure that computer programs use the correct files for data processing. Control procedures are also needed for the purpose of creating backup copies of critical files in the event that original copies of a file are lost, stolen, damaged, or vandalized. Figure 10-9 provides examples of file security control procedures to verify that the correct file is being updated and to prevent accidental destruction of files.

Business Continuity Planning.   Organizations develop and test business continuity plans to be reasonably certain that they will be able to operate in spite of any interruptions—such as power failures, IT system crashes, natural disasters, supply chain problems, and others. Although the distinction between business continuity plans and disaster recovery is not always obvious, they are different. **Business continuity planning (BCP)** is a more comprehensive approach to making sure organizational activities continue normally, whereas **disaster recovery** involves the processes and procedures that organizations follow to resume business after a disruptive event such as an earthquake, a terrorist attack, or a serious computer virus. In this section, we discuss disaster recovery controls, controls to ensure fault-tolerant systems, and controls to back up data.

Disaster Recovery.   Examples of natural disasters include such events as fires, floods, hurricanes, and earthquakes, as well as man-made catastrophes (such as terrorist attacks). An organization's disaster recovery plan describes the procedures to be followed in the

File Security Control	Purpose of File Security Control
External file labels	• Identify contents of a computer file and help prevent an individual from accidentally writing over a disk file.

Internal file labels	• Record name of a file, date file created, and other identifying data on the file medium that will be read and verified by the computer.
	
	• Internal file labels include *header labels* and *trailer labels*.
	
	  • Header label is a file description at the beginning of a file.
	
	  • Trailer label indicates end of a file and contains summary data on contents of file.

Lockout procedures	• Use to prevent two applications from updating the same record or data item at the same time.
Read-only file designation	• Use to earmark data on floppy disks so that data is available for reading only, data cannot be altered by users, nor can new data be stored on the file.

FIGURE 10-9   Examples of file security control procedures.

event of an emergency, as well as the role of every member of the *disaster recovery team* (which is made up of specific company employees). The company's management should appoint one person to be in charge of disaster recovery and one person to be second-in-command.

An important part of any disaster recovery plan is the designation of specific backup sites to use for alternate computer processing. These backup sites may be other locations owned by the company, such as another branch of the same bank, or a site that is owned by other organizations, which it can use for short-term periods in the event of a disaster. It is a good idea for the various hardware locations for data processing to be some distance away from the original processing sites in case a disaster affects a regional location.

Case-in-Point 10.7   USAA, a large insurance company in San Antonio, TX, engaged outside consultants to help determine where the company should locate an alternate data processing center for operations in the event of an emergency. The consulting firm suggested the company build a second data center in the area as a backup. After weighing the costs and benefits of such a project, USAA initially concluded that it would be more efficient to rent space on the East Coast. Ironically, USAA was set to sign the lease contract the week of September 11, 2001. Instead, USAA built a center in Texas, only *200 miles* away from its offices—close enough to drive between locations, but far enough away to pull power from a different grid and water from a different source.[10]

Disaster recovery sites may be either hot sites or cold sites. A **hot site** has a computer system with capabilities similar to the system it will replace. A hot site that also includes up-to-date backup data is called a **flying-start site** because it can assume full data processing operations within a matter of seconds or minutes. A **cold site** is a location where power and environmentally controlled space are available to install processing equipment on short notice. If a disaster recovery plan designates a cold site, then arrangements are also necessary to obtain computer equipment matching the configuration of equipment lost in the disaster. In practice, the type of disaster recovery site used by a company should be determined by a cost-benefit analysis. Finally, simply preparing a disaster recovery plan

---

[10] http://www.csoonline.com/article/print/204450

does not provide assurance that the plan will work when needed. It is also important to periodically test the disaster recovery plan by simulating a disaster, thereby uncovering weaknesses in the plan as well as preparing employees for such emergencies.

Copies of a disaster recovery plan will not be of much use if they are located only in computer systems that are destroyed by a disaster. For this reason, members of a company's disaster recovery team should each keep current copies of the plan at their homes. Finally, in addition to periodic testing, a disaster recovery plan should be reviewed on a *continuous* basis and revised when necessary. This process is an integral part of business continuity planning.

Case-in-Point 10.8   A 2010 survey by CDW found that most companies report having a business continuity plan in place, but almost all of these same companies took a hit when there was a network disruption. Although 82 percent of the respondents felt confident that their IT resources could sustain disruptions and support operations effectively, 97 percent admitted that network disruptions had detrimental effects on their businesses in the last year. Power loss ranked as the top cause of business disruptions over the past year. Hardware failures caused 29 percent of network outages, and 21 percent of the problems were a loss of telecom services to facilities.[11]

Fault-Tolerant Systems.   Organizations use **fault-tolerant systems** to deal with computer errors and keep functioning so that data is accurate and complete. Fault-tolerant systems are often based on the concept of *redundancy.* Computer systems can be made fault-tolerant with duplicate communication paths or processors. Two major approaches are as follows: (1) Systems with **consensus-based protocols** contain an odd number of processors; if one processor disagrees with the others, it is thereafter ignored. (2) Some systems use a second **watchdog processor**. If something happens to the first processor, the watchdog processor then takes over the processing work.

Disks can be made fault tolerant through a process called **disk mirroring** (also known as **disk shadowing**). This process involves writing all data in parallel to multiple disks. Should one disk fail, the application program can automatically continue using a good disk. At the transaction level, a fault-tolerant system can use **rollback processing**, in which transactions are never written to disk until they are complete. Should there be a power failure or should another fault occur while a transaction is being written, the database program, at its first opportunity, automatically *rolls* itself back (reverts) to its prefault state.

Backup.   Backup is similar to the redundancy concept in fault-tolerant systems. For example, if you write a research paper on a computer, you would be wise to backup your work on a flash drive. As we know, a variety of unfortunate events could occur, and you might lose all of your work! If you used a computer in a lab on campus, you are probably aware of the fact that the hard drives are automatically cleaned every night, so your paper would not be on the hard drive of that computer the next day. And of course, other events such as a power failure or human error might occur and—your paper is gone. However, if you copied your paper on a flash drive, you created redundancy so that a problem will not cause you to lose your work.

Because of the risk of losing data before, during, or after processing, organizations have an even greater need to establish backup procedures for their files. The backup and reconstruction procedure typically used under batch processing is called the grandfather-parent-child procedure. Very large organizations might store more than three such copies

---

[11] http://www.csoonline.com/article/621192/survey-business-continuity-plans-still-need-work

(i.e., great-grandfather, great-great-grandfather), and banks typically keep many more copies because of the nature of their business.

Three generations of reference data (i.e., previously processed data stored on master files) are retained with the transaction data used during the general ledger updating process. If the most recent master file, the "child" copy, is destroyed, the data are reconstructed by rerunning the pertinent transaction data against the prior copy of the reference data (the "parent" master file). Should a problem occur during this reconstruction run, there is still one more set of backup data (the "grandfather" master file) to reconstruct the parent. The "parent" master file is then used to reconstruct the "child" master file. Figure 10-10 depicts this procedure.

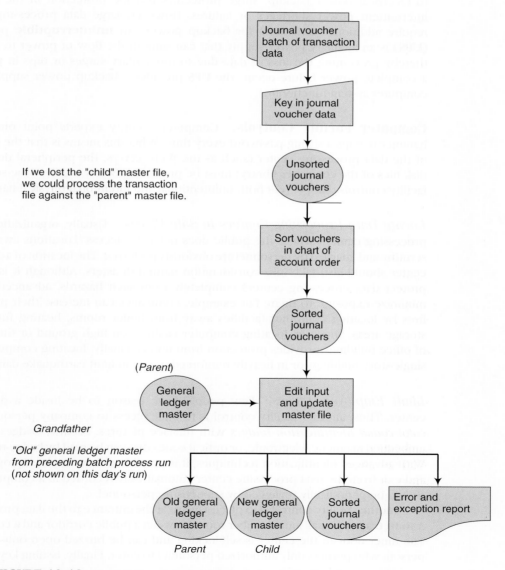

If we lost the "child" master file, we could process the transaction file against the "parent" master file.

FIGURE 10-10   Grandfather-parent-child procedure under batch processing.

With the sophisticated real-time systems widely used today, online backups are common. A **hot backup** is a backup performed while the database is online and available for read/write, whereas a **cold backup** is performed while the database is off-line and unavailable to its users. During processing, the reference data (master files) are periodically copied on a backup medium. A copy of all transaction data is stored as a *transaction log* as these data are entered into the system. The backup copies are stored at a remote site, which allows data to be recovered in the event a disaster occurs. Through a process called **electronic vaulting**, the data on backup media can be electronically transmitted to a remote site. Should the master file be destroyed or damaged, computer operations will *roll back* to the most recent backup copy of the master file. Recovery is then achieved by reprocessing the contents of the data transaction log against this master file backup copy.

A good disaster recovery plan also includes backups for hardware. With regard to electrical power backup, surge protectors provide protection in the case of short, intermittent power shortages or failures. However, large data processing centers may require additional generators for backup power. An **uninterruptible power system (UPS)** is an auxiliary power supply that can smooth the flow of power to the computer, thereby preventing the loss of data due to momentary surges or dips in power. Should a complete power failure occur, the UPS provides a backup power supply to keep the computer system functioning.

Computer Facility Controls.   Computer security experts point out that a blunt hammer trumps a strong password every time. What this means is that the physical assets of the data processing center (such as the Web servers, the peripheral devices, and the disk files of the computer library) must be protected. Below we describe some computer facility controls that prevent both unintentional and intentional physical harm to systems.

Locate Data Processing Centers in Safe Places.   Usually, organizations locate data processing centers where the public does not have access. Locations away from public scrutiny and guarded by personnel are obviously preferred. The location of a data processing center should also take into consideration natural disasters. Although it is impossible to protect data processing centers completely from such hazards, advanced planning can minimize exposure to them. For example, companies can increase their protection from fires by locating computer facilities away from boiler rooms, heating furnaces, or fuel storage areas. Similarly, locating computer facilities on high ground or the upper stories of office buildings provides protection from floods. Finally, locating computer facilities in single-story buildings or in heavily reinforced ones can limit earthquake damage.

Limit Employee Access.   Few people have reason to be inside a data processing center. Thus, another facility control is to limit access to company personnel who wear *color-coded identification badges* with full-face pictures. Security badges typically have embedded magnetic, electronic, or optical codes that can be read by badge-reading devices. With advanced identification techniques, it is possible to have each employee's entry into and exit from the data processing center automatically recorded in a computer log, which should be periodically reviewed by supervisory personnel.

Another facility control is to place a guard at the entrance to the data processing center. A **man trap** is a small antechamber room between a public corridor and a controlled room. The inner door to the center is self-locking and can be buzzed open only by the control person, who permits only authorized personnel to enter. Finally, issuing keys to authorized personnel or using dial-lock combinations limits access to the data processing center. With regard to this last control, it is also a good idea to change locks or lock combinations often and to use keys that cannot easily be duplicated.

Buy Insurance. Although insurance is usually thought to be an important method of protection for computer systems, it is actually the protection of last resort. Insurance does not protect the purchaser from loss, it merely compensates for losses if they occur. Insurance policies for computer damages are usually limited in coverage, which means that not all instances of loss may be recoverable by the policyholder. Furthermore, compensation usually is restricted to the actual losses suffered by a company. As you might imagine, a fair estimate of the value of data losses is not an easy matter.

APPLICATION CONTROLS FOR TRANSACTION PROCESSING

Enterprise-level controls focus on firm-wide issues, while IT general controls apply to all information systems. The purpose of **application controls** is to prevent, detect, and correct errors and irregularities in processing transactions. IT general controls and application controls are becoming more integrated because IT general controls support application controls, and together, they ensure complete and accurate information processing.

Application controls are those controls that are embedded in business process applications. The three major stages of data processing are inputting data, processing the data, and reporting the processed data in some form of output (e.g., a performance report). We discuss various application control procedures for AISs based on these three stages. First, we examine application controls over data input (called *input controls*). Next, we identify application controls that are intended to protect the processing of data (called *processing controls*), and finally, we survey application controls related to data output (called *output controls*).

Figure 10-11 emphasizes the important point that a company's application controls consist of input, processing, and output controls. Since every company's system is somewhat different, each company must consider the risk of errors and irregularities going undetected in processing its accounting data. The company must then design and implement its own cost-effective combination of input, processing, and output application controls.

Input Controls

Although many organizations are now using automated systems to collect data (e.g., bar code scanners), some applications still require employees to manually enter data in the information system. As a result, the risk of undetected errors and irregularities is typically

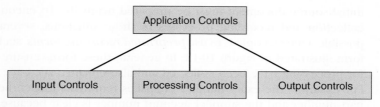

FIGURE 10-11 The composition of a company's application controls.

higher in this stage compared to the processing and output stages. In an attempt to reduce this risk factor, the strongest application controls are commonly found in the input stage of data processing.

Input controls help ensure the validity, accuracy, and completeness of the data entered into an AIS. It is usually cost-effective to test input data for the attributes of validity, accuracy, and completeness as early as possible. There are at least four reasons for this:

1. Data that are rejected at the time they are input can be more easily corrected—for example, by reference to a source document.

2. It is not cost-effective to screen accounting data continuously throughout the processing cycles of an AIS. Past some point in the job stream, all data are considered valid and error-free.

3. It is vital that an AIS use accurate data in later data processing operations. This protects master files from inaccuracies and safeguards computer processing in subsequent stages of the data processing work.

4. An AIS cannot provide good outputs if it does not start with good inputs.

For discussion purposes, it is useful to divide the topic of input application controls into three categories: (1) observation, recording, and transcription of data; (2) edit tests; and (3) additional input controls.

Observation, Recording, and Transcription of Data.

In general, data enter an AIS when business transactions are recorded. An organization often finds it useful to install one or more observation control procedures to assist in collecting data that will be recorded. One such control procedure is the introduction of a *confirmation mechanism*—for example, requiring a customer to sign, and therefore confirm, a sales order.

The data observation process can also make use of *dual observation*. Under this control procedure, the accuracy of the data observation process is enhanced because more than one employee participates in the process. In some organizations, the dual observation control procedure is *supervisory*. Here, the supervisor of the employee (or employees) involved in collecting data is required to confirm the accuracy of the data gathered by the employee.

Once accounting data have been collected, they must be recorded. Data collection and the subsequent recording of these data are areas in which a great deal of automation has taken place. For example, the use of *point-of-sale (POS) devices* (such as *bar code readers* that interpret the universal product code (UPC) commonly printed on store products and *smart cash registers* that are connected to off-site computers) to encode data have been found to substantially decrease error rates in the recording process as well as to eliminate the expense involved in rekeying data.

In some instances, automated data collection and recording are not feasible, and an initial source document must be prepared manually. To encourage accuracy in the data collection and recording processes in these situations, several control procedures are possible. One example is to use *preprinted recording forms,* such as the inventory receipts form illustrated in Figure 10-12. In general, these forms ensure that all the data required for processing have been collected and also enhance accuracy in the recording process. For example, the exact number of spaces required for such field items as the inventory part number and the supplier account number is clear because a box has been provided for each numerical digit, thus guarding against the loss or addition of digits in these fields. Organizations can use similar controls on Web pages.

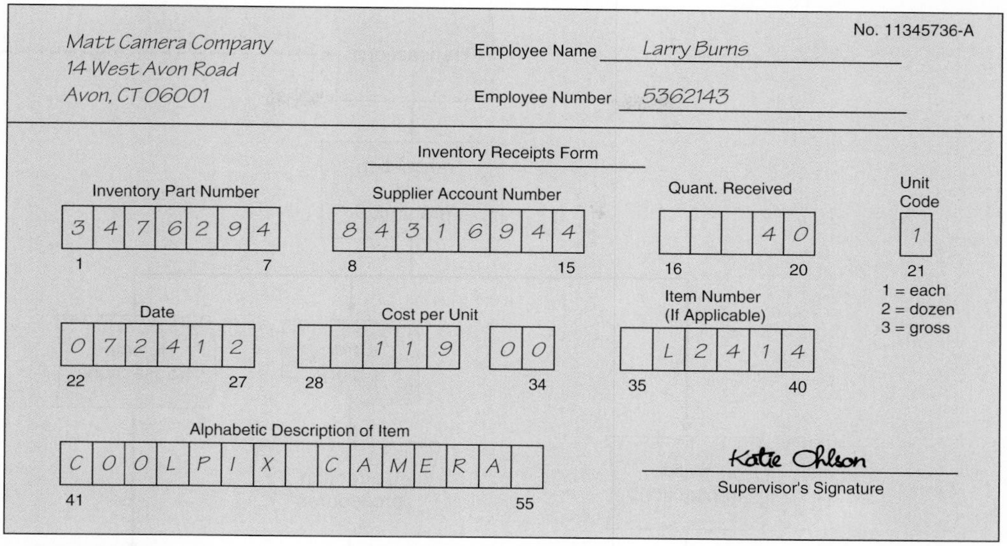

Matt Camera Company
14 West Avon Road
Avon, CT 06001

No. 11345736-A

Employee Name Larry Burns

Employee Number 5362143

Inventory Receipts Form

Inventory Part Number: 3 4 7 6 2 9 4 (1–7)

Supplier Account Number: 8 4 3 1 6 9 4 4 (8–15)

Quant. Received: 4 0 (16–20)

Unit Code: 1 (21)
1 = each
2 = dozen
3 = gross

Date: 0 7 2 4 1 2 (22–27)

Cost per Unit: 1 1 9 0 0 (28–34)

Item Number (If Applicable): L 2 4 1 4 (35–40)

Alphabetic Description of Item: C O O L P I X C A M E R A (41–55)

Katie Ohlson
Supervisor's Signature

FIGURE 10-12 A preprinted recording form for inventory receipts.

When using transcription, the data on source documents should be organized to facilitate the transcription process. Thus, well-designed, preprinted source-document forms are an important input control because they encourage adherence to the general principle of source-document and computer-input compatibility. Specially designed input forms are the most commonly used method to enter data in a database. Some advantages of database forms are that they can be designed to lock certain fields to prevent changes, to control certain fields so that a user cannot enter an unreasonable value, and to limit data values in certain fields.

Edit Tests. Programs or subroutines that check the validity and accuracy of input data after the data have been entered and recorded on a machine-readable file are called **input validation routines** (or **edit programs**). The specific types of validity and accuracy checks that input validation routines perform are called *edit tests* (or *edit checks*). **Edit tests** examine selected fields of input data and reject those transactions (or other types of data input) whose data fields do not meet the preestablished standards of data quality. Real-time processing systems perform edit tests during the data-entry process. Batch processing systems (illustrated in Figure 10-13) execute edit tests before regular data processing.

Edit tests can also be coordinated in what is called a *redundant data check* to ensure data accuracy. The idea is to encode repetitious data on a file or transaction record, thereby enabling a later processing test to compare the two data items for compatibility. For example, the reason you are always asked for the expiration date of your credit card is because that value is also encoded in the credit card number. Examples of edit tests are listed in Figure 10-14.

Additional Input Controls. It is possible for a data field to pass all of the edit tests previously described and still be invalid. To illustrate, a bank might use the incorrect

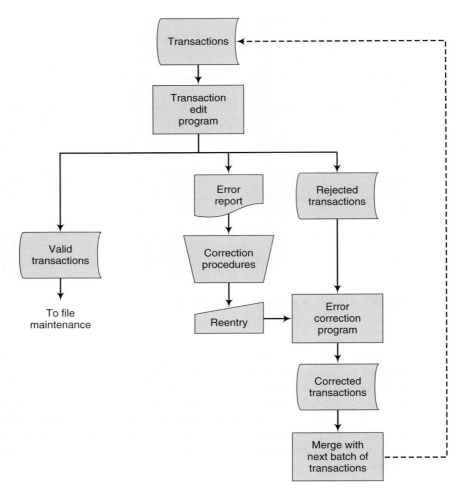

FIGURE 10-13 Use of edit program to execute edit tests under batch processing.

account number 537627 (instead of the proper account number 537621) when processing a customer's transaction. When the incorrect account number is keyed into a remote terminal and submitted to edit tests, it will, for example, (1) pass a test of numeric field content ensuring that all digits were numeric, (2) pass a test of reasonableness ensuring that the account number itself fell within a valid range of values (e.g., account number greater than 100,000 and less than 800,000), (3) pass a test of sign (i.e., account number positive), and (4) pass a test of completeness (i.e., no blanks in fields).

Thus, additional control procedures are required for this error to be detected. One control procedure is to incorporate a **validity test** into the data processing routine used to update the master file of bank records. With this approach, any transaction for which there is no corresponding master file record would be recognized as invalid and rejected from the transaction sequence (it would be returned for correction). But what if a master file record did exist for account 537627—the incorrect account number? This would indeed be unfortunate because our ''unfound-record'' control procedure would not detect the error,

Tests	Purpose
Numeric field content	To make sure that data fields such as Social Security number, sales invoice number, and date contain only numbers
Alphabetic field content	To make sure fields such as customer name contain only alphabetic letters
Alphanumeric field content	To make sure that fields such as inventory parts descriptions contain letters and/or numbers, but no special characters
Valid codes	For example, 1 = cash sale; 2 = credit sale
Reasonableness	For example, total hours worked by an employee during a weekly pay period does not exceed 50
Sign	For example, paycheck amounts always positive
Completeness	To check that there are no blanks in fields that require data
Sequence	To make sure that successive input data are in some prescribed order (e.g., ascending, descending, chronological, and alphabetical)
Consistency	For example, all transactions for the same sales office have the same office code number

FIGURE 10-14 Examples of edit tests.

and, even worse, the legitimate master file record with account number 537627 would be updated with the transaction data generated by another customer.

Continuing with our bank example, an alternative to this unfound-record test is to expand the six-digit data field of customer bank account numbers to seven digits with a *check-digit control procedure.* Normally, the check digit is computed as a mathematical function of the other digits in a numeric field, and its sole purpose is to test the validity of the associated data. To illustrate, consider the original (correct) account number 537621. The sum of these six digits is $5 + 3 + 7 + 6 + 2 + 1 = 24$. One type of check digit would append the low-order digit of this sum "4" to the account number. The seven-digit value 5376214 would be used instead of the six-digit series 537621 to represent the account number. The computer program would duplicate this computational procedure at the time of data access and therefore validate the accuracy of the data before the transaction data were used to update a master file record.

A check digit does not guarantee data validity. For example, the check-digit procedure described here would be unable to distinguish between the correct account number 5376214 and the transposed number 5736214 because the transposition of digits does not affect the sum. There are, however, check-digit techniques that do include "ordering of digits" in the construction of check-digit values. However, these and other very detailed computer checks are beyond the scope of this textbook, so we'll move on now to processing controls.

Processing Controls

Processing controls focus on the manipulation of accounting data after they are input to the computer system. An important objective of processing controls is to contribute to a good audit trail. A clear audit trail is essential, for example, to enable individual transactions to trace, to provide documentation for changes in general ledger account balances, to prepare financial reports, and to correct errors in transactions. To achieve a good audit trail, some systems require a printed *transaction listing* during each file update by batch processing systems and at the end of every day by online processing systems.

Furthermore, use of a unique and sequentially assigned transaction reference designator to identify each transaction in a listing promotes better audit trails. These transaction reference designators should be posted to the general ledger account records and recorded on the specific source documents pertaining to the transactions. Figure 10-15 illustrates an audit trail for a computer-based system, showing how source documents can be easily located by tracing back from an activity (or proof) listing, which is discussed shortly under output controls.

Control Totals. Suppose you were the data processing manager at a bank that processed over 100,000 bank checks per day. How would you make sure that all these checks are correctly processed by the computer? One procedure is to batch the checks in separate bundles of, say 200 checks, and prepare a special *batch control document* to serve as a control on the contents of each bundle. The information on this document might include the bundle number, today's date, and the total dollar amount for the checks themselves. The total dollar amount represents the **batch control total.** When computer processing commences, the special information on the lead control record (i.e., the batch control document) is accessed first and the batch control total is stored in computer memory. As the checks are accessed individually, their amounts are also accumulated in computer memory. Once all the checks in the batch are read, the accumulated total is compared with the batch control total. A match signals acceptable processing. A nonmatch signals an error, which may then be traced either to an error in the batch control total or to some difficulty in processing—for example, the inability of the MICR reader to understand the data on one or more checks.

In fact, MICR readers are themselves a form of control. An original check has a line of magnetic ink with specific information that is recognized by highly reliable MICR readers. Even the best printers do not use this magnetic ink and copied checks can therefore be detected immediately.[12]

A control total that involves a dollar amount is called a *financial control total.* Other examples of financial control totals include the sum of cash receipts in an accounts receivable application, the sum of cash disbursements in an accounts payable application, and the sum of net pay in a payroll application.

AISs also use *nonfinancial control totals,* which compute nondollar sums. For example, controls could compute the sum of the total number of hours worked by employees in

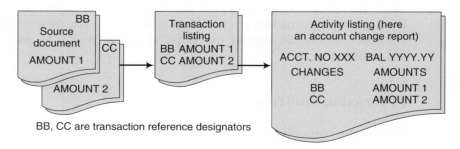

BB, CC are transaction reference designators

FIGURE 10-15 An audit trail for a computer-based system.

---

[12] http://www.pointofsale.com

a payroll application. A similar control is a *record count.* With this control procedure, the number of transaction items is counted twice: once when preparing transactions in a batch and again when actually performing the data processing. Yet a third example is the exact byte count of a legitimate computer program, which IT personnel can use to detect tampering.

Control totals do not have to make sense to be useful. For example, when cash receipts from customers are processed, the manual sum of the customers' account numbers in a batch of transactions might be computed to form a **hash total**. This sum is meaningless, but is useful as a check against an "internal" tally of this same hash total by the computer at the time of data access.

Data Manipulation Controls.   Once data have been validated by earlier portions of data processing, they usually must be manipulated (i.e., processed) in some way by computer programs to produce decision-useful information, such as a report. One processing control procedure is to make sure that the computer programs are complete and thorough in their data manipulation. Ordinarily, this is accomplished by examining *software documentation.* System flowcharts, program flowcharts, data flow diagrams, and decision tables can also function as controls because they help systems analysts do a thorough job in planning data processing functions.

After computer programs have been coded, they are translated into machine language by an error-testing *compiler.* The compiler controls the possibility that a computer program contains programming language errors. A computer program can also be tested with specially designed *test data* that expose the program to the exception conditions likely to occur during its actual use.

Output Controls

Once data have been processed internally by a computer system, they are usually transferred to some form of output medium for storage, screen display, or, in the case of printed output, prepared as a report. The objective of **output controls** is to ensure the output's validity, accuracy, and completeness. Two major types of output application controls within IT environments are (1) validating processing results and (2) regulating the distribution and use of printed output.

Validating Processing Results.   The validity, accuracy, and completeness of computerized output in AISs can be established through the preparation of *activity (or proof) listings* that document processing activity. These listings provide complete, detailed information about all changes to master files and thus contribute to a good audit trail. Organizational employees use such activity listings to trace file changes back to the events or documents that triggered these changes and thereby verify current file information or printed information as valid, accurate, and complete output.

Regulating Distribution and Use of Printed Output.   One of the more compelling aspects of output control deals with the subject of *forms control.* Perhaps the most interesting situations involve computerized check-writing applications in which MICR forms or perforated printer forms become the encoding media for preparing a company's checks. Usually, these forms are preprinted with the company's name, address, and bank account number. Control over the forms associated with check writing is vital.

The most common type of control used with computer-generated check-writing procedures is the coordination of a preprinted check number on the printer form with a computer-generated number that is printed on the same form at run time. The numbers on these *prenumbered forms* advance sequentially and are prepared by the forms' supplier according to the specifications of an organization. The computer-generated numbers also run sequentially and are initialized by adding 1 to the check sequence number stored from the last processing run. The numbers on the prenumbered forms and the computer-generated numbers should match during normal processing. Discrepancies should be examined carefully, and the causes fully resolved. Other examples of forms that employ prenumbering methods include reports containing sensitive corporate information and computer-generated lottery and athletic event tickets.

Computer reports often contain sensitive information and it is important that such information be restricted. Thus, for example, a payroll register, indicating the earnings of each employee during a given pay period, is a type of report whose distribution should be restricted. The most common approach to distributional control is through an *authorized distribution list.* For each output report (hard copy or electronic), distribution is limited to authorized users only. Where data processing activities are centralized, it is sometimes the case that the user will physically visit the computer facility to pick up a copy of a sensitive report. In these instances, a notebook, or log, of pickups can be maintained and the pickup employee asked to sign the book. The employee's identification number is recorded for security purposes at the time the report is taken.

In situations where it is not possible to have representatives from user groups pick up reports, bonded employees can be authorized to deliver the reports to users. Subsequently, random checks on the distribution of these reports can be made by the bonded employees' supervisors to verify distribution. After sensitive reports are no longer needed, it is important to properly destroy them (i.e., use a document shredder). Shredding reports is a stronger control than throwing them away because discarded reports can be retrieved from trash bins.

AIS AT WORK
Biometrics Used to Prevent Fraud[13]

Many firms failed in 2009 and 2010 because of the economic crisis. In addition, investors lost billions of dollars as a result of fraud perpetrated by employees and executives. SAP is expanding the use of biometrics in its enterprise systems in order to better prevent and detect fraud. The idea is to combine biometric identification with passwords such that system users must first be identified with fingerprints and then must supply a password before the user can gain access to any system. In addition, biometric and password combinations are specific to applications and subsets of major systems, which prevents employees from accessing anything that they are not specifically authorized to access.

A recent fraud at Societe Generale Bank could have been prevented with biometric internal controls. One of the bank's traders used his knowledge of the bank's ERP system to engage in secret trading activity. The trader had been trained in using the bank's ERP system prior to becoming a trader and he used his knowledge of the system to commit fraud. The trader was able to create e-mails in the system to establish fake authorizations,

---

[13] http://en.sap.info/biometric-security-for-financial-meltdown-solutions/10874

use his colleagues' log-in passwords to conduct trades in other employees' names, and delete records within the accounting system because he had access to more data within the AIS than he was authorized to have. Simple changes in IT general controls would have prevented the traders' fraud. For example, biometric identification would have prevented him from logging in as other employees, and biometric identification in combination with password access to only the trading system would have prevented him from changing accounting records to cover his tracks. In brief, biometric identification systems would have stopped the trader from making secret trades and eliminated his ability to cover his tracks. New versions of SAP emphasize the combination of biometrics and passwords. These systems also solve problems related to lost and stolen passwords. If a hacker is able to steal employees' passwords, the passwords are useless without fingerprints or iris scans.

 ## SUMMARY

✓ Enterprise-level controls are so important because they often have a pervasive impact on many other controls, such as IT general controls and application-level controls.

✓ At the organizational level, examples of important controls are management's ethical values, philosophy, assignment of authority and responsibility, and the effectiveness of the board of directors.

✓ Firms are using an integrated approach to security by combining a number of technologies, including firewalls, intrusion detection systems, content filtering, vulnerability management, virus protection, and virtual private networks.

✓ An integrated security system, supported by a comprehensive security policy, can significantly reduce the risk of attack because it increases the costs and resources needed by an intruder.

✓ IT general controls are controls that are applied to all IT service activities. These controls are critical for reliance on application controls.

✓ Senior management must have controls over human resources and data resources.

✓ Business continuity planning is essential for surviving natural disasters and other business disruptions.

✓ Organizations are increasingly relying on wireless networks and must recognize the need for a virtual private network (VPN) so that users may safely access entity data and other online resources.

✓ Due to increased mobility of employees, organizations must also develop controls for laptop computers to protect those assets as well as the data that resides on them.

✓ Three major types of application controls are: (1) input controls, (2) processing controls, and (3) output controls.

KEY TERMS YOU SHOULD KNOW

application controls	consensus-based protocols
batch control total	data encryption
biometric identification	data manipulation controls
business continuity planning (BCP)	disaster recovery
checkpoint	disk mirroring
cold backup	disk shadowing
cold site	edit programs

edit tests	message acknowledgment procedures
electronic eavesdropping	output controls
electronic vaulting	physical security
fault-tolerant systems	processing controls
flying-start site	red flags
hash total	rollback processing
hot backup	routing verification procedures
hot site	security policy
input controls	strong passwords
input validation routines	uninterruptible power system (UPS)
integrated security	validity test
IT general controls	virtual private network (VPN)
logical security	watchdog processor
man trap	

DISCUSSION QUESTIONS

10-1. What is a security policy? What do we mean when we say organizations should have an integrated security plan?

10-2. What do we mean when we talk about convergence of physical and logical security? Why might this be important to an organization?

10-3. What guidance or framework would you use to establish IT governance if you were a senior executive in a firm? If you were a midlevel IT manager who was designing IT general controls? A manager who was responsible for identifying the appropriate application controls?

10-4. What controls must be used to protect data that is transmitted across wireless networks?

10-5. Why is business continuity planning so important? Identify several reasons why testing the plan is a good idea.

10-6. What is backup and why is it important when operating an accounting system?

10-7. Discuss some of the unique control risks associated with the use of PCs and laptop computers compared to using mainframes. List what you consider to be three of the most important control procedures that should be implemented for PCs. For each control procedure, give your reason for including this procedure as an important control.

10-8. Jean & Joan Cosmetics has a complete line of beauty products for women and maintains a computerized inventory system. An eight-digit product number identifies inventory items, of which the first four digits classify the beauty product by major category (hair, face, skin, eyes, etc.) and the last four digits identify the product itself. Identify as many controls as you can that the company might use to ensure accuracy in this eight-digit number when updating its inventory-balance file.

10-9. Explain how each of the following can be used to control the input, processing, or output of accounting data: (a) edit tests, (b) check digits, (c) passwords, (d) activity listings, and (e) control totals.

10-10. What is the difference between *logical* access to the computer and *physical* access to the computer? Why is the security of both important?

10-11. Discuss the following statement: "The separation of duties control is very difficult in computerized accounting information systems because computers often integrate functions when performing data processing tasks. Therefore, such a control is not advisable for those organizations using computers to perform their accounting functions."

10-12. Discuss the role of the *hash total* in accounting information systems.

PROBLEMS

10-13. E. Wilson & Sons, Inc. hired a consulting team from Chesapeake and Associates to discuss application controls for the company's accounting data processing. In one of the workshops, the seminar leader stated, "We can classify all errors in processing accounting data as either accidental or intentional. Controls such as edit tests are primarily aimed at the former type of error, whereas personnel controls are primarily aimed at the latter type of error." Comment on the leader's statement.

10-14. Mark Goodwin, a computer programmer, had a grudge against his company. To get even, he coded a special routine in the mortgage loan program that erased a small, random number of accounts on the disk file every time the program was run. The company did not detect the routine until almost all of its records had been erased. Discuss what controls might have protected this company from its own programmer.

10-15. Jack Drucker, an accountant working for a medium-size company, set up several dummy companies and began directing the computer to write checks to them for fictitious merchandise. He was apprehended only when several of the company executives began to wonder how he could afford a ski vacation in the Alps every year. What controls might have prevented this fraudulent activity?

10-16. Identify one or more *control procedures* (either *general* or *application* controls, or both) that would guard against each of the following errors or problems.

    a. Leslie Thomas, a secretary at the university, indicated that she had worked 40 hours on her regular time card. The university paid her for 400 hours worked that week.

    b. The aging analysis indicated that the Grab and Run Electronics Company account was so far in arrears that the credit manager decided to cut off any further credit sales to the company until it cleared up its account. Yet, the following week, the manager noted that three new sales had been made to that company—all on credit.

    c. The Small Company employed Mr. Fineus Eyeshade to perform all its accounts receivable data processing. Mr. Eyeshade's 25 years with the company and his unassuming appearance helped him conceal the fact that he was embezzling cash collections from accounts receivable to cover his gambling losses at the racetrack.

    d. The Blue Mountain Utility Company was having difficulty with its customer payments. The payment amounts were entered directly onto a terminal, and the transaction file thus created was used to update the customer master file. Among the problems encountered with this system were the application of customer payments to the wrong accounts and the creation of multiple customer master file records for the same account.

    e. The Landsford brothers had lived in Center County all their lives. Ben worked for the local mill in the accounts payable department and Tom owned the local hardware store. The sheriff couldn't believe that the brothers had created several dummy companies that sold fictitious merchandise to the mill. Ben had the mill pay for this merchandise in its usual fashion, and he wrote off the missing goods as "damaged inventory."

10-17. Identify one or more *control procedures* (either *general* or *application* controls or both) that would guard against each of the following errors or problems.

    a. A bank deposit transaction was accidentally coded with a withdrawal code.

    b. The key-entry operator keyed in the purchase order number as a nine-digit number instead of an eight-digit number.

    c. The date of a customer payment was keyed 2001 instead of 2010.

    d. A company employee was issued a check in the amount of $-135.65 because he had not worked a certain week, but most of his payroll deductions were automatic each week.

    e. A patient filled out her medical insurance number as 123465 instead of 123456.

    f. An applicant for the company stock option plan filled out her employee number as 84-7634-21. The first two digits are a department code. There is no department 84.

g. A high school student was able to log onto the telephone company's computer as soon as he learned what telephone number to call.

h. The accounts receivable department sent 87 checks to the computer center for processing. No one realized that one check was dropped along the way and that the computer therefore processed only 86 checks.

10-18. To achieve effective separation of duties within a company's IT environment, the company's accounting and information processing subsystems should be separate from the departments that use data and perform operational activities. Discuss some of the ways this "separation of duties" is achieved.

10-19. Bristol Company has a high turnover rate among its employees. It maintains a very large computer system that supports approximately 225 networked PCs. The company maintains fairly extensive databases regarding its customers. These databases include customer profiles, past purchasing patterns, and prices charged. Recently, Bristol Company has been having major problems with competitors. It appears that one competitor seems to be very effective at taking away the company's customers. This competitor has visited most of Bristol Company's customers, and identical products have been offered to these customers at lower prices in every case.

a. What do you feel is the possible security problem at Bristol Company?

b. What can be done about this problem?

10-20. The Blatz Furniture Company uses an online data input system for processing its sales invoice data, salesperson data, inventory control, and purchase order data. Representative data for each of these applications are shown in Figure 10-16. Identify specific edit tests that might be used to ensure the accuracy and completeness of the information in each data set.

Application	Field Name	Field Length	Example
Invoicing	Customer number	6	123456
	Customer name	23	Al's Department Store
	Salesperson number	3	477
	Invoice number	6	123456
	Item catalog number	10	9578572355
	Quantity sold	8	13
	Unit price	7	10.50
	Total price	12	136.50
Salesperson activity	Salesperson number	3	477
	Salesperson name	20	Kathryn Wilson
	Store department number	8	10314201
	Week's sales volume	12	1043.75
	Regular hours worked	5	39.75
	Overtime hours worked	4	0.75
Inventory control	Inventory item number	10	9578572355
	Item description	15	Desk lamp
	Unit cost	7	8.50
	Number of units dispersed this week	4	14
	Number of units added to inventory	4	20
Purchasing	Vendor catalog number	12	059689584996
	Item description	18	Desk pad
	Vendor number	10	8276110438
	Number of units ordered	7	45
	Price per unit	7	8.75
	Total cost of purchase	14	313.75

FIGURE 10-16 Data for the Blatz Furniture Company's applications.

CASE STUDIES

The Big Corporation (Controls in Large, Integrated Systems)

The Big Corporation has recently grown substantially and must upgrade its information systems. The company is developing a new, integrated, computer-based information system. In conjunction with the design of the new system, management is reviewing the data processing security to determine what new control features should be incorporated. Two areas of concern are (1) confidentiality of company and customer records, and (2) protection of data, computer equipment, and facilities.

The new information system will process all company records, including sales, purchases, budgeting, customer, creditor, and personnel information. The stores and warehouses will be linked to the main computer at corporate headquarters by a system of remote terminals. This will permit data to be communicated directly to corporate headquarters or to any other location from each location within the terminal network. Employees will also be able to access the system with laptops and handheld devices via a secured wireless network.

At the current time, certain reports have restricted distribution because not all levels of management need to receive them or because they contain confidential information. The introduction of remote terminals in the new system may provide access to these restricted data by unauthorized personnel. Management is concerned that confidential information may become accessible and be used improperly.

The company's management is also concerned with potential physical threats to the system, such as sabotage, fire damage, water damage, or power failure. With the new system, a computer shutdown would severely limit company activities until the system is operational again.

Requirements

1. Identify and briefly explain the problems The Big Corporation could experience with respect to the confidentiality of information and records in the new system.

2. Recommend measures The Big Corporation could incorporate into the new system that would ensure the confidentiality of information and records in this new system.

3. What safeguards can The Big Corporation develop to provide physical security for its (a) computer equipment, (b) data, and (c) data processing center facilities?

Bad Bad Benny: A True Story (Identifying Controls for a System)[14]

In the early twentieth, century, there was an ambitious young man named Arthur who started working at a company in Chicago as a mailroom clerk. He was a hard worker and very smart, eventually ending up as the president of the company, the James H. Rhodes Company. The firm produced steel wool and harvested sea sponges in Tarpon Springs, Florida, for household and industrial use. The company was very successful, and Arthur decided that the best way to assure the continued success of the company was to hire trusted family members for key management positions—because you can always count on your family. Arthur decided to hire his brother Benny to be his Chief Financial Officer (CFO) and placed other members of the family in key management positions. He also

---

[14] Used with permission, Professor Constance Lehmann, Department of Accounting, University of Houston-Clear Lake.

started his eldest son, Arthur Junior (an accountant by training), in a management training program, hoping that he would eventually succeed him as president.

As the company moved into the 1920s, Benny was a model employee; he worked long hours, never took vacations, and made sure that he personally managed all aspects of the cash function. For example, he handled the entire purchasing process—from issuing purchase orders through the disbursement of cash to pay bills. He also handled the cash side of the revenue process by collecting cash payments, preparing the daily bank deposits, and reconciling the monthly bank statement.

The end of the 1920s saw the United States entering its worst Depression since the beginning of the Industrial Age. Because of this, Arthur and other managers did not get raises, and, in fact, took pay cuts to keep the company going and avoid layoffs. Arthur and other top management officials made ''lifestyle'' adjustments as well—for example, reducing the number of their household servants and keeping their old cars, rather than purchasing new ones. Benny, however, was able to build a new house on the shore of Lake Michigan and purchased a new car. He dressed impeccably and seemed impervious to the economic downturn. His family continued to enjoy the theater, new cars, and nice clothes.

Arthur's wife became suspicious of Benny's good fortune in the face of others' hardships, so she and Arthur hired an accountant to review the books. External audits were not yet required for publicly held companies, and the Securities and Exchange Commission (SEC) had not yet been formed (that would happen in 1933–1934). Jim, the accountant, was eventually able to determine that Benny had diverted company funds to himself by setting up false vendors and having checks mailed to himself. He also diverted some of the cash payments received from customers and was able to hide it by handling the bank deposits and the reconciliation of the company's bank accounts. Eventually, Jim determined that Benny had embezzled about $500,000 (in 1930 dollars).

If we assume annual compounding of 5 percent for 72 years, the value in today's dollars would be about $17.61 million! Arthur was furious and sent Benny away. Arthur sold most of his personal stock holdings in the company to repay Benny's embezzlement, which caused him to lose his controlling interest in the company and, eventually, was voted out of office by the Board of Directors.

Jim, the accountant, wrote a paper about his experience with Benny (now referred to as ''Bad Bad Benny'' by the family). Jim's paper contributed to the increasing call for required annual external audits for publicly held companies. Arthur eventually reestablished himself as a successful stockbroker and financial planner. Benny disappeared and was never heard from again.

Requirements

1. Identify the control weaknesses in the revenue and purchasing processes.
2. Identify any general controls Arthur should have implemented to help protect the company.
3. From Chapter 9, identify the internal control activities that Arthur should have considered (or implemented) that would have thwarted Benny's bad behavior.

Chapter 11

Computer Crime, Fraud, Ethics, and Privacy

INTRODUCTION

The connection between AISs and computer crime and fraud is both straightforward and important. Managers, accountants, and investors all use computerized information to control valuable resources, help sell products, authenticate accounting transactions, and make investment decisions. But the effectiveness of these activities can be lost if the underlying information is wrong, incomplete, or seriously compromised. This is why digital information is itself a valuable asset that must be protected. The more managers and accountants know about computer crime and fraud, the better they can assess risks and implement controls to protect organizational assets.

This chapter describes computer crime, fraud, and other irregularities that have occurred in the past and that may also occur in the future. In the first section, we take a closer look at computer crime, abuse, and fraud. In the second section, we examine three specific cases involving computer crime. The third section of this chapter identifies what organizations can do to protect themselves from computer crime and abuse—that is, what they can do to recognize potential problems and what they can do to control them.

Not all computer-related offenses are illegal—some are just unethical. Because of the importance of ethical behavior within the environment of computerized AISs, we also discuss the topic of computers and ethical behavior. Finally, the last section of our chapter addresses the importance of privacy and identity theft. The dramatic increase in the number of individuals, companies, and organizations using the Internet draws our attention to the question of personal privacy. What information is collected about us and how much of it is authorized? Also, how much of it is freely provided by individuals who do not realize that others will store and use the information for purposes other than what was intended? Accordingly, we focus on the issue of collection and protection of information.

COMPUTER CRIME, ABUSE, AND FRAUD

Articles in *Fortune, Business Week*, the *Wall Street Journal, Computerworld, Security Focus,* and *WIRED* all testify to the high level of public interest in computer crime, abuse, and fraud. Although data on computer crime and fraud are limited, at least three reputable organizations conduct surveys that help us understand the breadth and depth of these crimes. First, the **Computer Security Institute (CSI)** conducts an annual survey to help determine the scope of computer crime in the United States. The respondents to this survey are computer security practitioners in U.S. corporations, government agencies, financial institutions, medical institutions, and universities.

Second, KPMG, a global network of professional firms providing audit, tax, and advisory services, conducts surveys on fraud and business integrity. Survey participants are the business professionals who work for one of the top 2,000 companies listed in Dun and Bradstreet. Third, the **Association of Certified Fraud Examiners (ACFE)**—an international professional organization committed to detecting, deterring, and preventing fraud and white-collar crime—conducts a biannual survey and publishes the results in its *Report to the Nation on Occupational Fraud and Abuse*. The participants in this survey are its members, each of whom provides detailed information on one occupational fraud case he or she had personally investigated within the past two years.

Distinguishing Between Computer Crime, Computer Abuse, and Fraud

While the terms "computer crime" and "computer abuse" seem to describe the same problem, there is a subtle difference between them. **Computer crime** means that someone manipulates a computer or computer data, by whatever method, to dishonestly obtain money, property, or some other advantage—or cause significant loss. In contrast, **computer abuse** means that someone, who does not have permission, uses or accesses someone else's computer. So, a perpetrator commits a computer crime when he or she gains an illegal financial advantage or causes measurable loss to a person, company, or organization, while computer abusers are mischievous pests with such motives as a challenge or revenge. Then, too, there are hackers who exploit the vulnerabilities of an organization's computer systems just because they can.

> *Case-in-Point 11.1* At age 22, Adrian Lamo was well known for exposing gaping security holes at large corporations and then voluntarily helping the companies fix the vulnerabilities he exploited. At the *New York Times* site, Lamo obtained access to the names and Social Security numbers of employees. Although Lamo described this vulnerability to the *New York Times*, the publisher's managers were not grateful and initiated an investigation. More recently, Lamo reported to federal authorities that it was Bradley Manning who leaked sensitive U.S. government documents to WikiLeaks.[1]

The term computer crime is really a misnomer because *computers* do not commit crimes—people do. Figure 11-1 describes several cases that might qualify as computer crimes or abuses. In the first case, the primary objective was to disrupt a computer network—not personal gain. The second case is neither a computer crime nor an abuse. Rather, "misrepresentation" would probably more accurately describe the problem. In the third case, a computer screen was damaged but the loss would probably not be a criminal charge. In the fourth case, the attempt to sell credit information would be a criminal offense. In the fifth case, no computer was used, so it is difficult to call this a "computer crime." Finally, although the sixth case involved a computer and resulted in personal gain, it is perhaps more accurate to describe this crime as a "misappropriation of assets," which is described below.

Another example of a computer offense, which could be either a crime or an abuse, is a **logic bomb**. This is a computer program that remains dormant until some specified circumstance or date triggers the program to action. Once "detonated," a logic bomb program sabotages a system by destroying data and/or disrupting computer operations. The following Case-in-Point describes the first person in America to be convicted of "harmful access to a computer" because of a logic bomb that he triggered on the day he was dismissed from USPA, a Fort Worth-based insurance company.[2]

---

[1] http://www.wired.com/threatlevel/2010/05/lamo/and http://en.wikipedia.org/wiki/Adrian_Lamo
[2] http://www.cheycobb.com/logic_bombs.html

1. A graduate student infected a computer network with a virus that eventually disrupted over 10,000 separate systems.

2. A company accused a computer-equipment vendor of fraudulently representing the capabilities of a computer system, charging that the full system was never delivered and that the software was inadequate.

3. In a fit of resentment, a keyboard operator shattered an LCD screen with her high-heeled shoe.

4. Some employees of a credit bureau sent notices to some of the individuals listed as bad risks in its files. For a fee, the employees would withhold the damaging information, thereby enhancing the credit worthiness of the applicants.

5. A computer dating service was sued because referrals for dates were few and inappropriate. The owner eventually admitted that no computer was used to match dates, even though the use of a computer was advertised.

6. A programmer changed a dividends-payment program to reduce the dividends of selected stock holders and to issue a check to himself for the sum of the reductions—$56,000.

FIGURE 11-1   Examples of computer crimes.

Case-in-Point 11.2   Donald Burleson was a disgruntled computer programmer who set off a logic bomb that erased 168,000 sales commission records. Consequently, company paychecks were held up for a month. He embedded the logic bomb in a legitimate program, which he designed to go off periodically to erase still more records. But a fellow programmer who was testing a new employee bonus system discovered the bomb before it could execute again. The company's computers were shut down for two days while the bomb was located and diffused.

The type of computer crime with which most professional accountants are familiar is financial fraud. Statement on Auditing Standards No. 99 identifies two types of such fraud: (1) fraudulent financial reporting and (2) misappropriation of assets.[3] *Fraudulent financial reporting* (called cooking the books) happens when corporate officials such as senior-ranking executives intentionally falsify accounting records to mislead analysts, creditors, or investors. As a result, the annual financial statements do not fairly represent the true financial condition of the firm. The corporate scandals discussed in Chapter 1 are examples of this type of fraud.

Misappropriation of assets is usually committed by employees within an organization, although individuals can collude with outside conspirators to perform such acts as well. The ACFE calls this type of crime *occupational fraud* and has developed a "fraud tree" to describe the many ways that employees can misappropriate assets from an organization. Examples include skimming, larceny, payroll tampering, and check tampering. Figure 11-2 gives several examples of asset misappropriation. Most of these activities directly involve accounting information systems.

Computer Crime Legislation

A strict definition of computer crime must be found in the law. Such definitions are important because they determine what law enforcement officials can prosecute as well as how statistics on such crimes are accumulated. Both federal and state statutes govern computer usage.

---

[3] AICPA. 2003. Statement on Auditing Standards No. 99, *Consideration of Fraud in a Financial Statement Audit*.

Asset Class	Type of Fraud	Example
Cash	Larceny	Direct theft or removal from bank deposit
	Skimming	Nonreporting or underreporting of sales
		Write-offs of legitimate receivables as bad debts
		Lapping schemes
	Fraudulent disbursements	Payments to ghost companies or employees
		Payments for fictitious goods or services
		Multiple payments for the same bill
		Forged checks
		Altered payee on legitimate check
		False refunds
Inventory and all other assets	Misuse	Use of corporate limousine or jet for personal travel
	Larceny	Theft of raw materials or finished goods
		Fictitious inventory adjustments
		Nonreporting or underreporting of received goods

FIGURE 11-2 Examples of asset misappropriation.

Federal Legislation. Figure 11-3 lists some important federal legislation governing activities involving computers. Of these acts, the most important is probably the **Computer Fraud and Abuse Act of 1986 (CFAA)**, which was amended in 1994 and 1996. This act defines computer fraud as any illegal act for which knowledge of computer technology is essential for its perpetration, investigation, or prosecution. The following paragraphs identify the fraudulent acts found in the Computer Fraud and Abuse Act and give examples of each type of crime.

1. *Unauthorized theft, use, access, modification, copying, or destruction of software or data.* The PC manager at a King Soopers supermarket in Colorado was called repeatedly to correct computer errors that were thought to be responsible for a large number of sales voids and other accounting errors. Eventually, the company discovered that this manager was in fact the cause of these problems. Over the course of five years or more, officials estimate that he and two head clerks used a number of simple methods to steal more than $2 million from the company—for example, by voiding sales transactions and pocketing the customers' cash payments.

2. *Theft of money by altering computer records or the theft of computer time.* To commit an inventory fraud, several employees at an east coast railroad entered data into their company's computer system to show that more than 200 railroad cars were scrapped or destroyed. These employees then removed the cars from the railroad system, repainted them, and sold them.

3. *Intent to illegally obtain information or tangible property through the use of computers.* One case of industrial espionage involved Reuters Analytics, whose employees were accused of breaking into the computers of their competitor, Bloomberg, and stealing lines of programming code. These instructions were supposedly used in software that provides financial institutions with the capability to analyze historical data on the stock market.

4. *Use, or the conspiracy to use, computer resources to commit a felony.* Paul Sjiem-Fat used desktop publishing technology to perpetrate one of the first cases of computer forgery. Sjiem-Fat created bogus cashier's checks and used these checks to buy computer

Fair Credit Reporting Act of 1970. This act requires that an individual be informed why he or she is denied credit. The act also entitles the individual to challenge information maintained by the credit-rating company and to add information if desired. Seven years after this law was put into effect, the annual number of complaints filed under it exceeded 200,000.

Freedom of Information Act of 1970. This is a federal "sunshine law" guaranteeing individuals the right to see any information gathered about them by federal agencies.

Federal Privacy Act of 1974. This act goes further than the Freedom of Information Act of 1970 by requiring that individuals be able to correct federal information about themselves, by requiring that agency information not be used for alternate purposes without the individual's consent, and by making the collecting agency responsible for the accuracy and use of the information. Under this act, an individual may ask a federal judge to order the correction of errors if the federal agency does not do so.

Small Business Computer Security and Education Act of 1984. This act created an educational council that meets annually to advise the Small Business Administration on a variety of computer crime and security issues affecting small businesses.

Computer Fraud and Abuse Act of 1986. This act makes it a federal crime to intentionally access a computer for purposes such as (1) obtaining top-secret military information or personal financial or credit information; (2) committing a fraud; or (3) altering or destroying federal information.

Computer Fraud and Abuse Act (1996 amendment). This act prohibits unauthorized access to a protected computer and illegal possession of stolen "access devices," which includes passwords and credit card numbers.

Computer Security Act of 1987. This act requires more than 550 federal agencies to develop computer security plans for each computer system that processes sensitive information. The plans are reviewed by the National Institute of Standards and Technology (NIST).

USA Patriot Act of 2001. This act gives federal authorities much wider latitude in monitoring Internet usage and expands the way such data is shared among different agencies. However, a judge must oversee the FBI's use of an e-mail wiretap, and the FBI must disclose what was collected, by whom, and who had access to the information that was collected.

Cyber Security Enhancement Act of 2002. This act permits the United States Sentencing Commission to review and, if appropriate, amend guidelines and policy statements applicable to persons convicted of a computer crime to reflect the serious nature of (1) the growing incidence of computer crimes, (2) the need for an effective deterrent, and (3) appropriate punishment to help prevent such offenses.

CAN-SPAM Act of 2003. This act requires unsolicited commercial e-mail messages to be labeled, to include opt-out instructions, and to include the sender's physical address. It prohibits the use of deceptive subject lines and false headers in messages. This law took effect on January 1, 2004.

FIGURE 11-3   Federal legislation affecting the use of computers.

equipment, which he subsequently sold in the Caribbean. He was caught while trying to steal $20,000 from the Bank of Boston. The bank called in the Secret Service, which raided his apartment and found nine bogus checks totaling almost $150,000. Sjiem-Fat was prosecuted and sent to prison.

5. *Theft, vandalism, or destruction of computer hardware.* A disgruntled tax payer became enraged over his tax bill. He was arrested for shooting at an IRS computer through an open window of the building.

6. *Trafficking in passwords or other log-in information for accessing a computer.* Two former software developers of Interactive Connection (now known as Screaming Media) were arrested for breaking into Interactive's computer system one night. They allegedly stayed on the system for about four hours and copied proprietary files and software.

7. *Extortion that uses a computer system as a target.* A disgruntled employee of a European company removed all of the company's tape files from the computer room. He then drove to an off-site storage location and demanded half a million dollars for

their return. He was arrested while trying to exchange the data files for the ransom money.

State Legislation.   Every state now has at least one computer-crime law. Most of the laws have provisions that (1) define computer terms (many of which vary from state to state), (2) define some acts as misdemeanors (minor crimes), and (3) declare other acts as felonies (major crimes). These laws also require willful intent for convictions. Thus, words like *maliciously, intentionally,* or *recklessly* often appear in the wording of the computer-crime laws, and willful intent must be established for a successful prosecution. The National Center for Computer Crime Data, a collector of computer-crime statistics, reports that 77 percent of computer cases brought to state courts end in guilty pleas and that another 8 percent of the defendants are found guilty at trials.

Computer Crime Statistics

No one really knows how much is lost each year as the result of computer crime and abuse. One reason for this is the fact that a large proportion of computer crime and abuse takes place in private companies, where it is handled as an internal matter. We have no laws that require organizations to report computer offenses. But the most important reason we know so little about computer offenses is because we believe that most of it is not discovered. Recently, for example, the FBI estimated that only 1 percent of all computer crime is detected. Other estimates of computer-crime detection are between 5 percent and 20 percent. We mostly catch computer criminals through luck, chance, or accident. This is why experts believe the computer crime that is detected is only the tip of the iceberg.

Despite our lack of complete statistics, there are several reasons why we believe computer crime is growing. One reason is the exponential growth in the use of computer resources—for example, microcomputers, computer networks, and the Internet. As more people become knowledgeable about how to use computers, more people are in a position to compromise computer systems.

Another reason why we believe computer crime is growing is because of continuing lax security. There are millions of computer users in the world, but many of them are not aware of, or conscientious about, computer security. Then, too, some users are dishonest and have a new tool with which to commit frauds. Lastly, many Web sites now give step-by-step instructions on how to perpetrate computer crimes. For example, an Internet search found more than 17,000 matches for "denial of service," and there are now thousands of Web sites that detail how to break into computer systems or disable Web servers.

Case-in-Point 11.3   Dan Farmer, who wrote SATAN (a network security testing tool), tested 2,200 high-profile Web sites at governmental institutions, banks, newspapers, and so forth. Only three of these Web sites detected his probes and contacted him to find out what he was trying to do. His conclusion: most Web sites have serious vulnerabilities, and most of the control procedures at these sites are ineffective.[4]

The FBI, in partnership with the National White Collar Crime Center, established the Internet Fraud Complaint Center (IFCC) in May 2000 to provide cybercrime victims a point of contact for reporting computer crime and abuses. The IFCC changed its name in December 2003 to the Internet Crime Complaint Center (IC3) to reflect the broad nature

---

[4] http://www.g4tv.com/techvvault/features/3392/Interview_SATANs_Dan_Farmer.html

of complaints that it handles, including international money laundering, online extortion, intellectual property theft, identity theft, online scams, and computer intrusions. In 2010, there were 303,809 online fraud complaints reported, compared to only 75,000 in 2002. The majority of the complaints in 2010 were received from individuals in California (38.1 percent), and the top crime type was nondelivery of merchandise and/or payment (21.1 percent of complaints), followed by identity theft (18.8 percent of complaints).[5]

The Importance of Computer Crime and Abuse to AISs

The absence of good computer-crime statistics does not detract from the importance of computer crime and abuse on accounting information systems. One reason for this is that AISs help control financial resources and thus are often the favored targets of computer abusers and criminals. Also, as noted previously, AISs are prized targets for disgruntled employees seeking to compromise computer systems for revenge. A third reason is that accountants are responsible for designing, selecting, or implementing the control procedures that protect AISs. Finally, computer crime is important because both the government and the investing public rely on internal and external auditors to vouch-safe the accuracy and completeness of the financial statements of the corporations and government agencies they audit.

Using a computer, fraud perpetrators are able to steal more, in much less time, with much less effort, and leave little or no evidence. Consequently, computer fraud is typically much more difficult to detect than other types of fraud. At any point in time, the FBI is investigating approximately 800 separate incidents of economic espionage, which is why this is such an important topic to accountants.

Computer crime and abuse are also significant because of the large proportion of firms that suffer million-dollar losses due to frauds, computer viruses, unauthorized access, and denial-of-service attacks. The 2008 ACFE Report to the Nation estimates that the annual total losses from occupational fraud are almost $1 trillion (not all of which is computer based). The 2008 annual survey of the Computer Security Institute estimates that the average cost to target organizations from a computer-abuse incident is about $500,000—an amount whose financial impact can range from "substantial" to "catastrophic" to the victim firm.

THREE EXAMPLES OF COMPUTER CRIMES

Computer crime is perhaps best understood by studying selected cases. As one reads the fascinating accounts of different computer crimes, a pattern begins to emerge. One type of crime depends mostly on the falsification of input data, while others depend on unauthorized access to computerized files. This section of the chapter examines three specific cases of computer crime.

Compromising Valuable Information

A major class of computer crime involves illegal access to, or misuse of, the information stored in an AIS and is thus valuable-information computer crime. In the TRW Credit Data case, the valuable information involved was computerized credit data. TRW (now called

---

[5] http://www.ic3.gov/media/annualreports.aspx

Experian) was one of several large, credit-rating companies in the United States. When the fraud was discovered, the company was collecting and disseminating credit information on approximately 50 million individuals. Clients of TRW included banks, retail stores, and such credit-conscious concerns as Diner's Club, American Express, MasterCard, Visa, Sears, Roebuck and Co., and several leasing establishments.

TRW advised its clients of bad credit risks on the basis of the information maintained in its databases. However, this information could be changed. The fraud began when six company employees, including a key TRW clerk in the consumer relations department, realized this fact and began selling good credit to individuals with bad credit ratings. The names and addresses of the bad credit risks were already on file. It merely remained to contact these individuals and inform them of a newfound method of altering their records. Accordingly, the perpetrators approached individuals with bad credit ratings and offered them a clean bill of health in return for a "management fee."

Those people who decided to buy good credit ratings paid TRW employees under the table, and the clerk in the consumer relations department then inserted into TRW's credit files whatever false information was required to reverse the individual's bad credit rating. In some cases, this required deleting unfavorable information that was already stored in the individual's credit record. In others, it required adding favorable information. Fees for such services varied from a few hundred dollars to $1,500 per individual. Ironically, the TRW clerk who ultimately input the false information to the computer system received only $50 for each altered record. However, the losses resulting from these activities were not so inconsequential. Independent estimates have placed this figure at close to $1 million.

The principal victims of the fraud were TRW's clients who acted on credit information that ultimately turned out to be inaccurate. Exactly how many file records were altered is difficult to say. Lawyers for the prosecution documented 16 known cases of altered file records but had reason to believe the number exceeded 100 cases. Paradoxically, the prosecution had difficulty acquiring testimonies because the buyers of good credit standing as well as the TRW sellers were technically in violation of the law by conspiring to falsify credit-rating information.

Analysis. **Data diddling** means changing data before, during, or after they are entered into a computer system. The change can delete, alter, or add important system data, especially the data stored in corporate databases. This is a problem because most such data are (1) proprietary, (2) may give a firm a competitive advantage, and (3) are sometimes an organization's most valuable asset (think eBay, for example). Finally, because the data processing tasks in most computerized AIS job streams are automated, the data that are input manually to a system are particularly vulnerable to compromise.

Case-in-Point 11.4 Data diddling is common. In one instance, a clerk for a Denver brokerage altered a transaction to record 1,700 shares of Loren Industries stock worth about $2,500 as shares in Long Island Lighting worth more than $25,000. In a second instance, a ring of travel agents in California received prison sentences for compromising an American Airlines reservations system and stealing $1.3 million worth of frequent-flier tickets.

The TRW case involves two key issues: (1) the propriety of the input information used in updating a specific AIS, and (2) the protection afforded both consumer and user in the accuracy and use of credit information that is gathered by a private company. With regard to the first point, it is clear that the fraud was successful only because the perpetrators were able to enter false information into the computer system. This observation points to the importance of control procedures (e.g., the authorization and validation of credit changes) that safeguard the accuracy and completeness of file information. As with many cases of computer crime, the six TRW employees involved in the fraud were caught only by chance: an individual approached with an offer to buy a good credit rating for $600 became angry and called the FBI. Later, the TRW clerk in the consumer relations department decided to confess to the crime.

The second point, which involves protection of the consumer and the user of credit information, encompasses a much larger issue. In 1970, Congress passed the **Fair Credit Reporting Act**, which requires that an individual be told why he or she is denied credit. The consumer also has the right to contest the information maintained by the credit-rating company, although there is clearly a vast difference between the right to *challenge* and the right to *change* credit information.

Directly after the Fair Credit Reporting Act went into effect, TRW reported that consumer inquiries increased a hundred fold, and at the time the fraud was detected, approximately 200,000 consumers annually were complaining about their credit ratings. The fact that, by TRW's own admission, fully one-third of these inquiries resulted in a file change or update is unsettling. Moreover, it is not known how much more information collected by TRW is still inaccurate but simply not challenged—for example, because an individual is not aware of an inaccuracy or because the consumer does not know his or her rights under the law.

Wire Fraud and Computer Hacking[6]

Voice over Internet Protocol (VoIP) is a technology that allows you to make telephone calls using a broadband Internet connection instead of a regular telephone line. This technology converts your voice signal into digital signals that travel over the Internet and are then converted back to audio signals at the receiver's end.

Edwin Pena, who owned two Florida VoIP wholesale companies, was arrested for hacking into other providers' networks, routing his customers' calls onto those platforms, billing those companies, and then pocketing the proceeds. He was charged with one count of wire fraud and one count of computer hacking. The government claimed that Pena embezzled over $1 million from this scheme, which he used to purchase real estate, cars, and a 40-foot boat. To avoid attention, Pena apparently purchased these items in someone else's name.

The federal government also filed a criminal complaint against Robert Moore of Spokane, Washington, the professional **hacker** who penetrated the networks for Pena. However, Moore admitted his part in the fraud, disclosing that Pena paid him $20,000 for his work. Apparently, Moore scanned a lot of other companies' computer networks searching for vulnerable network ports to use to route calls. For instance, he made over 6 million scans of just AT&T ports over a five-month period. After Moore obtained proprietary codes (known as prefixes), he and Pena allegedly flooded providers with test calls until they were able to match up prefixes. Once they matched prefixes, Pena programmed the networks of other companies to use his prefix to route his customers' calls.

Analysis.   Hacking is a widespread problem. This is due, in part, to the fact that many computer applications now run on local and wide area networks, where computer files become accessible to unauthorized users. Then, too, the Internet enables users to log onto computers from remote sites, again increasing vulnerability to hacking.

---

[6] http://www.technologynewsdaily.com/node/3252

Computer hacking is common in universities, where students often view the activity as a harmless game of beating the system, although sometimes it's not so harmless, as the following Case-in-Point explains. Educational institutions view hacking as a particularly perplexing problem because the need for tight system security conflicts with the objective of providing easy and simple computer access to bona fide users.

Case-in-Point 11.5 At the University of Central Missouri, investigators traced a computer hacking scheme to two students and then raided the dorm room where the plot was hatched—only to find a Post-It note stuck to a computer monitor that read "too late!" with a smiley face on it. However, the students were apprehended and have been charged with computer intrusion causing damage, computer intrusion to further a fraud scheme, computer intrusion to obtain information, intercepting electronic communication, and two counts of aggravated identity theft.[7]

Many hackers brag that they can compromise any type of file information once they have successfully logged into a computer system. One way they achieve this is to elevate their system status to that of a "privileged user" or "network manager," which is a security level that gains the hackers access to password files, system control data, and other high-security information. These activities are thwarted by using system programming routines that test for, and deny, such bootstrapping and that also immediately communicate such attempts to computer supervisors as possible security violations.

Case-in-Point 11.6 When hackers invaded NDA (a consulting firm in Woburn, Massachusetts), the hackers installed a program that enabled them to record users' passwords and access the network freely. The invaders copied files containing ID codes for cell phones, gathered sensitive information on NDA's business customers, and then launched similar attacks on those companies.[8]

The maximum penalty for wire fraud is 20 years in prison and a $250,000 fine; the penalty for computer hacking is a maximum of five years in prison and a $250,000 fine. Provisions of the **USA PATRIOT Act (2001)** may help discourage computer hacking by helping Federal authorities locate and prosecute hackers.

Perhaps the most useful protection against hacking is encryption. For example, this protects transmitted data that might be intercepted en route. Encryption also protects stored data, which are then rendered useless to a hacker even if he or she manages to gain access to files that are protected by other means. Finally, encryption is useful in networking situations because a properly encrypted password further ensures that an authentic user sent it.

Another way to identify an organization's vulnerability to hacking is by hiring **ethical hackers**. These are network and computer experts who purposefully attack a secured system to help its owners find any vulnerabilities that could be exploited by a malicious hacker. Ethical hackers use the same methods as a malicious hacker to test a security system, but instead of taking advantage of these vulnerabilities, they report them to management. Ethical hacking is also referred to as **intrusion testing**, penetration testing, and red teaming. There is even a certification for this line of work, called a Certified Ethical Hacker.[9]

Another helpful practice is *user education*—that is, making potential hackers aware of the ethics of computer usage and the inconvenience, lost time, and costs incurred by victim

---

[7] http://blogs.pitch.com/plog/2010/11/joseph_camp_daniel_fowler_computer_hackers.php

[8] http://findarticles.com/p/articles/mi_m1154/is_n11_v85/ai_19969629

[9] https://www.eccouncil.org/certification/certified_ethical_hacker.aspx

organizations. Strong passwords are also helpful, but passwords are not foolproof mechanisms because, at present, computers cannot distinguish between authorized employees using their own passwords and unauthorized users entering compromised passwords. Thus, until biometric authentications such as retina scans or other cost-effective intrusion detection systems become widely available, protecting passwords is paramount. We will review some methods for this in a later section of the chapter.

Denial of Service[10]

A number of computer viruses and computer worms have gained media attention, but none have been as swift or as "deadly" as the Slammer worm. In 2003, this computer worm nearly shut down the Internet in less than 15 minutes. Internet service providers (ISPs) on the east coast of the United States were the first to recognize the problem, but the full impact of this computer worm quickly spread to other countries.

How did this happen? The Slammer worm took advantage of a weakness in Microsoft's SQL Server 2000 software—a weakness that allowed applications to automatically locate a specific database. As a result, just after midnight on January 25, 2003, over 55 million meaningless database server requests were crossing the globe. The Slammer worm was able to spread hundreds of times faster than any prior worm attack. The unfortunate part is that the total cost to fix the problem was estimated at over $1 billion, and we still do not know who did it or when it might happen again.

Analysis. **Denial-of-service (DOS) attacks** take many forms, including (1) computer viruses, (2) computer worms, or (3) distributed systems. A **computer virus** is an attachment to other files or programs that destroys computer files, disrupts operating system activities, or damages program software. As suggested by Figure 11-4, "viruses" continue to be the number one security problem for modern organizations. A recent survey of 300 private and public computer sites conducted by the International Computer Security Association, in Carlisle, Pennsylvania, found viruses in more than 3 percent of the survey sites.

Computer worms do not actually destroy data, but merely replicate themselves repeatedly until the user runs out of internal memory or disk space. Unfortunately, the Internet facilitates the spread of virus or computer worms from one system to another, making them the most popular form of computer crime or abuse. Finally with distributed denial-of-service attacks, a single virus or **worm program** enlists the aid of innocent "zombie computers," which then send e-mail messages to, or to request services from, the target system. The barrage of incoming mail or service requests then overwhelms the target system, typically requiring its owners to disable it.

Most computer viruses reside on secondary storage media, where they hide until finding an opportunity to execute. There are several variations of these viruses. **Boot-sector viruses** hide in the boot sectors of a disk, where the operating system accesses them every time it accesses the disk itself. **Trojan horse programs** reside in the disk space occupied by legitimate copies of computer programs, for example, spreadsheet programs. Logic bomb programs are similar to Trojan horse programs, except that they remain dormant until the computer system encounters a specific condition, such as a particular day of the year or a particular Social Security number in a file. Trojan horse and logic bomb programs are termed "programs" rather than "viruses" because they

---

[10] Boutin, P. 2003. *WIRED* 11 (July). Retrieved from http://www.wired.com

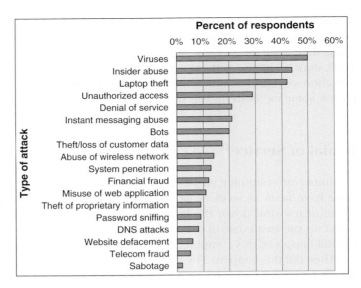

FIGURE 11-4 Percentage of respondents experiencing common types of computer crime and abuse. Source: 2008 CSI Survey.

sometimes contain code to defraud users as opposed to viruses that destroy or disrupt computer resources.

The Internet is a perfect environment for computer viruses because so many people use it for e-mail, conducting research, and downloading files or software. For example, a virus might be stored in a java **applet** (i.e., a small program stored in a Web page file and designed to run by Web browser software). Friendly applets animate Web pages, allow users to play games, or perform processing tasks. But unfriendly applets contain viruses that can infect computers and cause damage.

A computer virus that is lodged on a file server can affect thousands of other computers or servers before it is detected and eliminated. Estimating the business costs of recovering from a virus infection is difficult. The costs can be small—for example, limited to the inconveniences of reformatting a hard disk and reloading a few software programs, or the costs can be huge—by some estimates, billions of dollars annually.

There are a number of ways to prevent computer viruses. These include (1) **firewalls**, which limit external access to company computers, (2) antivirus software, and (3) antivirus control procedures. **Antivirus software** are computer programs that scan inputs for virus-like coding, identify active viruses already lodged in computer systems, clean infected systems, or perform some combination of these activities. Recent versions of Microsoft's Windows operating system incorporate software of this type. Generally speaking, however, antivirus programs provide less than complete protection because misguided individuals continuously write new, more powerful viruses that can avoid current detection schemes. Even worse, some antivirus programs have, themselves, contained viruses.

Perhaps one of the most vulnerable areas for many firms and universities is e-mails. Consider the number of e-mails you send and receive every day, and then multiply that by the number of people at your university, and you can understand why the risk of passing a virus around is very high. Unfortunately, viruses can hide in e-mails from friends and colleagues because their computer systems have been infected. To help mitigate this problem, your university most likely uses an antispam software solution in addition to antivirus software.

For many microcomputer users, antivirus control procedures are often better safeguards. These include (1) buying shrink-wrapped software from reputable sources, (2) avoiding illegal software copying, (3) not downloading suspicious Internet files, (4) deleting e-mail messages from unknown sources before opening them, and (5) maintaining complete backup files in the event you must rebuild your system from scratch. Additional safeguards include loading operating systems only from your own disks, being wary of public-domain software available on Internet bulletin boards and being suspicious of unusual activity on your computer system—for example, spontaneous disk writing that you did not initiate.

In organizational settings, effective control procedures against computer viruses include educating users about viruses and encouraging computer users to follow the virus prevention and detection techniques just discussed. Additional control procedures include (1) adopting policies that discourage the free exchange of computer disks or externally acquired computer programs, (2) requiring strong passwords that limit unauthorized access to computing resources, and (3) using antivirus filters on local and wide area networks.

PREVENTING COMPUTER CRIME AND FRAUD

What can organizations do to protect themselves against computer abuse? Experts note that, for all their intricacy and mystique, we can protect computer systems from crimes, abuses, and fraud just as well as we can manual systems, and sometimes better. For example, computers can be programmed to automatically search for anomalies and to print exception conditions on control reports. These computerized monitoring systems are often superior to manual surveillance methods because they are automatic and can screen 100 percent, instead of merely a sample, of the target population data. For example, the New York Stock Exchange now uses an **Integrated Computer-Assisted Surveillance System (ICASS)** to search for insider trading activities. This section of the chapter discusses several methods for preventing computer crimes, abuses, and fraud.

Enlist Top-Management Support

Most employees do not automatically follow organizational security policies and procedures—they are rarely rewarded for it, and such tasks take time away from those activities for which they are rewarded. This is why experts agree that computer security begins (or ends) with the top management and security policies. Without such policies, for example, organizations can only expect limited employee (1) compliance with security procedures, (2) sensitivity to potential problems, or (3) awareness of why computer abuse is important. Unfortunately, many top managers are not fully aware of the dangers of computer crime, abuse, and fraud and therefore are not sufficiently concerned about this type of offense. This is why security safeguards are effective only if top management takes computer crime seriously and chooses to financially support and enforce control procedures to stop, or at least minimize, computer crimes. The complaint of many midlevel security managers is that they must be able to justify their funding requests for investments in appropriate levels of computer security for a firm. Thus, the importance that top managers place on computer safeguards might be measured by the level of funding they allocate to IT security.

Increase Employee Awareness and Education

Ultimately, controlling computer crime means controlling people. But which people? The idea that computer crimes are outside jobs is a myth. With the exception of hackers, most computer abusers are the employees of the same companies at which the crimes take place. Many retail firms have clear prosecution policies regarding shoplifting. In contrast, prosecution policies associated with other types of employee fraud are notable for their absence in many organizations. Yet, evidence suggests that prosecuting computer crimes may be one of the most effective restraints on computer crime.

In fairness, employees cannot be expected to automatically understand the problems or ramifications of computer crime. Thus, another dimension of preventing computer crime is employee education. Informing employees of the significance of computer crime and abuse, the amount it costs, and the work disruption it creates helps employees understand why computer offenses are a serious matter. Studies suggest that informal discussions, periodic departmental memos, and formal guidelines are among the most popular educational tools for informing employees about computer crime and abuse. Requiring new hires to sign security statements indicating that they have received, read, and understand policy statements can also help.

According to the 2008–2009 KPMG Integrity Survey, employees who work in companies with comprehensive ethics and compliance programs reported more favorable results across the board than those employees who work in companies without such programs. For example, employees who work in organizations with these programs reported fewer instances of misconduct and higher levels of confidence in management's integrity, believing that the CEO and other senior executives set the right tone at the top. The report's authors also believe that these programs eliminate a number of conditions that might foster misconduct—for example, (1) pressure to do whatever it takes to meet targets, (2) the idea that policies and procedures are easy to bypass or override, and (3) the conviction that rewards are based on results, regardless of the method used.

One final idea regarding employee conduct comes from the 2008 Association of Certified Fraud Examiners *Report to the Nation*. This survey revealed that almost half of all the fraud reported by the survey's respondents was not detected by internal controls or audits, but rather from tips obtained from fellow employees, customers, or vendors. Given the value of such information, a prudent managerial policy is to provide channels that employees can use to report suspicious activity—for example, by allowing them to communicate with management anonymously through company Web sites. This and rewarding employees for providing such information may be two of the most effective things that organizations can do to curb occupational fraud and embezzlement.

Assess Security Policies and Protect Passwords

Common sense dictates that organizations should regularly survey their computer security measures and assess potential areas of vulnerability. Nearly all organizations use firewalls, antivirus software, and access controls, but many are not as conscientious about performing periodic security reviews. An important security process that organizations should consider is evaluating employee practices and educating users to protect their own computers. Figure 11-5 provides a list of 10 recommended steps for safeguarding personal computers. Similar safeguards apply to laptop computers, tablets, iPads, smart phones, and other mobile devices.

1. **Keep your firewall turned on**. Firewalls help protect your computer from hackers who might try to gain access to it, delete information, or steal passwords or other sensitive information.

2. **Install or update your antivirus software**. Antivirus software helps protect your computer from malicious code such as viruses or worms and can be set to update automatically.

3. **Install or update your antispyware technology**. Spyware is just software that is secretly installed on your computer and that allows others to observe your activities on it. Inexpensive antispyware software is readily available for download on the Internet or at local computer stores.

4. **Keep your operating system up to date**. Software developers regularly update their operating systems to stay current with technology requirements and fix security holes.

5. **Do not provide personal information online**. Hackers create phishing Web sites to lure visitors into providing their personal information and therefore steal their identity. Most companies will not ask you to provide your login name, password, account number, or similar personal information online.

6. **Be careful what you download**. Downloading e-mail attachments can thwart even the most vigilant antivirus software. Never open an e-mail attachment from someone you don't know, and be wary of forwarded attachments from anyone.

7. **Turn off your computer at night**. Although it's nice to always have your computer ready for action, the downside of "always on" is that it makes it more susceptible to hacker attacks. The safest computer is one that isn't on.

8. **Create backups often**. Computers are not infallible, and all hard disk drives eventually fail. Creating duplicate copies of your important files and storing them off-site enables you to easily recover from such problems. The authors recommend the automated backup services of a cloud service provider, as discussed in Chapter 2.

9. **Use surge protectors**. Power surges can "fry" your computer, but even the least expensive surge protector can guard against most such events.

10. **Protect passwords**. Many Web sites and computer systems now require logon names and passwords, but writing them on sticky notes stuck to your computer's monitor or keyboard is not a good idea. Try to find safer places to store the ones you can't commit to memory.

FIGURE 11-5   Ten simple steps to safer personal computers.

Protecting passwords is an important dimension of computer security because they are the *keys to the kingdom* (of valuable corporate data). Hackers use a variety of tactics to steal such passwords, including (1) posing as a legitimate user and "borrowing" them from unsuspecting employees, (2) creating phishing Web sites that ask users to input their passwords "for security purposes," or (3) using simulation programs that try all the words in a standard dictionary as potential passwords. To help obstruct these tactics, users should (1) be trained to not "loan" their passwords to others or tape them to their monitors, (2) understand that most businesses will not ask for their passwords on a Web screen, and (3) use strong passwords—that is, passwords that are difficult to guess. Examples of strong passwords are long terms (e.g., 20 characters), nonsense words (e.g., words not found in dictionaries), or words with embedded capitals or random numbers. Another control is to install password-checking software in file servers that test passwords for such requirements. A third control is to require employees to change their passwords periodically.

Hackers often use a tactic called **social engineering** to gain access to passwords. Sometimes, this means posing as bona fide employees and convincing network administrators to give them passwords over the phone. In other cases, the social engineer poses as a new, helpless employee who appears desperate and borrows a password from a fellow worker in order to accommodate a fictitious emergency. While it is advisable to distribute new passwords through external channels rather than through computer systems themselves, the practice of giving passwords to unknown employees compromises standard security procedures and should never be allowed.

Two additional password safeguards are lockout systems and dial-back systems. **Lockout systems** disconnect telephone users after a set number of unsuccessful log-in attempts, thereby preventing microcomputer users from using dictionary programs. Similarly, **dial-back systems** first disconnect all log-in users but reconnect legitimate users after checking their passwords against lists of bona fide user codes. Dial-back systems may be even more effective than lockout systems because only authorized users at already-recognized stations are reconnected. Dial-back security is also a useful strategy against social engineering, because hackers are unwilling to reveal their identities when making bogus requests for passwords.

Implement Controls

Most computer crime and abuse succeeds because of the *absence* of controls rather than the *failure* of controls. There are many reasons why businesses do not implement control procedures to deter computer crime. One is the all-too-common belief of those managers who have not suffered a computer crime that they have nothing to fear. Further, charities and not-for-profit organizations often believe that their mission somehow insulates them from such crimes. Then, too, those businesses that do not have a specific computer security officer have no one to articulate this concern or argue for specific control procedures. Finally, at least some businesses do not feel that security measures are cost-effective—until their organization is a victim of computer crime or abuse!

Case-in-Point 11.7 To execute a disbursement fraud, one man used a desktop publishing package to prepare fictitious bills for office supplies that he then mailed to companies across the country. He kept the dollar amount on each bill less than $300 and found that an amazingly large percentage of the companies paid the bills without question—probably because many organizations automatically pay vendor invoices for small amounts.

The solution to the computer security problems of most organizations is straightforward: design and implement controls. This means that organizations should install control procedures to deter computer crime, managers should enforce them, and both internal and external auditors should test them. Experts also suggest that employee awareness of computer controls and the certainty of prosecution may also act as deterrents to computer crime. Certainly, the enactment of the Sarbanes-Oxley Act of 2002 has placed a much greater emphasis on strong internal controls, including criminal offenses for senior executives who knowingly disregard such precautions. We talked more about internal controls in Chapters 9 and 10 and cover the Sarbanes-Oxley Act in more depth in Chapter 12.

In the United States, a disproportionate amount of security break-ins occur during the end-of-the-year holiday season. Reasons for this include (1) extended employee vacations and therefore fewer people to "mind the store," (2) students are out of school and consequently have more free time on their hands, and (3) counterculture hackers get lonely at year-end and increase their attacks on computer systems. Thus, it is especially important to make sure that effective control procedures are in place during the holidays.

Identify Computer Criminals

To prevent specific types of crimes, criminologists often look for common character traits with which to screen potential culprits. What are the characteristics of individuals who commit computer crimes or abuse, and what can be done to create a composite profile that organizations can use to evaluate job applicants?

Nontechnical Backgrounds. A company's own employees—not external hackers—perpetrate most computer crime and abuse. How technically competent are such employees? Figure 11-6 identifies the job occupations of computer criminals and abusers from a survey performed by Hoffer and Straub. Although this figure suggests that some computer offenses are committed by those with strong technical backgrounds, this study found that almost as many computer offenses are perpetrated by clerical personnel, data-entry clerks, and similar individuals with limited technical skills. A similar study by the U.S. Sentencing Commission (USSC) found that most of the 174 computer criminals convicted under the Computer Crime and Abuse Act of 1986 were corporate insiders with only "pedestrian levels" of computer expertise. There is good reason for this. It is usually easier and safer to alter data before they enter a computer than midway through automated processing cycles. Then too, input data can often be changed anonymously, whereas most computerized data cannot. These facts explain why many computer criminals are not even computer literate and also why computer security must extend beyond IT personnel.

Noncriminal Backgrounds. The USSC study also found that most of the convicted computer criminals had no prior criminal backgrounds. In addition, most computer criminals tend to view themselves as relatively honest. They argue, for example, that beating the system is not the same as stealing from another person—or that they are merely using a computer to take what other employees take from the supply cabinet. Furthermore, many perpetrators think of themselves as long-term borrowers rather than thieves, and several have exercised great care to avoid harming individuals when they committed their computer offenses.

Education, Gender, and Age. Although most media reports suggest that computer offenders are uniformly bright, motivated, talented, and college-educated individuals, the average computer criminal often does not fit this profile. In the ACFE 2008 Report to the Nation, for example, over half of the perpetrators did not have a college degree. But, according to the report, highly educated fraudsters were able to steal more—see

Programmers and systems analysts	27%
Clerical, data entry, and machine operators	23%
Managers and top executives	15%
Other system users	14%
Students	12%
Consultants	3%
Other information processing staff	3%
All others	3%
Total	100%

FIGURE 11-6 Occupations of computer-abuse offenders.

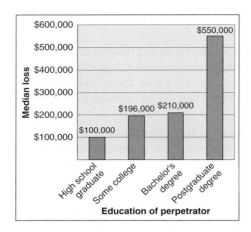

FIGURE 11-7 Median fraud losses, classified by the education level of the perpetrator. Source: *2008 ACFE Report to the Nation.*

Figure 11-7. However, because we believe that most computer crime and abuse are not detected—or prosecuted when it is detected—we do not know how representative these observations are for the general population of computer offenders.

Don't Forget Physical Security

An old adage in the computer security industry is that "a good hammer beats a strong password every time." What this means is that physical safeguards can be even more important than logical ones in deterring computer crime and abuse. For example, did you know that the most common security problem with laptop computers is simple theft? Other examples of physical security include protecting LAN servers and administrative work stations, enforcing "clean-desk policies" for employees, and protecting employee laptops against theft (see again Figure 11-5).

> *Case-in-Point 11.8* The administrators at one university believed that their desktop computers were safe as long as employees locked their individual office doors at night. But the university usually kept the buildings unlocked. The folly of this thinking became clear one morning when officials discovered that thieves had simply brought a ladder that allowed them to climb through the false ceiling of a building to steal over 30 PCs from one of the computer labs on campus.[11]

Organizations must also be able to recover from computer security breaches or losses when they do occur. One safeguard is to implement backup procedures. Another safeguard is to develop and test a disaster recovery plan that enables a business to replace its critical computer systems in a timely fashion. As suggested by the Case-in-Point above, monitoring cameras, motion detectors, and insurance are also important security measures.

Finally, organizations should be careful about how they dispose of outdated computers or copier machines. While state and federal environmental laws affect such disposals, our primary concern is the sensitive data stored on the hard drives of these devices. Reformatting these drives is usually not enough—the data may still be retrieved with

---

[11] From the authors.

software tools available on the Web. A better approach is either to use specialized file deletion software programs or to physically destroy the disk drives themselves.

Case-in-Point 11.9   Two MIT graduate students reported in an industry journal that after purchasing 129 used hard drives, they found more than a third of them still contained "significant personal information," such as credit card numbers and a year's worth of transactions and account numbers from an ATM.[12]

Recognize the Symptoms of Employee Fraud

The clues that signal some computer offenses can be subtle and ambiguous, but many are rather obvious. For example, the study conducted by KPMG concluded that nearly half the employee fraud would have been detected more quickly if obvious telltale symptoms had not been ignored. Although recognizing the symptoms of computer offenses will not prevent computer crime, knowing the telltale signs may help individuals detect and report it, which can help limit the potential damage to the victim organization. Consider, for example, the following Case-in-Point.

Case-in-Point 11.10   The Comfortable Shoe (TCS), a fashionable, high-end retail chain created its own health care plan for its employees. The plan was self-insured for medical claims under $30,000, which it handled internally, but plan administrators forwarded claims for larger amounts to an independent insurance company. The managers of TCS believed that the company had excellent control procedures for its system, which included both internal and external audits. Yet, over a period of four years, the manager of the medical claims department was able to embezzle more than $12 million from the company!

Although the name of the company has been changed, the events described above actually happened to a large company. However, you may be asking yourself how such a huge fraud could occur if the company had an excellent internal control system. From Chapter 9, we know that there are a number of practices and procedures that firms should use to protect against employee wrongdoing. The following internal control weaknesses were present at TCS and are typical warnings of computer fraud.

Accounting Irregularities.   To embezzle funds successfully, employees commonly alter, forge, or destroy input documents or perform suspicious accounting adjustments. An unusually high number of such irregularities are cause for concern. At TCS, no one noticed that payments to 22 of the physicians submitting claims to the company were sent to the same two addresses. While it is not uncommon for several physicians to form a group practice, it still should have caused TCS management concern that such a large number of doctors were at two addresses.

Internal Control Weaknesses.   Control procedures are often absent, weak, or ignored in computer fraud. At TCS, the medical claims manager had not taken a vacation for years, those employees submitting claims were never sent confirmation notices of the medical payments made on their behalf, and the physicians receiving these payments were never first investigated or approved. Here again, we recognize obvious internal control problems! Managers should require all employees to take vacations. Similarly, management should require reports for all employee claims, and they should require payment confirmation notices to employees—who would almost certainly report erroneous payments

---

[12] http://www.whitecanyon.com/used-hard-drives-pc-05-2003.php

that were made on their behalf. And most certainly, TCS should have an approved list of vendors (i.e., physicians) for payments.

Unreasonable Anomalies.   Perhaps the most important clue to computer fraud is the presence of many odd or unusual anomalies that somehow go unchallenged. Examined critically, such anomalies are unreasonable and require observers to suspend common sense. At TCS, for example, why were 100 percent of the medical payments to those 22 physicians all paid from the self-insured portion of the company program? Why were checks to those 22 physicians always endorsed by hand and deposited in the same two checking accounts? And why did some of the medical claims include hysterectomies for male employees? Exception reports may have highlighted these unusual pieces of information.

Lifestyle Changes.   Employees who miraculously solve pressing financial problems or suddenly begin living extravagant lifestyles are sometimes merely broadcasting fraud. At TCS, why did the medical claims manager announce that she had inherited a lot of money but never took a vacation? And why did she treat her employees to lunches in chauffeured limousines? An alert supervisor should have recognized such behavior as a red flag.

Behavioral Changes.   Employees who experience guilt or remorse over their crimes, or who fear discovery, often express these feelings in unusual behavior. At TCS, employees joked that the medical claims manager had developed a ''Jekyll and Hyde personality,'' including intense mood swings that were unusual even for her.

Employ Forensic Accountants

When an organization suspects an ongoing computer crime or fraud, it can hire forensic accountants to investigate its problem, document findings, and make recommendations. Many such individuals are professional accountants who have passed the two-day certified fraud examiner (CFE) examination administered by the ACFE. We introduced this professional designation in Chapter 1 and also pointed out the increasing number of job opportunities in this particular area. Forensic accounting is one of the fastest growing areas of accounting, and there are now more than 27,000 CFEs working in organizations such as the FBI, CIA, law firms, and CPA firms. For more information about forensic accounting, visit the ACFE Web site: http://www.acfe.org.

Forensic accountants have the required technical and legal experience to research a given concern, follow leads, establish audit trails of questionable transactions, document their findings, organize evidence for external review and law enforcement bodies, and (if necessary) testify in court. Most use specialized software tools to help them perform their tasks—for example, **Audit Command Language (ACL)** for auditing tasks (to analyze data) and **EnCase** for documentation tasks (to analyze digital media).

ETHICAL ISSUES, PRIVACY, AND IDENTITY THEFT

Computerized AISs often raise ethical issues that we did not have to face under manual AISs. An example is the practice of unauthorized software copying. Thus, fighting computer crime, abuse, or fraud is sometimes more dependent on ethical behavior than observing legal restrictions. Ethics is a set of moral principles or values. Therefore, ethical behavior involves making choices and judgments that are morally acceptable and then acting accordingly. Ethics can govern organizations as well as individuals. In the context of an organization, an underlying ethical principle is that each individual in the organization has responsibility for the welfare of others within the organization, as well as for the organization itself. For example, the managers of a company should make decisions that are fair to the employees as well as beneficial to the organization.

Ethical Issues and Professional Associations

Ethical concerns are often the issue in instances of computer abuse. In cases involving hacking, for example, ignorance of proper conduct or misguided playfulness may be the problem. To some, the challenge of defrauding a computer system and avoiding detection is irresistible because success brings recognition, notoriety, and even heroism. In these cases, ethical issues are overlooked and the costs of recovering from the abuse are ignored. The acceptability of these motives often comes down to issues of morality.

Some argue that morality in corporate cultures is a relative term. But is it? In one case, for example, a man named Fred Darm stole a computer program from a rival firm through his computer terminal. At his trial, the defense argued that it was common practice for programmers of rival firms to ''snoop'' in each other's data files to obtain competitive information. Thus, when he was apprehended for his offense, Darm was not only surprised, he was quite offended! Similarly, some claim the Ethics Code of the Pharmaceutical Research and Manufacturers of America (PhRMA) isn't working, as explained in the following Case-in-Point.

> *Case-in-Point 11.11* While the PhMRA Code promises that marketing practices will comply with the highest ethical standards, whistle-blower lawsuits in the past three years have totaled $7 billion. Apparently, PhMRA has been using prominent physician speakers to push their drugs for uses that are not approved by the FDA.[13]

The accounting profession has a number of associations, such as the Institute of Internal Auditors (IIA), the Institute of Management Accountants (IMA), the American Institute of Certified Public Accountants (AICPA), and the Information Systems Audit and Control Association (ISACA) that have had codes of ethics or codes of professional conduct in force for a number of years. These professional accounting association codes are self-imposed and self-enforced rules of conduct. One of the most important goals of a code of ethics or conduct is to aid professionals in selecting among alternatives that are not clear-cut. Included within professional association codes are rules pertaining to independence, technical competence, and proper practices during audits and consulting engagements involving information systems. The certification programs of these associations increase awareness of the codes of ethics and are essential in developing professionalism.

In recent years, professional accounting associations at both the national and state level have established ethics committees to assist practitioners in the self-regulation process. These ethics committees provide their members with continuing education courses, advice on ethical issues, investigations of possible ethics violations, and instructional booklets covering a variety of ethics case studies. Some of the ethics committees provide their members with a hotline to advise them on the ethical and moral dilemmas experienced in the workplace. These committees also encourage the instruction of ethics in accounting curricula at colleges and universities.

---

[13] Verschoor, C. 2011. Pharma ethics code isn't working! *Strategic Finance* 92(8): 17–19.

Ethical Issue	Example in Computer Usage
Honesty	Organizations expect employees to perform their own work, to refrain from accessing unauthorized information, and to provide authentic results of program outputs.
Protecting computer systems	Examples include tying up network access ports with multiple log-ins, sending voluminous (but useless) e-mails and computer files to others, complaining to system administrators about fictitious hardware or software failures, introducing computer viruses into networks, or giving unauthorized users access to private computer systems.
Protecting confidential information	Allowing unauthorized individuals to view private information—for example, financial data on a mortgage loan application or the results of diagnostic medical tests stored in the files of local area networks.
Social responsibility	Sometimes, social responsibility conflicts with other organizational goals. For example, suppose a programmer discovers a possible error in a software program that controls a missile guidance system. His boss tells him to ignore it—the design team is already over budget and this is only a possible error.
Acceptable use	The availability of computer hardware and software in workplaces does not automatically convey unrestricted uses of them. At universities, for example, ethical conduct forbids downloading microcomputer software for personal applications or using free mainframe time for personal gain.
Rights of privacy	Do organizations have the right to read the personal e-mail of their employees? Do employees have the right to use their business e-mail accounts for personal correspondence? In 2002, the state of Montana decided that monitoring computer activity on state-owned computers at state universities is legal. Officials at colleges and universities in Montana are hoping to decrease the incidence of illegal activity by individuals who are using campus property.

FIGURE 11-8 Examples of ethical issues in computer usage.

Professional computer associations such as the Association of Information Technology Professionals (AITP) and the Association for Computing Machinery (ACM) have developed codes of ethics, ethics committees, and certification programs. The codes of these professional computer associations examine issues such as obligations to their professional associations, clients, and society. Figure 11-8 presents a few examples of ethical issues in computer usage.

Meeting the Ethical Challenges

Because a significant amount of business activity and data communications now takes place on the Internet, it is not surprising that an increasing amount of computer crime and abuse also happens within the Internet's environment. Examples include thieves supplying fake credit card numbers to buy everything from investment securities to Internet access time itself, copying Web pages without permission, denying legitimate users Internet access, and posing as someone else for any number of illegal or dishonest purposes.

How we respond to the ethical issues above is determined not so much by laws or organizational rules as by our own sense of "right" and "wrong." Ethical standards of behavior are a function of many things, including social expectations, culture, societal norms, and even the times in which we live. More than anything else, however, ethical behavior requires personal discipline and a commitment to do the right thing.

How can organizations encourage ethical behavior? Some argue that morals are only learned at an early age and in the home—they cannot be taught to adults. However, others suggest that it helps to (1) inform employees that ethics are important, (2) formally expose employees to relevant cases that teach them how to act responsibly in specific situations, (3) teach by example, that is, by managers acting responsibly, and (4) use job promotions and other benefits to reward those employees who act responsibly.

Case-in-Point 11.12 Are you familiar with the student code of conduct at your school? Some universities have very lengthy and detailed codes of conduct, while others, such as Texas A & M University, have a very short, direct one: An Aggie does not lie, cheat, or steal or tolerate those who do.

Privacy

Although Americans are concerned and aware of various privacy issues, the events of September 11, 2001, changed our focus in some respects. For example, we are willing to accept less privacy at airports and to submit to increased security measures at various points in airport terminals. On a day-to-day basis, we freely give our name, address, phone number and similar information to receive **value cards** at grocery stores, shoe stores, sporting goods stores, greeting card stores, and other retail establishments. In some cases we receive discounts, in other cases we receive points that may be exchanged for goods or services, and in some instances, we simply receive advance information for upcoming sales before the general public. These cards are credit card size or key-ring size and have a bar code on the back side for the merchant to track our purchases.

Privacy also affects our use of the Internet. For example, when we order a book from Amazon.com, the next time we visit that site, we're greeted by name and told about other books we might enjoy. A remarkable marketing tool, but how do they know? They know because most commercial Web sites deposit a **cookie** on your computer, which is a small text file that stores information about your browsing habits and interests, as well as other information that you may supply by logging onto the site. Of course, cookies are not necessarily bad. If you frequently purchase items from a particular online vendor, it is very convenient to have your credit card and shipping information automatically recalled so that you are not required to enter this information for every purchase.

Some individuals even claim that computers and privacy are mutually exclusive—that you can't have both. Then why would computer privacy be a concern? The defining issue is probably whether the invasion of our privacy is with or without our permission. That is, did we agree or authorize the information to be collected? For example, few object to Amazon.com tracking their browsing habits on their Web site, but if we ordered a book or other item from that Web site, we would most certainly object to unauthorized uses of our credit card information.

Company Policies with Respect to Privacy

Because of the widespread use of computers in business, coupled with the fact that many employees travel and use laptops, employers should develop and distribute a company policy with respect to privacy. The Fair Employment Practices Guidelines suggest that these policies cover issues such as (1) who owns the computer and the data stored on the computer, (2) what purposes the computer may be used (e.g., primarily for business purposes), and (3) what uses are unauthorized or prohibited. Further, employers should specifically identify the types of acceptable and unacceptable uses, with some examples.

Another idea is to have a screen pop-up each time an employee signs on that reminds the employee of the company policy. In general, companies would benefit from legal counsel on this topic. A very basic policy might sound like the following Case-in-Point.

> ***Case-in-Point 11.13***   The use of XYZ Company automation systems, including computers, fax machines, and all forms of Internet/intranet access, is for company business and is to be used for authorized purposes only. Brief and occasional personal use of the electronic mail system or the Internet is acceptable as long as it is not excessive or inappropriate, occurs during personal time (lunch or other breaks), and does not result in expense to the Company.[14]

Most commercial Web sites have a **privacy policy**, although they are sometimes difficult to find. For example, at Amazon.com you need to click on ''help'' and then scroll down to the bottom of the page to find the section on policies. However, your search is rewarded with a comprehensive list of information that is covered by their privacy policy—including information you give them, cookies they use, e-mail communications, and information Amazon.com receives about you from other sources. Another online merchant, Lands' End, provides an easy-to-find link to its privacy policy on its home page. Its privacy policy states the information it does and does not collect and offers advice about managing cookies.

An important point to remember is that companies typically are very careful about protecting your personal information. They understand that their future viability depends, in part, on the security of both your information and their proprietary data.

Identity Theft

Identity theft refers to an act in which someone wrongfully obtains and uses another person's personal data for fraud or deception. Unlike your fingerprints, which are unique to you and cannot be used by someone else, your personal data can certainly be used by another individual if they have a mind to use it. Your personal data may be any one or a combination of the following pieces of information: your Social Security number, your bank account, your debit card number, your credit card number, your birth date, your mailing address. It was not until 1998 that Congress passed legislation making identity theft a crime.

Thieves steal identities in a number of ways including **dumpster diving** (stealing personal information from garbage cans), taking delivered or outgoing mail from house mail boxes, or making telephone solicitations that ask for personal information. **Phishing** scams use e-mails or Web sites that claim to be legitimate but that ask you to provide or update your personal information such as account number, credit card number, or password. **Smishing** is a similar scam using text messages on cell phones.

> ***Case-in-Point 11.14***   CD Universe's Web site was breached, and the hacker gained access to 350,000 credit card numbers. More recently, the Web site of furniture retailer IKEA was compromised, exposing thousands of customers' personal information. Several days after the IKEA incident, hackers entered Western Union's Web site and left evidence of having made electronic copies of the credit and debit card information of over 15,000 customers.[15]

In the United States and Canada, many people have reported that unauthorized persons have taken funds out of their bank or financial accounts. Even worse, some unscrupulous

---

[14] http://www.employmentlawadvisors.com/resources/policies/computerpolicy.html
[15] http://www.crimes-of-persuasion.com/Crimes/Telemarketing/Inbound/MajorIn/id_theft.htm

Method	Examples
Shoulder surfing	• Watching you from a nearby location as you punch in your debit or credit card number
	• Listening to your conversation if you give your debit or credit card number over the telephone to a hotel or rental car company
Dumpster diving	• Going through your garbage can or a communal dumpster or trash bin to obtain copies of your checks, credit card or bank statements, or other records that typically have your name, address, and telephone number
Applications for "preapproved" credit cards	• If you discard them without tearing up the enclosed materials, criminals may retrieve them and try to activate the cards
	• If your mail is delivered to a place where others have access to it, criminals may simply intercept and redirect your mail to another location
Key logging software	• Loading this type of software on computers in general use areas, such as university computer labs or public libraries to obtain your personal data and other identifying data, such as passwords or banking information
Spam and other e-mails	• Many people respond to unsolicited e-mail that promises some benefit but requests identifying data, which criminals use to apply for loans, credit cards, fraudulent withdrawals from bank accounts, or other goods

FIGURE 11-9 Examples of methods used by criminals to obtain your personal data.

individuals have gone so far as to take over an individual's identity, incurring huge debts and committing all sorts of crimes. Victims can incur enormous costs attempting to restore their reputation in a community or correcting erroneous information. Figure 11-9 identifies a number of ways you can become a victim of identity theft if you are not careful.

The news media continues to report instances of compromised personal data. Some of these describe breaches in the computer system of an organization. Other reports suggest that a stolen laptop might have the personal data about thousands of individuals. Various Web sites claim that there is an increase in successful hacking activity, which results in the compromise of an organization's security systems.

AIS AT WORK
Fighting Computer Crime at the Bank[16]

When the judge asked Willie Sutton—a habitual bank robber—more than 100 years ago why he stole from banks, his answer became famous: "because that's where the money is." In some ways, little has changed. Banking frauds in the United States totaled an estimated $39 billion in 2006—and are growing. Credit card fraud touches one out of every 20 credit card users.

Having read this chapter, you are already familiar with the major types of computer crimes perpetrated against banks—phishing, identity theft, worms and Trojan horses, spyware, and denial-of-service attacks. Banks can fight computer crime by first performing risk assessments that analyze potential risks and then implementing policies and procedures

---
[16] Singleton, T., A. Singleton., and G. Gottlieb. 2006. Cyber threats facing the banking industry. *Accounting and Finance* 19(2): 26–32.

to mitigate or prevent potential losses. One important control is to develop *and test* a disaster recovery plan, especially a test of a general computer system failure. Another is to develop an incident response plan that includes identifying who should do what in the event of a breach of computer security.

Phishing is an especially important problem for banks because hackers often create bogus Web sites that trick bank customers into revealing their account numbers and passwords. Raising customer awareness to this problem—for example, in brochures that accompany monthly bank statements—is one possibility. Providing similar information on bank home pages, along with examples of spoofed e-mails, links to the FTC Web site on identify theft, and consumer alerts about new threats, is another way to counter this problem.

Because *people* are often the weakest link in computer security, banks should pay special attention to employee safeguards. One important practice is employee education, which includes periodic training and monthly reminders to employees about specific computer security issues—especially guarding against social engineering attacks. Another safeguard is stringent employee hiring practices, including drug and credit checks and requiring employees to acknowledge and follow current security policies. Memos that encourage employees to follow the simple security steps listed in Figure 11-5 to protect individual computers from harm can also help. Finally, of all factors to successfully fight computer crime, none is more important than identifying a security officer to champion and proactively manage all the activities discussed here.

 ## SUMMARY

- ✓ We know very little about computer crime because few cases are reported and many more cases go undetected.
- ✓ Computer crime is growing and is likely to be expensive for those organizations that suffer from it.
- ✓ The subjects of three cases of real-world computer crime included compromising valuable information, wire fraud and computer hacking, and denial of service.
- ✓ Organizations can use the following methods to protect themselves against computer offenses: (1) solicit top management support, (2) educate users about computer crime and abuse, (3) conduct a security inventory and protect passwords, (4) design and implement control procedures, and (5) recognize the symptoms of computer crime and abuse.
- ✓ Organizations can help themselves by knowing which employees are most likely to become computer offenders and by employing forensic accountants to investigate suspected problems.
- ✓ Managers can implement a program that focuses on ethical behavior. Examples of ethical behavior include protecting confidential information, being socially responsible, respecting rights of privacy, avoiding conflicts of interest, and understanding unacceptable uses of computer hardware and software.
- ✓ Organizations can encourage ethical behavior by educating employees about it, rewarding it, and encouraging employees to join professional associations with ethical codes of conduct.
- ✓ Identity theft is a growing problem, and individuals must adopt reasonable precautions to protect their personal data.

KEY TERMS YOU SHOULD KNOW

applet

Association of Certified Fraud Examiners (ACFE)

Audit Command Language (ACL)

boot-sector viruses

computer abuse

computer crime

Computer Fraud and Abuse Act of 1986 (CFAA)

Computer Security Institute (CSI)

computer virus

computer worms

cookie

data diddling

denial-of-service (DOS) attacks

dial-back systems

dumpster diving

EnCase

ethical hackers

Fair Credit Reporting Act

firewalls

hacker

identity theft

Integrated Computer-Assisted Surveillance System (ICASS)

intrusion testing

lockout systems

logic bomb

phishing

privacy policy

smishing

social engineering

Trojan horse programs

USA PATRIOT Act (2001)

value cards

voice over internet protocol (VoIP)

worm program

DISCUSSION QUESTIONS

11-1. The cases of computer crime that we know about have been described as just "the tip of the iceberg." Do you consider this description accurate? Why or why not?

11-2. Most computer crimes are not reported. Give as many reasons as you can why much of this crime is purposely downplayed. Do you consider these reasons valid?

11-3. Why have most computer experts suggested that computer crime is growing despite the fact that so little is known about it?

11-4. Does a company have the right to collect, store, and disseminate information about your purchasing activities without your permission?

11-5. What enabled the employees at TRW to get away with their crime? What controls might have prevented the crime from occurring?

11-6. What is hacking? What can be done to prevent hacking?

11-7. What is a computer virus?

11-8. How can educating employees help stop computer crime?

11-9. What computer crimes are committed on the Internet? What assets are involved? What can be done to safeguard these assets?

11-10. How would you define "ethics"? What types of ethical issues are involved in computerized accounting information systems? How can organizations encourage their employees to act ethically?

11-11. The Rivera Regional Bank uses a computerized data processing system to maintain both its checking accounts and its savings accounts. During the last three years, several customers have complained that their balances have been in error. Randy Allen, the information systems bank manager, has always treated these customers very courteously and has personally seen to it that the problems have been rectified quickly, sometimes by putting in extra hours after normal quitting time to make the necessary changes. This extra effort has been so helpful to the bank that this year, the bank's top management is planning to select Mr. Allen for the Employee-of-the-Year Award. Mr. Allen has never taken a vacation. Comment.

PROBLEMS

11-12. Comment on each of the following scenarios in light of chapter materials.

a. A legitimate student calls the computer help desk from her cell phone because she has forgotten her password to the university system. The "tech" on duty refuses to give it to her as a matter of university policy. The student is unable to complete her assignment and proceeds to file a formal complaint against the university.

b. An employee at a building supply company is caught downloading pornographic materials to his office computer. He is reprimanded by his boss, asked to remove the offending materials, and told never to do it again. The employee refuses on the grounds that (1) there is no company policy forbidding these activities, (2) he performed all his downloads during his lunch breaks, (3) his work reviews indicate that he is performing above average, and (4) the discoveries themselves were performed without a search warrant and therefore violate his right to privacy.

c. The local community college installed a new, campus-wide local area network that requires all staff members to enter a log-in name and password. Users can choose their own passwords. Some pick the names of their pets or spouses as passwords, while others tape their passwords to their computer monitors to help remember them.

d. An employee in a hospital was hardly ever at his desk, but almost always reachable through his cell phone. When the department replaced his old computer with a new one, his boss scanned the old hard drive and made the startling discovery that this employee had a full-time second job as a beer distributor.

e. A routine audit of the computer payroll records of the local manufacturing plant reveals that the address of over 20 employees in different departments is the same empty lot in the city.

f. An analysis of online bidding on eBay reveals that one seller has bid on several of his own merchandise in an effort to increase the final sales price of his items.

g. A retailer sues a Web hosting company when it discovers that the employees of the Web company have been visiting sites on which the retailer advertises. The retailer pays a fee of $1 every time someone clicks on these advertising links.

11-13. (Library or Online Journal Research) Newspapers and journals such as *Datamation* and *Computerworld* are prime sources of computer-crime articles. Find a description of a computer crime not already discussed in this chapter, and prepare an analysis of the crime similar to the ones in the second section of this chapter.

11-14. Recall that the salami technique means using a computer to skim a small amount of money from hundreds or thousands of accounts and then diverting the proceeds for personal gain. Suppose that a computer programmer uses this technique to skim a penny from each customer's account at a small bank. Over the course of three months, he takes $200,000 and is never caught. Assuming that this hacker took only one penny per month from each customer, how many accounts did the bank have? If the bank had 100,000 accounts and the hacker stole one penny from each account's interest (which was computed daily), how much could the hacker steal in three months?

11-15. What company policies or procedures would you recommend to prevent each of the following activities?

a. A clerk at the Paul Yelverton Company faxes a fictitious sales invoice to a company that purchases a large quantity of goods from it. The clerk plans to intercept that particular payment check and pocket the money.

b. The bookkeeper at a construction company has each of the three owners sign a paycheck for her. Each check is drawn from a separate account of the company.

c. A clerk in the human relations department creates a fictitious employee in the personnel computer file. When this employee's payroll check is received for distribution, the clerk takes and cashes it.

d. A clerk in the accounts receivable department steals $250 in cash from a customer payment and then prepares a computer credit memo that reduces the customer's account balance by the same amount.

e. A purchasing agent prepares an invoice for goods received from a fictitious supplier. She sends a check for the goods to this supplier, in care of her mother's post-office box.

f. A hacker manages to break into a company's computer system by guessing the password of his friend—Champ, the name of the friend's dog.

g. An accounts receivable clerk manages to embezzle more than $1 million from the company by diligently lapping the accounts every day for three consecutive years.

h. A computer virus on the company's local area network is traced to an individual who accidentally introduced it when he loaded a computer game onto his microcomputer.

i. A clerk at a medical lab recognizes the name of an acquaintance as one of those whose lab tests are "positive" for an infectious disease. She mentions it to a mutual friend, and before long, the entire town knows about it.

11-16. Download a copy of the Association of Certified Fraud Examiners Fraud Prevention Checkup, which is available at http://www.acfe.com/documents/Fraud_Prev_Checkup_IA.pdf. On a separate piece of paper, list the seven areas and the maximum number of points suggested for each one. An example is

1. Fraud Risk Oversight (20 points).

Do you think that this checklist is likely to enable organizations to prevent most types of fraud? Why or why not?

11-17. Download a copy of the *ACFE Compensation Guide for Antifraud Professionals*, which is available at no charge at http://www.acfe.com/documents/2008-comp-guide.pdf. On the basis of this resource, answer the following questions:

a. How many people participated in the 2008 survey?

b. What is the median total compensation for certified forensic examiners (CFEs) and for non-CFEs?

c. What is the modal years of experience for CFEs and for non-CFEs?

d. What is the modal highest level of education completed for CFEs and for non-CFEs?

e. What is the median total annual compensation for females and males holding CFE certification and for CFEs versus non-CFEs? How can you explain these differences?

f. Do fraud examiners earn more if they work in one type of industry (e.g., health care) than another? How about internal auditors?

g. Do antifraud practitioners tend to earn more in some areas of the country than in others? If so, what explains these differences?

CASE STUDIES

The Magnificent Four Seasons Resort

The Four Seasons Resort Community is an elegant, thriving four-season resort and a community of over 1,200 single family homes, 1,000 time-share units, and a multimillion dollar ski business. Guests visiting the resort can enjoy the indoor/outdoor water park; play golf on one of the two 18-hole championship golf courses; ski, snowboard, or snow tube in the winter on 14 trails that are all lighted for night skiing; or relax at the full-service spa. There are also three dining rooms, card rooms, nightly movies, and live weekend entertainment.

The resort uses a computerized system to make room reservations and bill customers. Following standard policy for the industry, the resort also offers authorized travel agents a 10 percent commission on room bookings. Each week, the resort prints an exception report of bookings made by unrecognized travel agents. However, the managers usually pay the commissions anyway, partly because they don't want to anger the travel agencies and partly because the computer file that maintains the list of authorized agents is not kept up-to-date.

Although management has not discovered it, several employees are exploiting these circumstances. As often as possible, they call the resort from outside phones, pose as travel agents, book rooms for friends and relatives, and collect the commissions. The incentive is obvious: rooms costing as little as $100 per day result in payments of $10 per day to the "travel agencies" that book them. The scam has been going on for years, and several guests now book their rooms exclusively through these employees, finding these people particularly courteous and helpful.

Requirements

1. Would you say this is a computer crime? Why or why not?
2. What internal controls would you recommend that would enable the resort's managers to prevent such offenses?
3. Classify the controls that you just identified above as either preventive, detective, or corrective controls.
4. How does the matter of accountability (tracing transactions to specific agencies) affect the problem?

The Department of Taxation

The Department of Taxation of one state is developing a new computer system for processing state income tax returns of individuals and corporations. The new system features direct data input and inquiry capabilities. Identification of taxpayers is provided by using the Social Security numbers of individuals and federal identification numbers for corporations. The new system should be fully implemented in time for the next tax season. The new system will serve three primary purposes:

- Data will be input into the system directly from tax returns through CRT terminals located at the central headquarters of the Department of Taxation.

- The returns will be processed using the main computer facilities at central headquarters. The processing includes (1) verifying mathematical accuracy; (2) auditing the reasonableness of deductions, tax due, and so forth, through the use of edit routines (these routines also include a comparison of the current year's data with prior years' data); (3) identifying returns that should be considered for audit by revenue agents of the department; and (4) issuing refund checks to taxpayers.

- Inquiry service will be provided to taxpayers on request through the assistance of Tax Department personnel at five regional offices. A total of 50 CRT terminals will be placed at the regional offices.

A taxpayer will be able to determine the status of his or her return or get information from the last three years' returns by calling or visiting one of the department's regional offices. The state commissioner of taxation is concerned about data security during input and processing over and above protection against natural hazards such as fires or floods. This includes protection against the loss or damage of data during data input or processing and the improper input or processing of data. In addition, the tax commissioner and the state attorney general have discussed the general problem of data confidentiality that may arise from the nature and operation of the new system. Both individuals want to have all potential problems identified before the system is fully developed and implemented so that the proper controls can be incorporated into the new system.

Requirements

1. Describe the potential confidentiality problems that could arise in each of the following three areas of processing, and recommend the corrective action(s) to solve the problems: (a) data input, (b) processing of returns, and (c) data inquiry.

2. The State Tax Commission wants to incorporate controls to provide data security against the loss, damage, or improper input or use of data during data input and processing. Identify the potential problems (outside of natural hazards such as fires or floods) for which the Department of Taxation should develop controls, and recommend possible control procedures for each problem identified.

(CMA Adapted)

Chapter 12

Information Technology Auditing

INTRODUCTION

Chapters 9 and 10 stressed the importance of control procedures in the efficient operation of an AIS. To make sure that these controls are functioning properly and that additional controls are not needed, business organizations perform examinations or audits of their accounting systems. Auditing is usually taught in one or more separate courses within the typical accounting curriculum, and a single chapter of a book is not sufficient to cover the spectrum of topics involved in a complete audit of an organization. This chapter will be introductory and limited to areas of immediate consequence to AISs and the IT audit.

The discussion in this chapter is likely to complement, rather than repeat, the coverage within a financial auditing course. An accountant who specializes in auditing computerized AISs is referred to as either an *information systems (IS) auditor* or an *information technology (IT) auditor*. Both designations imply the same work, but we will use the term *IT auditor* in this chapter.

We begin our discussion with introductory comments about the nature of auditing, including a discussion that emphasizes the distinction between internal and external auditing. We then describe the relationship between an IT audit and a financial audit. Next, we discuss tools an IT auditor uses. To the surprise of many students, people and social skills are as important as technical skills. The chapter next describes a variety of approaches for evaluating internal controls in a computerized AIS.

We end Chapter 12 with several topics related to IT auditing today. These include discussion of information technology governance, fraud auditing, the effect of Sarbanes-Oxley and AS5 on IT audits, and discussion of third-party and systems reliability assurance services.

THE AUDIT FUNCTION

To audit is to examine and assure. The nature of auditing differs according to the subject under examination. This section discusses internal, external, and IT auditing.

Internal versus External Auditing

Conventionally, we distinguish between two types of audits: an internal audit and an external audit. In an *internal audit,* a company's own accounting employees perform the audit, whereas accountants working for an independent CPA firm conduct an *external audit*. Generally, internal auditing positions are staff positions reporting to top management and/or the Audit Committee of the Board of Directors. While an audit might be internal to a company, it is invariably *external* to the corporate department or division being audited. Thus, the auditing function preserves its objectivity and professionalism.

An internal audit involves evaluation of (1) employee compliance with organizational policies and procedures, (2) effectiveness of operations, (3) compliance with external laws and regulations, (4) reliability of financial reports, and (5) internal controls. It is relatively broad in scope, including activities such as auditing for fraud and ensuring that employees are not copying software programs illegally. Internal auditors can provide assurance to a company's top management and the board of directors about the efficiency and effectiveness of almost any aspect of its organization.

In contrast to the broad perspective of internal auditors, the chief purpose of an external audit is the attest function—that is, giving an opinion on the accuracy and fairness of financial statements. This fairness evaluation is conducted in the context of generally accepted accounting principles (GAAP) and requires application of generally accepted auditing standards (GAAS). In the past few years, the external auditor's role has expanded with respect to auditing for fraud. *Statement on Auditing Standards (SAS) No. 99 Consideration of Fraud in a Financial Statement Audit* requires auditors working for public accounting firms to undertake a number of specific actions to ensure that an organization's financial statements are free of erroneous or fraudulent material misstatements. Similarly, AS5 emphasizes the importance of evaluating controls designed to prevent fraud.

Today, there are specialized auditors called fraud auditors or forensic accountants (described in Chapters 1 and 11). These auditors specialize in investigating fraud, and they often work closely with internal auditors and attorneys. The fraud investigation units of the FBI, large public accounting firms, the IRS, insurance organizations, and other types of large corporations employ fraud auditors.

As mentioned in Chapter 1, external auditors have expanded the services they offer to include a wide variety of assurance services. Many of these services involve IT in some way. However, the attest function remains the external auditor's main responsibility. Although the primary goals of external and internal audits differ, they are complementary within the context of an AIS. For example, the controls that internal auditors examine within a company's IT environment are in part designed to ensure the accuracy of the external financial reports. External auditors evaluate these controls as part of their assurance function. Similarly, the use of an acceptable method of inventory valuation, as required by GAAP and evaluated by the external auditors, is likely to be an important corporate policy falling under the domain of the internal auditors.

Despite the differences in purpose between internal audits and external audits, internal auditors and external auditors perform a number of similar functions related to computerized AISs. Therefore, most of the following discussion applies to both internal and external auditors. We use the term *auditor* broadly to encompass both types of auditors. Even though internal and external auditors perform a number of similar functions, this is not to say that much audit work is duplicated. Instead, a large degree of cooperation and interaction often exists between a company's internal auditors and a public accounting firm's external auditors. For example, external auditors frequently review, and often rely on, the work of internal auditors as they assess an organization's financial statements.

Information Technology Auditing

IT auditing involves evaluating IT's role in achieving audit and control objectives. The assurance aspect of IT auditing involves ensuring that data and information are reliable,

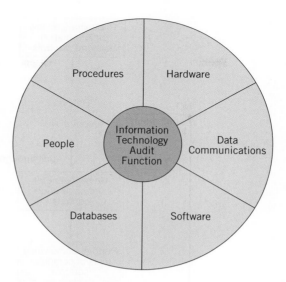

FIGURE 12-1   The six components of a computer-based AIS examined in an information technology audit.

confidential, secure, and available as needed. Traditional financial audit objectives are also present in information technology auditing. These include attest objectives such as the safeguarding of assets and data integrity, and management objectives such as operational effectiveness.

The Information Technology Audit Process.   As illustrated in Figure 12-1, the IT audit function encompasses all components of a computer-based AIS: people, procedures, hardware, data communications, software, and databases.

External auditors examine an organization's computer-based AIS primarily to evaluate how the organization's control procedures over computer processing affect the financial statements (attest objectives). The controls in place will directly influence the scope of the audit. For instance, if computer controls are weak or nonexistent, auditors will need to do more *substantive testing*—that is, detailed tests of transactions and account balances. An example of substantive testing is the confirmation of accounts receivable with customers. If the control procedures over a company's computerized financial accounting system are strong, the auditors may limit the scope of their audit by examining fewer transactions underlying accounts receivable account balances. For our example, this would mean contacting fewer customers to confirm accounts receivable than would be the case if little or no reliance could be placed on the computer-based controls.

Figure 12-2 shows a flowchart of the steps that generally take place in IT auditing. These steps are similar to those performed in any financial audit. What is different is that the auditor's examination in this case concerns a computer-based AIS. In Figure 12-2, the process begins with a preliminary evaluation of the system. The auditor will first decide if computer processing of accounting data is significant or complex enough to warrant an examination of the computer-based information system itself. Sometimes, if the system is neither large nor complex, the audit might proceed as it would in a manual data processing environment. Most often, computer-based processing warrants a preliminary review by the IT auditor to make an assessment of the control environment.

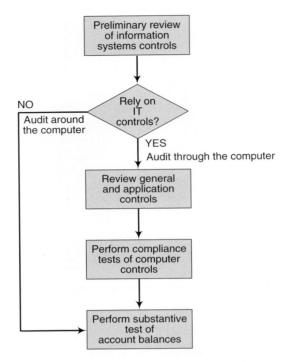

FIGURE 12-2   Flowchart of information technology audit process. Auditing through and around the computer are discussed later in the chapter.

Typically, an auditor will find enough computer-based controls in place to warrant further examination. In this situation, an auditor will want to make a more detailed analysis of both *general* and *application controls* (discussed in Chapter 10). After examining these controls in some detail, the auditors will perform **compliance testing** to ensure that the controls are in place and working as prescribed. This may entail using some **computer-assisted audit techniques (CAATs)** to audit the computerized AIS. These involve the use of computer processes or controls to perform audit functions, such as sorting data to detect duplicate accounts payable invoice numbers. Finally, the auditor will need to substantively test some account balances. As explained earlier, the results of the previous analysis and testing affect the scope of this testing.

Careers in Information Technology Auditing.   As organizations increasingly rely on computer-based AISs and as these systems become more technologically complex, the demand for IT auditors is growing. The passage of the Sarbanes-Oxley Act also created a need for more IT auditors. IT auditing requires a variety of skills. Some information technology auditors have college degrees in computer science or information systems, while others have accounting degrees and general audit experience. The ideal background includes a combination of accounting, auditing, and information systems or computer science skills.

As Chapter 1 noted, IT auditors may choose to obtain a professional certification such as Certified Information System Auditor (CISA). Applicants achieve this certification by successfully completing an examination given by the Information Systems Audit and Control Association (ISACA), meeting experience requirements, complying with a Code of Professional Ethics, undergoing continuing professional education, and complying with the Information Systems Auditing Standards. Figure 12-3 describes the content areas covered

Job Practice Domains	Coverage
IS Audit Process	10(%)
IT Governance	15(%)
Systems and Infrastructure Lifecycle Management	16(%)
IT Service Delivery and Support	14(%)
Protection of Information Assets	31(%)
Business Continuity and Disaster Recovery	14(%)

FIGURE 12-3 Job practice domains covered on the Certified Information Systems Auditor examination. Source: *CISA Job Practice Areas, CISA Task and Knowledge Statements* taken from the *2011 Candidate's Guide to the CISA® Exam and Certification* © 2011 ISACA®. All rights reserved. Used by permission.

on the CISA examination. Notice that they involve evaluation of IT, IT governance, and the protection of IT assets.

A more general certification for experienced information security professionals is the *Certified Information Security Manager (CISM)*, also granted by ISACA. Those seeking a CISM designation need to have a business orientation and understand risk management and security from a conceptual viewpoint. A CISM evaluates knowledge in information security governance, information security program management, risk management, information security management, and response management. The CISA designation has been granted since 1978, and the CISM is relatively new.

IT auditors may be employed as either internal or external auditors. In both cases, these professionals focus on evaluating control procedures rather than substantive testing. Evaluating controls over information systems hardware and various AIS applications requires a high level of expertise. As an example, an IT auditor evaluating controls that limit access to certain information needs to be familiar with the way a particular application organizes its access security. Compared to external auditors, internal auditors can more easily specialize in knowledge about their particular organization's hardware, operating system platform, and application programs.

An external auditor is likely to audit the information systems of many different client organizations. The external information systems auditor may or may not be part of the regular financial audit team. In some cases, the financial audit team only calls on external information systems auditors when a special risk assessment appears warranted. The Big Four public accounting firms all employ IT auditors and perform a variety of assurance-related IT services for clients.

Case-in-Point 12.1 Some IT auditors at Ernst & Young LLP work in the Technology and Security Risk Services (TSRS) practice within the Assurance and Business Advisory Services area. These professionals help clients to evaluate their IT risk, improve the value of IT, and provide IT security. Ernst & Young also offers specialized services that protect data and systems from threats, such as cyber terrorism.

Evaluating the Effectiveness of Information Systems Controls

The more confidence auditors have (as a result of strong controls) that data are input and processed accurately in a computer-based system, the less substantive testing they perform. On the other hand, if a computer-based system has weak controls over data input and processing, there is more need for detailed testing of financial transactions.

Risk Assessment. An external auditor's main objective in reviewing information systems control procedures is to evaluate the *risks* (associated with any control weaknesses) to the integrity of accounting data presented in financial reports. Control strengths and weaknesses will affect the scope of the audit. A second objective of the external auditor's review is to make recommendations to managers about improving these controls. Improving controls is also an objective of internal auditors.

The following four steps provide a logical framework for performing a **risk-based audit** of a company's AIS:

1. Determine the threats (i.e., errors and irregularities) facing the AIS.

2. Identify the control procedures that should be in place to minimize each of these threats and thereby prevent or detect the errors and irregularities.

3. Evaluate the control procedures within the AIS. The process of reviewing system documentation and interviewing appropriate personnel to determine whether the necessary control procedures are in place is called a *systems review*. In addition, auditors investigate whether these control procedures are satisfactorily followed. The tests include activities such as observing system operations; inspecting documents, records, and reports; checking samples of system inputs and outputs; and tracing transactions through the system.

4. Evaluate weaknesses (i.e., errors and irregularities not covered by control procedures) within the AIS to determine their effect on the nature, timing, or extent of auditing procedures. This step focuses on the *control risks* and on whether a company's control system as a whole adequately addresses the risks. If a control deficiency is identified, the auditor should determine whether there are compensating controls or procedures that make up for the deficiency. Control weaknesses in one area of an AIS may be acceptable if control strengths in other areas of the AIS compensate for them.

The risk-based audit approach provides auditors with a good understanding of the errors and irregularities that can occur in a company's AIS environment and the related risks and exposures. This understanding provides a sound basis for the auditors' development of recommendations to the company's management regarding how its controls can be improved.

The desirability of an internal control procedure is a function of its ability to reduce business risk. In fact, it is the business risk itself that is important, not the internal control system. For example, natural disasters such as floods or earthquakes pose a risk to an organization's ability to continue its business without interruption. A disaster recovery or business continuity plan is an internal control procedure designed to reduce this risk. Focusing on business risk focuses attention on those controls that are absolutely necessary and also cost-effective. One method by which an auditor can evaluate the desirability of IT-related controls for a particular aspect of business risk is through an **information systems risk assessment**.

In addition to the risk of fraud or intentional manipulation, auditors must also consider risk with respect to errors or accidents. For instance, inputting asset purchases incorrectly could lead to financial statement misrepresentations in the form of incorrect asset valuations. The loss of company secrets, unauthorized manipulation of company files, and interrupted computer access are also important risks in accounting systems with significant IT components. Auditors must assess the probability of data losses and recommend the implementation of control procedures to reduce threats to the integrity and security of data. In cases where the costs of protection are greater than potential losses, the auditor may recommend against implementing costly controls.

Sometimes companies assess their information systems risks by employing ethical hackers to conduct penetration testing. We discussed hacking in Chapter 11 as a computer crime. However, when an IT auditor employs "white hat" hacking techniques, the purpose is to evaluate risk and design controls to protect against unauthorized access. We call this type of ethical hacking penetration testing because the auditor is trying to penetrate the system to gain access to resources or sensitive information.

Chapters 9 and 10 pointed out that the Information Systems Audit and Control Foundation developed the Control Objectives for Information and related Technology (COBIT) framework. This framework provides auditors and businesses with guidance in managing and controlling for business risk associated with IT environments. COBIT includes control objectives and control outcomes tests for evaluating the effectiveness of IT controls. Using the framework, management and auditors can design a cost-effective control system for IT resources and processes. COBIT benefits business and IT managers, as well as auditors. For auditors, the model helps in advising management on internal controls and can provide substantive support for audit opinions. The next case describes one company's use of COBIT.

Case-in-Point 12.2   Sun Microsystems is a worldwide provider of hardware and software solutions. In order to improve the strategic value of IT and to comply with the Sarbanes-Oxley Act, Sun's IT department decided to use the COBIT framework to evaluate and measure the relationship of IT to corporate strategy. The framework enabled Sun to successfully evaluate six data centers and more than 600 IT applications and enabled senior IT executives to create a Sun IT/COBIT Activities Listing that mapped Sun's IT processes and activities to COBIT.[1]

THE INFORMATION TECHNOLOGY AUDITOR'S TOOLKIT

Auditors can use computer-assisted audit techniques (CAATs) to help them in various auditing tasks. In an automated AIS, **auditing with the computer** (i.e., using the computer itself as an audit tool) is virtually mandatory because data are stored on computer media and manual access is impossible. However, there are many reasons for auditing with the computer beyond the need to access computerized accounting data. One of the most important is that computer-based AISs are rapidly increasing in sophistication. Another is that CAATs save time. Imagine footing and cross-footing large spreadsheets or schedules without using a computer.

Auditing Software

Auditors can use a variety of software when auditing with the computer. Examples include general-use software (such as word processing programs, spreadsheet software, and database management systems). Other software that we discuss, such as generalized audit software (GAS) and automated workpaper software, are more specifically oriented toward auditor tasks.

General-Use Software.   Auditors employ **general-use software** as productivity tools that can improve their work. For instance, word processing programs improve effectiveness when writing reports because built-in spell checks can significantly reduce spelling errors.

---

[1] http://www.isaca.org/Knowledge-Center/cobit/Pages/Sun-Microsystems.aspx

Similarly, an auditor can write a customer confirmation letter with a word processing program and mail-merge it with an address file so that each letter appears to have been individually prepared.

Spreadsheet software allows both accountants and auditors to make complex calculations automatically. It also allows the user to change one number and update all related numbers at the click of a mouse. One of the most common uses of electronic spreadsheets by accountants and auditors is for making mathematical calculations, such as interest and depreciation. Spreadsheet software can also be used to perform analytical procedures, such as computing ratios. Different presentation formats for data contained in spreadsheets contribute to the usefulness of these data for management decision making and other managerial functions.

Accountants and auditors can use a database management system (DBMS) to perform some of the same functions as spreadsheet software. For instance, DBMSs can sort data and make certain mathematical computations. However, they are distinguished from spreadsheet software by their ability to manipulate large sets of data in fairly simple ways. As a general rule, accountants and auditors use spreadsheet software to make complex calculations with relatively small sets of data, whereas they will use DBMSs for simpler calculations or manipulations, such as sorting, on large data sets.

A DBMS is the backbone of almost all organizational accounting systems. The auditor can select subsets of a client company's data for manipulation purposes. This can be done either on the client's computer system or on the auditor's computer after the data are downloaded. A valuable tool for retrieving and manipulating data is structured query language (SQL), a popular data manipulation language. Auditors can use SQL to retrieve a client's data and display these data in a variety of formats for audit purposes. As an example, an auditor may use the SELECT command to retrieve inventory items meeting certain criteria, such as minimum dollar amount. Other data manipulation capabilities of SQL include (1) selecting records matching specified criteria, (2) deleting records from a file based on established criteria, (3) generating customized reports based on all or a subset of data, and (4) rearranging file records in sequential order.

Generalized Audit Software. **Generalized audit software (GAS)** packages enable auditors to review computer files without continually rewriting processing programs. Large CPA firms have developed some of these packages in-house, and many other programs are available from various software suppliers. GAS packages are available to run on microcomputers, minicomputers, or mainframes. GAS programs are capable of the basic data manipulation tasks that spreadsheet or DBMS software might also perform. These include mathematical computations, cross footing, categorizing, summarizing, merging files, sorting records, statistical sampling, and printing reports. One advantage GAS packages have over other software is that these programs are specifically tailored to audit tasks. Auditors can use GAS programs in a variety of ways in specific application areas, such as accounts receivable, inventory, and accounts payable. Figure 12-4 shows some of the ways auditors might use GAS to audit inventory applications.

Two popular GAS packages used by auditors are Audit Command Language (ACL) and Interactive Data Extraction and Analysis (IDEA). These programs allow auditors to examine a company's data in a variety of formats. They include commands such as STRATIFY, EXTRACT, and JOIN. Each of these commands provides an auditor with a different view of the data. For example, the STRATIFY command lets an auditor group data into categories. This is useful, for example, in sorting inventories into various classes based on their cost. Stratification lets an auditor concentrate on high-dollar-value inventory items.

- Merge last year's inventory file with this year's, and list those items with unit costs greater than a certain dollar amount and that have increased by more than a specified percentage.
- List inventory quantities on hand in excess of units sold during a specified period, and list those inventory items with a last sales date prior to a specified date to identify possible obsolete inventory items.
- Select a sample of inventory tag numbers and print the sample selection.
- Scan the sequence of inventory tag numbers and print any missing or duplicate numbers.
- Select a random sample of inventory items for price testing on a dollar-value basis, and list all items with an extended value in excess of a specified amount.
- Perform a net-realizable-value test on year-end inventory quantities, and list any items where inventory cost exceeds net-realizable value.

FIGURE 12-4 Various ways to use generalized audit software packages to audit inventory.

Another example of data stratification is related to auditing accounts receivable. Auditors will want to verify large receivable balances in greater proportion than small accounts receivable balances. Most GAS packages allow auditors to *extract* data according to some specification. Auditors can extract data to detect a variety of exception conditions, such as duplicate invoice numbers, inventory items that have not been sold in more than one year, and customers with negative accounts receivable balances. By joining files, auditors can compare data. For example, combining the employee file with the vendor file may show that an employee has perpetrated a fraud by creating a fictitious vendor. The following case describes how Stanford University used ACL to detect errors and improve security.

Case-in-Point 12.3 Stanford University uses ACL to analyze data from many different systems and its large ERP system. Stanford recently analyzed its payment transactions and identified $480,000 in annual duplicate payments to vendors. The university also detected a programming error in its ERP system that created a data security threat.[2]

Automated Workpapers. **Automated workpapers** allow internal and external auditors to automate and standardize specific audit tests and audit documentation. Some of the capabilities of automated workpapers are to (1) generate trial balances, (2) make adjusting entries, (3) perform consolidations, (4) conduct analytical procedures, and (5) document audit procedures and conclusions. One advantage of using automated workpapers is the automation of footing, cross footing, and reconciliation to schedules. Auditors can use this software to prepare consolidated trial balances and financial statements (that combine accounts of multiple companies). Automated workpapers can also help auditors create common-size income statements and balance sheets that show account balances as percentages. In addition, automated workpapers can easily calculate financial statement ratios and measurements, such as the current ratio, the working capital, the inventory turnover rate, and the price-earnings ratio.

The Internet can also be a valuable resource for IT auditors. There are many Web sites that offer useful advice and guidance. These include software vendor sites with patches for software security holes, sites with alerts about security threats, and Web sites that have special tools that may be used free of charge or purchased.

---

[2] http://www.acl.com/customers/

Case-in-Point 12.4 *AuditNet* describes itself as a "global resource for auditors." Registered users can subscribe to download audit programs for a variety of application areas, such as accounts payable. These programs include detailed audit procedures. There is also a Sarbanes-Oxley resource center, a discussion forum, a virtual library, and a list of audit terminology and definitions.[3]

People Skills

Arguably the most important skills that auditors require are people skills. After all, auditors must work as a team and be able to interact with clients. For example, to understand the organizational structure of the IT function, the IT auditor will need to interview the CIO. Interviews are a mainstay of IT auditing. Similarly, IT auditors are also likely to find that many of the audit steps in their evaluation of internal controls have more to do with human behavior than technology. For example, one of the best protections against programmed threats such as viruses and worms is regularly updated antivirus software. It may be important to understand the capabilities of the software, but it is even more important to see if the security administrator is checking for virus updates and patches on a regular basis.

AUDITING COMPUTERIZED ACCOUNTING INFORMATION SYSTEMS

When computers were first used for accounting data processing functions, the typical auditor knew very little about automated data processing. The basic auditing approach, therefore, was to follow the audit trail up to the point at which accounting data entered the computer and to pick these data up again when they reappeared in processed form as computer output. This is called **auditing around the computer**. It assumes that the presence of accurate output verifies proper processing operations. This type of auditing pays little or no attention to the control procedures within the IT environment. Auditing around the computer is not generally an effective approach for auditing in a computerized environment, in part because it tests normal transactions but ignores exceptions. It is the exceptions that are of primary interest to the auditor.

When auditing a computerized AIS, an auditor should follow the audit trail through the internal computer operations phase of automated data processing. This approach, **auditing through the computer**, attempts to verify that the processing controls involved in the AIS programs are functioning properly. It also attempts to verify that the accounting data processed are accurate. Because this type of auditing tests the existence and functioning of control procedures, it normally occurs during the compliance phase of the flowchart in Figure 12-2.

Auditing through the computer usually assumes that the CPU and other hardware are functioning properly. This leaves the auditor the principal task of verifying processing and control logic as opposed to computer accuracy. Five techniques that auditors use to audit a computerized AIS are (1) use of test data, integrated test facility, and parallel simulation to *test programs*, (2) use of audit techniques to *validate computer programs*, (3) use of logs and specialized control software to *review systems software*, (4) use of documentation and CAATs to validate user accounts and access privileges, and (5) use of embedded audit modules to achieve *continuous auditing*.

---

[3] http://www.auditnet.org

Testing Computer Programs

In testing computer programs, the objective is to ensure that the programs accomplish their goals and that the data are input and processed accurately. Three techniques that auditors may employ to test computer programs are (1) test data, (2) integrated test facilities, and (3) parallel simulation.

Test Data. It is the auditor's responsibility to develop a set of transactions that tests, as completely as possible, the range of exception situations that might occur. Conventionally, these transactions are called **test data**. Possible exception situations for a payroll application, for example, include out-of-sequence payroll checks, duplicate time cards, negative hours worked, invalid employee numbers, invalid dates, invalid pay rates, invalid deduction codes, and use of alphabetic data in numeric codes.

To conduct audit testing, an auditor will compare the results obtained from processing test data with a predetermined set of answers on an audit worksheet. If processing results and worksheet results do not agree, further investigation is necessary. A sample set of program edit tests and test data appears in Figure 12-5.

Integrated Test Facility. Although test data work well in validating an application's *input controls*, they are not as effective for evaluating integrated online systems or complex programming logic. In these situations, it may be better to use a more comprehensive test technique such as an **integrated test facility (ITF)**. The purpose of an ITF is to audit an AIS in an operational setting. This involves (1) establishing a fictitious entity such as a department, branch, customer, or employee; (2) entering transactions for that entity; and (3) observing how these transactions are processed. For example, an auditor might create a number of fictitious credit customers and place appropriate accounts receivable master records in the company's accounts receivable computer files. From the standpoint of the auditor, of course, the information contained on these records is for test purposes only. To most of the employees of the company, however, these records represent bona fide customers entitled to purchase company merchandise inventory or services on credit.

To use an ITF, an auditor will introduce artificial transactions into the data processing stream of the AIS and have the company routinely handle the business involved. In a truly integrated test facility, this may mean actually shipping merchandise (not ordered by anyone) to designated addresses or billing customers for services not rendered. Because of the amount of work involved, however, it may be necessary to intercept the ordered merchandise at the shipping department and reverse the billing transactions at the managerial level.

Program Edit Test	Required by Program	Test Data
Completeness	6 characters required	12345
Numeric field	Numeric characters only	123C45
Sign	Positive numbers only	−123456
Reasonableness	Hours worked should not exceed 80 per week	110
Valid code	Accept only I (invoice), P (payment), M (memo)	C
Range	Accept only dates between 01/01/10 and 12/31/11	02/05/13

FIGURE 12-5 Program edit tests and test data.

Parallel Simulation.   With **parallel simulation**, the auditor creates a second system that duplicates a portion of the client's system. The auditor's system runs at the same time as the client's system, and the auditor processes *live* data, rather than test data. The auditor can compare the processing and outputs from their own system to the client's system. Differences between the processing and outputs of the client system, relative to the auditor's duplicate (or parallel) system, indicate problems with the client's system.

In order for this method to be effective, an auditor must thoroughly understand the audited organization's computer system and know-how to predict the results. As you might imagine, it can be very time consuming and thus cost-prohibitive for an auditor to write computer programs entirely replicating those of the client. For this reason, parallel simulation usually involves replicating only certain critical functions of a program. For example, a program that replicates payroll processing might just calculate net pay for employees rather than making all the payroll calculations in the entire payroll program.

Validating Computer Programs

A clever programmer can thwart the use of test data by changing programs just before an auditor asks for the processing routine(s) required for the audit. Therefore, an auditor must validate any program that he or she is given by a client. Although there is no 100 percent foolproof way of validating a computer program, several procedures may be used to assist in this task, including tests of program change controls and program comparisons.

Tests of Program Change Controls.   The process by which a newly developed program or program modification is put into actual use should be subject to **program change controls**. These are internal control procedures developed to protect against unauthorized program changes. Sound program change control requires documentation of every request for application program changes. It also requires computer programmers to develop and implement changes in a separate test environment rather than a live processing environment.

Depending on the size of an organization, the change control process might be one of many duties performed by one individual. Alternatively, responsibility might be assigned to more than one individual. The basic procedures in program change control include testing program changes and obtaining proper authorizations as programs move from a testing stage to actual production (live) use. The auditor's responsibility is to ensure that a company's management establishes and executes proper authorization procedures and that the company's employees observe these procedures.

A test of program change controls begins with an inspection of the documentation maintained by the information processing subsystem. Many organizations create flowcharts of their change control processes. The organization should also have special forms that authorize changes to existing programs or the development of new programs. Included on these *program authorization forms* should be the name of the individual responsible for the work and the signature of the supervisor responsible for approving the final programs. Similarly, there should be forms that show the work has been completed and a signature authorizing the use of the program(s) for data processing. These authorizing signatures affix responsibility for the data processing routines and ensure accountability when problems arise. We call this a responsibility system of computer program development and maintenance. Figure 12-6 describes the processes that an auditor should validate.

The chief purpose of a responsibility system at the computer center is not to affix blame in the event of program failures but to ensure accountability and adequate supervisory controls in the critical area of data processing. Tighter control over both the development

- Programmers document all program changes on the proper change-request forms.
- Users and accountants properly cost all program change requests and the planning committee reviews high-cost projects.
- Both computer development committee personnel and users sign the outline specification form, thereby establishing authorization for the programming work.
- Program changes match those in the programs in the production load library (where currently used programs are stored).
- Documentation matches the production version of a computer program.
- Information systems personnel properly carry out librarian functions, especially a review of the paperwork involved with the documentation of program change requests.

FIGURE 12-6 Each of the above processes is checked by an auditor in reviewing a responsibility system of computer program development and maintenance.

of new programs and changes to existing programs is likely to result in better computer software, since individuals tend to exert more effort when they are held responsible for a given piece of work.

Program Comparison. To guard against unauthorized program tampering, such as the insertion of malicious code, it is possible to perform certain *control total tests* of program authenticity. One is a *test of length*. To perform this test, an auditor obtains the latest version of an accounting computer program to be verified and compares the number of bytes of computer memory it requires with an entry in a security table of length counts of all valid accounting programs. If the accounting program's length count fails to match its control total, the program is then further scrutinized. (This process is similar to comparing the word count in two similar documents produced by Microsoft Word.)

Another way to ensure consistency between the authorized version of an accounting computer program and the program version currently in use is to compare the code directly on a line-by-line basis using a *comparison program*. A comparison program will detect any changes that a programmer might have made, even if the programmer has been clever enough to ensure that the program length for the two versions is the same. Auditors must evaluate the trade-off between efficiency and effectiveness in choosing whether to use control totals, perform detailed program comparison, or rely on general controls over program changes to prevent unauthorized tampering with computer programs.

Review of Systems Software

Systems software controls include (1) operating system software, (2) utility programs that do basic "housekeeping" chores such as sorting and copying, (3) program library software that controls and monitors storage of programs, and (4) access control software that controls logical access to programs and data files.

When auditing through the computer, auditors will want to review the systems software documentation. In addition, auditors will request management to provide certain output or runs from the software. For instance, the auditor, in reviewing how passwords within the system are set, will ask the information systems manager for a listing of all parameters or password characteristics designated in the system. Figure 12-7 lists some of the characteristics of passwords that the auditor typically examines.

Auditors may choose to use software tools to review systems software. A number of tools are available, ranging from user-written programs to commercial packages such as

Parameter	Definition	Sample Setting	Risk
Minimum password length	Minimum number of characters required	6 digits	Short passwords are more easily guessed
Required password change	Require users to change passwords at specific intervals	60 days	Compromised passwords can be used forever
Minimum interval before password change	Minimum number of days before user can change password	1 day	If a user believes someone has learned the password, how much time must pass before it can be changed?
Maximum number of repeating characters allowed	Specifies how many characters may be repeated within the password	2 characters	Passwords such as "AAAAAA" are easily guessed
Alphabetic characters	Passwords may not consist of only numbers	Alpha	Protects against use of birthdates or other easily guessed numbers
Dictionary entries	Passwords cannot be dictionary words	ROOTTOOT	Hackers use standard dictionaries to find passwords
Assignment	Only bona fide users are given passwords	Employee	Passwords ensure accountability in addition to providing access

FIGURE 12-7   Examples of parameters that might be set to control passwords.

CA-Examine. There are also general analysis software tools, such as *SAS, SPSS,* and *FOCUS.* These software tools can query operating system files to analyze the system parameters.

Systems software usually generates automatic outputs that are important for monitoring a company's computer system. In auditing the company's system, an auditor will want to inspect these outputs, which include logs and incident reports. The company's management uses logs for accounting purposes and for scheduling the use of computer resources efficiently. Auditors will make use of these logs to evaluate system security. Unusual occurrences, such as programs run at odd times or programs run with greater frequency than usual, are noted and subsequently investigated. Management may manually maintain incident reports, or systems software may automatically generate these reports. The reports list events encountered by the system that are unusual or interrupt operations. Examples of incidents commonly recorded are security violations (such as unauthorized access attempts), hardware failures, and software failures.

Validating Users and Access Privileges

An IT auditor needs to make sure that all computer-system users are valid and that each has access privileges appropriate to his or her job responsibilities. Systems software generally includes access control software that determines how the system administrator sets up and controls user IDs, user profiles, and passwords. The IT auditor should verify that the software parameters are set appropriately and that IT staff are using them appropriately. For example, one audit task is to make sure that employee accounts are closed immediately after someone leaves the organization. To accomplish this, the IT auditor might request a list of current personnel from Human Resources. Another approach would be to obtain a current phone directory and compare names with those in the listing of user accounts.

IT auditors should also look at user listings to see if there are any Group IDs assigned. For example, there may be an ID named AP_Clerk. Sometimes managers decide to issue these IDs to cut down on paperwork when making personnel changes. However, this type of ID prevents assigning responsibility to an individual. If one AP clerk were to make a mistake or commit fraud, the use of a Group ID would make it difficult to identify which of the accounts payable clerks was responsible.

An IT auditor can visually inspect printouts from databases and software documentation to verify users, appropriateness of passwords, and spot Group IDs. However, a variety of auditor software tools are available to make the work more efficient. As an example, such software might examine log-in times. If a user has not logged in for several months, it may be that the account should have been deleted. Users logging in at odd hours may also provide information that something is not right. As we noted earlier in the chapter, IT auditors need to identify exception conditions and irregularities.

Continuous Auditing

Some audit tools can be installed within an information system itself to achieve **continuous auditing** or real-time assurance. Continuous auditing is increasingly important as we move toward real-time financial reporting. There is also increasing pressure to reduce the time span between the production of financial information and the audit of the information, known as the audit cycle. Stakeholders want audited information quickly. Many businesses report their financial information over the Internet, and many more are likely to do so as XBRL enhances this form of reporting.

Five specific approaches for continuous auditing are (1) embedded audit modules or audit hooks, (2) exception reporting, (3) transaction tagging, (4) the snapshot technique, and (5) continuous and intermittent simulation. These tools allow auditing to occur even when an auditor is not present. With embedded audit modules, application subroutines capture data for audit purposes. These data usually are related to a high-risk area. For example, an application program for payroll could include program code that causes transactions meeting prespecified criteria to be written to a special log. Possible transactions that might be recorded in a log include those affecting inactive accounts, deviating from company policy, or involving write-downs of asset values. For payroll applications, these transactions could reflect situations where, for instance, employees worked more hours than are allowed. Another example might be recording related transactions occurring in a particular sequence.

The practice of *exception reporting* is also a form of continuous auditing. If the information system includes mechanisms to reject certain transactions that fall outside predefined specifications (such as an unusually large payment to a vendor), then the ongoing reporting of exception transactions allows the system to continually monitor itself.

Using transaction tagging, auditors can tag certain transactions with special identifiers such that the transactions can be traced through processing steps in the AIS and logged for review. For example, if a large payment is tagged by the AIS, the auditor will be able to review how this transaction entered the system, how it was processed, and what output it produced. Tagging in this instance could also check to see that controls within the system are operating. Suppose that a control procedure requires rejection of vendor payment if it exceeds a predetermined level. Auditors can review tagged transactions to make sure that the control procedure is functioning properly or determine if someone is overriding the control.

The snapshot technique examines the way transactions are processed. Selected transactions are marked with code that triggers the snapshot process. Audit modules in the computer program record these transactions and their master file records before and after processing activities. Snapshot data are recorded in a special file and reviewed by the auditor to verify that all processing steps have been properly performed.

Continuous and intermittent simulation (CIS) embeds an audit module in a database management system (DBMS). The CIS module examines all transactions that update the DBMS. If a transaction has special audit significance, the audit module independently processes the data (in a manner similar to parallel simulation), records the results, and compares them with those results obtained by the DBMS. If any discrepancies exist, the details of these discrepancies are written to an audit log for subsequent investigation. If serious discrepancies are discovered, the CIS may prevent the DBMS from executing the update process. A challenge for continuous auditing is that the data in complex organizations may be located in multiple DBMSs. To effectively conduct real-time assurance, auditors may need to create a data mart or subset of the data warehouse specifically for audit purposes.

An example of continuous auditing on a smaller scale is embedding audit modules in spreadsheets. For example, the *Excel* payroll spreadsheet in Figure 12-8 computes the regular and overtime earnings for the employees of a construction company. Most spreadsheets of this type would only include the first few lines shown in the figure, plus perhaps the "Total" line in row 11. But this spreadsheet includes an auditing module that

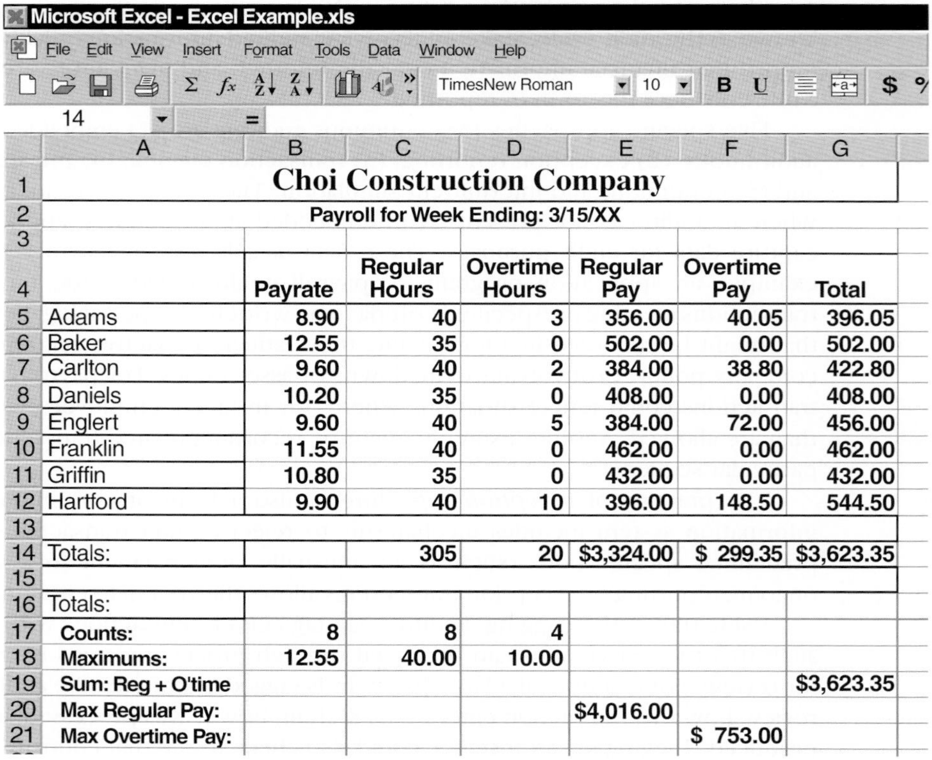

	A	B	C	D	E	F	G
1	**Choi Construction Company**						
2	**Payroll for Week Ending: 3/15/XX**						
3							
4		**Payrate**	**Regular Hours**	**Overtime Hours**	**Regular Pay**	**Overtime Pay**	**Total**
5	Adams	8.90	40	3	356.00	40.05	396.05
6	Baker	12.55	35	0	502.00	0.00	502.00
7	Carlton	9.60	40	2	384.00	38.80	422.80
8	Daniels	10.20	35	0	408.00	0.00	408.00
9	Englert	9.60	40	5	384.00	72.00	456.00
10	Franklin	11.55	40	0	462.00	0.00	462.00
11	Griffin	10.80	35	0	432.00	0.00	432.00
12	Hartford	9.90	40	10	396.00	148.50	544.50
13							
14	Totals:		305	20	$3,324.00	$ 299.35	$3,623.35
15							
16	Totals:						
17	**Counts:**	8	8	4			
18	**Maximums:**	12.55	40.00	10.00			
19	**Sum: Reg + O'time**						$3,623.35
20	**Max Regular Pay:**				$4,016.00		
21	**Max Overtime Pay:**					$ 753.00	

FIGURE 12-8 This simple spreadsheet to compute regular and overtime payments contains several errors.

can help an accountant audit the application and check its validity and accuracy. The figure in the "Counts" row uses Excel's COUNTIF function to count the number of positive values in columns B, C, and D of the spreadsheet. An auditor can compare the largest of these numbers to the total number of employees known to work for the company. If we assume that this company has upper limits for the pay rate ($13), regular hours (40), and overtime hours (10), an auditor can also compare the values in the "Maximums" row against these upper limits to determine if any entry is too large.

INFORMATION TECHNOLOGY AUDITING TODAY

IT auditing is actually a component of information technology (IT) governance. In this section, we discuss the issue of IT governance and other important recent developments that affect IT auditing. These include the use of technology to deter fraud, the effects of the Sarbanes-Oxley Act of 2002 and AS5 on IT auditing, and third-party and systems reliability assurance.

Information Technology Governance

Information technology (IT) governance is the process of using IT resources effectively to meet organizational objectives. It includes using IT efficiently, responsibly, and strategically. The IT Governance Institute, an affiliation of the Information Systems Audit and Control Association (ISACA), was created to help organizations ensure that IT resources are properly allocated, that IT risks are mitigated, and that IT delivers value to the organization.

There are two primary objectives of IT governance. The first set of objectives focus on using IT strategically to fulfill the organizational mission and to compete effectively. Top management and the Board of Directors are responsible for ensuring these IT governance objectives. The second set of IT governance objectives involves making sure that the organization's IT resources are managed effectively and that management controls IT-related risks. Meeting these objectives is the concern of the chief information officer (CIO), the auditors, and top management.

Case-in-Point 12.5   A survey of public CIOs from the United States indicates that CIOs see a need for improved IT governance. CIOs are turning to new technologies such as cloud computing and social media to manage technology. Tighter state budgets are forcing CIOs to search for increased efficiency in the use of IT.[4]

Auditing for Fraud—Statement on Auditing Standards No. 99

The financial statement audits mandated by the Securities and Exchange Commission require auditors to attest to the fairness of a company's financial statements. They do not require auditors to detect fraudulent activities. This has long been seen as a problem by many investors and other business stakeholders who believe that an auditor's report indicates that a company is clean or that there is no fraud being committed by management or other employees. As a result, the AICPA's Auditing Standards Board issued *Statement on Auditing Standards (SAS) No. 99 Consideration of Fraud in a Financial Statement Audit*.

---

[4] http://www.govtech.com/pcio/State-CIOs-Want-Better-IT-Governance.html

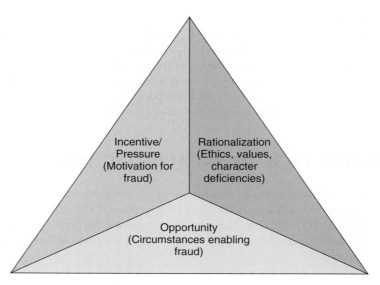

FIGURE 12-9   The fraud triangle. Three conditions required for fraud.

SAS No. 99 superseded SAS No. 82. While the earlier rule had the same name, the 2002 fraud standard provides more guidance for auditors to proactively prevent and deter fraud. The standard is part of a corporate responsibility and antifraud initiative of the AICPA. It encourages auditors to adopt professional skepticism and remain alert for signs of fraud, such as those in the **fraud triangle** depicted in Figure 12-9. This triangle includes three elements that indicate potential fraud. These are the motive for committing the fraud, the opportunity that allows the fraud to occur, and the rationalization by the individual perpetrating the fraud that the behavior is appropriate or justified.

The Sarbanes-Oxley Act of 2002

In 2002, the United States Congress passed the Sarbanes-Oxley Act (SOX), the most sweeping piece of legislation to affect financial reporting and the accounting profession since the SEC Acts of 1933 and 1934. As noted in Chapter 1, the bill was a response to the wave of corporate accounting scandals that took down many long-time business icons, including Enron and Arthur Andersen. Figure 12-10 describes several of the major provisions of the act. For example, *Section 201: Services Outside the Scope of Practice of Auditors; Prohibited Activities* prohibits public accounting firms from offering nonaudit services to a client at the same time they are conducting an audit. This means that, for example, one Big Four firm might be the external auditors of Company A and a different Big Four firm could be the outsourced internal auditors for Company A. (They may, however, provide these services to nonaudit clients.)

SOX has four basic groups of compliance requirements: (1) audit committee/corporate governance requirements, (2) issues regarding certification, disclosure, and internal controls, (3) rules about financial statement reporting, and (4) regulations governing executive reporting and conduct. However, Section 302 and Section 404 of the Act are sometimes called full-employment acts for IT auditors! The cost of complying with the legislation, particularly the requirement to document and attest to internal controls, runs into millions of dollars for large public companies.

Section 201: Services Outside the Scope of Practice of Auditors: Prohibited Activities

- Bookkeeping or other services related to accounting records of financial statements
- Financial information systems design and implementation
- Appraisal or valuation services, fairness opinions, or contribution-in-kind reports
- Actuarial services
- Internal audit outsourcing services
- Management functions or human resources
- Broker or dealer, investment adviser, or investment banking services
- Legal services and expert services unrelated to the audit
- Any other service determined by the Public Company Accounting Oversight Board as unallowable

Section 302: Corporate Responsibility for Financial Reports

The CEO and CFO of each public company issuing financial reports must prepare a statement that accompanies the audit report to certify the "appropriateness of the financial statements and disclosures contained in the periodic report, and that those financial statements and disclosures fairly present, in all material respects, the operations and financial condition of the issuer." The CEO and CFO must knowingly and intentionally violate this requirement in order to be liable.

Section 404: Management Assessment of Internal Controls

Public company annual reports must contain an internal control report, which should state the responsibility of management for establishing and maintaining an adequate internal control structure and procedures for financial reporting; and contain an assessment, as of the end of the issuer's fiscal year, of the effectiveness of the internal control structure and procedures of the issuer for financial reporting. Each issuer's auditor must attest to, and report on, management's assessment.

FIGURE 12-10   A summary of key provisions of the Sarbanes-Oxley Act of 2002.

When Jeffrey Skilling, Enron's chief executive officer (CEO), testified before the Senate Banking and Commerce Committee in 2002, he claimed ignorance with respect to Enron's accounting. Later, Bernie Ebbers, CEO of WorldCom, claimed a similar lack of knowledge about his company's financial records. Shocked that corporate leaders might not understand the financial activities of their own companies, lawmakers included Section 302. This SOX provision requires both chief financial officers (CFOs) and CEOs to certify personally that their company's financial statements are accurate and complete and also that internal controls and disclosures are adequate. Thus, SOX requires top management in public companies to understand their internal controls and makes them legally liable if they knowingly misrepresent the condition of these controls.

Section 404 of SOX requires both the CEO and CFO to assess their organization's internal controls over financial reporting and attest to them. They do so in an internal control report that is filed with the annual report. This section also requires that the external auditors report on management's internal control assessment. This is the work that is keeping management and a company's internal and external auditors the busiest.

To assess internal financial controls requires documenting business processes and internal controls. Large public companies are likely to make heavy use of IT in their processes and financial reporting, which means that they'll need an IT auditor to document the processes and controls. This can be a daunting task but useful for companies to undertake. Consider that you may have a large financial services firm, for example, with literally hundreds of software applications and very complex business processes. Who has the big picture? Probably no one, unless the internal audit staff takes the time to fit the pieces together and create a map of the entire company's processes and applications.

The auditors can use this map to examine the internal controls in general and for each application. For example, one general type of internal control is separation of duties (see Chapter 9). Employees' duties should be clearer after the documentation of processes. Various applications will each have internal controls unique to them as well, such as a control over a procurement application concerning who may enter invoices.

An interesting by-product of SOX is the emergence of software to facilitate compliance with the new rules. The main uses of software for SOX are for managing communication, workflow, and documentation. Many accounting software packages, such as *ACCPAC* or *Peoplesoft* include features to document internal controls. However, there are also specialized programs designed specifically to adhere to the requirements of the Sarbanes-Oxley Act.

Case-in-Point 12.6 S-O Comply® was one of the earliest software tools created to assist with Sarbanes-Oxley compliance, and it includes document management and audit tools. One of the primary requirements of the act is for companies to disclose all material information that might affect the company's financial performance over time. The software includes a Compliance Manager that manages controls, issues, and tasks; discloses documents and work flow; and maintains an audit trail.[5]

SOX regulations do not require companies to automate their controls or processes in order to be compliant. So a company may have many manual processes and manual controls over those processes, in addition to the computerized processes and controls that are of primary interest to the IT auditor. IT auditors must work closely with financial auditors to complete the thorough internal control review mandated by Section 404.

Auditing Standard No. 5 (AS5)

As a result of the substantial burdens created by Section 404 and the uncertainty surrounding the specific requirements of Section 404, the Public Company Accounting Oversight Board provided guidance in Auditing Standard No. 5 (AS5) that helps internal and external auditors reduce control testing and focus on the most critical controls.

One of the major effects of AS5 is what has been called a rebalancing of internal auditors' work. Decreasing the volume of control testing allows internal auditors to spend more time on issues such as advising the board of directors and ensuring compliance with laws and regulations. AS5 also allows external auditors to increase their reliance on the test performed by internal audit functions, which reduces redundant tests. Of course, this has also resulted in decreased audit fees after the passage of AS5, but control testing and documentation is still much more substantial than it was in periods prior to SOX.

Third-Party and Information Systems Reliability Assurances

Auditing e-commerce is a specialized field—in part because of the skill level involved and in part because many of the safeguards found in non-e-commerce systems are absent. One problem is the lack of hard-copy documents with which to verify the existence of accounts, purchases, or payments—a characteristic of electronic communications. Similarly, the arrival of an electronic transaction on a server does not guarantee its validity or authenticity—only that something was transmitted. As an increasing number of companies publish their financial statements online, auditors need to attest to this type

---

[5] http://www.onproject.com/soa

of format. An audit report or digital signature can provide those viewing online financial information with the same assurances as found in a traditional audit report.

In recent years, auditors have shifted away from audits of transactions to examinations of business risks. Because Internet systems and Web sites are sources of such risks, specialized audits of these systems, particularly in terms of security and privacy, are becoming commonplace. In fact, the risks introduced by a business' Internet presence have created a market for **third-party assurance services**. Independent third parties may provide business users and individual consumers with some level of comfort over their Internet transactions. The comfort level varies with the type of assurance services offered. In some cases, third-party assurance is limited to data privacy. The TRUSTe assurance seal is an example of privacy assurance. TRUSTe is a nonprofit organization that issues a privacy seal.

Case-in-Point 12.7 Monster® offers online career connection services. It matches employers with prospective employees and also offers career advice. Since job seekers post personal information at the site, privacy is particularly important. Monster displays the TRUSTe privacy seal at its Web site, along with a privacy statement that includes information about how the company uses the data it collects. The seal is a symbol of assurance to the site users that Monster complies with TRUSTe's privacy practice requirement.[6]

Other assurance services offer different kinds of protection. Consumers and business partners are not only concerned about privacy and security of data transmissions. They also worry about the business policies of an Internet company, its ability to deliver goods and services in a timely fashion, its billing procedures, and its integrity in using a customer's e-mail address. The Better Business Bureau's BBBOnline seeks to verify the business policies of Internet businesses. **CPA WebTrust**, offered by the AICPA, is a third-party assurance seal that promises data privacy and security, in addition to reliable business practices and integrity in processing transactions. Concerns about e-mail spamming and phishing (discussed in Chapters 11 and 14) have led to the development of e-mail assurance or accreditation. In addition to privacy protection, *TRUSTe* now offers a specialized seal to businesses that assures customers that a company will not spam them or misuse their e-mail address.

Auditors must consider information systems risks with respect to their possible effects on financial statements. In addition, many businesses seek assurance as to the *reliability* of their information systems. AICPA members may offer **Trust Services** that include both *WebTrust* and *SysTrust,* an assurance service that evaluates the reliability of information systems with respect to their availability, security, integrity, and maintainability. CPAs offering *SysTrust* services to their clients may evaluate all or some of these reliability characteristics. For instance, a company may have concerns about the security of its information systems. As increasing numbers of parties rely on organizations' information systems, assurance over the reliability of those systems is likely to grow in importance.

The principles of the AICPA's Trust Services are (1) security (protection against unauthorized access), (2) availability (the information system is available for use), (3) processing integrity (processing is complete, timely, authorized, and accurate), (4) online privacy (protection of personal information), and (5) confidentiality (protection of information designated as secret or confidential). Trust Services consists of these principles, together with specific criteria and illustrative controls. The structure provides guidance to practitioners who are evaluating organizations in terms of their reliability, privacy, and security.

---

[6] http://www.truste.com/pdf/Monster_Case_Study.pdf

AIS AT WORK
Future of Information Technology Auditing[7]

One of the author's graduate accounting students recently visited her former professor after working for two years with a Big Four public accounting firm. She indicated that her work involved much more information technology auditing than she ever expected. In fact, her very first assignment in public accounting was to audit the passwords and access controls of an operating system. The student was amazed that most of her work during the first year involved both the use and analysis of sophisticated technology. Recent research of the audit profession suggests that information technology auditing will only continue to grow in importance.

A 2010 study collected survey responses from 1,029 chief audit executives (CAEs) from Australia, Canada, New Zealand, the United Kingdom/Ireland, and the United States. The study found that internal audit functions are spending more and more of their time on information technology audits. The CAEs stated that internal audit functions spent 7.9 percent of their time on IT audits in 2003, but this percentage grew to 13.4 in 2009. The increased need for IT audits is being driven by substantial increases in IT spending over the past decade.

The study also revealed that there is a need to increase efforts to recruit auditors with IT skills and a need to increase spending on IT training. Thus, we should expect to see an increased demand for students with both IT and audit skills and knowledge. A final conclusion of the study involves the need for firms to seek more auditors with the CISA certification when the firms expect to engage in more IT auditing in the future. This suggests an increased demand for the CISA certification as firms continue to increase their investments in IT and move to more complex, integrated systems.

SUMMARY

- ✓ Although both internal and external auditors are concerned with computerized systems, there are important differences in the goals of each type of auditor.
- ✓ IT auditing may complement the financial audit by providing a basis for determining the appropriate scope of the financial audit.
- ✓ Auditors today have some special tools available to them for designing and evaluating internal controls in IT environments, including general-use software and GAS.
- ✓ People skills, including team building and interpersonal skills, are important for an IT auditor.
- ✓ IT auditors use a risk assessment approach in designing their audit programs to ensure that the costs of control procedures do not outweigh their value.
- ✓ Auditing through the computer involves both testing and validating computer programs, as well as reviewing systems software and validating user accounts and access privileges.
- ✓ Embedded audit modules are an example of one tool available to perform a continuous audit.
- ✓ Proper IT governance mandates that managers not only control risks associated with IT but that they also use IT strategically.

[7] Abdolmohammadi, M., and S. Boss. 2010. Factors associated with IT audits by the internal audit function. *International Journal of Accounting Information Systems* 11(3): 140–151.

✓ An increase in attention to fraud and internal controls, as mandated by SAS No. 99 and the Sarbanes-Oxley Act of 2002, has increased the need for the type of work done by IT auditors.

✓ IT auditors may also offer assurance services unrelated to financial audits, such as third-party and systems reliability assurance.

KEY TERMS YOU SHOULD KNOW

auditing around the computer	generalized audit software (GAS)
auditing through the computer	information systems risk assessment
auditing with the computer	information technology (IT) governance
automated workpaper	integrated test facility (ITF)
compliance testing	parallel simulation
computer-assisted audit techniques (CAATs)	program change control
continuous auditing	risk-based audit
CPA WebTrust	test data
fraud triangle	third-party assurance services
general-use software	Trust Services

DISCUSSION QUESTIONS

12-1. Distinguish between the roles of an internal and an external auditor. Cite at least two examples of auditing procedures that might reasonably be expected of an internal auditor but not an external auditor. Which type of auditor would you rather be? Why?

12-2. How does information technology auditing differ from financial auditing? Make a list of the skills you think are important for financial auditors and for IT auditors. Do you think all auditors should have all the skills on both lists? Why or why not?

12-3. Describe the differences between general-use software and generalized audit software. How might you use spreadsheet software, database software, and word processing software in conducting an audit of fixed assets?

12-4. IT auditors need people skills as well as technical skills. One such skill is the ability to interview effectively. Discuss some techniques or tools that might help an interviewer get the best information from an interviewee, including sensitive information.

12-5. Describe how an auditor might use through-the-computer techniques such as test data, an integrated test facility, parallel simulation, or validation of computer programs to accomplish audit objectives relative to accounts payable.

12-6. Jose Rodriguez was the only internal auditor of a medium-size communications firm. The company used a computer for most of its accounting applications, and recently, several new software packages had been implemented to handle the increased volume of the company's business. To evaluate the packages' control capabilities, Jose performed a cost-benefit analysis and found that many of the control procedures were potentially useful but not clearly cost-effective. The problem, therefore, was what to say in his report to management. After pondering this question for some time, he decided to recommend almost all the controls based on the idea that a company was "better to be safe than sorry." Comment on the wisdom of this idea.

12-7. This chapter described several third-party assurance seals, including CPA WebTrust, BBB-Online, and TRUSTe. Explain the differences among them. Identify at least one other third-party assurance seal available for companies that allows them to demonstrate to their customers that they may be trusted in business transactions.

PROBLEMS

12-8. The Espy Company recently had an outside consulting firm perform an audit of its information systems department. One of the consultants identified some business risks and their probability of occurrence. Estimates of the potential losses and estimated control costs are given in Figure 12-11.

    a. Using information in Figure 12-11, develop a risk assessment for the Espy Company.

    b. If you were the manager responsible for the Espy Company's information processing system, which controls would you implement and why?

12-9. Visit http://www.isaca.org, the Web site for the Information Systems Audit and Control Association. Investigate the Certified Information Systems Auditor (CISA) credential. Describe the purpose of the credential and the types of auditing CISAs perform.

12-10. Information systems auditors sometimes use tools or information they can download from the Internet. These tools or information may include software, audit guides, or computer security advisories. Locate some examples from the Internet of audit tools, audit guides, or computer security advisories that you would find useful in conducting an audit of a client's computer system.

12-11. Continuous auditing has the potential to reduce labor costs associated with auditing. It also can provide audit assurance closer to the occurrence of a transaction, which improves the reliability of frequent or real-time financial reports. Using an Internet search engine, find an example of an organization's usage of continuous auditing.

CASE STUDIES

Basic Requirements (Systems Reliability Assurance)

Kara and Scott Baker own a small retail company, Basic Requirements, with one store located in a small college town and a Web site through which customers can make purchases. The store sells traditional but up-to-date clothing for young women such as tee shirts, jeans, chinos, and skirts. The store has been open for 10 years, and the owners added the online shopping capability just last year. Online business has been slow, but

Hazard	Probability That Loss Will Occur	Losses ($)		Estimated Control Costs ($)
		Low Estimate	High Estimate	
Equipment failure	.08	50,000	150,000	2,000
Software failure	.10	4,000	18,000	1,400
Vandalism	.65	1,000	15,000	8,000
Embezzlement	.05	3,000	9,000	1,000
Brownout	.40	850	2,000	250
Power surge	.40	850	2,000	300
Flood	.15	250,000	500,000	2,500
Fire	.10	150,000	300,000	4,000

FIGURE 12-11 A risk analysis for the Espy Company.

Kara and Scott believe that as student customers graduate from the university, they will use the online site to continue to have access to their favorite store from their college days.

The store's Web site has many features. It classifies clothing by type, and customers can view items in various colors. To purchase an item, the user clicks on the icon depicting the desired product and adds it to an individual online shopping basket. The customer can view the basket and make a purchase at any time while browsing the site. When checking out at the site, a new customer must first register, providing billing and shipping information, as well as credit card data. Returning customers log in with the identification code and password they created when they registered. They also use that method to check on an order status. If a customer forgets their login information, they can simply click on a link to have it e-mailed to them. Once a user registers, Basic Requirements' system will automatically add their e-mail address to a file that they use to regularly send out e-mails about sales and other promotions.

Kara and Scott are concerned about internal controls in their business. They especially worry because they know that their Web access creates some special risks. They have asked one of their customers who is an accounting student at the university to evaluate the reliability of their information system, with respect to security, availability, and privacy.

Requirements

1. Identify two security, availability, and privacy risks that Basic Requirements faces.
2. For each risk identified above, describe two internal controls Basic Requirements should use to protect against these risks.
3. The accounting student who is evaluating the reliability of Basic Requirements' information system is interested in becoming an IT auditor. Describe some of the specific actions an IT auditor would take to verify that Kara and Scott have adequate controls in place concerning privacy.

Tiffany Martin, CPA (Information Technology Audit Skills)

Tiffany Martin is an audit manager in a medium-size public accounting firm. Tiffany graduated from college seven years ago with a degree in accounting. She obtained her CPA certification soon after she joined the firm where she currently works. Tiffany is a financial auditor; she has had little training in auditing computerized information systems.

The current engagement Tiffany is working on includes a complex information processing system with multiple applications. The financial accounting transactions are processed on a server. The IT department employs 25 personnel, including programmers, systems analysts, a database administrator, computer operators, technical support, and a director. Tiffany has not spoken with anyone in the department because she is fearful that her lack of technical knowledge relative to IT will cause some concern with the client.

Because Tiffany does not understand the complexities of the computer processing environment, she is unable to determine what risks might result from the computerized system's operations. She is particularly worried about unauthorized changes to programs and data that would affect the reliability of the financial statements.

Tiffany has spoken to Dick Stanton, the partner who has responsibility for this audit client, about her concerns. Dick has suggested that Tiffany conduct more substantive testing than she would undertake in a less complex processing environment. This additional testing will hopefully ensure that there are no errors or fraud associated with the computer processing of the financial statements.

Requirements

1. Do you think that Dick Stanton's suggested approach is the most efficient way to control risks associated with complex computer environments?

2. How should Tiffany respond to Dick's suggestion?

3. What can a public accounting firm, such as the one in which Tiffany works, do to ensure that audits of computerized accounting information systems are conducted efficiently and effectively?

4. Should Tiffany be allowed to conduct this audit given her limited skill level? How might she acquire the necessary skills?

Consolidated Company (Audit Program for Access Controls)

Jason Saving is an IT auditor for a large, public accounting firm. His manager has assigned him to the Consolidated Company audit. The IT auditors must complete several evaluating and testing procedures in order to help determine the scope of the financial audit. The IT auditors also need to evaluate IT controls to provide the financial auditors with information in order to form an opinion on internal controls as part of Sarbanes-Oxley compliance.

Consolidated Company manufactures automotive parts and supplies them to the largest auto makers. The company has approximately 1,500 employees and has manufacturing operations and offices in three locations. Consolidated uses a midsized ERP software program for manufacturers that they acquired and implemented two years ago.

You need to develop an audit program to examine logical access to the ERP system. According to the Security Administrator at Consolidated, each employee is assigned a unique User ID and password when they join the company. The company is very concerned about security, so there is no remote access to the ERP system. The ERP system requires that users change their passwords every six months. System and group settings assigned to each User ID determine what parts of the ERP systems are available to each user.

Requirements

1. Explain how a deficiency in controls over User IDs and passwords might affect the financial statements.

2. Why is it necessary to examine User IDs and passwords?

3. Describe at least four control procedures that Consolidated should have in place to ensure that only authorized users access the system and that user access is limited according to their responsibilities.

Chapter 13

Developing and Implementing Effective Accounting Information Systems

INTRODUCTION

Part of an organization's overall mission is ensuring that it uses its IT resources effectively, efficiently, and strategically. A comprehensive IT strategy requires careful planning that prioritizes the acquisition or development of various information systems, including application systems such as accounting information systems. In turn, developing effective, strategic information systems requires the collaboration of a wide range of individuals, including computer programmers, analysts, designers, and managers. Accountants, both as auditors and as general information users, should be part of all IT studies involving accounting information systems.

This chapter is about systems studies—that is, the planning, analysis, design, development, implementation, and maintenance of AIS applications. As you might imagine, sometimes an organization might choose to design some of its applications in-house, and at other times, it might decide that the best alternative is to purchase, lease, or outsource the work to others. Selecting the best choice from among these alternatives is part of the IT systems study process.

THE SYSTEMS DEVELOPMENT LIFE CYCLE

As you might imagine, acquiring IT resources, implementing systems, and training people to use a large AIS is a difficult task. A **systems study** (also called *systems development work*) begins with a formal investigation of an existing information system to identify strengths and weaknesses.

Who actually performs a systems study? This varies from company to company as well as from project to project. Many large organizations have IT professionals to perform this work. In contrast, smaller organizations with limited technical expertise as well as larger organizations with other priorities are more likely to hire outside consultants for this work. (Note: The Sarbanes-Oxley Act of 2002 expressly forbids CPA firms from performing such systems work for a client with whom it already has an audit relationship.) Our discussion assumes that most of the work is performed by a generic "study team" of experts who may or may not be outside consultants.

Four Stages in the Systems Development Life Cycle

Traditionally, we can identify four major steps or phases of a systems study:

1. *Planning and investigation.* This step involves organizing a systems study team, performing a preliminary investigation of the existing system, and developing strategic plans for the remainder of the study.

2. *Analysis.* This step involves analyzing the company's current system to identify the information needs, strengths, and weaknesses of the existing system.

3. *Design.* In this step, an organization designs changes that eliminate (or minimize) the current system's weak points while preserving its strengths.

4. *Implementation, follow-up, and maintenance.* This phase includes acquiring resources for the new system as well as training new or existing employees to use it. Companies conduct follow-up studies to determine whether the new system is successful and, of course, to identify any new problems with it. Finally, businesses must maintain the system, which means that they correct minor flaws and update the system as required.

These four phases are the **system development life cycle (SDLC)** of a business information system. Logically, the activities in these phases flow from stage to stage in only one direction, like water flowing in a stream. This is why earlier descriptions of the SDLC referred to it as the **waterfall model**. In practice, there is usually much overlap between phases in the life cycle, and the steps in a systems study don't necessarily occur in sequence. Instead, system developers often perform two or more stages in parallel with each other.

> *Case-in-Point 13.1* After purchasing the rights to a medical practice billing system from another company, Allscript (a software provider for the medical field) decided to enhance it to fit better with its other products. But the system requirements were not clear because Allscript's customers weren't sure what *they* wanted. For this reason, the company used an **agile development methodology** based on iterative revisions and customer collaboration. "Agile is perfect when you're not sure what you're getting into" said an Allscript representative. "If you run into a big roadblock, you're only derailed on average a week's worth of work."[1]

Figure 13-1 illustrates that this life cycle spans the time during which a company's system is operating normally and is subsequently revised as a result of some problem (or problems). Each time a newly revised system takes over the company's daily operating activities, a new life cycle begins.

The dashed arrows in Figure 13-1 emphasize that follow-up studies of a system should be a continuous process. An organization reevaluates systems regularly to confirm they

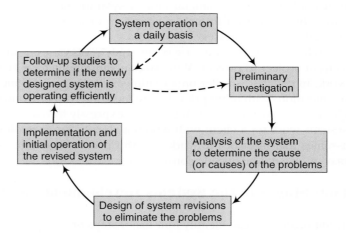

FIGURE 13-1   System development life cycle of a business information system.

---

[1] http://www.projecttimes.com/agile/agile-processes-go-lean.html

are still working well. If follow-up studies indicate that previous problems have recurred or new ones have developed, an organization should take the dashed-arrow route from the follow-up studies to the recognition of systems problems and begin a new systems study.

Systems Studies and Accounting Information Systems

A systems study looks at all IT in an entity's **applications portfolio**. This portfolio may include an enterprise system, along with other specialized information systems, or it may consist of many separate systems for functional areas such as accounting, marketing, and human resources. Accounting information systems (AISs) are prime targets for systems studies—for example, because they may not currently support e-commerce or may not comply with new governmental regulations. But, in general, a systems study means more than just replacing or modifying existing information systems. Typically, altering an accounting information system also affects work flows, data gathering and recording tasks, employee responsibilities, and even the way an organization rewards its managers. Thus, one reason why organizations perform systems studies is because such studies are part of the greater task of business process reengineering (BPR)—that is, the task of making major modifications to one of an organization's core systems. Because the accommodation involves so many changes, it is also a major reason why so many new systems fail. We discussed BPR in more depth in Chapter 8.

> *Case-in-Point 13.2* On average, almost 75 percent of all systems fail. The most common reason for such failures: a lack of user involvement and/or user commitment. A second common factor: incomplete or changing system requirements. A surprising statistic: system analysts have known about such problems for the last 35 years.[2]

SYSTEMS PLANNING

The first phase of a systems study involves systems planning and an initial investigation.

Planning for Success

In large organizations, system redesigns (or new development work) typically involve millions of dollars, making mistakes very costly. In smaller organizations, major errors can be catastrophic, leading a firm to bankruptcy. What else can happen when organizations do not plan carefully? Here are some examples:

- Systems do not meet users' needs, causing employee frustration, resistance, and even sabotage.
- Systems are not flexible enough to meet the business needs for which they were designed and are ultimately scrapped.
- Project expenditures significantly overrun what once seemed like very adequate budgets.
- The time required to complete the new system vastly exceeds the development schedule—often by years.

---

[2] Kroenke, D. 2011. *Using MIS*. Boston: Prentice Hall, p. 406.

- Systems solve the wrong problems.
- Top management does not approve or support the new systems.
- Systems are difficult and costly to maintain.

Studies of unsuccessful information systems projects suggest that mistakes made at the outset of a systems study are a common reason why such projects ultimately fail. Careful systems planning and an initial investigation can avoid critical missteps that lead to disaster. "Planning for success" means beginning a systems study with a focused investigation that (1) approaches specific organizational problems from a broad point of view, (2) uses an interdisciplinary study team to evaluate an organization's information systems, and (3) makes sure the company's study team works closely with a steering committee (described below) and end users in all phases of the work.

Broad Viewpoint in a Systems Study.   When performing a systems study, the participants should use a **systems approach**, that is, a broad point of view. This approach aligns the systems study with the organization's mission and strategic planning goals and objectives. For example, if a company plans to consolidate divisions or discontinue unprofitable product lines, new IT systems will need to reflect these plans. In another scenario, a company that is embarking on a growth strategy through merger and acquisition should think twice about implementing a new enterprise system that might not be compatible with newly acquired companies. Also, management should think strategically about whether a potential new system could accommodate acquired businesses operating in different industries.

The Study Team and the Steering Committee.   Using an interdisciplinary study team (Figure 13-2) follows from the need for a broad viewpoint when performing a systems study. It also serves to correct the thinking that the system belongs only to the IT staff. Because most accounting and computer professionals are specialists, it is unlikely that any one or two people will have the broad background and experience necessary to understand and change a large AIS. For this reason, the recommended approach is to form (or hire) a team of specialists—a "study team"—to perform the systems study.

It is important that the study team communicate closely and meaningfully with the company's top managers. To provide this continuous interface, the company's top management should also appoint a **steering committee** to work with each study team as

FIGURE 13-2   An interdisciplinary study team usually includes representatives from several business areas to help achieve a broad point of view. Source: iStockphoto.

it performs its tasks. Ideally, the committee will include top management personnel—for example, the controller, the vice president of finance, the top-level IT manager (i.e., the CIO), perhaps one or more staff auditors, and (for very important projects) even the chief executive officer of the company. The rationale for such involvement is straightforward: top-management commitment is critical to the ultimate success of a new or revised system.

Investigating Current Systems

Planning for IT includes constant monitoring of current systems. When a system appears to have problems, the systems study team performs a **preliminary investigation** of the system in question and advises the steering committee of its findings. One important part of this work is to separate symptoms from causes. In its deliberations, the study team may consider alternatives to the current system, attempt to estimate the costs and benefits of its proposed solutions, or make recommendations for desired alternatives. In this phase of the project, the study team enjoys wide latitude in what it can choose to examine, and it is usually encouraged to "think outside the box" (i.e., to consider vastly different and innovative approaches to address current problems).

The duration of a preliminary investigation is comparatively brief—typically, a matter of a few weeks. The deliverable from this phase of the systems study is a preliminary investigation report describing the problems or objectives the study team identified, the solutions or alternatives it investigated, and the course(s) of action it recommends. The study team submits this report to the company steering committee for a final determination. The steering committee may decide to (1) disband the study team and do nothing, (2) perform additional preliminary investigations, or (3) proceed to the formal systems analysis stage of the systems study.

SYSTEMS ANALYSIS

The basic purpose of the **systems analysis** phase is to examine a system in depth. The study team will familiarize itself with the company's current accounting system, identify specific inputs and outputs, identify system strengths and weaknesses, and eventually make recommendations for supplementary work. Figure 13-3 shows the logical procedures that the team should follow.

In performing its work, the study team should strive to avoid overanalyzing a company's system. Instead, the team should try to identify and understand the organization's goals for the system, perform a systems survey, and prepare one or more reports that describe its findings.

Understand the systems goals

↓

Systems survey to acquire sufficient information
relating to current systems problems

↓

Suggest possible solutions to solve the systems
problems through a systems analysis report

FIGURE 13-3 Systems analysis procedures.

Understanding Organizational Goals

For the study team to do an adequate job—for example, determine the real problems within a company's information system—its members must first understand the system's goals. Of special importance is determining which goals are not being achieved under the present system and why this happens. Organization goals include (1) general systems goals, (2) top management systems goals, and (3) operating management systems goals.

General Systems Goals.   General systems goals apply to most organization's information systems and help an AIS contribute to an efficient and effective organization. Principles contributing to these goals are (1) awareness that the benefits of the new system should exceed the system's costs, (2) concern that the outputs of the system help managers make better decisions, (3) commitment to designing a system that allows optimal access to information, and (4) flexibility so that the system can accommodate changing information needs.

The study team must determine whether the current information system helps to achieve general systems goals. For example, if an AIS has excessive costs associated with using traditional paper documents (e.g., purchase orders, receiving reports, and vendor invoices), this will violate goal number one (cost awareness), and the study team might recommend that the company use a Web-based system instead.

Top Management Systems Goals.   AISs typically play key roles in satisfying top management goals. For instance, AISs usually provide top managers with long-range budget planning data so they can make effective strategic decisions regarding future product-line sales or similar business activities. Similarly, periodic performance reports provide top management with vital control information about corporate operations—such as, how sales of new product lines are doing. Finally, top management needs to know about the short-range operating performance of its organization's subsystems—for example, summary information about individual department operating results and how these results compare with budgetary projections.

Operating Management Systems Goals.   Compared to top management, the information needs of operating managers (i.e., managers working within specific organizational subsystems) are normally easier to determine. This is because the decision-making functions of operating managers typically relate to well-defined and narrower organizational areas. In addition, the majority of operating managers' decisions is for the current business year (in contrast to top management's long-range decision-making functions). Much of the information required for operating managers' decisions is generated internally as a by-product of processing a company's accounting data.

> **Case-in-Point 13.3**   Grupo Financiero Bital is a Mexican bank with almost 1,200 branches, 3 million customers, and $9 billion in assets. To work effectively, branch managers need access to information about customer accounts at other branches. A redesign of its information system resulted in a corporate intranet that let branch managers and top managers access exactly the data they needed to view performance measures of the individual branches. The company is realizing many indirect benefits from the new system and saves almost $6,000 per month in printing costs alone![3]

---

[3] http://itmanagement.earthweb.com/erp/article.php/602201

Systems Survey Work

The objective of a **systems survey** is to enable the study team to obtain a more complete understanding of the company's current operational information system and its environment. Of special importance is identifying the strengths and weaknesses of the current system. The overall objective is to retain the system's strengths while eliminating the system's weaknesses, especially those weaknesses causing problems in the current system. These weaknesses will likely relate to specific goals that the current system does not now accomplish.

Understanding the Human Element and Potential Behavioral Problems.

Because the appearance of a study team on the work scene usually signals change, employees are often resistant to help. Unless the study team deals directly with this problem at the beginning, there is a good chance that employees will oppose the changes that the team recommends. In short, a systems study must gain the full cooperation and support of those employees who are crucial to the effectiveness of a new system. The best designed system on paper is likely to cause behavioral problems when implemented if the system does not have wide user support.

Data Gathering.

A systems survey requires the study team to gather data about the existing system. There are several ways of doing this, including:

- *Review existing documentation or create new materials.* This documentation includes descriptive data such as organizational charts, strategic plans, budgets, policy and procedure manuals, job descriptions, and charts of accounts, as well as technical documentation such as flowcharts, process maps, and training manuals (see Chapter 6 to refresh your memory on flowcharts and process diagrams).

- *Observe the current system in operation.* Visiting various parts of the operation on a surprise schedule and asking workers questions about their jobs can be extremely helpful in learning whether the system works as described, or about the morale of employees, the frequency of down-time, and workload cycles.

- *Use questionnaires and surveys.* These can be anonymous so that respondents share their views openly about sensitive issues. *Open-ended questionnaires* provide an unstructured free-flow of ideas that may bring new issues to light. *Close-ended questionnaires* (Figure 13-4), on the other hand, are efficient and allow for easy tabulation of results.

- *Review internal control procedures.* In earlier chapters of this book, we discussed the importance of internal control systems. Weaknesses in these procedures can cause major problems for a company. The study team should identify high-risk areas and strengths and weaknesses of the specific procedures.

- *Interview system participants.* Face-to-face interviews allow the study team to gather system information in the greatest depth and can sometimes reveal surprises. For example, an interview might reveal that a manager's decisions don't really require input from several existing reports.

Data Analysis

Once the study team completes its survey work, it must analyze the results. Often, this means nothing more than creating summary statistics, but it can also involve developing

---

Example of an open-ended question on a systems study questionnaire:

1. Please use the space in this box to explain why you are either satisfied or dissatisfied with the current general ledger system.

> *The system is ok, but finding the right account requires a lot of drill down. Some account definitions are also unclear to newbies.*

Example of a closed-ended question on a systems study questionnaire:

2. Please indicate your level of satisfaction with the current general ledger system by checking the appropriate button:

Very satisfied	Somewhat satisfied	Neither satisfied nor dissatisfied	Somewhat dissatisfied	Very dissatisfied
○	○	○	○	◉

FIGURE 13-4 Sample questions and illustrative answers on a systems survey questionnaire. Note that such a questionnaire could be conducted on the Web.

flowcharts and/or process maps that can highlight bottlenecks in information flows, redundant reporting, and missing information links.

Systems analysis work necessarily takes longer than a preliminary investigation, typically months. Where required, the study team will provide interim reports to the steering committee about its progress. The most important deliverable from the analysis portion of the systems study, however, is the *final systems analysis report*, which signals the end of the analysis phase of the system study. Like other reports, the study team submits this report to the steering committee, which then considers the report's findings and debates the recommendations it contains.

As representatives of top management, the steering committee has, within limits, the ability to do whatever it wants. For example, it can abandon the project, ask for additional analyses and a set of revised recommendations, or vote to proceed to the systems design phase of the project.

Evaluating System Feasibility

After obtaining a positive response from the steering committee, the design team must perform a detailed investigation of different potential systems. Figure 13-5 shows that this work involves five major procedures or activities. The first of these is a **feasibility evaluation**, in which the design team determines the practicality of alternative proposals. Only after this step is completed can the design team tackle the other steps. For each system alternative, the design team must examine five feasibility areas: (1) technical feasibility, (2) operational feasibility, (3) schedule feasibility, (4) legal feasibility, and (5) economic feasibility.

Technical Feasibility. The **technical feasibility** of any proposed system attempts to answer the question, "What technical resources are required by a particular system?" Hardware and software are obvious components. A proposed system that can interface with critical existing software is more desirable than one requiring the organization to buy new software. Computer experts typically work on this phase of the feasibility evaluation because a thorough understanding of IT is essential.

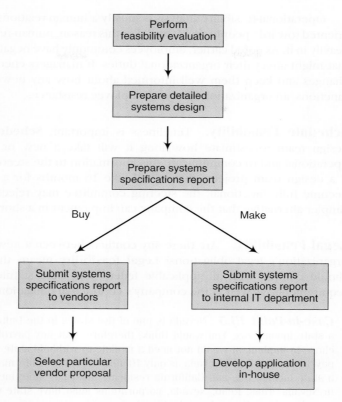

FIGURE 13-5   Steps in the systems design phase of a systems study.

In addition to developing a preliminary hardware or software configuration for a proposed system, the design team must also determine whether current employees have the technical skills to use it. If a specific computerized system is too sophisticated for a company's employees, it is unlikely that requiring employees to use it in subsequent daily operations will be very successful.

Operational Feasibility.   The **operational feasibility** of a proposed system examines its compatibility with the current operating environment. That is, how consistent will the tasks and procedures required by the new system be with those of the old system? The design team must also analyze the capabilities of current employees to perform the specific functions required by each proposed system and determine to what extent employees will require specialized training.

Case-in-Point 13.4   According to the Small Business Administration of the U.S. Government, 10 percent of the 6 million businesses in the United States are not-for-profit organizations. The accounting software for such enterprises often has special requirements, including fund accounting, the ability to interface with donation accounting software, the ability to maintain donor histories, and perhaps an automated tool for interfacing with gifts collected via the Web.[4]

[4] Johnson, R. 2009. Helping not-for-profits with better accounting. *CPA Technology Advisor* 19(8): 42.

Operational-feasibility analysis is mostly a human-relations study because it is strongly oriented toward "people problems." For this reason, human-relations specialists participate heavily in it. As noted earlier, employees commonly have negative attitudes toward changes that might affect their organizational duties. If managers encourage employees to suggest changes and keep them well informed about how any new system will affect their job functions, an organization can limit employee resistance.

Schedule Feasibility.   Timeliness is important. **Schedule feasibility** requires the design team to estimate how long it will take a new or revised system to become operational and to communicate this information to the steering committee. For example, if a design team projects that it will take 16 months for a particular system design to become fully functional, the steering committee may reject the proposal in favor of a simpler alternative that the company can implement in a shorter time frame.

Legal Feasibility.   Are there any conflicts between a newly proposed system and the organization's legal obligations? **Legal feasibility** means that a new or revised system should comply with all applicable federal and state statutes about financial reporting requirements, as well as the company's contractual obligations.

Case-in-Point 13.5   Nevada is one of five states in the United States that does not have a state income tax. You would think, therefore, that any payroll system a Nevada company chose to implement would not need a module to withhold state income taxes from employee paychecks. But Reno, Nevada, is only 10 miles from the California border, California does have a state income tax, and California residents must pay state income taxes even if they work in Nevada. Thus, Reno, Nevada, corporations must have state withholding modules in their payroll systems for such employees.

Economic Feasibility.   Through **economic feasibility** evaluation, the design team attempts to evaluate whether the anticipated benefits of the system exceed its projected costs. This requires accountants to perform a cost-benefit analysis. This analysis should consider all costs, including indirect costs such as time spent by current employees on implementing the new system. It also considers benefits, which are sometimes difficult to foresee or estimate. A mistake frequently made in thinking about new systems is underestimating costs for implementation and continuing operations. The accountants conducting the analysis need to separately identify one-time costs versus recurring ones. The point of the economic feasibility analysis is to get a "best estimate" of the economic worthiness of a project.

DETAILED SYSTEMS DESIGN

Once the steering committee approves the feasibility of a general system plan (project), the design team can begin work on a **detailed systems design**. This involves specifying the outputs, processing procedures, and inputs for the new system. Just as construction blueprints create the detailed plans for building a house, the detailed design of a new system becomes the specification for creating or acquiring a new information system. Figure 13-6 provides examples of the detailed requirements that the design team must create, and these requirements in turn explain specifically what the proposed system must produce.

Requirements	Discussion
Processes	Descriptions of the various processes to be performed in the revised system, stressing what is to be done and by whom.
Data elements	Descriptions of the required data elements, including their name, size, format, source, and importance.
Data structure	Preliminary data structure that indicates how the data elements will be organized into logical records.
Inputs	Copies of system inputs and descriptions of their contents, sources, and who is responsible for them.
Outputs	Copies of system outputs and descriptions of their purpose, frequency, and distribution.
Documentation	Descriptions of how the revised system and each subsystem will operate.
Constraints	Descriptions of constraints such as staffing limitations and regulatory requirements.
Controls	Controls to reduce the risk of undetected errors and irregularities in the input, processing, and output stages of data processing work.
Reorganizations	Necessary changes such as increasing staff levels, adding new job functions, and terminating certain existing positions.

FIGURE 13-6   Examples of detailed requirements for a system proposal.

From an accounting standpoint, one of the most important elements in a new system is its control requirements. In this matter, the design team should have a "built-in mentality" when designing control procedures for a system. In other words, rather than adding controls after a system has been developed and installed, the team should design cost-effective general and application control procedures into the system as integrated components. The Committee of Sponsoring Organizations of the Treadway Commission (introduced in Chapter 9) emphasizes the importance of this view:

> *Whenever management considers changes to its company's operations or activities, the concept that it's better to "build-in" rather than "build-on" controls, and to do it right the first time, should be the fundamental guiding premise.*[5]

Designing System Outputs, Processes, and Inputs

Once the design team determines that a system is feasible and creates a general design, it can focus on developing the system's input, processing, and output requirements. When performing design tasks, it is perhaps curious that the design team first focuses on the outputs—not the inputs or processing requirements—of the new system. The reason for this is that the most important objective of an AIS is to satisfy users' needs. Preparing output specifications first lets these requirements dictate the inputs and processing tasks required to produce them.

During the analysis phase and general system design, the study team develops boundaries for the new system. These boundaries define the project's scope. However, as the design team works with users, they are likely to be asked to do additional work. This is called **scope creep**—that is, expanding the boundaries of a project beyond the initial scope of the project. Outside consultants often handle these requests by drafting proposals

[5] http://www.coso.org

showing the additional costs associated with them. These costs can include delays in meeting the schedule for delivering the project.

> *Case-in-Point 13.6* Universities are large, complex organizations with many specialized processes. These entities are good candidates for enterprise systems, but scope creep and other problems can send these projects off track. The North Dakota University System had troubles as they worked to implement *PeopleSoft ERP*. The final software project cost was $49 million ($14 million over budget) and over three years behind planned rollout. Extensive customized computing needs appeared to be one source of the overruns for North Dakota's ERP.[6]

System Outputs. The design team will use the data gathered from the prior systems analysis work to help it decide what kinds of outputs are needed as well as the formats that these outputs should have. Although it is possible for the design team to merely copy the outputs of an older system, this would make little sense—the new system would be just like the old one. Instead, the team will attempt to create better outputs—that is, design outputs that will better satisfy their users' information needs than did the old system.

Outputs may be classified according to which functional area uses them (e.g., marketing, human resources, accounting, or manufacturing) as well as how frequently they must be produced (e.g., daily or weekly). Where a specific report is not needed on a regular basis, the system should be able to provide it when requested (a *demand report*) or triggered when a certain condition is met (an *exception report*). For example, an accounts receivable report on a specific customer's payment history might be issued on demand, or generated automatically when a customer owes more than a specified amount. Although many organizations still rely heavily on hard-copy (printed) reports, systems designers should also consider the possibility of creating soft-copy (screen) reports as an alternative, which use less paper and, of course, do not require a printer for viewing.

Process Design. Until now, the system designers have focused on *what the system must provide* rather than *how the system can provide it.* After designing the outputs, their next step is to identify the processing procedures required to produce them. This involves deciding which application programs are necessary and what data processing tasks each program should perform.

There are a large number of tools for modeling computer processes. Among them are the system flowcharts, data flow diagrams, program flowcharts, process maps, and decision tables discussed in Chapter 6. Another popular tool is the entity-relationship (E-R) diagram discussed in Chapter 3. Common to all these design methodologies is the idea of **structured, top-down design**, in which system designers begin at the highest level of abstraction and then ''drill down'' to lower, more detailed levels until the system is completely specified.

Designing System Inputs. Once the design team has specified the outputs and processing procedures for a new project, its members can think about what data the system must collect to satisfy these output and processing requirements. Thus, the team must identify and describe each data element in the systems design (e.g., alphabetic, maximum number of characters, and default value) as well as specify the way data items must be coded. This is no easy task, because there are usually a large number of data items

---

[6] Songini, M. L. 2006. PeopleSoft apps vex N.D. colleges (June 23), Retrieved from http://www.computerworld.com/s/article/9001396/PeopleSoft_apps_vex_N.D._colleges

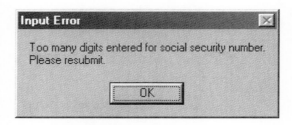

FIGURE 13-7 An AIS might display this error message if the user made a mistake entering a Social Security number in a dialogue box.

in even a small business application. Chapter 4 discusses the subject of data modeling in detail.

After the design team identifies and describes the input data, it can determine the source of each data element. For example, customer information such as name, address, and telephone numbers may be gathered directly from Web screens, while the current date can be accessed from the computer system itself. Wherever possible, the design team will attempt to capture data in computer-readable formats, as noted in Chapter 2. This avoids costly, time-consuming data transcription as well as the errors such transcription typically introduce into the job stream.

Finally, system designers try to create systems that streamline data-entry tasks because this facilitates the process and helps users avoid errors. Examples include substituting system default values, screen menus, and mouse clicks for system commands or other inputs that must otherwise be entered manually. Additional examples include using dialogue boxes for special user inputs and message boxes that help explain why a particular input value is unacceptable (Figure 13-7).

Prototyping

Prototyping means developing a simplified model of a proposed information system. A prototype is a scaled-down, experimental version of a nonexistent information system that a design team can develop cheaply and quickly for user-evaluation purposes. The prototype model does not run, but presents users with the look and feel of a completed system. By allowing users to experiment with the prototype, the designers can learn what users like and dislike in the mockup. They can then modify the system's design in response to this feedback. Thus, prototyping is an iterative process of trial-use-and-modification that continues until users are satisfied. Prototyping has four steps, as illustrated in Figure 13-8.

Case-in-Point 13.7 A company hired a consulting firm to develop a large-scale student management information system to manage its training and continuing education programs. The consulting firm developed a prototype that showed the primary input screens and reports and used it to obtain user feedback on how to modify the system. For instance, users experimented with the screens and considered how easy it would be to input data through them. Users also decided whether the reports would give them the information they needed, such as a listing of all students in a class and all classes taken by a student. The programming to activate the screens and enable the processing, along with the database functionality, came later. This prototyping approach ensured that the completed system would satisfy user needs.

Prototyping is useful when end users do not understand their informational needs very well, system requirements are hard to define, the new system is mission-critical or

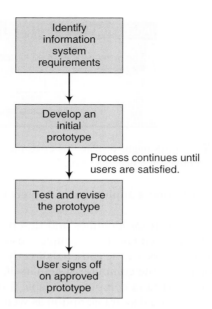

FIGURE 13-8 Steps in prototyping an accounting information system.

needed quickly, past interactions have resulted in misunderstandings between end users and designers, and/or there are high risks associated with developing and implementing the wrong system. However, prototyping is not always the best systems design approach. For example, both managers and IT professionals can distrust it—the managers, if they perceive prototyping as "too experimental" and the IT professionals, if they harbor fears that the results lead to poor design solutions. Then, too, a design team can be misled if it relies on a small portion of the user population for developing its models and thus satisfies the informational needs of nonrepresentative employees. For this reason, prototyping is not normally appropriate for designing large or complex information systems that serve many users with significantly different information needs. Finally, IT professionals do not recommend prototyping for developing traditional AIS applications such as accounts receivable, accounts payable, payroll, or inventory management, where the inputs, processing, and outputs are already well known and clearly defined.

The System Specifications Report

After the design team completes its work of specifying the inputs, outputs, and processing requirements of the new system, the members will summarize their findings in a (typically large) **systems specification report**. Figure 13-9 provides some representative information in such a report. The design team submits this report to the steering committee for review, comment, and approval.

The Make-or-Buy Decision. The project is now at a critical juncture. If the steering committee approves the detailed design work, it then faces a **make-or-buy decision**. In large organizations, one possibility is to use internal IT staff to develop the system. This choice offers the tightest control over project development, the best security over sensitive data, the benefits of a custom product that has been tailor-made for the exact requirements

1. *Historical background information about the company's operating activities.* Included here would be facts about the types of products manufactured and sold by the company, the financial condition of the company, the company's current data processing methods, the peak volume of data processing activities, and the types of equipment currently being used in the company's data processing system.

2. *Detailed information about the problems in the company's current system.* By understanding the present systems problems, the computer vendors should have a better idea of what type of specific computer application will eliminate the company's system weaknesses. The design team may also include information about how soon they would like to receive the vendors' recommendations and the approximate date that the final decision will be made by their client regarding which computerized system will be purchased (or leased).

3. *Detailed descriptions of the systems design proposals.* For every design proposal, information should be included about things such as the data input and output of specific computer processing runs, the types of master files needed and the approximate volume of each file, the frequency of updating each master file, the format of each output report, the approximate length of each output report, the types of information included in each report and how often the various reports will be prepared, the organizational managers to whom every report will be distributed, and the company's available space for computer facilities.

4. *Indication of what the vendors should include in their proposals to the company.* This section of the systems specifications report, in effect, tells the vendors how detailed they should make their proposals. The company might request information regarding the speed and size of the central processing unit needed, the type of PCs needed for the company's local area network, the type and quantity of input and output devices as well as the capabilities of these devices, the availability of prewritten software packages for specific processing activities, the training sessions offered by the vendors on the operating details of the new system, the help provided by the vendors in implementing and testing the new system, the maintenance services available from the vendors, and the vendors' provisions for backup data processing facilities.

5. *Time schedule for implementing the new system.* This final section of the report will request the computer vendors to estimate the number of weeks, months, or years that will be necessary to implement their recommended computer system within the company.

FIGURE 13-9 Systems specifications report information.

of the application, the luxury of replacing the old system piecemeal as modules become available, and a vote of confidence for the organization's IT staff. But this choice also uses valuable employee time and can divert the organization's resources from its main objectives—for example, manufacturing products.

Another possibility is to outsource the project's development to a contractor. This choice is useful when an organization lacks internal expertise to do the work or simply wishes to avoid the headaches of internal project development. Alternatively, the steering committee can purchase prewritten software (commonly called **canned software**) and perhaps modify it to suit the organization's needs. If the organization requires both hardware and software, the committee may also choose to shop for a complete, "ready-to-go" **turnkey system**. The steering committee can ask the computer vendors to submit bid proposals for such a complete system, or alternatively, can ask each vendor to provide separate bids for hardware and software. Finally, the committee can outsource the entire processing job to an external service provider.

Choosing an Accounting Information System

Because internal project management and systems development are beyond the scope of this text, we'll assume here that the steering committee opts to acquire most of its system resources from outside vendors. This is the most common choice. If the committee takes this course of action, the systems specifications report helps them create a **request for proposal (RFP)** outlining the specific requirements of the desired system. After finalizing the systems specifications, the steering committee (with the help of the design team and perhaps outside consultants) will send a copy to appropriate vendors. Typically, the RFP also contains a deadline for bidding, the length of which varies—for example, just a few weeks for hardware, and longer periods for systems requiring custom development tasks.

After the deadline has passed, an evaluation committee supervised by the steering committee will review vendor submissions and schedule separate meetings with those vendors who provide viable system proposals. The participants at each meeting include representatives from the vendor, representatives from the steering committee, and representatives from the design team. The vendor's role is to present its proposal and answer questions from the other participants. The evaluation committee's role is to listen to the vendor proposals, ask questions, provide input to the steering committee about the pros and cons of each one, and perhaps make a recommendation for a preferred provider.

Selection Criteria. The steering committee's responsibility is to make a final selection, and is not restricted in its choices. It can accept one bid totally, negotiate with one vendor for specific resources, or spread its purchases among two or more providers. Here are some key factors that a steering committee should consider when evaluating vendor proposals:

- *The performance capability of each proposed system.* A vendor system must be able to process the organization's data so that management will receive outputs when they need them. There are many measures of performance, including speed, response time, number of users supported, and system reliability. One way to examine the operating efficiency of a particular system is to use a **benchmark test**. With this approach, the vendor's system performs a data processing task that the new system must perform (e.g., payroll processing), and representatives of the organization then examine the outputs for accuracy, consistency, and efficiency.

- *Costs and benefits of each proposed system.* The accountants on the design team will analyze the costs of every vendor's proposed system in relation to the system's anticipated performance benefits. They will also consider the differences between purchasing and leasing each vendor's system. If the steering committee elects to purchase a system, the accountants should then advise the committee on a realistic depreciation schedule for the new system.

- *Maintainability of each proposed system.* Maintainability refers to the ease with which a proposed computer system can be modified. For example, this flexibility enables a firm to alter a portion of a payroll system to reflect new federal tax laws. Because the costs of maintaining a large information system are typically five times as much as the costs of initially acquiring or developing a system, the evaluators should place considerable emphasis on this dimension.

- *Compatibility of each proposed system with existing systems.* The new system must interface and work with existing computer hardware, software, and operating procedures. In some instances, this comes down to hardware issues. For example, it may not be possible to run specific software modules of the new system on some of the company's older local area network servers, which will consequently have to be upgraded. But compatibility issues can also involve the operating system, existing application software, or operational concerns as well—for instance, the requirement that employees learn a whole new set of procedures for inputting or accessing data.

- *Vendor support.* Vendor support includes (1) training classes that familiarize employees with the operating characteristics of the new system, (2) help in implementing and testing the new system, (3) assistance in maintaining the new system through a maintenance contract, (4) backup systems for temporarily processing company data if required, and (5) telephone assistance for answering user questions. The availability of "business-hours-only" versus "round-the-clock" support and the availability of domestic versus offshore customer support are other considerations. Most vendors charge extra for enhanced services.

Making a Final Decision.

Because this book is about accounting information systems, our focus here will be on acquiring accounting software. Selecting an accounting system is a major responsibility that requires careful planning. After all, a software package that fails to meet the needs of a company or its accounting staff can throw an organization into turmoil, losing time and money. We also discuss the topic of choosing software in Chapter 15. Here we discuss an analytical approach to choosing hardware and software vendors of accounting information systems.

Point-Scoring Analysis.

A technical approach for evaluating hardware or software that meets most of a company's major requirements is a **point-scoring analysis**, such as the one illustrated in Figure 13-10. To illustrate, assume that in the process of selecting an accounts payable system, an organization finds three independent vendors whose packages appear to satisfy current needs. Figure 13-10 shows the results of the analysis. Because the cost to purchase or lease each vendor's accounts payable software package is about the same, "cost" is not an issue in this selection process.

When performing a point-scoring analysis, the evaluation committee first assigns potential points to each of the evaluation criteria based on its relative importance. In

Software Evaluation Criteria	Possible Points	Vendor A	Vendor B	Vendor C
Does the software meet all mandatory specifications?	10	7	9	6
Will program modifications, if any, be minimal to meet company needs?	10	8	9	7
Does the software contain adequate controls?	10	9	9	8
Is the performance (speed, accuracy, reliability, etc.) adequate?	10	7	8	6
Are users satisfied with the software?	8	6	7	5
Is the software well documented?	10	8	8	7
Is the software compatible with existing company software?	10	7	9	8
Is the software user friendly?	10	7	8	6
Can the software be demonstrated and test driven?	9	8	8	7
Does the software have an adequate warranty?	8	6	7	6
Is the software flexible and easily maintained?	8	5	7	5
Is online inquiry of files and records possible?	10	8	9	7
Will the vendor keep the software up to date?	10	8	8	7
Totals	123	94	106	85

FIGURE 13-10 A point-scoring analysis for evaluating three independent vendors' accounts payable software packages.

Figure 13-10, for example, the committee feels that "adequate controls" (10 possible points) is more important than whether users are satisfied with the software (8 possible points). After developing these selection criteria, the evaluation committee proceeds to rate each vendor or package, awarding points as it deems fit. The highest point total determines the winner. In Figure 13-10, the evaluation indicates that Vendor B's accounts payable software package has the highest total score (106 points), and the committee should therefore acquire this vendor's system.

Although point-scoring analyses can provide an objective means of selecting a final system, many experts believe that evaluating accounting software is more art than science. There are no absolute rules in the selection process, only guidelines for matching user needs with software capabilities. Even for a small business, evaluators must consider issues such as the company's data processing needs, the computer skills of its employees, vendor reputations, software costs, and so forth.

Selecting a Finalist.   After each vendor presents its proposal to the organization, the steering committee must select the best one. Although a vendor's reputation is relative, a buyer can obtain clues by checking with the Better Business Bureau and speaking with some of the vendor's other clients. It is also possible that none of the computer vendors' proposals is satisfactory. (At the time the design team performed their economic feasibility study, the results were favorable, but the subsequent detailed design specifications result in actual costs that are considerably higher than anticipated.) At this point, the organization's steering committee can (1) request the design team to obtain additional systems proposals from other vendors, (2) abandon the project, or (3) outsource needed services.

Outsourcing

An alternative to developing and installing accounting information systems is to outsource them. As we discussed in Chapter 7, outsourcing occurs when a company hires an outside organization to handle all or part of the operations for a specific business function. Accounting tasks have long been a target for outsourcing, including accounts payable, accounts receivable, payroll, general ledger, accounting for fixed assets, and financial reporting. Even preparing U.S. tax returns are outsourced, typically to English-speaking countries such as India. Two popular types of outsourcing are business process outsourcing (BPO) and **knowledge process outsourcing (KPO)**.

Business Process Outsourcing.   In the accounting area, the degree to which a company outsources its processing operations can range from routine assistance with a single application such as payroll or tax compliance to performing almost all the accounting functions of the organization. Outsourcing contracts are typically signed for five to ten years. Annual costs depend on the amount of data processing work to be performed and range from "thousands" to "millions" of dollars. When a large company decides to outsource its IT functions, it is not uncommon for the vendor to purchase all of its clients' hardware and software and hire almost all of that company's IT employees. The outsourcing organization then operates and manages the client company's entire information systems, either on the client's site or by migrating the client's systems to its own computers.

Knowledge Process Outsourcing.   Businesses have been outsourcing various processes, such as sales order processes, for several years. A new development is KPO, where a business or an individual contracts with someone, often in another country, to perform research or other knowledge-related work. The growth of outsourcing in this area is expected to be as much as 46 percent a year, with India doing much of the work. Three high-potential areas for this type of outsourcing are intellectual property research related to developing and filing a patent application, data mining of consumer data, and research and development related to medical drugs and biotechnology. Individuals, small businesses, and other organizations may also use KPO services. This could involve contracting with someone in another country, where labor rates are low and technical and research skills high, to conduct basic research for a project and prepare a report, complete with PowerPoint slides!

Advantages and Disadvantages of Outsourcing.   Often, making a decision to outsource a process or knowledge activity is not an easy one. One advantage is that an organization can focus on its core competencies while experts do the other work. For example, hospitals often outsource their data processing functions so they can focus on better patient care. Outsourcing also frees managerial time, financial assets, and related resources for other purposes, and an organization doesn't need to worry about keeping up with technology.

A primary motivator for outsourcing is cost savings. For example, these can come from economies of scale where the process provider is able to spread costs among several clients. Other cost savings can come from moving selected operations to areas where real estate prices, building rents, or labor costs are less—for example, to offshore sites. This also enables a company to reduce its own labor force, save money, and remain competitive.

Although the advantages of outsourcing are compelling, outsourcing is not always the best alternative. One disadvantage is inflexibility. The typical outsourcing contract requires a company to commit to services for an extended time period—10-year contracts are common. Should the contracting company become dissatisfied with the services it receives during this period, however, it is usually difficult to break the agreement. Even with a termination clause, the company may still be locked into outsourcing—for example, because it has already sold its data processing centers and terminated its IT staff.

Loss of control is another potential disadvantage. When an outsourcing vendor performs a significant portion of an organization's data processing, that organization loses control of its information systems. For example, the contracting company can no longer control its data, data errors, or other processing irregularities that occur from the outsourcer's processing work. Finally, outsourcing can cause an organization to lose competitive advantage. That is, when a company outsources its IT functions, it can also lose a basic understanding of its own information system needs or how its information systems provide it with competitive advantages.

IMPLEMENTATION, FOLLOW-UP, AND MAINTENANCE

Systems implementation is often called the action phase of a systems study because the recommended changes from the prior analysis, design, and development work are now put into operation. But systems implementation can also be a stressful time. As the time draws near for installing a new system, end users and clerical personnel become nervous about their jobs, middle managers wonder if the new system will deliver the benefits as promised, and top managers become impatient when installations run longer than anticipated or go over budget. Even if an organization did a perfect job of analyzing, designing, and developing a new system, the entire project can fail if its implementation is poor.

Implementation Activities

Implementing a new accounting information system involves many activities and tasks that will vary in number and complexity depending on the scale of the system and the development approach. Some of the steps that may be involved are

A. *Prepare the physical site.* An organization must have physical space for any new hardware and personnel.

B. *Determine functional changes.* Whenever a company makes changes to a major accounting system, it must also consider the effects of such changes on its reporting structure and personnel relationships.

C. *Select and assign personnel.* Because the design team has developed detailed specifications for the new system, the organization should now have a firm idea about the job descriptions of system users.

D. *Train personnel.* Both the implementation team and computer vendors can help train company employees to work with the new system, while seminars can acquaint other employees with the new system's advantages and capabilities. Vendors may provide technical training for free, or at reduced costs, to corporate users as incentives to use their products.

E. *Acquire and install computer equipment.* After preparing the physical site location for the new computer system, the company must acquire computer equipment such as microcomputers, Web servers, routers, modems, and printers from outside vendors.

F. *Establish internal controls.* Chapters 9 and 10 described why an organization must install control procedures that safeguard its assets, ensure the accuracy and reliability of accounting data, promote operating efficiency, and encourage employee compliance with prescribed managerial policies. Again, these controls should be built into a system rather than added later.

G. *Convert data files.* When converting to a new system, an organization may have to convert its data files to alternate, more useful formats. This activity is also common when merging two systems—for example, when consolidating formerly separate divisions of a company or merging the systems from two separate companies into one.

H. *Acquire computer software.* The implementation team must also install the software that was acquired or developed for the project. The software from independent vendors is often called canned software, which sometimes comes bundled (i.e., combined) with hardware in complete turnkey systems. In general, the process of acquiring (and possibly making modifications to) computer software from an independent vendor takes considerably less time than developing the programs in-house.

I. *Test computer software.* Programs must be tested regardless of where they came from to ensure day-to-day processing accuracy and completeness.

J. *Convert to the new system.* In switching to the new system, the firm may choose to make a **direct conversion** by immediately discontinuing use of the old system and letting the new system "sink or swim." An alternative is **parallel conversion**, where the organization operates both the new and the old system for some period of time. Another choice is **modular conversion**, where the new system is implemented in stages, one process or module at a time. An example would be first implementing the inventory module, then order processing, and so on.

The most difficult issue in implementing a new system is **change management**. The new system will bring with it changes to employee job descriptions and, in some cases, new jobs and no jobs. Members of the implementation team and steering committee should communicate openly with affected workers about how the new system will impact them. Organizations should give those employees whose jobs are either eliminated or materially altered an opportunity to apply for the new jobs and obtain retraining, if necessary. Similarly, terminated employees should receive ample notice to enable them to apply for other jobs before their employment ends. Some companies even set up internal outplacement offices for displaced employees or create early retirement plans for qualified employees.

Managing IT Implementation Projects

The preceding section made clear that there are many tasks involved in implementing a new accounting system. Moreover, an organization cannot perform these tasks randomly, but rather, must complete them in a logical sequence. A good analogy is the process of building a house, which requires completing the foundation, subfloors, and load-bearing walls before putting on the roof. Similarly, if an organization does not plan its systems implementation in an orderly fashion, the project's coordination is almost sure to suffer and its completion may be prolonged unreasonably.

There are many tools available to help manage projects. Two of these, **Program Evaluation and Review Technique (PERT)** and **Gantt charts**, help managers schedule and monitor the activities involved in large projects, such as the implementation of a large-scale information system. There are also software solutions that may be used for project management, which we discuss below.

Program Evaluation and Review Technique. With PERT, a project leader first prepares a list of systems implementation activities, identifies the prerequisite activities that must be completed before others can start, and estimates the amount of time required to complete each activity. Figure 13-11 shows what a PERT diagram might look like for the implementation tasks outlined above. The lines with arrows in this diagram conventionally flow from left to right and represent the activities required to implement the system. Thus, for example, activity A takes 17 weeks and the diagram indicates that it must be completed before activity E. The circles (called *nodes*) in the diagram represent project milestones—that is, the starting points or completions of specific activities—and therefore do not require any time.

Top managers may not be interested in PERT analyses, but they are usually very concerned about the time required to finish the entire project. The project leader can estimate this completion time by examining the various paths in the PERT network. For example, the activities A-E-H-I-J together would take 55 weeks. Because all activities must be completed before the project is done, the answer to the question "when will this project be finished" is equivalent to finding the longest path—termed the **critical path**—through the network. By examining all the possibilities, this is path B-F-H-I-J, which takes 58 weeks.

Because PERT diagrams in actual practice are so large (often covering entire walls when drawn on paper), project leaders normally use computer software to identify the critical path. The project leader will closely monitor the work on each critical-path activity to avoid setbacks. **Slack time** describes the amount of delay time that can occur in each noncritical activity and still not delay the project. Thus, slack time is the extra time that noncritical activities have before they must get started. By definition, the slack time for

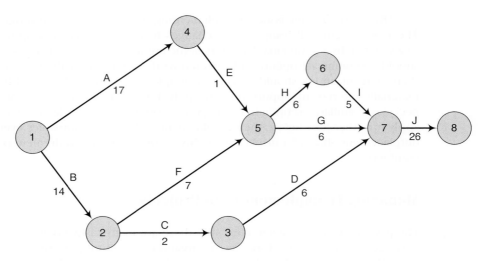

FIGURE 13-11   PERT network diagram for a systems implementation project.

each activity along the critical path is zero. There is no extra time for any of them, and any delays will automatically extend the completion time of the entire project.

PERT is a useful project management tool because of its ability to help managers identify critical paths and areas where slack time occurs. For example, can you understand why activity J (on the critical path) has no slack time, while activity D (not on the critical path) has four weeks of slack? (Hint: subtract the earliest start time from the latest start time of this activity.)

As the implementation team performs specific activities, it also provides feedback reports to the steering committee that compare actual implementation times with planned times. These reports enable both parties to focus on delays in completing specific activities and to estimate what effect these delays may have on the entire installation project. If a specific critical activity is behind schedule, the project leader may allocate additional resources to speed its completion. Alternately, if another activity is ahead of schedule, the project leader may reduce the resources assigned to it and use them elsewhere.

Gantt Charts.   Another tool that an organization can use in planning and controlling a systems implementation project is a Gantt chart (Figure 13-12). Gantt charts are useful for both scheduling and tracking the activities of systems implementation projects because actual progress can be indicated directly on the Gantt chart and contrasted with the planned progress.

> ***Case-in-Point 13.8***   When it ran 15 months late on the completion of a construction project, a building company incurred extensive penalty charges that eventually led to its closure. The original contract for the construction of a block of flats did not include a dated project plan showing the critical path. When the customer made changes to the specification, the contractor failed to also create plan revisions to show how these changes would affect the project's completion date. If it had created a Gantt chart at the contract stage, it also would have had a baseline plan against which to monitor progress.[7]

---

[7] http://www.projectsmart.co.uk/how-gantt-charts-can-help-avoid-disaster.html

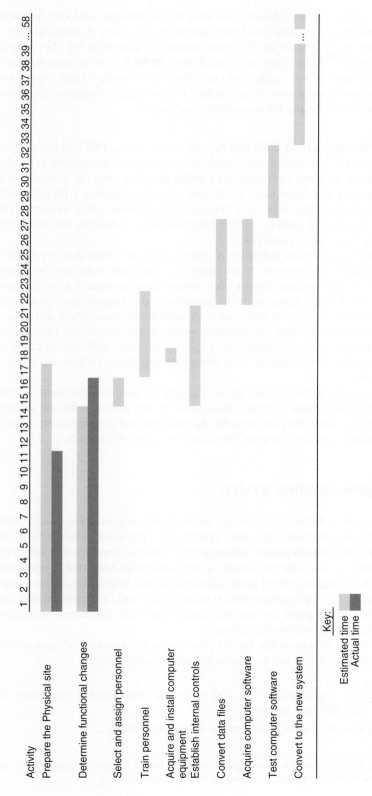

FIGURE 13-12 A Gantt chart depicting systems implementation activities.

Gantt charts are straightforward, easy to understand, and can be used with PERT to compare estimated completion times against actual ones. A disadvantage of Gantt charts is that they do not indicate the precedence of activities for the project, as do PERT charts. Rather, a Gantt chart treats each activity as if it were independent of the others, which of course is not really the case. For this reason, Gantt charts are better suited for systems implementation projects that are not highly complex and have relatively few interrelationships among implementation activities.

Project Management Software. As noted above, PERT diagrams can become complex, making the calculations required to compute and recompute critical paths and slack times difficult. **Project management software** that runs on desktop or notebook computers can perform these tasks easily and quickly, enabling a project leader to plan and control implementation tasks and helping a team install a new system on time and within budget. Examples of project management software solutions include *eProject, Microsoft Project, PlanBee*, and *Time Line.*

Project management software requires users to break down complex projects into smaller, simpler activities and to estimate the time, cost, and other resources required for each of them. The project leader then enters these estimates into the computer running the project software, along with the priority of the various activities of the project. The software can then schedule tasks, identify critical and noncritical activities, compute slack times, and so forth. Project management software also allows the project leader to perform **what-if analyses**—for example, to experiment with different systems implementation work schedules or determine how delays in specific activities are likely to affect other project tasks.

Interestingly, some of the more current project management information systems (PMISs) are much more complex than some of the earlier software solutions. These new systems are not limited to just scheduling and resource management—they are much more comprehensive and can support the entire life cycle of projects.[8]

Postimplementation Review

Regardless of which conversion method an organization uses, the new system will eventually become the sole system in operation. This brings us to the final, **follow-up and maintenance phase** of our systems development life cycle. The purpose of this phase is to monitor the new system and make sure that it continues to satisfy the three levels of organizational goals discussed at the beginning of this chapter: (1) general systems goals, (2) top management systems goals, and (3) operating management systems goals. When these goals are not adequately satisfied, problems normally occur and the system requires further modifications.

After the new system has been in operation for a period of time, the implementation team should reevaluate the new system's effectiveness by:

- Talking with top management and operating management personnel about their satisfaction with the new system.
- Talking with end users to determine their satisfaction.

---

[8] Ahlemann, F. 2009. Towards a conceptual reference model for project management information systems. *International Journal of Project Management* (January): 19–30.

- Evaluating the control procedures of the system to verify whether they are functioning properly.
- Observing work performance to determine whether the employees can accomplish their job functions efficiently and effectively.
- Evaluating whether computer processing functions, including data capture and preparation, are performed efficiently and effectively.
- Determining whether output schedules for both internal and external reports are met with the new computer system.

At the conclusion of the initial follow-up study, the team will prepare a *postimplementation review report* for the steering committee that summarizes the implementation team's findings. If the team is satisfied that the new system is working satisfactorily, no further revisions are required. If follow-up studies reveal that problems still exist in the new system, the team will communicate these findings to the steering committee and perhaps recommend further systems studies. On receiving approval from the steering committee, the organization will perform the systems study steps again with the objective of making revisions to the system.

A post-implementation review is also beneficial to the implementation team. At this point in the systems development life cycle, the team members are in a position to evaluate their own work, learn from the mistakes they made or successfully avoided, and become more skilled "systems people" in future engagements.

System Maintenance

In practice, implementation teams do not normally perform follow-up studies of their company's new information system. Instead, the team turns over control of the system to the company's IT department, which then shoulders the responsibility for maintaining it. In effect, **system maintenance** continues the tasks created by the initial follow-up study, except that experts from the company's IT subsystem now perform the monitoring and perhaps modifications. For example, when users complain about errors or anomalies in the new system, it becomes the IT subsystem's responsibility to respond to these needs, estimate the cost of fixing them, and (often) perform the necessary modifications—or communicate with the vendor to perform needed modifications. The IT departments of even medium-size companies typically have forms for such requests, policies for prioritizing maintenance tasks, and formulas for allocating maintenance costs among the various user departments.

It is common for business systems to require continuous revisions. Some reasons for this include competition, new governmental laws or regulations, or the changing information needs of top management (or other levels of management). In fact, studies show that, over the life of a typical information system, organizations spend only about 20 to 30 percent of the total system costs developing and implementing it. They spend the remaining 70 to 80 percent maintaining it, typically on further modifications or software updates. In other words, "maintenance" may not be the most glamorous part of a systems development life cycle, but it is almost always the most expensive part (Figure 13-13). For this reason, organizations try to develop or acquire scalable systems (that can handle larger volumes of transactions in the future) as well as ones that are easily modified. Such systems save businesses money in the long run, even if they cost more in the short run.

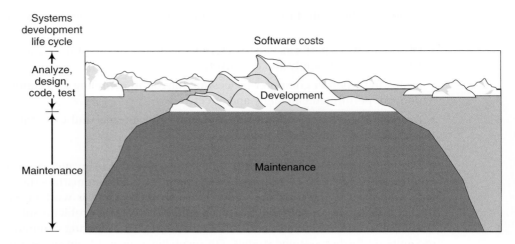

FIGURE 13-13   In the systems development life cycle, the costs of analysis, design, development, and implementation are often just the tip of the iceberg: software maintenance costs are the most expensive part.

AIS AT WORK
Outsourcing IT to India, Sort Of[9]

A recent research survey of 420 IT professionals found "cost savings" to be the primary reason companies choose to outsource their IT. Some cost savings stem from increased flexibility, but most of the savings are the result of avoiding personnel costs (i.e., health care, pensions, and other benefits). The company using the outsourced IT services has the ability to be more flexible and can adapt quickly to ebbs and flows in business and demands for IT services.

In addition to flexibility, cost savings from outsourced IT also can result from lower labor costs, achievable by sending the work to countries with lower wages. One-quarter of all outsourced IT dollars is spent on offshore IT, with much of that work going to service providers in India. Vendor selection reflects the emphasis on cost cutting. In evaluating IT service providers domestically, reliability is the most important criterion. When choosing an offshore vendor, it's all about cost.

Domestic U.S. companies, including IBM and Accenture, are benefiting from the trend to outsource IT services. But so are Indian companies, such as Infosys, Wipro Consulting Services, Satyam Computer Services, Tata Consultancy Services (TCS), and Cognizant Technology Solutions (CTS).

CTS demonstrates the complex relationships in global business. The company was founded to take advantage of India's large labor pool and low labor costs. Just as U.S. companies once moved among states—American, Indian, Chinese, and European companies now look at earth's whole map and do the work where it can be done best or costs the least. In 2010, CTS employed over 100,000 employees and earned $4.6 billion

---

[9] McDougall, P. 2006. Cost conscious, but demanding. *InformationWeek* (June 19): 43–48; and Varadarajan, N. 2006. IT's new billion dollar baby. *Business Today* (February 10): 70.

in revenues. Its fast growth may be partly due to its "Americanism." CTS is not purely an American company, nor is it Indian. It's a hybrid company that may be considered either American-Indian, or Indian-American. For example, the CEO resides in the company's New Jersey headquarters, and the company uses an American approach to attracting customers by developing strategic solutions. It emphasizes specialization in business applications, primarily in the financial services and health care industries.

SUMMARY

✓ The four stages in a systems development life cycle are (1) planning and investigating, (2) analysis, (3) design, and (4) implementing, follow-up, and maintenance.

✓ Planning requires creating a team to investigate the current system and making recommendations to a steering committee.

✓ Systems analysis requires identifying general systems goals, top management systems goals, and operating management systems goals.

✓ A systems survey uses a variety of data gathering techniques to understand and document the system.

✓ The systems analysis report contains the study team recommendations.

✓ The components of a feasibility evaluation are technical, operational, legal, and economic feasibility.

✓ Detailed systems design begins with the design of outputs, followed by inputs and processes. Designers may choose a prototyping approach to create the new system.

✓ A systems specification report contains detailed information about the organization and its desired system.

✓ Choosing a system requires evaluating system performance capabilities, costs and benefits, system maintainability, system compatibility with other systems, and vendor support.

✓ An organization may choose to outsource its IT operations, accounting processes, or research-related (knowledge) tasks.

✓ Organizations use PERT, Gantt charts, and project management software to manage the implementation of complex information systems.

✓ Organizations need to follow up to find out if new systems are working as planned.

KEY TERMS YOU SHOULD KNOW

agile development methodology

applications portfolio

benchmark test

canned software

change management

critical path

detailed systems design

direct conversion

economic feasibility

feasibility evaluation

follow-up and maintenance phase

Gantt charts

knowledge process outsourcing (KPO)

legal feasibility

make-or-buy decision

modular conversion

operational feasibility

parallel conversion

point-scoring analysis

preliminary investigation

Program Evaluation and Review Technique (PERT)

project management software

prototyping

request for proposal (RFP)

schedule feasibility

scope creep

slack time

steering committee

structured, top-down design

system development life cycle (SDLC)

system maintenance

systems analysis

systems approach

systems implementation

systems specification report

systems study

systems survey

technical feasibility

turnkey system

waterfall model

what-if analyses

DISCUSSION QUESTIONS

13-1. Discuss the major differences between the planning, analysis, and design phase of a systems study.

13-2. What is a steering committee? Discuss its role in a systems study performed by a consulting firm.

13-3. A systems study team should understand three levels of corporate goals: general systems goals, top management systems goals, and operating management systems goals. If you had to select one of these categories of systems goals as the most important to the effective operation of an organization's information system, which one would you choose? Explain the reasons for your choice.

13-4. What is the purpose of a systems feasibility evaluation? Should this activity precede or follow the preparation of a systems specifications report for computer vendor evaluation? Explain.

13-5. Discuss some of the annual cash benefits and annual cash costs that a company might have when it creates an online ordering system on the World Wide Web.

13-6. What is prototyping? Under what circumstances should prototyping be used? Under what circumstances should it not be used?

13-7. What is the purpose of a systems specifications report? In what ways, if any, do the data included in this report differ from the data accumulated by the design team during their feasibility evaluation work?

13-8. When implementing a new computer system, two required activities are (1) establishing controls and (2) converting data files. What is the rationale for performing activity 1 before activity 2?

13-9. Three methods for implementing a new system in an organization are direct conversion, parallel conversion, and modular conversion. Discuss the advantages and disadvantages of using each of these three systems implementation methods.

13-10. What is a PERT chart? What is a Gantt chart? Discuss the advantages and disadvantages of using PERT network diagrams versus Gantt charts for planning and controlling the activities involved in implementing an information system.

13-11. What is the purpose of follow-up in a systems study? Describe some of the specific activities that the management implementation team would perform in their follow-up work.

13-12. Discuss the two major ways that a company's software can be acquired. Which of these ways for acquiring software do you recommend? Explain your reasoning.

13-13. What is the difference between business process outsourcing (BPO) and knowledge process outsourcing (KPO)? Why do firms outsource their IT functions?

PROBLEMS

13-14. The Chris Hall Company manufactures and distributes low-priced bottled wines to retailers. You are hired as a management consultant to help this company solve some of its systems problems. Describe the types of decision-making information that probably would be needed by the company's (a) supervisor of the production plant, (b) top management, and (c) marketing manager.

13-15. Lilly Li Apparel is a manufacturer of fashion apparel that has just opened its first large retail store for selling high-fashion clothes at high-fashion prices. The company's competitive strategy depends on a comprehensive point-of-sale (POS) system supporting online, up-to-the-minute sales totals, day-to-day tracking of stock information, and quick checkout of customer purchases. Because cashiers were already familiar with electronic cash registers, management decided that only minimal training was required. Cashiers enter four-digit stock tracking numbers (STNs) into one of the POS terminals that retrieves price and description data, computes the tax and total amount due, accepts the type of payment, and controls the cash drawer. A unique STN identifies each of the 9,500 pieces of merchandise. The central microcomputer server maintains stock information.

In the first month of operation, new cashiers were awkward using the new system. They eventually became proficient users but were frustrated with the slow printing of sales tickets and the unpredictable action of their cash drawers. Each checkout stand has a telephone that cashiers use to call for approval of credit-card transactions. Customers became impatient when credit approvals delayed the checkout process or when the microcomputer was down, thus stopping all sales, including cash sales. Identify four problems with the system and describe how you would remedy each of them.

13-16. Jay Beck works for the AAZ Consulting Firm. His friend, Hank Henley, is the general manager and majority stockholder of the Pacific Worldwinds, a professional football team. Hank asked Jay to design an online, real-time computer system for "the efficient operation of the football franchise." Jay was quite confused because he could not think of any possible uses for an online, real-time system within the operational activities of a football team (or any other type of athletic team). Assume that you are also employed at the AAZ Consulting Firm. Provide several suggestions to Jay concerning specific areas of athletic teams' (football teams, baseball teams, etc.) information systems, where an online, real-time computer configuration might be beneficial to managerial decision making.

13-17. Cook Consultants is currently in the process of completing the systems implementation activities for converting Samuel Company's old system to a new one. Because of unexpected delays in performing specific implementation activities, Jerry Hazen, the project manager, is concerned about finishing the project on time. The one remaining activity is testing the new computer system and subsequently eliminating the old one. Jerry's assistant, May Fong, suggests that they can still meet their completion deadline if they use *direct conversion* rather than *parallel conversion*. Assuming that you are the CIO of the company, how would you react to May Fong's suggestion? Discuss.

13-18. With the help of your instructor, identify a particular information system that is not working very well and perform a preliminary investigation of it. In your work, be sure to talk to (1) at least one external customer who is affected by the system, (2) one employee who uses the system daily, and (3) one person who manages this type of employee. For example, at a university, you might study the student parking information system. The customers are those car owners who purchase parking permits (e.g., students, faculty, and university staff members), data input clerks are the employees who use the system daily, and the parking manager is the person who supervises these employees. Ask each such person what he or she feels are the problems of the system and what they think should be done to address these problems.

Prepare a preliminary investigation report that describes your system and outlines the following items: (a) the problems that each person experiences with the system, (b) the actions that each person thinks might solve the problems, and (c) your opinion of which difficulties are the real problems and which are just symptoms of these problems. Also include some recommendations. Should the present system be replaced, or are just minor modifications required?

13-19. Do you understand PERT charts? Refer back to Figure 13-11 and answer the following questions:

    a. Which activity or activities must be completed before activity C can begin?

    b. Which activity or activities must be completed before activity G can begin?

    c. Which activity or activities must be completed before activity J can begin?

    d. What are the five paths through the network? Which one is the critical path?

    e. What is the earliest projected start time for activity F?

    f. What is the earliest projected start time for activity G?

    g. What is the latest time that activity J can begin without delaying the entire project?

    h. What is the latest time that activity G can begin without delaying the entire project?

    i. What is the slack time for activity G? (Hint: it's the difference between the early and late start times.)

13-20. Do you understand Gantt charts? Use Figure 13-12 and test your understanding by answering the following questions. (Hint: you might also want to look at the PERT chart in Figure 13-11.)

    a. When is the activity *convert data files* scheduled to begin and end?

    b. When is the activity *test computer software* scheduled to begin and end?

    c. How much time did it actually take the company to complete the task *prepare the physical site*? Was this more or less time than planned?

    d. How much time did it actually take the company to complete the task *determine the functional changes*? Was this more or less time than planned?

    e. Given what has happened so far, when can the activity *acquire and install computer equipment* actually begin?

    f. Given what has happened so far, when can the activity *select and assign personnel* actually begin?

CASE STUDIES

Prado Roberts Manufacturing (What Type of Computer System to Implement?)

Prado Roberts Manufacturing is a medium-size company with regional offices in several western states and manufacturing facilities in both California and Nevada. The company performs most of its important data processing tasks, such as payroll, accounting, marketing, and inventory control, on a mainframe computer at corporate headquarters. However, almost all the managers at this company also have personal computers, which they use for such personal productivity tasks as word processing, analyzing budgets (using spreadsheets), and managing the data in small databases.

The IT manager, Tonya Fisher, realizes that there are both advantages and disadvantages of using different types of systems to meet the processing needs of her company. While she acknowledges that many companies are racing ahead to install microcomputers and client/server systems, she also knows that the corporate mainframe system has provided her company with some advantages that smaller systems cannot match. Tonya knows that American companies annually purchase over $5 billion in used computers, primarily mainframes.

Requirements

1. Identify several advantages and disadvantages of operating a mainframe computer system that are likely to be present at Prado Roberts Manufacturing. Are these advantages and disadvantages likely to parallel those at other manufacturing companies?
2. Identify at least two factors or actions that companies experience or do to prolong the lives of their legacy systems. Are these factors or actions likely to apply to Prado Roberts Manufacturing?
3. Identify several advantages and disadvantages of microcomputer/client server systems. Would these advantages apply to Prado Roberts Manufacturing?

(CMA Adapted)

Wright Company (Analyzing System Reports)

Wright Company employs a computer-based data processing system for maintaining all company records. The current system was developed in stages over the past five years and has been fully operational for the last 24 months.

When the system was being designed, all department heads were asked to specify the types of information and reports they would need for planning and controlling operations. The systems department attempted to meet the specifications of each department head. Company management specified that certain other reports be prepared for department heads. During the five years of systems development and operation, there have been several changes in the department head positions because of attrition and promotions. The new department heads often made requests for additional reports according to their specifications. The systems department complied with all of these requests. Reports were discontinued only on request by a department head, and then only if it was not a standard report required by top management.

As a result, few reports were discontinued and the information processing subsystem continued to generate a large quantity of reports each reporting period. Company management became concerned about the quantity of report information produced by the system, and therefore asked the internal audit department to evaluate their effectiveness. The audit staff determined early in the study that more information was being generated by the information processing subsystem than could be used effectively. They noted the following reactions to this information overload:

- Many department heads would not act on certain reports during periods of peak activity. The department heads would let these reports accumulate with the hope of catching up during subsequent lulls.
- Some department heads had so many reports that they did not act at all on the information, or they made incorrect decisions because of misuse of the information.
- Frequently, actions required by the nature of the report data were not taken until the department heads were reminded by others who needed the decisions. These department heads did not appear to have developed a priority system for acting on the information produced by the information processing subsystem.

- Department heads often would develop the information they needed from alternative, independent sources, rather than use the reports generated by the information processing subsystem. This was often easier than trying to search among the reports for the needed data.

Requirements

1. Indicate whether each of the foregoing four reactions contributes positively or negatively to the Wright Company's operating effectiveness. Explain your answer for every one of the four reactions.
2. For each reaction that you indicated as negative, recommend alternative procedures the Wright Company could employ to eliminate this negative contribution to operating effectiveness.

(CMA Adapted)

Kenbart Company (Redesigning Profit Plan Reports)

The managers at Kenbart Company have decided that increased emphasis must be placed on profit planning and comparing *results* to *plans*. A new profit planning system was implemented to help with this objective. The company uses contribution margin reporting for internal reporting purposes and applies the concept of flexible budgeting for estimating variable costs. Kenbart's executive management uses the following terms when reviewing and analyzing actual results and the profit plan.

- *Original plan.* Profit plan approved and adopted by management for the year
- *Revised plan.* Original plan modified as a consequence of action taken during the year (usually quarterly) by executive management
- *Flexed revised plan.* The most current plan (i.e., either original plan or revised plan, if one has been prepared) adjusted for changes in volume and variable expense rates
- *YTD actual results.* The actual results of operations for the year
- *Current outlook.* The summation of the actual year-to-date results of operations plus the flexed revised plan for the remaining months of the year

Executive management meets monthly to review the actual results compared with the profit plan. Any assumptions or major changes in the profit plan usually are incorporated on a quarterly basis once the first quarter is completed. Figure 13-14 provides an outline of the basic Profit Plan Report designed by the information processing subsystem. The current system produces this report at the end of the month, and whenever executive management initiates a change or modification in its plans. Consequently, many different versions of the firm's profit plan exist, which makes analysis difficult and confusing.

Several members of the executive management have voiced disapproval of the Profit Plan Report because the "Plan" column is not well defined and varies in meaning from one report to another. Furthermore, the report does not include a current-outlook column. Therefore, the accounting subsystem has been asked to work with the information processing subsystem in modifying the report so that users can better understand the information being conveyed and the reference points for comparison of results.

Kenbert Company Profit Plan Report
Month, Year-to-Date

	Month				Year-to-Date			
			Over/ (Under)				Over/ (Under)	
	Actual	Plan	$	%	Actual	Plan	$	%
Sales								
Variable manufacturing costs								
Raw materials								
Direct labor								
Variable overhead								
Total variable manufacturing costs								
Manufacturing margin								
Variable selling expenses								
Contribution margin								
Fixed costs								
Manufacturing								
Sales								
General administration								
Income before taxes								
Income taxes								
Net income								

FIGURE 13-14 Basic profit plan report outline.

Requirements

1. Redesign the layout of the Profit Plan Report so that it will be more useful to Kenbart's executive management in its task of reviewing results and planning operations.
2. Explain the reason for each modification you make in the report.

Chapter 14

Accounting on the Internet

INTRODUCTION

Most accountants use the Internet for research, education, and e-mail on a daily basis. Auditors regularly evaluate their client's internal controls to ensure complete, accurate, and authentic transmissions of transactions over the Internet. In fact, it's nearly impossible to imagine how accountants would accomplish their various job responsibilities without the many Internet technologies that support today's businesses.

This chapter describes some accounting applications of the Internet in detail. The first section describes Internet components such as Internet addresses and software. This section also discusses some Internet concepts of special importance to accountants (i.e., intranets and extranets). We also discuss XBRL, a financial reporting language, in this section.

One of the most important uses of the Internet is for electronic business (e-business) —the topic of the next section of this chapter. While the terms e-commerce and e-business are often used interchangeably, some experts prefer to view them as different concepts. E-commerce involves buying or selling goods and services electronically. This activity can be between two businesses, between a profit-seeking company and a governmental entity, or between a business and a customer. In contrast, e-business goes beyond e-commerce and deep into the processes and cultures of an enterprise. This could include, for example, e-mail, soliciting vendor bids electronically, making e-payments, exchanging data electronically, and a host of specialized cloud-computing services. Thus, it is the powerful business environment that organizations create when they connect their critical business systems directly to customers, employees, vendors, and business partners, using intranets, extranets, e-commerce technologies, collaborative applications, and the Web.[1] We discuss some of these topics in the third section of this chapter.

As more organizations conduct at least some business on the Internet, it is only natural that managers increasingly recognize the importance of Internet privacy and security. This includes protecting consumers' personal privacy, protecting proprietary data from hackers, and safeguarding information that businesses send to one another over the Internet. The final section of this chapter discusses these topics in detail.

THE INTERNET AND WORLD WIDE WEB

The **Internet** is a collection of local and wide area networks that are connected together via the Internet backbone—that is, the main electronic connections of the system. Describing the Internet as an "information superhighway" makes sense because over two billion

---

[1] http://www.ebusinessprogrammers.com/ebusiness/ecommerce_and_ebusiness.asp

people from around the world now use it, just as a set of state, interstate, and international highways connect people physically.[2] Almost all universities are connected to the Internet, as are most commercial information services, businesses, government agencies, and not-for-profit organizations. This section of the chapter discusses Internet basics, including Internet addresses and software, intranets and extranets, the World Wide Web (WWW), IDEA, groupware, electronic conferencing, and Web logs.

Internet Addresses and Software

To transmit data over the Internet, computers use an Internet address and a forwarding system that works much the same way as the post office system. On the Internet, the initial computer transmits a message to other computers along the Internet's backbone, which, in turn, relay the message from site to site until it reaches its final destination. If the message is large, Internet computers can divide it into smaller pieces called *data packets* and send each of them along different routes. The receiving computer then reassembles the packets into a complete message at the final destination.

An Internet address begins as a **domain address**, which is also called a **uniform resource locator (URL)**. This is a text address such as www.name.com.uk. As suggested by this generic example, the lead item indicates the World Wide Web. The second entry designates the site name, and the third entry ("com" for commercial user) is the organization code. Other organization codes are "edu" (education), "gov" (government), "mil" (military), "net" (network service organization), "org" (miscellaneous organization), and "int" (international treaty organization). Finally, a domain address can include a country code as well—for example, "ca" for Canada, "uk" for the United Kingdom, or "nz" for New Zealand.

For transmission purposes, Internet computers use tables of domain names that enable them to translate a text-based domain address such as www.wikipedia.org into a numeric Internet protocol (IP) address such as 207.142.131.248. The elements in this address contain a geographic region ("207"), an organization number ("142"), a computer group ("131"), and a specific computer ("248"). The IP address enables Internet computers to deliver a specific message to a specific computer at a specific computer site—for example, send an e-mail message to a friend at another university using the common **Transmission Control Protocol/Internet Protocol** standard—commonly called **(TCP/IP)**. IP addresses are useful to auditors because they help identify the sender, which is an important control in e-commerce applications.

Intranets and Extranets

Because Internet software is so convenient to use, many companies also create their own **intranets** for internal communications purposes. These computer networks use the same software as the Internet but are internal to the organization that created them. Thus, outsiders cannot access the information on intranet networks—a convenient security feature.

One common use of intranets is to allow users to access one or more internal databases. Advanced search engine technology coupled with an intranet can deliver user-defined information when needed. For example, a purchasing agent can access a centralized listing

---

[2] http://www.internetworldstats.com/stats.htm

of approved vendors using his or her Web browser and a local area network. Another valuable use of an intranet is for gathering and disseminating information to internal users. For example, employees can collaborate with each other by posting messages and data on the internal network, update records, check out job postings, complete forms to request office supplies, and enter travel expenses through their organization's intranet. Universities offer many of the same services to their employees, as well as a similar variety of services and educational opportunities to students.

Extranets enable selected outside users to access corporate intranets. Users connect through the Internet itself via passwords or private data communications channels. The following is an example.

Case-in-Point 14.1 Chamberlain Group, Inc., distributes door operators, gate operators, and telephone entry systems. The firm's extranet helps the independent dealers who sell its products place orders, view invoices, obtain return authorizations, track warranty claims, and download manuals in PDF format. The company is particularly proud of its "resource center"—a separate portion of its Web site—which allows dealers to obtain advertising assistance, download high-resolution logos and pictures of products and even TV and radio commercials.[3]

The World Wide Web and HTML

The multimedia portion of the Internet is commonly called the World Wide Web or just "the Web." As you probably already know, you view these graphics using a **Web browser** such as Microsoft's Internet Explorer. A typical entity on the Web is a Web page—that is, a collection of text, graphics, and links to other Web pages stored on Internet-connected computers.

Developers typically create Web pages in an editing language such as **hypertext markup language (HTML)**—see Figure 14-1a. Web designers store these instructions in one or more files and use the Internet to transfer these pages from a source computer to a recipient computer using a communications protocol such as **hypertext transfer protocol (HTTP)**. Your Web browser then deciphers the editing language and displays the text, graphics, and other items of the Web page on your screen (Figure 14-1b).

Because HTML is an editing language, many of its instructions are simply pairs of tags that instruct a Web browser how to display the information bracketed by these tags. Thus, in Figure 14-1a, note that the entire file begins with an <html> tag and ends with a closing tag </html>. Similarly, the <b> and </b> tags bold and unbold text, and the <i> and </i> tags begin and end italicized text. Using Figure 14-1b, you can probably guess the purpose of anchor tags (beginning with <a>), ordered list tags (beginning with <ol>), and list item tags (beginning with <li>). Problem 14-18 is an exercise to help you understand HTML tags.

Groupware, Electronic Conferencing, and Blogs

Groupware allows users to send and receive e-mail, plus perform a wide range of other document-editing tasks. In addition to e-mail support, these network packages allow users to collaborate on work tasks, make revisions to the same document, schedule appointments on each other's calendars, share files and databases, conduct electronic meetings, and develop

---

[3] Anonymous. 2007. The Chamberlain Group updates its extranet. *Security Distributing and Marketing* 37(10): 26–27.

```html
<html>
<title>Some examples of HTML tags</title>
<body lang=EN-US style='tab-interval:.5in'>
<h1>Some Examples of HTML Tags</h1>
<p><b>This sentence is bold.</b></p>
<p><i>This sentence is in italics.</i></p>
<p><span style=font-size:14.0pt>
This sentence uses 14-point type
</span>
</p>
<p><a href="http://www.wiley.com">John
   Wiley web site</a></p>
<p>This is an ordered list.</p>
<ol><li>This is item #1.</li>
<li>This is item #2.</li>
</body>
</html>
```

(a) HTML code

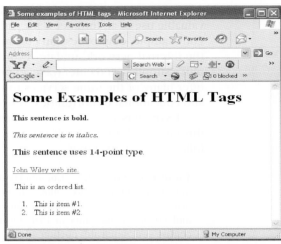

(b) What the code in part (a) displays

FIGURE 14-1 An example of HTML code and what that code displays in a Web browser. Note the anchor tag <a>, which allows you to create a link to another Web page—in this case, the Wiley Web site.

custom applications. Examples of such software include *Exchange* (Microsoft), *Groupwise* (Novell), *Lotus Notes* (Lotus Development Corporation), and *Outlook* (Microsoft).

Instant messaging software enables remote users to communicate with each other in real time via the Internet. You are probably already familiar with such software if you use MSN Messenger, Yahoo Messenger, or Skype to chat with distant friends. Many of these packages also support audio, video, and **electronic conferencing** (enabling several users to join a discussion, instead of just two). Accounting applications include the ability to interview job applicants remotely, consult with clients about tax or audit problems, discuss projects with individuals at several international branch offices, or plan corporate budgets.

Large consulting and accounting firms have access to a wealth of information within their organizations. Groupware is one of the technologies behind **knowledge management** that many professional service firms (such as accounting and consulting firms) use to distribute expertise within the organization (frequently on its intranet). This information includes descriptions of clients' best practices, research findings, links to business Web sites, and customized news. For example, an accountant with a client issue can access the knowledge database to learn how others handled similar issues.

Web logs or **blogs** are collaboration tools that allow users with Web browsers and easy-to-use software to publish a personalized diary online. Blogging introduces a new way to create, share, and leverage knowledge in an organization and therefore can be valuable to accountants. Enterprise blogs provide companies with easy-to-use tools to manage internal and external information, which in turn affects relationships with customers, partners, and investors, as well as internal decision makers.

XBRL—FINANCIAL REPORTING ON THE INTERNET

While the Internet supports general financial reporting, exchanging financial information between trading partners often requires more detailed specifications. **Extensible markup language (XML)** is similar to HTML in that it also uses tags such as <b> and </b> to format data. But there are two important differences between HTML and XML. One is that XML tags are "extensible," allowing users to define their own tags, such as <SalesRevenue>. The other difference is that the XML tags actually *describe* the data rather than simply indicate how to display it. For example, if a business wants to report sales revenue of $1 million, it could use the XML tags: <SalesRevenue>$1,000,000</SalesRevenue>. Now, this data item has meaning.

A problem with XML tags is a potential lack of consistency among users. For example, one company might use the XML tag <SalesRevenue>, but another company might choose <Revenues>. Without standardized markers (tags), users cannot exchange financial information or extract data from XML files for comparison purposes. Extensible business reporting language (XBRL) solves this problem by standardizing the tags that describe financial information in documents for both profit and not-for-profit organizations. In short, XBRL is a specialized subset of XML for reporting financial information. Figure 14-2 provides an example of XBRL code and what that code creates.

The XBRL International Consortium (discussed below) creates XBRL standards that anyone can use, license free. In addition, many accounting software packages are now *XBRL-enabled*, meaning that they can insert appropriate XBRL tags automatically in user financial files. Because of its growing importance, some authorities now suggest that XBRL become an integral part of the general accounting curriculum—not just a subject to be studied by AIS students.

XBRL Instance Documents and Taxonomies

XBRL documents are called **XBRL instance documents** because they are examples (instances) of a class of documents defined by a standard or specification. Figure 14-2 shows an example—a portion of an income statement in XBRL. In this example, note that XBRL tags follow conventional HTML and XML coding rules that use a beginning tag such as <ifrs-gp:OtherAssetsCurrent> and an ending tag such as </ifrs-gp:OtherAssetsCurrent> to define a value. The number itself sits between these two tags. XBRL tags identify financial values uniquely. For example, the term "CashCashEquivalents" within a tag unambiguously

```
XBRL code:

<ifrs-gp:CashCashEquivalents contextRef="Current_AsOf" unitRef="U-Euros"
     decimals="0">1000000</ifrs-gp: CashCashEquivalents>
<ifrs-gp:OtherAssetsCurrent contextRef="Current_AsOf" unitRef="U-Euros"
     decimals="0">200000</ifrs-gp: OtherAssetsCurrent>
<ifrs-gp:AssetsCurrentTotal contextRef="Current_AsOf" unitRef="U-Euros"
     decimals="0">1200000</ifrs-gp:AssetsCurrentTotal>


What the XBRL code displays in a Web browser:

   Current Assets:
          Cash and Cash Equivalents      1,000,000
          Other Assets, Current            200,000
      Current Assets, Total:             1,200,000
```

FIGURE 14-2 An example of XBRL code and what that code creates.

- Due to corporate scandals, shareholders, analysts, and reporters are demanding more transparent reporting. XBRL allows readers to quickly access the information they need.
- XBRL permits the automatic and reliable exchange of financial information across all software formats and technologies, including the Internet.
- XBRL does not require a change to existing accounting standards of corporate disclosure policies.
- XBRL improves access to financial information because data is in a digital, reusable form.
- XBRL eliminates the need to reenter financial data for different users, which reduces risks associated with data entry and lowers the cost to prepare and distribute financial statements.
- XBRL improves investor and analyst access to information.
- XBRL allows accountants to more quickly and easily consolidate and scrutinize internal data for use in financial reports.
- XBRL allows CEOs and CFOs to deliver more transparent information to investors and analysts, and allows a vehicle for control within the firm.

FIGURE 14-3 How does XBRL affect accountants? Source: Charles Hoffman and Carolyn Strand, *XBRL Essentials* (New York: AICPA), 2001; and www.xbrl.org

defines "cash and cash equivalents." Finally, you can use optional entries in each tag to identify currency units (e.g., euros) and the number of decimal places (e.g., 0).

To create an XBRL instance document, you need to know: (1) the standard tags that define familiar items such as net revenues and operating expenses and (2) the rules that govern how to use these tags. XBRL Specification 2.1 currently defines the rules and syntax for XBRL taxonomies and XBRL documents. XBRL taxonomies define the tags that represent accounting and financial terms used in XBRL instance documents. With standard tags for each piece of common financial data, accounting software can create instance documents for income statements, balance sheets, and similar financial statements in a straightforward manner. Figure 14-3 lists a number of ways that XBRL affects accountants.

The Benefits and Drawbacks of XBRL

Perhaps the most obvious benefit of XBRL is the ability to transmit financial information in a standard format. This facilitates communication between suppliers and their buyers, companies and their shippers, and even retailers and their customers. The same standardization applies to financial filings. For example, the Securities and Exchange Commission (SEC) now requires XBRL-formatted financial statement reports such as 10-Q and 10K reports and has mandated that all U.S. publicly traded companies file all their financial statements in XBRL by 2011.

Another important advantage of XBRL is that it defines data items uniquely. Consider, for example, how a spreadsheet stores financial information. The only way we know that a particular number *in* a spreadsheet is, say, "net revenue" is because we also see a label that identifies it as such. Move the number somewhere else in the spreadsheet and you also lose its meaning. In contrast, a "net revenue" figure remains "net revenue" no matter where it appears in XBRL instance documents as long as it remains within its tags. It is for this reason that some experts predict that some accounting systems will begin *collecting and storing* their data in XBRL formats, redefining XBRL as a *formatting* language as much as a *reporting* language.

XBRL's standardized tags also make searching for items in XBRL financial documents relatively easy. If you know the standard tag for an item of interest, you can unambiguously find and extract the number in question from those documents. One repository of such financial information is the Security and Exchange Commission's new **interactive data and electronic applications (IDEA)**, which the agency unveiled in August 2008 and now contains XBRL data for over 10,000 companies—a particularly important source of financial information and a particularly important reason why standardized reporting is useful.

In business environments, the term *semantic meaning* refers to the fact that the financial data are related to one another through formulas such as "Assets = Liabilities + Equity." An additional advantage of XBRL is its ability to express such relationships in formulas, thereby making the data self checking. This is important because organizations often need to transmit financial data to others, and XBRL provides a means of internal control.

> **Case-in-Point 14.2** The Federal Deposit Insurance Corporation (FDIC) insures banks and similar financial institutions throughout the United States. The FDIC exchanges financial information with member institutions all the time and uses a set of 1,800 rules to validate such data. The FDIC was an early adopter of XBRL, in part because this language has the ability to perform data validation tasks automatically.[4]

Companies using XBRL-enabled software can save their financial information in standard XBRL format, thus avoiding the errors that may come from reentering data multiple times from multiple sources. Companies can then directly upload their business information in this format onto their Web sites. This is important because a recent study by Forrester Research estimated the cost of rekeying information at $402 billion per year.[5]

Another advantage is that XBRL permits the automatic and reliable exchange of financial information across all software platforms and technologies, including the Internet. Thus, anyone interested in comparing the cash and cash equivalents of several companies can search for the data and export it to a spreadsheet for analysis purposes.

Finally, it is important to note that XBRL does not constrain companies to a particular *format* for their financial reports. On the contrary, the language is flexible and therefore intentionally constructed to support financial reporting by companies in different industries or from different countries. The hope is that both the extensible capabilities of the language as well as this flexibility are great enough to meet business and governmental needs at all levels. Problem 14-20 invites you to explore the benefits of XBRL in further detail.

XBRL also has several disadvantages. Perhaps the most important is the fact that a common reporting language requires its users to learn, and conform to, the standards of that language. Usually, accountants achieve this task by acquiring software that can output data in XBRL formats. Another problem is that evolving XBRL standards require users to conform to changing specifications—a drawback, for example, that may require organizations to update their accounting software more often. A third concern is that, at present, there is no requirement for auditors to provide assurance on the XBRL filings. Finally, the transition to XBRL reporting is not without costs.

> **Case-in-Point 14.3** A survey by the SEC of XBRL filers revealed that the additional costs of the requirement averaged between $30,000 and $40,000, but in some cases ran as high as $82,000. However, these costs tended to diminish over time as organizations gained experience with the language and were able to reuse their software.[6]

---

[4] http://www.ubmatrix.com/Documents/XBRLComparedToXML-2005-07-06%20(4).pdf
[5] http://accounting.smartpros.com/x37643.xml; "How XBRL Is Transforming Financial Reporting"
[6] Gray, G. and D. Miller. 2009. XBRL: Solving real-world problems. *International Journal of Disclosure & Governance* 6(3): 207–223.

The Current Status of XBRL

The **XBRL International Consortium** has about 450 members and is in charge of developing XBRL standards. Many U.S. accounting firms are members of this consortium, as is the American Institute of Certified Public Accountants and parallel accounting organizations around the world. The specifications for version 2.1 of XBRL were issued in July 2008. The Web site at http://www.xbrl.org provides additional information on both current and proposed standards, as well as lists of recent papers about XBRL best practices.

As you might imagine, developing global standards for financial reporting is a massive undertaking. The language specifications require classification systems for different countries, different reporting segments (e.g., different industries), and even different organizational standards, such as the United States Generally Accepted Accounting Principles (GAAP). For example, oil and gas companies require specialized tags to identify reserve balances, casinos require specialized tags to identify allowances for unclaimed gambling chips, and so forth. Then too, the language requires standard tags for formulas (e.g., a Price/Earnings ratio) and different functions. For this reason, XBRL is best viewed as a dynamic language still in development.

Most accounting software vendors now support XBRL in one or more of their software packages, and the worldwide adoption of XBRL is moving along quickly. For example, in Germany, it's universal—XBRL is already built into a software package used by 80 percent of the accountants in that country. The XBRL International consortium publishes a progress report three times a year, available on its Web site that contains current information about XBRL.

ELECTRONIC BUSINESS

The term electronic business or e-business refers to conducting business with computers and data communications. Often, e-business is performed over the Internet, but businesses can also conduct e-business over proprietary data transmission lines. Recent surveys estimate that the total annual revenues for e-commerce in the United States exceeds $1 trillion, and the FBI estimates that the banking industry transfers over $1 trillion each week by electronic means. Some general categories of electronic business are (1) retail sales, (2) e-payments and e-wallets, (3) electronic data interchange, and (4) a variety of cloud-computing services, each of which we examine briefly in the paragraphs that follow.

Retail Sales

The World Wide Web offers businesses the opportunity to create virtual stores (''shopping-cart applications'') for selling merchandise directly to customers. At the retail level, it is clear that such Web sites are really automated AISs that allow customers to create their own order forms, shipping forms, and payment documents. Testimony to the success of such retail e-commerce abounds. The number of online shoppers has increased steadily over the past decade. About 80 percent of the U.S. population is now connected to the Internet, many of whom make online purchases on a regular basis. For example, consumers now reserve most of their domestic airline tickets, rental cars, and hotel rooms over the Internet. Figure 14-4 lists some of the advantages of virtual stores. Note how many of these advantages relate directly to AISs.

Internet retail sales also introduce special issues. One problem is that customers usually cannot determine whether a retail Web site is legitimate. Similarly, consumers must usually

1. Web pages are much cheaper to create than creating and mailing catalogs.
2. Distribution is global.
3. Sales can occur around the clock.
4. Customers can search for specific products or services electronically, either within a particular Web site or as a hit from another site.
5. A business can easily outsource its Web business to others, enabling it to focus on core processes.
6. The Web sites themselves can use automated tools to verify customer credit cards.
7. Businesses can send e-mails to confirm orders or advise customers about shipping dates.
8. Businesses can update product descriptions, sales prices, and information on merchandise availability immediately.
9. Customers create their own sales orders online.
10. Customers can track their own orders, freeing business personnel for other tasks.
11. The sales and customer-relations personnel required for virtual stores is minimal, thus reducing labor costs per dollar of sales.

FIGURE 14-4 Some advantages of virtual stores on the Internet.

rely on e-mails to voice their complaints (rather than speaking to someone in person), and returns are sometimes problematic. A third problem is that online stores frequently rely on suppliers rather than their own shelves for merchandise to satisfy orders, creating the potential for stock-out and backorder problems. Finally, a growing e-commerce problem is **click fraud**, in which dishonest managers inflate the number of clicks viewers make on an advertisement on a Web page and therefore bill the linked company for more referrals than actually occurred.

Internet retail sales also provide retailers with a wealth of data about their customers, raising issues about privacy. For example, you might be concerned about the fact that your Web purchase also means that a retailer now has (1) your e-mail address (which it can use to send additional annoying e-mails or sell to others), (2) your credit card information (which it may or may not protect as well as you would like), and (3) sensitive information about your purchase patterns (e.g., prescription drugs). A later section of this chapter addresses these privacy and security issues in greater detail.

E-Payments and E-Wallets

Most customers pay for the merchandise they order over the Internet with a credit card, requiring vendors to use third-party affiliates to authenticate user credit card numbers. This is a problem because such credit card verification systems only indicate that a card is valid, not that the online customer is authorized to use it. A related problem with online payments is that, while online customers might not mind giving their credit card numbers to trusted merchants, they may not wish to share the number with unfamiliar businesses or unknown sellers on mass auction sites.

Some merchants and auction sites solve these problems with **electronic payments (e-payments)**, which proponents claim are a faster, easier, and safer way for both customers and sellers to handle online transactions. The e-payment service acts as a trusted intermediary because it collects a payment from a buyer and pays that amount to the seller.

Case-in-Point 14.4 Consumers who buy products on eBay or other online auction sites may be familiar with PayPal (http://www.paypal.com), an e-payment system that operates via

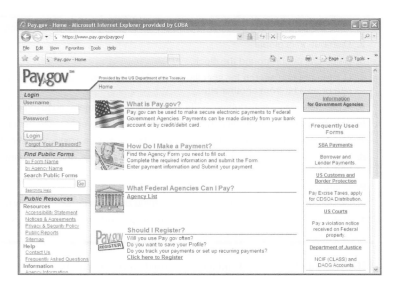

FIGURE 14-5 The home page for Pay.gov—an e-payment system supported by the U.S. government.

the Internet. Customers who want to bid for items in online auctions, but who don't wish to share their credit card number with unknown sellers, may open an account with PayPal. Account holders can deposit cash in their PayPal account using credit cards, debit cards, or bank checks. When consumers purchase items, PayPal acts as an intermediary bank, withdrawing money from the purchaser's account and depositing similar funds into the seller's account (or sending a check).[7]

Businesses are not the only entities that can enjoy the convenience of e-payments. The U.S. government has its own system to conduct financial transactions online:

Case-in-Point 14.5 Pay.gov (Figure 14-5) enables businesses and individuals to make payments to the U.S. government electronically. Developed by the U.S. Treasury Department's Financial Management Services (FMS), Pay.gov is a central location through which businesses and individuals can make payments, submit forms, and send bills to federal agencies. This portal provides authentication services for secure transactions. FMS expects Pay.gov to handle approximately 80 million transactions worth over $125 billion a year, reduce paperwork, and save agencies over 5 percent in processing costs.[8]

Another Internet payment option is an **e-wallet**. E-wallets are software applications that store a consumer's personal information, including credit card numbers, e-mail addresses, and shipping addresses. Shoppers pay for online purchases by providing their e-wallet account numbers to online vendors that also subscribe to the system.

An advantage of an e-wallet is that you can use it whenever you visit subscriber Web sites. These systems spare you the trouble of entering your personal information each time you make an online purchase. Also, because your e-wallet information is usually stored on your own hard drive, you control it. This maintains your e-mail privacy as well. E-wallets may be as important for retailers as they are for consumers because many consumers

---

[7] To learn more about PayPal, log onto its Web site at http://www.paypal.com
[8] To learn more about this program, log onto its Web site at http://fms.treas.gov/index.html

cancel e-commerce transactions before they complete them, often because of frustration with online forms.

Business-to-Business E-Commerce

While there has been tremendous growth in retail e-commerce, it is dwarfed by **business-to-business (B2B) e-commerce**—that is, businesses buying and selling goods and services to each other over the Internet. Buying goods online shortens the time from purchase to delivery and also allows businesses to shop from vendors all over the world. Like retail consumers, corporate purchasing agents using B2B e-commerce tools can select items from online catalogs, confirm purchases, track shipments, and pay bills electronically. E-commerce software can also expedite internal paperwork by first sending purchase orders to the appropriate managers for approvals and then forwarding them to the vendor, thus reducing the costs of processing purchase requisitions.

> *Case-in-Point 14.6* BASF is one of the world's largest chemical, plastics, and energy companies, with sales of €20.7 billion in 2010 and 109,000 employees on five continents. Company managers credit much of its recent 47 percent growth in revenues to its new e-commerce initiatives. According to Herbert Fisch, head of global e-commerce, "In addition to order management, e-commerce provides our customers with information and service tools. Customers benefit from greater transparency and we gain valuable time to better serve them."[9]

Further back in the supply chain, the Internet affects accounting activities just as strongly. Another feature of B2B e-commerce is the wider availability of real-time data that allows managers to view up-to-the-minute information. Take, for instance, a distributor whose business customers in turn sell products to end users. With current data about its customers' retail sales, the supplier could quickly increase or decrease its operations as required. Similar online information can determine the location of specific trucks (using GPS systems), check the estimated arrival date of incoming cargo ships, or determine the current status of finished products, parts inventories, or even working assembly lines.

Even vendors of inexpensive accounting software now include an e-commerce interface with their products. An example is *Peachtree* software's *Peachlink* feature that provides users with tools to create and use a shopping cart Web site and accept Internet orders.

While the Internet has streamlined procurement and inventory tracking operations, it has been slow to impact accounts payable or accounts receivable. In part, this is because companies like to hold their money as long as possible. However, delayed bill payment works *against* these same businesses who want to *collect* on their own accounts receivable. Software from companies such as Time Capital allows vendors and customers to view purchase and shipping documents so that they can resolve discrepancies quickly and cut checks or make electronic payments as needed.

Electronic Data Interchange

Electronic data interchange (EDI) means transmitting information over high-speed data communication channels. Literally thousands of companies use EDI to electronically exchange billions of dollars every year as well as many business documents. Examples of EDI business documents include requests for quotes (RFQs), purchase orders, bills of

---

[9] Burridge, E. 2005. E-commerce revenues boost achieved by BASF. *European Chemical News* 83(2174): 14; and http://www.basf.com/group/corporate/en/function/conversions:/publish/content/about-basf/facts-reports/reports/2010/Financial_Statements_BASF_SE_2010.pdf

lading, freight bills, sales invoices, customs documents, payment remittance forms, and credit memos. Thus, EDI automates the exchange of business information and permits organizations to conduct many forms of commerce electronically.

> ***Case-in-Point 14.7***   Pratt and Whitney is a large-engine manufacturer that buys over 26,000 parts from more than 700 suppliers. This company now transmits over 50,000 EDI documents per month, including purchase orders, procurement schedules, and sales invoices. The company estimates savings between $10 and $20 on every purchase order—over $6 million per year.

Government agencies also depend heavily on EDI. One example is the U.S. Customs Service, which uses it to identify and streamline the processing of import merchandise and customs declarations.

One potential advantage of EDI compared to Internet e-commerce is that many business documents are simply faxed over telephone lines, avoiding computers completely. This does not mean that EDI documents are not delivered via the Internet. Many businesses now have telephone systems that use Internet lines for both voice and digital transmissions. Another advantage is that many EDI documents include handwritten signatures, providing assurance of their authenticity. A third advantage is that EDI includes the exchange of graphic and photographic documents—media that can be scanned and captured electronically, but at additional time or cost.

Cloud Computing

As explained in Chapter 1, cloud computing refers to purchasing services from vendors over the Internet. The term derives its name from the cloud-like symbol often used to depict the Internet in networking diagrams. A host of activities fall into this category, including Web hosting, payroll processing, backup provisioning, e-mailing, and even outsourcing business phone systems. Here, we briefly discuss some examples of these services.

Processing Services.   Companies that access specialized software (e.g., tax-preparation applications) purchase software as a service (SaaS). In contrast, Web hosting is an example of **platform as a service (PaaS)**. Examples of cloud vendors include Amazon.com (data storage), Oracle (database software), and Intuit (both tax and payroll processing).

Cloud computing closely resembles other forms of outsourcing and therefore enjoys the same advantages. For example, when a hospital contracts with a second company to do its payroll, it can focus on its core mission and shift the burdensome details of payroll processing (e.g., how much taxes to withhold for out-of-state employees) to the contractor. But cloud computing also differs from traditional forms of outsourcing. For example, the data communications in cloud computing takes place over the Internet and are therefore instantaneous. Another important difference is that transaction volumes are usually charged by the day, hour, or even minute—and are billed accordingly—not by peak load.

> ***Case-in-Point 14.8***   The heaviest demands on the Web sites of most textbook publishers are in the weeks just before final examinations—not uniformly distributed over a semester or quarter (as you might expect). This is the main reason why publishers such as John Wiley & Sons, Inc., the publisher of this textbook, might contract with a cloud computing company like Amazon.com to host its Web services. This allows Wiley to not worry about such peak demands, but simply pays the cloud vendor for only the resources used.[10]

---

[10] Kroenke, D. 2011. *Using MIS.* Boston, MA: Prentice Hall, p. 432.

Advantage	Example
Access to specialized expertise	In a payroll application, the vendor keeps up to date with the most recent tax-withholding requirements.
Cost savings	The contracting company avoids the hardware, software, and training costs involved in performing the service in-house, and pays only for the services actually consumed.
Speed	In a tax-preparation application, all communications take place electronically and therefore nearly instantaneously, thereby avoiding the data-transfer delays in, say, post-office options.
Access to distant vendors	In an e-mail application, the least costly vendor might be thousands of miles away—a factor of no consequence to the contracting company.
Avoiding peak loading problems	Sales often spike during the Christmas season. The retailer offloads these volume problems to the vendor.
Virtual remote backup	A company makes a copy of its critical data at the same time it updates the initial database. This increases security because the backup copy is, by definition, off-premises.
Pay as you go	The outsourcing company avoids the initial investments in hardware, software, or personnel. This can be similar to the difference between owning a car and renting a taxi.

FIGURE 14-6 Some advantages of cloud computing

Cloud computing offers many advantages to companies, which explains why so many organizations now contract with cloud vendors. Figure 14-6 outlines some of these advantages. Cloud computing also has several disadvantages. Perhaps the most important is the loss of control that client firms experience when another company assumes responsibility for their data and data processing—a security concern at the very least. Language barriers, quality control, and time differentials are additional potential concerns when contracting with overseas vendors. A third concern is that backup service providers typically require large bandwidths, and the timing of automatic backups is not always convenient to individual subscribers. Finally, cloud computing often promises cost savings but does not guarantee it, and performing the same work within the organization and dealing with all its attendant problems may be the cheaper option.

Backup Services.   One of the most important types of cloud computing is creating and maintaining backup copies of critical data for organizations. Vendors include Amazon, Backblaze, Carbonite, Drop Box, JungleDisk, and MozyHome (Figure 14-7). Most of these vendors provide low-cost, and even free, backup services for individual customers. In commercial, fee-for-service settings, most backups are synchronized and therefore occur at the same time a computerized system gathers and stores the original data, thereby creating mirror, off-site copies of vital accounting data. Additional, and usually optional, services for home computing applications include encryption, fixed-time backup schedules, expandable storage options, and Mac computer support.

Educational Services.   You probably already use Web search engines such as Google or Bing to answer personal questions of interest. Professional accountants do the same thing, using these same engines to answer asset classification, depreciation, or tax questions. In addition, the Internet provides a host of specialized educational services. One category is "software tutorials." For example, you can find explanations and videos explaining how to perform a wide variety of spreadsheet tasks by searching the term "Excel Tutorials."

FIGURE 14-7 A screen from MozyHome—a cloud backup service provider. Source: www.MozyHome.com

Similar tutorials also explain how to use Microsoft Access, complete specific schedules of IRS tax returns, or create PowerPoint presentations.

As suggested by the opening quote to this chapter, another category of online educational services are complete degree programs—that is, institutions of higher education that offer online courses of study leading to accounting degrees. You can earn an associate's degree, bachelor's degree, and even a master's of science degree in accounting through such distance-learning offerings. A partial listing of them may be found at http://www.elearners.com/online-degrees/accounting.htm.

PRIVACY AND SECURITY ON THE INTERNET

The most important advantage of the Internet and World Wide Web—*accessibility*—is also its greatest weakness—*vulnerability*. This means that someone who *poses* as an authorized user may be able to access any e-mail, Web page, or computer file that an authorized user can access through the Internet. This section of the chapter discusses Internet privacy and security in detail.

Privacy and Identity Theft

E-mailers do not want their messages read by strangers. Businesses need to protect the payroll data they send to service providers electronically. Online shoppers want to know that their privacy is protected. But these needs often conflict with other objectives. For example, managers feel they have the right to view all the e-mail messages of employees who use company computers during working hours, and companies doing business on the Web are sometimes hard-pressed not to use the wealth of data that online shoppers provide them.

Most Web sites accessed by online users collect personal information. What they collect and how they use it are dictated by their privacy policy. Because businesses vary widely in the amount of privacy protection for customers, it is important to read a company's privacy policy carefully. State governments, prompted by concerns over consumer privacy rights, particularly in the financial and health care industries, are introducing a variety of privacy legislation. Groups such as the Electronic Frontier Foundation and the Online Privacy Alliance are also working to protect the privacy of data transmitted over the Internet.

Of course, the concern is that companies might not properly protect the personal and financial information they collect from customers. Identity theft refers to all types of crime in which someone uses another person's personal data in some way that involves fraud or deception (usually for economic benefit).[11] Statistics released by Javelin Strategy and Research indicate that 11.1 million Americans were identity theft victims in 2010 and experienced losses totaling $54 billion.[12] After nearly tripling in reported cases from 2001 to 2004, the Federal Trade Commission found only small increases in ID theft in recent years—still, an important trend when applied to a multibillion-dollar base.

The most common complaint related to identity theft is credit card fraud. The Department of Justice prosecutes ID theft violations under the **Identity Theft and Assumption Deterrence Act (ITADA) of 1998**. The punishment can be a prison term of 15 years, a fine, and forfeiture of any personal property used to commit the crime.

While companies need strong preventive controls to help protect customer information, individuals should also exercise reasonable caution in protecting personal information. Unscrupulous individuals, posing as a company or bank employee, might call or send e-mail messages to solicit personal information. Use your professional skepticism. If you are uncertain about the authenticity of the request, ask the person to send the request in writing on company letterhead. If you question the authenticity of a particular Web site, do more research on the company before purchasing goods or services through it—especially if you must give your credit card number. Figure 14-8 outlines some additional steps that you can take to better protect your personal information—almost all of them accounting related.

Security

Security policies and procedures safeguard an organization's electronic resources and limit their access to authorized users. As noted in Chapter 1, **information security** has been the number one technology in each of the last five years in the AICPA's survey of the "Top 10 Technologies" expected to have a powerful influence over business.

Case-in-Point 14.9 Richard Farina of AirTight Networks was traveling on an American Airlines flight in October 2008, which supported Internet access for its passengers. As an experiment, he used some of his company's intrusion protection software and found that he could view all his fellow passenger's Internet activities because of the airline's poor security.[13]

Of special importance to AISs is **access security**—for example, restricting access to bona fide users. *Access authentication* requires individuals to prove they are who they say they are. The three types of authentication are based on (1) what you *have,* (2) what you *know,* and (3) who you *are.* What you *have* may be a plastic card that provides you physical access to information or a restricted area. Examples are your ATM card, debit

---

[11] http://www.usdoj.gov/criminal/fraud/idtheft.html
[12] Irbey, L. (2011). ID theft statistics: Javelin 2010 Identity Theft Report (February 24). Accessed at: http://www.spendonlife.com/blog/2010-identity-theft-statistics
[13] Buley, T. 2008. Phishing at gate B22. *Forbes* 182(12): 52.

1. Only give personal information such as Social Security numbers and dates of birth to those absolutely needing it.

2. Mail checks, credit applications, and similar materials directly in locked outgoing mail boxes, not in front-yard mail boxes with red, "steal me" flags on their sides.

3. Do not leave purses, wallets, or similar carrying cases unattended—for example, in unlocked gym lockers.

4. When asked by a legitimate business person such as a bank teller for your personal information, write it down for them—do not recite it verbally.

5. Be wary of unsolicited calls from individuals claiming to be bank representatives, credit card issuers, or others, especially if they ask for personal information. A similar rule applies to e-mails from unknown agents.

6. Do not "lend" personal information to others—for example, a password.

7. Do not simply toss sensitive information in trash cans where others can retrieve it. Shred or burn it first.

8. Be wary of relatives in financial difficulties. Sadly, family members who are well known by the victims account for a high percentage of identity theft.

9. Phishing describes a Web site that appears to be from a well-known company but that gathers personal data for illegal purposes. Don't fall for them.

10. Key-logging software is software that captures your keystrokes—usually for illicit purposes. Use security software to guard against it.

FIGURE 14-8   Steps that you can take to safeguard your personal data from identity theft.

card, or employee card that gives you access to certain premises. What you *know* refers to unique information you possess, such as a password or your mother's maiden name. Finally, you can authenticate who you *are* with a unique physical characteristic such as your fingerprint or the pattern of the retina in your eye. As you might guess, using security that forces a user to prove who they are is the highest level of authentication. Some security systems require a combination of authentication techniques—for example, using both your debit card and your password to withdraw cash from an ATM.

Spam and Phishing

A current Internet problem is the increasing amount of **spam**—those annoying, unsolicited e-mail messages that clog your e-mail inbox. However, spam is more than a simple bother—it is distracting, often illegal, and increasingly costly to organizations. AOL and Microsoft, two of the biggest Internet service providers, estimate that they each block over 2 billion spam e-mails per day.

> *Case-in-Point 14.10*   According to a 2010 McAfee report, worldwide spam exceeded 62 trillion e-mails in 2008. The estimated electrical energy required for such e-mails totaled 33 billion kilowatt hours—the amount of energy equivalent to that stored in 2 billion gallons of gasoline. The report estimates that one out of every five e-mails is spam.[14]

Although about 35 percent of spam messages are harmless advertising, a greater percentage contains pornographic solicitations, attempts to steal identities, or fictitious stories asking recipients for money. Clicking on the "unsubscribe button" in such messages usually accomplishes the exact opposite effect because it tells the sender that you are a

[14] http://img.en25.com/Web/McAfee/CarbonFootprint_web_final2.pdf

legitimate user who actually reads such e-mails. Spammers sell lists of such prized, active e-mail accounts to one another, furthering the problem.

Case-in-Point 14.11 The Radicati Group has 21 Exchange e-mail servers, of which five handle nothing but junk mail. The company estimates that it spends almost half a million dollars annually on such server capacity to process spam transmissions.[15]

Although some spam e-mail contains legitimate sales offers, many more are bogus. In such cases, the spammers advertise products at "too-good-to-believe prices," take credit card orders, collect the money, and then quickly fold up shop before consumers realize they've been victimized.

Case-in-Point 14.12 In 2008, New Zealand brothers Shane and Lance Atkinson were in federal court as a result of a suit filed by the Federal Trade Commission (FTC) for "deceptive and fraudulent practices." The FTC claim is that, in less than nine months in 2007, the team used a botnet-driven spam network to defraud victims of more than $7 million.[16]

As we described in Chapter 10, phishing Web sites trick users into providing personal information such as Social Security numbers, debit card PIN numbers, or similar personal information—for example, for "routine security purposes" or even "because we believe your account has been compromised." Phishing activity is growing. For 2008, the Gartner research group estimated that 5 million Americans were victims of phishing—a 40 percent increase over the previous year—and that total losses were more than $3.2 billion. According to a banking group in the United Kingdom, the comparable growth figure is 180 percent. These statistics are especially relevant to accounting information systems because most phishers want personal information that in turn provides access to financial resources. In 2010, for example, the Anti-Phishing Working Group found that over 80 percent of the targeted companies were financial or payment service companies.

Social Networking

Social networking options like Twitter, Facebook, MySpace, and YouTube mostly began for similar reasons—to create Internet options that allow individuals to post, store, and view their own messages, photos, and videos. Today, however, such sites also have important commercial applications and privacy implications. For example, when businesses launch a new product or service, they now often scan such sites in search of honest reactions to the new offerings.

Another important commercial application of social networking is for individuals to develop an online presence. This is important for both individuals who might be seeking employment and for businesses that might be seeking qualified applicants. For those professionals who have lost their jobs in the recent recession, employment counselors consider an online identity a must-have.

Social networks also pose interesting privacy concerns. For example, employers often check postings on social networking sites to search for "red-flags"—for example, substance abuse, large amounts of debt, criminal activity, or membership in fanatical groups—which they use to help them evaluate employees or disqualify job applicants. Like it or not, bosses regularly screen the postings of their subordinates, and more than one person has lost

---

[15] http://www.radicati.com/?p=3237
[16] http://www.scmagazineus.com/SC-World-Congress-Anatomy-of-a-spam-business/article/122708/

his job by posting candid or offensive materials where the boss could see it. This is more common than you might think—a Google search by one of the authors on the terms "social networking" and "lost jobs" yielded 20 million hits! Even if you allow for duplications, that's a big incentive to be cautious about what you post!

> ***Case-in-Point 14.13*** One new employee forgot that she had accepted her boss's invitation to add him as a friend on Facebook. She later posted a note saying that she hated her job and added several additional, unflattering comments about him. He fired her on the spot.[17]

Firewalls, Intrusion Detection Systems, Value-Added Networks, and Proxy Servers

To gain access to a company's files, a computer hacker must first obtain access to that company's computers. The firewalls, intrusion detection systems, and proxy servers discussed here protect against unwarranted intrusions from external parties.

Firewalls. A firewall (Figure 14-9a) guards against unauthorized access to sensitive file information from external Internet users. On networked systems, firewalls are often stand-alone devices with built-in, protective software (Figure 14-9b). On mainframe or host systems, firewalls are usually software.

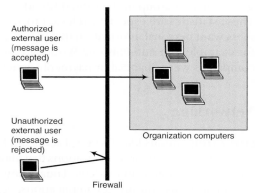

(a) Firewalls accept messages from bona fide users but reject messages from unauthorized users.

(b) This hardware-based firewall from Sonicwall can support an unlimited number of users and 8 gigabytes of traffic per second.

FIGURE 14-9 A firewall acts as a barrier between unauthorized external users and organizational (internal) computers and files.

---

[17] http://open.salon.com/blog/trudge164/2009/08/18/social_networking_101_how_to_lose_your_job_on_facebook

The two primary methods of firewall protection are *by inclusion* or *by exclusion*. When firewalls protect internal systems by inclusion, the software examines packets of incoming messages and limits entry to authorized ("included") users. To do this, the software maintains an **access control list (ACL)** of bona fide IP addresses that network administrators create for this purpose. If the software does not recognize the IP address of an external user, it refuses that user access to the files he or she requested. When firewalls protect internal systems by exclusion, the software compares the incoming packet IP address to a list of known threat addresses, rejecting messages from these sources but accepting all others.

Firewalls are useful Internet security controls but (like most security features) are not foolproof. One problem is that they cannot protect against denial-of-service (DOS) attacks, which overwhelm system resources with a volume of service requests. Another problem is **spoofing** (i.e., masquerading as an authorized user with a recognizable IP address). A similar, but less obvious, problem is the ability of a determined hacker to alter the contents of the access control list itself—a security breach that is especially difficult to overcome. A final problem is that most firewalls can only protect against external attacks, not internal (authorized) users bent on mischief.

Intrusion Detection Systems. Firewalls simply reject unauthorized users from access, whereas **intrusion detection systems (IDSs)** create records of such events. *Passive IDSs* create logs of potential intrusions and alert network administrators to them either via console messages, alarms, or beepers. *Reactive IDSs* have the ability to detect potential intrusions dynamically (e.g., by examining traffic flows), log off potentially malicious users, and even reprogram a firewall to block further messages from the suspected source.

Perhaps the most important advantage of an IDS is its ability to both prevent unauthorized accesses to sensitive information and to alert system administrators to potential violations. This may also increase the perceived risk of discovery, dissuading would-be hackers. IDSs may also be able to detect preambles to attacks, forestalling their effectiveness. Finally, an IDS is an important tool for documenting an attack, thereby generating invaluable information to both network administrators and investigators.

Value-Added Networks. Message-routing is important to accountants because the security of a data transmission partially rests on the security of all the intermediate computers along a given communications pathway. Thus, the greater the distance between the sending station and the destination computer, the more intermediary routing computers there are and the more vulnerable a message becomes to interception and abuse. This is one reason why businesses often prefer to create their own (proprietary) networks to transmit data electronically.

Value-added networks (VANs) are private, point-to-point communication channels that large organizations create for themselves—usually for security reasons (Figure 14-10). When it first implements a VAN, the business assigns each user a unique account code that simultaneously identifies the external entity and authenticates the organization's subsequent electronic transactions.

There are at least three ways to create secure networks. One way is to start with a blank slate and create everything from scratch—an approach first used by the military and later by Walmart. A second way is to lease secure, dedicated transmission lines from conventional long-distance carriers such as AT&T—the approach used by IGT's Megabucks system (see Chapter 2).

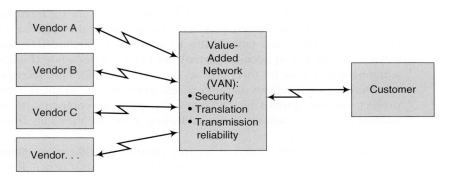

FIGURE 14-10 A VAN-based EDI system.

A third alternative is to create a virtual private network (VPN) on the Internet (see Chapter 10). As the name suggests, a VPN mimics a VAN in many of its security features but enjoys the benefit of transmitting messages cheaply over existing Internet connections. A VPN creates secure data transmissions by (1) using "tunneling" security protocols embedded in the message frames sent to, and received by, the organization, (2) encrypting all transmitted data, and (3) authenticating the remote computer, and perhaps, also the individual sender as well, before permitting further data transmissions. Most AIS VANs use this approach.

Proxy Servers. Given the large amount of information now available on the Web, some organizations seek to limit the number of sites that employees can access—for example, to ensure that employees do not use Web-access privileges for frivolous or counterproductive purposes. A **proxy server** is a network server and related software that creates a transparent gateway to and from the Internet and controls Web access. In a typical application, users log onto their familiar file server as before. But when they attempt to access a Web page, the initial network server contacts the proxy server to perform the requested task.

One advantage of using a proxy server is the ability to funnel all incoming and outgoing Internet requests through a single server. This can make Web access more efficient because the proxy server is specifically designed to handle requests for Internet information. A second advantage is the proxy server's ability to examine all incoming requests for information and test them for authenticity (i.e., the ability to act as a firewall). A third advantage is that a proxy server can limit employee Internet access to approved Web sites (i.e., to only those IP addresses contained in an access control list). This enables an organization to deny employees access to gambling, pornographic, or game-playing Web sites that are unlikely to have any productive benefits.

A fourth advantage is the ability to limit the information that is stored on the proxy server to information that the company can afford to lose. If this server fails or is compromised by hackers, the organization is only marginally inconvenienced because its main servers remain functional. To recover, the company can simply restart the system and reinitialize the server with backup data.

Netscape Communications estimates that between 30 and 60 percent of Internet requests are redundant. A final advantage of proxy servers is the ability to store ("cache") frequently accessed Web pages on its hard drive—for example, the Web pages of preferred vendors. This enables the server to respond quickly to user requests for information because the Web page data are available locally. This feature also enables managers to obtain some idea of what information employees need most and perhaps take steps to provide it internally (rather than through Web sources).

Data Encryption

To safeguard transmitted data, businesses often use data encryption techniques that transform original, plaintext messages into unintelligible cyphertext ones. The receiving station then decodes the encrypted messages back into plaintext for use. There are many encryption techniques and standards. The simple method shown in Figure 14-11 uses a *cyclic substitution* of the alphabet with a displacement value of "5" to transform the letters of a plaintext message into alternate letters of the alphabet. To decode the message, the recipient's computer performs the encryption process in reverse, decrypting the coded message back into readable text. To make things more secure, the sender can use a different displacement value for each coded message.

The method that computers use to transform plaintext into cyphertext is called the **encryption key**. This is typically a mathematical function that depends on a large prime number. The **data encryption standard (DES)** system used by the U.S. government to encode documents employs such a system. DES uses a number with 56 binary digits to encode information, a value equal to approximately 72 quadrillion. Thus, to crack the code, a hacker must guess which of 72 quadrillion values was used to encrypt the message.

The data encryption method illustrated in Figure 14-11 uses a single cryptographic key that is shared by the two communicating parties and is called **secret key cryptography**. This system derives its name from the fact that its users must keep the key secret and not share the key with other parties. The most common encryption methods today use **public key encryption**, a technique that requires each party to use a pair of public/private encryption keys. Two examples are *Secure Socket Layer (SSL)* and *Secure Hypertext Transport Protocol (S-HTTP)*.

To employ public key encryption, the sending party uses a public key to encode the message and the receiving party uses a second, private key to decode it. A major advantage of public key encryption is that the same public key cannot both encode and decode a message. Data transmissions using public key encryption are likely to be secure because the transmitted message itself is scrambled and because neither party knows the other's key. This is the main reason why most Web applications use public key encryption systems.

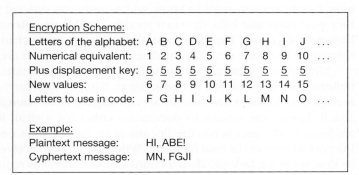

```
Encryption Scheme:
Letters of the alphabet:   A   B   C   D   E    F    G    H    I    J   ...
Numerical equivalent:      1   2   3   4   5    6    7    8    9   10   ...
Plus displacement key:     5   5   5   5   5    5    5    5    5    5
New values:                6   7   8   9  10   11   12   13   14   15
Letters to use in code:    F   G   H   I   J    K    L    M    N    O   ...


Example:
Plaintext message:        HI, ABE!
Cyphertext message:       MN, FGJI
```

FIGURE 14-11   A simple data encryption method.

Digital Signatures and Digital Time Stamping

Many businesses want proof that the accounting documents they transmit or receive over the Internet are authentic. Examples include purchase orders, bids for contracts, and acceptance letters. To authenticate such documents, a company can transmit a complete document in plaintext and then also include a portion of that same message or some other standard text in an encrypted format—that is, a company can include a **digital signature**.

In 1994, the National Institute of Standards and Technology adopted Federal Information Processing Standard 186—the **digital signature standard (DSS)**. The presence of a digital signature authenticates a document. The reasoning is straightforward: if a company's public key decodes a message, then the authentic sender must have created the message. Thus, some experts consider digital signatures even more secure than written signatures (which can be forged). Further, if the sender includes a complete message in both plaintext and cyphertext, the encrypted message provides assurance that no one has altered the readable copy. If someone has altered the plaintext, the two copies will not match.

Another authentication technique is a **digital certificate**—an authenticating document issued by an independent third party called a **certificate authority** (e.g., Thawte or VeriSign). The certificates themselves are signed documents with sender names and public key information. Certificates are generally encoded, possibly in a certificate standard such as the X.509 certificate format. Customers can also use digital certificates to assure themselves that a Web site is real.

Case-in-Point 14.14 In the future, each U.S. citizen may have a taxpayer's digital certificate within a smart card. Citizens could use the smart card for all their transactions with the federal government. The government program responsible for developing this card is called Access Certificates for Electronics Services project, or ACES. While the intent of ACES is to ensure secure communications, privacy advocates are afraid that maybe the cards are *too* smart because they contain *all* your personal information in one place. ACES cards are only available to a federal or authorized agency but those concerned with privacy worry that the existence of the card will prove tempting for unintended uses.

Many important business documents are time sensitive. Examples include bidding documents that must be submitted by a deadline, deposit slips that must be presented to banks before the close of business, buy orders for stock purchases that depend on the date and time of issue, and legal documents that must be filed in a timely fashion. Then, too, most businesses also want to know when customers ordered particular purchases, when they paid particular bills, or when specific employees entered or modified data items in important databases. Finally, a good way to protect intellectual property such as computer software is to clearly establish the date and time it was first created or distributed.

What these items have in common is the need for a time stamp that unambiguously indicates the date and time of transmission, filing, or data entry. PGP Digital Time Stamping Service and Verisign are two of several **digital time-stamping services (DTSSs)** that attach digital time stamps to documents either for a small fee or for free. In a typical application, the user sends the document to the service's e-mail address along with the Internet address of the final recipient. When the service receives the document, it performs its time-stamping task and then forwards the document as required.

Digital time stamping performs the same task electronically that official seals and other time stamps perform manually: authenticate the date, time, and perhaps place of a business transaction. This can be important over the Internet. Although most documents are transmitted almost instantaneously, time delays can occur when file servers temporarily falter or power failures disrupt wide area networks. DTSSs enable businesses to overcome these problems.

AIS AT WORK
The Benefits of Online Accounting Outsourcing[18]

The advantages of outsourcing accounting functions such as payroll or tax preparation are well known, but outsourcing additional accounting tasks to online providers is a different matter. Can a cloud provider, perhaps located offshore, perform general ledger or deprecation computations as well? A growing number of businesses say "yes!"

The most common reason why organizations outsource a given business process is "to reduce costs," and this applies to accounting applications as well. Additional benefits include faster turnaround, improved quality, enhanced access to expertise, improved ability to handle peak processing volumes, and reduced capital expenditures (e.g., realized savings in computer hardware and software). Experts note that outsourcing also enables clients to reduce in-house labor costs, pay only for the services they need, and instead focus on their core businesses.

Perhaps the most commonly cited objection to outsourcing is a loss of control. In a recent survey of more than 800 businesses by Accenture, however, more than 85 percent of the respondents said that outsourcing actually gave them more control—especially in the ability to plan. In addition, more than 55 percent thought that accounting outsourcing enabled them to implement strategic changes faster and at more controlled rates. But the biggest benefit of outsourcing may be the increased business for those accounting companies providing these services—yet one more opportunity made possible by the Internet.

SUMMARY

✓ The Internet is a collection of local, wide area, and international networks that accountants can use for communication, research, and business purposes. Most accountants also use the World Wide Web—the multimedia portion of the Internet—for similar purposes.

✓ Intranets are private networks that businesses create for internal purposes such as distributing e-mail. Extranets are similar to intranets, except that they allow external parties to access internal network files and databases.

✓ Groupware is software that supports e-mail on business networks, plus allows users to share computer files, schedule appointments, video conference, and develop custom applications.

✓ To exchange financial information on the Internet, businesses can use XBRL—a standardized form of XML that provides a common format for financial data and allows searches of the data and extraction for comparison purposes. The XBRL International Consortium develops XBRL standards.

✓ Electronic business includes retail sales on the Internet, electronic data interchange (EDI), and business-to-business (B2B) applications. In addition to credit and debit cards, consumers use e-payment and e-wallet systems to pay for Internet purchases.

---

[18] http://www.articlesbase.com/outsourcing-articles/why-outsourcing-accounting-is-a-good-idea-for-you-591876.html

✓ For security reasons, some businesses prefer to use expensive, but private, value-added networks (VANs) rather than the Internet to support e-commerce applications.

✓ Cloud computing means providing data processing, data storage, backup, and even educational services on the Internet. Many of these services are especially important to AISs.

✓ Internet privacy and security concerns include hacking, identity theft, spam, and phishing, all of which impact AISs. These concerns prompt many businesses to use firewalls, intrusion detection systems, proxy servers, data encryption techniques, digital signatures, and digital time stamping to achieve control objectives.

✓ Authentication requires users to prove they are who they say they are. Privacy concerns also include the need to protect users' private information and the growing threat of identity theft.

KEY TERMS YOU SHOULD KNOW

access control list (ACL)

access security

blogs

business-to-business (B2B) e-commerce

certificate authority

click fraud

data encryption standard (DES)

digital certificate

digital signature

digital signature standard (DSS)

digital time stamping service (DTSS)

domain address

electronic conferencing

electronic data interchange (EDI)

electronic payments (e-payments)

encryption key

e-wallet

extensible markup language (XML)

extranets

groupware

hypertext markup language (HTML)

hypertext transfer protocol (HTTP)

Identity Theft and Assumption Deterrence Act
  (ITADA) of 1998

information security

instant messaging software

interactive data and electronic applications
  (IDEA)

Internet

intranets

intrusion detection system (IDS)

knowledge management

platform as a service (PaaS)

proxy server

public key encryption

secret key cryptography

social networking

spam

spoofing

Transmission Control Protocol/Internet
  Protocol (TCP/IP)

uniform resource locator (URL)

value-added networks (VANs)

Web browser

XBRL instance documents

XBRL International Consortium

DISCUSSION QUESTIONS

14-1. What are intranets? What are extranets? Why are intranets and extranets important to accountants?

14-2. What are blogs? How are they used? Who is using them?

14-3. What is hypertext markup language? How does it differ from XML and XBRL? (Note: for a more comprehensive description of the differences, you may want to search the Internet.)

14-4. How does XBRL compare to the IDEA database?

14-5. Describe some important uses of e-commerce and explain why it is important to accountants.

14-6. What are electronic payments? How are they different from credit card payments?

14-7. What is electronic data interchange? Why do companies use EDI?

14-8. Most retail sales Web sites require customers to use their credit cards to make purchases online. How comfortable are you in providing your credit card number in such applications? Why do you feel this way?

14-9. What is click fraud? Who benefits and who loses when click fraud occurs?

14-10. What is spamming? How is spam related to accounting information systems? Should all spamming be illegal? Why or why not?

14-11. What are Internet firewalls and proxy servers? How are they created? How do businesses use them for Internet security?

14-12. What is data encryption? What techniques are used for data encryption?

14-13. Describe and contrast the three types of authentications. Can you think of a business situation where someone would need to use a combination of all three levels to gain access to information?

14-14. What are digital signatures? Why do businesses use them? How can businesses use a digital certificate for Internet security?

14-15. Analysts claim that businesses can increase sales on the Internet, but not profits. What evidence does this chapter provide to support or refute this claim? Discuss.

PROBLEMS

14-16. The Internet uses many acronyms. Within the context of the present chapter, what words were used to form each of the following?

a. blog	**f.** IDS	**k.** VANs
b. e-commerce	**g.** IP address	**l.** VPN
c. EDI	**h.** SaaS	**m.** WWW
d. e-mail	**i.** TCP/IP	**n.** XBRL
e. HTTP	**j.** URL	**o.** XML

14-17. In Discussion Question 14-1 above, you discussed intranets and extranets, and identified the importance of each to accountants. Now, assume that you are a partner in a medium-size, local CPA firm. Your firm has four partners, ten staff accountants, one research assistant, and an administrative assistant. Your firm is considered a technology leader in the local area, and this is considered a competitive advantage for your firm. At the weekly staff meeting next Friday, you want to discuss the topic of developing an intranet for the firm. To be sure everyone is prepared to discuss this topic, you want to develop a "talking paper," which is a one-page summary of salient points that you want to be sure you cover in your presentation to everyone. What would you include in this one-page discussion aid?

14-18. Create an HTML document of your own, using the example in Figure 14-1 to guide you. Put the name of this assignment in the <h1> tag for the heading. Put your name in bold. Include at least one hyperlink to a favorite Web page using the anchor <a> tag. Finally, include an ordered list in your Web page with at least three items—for example, a list of your favorite books, favorite restaurants, or the courses you're taking this semester. You will find it easiest to work in Notepad for this problem, but you can also use a word processor—as long as you save your document as "text." Also, be sure to add the extension "html" to the end of your file name. View your completed document in your Web browser—for example, by selecting File/Open in Microsoft Internet Explorer—and screen capture your work.

14-19. At the time this book was written, the U.S. Securities and Exchange Commission still supported Edgar—a depository of corporate accounting filings. Log onto Edgar at http://www.sec.gov/edgar.shtml, click on "Search for Company Filings," click on "Companies and Other Filers," and finally, select two companies in the same industry (either your instructor's choice or your choice) so that you can compare various financial data. Note that you can select either "text" or "html" formats. Compare these formats to Figure 14-1. Are they similar? Looking at either image, can you download the financial information into a spreadsheet? Can you easily do financial comparisons such as ratio analysis? What do you have to do if you want to make financial comparisons?

14-20. Visit the XBRL home page at http://www.XBRL.org, and read the section entitled "What is XBRL." Then, do each of the following:

a. Select the option "Latest News" from the home page, which lists several articles that describe recent developments. Choose one of these and write a one-page summary of your findings.

b. Select "Benefits Across Business" at http://www.xbrl.org/BenefitsAcrossBusiness/. This site contains a set of articles describing the various benefits of XBRL to different types of businesses. Select one article from this list, and write a one-page summary of it.

14-21. Write a one-page paper on each of the following topics as they relate to XBRL:

a. What is the history of XBRL? What professional accounting organization helped in the early stages of this concept?

b. What is an XBRL specification, and what is the latest version? When was it released? By whom?

c. How could XBRL help a company engage in "continuous reporting"? Find a Web site or an e-journal (an article) that discusses XBRL and continuous reporting. What are the main points of the article?

d. Find at least two other companies (other than Microsoft) that are publishing their financial statements on the Internet using XBRL. What business are they in (what industry)?

14-22. Examine the data encryption technique illustrated in Figure 14-11. Use a displacement value of "8" to encrypt the following message. Hint: This task becomes easy if you use an Excel spreadsheet and VLookUp formulas that reference a table of letters and their numeric equivalencies.

"Those who ignore history are forced to repeat it."

14-23. The messages below were encrypted using the technique illustrated in Figure 14-11 (using displacement keys other than 5). Using trial and error, decode them. Hint: This task becomes easy if you use an Excel spreadsheet and VLookUp formulas that reference a table of letters and their numeric equivalencies.

Message 1: OZ OY TUZ CNGZ CK JUTZ QTUC ZNGZ NAXZY AY
OZ OY CNGZ CK JU QTUC ZNGZ PAYZ GOTZ YU

Message 2: QBZAPJL KLSHFLK PZ QBZAPJL KLUPLK

Message 3: FAA YMZK OAAWE EBAUX FTQ NDAFT

14-24. A number of accounting journals now post back issues, or even publish their entire journals, online. Access the *Journal of Accountancy* Web site at http://www.aicpa.org (or another Web site selected by your instructor). Select an article that pertains to a topic in this chapter, and write a one-page report on it. Be careful to correctly cite any information that you use from this article!

14-25. The following stated policies pertain to the e-commerce Web site for Small Computers, Inc., a personal and handheld computer manufacturer and seller.

Privacy statement

- We will only use information collected on this Web site for legitimate business purposes. We do not give away or rent any information to third parties.

- We will only contact you for legitimate business purposes, possibly from time to time, as needed. Please be 100 percent assured that we hold all transactions between you and our company in the strictest confidence.

Disclosure of business practices, shipping, and billing

- We will ship all items at the earliest possible date.
- We will not require you to accept items that you did not order.
- We will accept any returns from you of damaged or defective merchandise.
- In the event that we should accidentally bill you more than once for the same item, we will immediately issue you a refund.

Evaluate these stated policies in terms of how well they promote customer trust and confidence in Small Computers, Inc.'s electronic business operations.

CASE STUDIES

Hammaker Manufacturing IV (XBRL-Enabled Software)

Recall, from Chapter 8, the Hammaker Manufacturing Company (HMC) is located in Burke, Virginia, and manufactures specialty parts for Corvettes. The company implemented a new AIS with the help of a consulting firm. At the time, Hammaker was especially interested in collecting data about inventories. Then, HMC decided to accept the consulting firm's recommendation to reengineer some processes in the production departments, rather than outsource these processes. Generally speaking, the BPR project is considered a success, based on the results that have been achieved—increased profits and more satisfied customers. To Denise's credit, she kept the employees informed throughout the study phase so that they understood the need for change. As a result of employee involvement, many useful changes were made and no employees were terminated.

Now, with increased profits and a very optimistic view of future growth, Hammaker meets with Denise and Lloyd to discuss the advantages and disadvantages of a new, more powerful AIS. Lloyd's area of expertise is implementing ERPs, and he is eager to inform HMC about the advantages of selecting an XBRL-enabled software solution for the firm.

Requirements

1. What does it mean when software is ''XBRL-enabled''?
2. Identify at least five advantages that Lloyd might discuss with Dick and Denise regarding an XBRL-enabled software solution. Identify any disadvantages that might also be relevant for HMC.
3. Assume that you are Lloyd's research assistant. Draft a memo for Lloyd to give to HMC that explains how XBRL works. Remember to keep in mind your audience. This should be an executive-level piece of correspondence.

4. Now, as the research assistant, develop a PowerPoint presentation for Lloyd to give to Dick and Denise explaining exactly what sorts of benefits they could realize with an XBRL-enabled software solution. Be creative, and use diagrams and examples where appropriate.

DeGraaf Office Supplies (Business Web Sites and Security)

DeGraaf Office Supplies is a national retailer of office supplies, equipment, and furnishings. The company opened its first store in 1932, in Columbus, Ohio. Currently, DeGraaf has 300 stores nationwide. Owner-managers purchase and run franchised stores. Kim DeGraaf, the founder's daughter, currently is president and CEO of the corporation.

Sales revenues grew steadily during the past decade, but 2011 sales were quite disappointing, down 8 percent from 2010. The company's stock price has also taken a big hit during the past few months. Kim resisted developing an Internet presence for the company, and it appears now that this was a mistake. Online sales of office supplies are growing rapidly, particularly in the business-to-business sector as business organizations are finding it faster and more efficient to enter their office supply orders electronically. The following is a conversation between Kim and Peter Brewer, vice president of marketing.

Peter: "Kim, I warned you that we were going to see sales decline if we didn't hurry up and get on the Internet. The established brick-and-mortar businesses in many industries are suffering."

Kim: "You were right, Peter. I think I've been overly concerned about security and privacy issues. I also didn't really believe that online sales in our industry would take off the way they have. I hope we're not too late, because I want to move ahead immediately in developing a Web site. I know other companies have a jump start but hopefully our brand name recognition and reputation for quality will help us. I have contracted with a consulting firm to start the Web site development and am going to give a press release this afternoon about our plans. Fortunately, our current enterprise software has e-commerce features, and the consultants tell me that our Internet site should be ready for business in about six months. I need you to have your staff prepare an analysis of our competitor Web sites. I would also like as much information as possible related to providing retail and business customers with security and privacy over online transactions with us."

Peter: "This is great news! I will get my staff busy at once, providing you and the consulting team with the information they need. There will be a lot of decisions to make. I've studied all the office supply Web sites and they are organized in a variety of ways. For instance, some sites provide customers with the option to select a type of product such as ballpoint pens and then show the vendor options in that category, while other sites are organized around the vendors. This type of site allows customers to select a vendor name, such as PaperMate, and then lists all the product offerings from that vendor. Hopefully, the consultants have a lot of experience with business Web sites and they can help us with many of these issues."

Requirements

1. Visit the Web sites of two office supply stores on the Internet. Develop a set of four to five criteria for evaluating their Web site.

2. Evaluate DeGraaf's chances for catching up to competitors in the online marketplace.

3. Discuss the privacy and security concerns for companies doing business electronically. Make recommendations to DeGraaf Office Supplies for addressing these concerns.

Barra Concrete (XOR Encryption)

Barra Concrete specializes in creating driveways and curbs for the residential market. Its accounting software uses exclusive OR (XOR) operations to convert the individual bits of a plaintext message into cyphertext. The rules are as follows:

	Exclusive OR rules			
	Rule 1	Rule 2	Rule 3	Rule 4
Plaintext bit	0	0	1	1
Bit in key	0	1	0	1
Cypertext result	0	1	1	0

In other words, exactly one of the bits must be a "1" and the other a "0" for the result of an XOR operation to be a "1." To illustrate, suppose that the bits representing a single plaintext character were 1010 0101 and the secret key used just the four bits 1110. Here are the results of the XOR operation, using this key:

Plaintext bits	1010	0101
Key (repeated)	1110	1110
Cypher text result	0100	1011

The encrypted bits are the cypher text, or 0100 1011, as shown. These (encrypted) bits are what the software would transmit to the final recipient.

Requirements

1. Decrypting the cipher text created by an XOR operation is easy—just use the same XOR operation on the encrypted bits! Demonstrate this for the example above.

2. Suppose the secret key were longer—the eight bits 1100 0011. Using this key and an XOR, what is the cipher text for the plaintext message "Go, team" if the bit configuration for these letters is as shown below? (Hint: the final answer consists of seven sets of data, each containing eight bits.)

Message	G	O	,	T	E	A	M
Binary	0100 0111	0100 1111	0010 1100	0101 0100	0100 0101	0100 0001	0100 1101

Chapter 15

Accounting and Enterprise Software

INTRODUCTION

Because of the repetitive nature of many tasks in accounting, it is not surprising that these tasks have been automated. With advances in hardware and software technology, accounting software has become increasingly sophisticated and customized for specific industry needs. This chapter describes various types of accounting and enterprise software. Initially, accounting software packages were simple bookkeeping systems. Today, accounting and enterprise-wide software are incredibly powerful and complex, and they are capable of collecting a wide variety of data to support business decisions for large, multinational firms. Further, specialized accounting software packages can accommodate the specific needs of various industries that have unique business processes (such as those described in Chapter 8).

For many large firms, accounting software has evolved to become a module within integrated enterprise software called enterprise resource planning (ERP) systems. These ERP systems encompass the needs of an entire organization and have large databases at their core. In ERP systems, the accounting functions interface with manufacturing, sales and distribution, human resources applications, and other systems. The largest enterprises today, realizing the benefits of integrating their information systems, extend their ERP systems up and down their supply chains. This chapter discusses various aspects of integrated accounting software and enterprise-wide systems in some detail, including their functionality, architecture, effects on business processes, costs, and benefits. Because the effects of enterprise-wide software packages are so important to accountants, we cover this software in more depth.

Knowing when to upgrade to a new accounting information system can be a challenge. In some cases, changes in an organization's external environment, such as increased competition, may force an upgrade. In other cases, management must identify and assess current business processes to determine whether new accounting systems are needed to improve processes. As we point out with the opening quote for this chapter, selecting the right software for an organization is both critical and challenging. The last section of the chapter discusses the topic of software selection.

INTEGRATED ACCOUNTING SOFTWARE

Integrated accounting software can process all types of accounting transactions. These include transactions affecting accounts in both general and special journals, such as sales and purchases. Integrated accounting software programs organize transaction processing in modules and provide links among these modules. The general ledger module, which includes the chart of accounts, is the foundation for the system. Other modules typically

417

- Audit trails
- Budgeting capability
- Check and invoice printing
- E-commerce features
- Financial analysis tools
- Graphic reports
- Inventory management
- Recurring journal entries
- Ability to handle multiple users
- Ability to handle multiple companies
- Customizable financial reporting
- Cash-based and accrual-based accounting options
- Scalability (accommodates business growth)
- Variance analysis (budget to actual)

FIGURE 15-1   A sample of features commonly found in integrated accounting software programs.

found in integrated accounting software programs include accounts receivable, accounts payable, inventory, and payroll. These modules correspond to the business processes we discussed in Chapters 7 and 8.

Journal entries recorded in accounting software modules update the general ledger module on a periodic or real-time basis. Depending on an accounting program's level of sophistication, it may include additional modules such as job costing, purchasing, billing, invoicing, and fixed assets. Figure 15-1 lists several features commonly found in integrated accounting software programs.

Small Business Accounting Software

At the low end, commercial accounting software programs are available at very low costs. Microsoft even offers a very basic package for free. Two popular examples of inexpensive small business accounting software are Quickbooks by Intuit and Peachtree products. Even the most basic accounting software typically includes a chart of accounts and modules for the general ledger, accounts receivable, and accounts payable. They produce many kinds of accounting reports, including basic financial statements and budget reports as well as bar graphs and pie charts. Even low-end accounting software generally has several sample charts of accounts for different types of organizations. Users can select one of these charts of accounts and then customize the selection to match their organizations' account structures.

Because there are so many low-end accounting software packages readily available to small businesses, you might think that all small businesses already have one. However, even though the software itself is inexpensive, the challenge is for the owner and employees to learn how to use the software and get the greatest value from their product. For example, how many features are there in Microsoft Word that you don't use—or don't even know are available? Similarly, to gain the most benefit from any accounting software, a business owner should consider discussing options with the firm's CPA firm or a local software consultant who can help select the software, train employees, help the firm identify useful reports for decision making, or possibly even help with rescue and recovery needs, should a disaster occur.

A trend in low-end and midlevel accounting software has been the consolidation of vendors and more extensive product lines from the remaining ones. For example, Intuit sells over 20 different versions of its accounting software, and you can select from 10 different Peachtree offerings. The variety of features offered in these software packages also continues to grow. One feature that even low-end packages incorporate today is

Internet connectivity, which permits small businesses to create Web sites and engage in e-commerce. For example, Peachtree Accounting has a special link that allows companies to take orders and receive payments over the Internet. Another software feature is the ability to export accounting data in XBRL format.

Small business accounting software may be adequate for businesses with less than $5 million in revenue and few employees. One factor to consider in choosing a package is the number of transactions that the system can process during a given period of time (for example, each month). For example, if a company processes only a few accounts receivable transactions daily, an inexpensive package should handle this processing satisfactorily. It is also very useful if a small business accounting package is **scalable**, meaning that the software can grow as the business grows (i.e., the organization can add modules to the software or upgrade to more powerful software without reinstalling or reconfiguring data). For example, the Quickbooks product line includes a low-end package with very basic financial accounting features for about $100. However, a company can upgrade to an enterprise-wide software package that sells for several thousand dollars when it grows.

Scalability is also important because the cost of the software package itself is small compared to the costs of implementing and using the package. Each time a company changes software, for example, employees may need to reenter historical and current transaction data; create new codes for customers, employees, or products; and redefine its chart of accounts. Understandably, cost savings are significant when the software vendor offers packages that allow users to avoid these tasks.

Midrange and Large-Scale Accounting Software

When transaction processing needs to grow in volume and complexity, a midrange (see Figure 15-2) or large-scale software package may be necessary. Some examples are Microsoft Dynamics GP, SAP Business One, Epicor, Sage software's MAS 90 and MAS200, Everest, Made2Manage, and Accpac. These software packages range in cost from $2,000 to well over $300,000 and offer many features needed by midsize and larger companies. One capability required by international companies, for example, is the ability to process transactions in multiple currencies. Some software packages can convert transactions from one currency to another and can write checks in foreign currencies. Another example is the ability to split commissions among multiple salespersons.

Case-in-Point 15.1 Midrange and large-scale accounting software also may handle more than just accounting functions. Sage software's Accpac product line includes modules for financial accounting, purchasing, sales and receivables, inventory management, project management, and payroll. The software can integrate with other solutions, extending its usefulness for customer relationship management (CRM), business intelligence, e-commerce, human resource management, point-of-sale, management of fixed assets, and supply chain (warehouse) management. Accpac's Extended Enterprise Suite now includes dashboards, a fixed asset management module, and other desirable features.[1]

In addition to offering a variety of modules and interfaces, midlevel and large-scale software vendors allow customers to choose from an array of deployment options. For example, the software can be made available on a desktop computer or through a Web browser or hosted by a cloud service provider—a **hosted solution**. Both Peachtree and Accpac provide such services. Three advantages of a hosted solution are (1) processing is

---

[1] http://www.sageaccpac.com

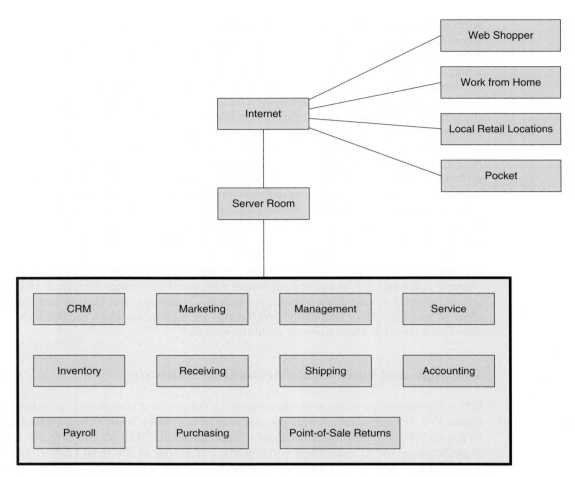

FIGURE 15-2 An example of midrange accounting software's integration of business processes.

easily scalable; (2) the host performs software maintenance, backup, and upgrades; and (3) the programs and data are accessible anywhere, anytime.

Specialized Accounting Information Systems

There are literally thousands of vendors that sell accounting software designed to fit a particular industry or even a small niche within an industry. Some examples are accounting software for dental offices, pet retailers, and grammar schools. In addition, many accounting software developers offer add-on modules that firms can use to process special information. These extra modules might be job-cost modules used by construction companies or point-of-sale features tailored to retailers. For instance, the hotel industry needs software that includes many specialized functions. Execu/Suite by Execu/Tech integrates accounting, property management functions, reservations systems, housekeeping management, sales and marketing, online booking, event management, dining reservations, and in-room movie accounting.

Case-in-Point 15.2 Not-for-profit accounting software allows users to track records by individual donations, which is sometimes required by the agency or its contributors. The software also allows users to track projects and grants. Cougar Mountain Fund Suite is an example of this type of software. This package can handle transfers among funds, deal with multiple grants with varying year-ends, and track restricted, temporarily restricted, and unrestricted contributions and assets in separate categories.[2]

Some integrated accounting packages contain programs written by independent developers to interface with their packages and provide features needed by customers in specialized industries. Other software vendors include the source code with their programs so that businesses can customize the software for themselves. Customizing software is a good business for value-added resellers or consultants who have programming skills and an understanding of the specific needs of specialized businesses.

ENTERPRISE-WIDE INFORMATION SYSTEMS

An organization's information systems must do more than process financial data. The capabilities of accounting software programs to process enterprise-wide data expand with the price and complexity of the software. Examples of software in this category, known as enterprise resource planning (ERP) systems, **enterprise software**, and **business application suites** include Microsoft Dynamics AX, SAP All-in-One, Sage MAS 500, NetSuite Enterprise Solution, Infor Enterprise Solutions, Epicor, and Oracle. Two important features of this type of technology are integration and a central database. Typically, the software integrates the financial or accounting subsystem with CRM, business services, human resources (HR), and supply chain management (SCM)—see Figure 15-3.

FIGURE 15-3   ERP system integration.

[2] http://www.cougarmtn.com

Because SAP's high-end products can cost hundreds of millions of dollars to implement, they are mostly used by the world's largest business organizations. In addition, large-scale ERP software typically forces companies to reengineer or redesign their business processes for maximum efficiency. Multinational corporations such as Eastman Kodak Company, Owens-Corning Fiberglass Corporation, and Procter and Gamble have spent millions of dollars implementing SAP for its potential cost savings. Cost savings (discussed in detail later in the chapter) often come from streamlining, speeding, or consolidating processes.

Case-in-Point 15.3 A 2010 study indicates that the U.S. Department of Agriculture saved $18 million per year by implementing SAP to consolidate its financial management, budget, and purchasing processes.[3]

Enterprise System Functionality

Basic ERP Functions. Today's ERP systems provide integration among many of an organization's major business processes—for example, order processing and fulfillment, manufacturing, purchasing, and human resources functions—all of which provide data to each other and to the financial system. This integration means, for example, that a salesperson taking an order for a manufacturing company is able to check inventory availability immediately. If inventory exists, the information system will notify shipping to pick the goods and fill the order. If no inventory is on hand (and the customer is important), the ERP system can trigger the manufacturing subsystem to make more product. The integration between the customer order and manufacturing subsystems can result in a revision to production schedules to accommodate the new orders. Human resources may also be involved if the new order requires extra workers or workers to be reassigned. In short, all functional areas of the organization can use the same information to perform their tasks efficiently to meet customer needs.

Extended ERP Systems. The business processes integrated by ERP systems are known as **back-office** functions because they primarily concern an enterprise's internal systems. Traditional ERP systems focus on internal data, generated primarily by internal processes (e.g., human resources and manufacturing) and an enterprise's own decision makers. Today's ERP systems are extended with e-business and other **front-office** capabilities. Extended enterprise systems bring customers, suppliers, and other business partners, such as investors and strategic business relations, into the picture.

ERP systems also interface with suppliers and customers through **supply chain management (SCM)** applications. The supply chain for a single enterprise extends from its suppliers to its customers. However, the supply chain of one company is only one part of a *linked* supply chain. Figure 15-4 demonstrates this concept for an automotive manufacturer. Note that goods and money are not the only commodities exchanged by partners along the chain. Information flows backward from customers to suppliers. SCM applications provide suppliers with access to the buyer's internal data, including inventory levels and sales orders. These data allow a business to reduce the cycle time for procuring goods for manufacture and sale. At the same time, the customer is able to view the supplier's information related to his or her order.

Another tool that helps companies optimize their supply chain is **customer relationship management (CRM)**. CRM is a collection of applications including databases,

---

[3] http://www.sap.com/solutions/business-suite/erp/customers/index.epx

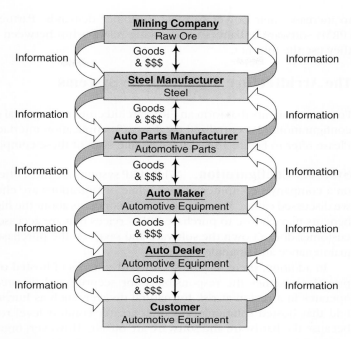

FIGURE 15-4 The supply chain for a component of the automotive industry.

sales order and customer service systems, and financial packages. The integrated CRM collects the data from these disparate applications and integrates them for decision-making purposes. Businesses also use CRM to analyze customer data—for example, find trends and buying patterns. This analysis can improve customer relations when the business uses the information to better meet customer needs.

Business intelligence (BI) tools help managers analyze and report data from their CRM and other systems. Combined with BI tools, CRM enables businesses to serve their customers better and also improve the bottom line. For example, CRM combined with BI can help a company learn which of their customers are most profitable and can direct sales efforts toward those customers. Analysis of buying trends and special customer features can increase sales revenues and cut costs.

Case-in-Point 15.4 Cartridge World, the leader in printer cartridge refilling and recycling, is the fastest growing franchise in the $80 billion printer cartridge industry. Recently, it successfully integrated NetSuite into its operations to oversee hundreds of its 1,650 worldwide franchise locations and manage a rapidly growing business. The company saved about $200,000 in annual IT and administrative costs. Their B2B e-commerce capabilities supported a 200 percent increase in sales across their 1,650 stores worldwide.[4]

Other ERP applications link strategic partners to an enterprise. Of course, many of these partners are suppliers and customers, but others include investors, creditors, and other channel partners with whom the enterprise might "team up with" to offer special services. **Collaborative business partnerships** are becoming more common as organizations find that there are often advantages to working with other businesses, even their competitors,

---

[4] http://www.netsuite.com/portal/customers/main.shtml

to increase their power to meet customer demands. Partner relationship management (PRM) software enhances the working relationship between partners, particularly when they use the Internet.

The Architecture of Enterprise Systems

Four components that form an ERP's architecture or technical structure are the (1) systems configuration, (2) centralized database, (3) application interfaces, and (4) Internet portals. Please refer to Figure 15-5 as we examine each of these components in greater detail.

Systems Configuration.   While ERP systems are most often licensed software that run on a company's computer system, some organizations are choosing hosted solutions that we discussed earlier. Organizations with concerns about the high cost of ERP and uncertain benefits may choose to purchase ERP services that are accessed through the Internet. The customer doesn't own the software and saves on the purchase price, hardware costs, and maintenance and upgrade expenses.

In addition, there may be security advantages of hosted options because the software provider assumes the responsibility for security and disaster recovery. A business that operates in a region at risk for natural disaster, such as hurricanes and earthquakes, may find that hosted solutions provide a greater comfort level regarding business continuity because the hardware and software are off-site. However, organizations in some industries where data security is especially important (e.g., health care and banking) may be concerned about a hosted solution because they give up control over their data and information.

Case-in-Point 15.5   Thermos, Inc., needed better information than it was getting from its current ERP system. However, the IT staff and others had invested heavily in the current system and were reluctant to upgrade. Management decided to take a risk and move to a hosted system, Oracle On Demand. The switch led to decreased needs for IT staffing, and the company expects benefits from the hosted solution to exceed $6 million.[5]

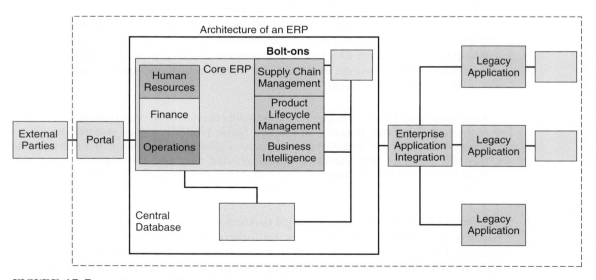

FIGURE 15-5   A diagram of the architecture of enterprise resource systems.

[5] http://www.cfo.com/article.cfm/5435396

A Centralized Database. To accomplish integration, ERP systems architecture is configured around a **central database**. The database stores information about each data item just once (thus avoiding data redundancy) and makes it immediately available to all functions in an organization. To appreciate the value of a central database, consider the following example.

Most businesses maintain price lists for their products. In firms where there is no centralized database, the price list may be duplicated many times. For example, the marketing department will set the prices, and it will also create and maintain a price list. Accounts receivable also keeps a price list to reference for invoicing, and the Web master uses a price list to update the selling prices displayed at the company's online store. Suppose the marketing department makes a price change. If the Web master and accounts receivable price lists are not updated, then products will be offered to customers at incorrect prices, and invoices may bill customers for incorrect amounts. The end result will be very dissatisfied customers.

Application Interfaces. Although an ERP system can integrate data from many business units within an organization, the flexibility of choosing the best software in different categories may argue for a **best-of-breed** approach. For instance, a company might implement an ERP system from SAP and then choose to interface it with a supply chain management or business intelligence product from another software manufacturer (these products are commonly called **bolt-ons**). Cost might be another reason for an organization to forgo the "one-system approach." For example, a company might run out of money during the implementation of an ERP and choose to complete its system with a module or two from another vendor.

Case-in-Point 15.6 Virginia Commonwealth University (VCU) in Richmond, Virginia, implemented Banner's ERP system in 2006, which is widely used in higher education. This ERP has modules to support student registrations and payments, course management, financial aid, finance, HR, and advancement. However, when the School of Business moved into its new building in the spring of 2008, decision makers determined that the CRM module in Banner did not have the functionality desired. Accordingly, they selected a bolt-on CRM called Intelliworks Program Management. This CRM helps current and prospective students through the initial exploration and inquiry stages of their searches and allows them to register for courses and submit payments online.[6]

Another useful method of combining multiple systems is **enterprise application integration (EAI)**. EAI allows companies with legacy applications and databases to integrate and continue to use those systems. This is particularly beneficial if these firms decide to implement an ERP or acquire new applications that exploit the Internet, e-commerce, extranet, and other technologies. EAI can accomplish this integration, and companies do not incur the cost of building their own custom interfaces to link their multiple applications together.

Internet Portals. Extended ERP systems interface with individuals inside and outside an organization through **portals**. A portal is a gateway to other Web sites or services that enhances communication and productivity among employees, customers, partners, and suppliers. For example, a company can allow its suppliers to see its price lists and

---

[6] http://www.intelliworks.com/news/press_releases/2008/VCU

also to learn the payment status of its invoices on a real-time basis. Similarly, university portals allow students and faculty to access a wide variety of university resources—such as university calendars, course information, and the library. Finally, organization portals provide users access to corporate-wide systems, data, and information from across the enterprise to connect people for meaningful collaboration.

Business Processes and Enterprise Systems

Accountants and others record an organization's accounting transactions in the financial modules of an ERP system, which, in turn, can interact with any subsystems supported by the ERP (e.g., human resources, manufacturing, customer relationship management, distribution, etc.). For example, a finance module can exchange payroll and tax data with the human resources subsystem. When a customer places an order, the distribution subsystem can check the customer's credit limit and accounts receivable balance in the finance module. A salesperson can check inventory levels and better manage the customer account through the CRM module.

Business Process Reengineering and ERPs.   An ERP system often requires organizations to adopt new ways of doing business. It entails reengineering procedures, hopefully to achieve the best practices of the industry. But implementing an ERP and reengineering business processes is expensive and very demanding on employees throughout an organization. Knowing the lessons learned from those who have been through the process is important to implementation success. While the VCU Case-in-Point identifies several key points about the business processing reengineering (BPR) efforts of one small university, a recent survey of 327 organizations (including over 13 major industry sectors) offers a more comprehensive understanding of BPR. The survey respondents identified the following as the most critical success factors in their BPR: (1) planning, where scope and roles were decided, (2) high-level review of current process, and (3) support from top management.[7] The continuous involvement of affected employees is also important. Figure 15-6 lists several additional key aspects that should be considered to help ensure successful BPR initiatives.

A company considering an ERP system may choose to conduct a BPR initiative before implementing the software, or it may undertake BPR concurrent with the implementation. Implementing an ERP system necessarily results in changes to the business because the software dictates certain business activities. For example, if the ERP system requires the collection of data about customers that have never been collected in the past, the business must adapt its processes in order to collect the new data. If a business does not examine and improve its processes prior to ERP implementation, the business will be forced to conform to the processes incorporated in the ERP software. Alternatively, a business may choose to first reengineer their processes and then customize the ERP system and any bolt-ons to better match their own processes.

Risks and Benefits of Enterprise Systems

Because ERP systems are expensive, require extensive training and consultation with change management specialists, and take a long time to implement, the potential risks

---

[7] http://www.prosci.com/bprbestpractices.htm

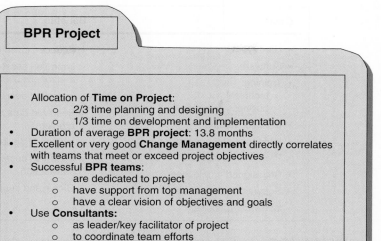

BPR Project

- Allocation of **Time on Project**:
  - 2/3 time planning and designing
  - 1/3 time on development and implementation
- Duration of average **BPR project**: 13.8 months
- Excellent or very good **Change Management** directly correlates with teams that meet or exceed project objectives
- Successful **BPR teams**:
  - are dedicated to project
  - have support from top management
  - have a clear vision of objectives and goals
- Use **Consultants**:
  - as leader/key facilitator of project
  - to coordinate team efforts
  - for IT or technical systems advice and expertise

FIGURE 15-6 Key aspects of a successful BPR project. Source: © Prosci 2002. All rights reserved. Reprinted with permission.

and rewards associated with these systems are substantial. Unfortunately, there are many examples of failed ERP implementations, and these failures often have disastrous effects on the financial statements of a business even if the business survives.

Case-in-Point 15.7 Waste Management was looking for a new revenue management system and selected SAP's ERP software. After two years and over $100 million in project expenses, Waste Management discovered that their ERP software had significant gaps between its functionality and Waste Management's business requirements. Waste Management determined that the system was a complete failure and sued SAP for fraud, claiming that the system was unstable and lacked promised functionality. SAP settled the lawsuit in 2010 for an undisclosed sum.[8]

Risks and Costs of ERPs. Sadly, many ERP systems fail, and many fail so badly as to affect the financial stability of the company that implemented the system. Besides the risks from failed implementations, ERP systems have many potential costs. Figure 15-7 identifies the costs and benefits normally associated with ERP systems. Implementation costs include hardware, software, and professional services. There are also costs for training, data conversion, and reengineering. Training costs involve technical training as well as training for those employees who are affected by the new business processes. Data conversion can be very expensive. Imagine a multinational corporation that is replacing more than 100 legacy systems with an ERP system. It is possible, for example, that each of the 100 systems represented an employee number in a different format. The new system will have just one uniform employee number. Management must agree on the format of the new employee number, and staff working on the implementation will have to convert all employee data to the new standard. Given the millions of potential decisions involving data

---

[8] http://www.computerworld.com/s/article/9176259/SAP_Waste_Management_settle_lawsuit

Costs	Benefits
• Hardware	• Reduced inventory investment
• Software	• Improved asset management (e.g., cash and receivables)
• Training:	• Improved decision making
– technical	
– business processes	• Resolved data redundancy and integrity problems
• Data conversion	
• Interfaces and customization	• Increased flexibility and responsiveness
• Professional services	• Improved customer service and satisfaction
• Reassigned employees	
• Software maintenance	• Global and supply chain integration
• Software upgrades	

FIGURE 15-7 A summary of costs and benefits typically associated with ERP systems.

naming and formatting alone, one can see how conversion of legacy systems can involve massive investments of time.

There are also many costs that don't always make it into the cost-benefit equation. These include internal staff costs. An ERP implementation will require some inside help, even if an organization hires specialized consultants for various aspects of the implementation. Company employees who are dedicated to the project cannot do their normal jobs. If they are assigned to the implementation, their salaries should be considered implementation costs.

Many ERP costs will continue, even after implementation. These include software maintenance and upgrade costs. One company noted that it had not realized how much it would cost for the highest level of vendor support, to constantly send their IT staff to training on the software, and to continually upgrade the system. ERP operating costs can vary from a hundred thousand to hundreds of millions of dollars.

Benefits of ERPs. Despite the high costs, there are many compelling reasons to implement an ERP system. These benefits can sometimes be difficult to quantify. For example, how can you estimate precisely what dollar benefit arises from improved decision making or more satisfied customers? Also, what is the dollar value of keeping up with competitors' IT and data analysis capabilities?

Most organizations make an attempt to identify the benefits they expect from the new ERP system. Many of the benefits result from cost reductions, such as reductions in inventory and employees. **Spend management** describes an approach to cutting expenses to their bare minimum. These include reducing employee travel expenses, procurement expenses, and even the costs associated with invoice processing.

Case-in-Point 15.8 Newell Rubermaid, a world leader in consumer products with business units throughout the world, implemented an SAP system to help it collect and interpret data across the entire company. Matt Stultz, vice president of Information Technology, said the following about the their ERP system and its spend management capabilities: "Whether it's analyzing our spend data or more efficiently managing our inventory, we have both the historical and up-to-date information we need to move our business forward."[9]

---

[9] http://www.iappnet.org/ViewItem-1761.do

Other benefits of ERP systems include better abilities to: (1) make enterprise-wide decisions, (2) identify trends, (3) understand interrelationships between business units, (4) eliminate redundant data, (5) increase the efficiency of financial reporting, and (6) monitor business processes in new and different ways—for example, with dashboards and mashups (explained below). In Chapter 1, we introduced the idea of dashboards and how they are used by senior management to monitor corporate performance with respect to the balanced scorecard. The use of dashboards is a major trend in business intelligence, and dashboards can be used successfully throughout the organization.

Digital dashboards and scorecards are essential tools for organizations to monitor a wide variety of business processes. For example, a sales dashboard could monitor key sales activities such that managers could identify sales trend information—such as best customers, products, and salespeople (and measure these by revenue, units, margin, or region). Figure 15-8 shows an example of a sales dashboard that managers might use. Production dashboards are used to monitor and compare real-time production figures with historical trends to put current events in perspective. Dashboards are used in universities by deans and department chairs to monitor processes, such as assessment data, student enrollments, budget status, and many other processes.

Managers often use dashboards that use data collected from within the organization. However, the VP for Emerging Internet Technologies at IBM is encouraging managers to experiment with **enterprise mashups**. Visualize a dashboard that collects data from a variety of sources both inside and outside the firm. That's a mashup. In a recent

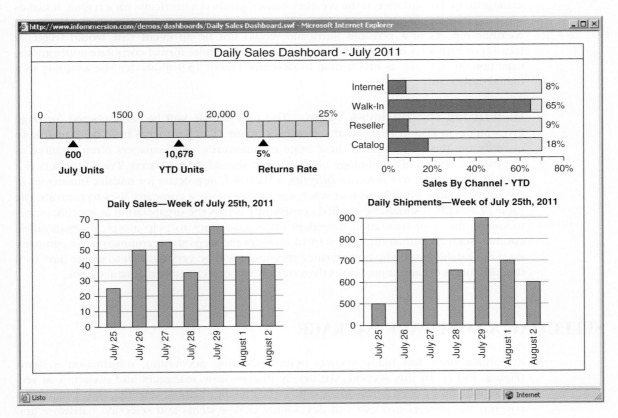

FIGURE 15-8 Example of a sales dashboard.

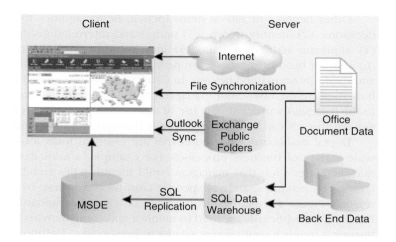

FIGURE 15-9 The anatomy of a digital dashboard. This dashboard has three possible data sources: the Internet, Microsoft Exchange, and relational data in a SQL server table. All of these sources are available offline as well as online. Source: Courtesy of MSDN Magazine.

pilot of a mashup, IBM developed a content-oriented application for one of the national home improvement retail chains. The idea was to merge weather reports with inventory management. For instance, if the weather service predicts a hurricane for a region, it makes sense to transfer inventories of plywood to stores near the area of the storm. Normally, weather reports of a possible hurricane would not be an event that would trigger a transfer of inventory in most ERP systems. And, unlike more formal corporate applications, mashups do not take as much time to develop. Figure 15-9 illustrates the anatomy of a digital dashboard.

Quantifying the Business Value. The past decade will be remembered for large investments in IT and ERP systems. However, many IT departments have been unable to quantify the business value of these huge expenditures, and managers often disagree as to how the effects of technology on firm value should be measured. Trish Saunders is a contributing author to *Customer Insights*, a Microsoft newsletter for midsize businesses in the United States. She claims that whatever methodology a company uses to measure the value of an ERP, it should be applied consistently across the organization at specific points following the implementation. Saunders offers guidelines to help a typical organization conduct such an evaluation. Figure 15-10 includes the steps she recommends if a company does not establish specific performance metrics, it will be very difficult to gauge how well the ERP meets organizational objectives or how to correct any performance gaps.

SELECTING A SOFTWARE PACKAGE

An organization has many choices when selecting accounting information systems (Figure 15-11). In this section, we briefly discuss how managers and owners can recognize when they need a new AIS and how they might go about selecting one. Chapter 13 covered the general processes of developing new systems and selecting hardware and software in more detail.

> 1. Determine how you will measure success.
>
> 2. Set up specific metrics based on your industry.
>
> 3. Perform regular postimplementation audits.
>
> 4. Analyze your performance numbers.
>
> 5. Set up universal processes.
>
> 6. Create a continuous learning loop.
>
> 7. Prepare for inevitable security failures.

FIGURE 15-10   Methodology for measuring the value of an ERP.

Software Type	Business Characteristics	Cost	Examples
Entry-level	Smaller businesses with less than 10 active users	Free–$1,000	MYOB, Sage Peachtree, Intuit Quickbooks
Small–medium business	Less than 100 active users	$5,000–$100,000	Sage MAS 90, Sage MAS 200, Quickbooks Enterprise
Small–medium business basic enterprise system	Over 100 active users	$20,000–$500,000	Sage MAS 500 ERP, Microsoft Dynamics AX
High-end enterprise system	Over 100 users and capable of handling the volume of Fortune 1000 firms	$500,000–hundreds of millions of dollars	JD Edwards, Oracle, PeopleSoft, SAP
Custom-built	Any size	$5,000–hundreds of millions of dollars	

FIGURE 15-11   Types of accounting and enterprise software.

When Is a New AIS Needed?

Believe it or not, there are still many small businesses that keep their (manual) accounting systems in a shoebox, a filing cabinet, or similar storage. This is because small business entrepreneurs often begin with an idea for a business, do not have accounting degrees, and therefore rely on others to perform their accounting tasks. The owner may deliver financial records to a bookkeeper or accountant periodically to prepare needed reports, file taxes, or see how well the business is doing. But manual accounting systems do not allow their users to thoroughly analyze their data, generate financial statements in a timely manner, or identify trends or opportunities to reduce costs or increase revenues.

For those already using computerized AISs, there are many signals to business owners or managers that a new accounting software package, or an upgrade in software, is a good idea. These signs may have nothing to do with the company itself, its vendors, or its customers. One example might be new regulations or legislation that changes the way companies must operate. Compliance with rules or laws, such as the Sarbanes-Oxley Act of 2002 (SOX), is often a reason to move to new software or to purchase a bolt-on to an ERP. SOX called for built-in controls, visible audit trails, workflow and documentation software

1. Late payment of vendor invoices, which means late fees and lost cash discounts.
2. Late deliveries to customers.
3. Growth in inventories, accompanied by an increase in stockouts.
4. Slowdown in inventory turnover.
5. Increased time in collecting on receivables.
6. Late periodic reports.
7. Increasing length of time to close out books at the end of a period.
8. Managers concerned about cash flows and financial picture of organization.
9. Manager complaints about lack of information needed for decision making.
10. Owner worries about cash flows, taxes, and profitability.

FIGURE 15-12   Indicators that a company needs a new (or upgraded) AIS.

features, and management alerts that many software packages did not offer prior to SOX. Figure 15-12 lists 10 such signals.

When a business owner or manager recognizes that it is time to purchase new (or more powerful) software, the next question is, "Which software should I select?" or "How do I know which software package is the best fit for my company?"

Selecting the Right Accounting Software

The approach to buying accounting software varies with the complexity of the business and the software. For small businesses, the selection process is obviously much quicker and less expensive than when a large company wants to select an ERP system. Large organizations with specialized accounting information needs may decide to build a customized AIS from scratch. While custom systems are difficult and expensive to develop, they are becoming less expensive with advances in object-oriented programming, client/server computing, and database technology. Custom systems often take longer to develop than management anticipates, which is why most firms retain consultants to help with the selection and implementation of AISs.

Consultants usually find that packaged software can handle about 80 percent of a client's processing needs. A company can ignore the other 20 percent, meet their needs with other software such as spreadsheet or database programs, and purchase bolt-on software or develop its own bolt-on modules to complete its system. However, today's accounting software is easy to use and feature-rich. Internet research and discussions with other business owners in a similar industry may be enough to help a business owner select a software package. A number of helpful sites are available on the Internet to help with this selection process.

Case-in-Point 15.9   Three Web sites, http://www.cpatechnologyadvisor, http://www.2020software.com, and http://www.ctsguides.com, list features in accounting software packages, describe these features, and allow individuals to compare the various features in the software packages. These sites offer software demos, make software recommendations, and provide detailed online software reviews.

Shopping-mall software retailers typically do not sell middle-range or high-end accounting software packages. Instead, business owners and managers at larger firms are most likely to purchase them from a value-added reseller (VAR) or a qualified installer. VARs and qualified installers make special arrangements with software vendors to sell their programs. They also provide buyers with services such as installation, customization, and training. These services are necessary because of the complexity of the middle-range accounting programs. A VAR offers a broader array of services for more software programs than a qualified installer. Chapter 13 elaborates on this topic and discusses tools available to help in making software selection decisions.

Because ERP system implementations can cost hundreds of millions of dollars and take many years, it is always advisable to get the help of an expert when choosing among them. Consultants can conduct a thorough analysis of your organization and its processes to determine which software vendor has the best solution and what customization might be needed. There are many types of ERP consultants, including those who work for the vendors, professionals who work in IT consulting firms, and specialists within large accounting and professional service firms. The best way to choose a consultant is to look for someone who has experience with your industry and who is familiar with more than one package. As you would expect, vendor consultants are unlikely to suggest any solution other than the one or ones offered by their employer.

AIS AT WORK
Sheldon Needle and CTS Guides

In 1983, Sheldon Needle left his full-time accounting job to start his own business, Computer Training Services (CTS). He knew a lot about accounting software and decided to create a company that would evaluate software and publish guides for various businesses. He published a paperback book that compared five small business software programs, advertised the book in the *Journal of Accountancy*, and waited for the orders. His phone quickly began ringing off the hook, and he knew that the service he offered was in high demand.

Sheldon next developed a spreadsheet rating system that compared the major features of top-selling accounting software programs. The program, called *Requirements Analyst*, also allowed users to determine whether a software feature was necessary, desirable, or optional. The program user, usually a software consultant, could then use Requirements Analyst to choose the best software for a given client. CTS grew, adding guides for special industries and different levels of accounting software. Competition came from other consultants and services that also offered software comparisons. But CTS had an advantage in that the evaluations were performed by Sheldon or the independent contractors he hired. Other comparison programs typically used vendors to supply the data about what their programs could and could not do.

The Internet began to impinge on the value proposition for CTS as search engines and vendor Web sites decreased the value of the software guides to users. For example, a decade ago, a business in the construction industry would need to do exhaustive research to find the top industry accounting software packages and lists of their features. Now, Internet search engines make this information accessible to anyone. Also, some consultants began to offer their services in helping companies select software for a low fee over the Internet. A small business owner could answer a few questions about the company—such as number of users; annual sales dollars; numbers of customers, employees, and suppliers; industry niche, and so on—and the Web site would instantly recommend a software package.

In 2003, CTS changed its business model so that most information is now available at no cost to visitors at http://www.ctsguides.com. Rather than earning profits from customers, the company now receives income from software vendors. The vendors use CTS for advertising and distributing information about their products. Sheldon shares his expertise personally and talks with clients, either on the phone or via e-mail. His company also continues to sell guides, tips on software selection, and tools such as one that helps users create a request for proposal (RFP). The new business model is working well, and CTS has successfully navigated the constantly changing world of technology and accounting software.

SUMMARY

- ✓ Categories of integrated accounting software include entry-level, small to medium business, ERP, special industry, and custom-built software.
- ✓ Integrated accounting software packages may include modules or transaction groupings for general ledger, accounts receivable or sales, accounts payable or purchasing, inventory, and payroll.
- ✓ Entry-level accounting programs usually include a chart of accounts that users can customize, along with the ability to produce a variety of accounting reports, including financial statements and budgets.
- ✓ Midrange and large-scale accounting software packages include special features and options, such as international currency translation.
- ✓ Deployment options for accounting software and high-end ERP systems include hosted solutions, where users lease software as a service and customer data resides on the vendors' hardware.
- ✓ ERP systems integrate both financial and nonfinancial information from an organization's business processes.
- ✓ Traditional ERP systems are back-office information systems, integrating financial, manufacturing, sales, distribution, and human resource systems. Extended ERP systems add front-office features to the traditional systems, helping an organization to integrate its supply chain.
- ✓ ERP systems have a central database that allows them to reduce data redundancy, enhance the integrity of the data, and make more information available for decision making.
- ✓ There are many costs and benefits associated with ERP systems, and managers need to consider all of them when making a decision about implementing such a large system. Savings often accrue from redesigned and more efficient business processes that lead to increases in revenues and cost savings.
- ✓ There are several warning signals that indicate when a company needs to upgrade its AIS, including dissatisfied vendors, customers, or employees. Sometimes the impetus is external, such as with the Sarbanes-Oxley Act or other regulations.
- ✓ The Internet provides many tools to help in selecting a new AIS, but the help of a consultant or VAR is often needed to select and implement a new system.

KEY TERMS YOU SHOULD KNOW

back-office
best-of-breed
bolt-ons
business application suites

business intelligence (BI) tools
central database
collaborative business partnerships
customer relationship management (CRM)

enterprise application integration (EAI)

enterprise mashups

enterprise software

front-office

hosted solution

integrated accounting software

Internet connectivity

portals

scalable

spend management

supply chain management (SCM)

DISCUSSION QUESTIONS

15-1. Which accounting software features are likely to be the most important for the following businesses? Search the Internet for an example of an AIS that you would recommend for each of these owners and include your rationale for that product.

    a. A boutique shop that sells trendy ladies clothing

    b. A small business specializing in custom golf clubs, replacement shafts for clubs, replacement grips for clubs, and similar repairs

    c. A local CPA firm with three partners, five associates, and two administrative employees

    d. A pet breeder that specializes in Burmese kittens

    e. A business that sells and rents Segways in Washington, DC, which is located on Constitution Avenue, near the Lincoln Memorial

    f. A high-end men's clothing business that has four stores that are all located in the same large metropolitan city (56 employees), and the owner is contemplating additional locations for stores in nearby cities

15-2. The difference between the price tag for middle-market accounting software versus an ERP system can be millions of dollars. What can these high-end systems do that the less expensive enterprise accounting packages cannot?

15-3. Discuss the differences between traditional ERP and extended enterprise systems.

15-4. Discuss some of the basic features of an ERP. How do these features distinguish an ERP from an integrated accounting software program?

15-5. What are some of the benefits of a centralized database architecture? What are some of the difficulties in moving from multiple databases or files to a centralized database structure?

15-6. A new company will have no business processes in place. How would the owner go about selecting an appropriate AIS for the new company? Should the owner consider acquiring an ERP package immediately?

15-7. Find an article about a company that has adopted a business application suite. Identify the company and its basic characteristics (such as location, products, and number of employees). What are some cost savings realized by the company? Were there specific efficiencies identified as a result of the ERP implementation? Were there problems implementing the system? How long did it take for the company to complete the implementation? Were there cost or time over-runs?

15-8. While you are likely to purchase a middle-end accounting software package from a value-added reseller (VAR), why should you be cautious about hiring one to recommend a software package for your business?

15-9. What are some of the consequences to a company that makes a poor decision in selecting a new AIS?

15-10. Why do businesses typically need to engage in business process reengineering when they adopt an ERP? Identify at least four key aspects of a successful BPR project.

PROBLEMS

15-11. Visit the software Web sites of two low-end accounting software package vendors and then two ERP vendors. Analyze the descriptions of the software and then describe the differences you see between the low-end packages and the ERP systems.

15-12. Define the concept of "scalability." Explain why it might be a good idea for owners of small businesses—and managers in larger businesses—to understand this concept.

15-13. Tom O'Neal always wanted to own his own business. When he was in high school, he worked evenings and most weekends at a neighborhood bicycle shop. When Tom went to college at the nearby State University, he still came home in the summers and worked at the bike shop. On graduation from college, with his accounting degree in hand, the sole proprietor (Steven Judson) of the bike shop invited Tom to become a full partner in the bike shop. Steven told Tom that he really wanted to grow the business and thought that Tom was just the person to help him do this. Tom decided to join Steven.

Over time, the business grew, and they opened two more bike shops in neighboring cities. Sales increased to more than $3.5 million during the past year, and the three bike shops now employ 14 full-time workers and another six part-time employees. Although Steven and Tom hired an accountant who was keeping their books for them and producing the financial statements each year, the partners thought they needed much more information to really run their business efficiently. They thought that they might need to make an investment in information technology to take their business to the next level.

a. Would you recommend that Steven and Tom consider an investment in IT?

b. Visit the Web sites of the vendors that offer the appropriate-size software packages for this business. What are some of the features of possible software packages that Steven and Tom should consider?

c. Would you advise Steven and Tom to hire a consultant? Support your recommendation with appropriate research citations (e.g., business articles that offer this type of advice—what rationale do they give?).

15-14. B&R, Inc., is one of the world's largest manufacturers and distributors of consumer products, including household cleaning supplies and health and beauty products. Last year, net sales revenues exceeded $5 billion. B&R has multiple information systems, including an integrated accounting system, a computerized manufacturing information system, and a supply chain management software system. The company is considering an ERP system to be able to conduct more of its business over the Internet.

B&R hired National Consulting Firm (NCF), and NCF recommended the move to an ERP system, which would have e-commerce interfaces that will allow B&R to sell its products to its business customers through its Web site. The cost-benefit justification for the new software, which comes with an estimated price tag of $100 million (including consultant fees and all implementation and training costs) shows that B&R can expect great cost savings from improved business processes that the ERP system will help the company to adopt. NCF implements the ERP, adopting the industry's *best practices* for many of the business processes.

a. What are the likely advantages of an ERP system for B&R?

b. Visit the Web sites of the major ERP vendors. What are some of the characteristics you notice about their customers?

c. B&R has heard some horror stories from other CEOs about ERP implementations. What are some of the concerns B&R should address as they move forward with this project?

CASE STUDIES

The RETAIL Cooperative (Creating an Enterprise Portal)

Over the past decade, The RETAIL Cooperative (TRC) successfully acquired a number of smaller retailers. These strategic acquisitions enabled TRC to grow significantly. In fact, TRC is now one of the largest retailers in Europe and employs over 230,000 people in 25 countries. The company has three primary business units: Department Stores, Hardware Stores, and Food Stores. TRC has many cross-division service companies in both Europe and Asia to support the three primary business units. These support companies provide a variety of services, such as purchasing, information technology, advertising, human resources, and others.

In early 2007, the CEO scheduled a full-day strategy session with the vice presidents of the business units. By the end of the day, these senior managers decided on a set of specific strategic objectives to continue the growth of the company. In particular, the CEO and vice presidents of TRC determined that the company needed to: (1) attract well-educated, skilled managers to succeed in future expansions and (2) focus on optimizing distribution channels so that managers at all levels of the organization would have immediate access to information for decision making. The goal was to link TRC's management expertise with the geographic area of operation so that the company would continue to be dynamic and responsive to customers 24/7. Essentially, the senior managers wanted TRC midlevel managers in each of the business units to have the ability to "Coordinate Globally—Act Locally."

The consensus was that the Human Resources support company would develop and implement appropriate procedures to find the quality of managers that TRC requires. However, the VPs of the business units wanted to be directly involved in the distribution channel optimization. As a result of TRC's rapid growth, the VPs of the business units were encountering a number of recurring problems—such as lapses in customer service, inability to respond to customer queries, and coordination problems with product availability and delivery dates. In addition, the manager for the travel department of the company noticed a significant increase in travel expenses for each of the business units and sent each of the VPs a memo. On the basis of these concerns, the VPs decide to meet with the controller and chief information officer (CIO) to discuss these problems and to identify possible options to resolve these issues.

To prepare for the meeting, Robin Frost (the CIO) talked with several top-level managers to collect their ideas and suggestions of the features that might be required of any new technology the firm might purchase. Each of the managers agreed that TRC would need an e-business application(s) that would give its managers a detailed online view of the status of the purchasing process that is shared among TRC's employees, suppliers, and customers. For example, each purchasing agent would like to access all the purchase prices, inventories, and selling prices that are in place in any store, no matter where it is located. He/she should also be able to see TRC's manufacturing prices for its own brands, the bids made by TRC's suppliers, and the comments or complaints made by TRC's customers.

In addition, the new technology would have to link TRC's suppliers, distributors, and resellers with the company's Logistic, Production, and Distribution departments. The Accounting and Finance departments would need access to information so they could track the status of TRC's sales, inventory, shipping, and invoicing in any TRC store, world wide. And finally, the Marketing and Sales departments would also need access to manage and update the company's product catalogs, price lists, and promotional information for any TRC outlet, regardless of its geographic location.

At the meeting with the VPs, Robin made a 10-minute presentation on Internet portals. Her research on this new technology leads her to believe this might help the VPs solve the problem of information asymmetries—that is, information not being readily available to midlevel managers working with customers. At this point, Robin just knows that there exist software packages that can make information available to company employees. She's not able to articulate all the pros and cons of the technology and has not yet called any outside consultants for advice. Robin believes that the primary challenge for this new technology will be to create a real-time "retail connectivity" that will allow vendor collaboration, multichannel integration, and public and private trading exchanges across the globe.

Requirements

(Note: Research is required to properly respond to the following case questions, which could include journal articles on enterprise portals, and Internet research that could include online journal articles as well as vendor Web sites for product information.)

1. Assume you are a consultant with one of the application platform vendors (e.g., IBM, Oracle, SAP, and Microsoft) and Robin called you for information regarding Enterprise Portals. Prepare a one-page summary of the advantages TRC might be able to achieve if they used an Enterprise Portal for each of the business units (and for TRC-wide operations).

2. After preparing the one-page summary, prepare a 10-minute PowerPoint presentation on Enterprise Portals, focusing on the advantages for TRC of implementing this technology. (Hint: As a minimum, be sure to address such issues as scalability of the portal, reliability, performance, and fault tolerance.)

3. What sort of implementation schedule would you recommend for TRC, that is, what steps are important in an orderly implementation of this technology? Explain.

4. On the basis of your research, which system do you recommend for TRC? Prepare a matrix that compares the different features of the different Enterprise Portal solutions that you considered.

Linda Stanley and State University (Transitioning from a Legacy System to an ERP)

Linda Stanley is the vice president for Computing and Information Services at State University (SU), a medium-size, urban university that has experienced a 3 percent growth in enrollments every year for more than a decade. The university now has almost 22,000 students, just under 12,000 faculty and staff, nearly $1 billion in revenues, and can currently accommodate 5,000 students in residence halls. In addition, the state legislature has financially supported infrastructure development for SU to help accommodate the sustained growth in enrollments. The campus has significantly and positively impacted the visual appearance and the economy of the city where it is located.

The number of legacy systems across campus has adequately served SU in the past, but with the growth in enrollments, the university has also increased the number of faculty, support staff, and services. Currently, the core applications at SU include Blackboard, Lotus Domino, Web self-service, and legacy administrative applications for all other purposes.

In recent meetings with the provost of the university, Linda and her staff have responded to a number of concerns and problems from the deans of academic departments on campus, as well as a number of the support departments, such as payroll, student financial aid, and HR. As Linda pointed out to the provost and deans, universities have unique technology challenges, such as an open technology environment 24 hours a day, 7 days a week, and that is 365 days a year, not just when school is in session. She also mentioned that SU has other factors that impact the effectiveness of IT services—such as their urban location and the rapid growth of the university over the past decade. Linda reminded the provost that she and her staff were diligently working on a number of major technology initiatives for SU, including network reengineering, e-mail consolidation, telephony modernization, helpdesk/customer care redesign, and classroom technology.

Last week, the provost called Linda and asked her to meet him at the coffee shop in the Student Commons—he wanted to ask her opinion about a technology issue. In the discussion, the provost reflected on the growth of SU and wondered aloud if the university might be at a stage of maturity where they really should consider the entire technology infrastructure of the university. He pointedly asked Linda what she thought—should they consider purchasing an ERP?

Of course, Linda was not prepared to discuss this question in great depth and told the provost that she would do some research and make an appointment in a couple of weeks to have a more meaningful discussion of the issue. When she returned to her office, she scheduled a meeting with her staff for the next day so that she could go over the provost's request with them and then assign different parts of this research project to them. Linda reminded everyone that they had a limited amount of time to pull the information together—that she needed to deliver the Executive Summary to the provost in the next few weeks.

Requirements

(Note: Some Internet research is required to properly respond to the following case questions.)

1. Search the Internet and find ERP solutions that might be suitable for a university, such as SU. What are the primary modules for this type of ERP? Briefly describe the functions of each module.

2. What business processes would most likely be affected if SU implemented an ERP?

3. Since this is a state university, the Board of Visitors and the State Legislature will need to see a report on the expected costs and benefits of an ERP, both tangible and intangible. Although you don't have any dollar amounts, identify some typical costs and benefits that Linda should include in her executive summary.

4. Should Linda use consultants? If so, what types of support should she expect from them?

5. Search the Internet—can you find an expected timeline for implementation of an ERP at a university? Do you think Linda should include a possible timeline in her report to the provost? Why or why not?

Glossary

1992 COSO Report a committee established by the Treadway Commission to develop a common definition for internal control and to provide guidance for judging the effectiveness of internal control as well as improving it.

Access control list (ACL) a list of bonafide IP addresses in devices such as firewalls.

Access security uses access authentication to require individuals to prove they are who they say they are.

Accounting information system (AIS) the application of information technology (IT) to accounting systems. It's a collection of data and processing procedures that creates needed information for its users.

Action query a query that manipulates, and typically alters, one or more tables in an Access database.

Activity-based costing (ABC) systems managers in a variety of manufacturing and service industries identify specific activities involved in a manufacturing or service task, and then assign overhead costs based on the resources directly consumed by each activity.

Agent the *who* associated with events. Agents are classified as either internal or external. Internal agents work within the firm for which a database is designed (e.g., salespeople), while external agents are outside of the firm (e.g., customers).

Agile development methodology uses iterative revisions and customer collaboration when developing a new software application.

Antivirus software computer programs such as Norton Antivirus or MacAffee that end users typically install in their microcomputers to guard against computer viruses.

Applet a small program that is stored in a Web page and is designed to run by Web browser software. Friendly applets animate Web pages, allow users to play games, or perform processing tasks. Unfriendly applets contain viruses that can infect other computers and cause damage.

Application controls a major category of computer controls that are designed and implemented to prevent, detect, and correct errors and irregularities in transactions as they flow through the input, processing, and output stages of data processing work.

Application software computer software that performs specific tasks such as accounting tasks, spreadsheet tasks, marketing tasks, or word-processing tasks.

Applications portfolio a set of software applications belonging to an organization.

Association of Certified Fraud Examiners (ACFE) an international professional organization committed to detecting, deterring, and preventing fraud and white-collar crime.

Attributes the data fields *describing* each entity in a database (i.e., the columns in each table).

Audit Command Language (ACL) specialized software tools to help auditors perform auditing tasks.

Audit trail enables information users within a company's system to follow the flow of data through the system.

Auditing around the computer audit approach whereby an auditor follows a company's audit trail up to the point at which accounting data enter the computer and then picks these data up again when they reappear in processed form as computer output; this audit approach pays little or no attention to the control procedures within the IT environment.

Auditing through the computer audit approach whereby an auditor follows a company's audit trail through the internal computer operations phase of automated data processing; this audit approach attempts to verify that the processing controls involved in the AIS programs are functioning properly.

Auditing with the computer audit approach whereby the auditor uses the computer to aid in performing various auditing procedures (e.g., selecting a sample of accounts receivable data for confirmation).

Automated workpaper allow internal and external auditors to automate and standardize specific audit tests and audit documentation. Some of the capabilities of automated workpapers are to (1) generate trial balances, (2) make adjusting entries, (3) perform consolidations, (4) conduct analytical procedures, and (5) document audit procedures and conclusions.

Back-office refers to internal functions and processing within an organization, such as human resources and accounting.

Balanced scorecard an approach to performance measurement that uses measures in four categories (financial performance, customer knowledge, internal business processes, and learning and growth) to evaluate and promote certain activities and behaviors.

Bar code reader a device that interprets the familiar barcode stripes printed on merchandise packages, shipping labels, and similar documents, and inputs the data into a computer.

Batch control total typically, a manual total that is compared to a computer total to determine whether data were processed correctly.

Benchmark test an approach for examining the operating efficiency of a particular system whereby a computer vendor's system performs a data processing task that a company's new system must perform and company representatives then examine the processing outputs for accuracy, consistency, and efficiency.

Best-of-breed an approach to systems development where each application may be acquired from a separate vendor and represents the best program in that category of need.

Biometric identification a form of intrusion protection. Currently, fingerprint authentication appears to be the most trusted, practical, and affordable method to eliminate the hassles and security vulnerabilities associated with employee and customer-driven password management.

Biometric scanner authenticates users based on who they are. Behavioral systems recognize signatures, voices, or keystroke dynamics. Physiological systems recognize fingerprints, irises, retinas, faces, and even ears. Most of these devices connect directly to computer USB ports or are integrated in computer keyboards, mice, or Web cams.

Blog collaboration tools that allow users with Web browsers and easy-to-use software to publish a personalized diary online.

Blu-ray disc writers encode the same-size disk medium as CDs and DVDs, but can store up to 25 gigabytes of data. Their name comes from the blue color of the shorter wavelength laser beams used to encode and read the disks. BD-Rs are read-only media that can be written only once, while BD-REs can be erased and re-recorded multiple times.

Bolt-ons software products that can be added to large ERP systems.

Boot-sector virus a virus that hides in the boot sector of a disk, where the operating system (OS) accesses the virus every time the OS accesses the disk itself.

Bound control a form control such as a textbox or label that displays the underlying data from a database table.

Business application suites is a type of software that integrates financial or accounting subsystem with CRM, business services, human resources (HR), and supply chain management (SCM).

Business continuity plan (BCP) management's policies and procedures to continue the organization. This includes risk identification, scenario planning, and practicing the plan so that employees can appropriately respond to whatever emergency or disaster occurs.

Business event an event that occurs in a business that does not directly affect the financial statements. For example, the hiring of a new manager or creation of a new product.

Business intelligence a need was recognized for integrated information and therefore business intelligence software was developed to meet this need. Along with the Internet, integrated systems, and other advanced technologies, balanced scorecards and other approaches to CPM are becoming increasingly valuable business intelligence tools.

Business intelligence (BI) tools data analysis software that helps managers obtain the most information from their customer relationship management systems.

Business process reengineering (BPR) techniques used by organizations to redesign their business processes from scratch.

Business-to-business (B2B) e-commerce refers to businesses buying and selling goods and services to each other over the Internet.

Calculated field a field in a database table that is calculated using data in other fields.

Canned software software acquired from independent vendors.

Cardinalities a notation reflecting the nature of relationships among entities as one-to-one, one-to-many, none-to-one, none-to-many, or many-to-many.

CD-ROM an acronym for "compact disk-read only memory." CD-ROM disks can store approximately 640 megabytes of data.

Central database a comprehensive database that holds all the data for multiple applications or processes.

Central processing unit (CPU) the component of a computer that performs that processing tasks of the system. The processor part of the CPU is typically a single silicon chip that can manipulate data—for example, perform mathematical functions such as addition as well as logic operations such as comparing text or number values.

Certificate authority an entity that issues digital certificates—for example, to authenticate the legitimacy of a bid or financial purchase.

Certified Fraud Examiner (CFE) a certification that requires individuals to meet certain qualifications set by the Association of Certified Fraud Examiners.

Certified Information Systems Auditor (CISA) a professional information systems auditor who meets certification requirements of the Information Systems Audit and Control Association.

Certified Information Technology Professional (CITP) a designation given by the AICPA for CPAs who meet specified additional requirements related to information technologies.

Change management a systematic approach to introducing dynamic change or disruption in an organization.

Change management consultants are outside consultants who help facilitate the complex process of business process reengineering to find areas for improvement and overcome potential negative reactions to change among employees.

Checkpoint a control that is performed at periodic intervals during processing. A company's computer network system temporarily does not accept new transactions. Instead, it completes updating procedures for all partially processed transactions and then generates an exact copy of all data values and other information needed to restart the system. The checkpoint is recorded on a separate tape or disk file. This process is executed several times per hour. Should a hardware failure occur, the system is restarted by reading in the last checkpoint and then reprocessing only those transactions that have occurred since the checkpoint.

Click fraud is a growing e-commerce problem in which dishonest managers inflate the number of clicks viewers make on an Web page advertisement and therefore bill the linked company for more referrals than actually occurred.

Client/server computing an alternate to mainframe computing in which processing tasks are shared between a centralized host computer called the "server" and a smaller microcomputer called the "client."

Cloud computing is a way of using business applications over the Internet. It is a way to increase IT capacity or add capabilities without investing in new infrastructure, training new people, or licensing new software.

Cold backup a backup that is performed while the database is off-line and unavailable to its users.

Cold site a location where power and environmentally controlled space are available to install processing equipment on short notice. If a disaster recovery plan designates a cold site, then separate arrangements are also necessary to obtain computer equipment matching the configuration of equipment lost in the disaster.

Collaborative business partnerships situations in which organizations work with other businesses, even their competitors, to increase their power to meet customer demands.

Compiler translates procedural-language programs (called source code) written, for example, in Java, into machine-language programs (called object code) that computers can execute immediately When end users buy application software packages, they buy compiled computer programs in machine language that are ready to execute on their specific computers.

Compliance testing procedures performed by auditors to ensure the general and application controls are in place and working as prescribed.

Computer abuse the unauthorized use of, or access to, a computer for purposes contrary to the wishes of the owner of the computer.

Computer crime involves the manipulation of a computer or computer data, by whatever method, to dishonestly obtain money, property, or some other advantage of value, or to cause loss.

Computer Fraud and Abuse Act of 1986 (CFAA) this act defines computer fraud as any illegal act for which knowledge of computer technology is essential for its perpetration, investigation, or prosecution.

Computer record a set of data fields about one file entity—for example, one employee, one inventory item, or one sales transaction.

Computer Security Institute (CSI) an organization that conducts an annual survey to help determine the scope of computer crime in the United States.

Computer software refers to any program that a computer can run. The two basic types of computer software are: (1) operating systems and (2) application software.

Computer tablet is a new category of portable computer systems—for example, iPads. Although many people buy these devices for personal uses, commercial applications are emerging.

Computer virus a computer program that rogue programmers embed in other programs, e-mails, or computer files, and that (when executed) typically perform such destructive acts as erasing files, disrupting e-mails, or interfering with operating system functions.

Computer worm a computer virus that does not actually destroy data, but merely replicates itself repeatedly until the user runs out of internal memory or disk space.

Computer-assisted audit techniques (CAATs) used by auditors when auditing through the computer; CAAT's can aid in the performance of compliance tests to ensure that a company's controls are in place and working as prescribed.

Concurrency controls prevents two or more users of a database to access the same record from the same file at the same time.

Consensus-based protocols a fault tolerant system that contains an odd number of processors. If one processor disagrees with the others, it is thereafter ignored.

Continuous auditing requires the use of tools (such as embedded audit modules) that allow auditing to occur even when an auditor is not present; it is particularly effective when most of an application's data are in electronic form.

Control activities are the policies and procedures that management develops to help protect the firm's assets.

Control break a change of value in an important data field (e.g., department number) of the records of a database table that requires additional computations in an output listing—for example, a subtotal.

Control environment A component of internal control that establishes the tone of a company, which influences the control awareness of the company's employees.

Control Objectives for Information and related Technology (COBIT) project undertaken by the IT Governance Institute to develop a framework for internal control relative to information technology.

Control Source property the link of a bound control to an underlying data field. Bound controls have a Control Source setting, whereas unbound controls do not.

Cookie a small text file that stores information about your browsing habits and interests, as well as other information that you may supply by logging onto a Web site.

Corporate governance managing an organization in a fair, transparent, and accountable manner to protect the interests of all the stakeholder groups.

Corrective controls control procedures within a company's internal control system that are designed to remedy problems discovered through detective controls.

Cost accounting is part of managerial accounting specifically assists management in measuring and controlling the costs associated with an organization's various acquisition, processing, distribution, and selling activities. In the broadest sense, these tasks focus on the value added by an organization to its goods or services.

Cost accounting subsystem generally associated with manufacturing firms, this subsystem provides important control information (such as variance reports) and is usually either job costing or process costing.

CPA Trust Services is a set of professional service areas built around a set of common principles and criteria related to the risks and opportunities presented by IT environments. Trust services include online privacy evaluations, security audits, tests of the integrity of information processing systems, verification of the availability of IT services, and tests of systems confidentiality.

CPA WebTrust a set of services offered through the AICPA where auditors provide third-party assurance over a client's Web site and Internet services.

Critical path is the longest path through a PERT network.

Customer relationship management (CRM) employed to gather, maintain, and use data about a company's customers with the objective of improving customer satisfaction and company profitability.

Dashboards a graphic technique that shows an organization's performance metrics and compares actual data with planned.

Data are raw facts about events that have little organization or meaning.

Data communications refers to transmitting data to and from different locations. Many accounting applications use data communications in normal business operations.

Data communications protocol the settings that create a communications standard for a specific data communications application. Examples of such settings include the transmission speed, parity bit, duplex setting, or synchronous-versus-asynchronous transmission type.

Data definition language (DDL) part of a DBMS that enables its users to define the record structure of any particular database table.

Data dictionary describes the data fields in each database record of a database system.

Data diddling changing data before, during, or after they are entered into a computer system.

Data encryption scrambling the data in a message in a systematic way in order to prevent competitors from electronically monitoring confidential data transmissions.

Data encryption standard (DES) an encryption methodology initially adopted in 1976 and enjoying widespread usage. It is now considered insecure because of a small (56-bit) key size.

Data field information that describes a person, event, or thing in the database.

Data flow diagram (DFD) primarily used in the systems development process to document the flow of data through an AIS.

Data hierarchy storing data electronically in the following ascending order: bit_character_data_field_record_table_database.

Data integrity controls internal controls that protect the databases from erroneous data entries. Examples include tests for data completeness, conformance to the data type specified for the data field, valid code tests, and reasonableness tests.

Data manipulation controls methods of controlling data processing, such as examining software documentation, system flowcharts, program flowcharts, data flow diagrams, and decision tables because they help systems analysts do a thorough job in planning data processing functions.

Data manipulation language (DML) commands that allow an end user to perform queries and similar tasks on the records in a database.

Data mart a form of data warehouse that allows users to perform predefined analytical tasks on the data.

Data mining a set of data analysis and statistical tools that enables companies to detect relationships, patterns, or trends among stored data within a database.

Data modeling term used to describe the process of designing databases.

Data transcription the task of converting manually prepared source documents such as credit-card application forms to computer-readable file records. Where possible, AIS developers try to avoid data transcription because it is costly, labor intensive, time-consuming, and likely to introduce errors into the data.

Data type is the data type that tells Access how to store the data—for example, as text, a number, yes/no, memo, or a date/time.

Data warehouses large collections of historical data that organizations use

to integrate their functions, thus allowing managers (and to some extent external parties) to obtain the information needed for planning, decision making, and control.

Database a large collection of related data that are typically stored in computerized, linked files and manipulated by specialized software packages called database management systems.

Database administrator the person responsible for supervising the design, development, and installation of a large database system; this person is also responsible for maintaining, securing, and revising the data within the database system.

Database management system (DBMS) a separate software system that enables users to create database records, delete records, access specific information, query records for viewing or analysis, alter database information, and reorganize records as needed.

Database-As-A-Service (DAAS) allows firms to outsource their databases to cloud service providers.

Datasheet screen the Access screen that displays the records in a table.

Default value specifies a default value for the data fields in new records to help control accuracy of the data entry.

Demand drafts commonly used to pay monthly bills by having money debited automatically from an individual's checking account.

Denial-of-service (DOS) attack an attack on an online company (such as eBay) when hackers "flood" the company's Web site with bogus traffic.

Detailed systems design the systems design work that involves specifying the outputs, processing procedures, and inputs for a new system.

Detective controls control procedures within a company's internal control system that provide feedback to management regarding whether or not operational efficiency and adherence to prescribed managerial policies have been achieved.

Dial-back systems a password safeguard that initially disconnects all login users but reconnects users after checking their passwords against lists of bonafide user codes.

Digital certificate is an authentication technique in which an authenticating document is issued by an independent third party called a certificate

authority. The certificates themselves are signed documents with sender names and public key information. Customers can also use digital certificates to assure themselves that a Web site is real.

Digital signature used, for example, to authenticate documents (such as purchase orders) by including a portion of a document's message in an encrypted format (which reflects the digital signature).

Digital signature standard (DSS) adopted by the National Institute of Standards and Technology in which digital signatures are used to authenticate a document.

Digital subscriber line (DSL) a set of technologies that enable users to send and receive digital messages over telephone lines. Transmission rates range between 128 and 24,000 kbits per second.

Digital time stamping service (DTSS) the process of attaching time stamps to business transactions to authenticate the time and possibly the place of individual transactions.

Direct conversion method of systems implementation in which a company's old system is immediately dropped and the new system takes over the complete processing of the company's transactions.

Disaster recovery part of contingency planning that describes the procedures to be followed if a company's data processing center becomes disabled.

Disk mirroring also known as disk shadowing. This process involves writing all data in parallel to two disks. Should one disk fail, the application program can automatically continue using the good disk.

Disk shadowing also known as disk mirroring. This process involves writing all data in parallel to two disks. Should one disk fail, the application program can automatically continue using the good disk.

Domain address an Internet address, also referred to as a universal resource locator (URL).

Dot-matrix printer an impact printer that uses a print head of tiny wires, arranged in a grid (e.g., 5 wires in each of 7 rows) to create our familiar letters and other printing characters. Many cash registers still use dot-matrix printers today.

Dumpster diving a method used by thieves to steal personal information from garbage cans or delivered or outgoing mail from house mail boxes.

DVD is a 5-inch plastic disk that uses a laser to encode microscopic pits in its substrate surface. A DVD can have as many as two layers on each of its two sides and results in a medium that can hold as much as 17 gigabytes of data that is writeable or even rewriteable.

Dynaset a subset of database information typically selected dynamically with a query. A dynaset can be a set of selected records from a single, large table, a limited number of data fields selected from each record in a table, a set of related data fields from the records in several tables, or a combination of these items.

E-business conducting business over the Internet or dedicated proprietary networks.

E-commerce largely buying and selling transactions within e-business.

Economic event events that affect an organization's financial statements. An example of an economic event is a sale on account.

Economic feasibility the process of analyzing the cost-effectiveness of a proposed system.

Edit programs also called "input validation routines." These are programs or subroutines that check the validity and accuracy of input data after the data have been entered and recorded on a machine-readable file.

Edit tests tests that examine selected fields of input data and reject those transactions (or other types of data input) whose data fields do not meet the preestablished standards of data quality.

Electronic conferencing enables accountants and others to use computers and phone lines to communicate with clients, etc., through the use of high-end groupware communications packages.

Electronic document and record management systems (EDRMs) enable businesses to systematically capture and store manual documents electronically. This helps companies manage the workflow of electronic documents during document development, provide collaborative tools that enable several users to work on the same document, and create and store multiple versions of documents.

Electronic data interchange (EDI) a communications technique that allows organizations to transmit standard business documents over high-speed data communications channels.

Electronic eavesdropping unauthorized access to a computer system and its data to observe transmissions intended for someone else.

Electronic funds transfer (EFT) a cash management technique whereby the transfer of funds is electronic or computer-to-computer.

Electronic payments (e-payments) a faster, easier, and safer way for both customers and sellers to handle online transactions. The e-payment service acts as a trusted intermediary because it collects a payment from a buyer and pays that amount to the seller.

Electronic vaulting backup copies of files that are electronically transmitted to a remote site rather than physically delivering these media to an off-site storage location.

EnCase specialized software tools to help auditors perform file copying, custody documentation, and other forensic activities.

Encryption key a (typically long) set of bits that is used to encrypt a message for transmission over public data transmission lines.

Enterprise application integration (EAI) method of combining multiple systems that allows companies with legacy applications and databases to integrate and continue to use those systems.

Enterprise asset management (EAM) systems are programs that automate the management of a broad spectrum of assets. These programs can be used to streamline purchasing, reduce inventory, trim machine downtime, and reduce maintenance costs.

Enterprise mashups a dashboard that managers use to quickly view critical business information that collects data from a variety of sources—both inside and outside the firm.

Enterprise network is typically a wide area network spanning an entire organization (i.e., connecting the employees in a large organization).

Enterprise resource management (ERP) software is application software that integrates the accounting, production, marketing, human resources, and similar functions of an organization in one large application. Thus, in particular, it enables businesses and government agencies to transmit and manipulate financial data on an organization-wide basis.

Enterprise resource planning (ERP) systems software (*e.g., Oracle*) that provides for integration among all of an organization's major business processes through the use of a central database; ERP II systems are extended with e-business and other front-office capabilities.

Enterprise risk management (ERM) also called the 2004 COSO Framework. ERM helps an organization determine if their objectives are aligned with their strategy and that goals are consistent with the level of risk the organization is willing to take.

Enterprise software a type of software that integrates financial or accounting subsystems with CRM, business services, human resources, and supply chain management.

Enterprise-wide database a large repository of organizational data that is available to a wide range of employees.

Entity objects of interest in a database. Database entities include business and economic events plus information about who (i.e., agents) and what (i.e., resources) were involved in those activities.

Entity-relationship (E-R) diagram graphical documentation technique used by database designers to depict database elements and their direct relationships.

Ethical hacker these are network and computer experts who purposefully attack a secured system to help its owners find any vulnerabilities that could be exploited by a malicious hacker.

Event-driven programming language a computer programming language such as Visual Basic, that enables a computer to respond to specific events (e.g., clicking on a menu choice).

E-wallet also known as a "digital wallet," e-wallets function like conventional wallets, but enable their users to buy and sell merchandise over the Internet.

Expected loss is based on estimates of risk and exposure.

Extensible business reporting language (XBRL) a standardized set of markup (editing) tags and rules created with XML used by the financial reporting industry.

Extranets enable selected outside users to access organizations' intranets.

Extensible markup language (XML) an extension of HTML that allows users to create their own markup (editing) tags.

Fair Credit Reporting Act a law that requires that an individual be told why he or she is denied credit.

Fault-tolerant system systems designed to tolerate faults or errors that are often based on the concept of redundancy.

Feasibility evaluation the first major procedure in systems design work whereby the design team determines the practicality of alternative proposals.

Fidelity bond insurance coverage that companies buy to reduce the risk of loss caused by employee theft of assets. The insurance company investigates the backgrounds of the employees that an organization wants to have bonded.

Field properties the settings for data fields in a database table such as field size, format, and input masks.

File server a computer whose principle task is to store and output the contents of computer files. For example, most Internet applications use file servers to store and output Web page files.

Financial accounting information system the component of an AIS in which the major objective is to provide relevant information (primarily economic) to individuals and groups outside an organization's boundaries.

Financial planning model information systems that aid financial managers in selecting an optimum strategy for acquiring and investing financial resources.

Financing process the process by which a company acquires and uses financial resources such as cash, other liquid assets, and investments.

Firewall a software program or hardware device designed to prevent unauthorized data communications between hackers and the information resources within an internal, trusted network.

First normal form (1NF) a level of normalization. A database is in first normal form (1NF) if all of a single record's attributes (data fields) are singular. That is, each attribute has only one value.

Fixed asset management management of the purchase, maintenance, valuation, and disposal of an organization's fixed assets.

Flash memory is solid-state memory that comes in various forms. Examples include the flash drives that use the USB ports of microcomputers, the PCMCIA memory, cards used with laptops, the memory sticks used in digital cameras, the memory cards used with video games, and the RAM of newer microcomputers.

Flying-start site a disaster recovery location that includes everything contained in a hot site plus up-to-date backup data and software.

Follow-up and maintenance phase the continued monitoring of a newly implemented system to ensure that the system continues to operate properly and meets the organization's information needs.

Foreign key data fields within some accounting records that enable these records to reference one or more records in other tables.

Forensic accounting combines the skills of investigation, accounting, and auditing to find and collect pieces of information that collectively provide evidence that criminal activity is in progress or has happened.

Form a user interface that typically uses text boxes, labels, and similar form controls to create or display records in a database table.

Form controls in Form Wizard, form controls are the objects such as textboxes and labels that appear on a form.

Form Wizard in Microsoft Access a Form Wizard can be used to rapidly design and create custom forms.

Fraud triangle the triangle includes three elements that indicate potential for fraud. These are the motive for committing the fraud, the opportunity that allows the fraud to occur, and the rationalization by the individual perpetrating the fraud that the behavior is appropriate or justified.

Front-office refers to external functions and processes of an organization, such as those that involve customers, suppliers, and other business partners.

Gantt chart a tool for planning and controlling a systems implementation project.

Generalized audit software (GAS) computer packages that enable auditors to review computer files without continually rewriting processing programs.

General-use software the software used by auditors as productivity tools for improving their work; For example,

the use of a word processing program by an auditor when writing an audit report.

Graphical user interface (GUI) one or more visual computer screens that enable an end user to communicate with a computer—typically by selecting items from menus or clicking on choices using a computer mouse. Computer programs that did not use GUIs typically were command-driven systems that required users to memorize and type in system commands and instructions.

Groupware allows users to send and receive e-mail, plus perform a wide range of other document-editing tasks. In addition to e-mail support, these network packages allow users to collaborate on work tasks, make revisions to the same document, schedule appointments on each other's calendars, share files and databases, conduct electronic meetings, and develop custom applications.

Hacker a person who breaks into the computer files of others for fun or personal gain.

Hard-copy output is printed output and is the opposite of soft-copy output such as found on computer screens. Accounting data are meaningless if they cannot be output in forms that are useful and convenient to end users.

Hash total a meaningless sum that is used to check for the completeness of data entry or processing.

Hosted solution an approach to acquisition of software where the package is rented over the Internet, rather than purchased.

Hot backup a backup performed while the database is online and available for read/write.

Hot site a disaster recovery location that includes a computer system configured similarly to the system currently in use by a company for its data processing activities.

Human resource (HR) management an activity of an organization that includes the personnel function and the payroll function.

Hypertext markup language (HTML) an acronym for hypertext markup language—the editing language that tells a Web browser how to display information from the World Wide Web.

Hypertext transfer protocol (HTTP) a communications protocol designed to transfer information on the World Wide Web.

I/O-bound a computer whose input speeds or output speeds are slower than its computational speed.

Ideal control a control procedure within a company's internal control system that reduces to practically zero the risk of an undetected error or irregularity.

Identity theft the intentional misuse of someone else's personal information with the intent to deceive another.

Identity Theft and Assumption Deterrence Act (ITADA) of 1998 the Department of Justice prosecutes ID theft violations under this act.

Image processing storing, manipulating, or outputting the graphical information that usually first appear on hard-copy documents such as contracts, architectural plans, machinery schematics, or real-estate photos.

Information data that is useful or meaningful because it has been sorted, manipulated, aggregated, and classified.

Information age where more workers are knowledge workers rather than production workers.

Information overload a situation where an individual has too much information, and especially too much trivial information, which can be overwhelming and possibly causing relevant information to be lost or overlooked.

Information security are policies and procedures that safeguard an organizations electronic resources and limit their access to authorized users.

Information Systems Audit and Control Association (ISACA) the professional association of information technology auditors.

Information systems risk assessment method used by an auditor to evaluate the desirability of IT-related controls for a particular aspect of business risk.

Information technology (IT) the hardware and software used in computerized information systems.

Information technology (IT) auditors auditors who concern themselves with analyzing the risks associated with all aspects of information technologies.

Information technology (IT) governance ensuring that information technology risks are controlled and also that IT in an organization is deployed strategically to meet objectives.

Ink-jet printer a printer that uses very small nozzles to spray ink onto blank pages to create printed outputs. An advantage of ink-jet printers over dot-matrix printers is their ability to print in color. But ink-jet printers are slower and more costly, per-page, than laser printers.

Input controls computer application controls that attempt to ensure the validity, accuracy, and completeness of the data entered into a company's AIS; for example, edit tests.

Input mask a set of characters that dictate the required format for input data. For example, in Microsoft Access, the mask ''(###)###-####'' specifies the sequence of numeric digits (represented by # signs) required for a phone number.

Input-processing-output cycle refers to the three phases of computer processing. Most accounting transactions are processed in a three-phase operation called the input-processing-output cycle.

Input validation routines programs or subroutines that check the validity and accuracy of input data after the data have been entered and recorded on a machine-readable file.

Instant messaging software enables remote users to communicate with each other in real time via the Internet.

Integrated accounting software software packages that can process all types of accounting transactions and provide a variety of reports, including financial statements and budgets.

Integrated Computer-Assisted Surveillance System (ICASS) a system used by the New York Stock Exchange to search for insider trading activities.

Integrated security an integrated approach to security involves managers combining a number of key security technologies to protect the organization. This might include the following: firewalls, intrusion detection systems, content filtering, vulnerability management, virus protection, and virtual private networks.

Integrated services digital network (ISDN) lines high speed data transmission lines, typically using fiber optics, that end users can rent from phone companies and that support transmission rates up to 1.5 million bits per second (Mbps).

Integrated test facility (ITF) used by auditors to test a company's computer programs; particularly useful for auditing in an operational setting and/or for evaluating integrated online systems or complex programming logic.

Interactive data data that can be re-used and carried seamlessly among a variety of applications or reports.

Interactive data and electronic applications (IDEA) is a respository for financial information that now contains XBRL data for over 10,000 companies.

Internal control as defined by the COSO, a process, effected by an entity's board of directors, management, and other personnel, designed to provide reasonable assurance regarding the achievement of objectives in the following categories—effectiveness and efficiency of operations, reliability of financial reporting, and compliance with applicable laws and regulations.

Internal control system consists of the various methods and measures designed into and implemented within an organization to achieve the following four objectives: (1) safeguard assets, (2) check the accuracy and reliability of accounting data, (3) promote operational efficiency, and (4) enforce prescribed managerial policies.

Internet a global collection of tens of thousands of interconnected business, government, military, and education networks that communicate with each other.

Internet connectivity software that permits small businesses to create Web sites and engage in electronic commerce.

Intranets networks using the same software as the Internet, but which are internal (for communications purposes) to the companies that created them.

Intrusion detection system (IDS) computer software that enables users to identify, document, and perhaps mislead hackers attempting to access a protected system.

Intrusion testing see penetration testing or ethical hacker.

IT general controls controls over data processing to provide reasonable assurance that (1) development of, and changes to, computer programs are authorized, tested, and approved before their usage, and (2) access to data files is restricted to authorized users and programs to increase the likelihood that processed accounting data are accurate and complete.

Job costing information system a system of costing that keeps track of the specific costs for raw materials, labor, and overhead associated with each product or group of products.

Just-in-time (JIT) inventory is a system used to minimize inventories at all levels. Sometimes JIT inventory is called a "make-to-order inventory system."

Key performance indicators (KPIs) important metrics that convey information about operational performance against plans or budgets.

Knowledge management uses professional service firms (such as accounting and consulting firms) to distribute expertise within the organization (frequently on its intranet).

Knowledge process outsourcing (KPO) an approach where an organization chooses to have some of its functions and activities related to research and acquisition of knowledge performed by an external organization.

Knowledge workers individuals who produce, analyze, manipulate, and distribute information *about* business activities.

Laser printer a type of printer that uses a laser to sensitize portions of a rotating drum. These sensitized portions attract small graphite particles called toner that can then be transferred to a blank piece of paper and permanently "fixed" to the page with heat.

Lean accounting is used by companies to measure and evaluate results by value stream management rather than by traditional departments (such as customer service, purchasing, etc.).

Lean production/manufacturing involves making the commitment to eliminate waste throughout the organization. Companies that practice lean production and manufacturing focus on the elimination or reduction of non-value-added waste to improve overall customer value and to increase the profitability of the products or services that the organization offers.

Legacy system a business's older, customized computer system that typically runs on a mainframe computer and that is often too large and expensive to replace.

Legal feasibility determining whether or not there will be any conflict between a newly proposed system and a company's legal obligations.

Local area network (LAN) a collection of microcomputers, printers, file servers, and similar electronic components that are physically located near one another—for example, in the same building—and connected together for communication purposes.

Lock-box system a tool used by a company to reduce the float period during which checks clear the bank.

Lock-out system a password safeguard that disconnects telephone users after a set number of unsuccessful login attempts.

Logic bomb a computer program that remains dormant until some specified circumstance or date triggers the program to action. Once "detonated," a logic bomb program sabotages a system by destroying data or disrupting computer operations.

Logical security uses technology such as password controls to limit access to only authorized individuals to the organization's systems and information.

Magnetic (hard) disk a secondary storage device that enables a computer to store billions of bytes of information. Unlike primary (RAM) memory, whose information is lost when its computer loses power, magnetic disk memory is permanent.

Magnetic ink character recognition (MICR) the technology used primarily by banks to encode magnetically readable symbols at the bottom of checks or similar financial documents. Because the magnetic flux of the ink used in these symbols loses strength over time, MICR is not widely used elsewhere.

Mainframe computer a large, multi-user computer that enables large companies to centralize processing power in a single device.

Make-or-buy decision determining whether it is more cost effective to purchase an AIS or develop one in-house.

Man trap is a building facility control. A small antechamber room between a public corridor and a controlled room that is designed to permit only authorized personnel to enter.

Mark-sense media documents such as academic test forms, surveys, and similar papers that users complete with simple pencils or pens but that can be read and evaluated by computerized input devices.

Master file a file that stores permanent information about file entities (e.g., employees, customers, or financial assets). Its opposite is a transaction file, which typically stores temporary information about the transactions for a limited period of time.

Message acknowledgment procedures a control for computer network systems that is useful in preventing the loss of part or all of a company's transactions or messages on a computer network system.

Metadata data in a database that described other data.

Microprocessor the portion of a CPU that performs the arithmetic and logic tasks of a computer, and that also interprets and executes computer instructions.

Minicomputer a multi-user computer with less processing power than a mainframe but typically more power than a personal, or microcomputer.

Modem (modulator-demodulator) a device for converting the digital data that a computer uses into sound pitches that can be transmitted over phone lines.

Modular conversion a method of systems implementation whereby the users involved in specific data processing tasks are divided into smaller units or modules; the data processing system is then installed module by module.

Multimedia combines video, text, graphics, animation, and sound to produce multidimensional output. By definition, multimedia presentations also require advanced processor chips, sound cards, and fast video cards to work properly.

Multiprocessing is a computer's ability to perform several tasks simultaneously. Computers achieve this in multiuser environments by apportioning computer time.

Near field communication (NFC) enables mobile devices such as cell phones, PDAs, and laptop computers to communicate with similar devices containing NFC chips.

Non-value-added waste part of the production/manufacturing process that does not contribute to overall profitability or customer satisfaction.

Normalization the process of examining and arranging file data in a way that helps avoid problems when these files are used or modified later; data can be in first, second, or third normal form.

Object-oriented programming language computer programming languages that have strict rules (particularly "inheritance" and "encapsulation") that govern the properties, attributes, and operations of language objects (such as variables and form controls). Object-oriented programming also includes the developer's ability to create new objects with these characteristics that can be used by other procedures and programs.

Online analytical processing (OLAP) allows database users to extract multidimensional information from one or more database tables for the purpose of making complex decisions.

Operating System (OS) a set of software programs that helps a computer run itself as well as the application programs designed to run under it. Examples include Windows 2000, Windows XP, and Unix.

Operational audits an audit performed by a company's internal audit staff that focuses on evaluating the efficiency and effectiveness of operations within a particular department.

Operational feasibility examining a proposed system's compatibility with the current operating environment (e.g., ensuring that the organizational structure would support the new system).

Optical character recognition (OCR) an older technique that enables computer input devices to interpret machine-printed (and to a limited extent, hand-written) data using optical technology.

Parallel conversion method of systems implementation where both the old and new system of a company operate simultaneously for a period of time.

Parallel simulation a control testing method used by auditors to create a second system that duplicates a portion of the client's system. The auditor's system runs at the same time as the client's system, and the auditor can verify that the client's system processes data correctly and that no unauthorized changes have been made to the client's system.

Payroll processing information system used to pay employees for their work, and also maintain employee earnings records (a payroll history), comply with various government tax and reporting requirements, report on various deduction categories (e.g., pension funds and group insurance), and interact with other personnel functions.

Penetration testing also sometimes called ethical hacking, auditors may use this approach to see if they can access resources within an information system.

Peripheral equipment devices such as keyboards, display monitors, and printers, that typically physically surround a computer processor.

Personal data assistant (PDA) device a computerized device that includes such functions as calculator, address book, memo storage, daily planner, and perhaps even provides wireless Internet access.

Personal productivity software software that typically runs on microcomputers (e.g., word processing and spreadsheet programs) and that helps individuals perform their jobs faster, easier, and more accurately.

Phishing an e-mail from someone who falsely claims to be an established, legitimate company.

Physical security is any measure that an organization uses to protect its facilities, resources, or its proprietary data that are stored on physical media.

Picture elements (pixels) are tiny, discrete dots of color that are arranged in a matrix in digital computer screens to create familiar letters in word documents or pictures in graphics applications.

Pivot tables a feature which enables a database user to create two-dimensional statistical summaries of database information.

Platform as a service (PaaS) refers to cloud computing vendors who provide hardware services over the Internet. An example is when a vendor supplies Web-server hardware, thereby enabling a company to avoid buying and maintaining the servers itself.

Point-of-sale (POS) device an input device such as a barcode reader that enables a user to input data directly into a computer from a checkout stand in a supermarket or merchandise store and avoid manual keystrokes.

Point-scoring analysis approach used to evaluate accounting software packages (as well as hardware) of vendors that meet most of a company's major IT requirements.

Ponzi scheme this type of fraud is named for Charles Ponzi and is a pyramid fraud in which new investment funds are used to pay returns to current investors.

Portals Web sites that allow outsiders with authorized access to view a company's internal information systems.

Predictive analytics a technique using data stored in data warehouses to improve performance.

Preliminary investigation the first task performed by a systems study team whereby the team, for example, investigates current needs or problems in a company's present system and reports findings to the steering committee.

Preventive controls control procedures that are designed and implemented within a company's internal control system to *prevent* some potential problem from occurring when an activity is performed.

Primary key the data field in each record that uniquely distinguishes one record from another in a database table. Primary keys are required for every record in a database, and they are unique.

Primary memory the internal random-access memory or RAM that a computer uses to temporarily store computer programs and immediate data.

Privacy policy a Web sites' policy that states the information it does and does not collect about you and how they might use that information.

Process costing information system a system that uses averages to calculate the costs associated with goods in process and finished goods produced.

Processing controls computer application controls that focus on the manipulation of accounting data after they are input to a company's computer system—for example, data-access controls.

Production process begins with a request for raw materials and ends with the transfer of finished goods to warehouses (also called the conversion process).

Program change control a set of internal control procedures developed to ensure against unauthorized program changes.

Program Evaluation and Review Technique (PERT) a technique for scheduling and monitoring the activities in large systems implementation projects.

Programming language a language such as Java or Visual Basic that enables a programmer to create instructions (called "code") that a computer can understand.

Project management software software that can aid in planning and controlling the tasks involved in a systems implementation project.

Property Sheet window in Form Wizard, Property Sheet window can be used to change individual settings for control objects.

Prototyping approach to systems design work that involves developing a simplified model of a proposed information system that is experimented with by the system's users.

Proxy server a computer and related software that creates a transparent gateway to and from the Internet which can be used to control Web access.

Public key encryption encrypting messages using a scrambling key assigned by a public entity.

Queries allow database users to create subschemas of interest to them.

Radio frequency identification (RFID) enables users to identify warehouse pallets or similar items without unpacking them from shipping crates. Passive RFID tags have no power source (and therefore cannot wear out) but can nonetheless "answer" energized inquiries from energized sources. Active RFID tags are actually chips with antennas that have their own power source, enjoy ranges of more than 100 meters, and are generally more reliable than passive tags.

REA accounting stores important nonfinancial information about resources, events, and agents in databases precisely because they are relevant to the decision-making processes of their users.

REA model an approach to data modeling that focuses on resources (R), events (E), and agents (A).

Record the second level of data hierarchy. A database record stores all of the information about one entity (i.e., person, event, or thing).

Record structure the specific data fields in each record of a database table; this structure is fixed in many accounting applications.

Red flag are certain signs and behaviors that coworkers and supervisors can look for and alert them to employees who are defrauding their organizations.

Redundant array of independent disks (RAIDs) a set of magnetic disks that act as a single hard drive.

Referential integrity a control that denies a user the ability to create a child record with no parent, or to

delete a parent record that has child records.

Relational database groups of related, two-dimensional tables.

Relationship table necessary to link two tables when you have many-to-many relationships. Without relationship tables, there would be fields in a database table that could contain many possible values.

Report database reports provide custom information to database users. Reports can be simple documents that display only the contents of a table or complex outputs that combine the information from several tables and show selected subsets of database information useful for decision making.

Report Wizard a tool available in Access that allows for rapid creation of reports.

Request for proposal (RFP) report sent to computer vendors in systems design work that outlines the specific requirements of a company's desired system.

Resources resources represent things of economic value. Common examples of resources are cash, raw materials, and inventory.

Responsibility accounting system a system where managers trace unfavorable performance to the department or individuals that caused the inefficiencies and each subsystem within an organization is only accountable for those items over which it has control.

Risk assessment a component of internal control that considers the risk factor when designing controls for a company.

Risk matrix a tool especially useful for prioritizing large risks. A risk matrix classifies each potential risk by mitigation cost and by likelihood of occurrence.

Risk-based audit an approach that provides auditors with a good understanding of the errors and irregularities that can occur in a company's AIS environment and the related risks and exposures. Using a risk-based approach, the extent of tests of controls and substantive tests are based upon risk assessments.

Rollback processing a fault-tolerant system, at the transaction level, in which transactions are never written to disk until they are complete.

Routing verification procedures a control for computer network systems that helps to ensure that no transactions or messages of a company are

routed to the wrong computer network system address.

Sarbanes-Oxley Act of 2002 sweeping financial legislation that emphasizes organizational internal controls and accountability.

(SAS) No. 94 "The Effect of Information Technology on the Auditor's Consideration of Internal Control in a Financial Statement Audit." This SAS cautions external auditors that the way firms use IT might impact any of the five internal control components.

Scalable ability for a software user to migrate easily to packages that handle increasingly large volumes of data and transactions.

Scenario planning under "Event Identification" (of ERM), management identifies scenarios of minor concern to major disasters that could occur.

Schedule feasibility an evaluation that involves estimating the time frame for a new or revised system to become operational.

Schema is a map or plan of the entire database. It is the totality of the information in a database and the relationships between its tables.

Scope creep a situation where the size of a task or project gradually becomes larger, and perhaps more complex and costly.

Second normal form (2NF) the second level of normalization. A database is in second normal form if it is in first normal form and all the attributes in each record depend entirely on the record's primary key.

Secondary storage computer equipment that stores data permanently (e.g., hard disks, CD-ROMS, and USB drives).

Secret key cryptography uses a single cryptographic key that is shared by the two communicating parties.

Section 404 a key provision of the Sarbanes-Oxley Act of 2002, which reaffirms that management is responsible for establishing and maintaining an adequate internal control structure.

Security policy a comprehensive plan that management must develop to help protect the enterprise from internal and external threats.

Select query creates a subset of database information based on two types of user-specified criteria: (1) criteria that determine which records to include and (2) criteria that determine which data fields to include from those records.

Separation of duties an activity of an internal control system that focuses on structuring work assignments among employees so that one employee's work activities serve as a check on those work activities of another employee.

Sizing handles appear on the border of an object in the Form Wizard and allow for resizing of the object.

Slack time describes the amount of delay time that can occur in the noncritical activity of a project and still not delay the completion time of the entire project itself.

Smishing a scam, using text messages on cell phones, that claims to be legitimate but asks you to provide or update your personal information such as account number, credit card number, or password.

Social engineering a tactic hackers use to gain access to passwords, such as posing as a bona fide employee to convince a network administrator to give passwords over the telephone.

Social networking occurs on Web sites such as Facebook or Linkin. These sites allow individuals to post, store, and view messages, photos, and videos.

Soft-copy output computer output on video screens, billboards, and similar devices; the opposite of hard copy (printed) output.

Software as a service (SAAS) is a cloud-computing service in which the client pays the vendor a fee for accessing and using application software—for example, tax preparation software.

Source document a piece of paper or an electronic form that becomes the source of subsequent computer records and processing activities. Examples of source documents include time cards in payroll systems, employee application forms, doctor medical diagnoses, insurance claim forms, and personal bank checks.

Spam illegal, unsolicited e-mail messages; can include such content as advertisements, pornographic solicitations, attempts to steal identities, or fictitious stories asking recipients for money.

Spend management a systematic approach to controlling an organization's expenses.

Spoofing masquerading as an authorized Internet user.

Steering committee a group consisting of a company's top management personnel and possibly one or more staff auditors that works with the systems study team throughout all phases of system development activities.

Strong passwords passwords that contain a variety of characters (letters, numbers, and symbols) and are 14 characters or longer. A 15-character password composed of random letters and numbers is about 33,000 times stronger than an 8-character password composed of characters from the entire keyboard.

Structured query language (SQL) a popular data manipulation language for retrieving and manipulating data; auditors can use SQL to retrieve a client's data and display these data in a variety of formats for audit purposes.

Structured, top-down design refers to a computer-application design methodology in which system designers begin at the highest level of abstraction and then drill down to lower, more detailed levels until the system is completely specified.

Subform is a form within a form that displays data related to the information in the main form.

Subschema a subset of the information in a database. Subschemas can be used to limit access to specific information.

Supercomputer a computer that is faster and more powerful than a mainframe, and capable of performing trillions of operations per second.

Supply chain management (SCM) applications that enable an ERP system or other software to interface with a company's suppliers and customers.

Suspicious activity reporting (SAR) laws that require accountants to report questionable financial transactions to the U.S. Treasury Department. Examples of such transactions are ones suggestive of money laundering, bribes, or wire transfers to terrorist organizations.

Sustainability reporting focuses on nonfinancial performance measures that might impact an organization's income, value, or future performance.

System development life cycle (SDLC) comprises the planning, analysis, design, and implementation phases of acquiring or developing a new information system.

System maintenance ensuring the continuing operations of a system.

Systems analysis phase of a systems study in which the study team thoroughly familiarizes itself with a company's current operating system by focusing on strengths and weaknesses within the system.

Systems approach using a broad point of view in performing a systems study.

Systems consultant provide help with issues concerning information systems.

Systems implementation the phase of a systems study in which the recommended changes from analysis, design, and development work are now put into operation.

Systems specification report a document that summarizes the findings of a design team regarding the needs for a new information system.

Systems study a formal investigation of a company's existing information systems.

Systems survey part of systems analysis in which the study team obtains a more complete understanding of a company's current operation information system and its environment.

Tab order the order in which each control becomes active on a form in run mode.

Technical feasibility an analysis of the technical resources required by a particular information system.

Test data a set of transactions that examine the range of exception situations that might occur under normal processing conditions.

Third normal form (3NF) the third level of normalization. A database is in third normal form if it is in second normal form and contains no transitive dependencies. This means that the same record does not contain any data fields where data field *A* determines data field *B*.

Third-party assurance services audit and assessment services offered by independent third parties to provide business users and individual consumers with some level of comfort over Internet transactions.

Third-party billing when an organization does not bill their customers directly for services received. Rather, they bill insurance companies or government agencies who in turn reimburse these service providers.

Time and billing information systems similar to job order costing systems, tracking hours and costs associated with each job (i.e., each client) and each employee (i.e., professional staff).

Transaction controls ensure that the database system performs each transaction accurately and completely.

Transaction file a temporary file of accounting records that typically stores the transactions for a specific period of time.

Transitive dependencies when the same record does not contain two data fields in which data field A determines data field B.

Transmission Control Protocol/Internet Protocol (TCP/IP) is commonly used to transmit e-mail and other text messages over the Internet.

Trojan horse program a destructive or deceptive computer program hidden inside an accepted program.

Trust Services third party assurance services offered through the AICPA, that provide guidance to practitioners to evaluate organizations in terms of their reliability, privacy, and security.

Turnaround document a hard-copy document such as a bank check or confirmation slip that a business creates, sends to a second party for completion or approval, and then receives back for further processing. For convenience, most turnaround documents are computer readable.

Turnkey system a computer system acquired from independent vendors that includes both software and hardware.

Unbound control are labels, pictures, and similar items on a form that are consistent from record to record in a form and do not display underlying database information.

Uniform resource locator (URL) is the text address of a Web site—for example, www.Wiley.com. The lead item indicates the World Wide Web, the second entry designates the site name, and the third entry ("com" for commercial user) is the organization code.

Uninterruptible power system (UPS) an auxiliary power supply that can smooth the flow of power to the computer, thereby preventing the loss of data due to momentary surges or dips in power.

USA PATRIOT Act a law that helps Federal authorities locate and prosecute hackers.

Utility program computer programs that are typically included with computer operating systems, but which perform specific end-user tasks. Examples include programs that format disks, transfer file data from one medium to another, or test e-mails for viruses.

Val IT is a formal statement of principles and processes for IT management that helps organizations understand if they are making the right IT investments and optimizing the returns from them.

Validation rule see data validation rule.

Validity test evaluates the validity of a transaction by checking for the existence of matching records in a master file.

Value card credit-card size or key-ring size cards from retailers that have a barcode on the back side for the merchant to track purchases. In some cases, the merchant offers discounts or points that may be exchanged for goods or services. In other cases, customers simply receive advance information for upcoming sales before the general public.

Value-added networks (VANs) proprietary networks that large IT organizations design and maintain for their customers in order to implement EDI or intranet applications.

Value-added resellers (VARs) special type of systems consultants who are licensed to sell particular software packages and provide organizations with consulting services related to those packages.

Value stream management a management process that controls activities that generate value in a product or service rather than by functional area.

Vertical markets are markets or industries that are distinct in terms of the services they provide or the goods they produce.

View controls security feature within a database system that limits each user's access to information on a need-to-know basis.

Virtual private network (VPN) a security appliance that runs behind an organization's firewall and allows remote users to access entity resources by using wireless, hand-held devices.

Virtual storage a computer operating system technique that uses magnetic disk storage as a virtual extension of primary storage.

Virus a computer program that rogue programmers embed in other programs, e-mails, or computer files, and that (when executed) typically perform such destructive acts as erasing files, disrupting e-mails, or interfering with operating system functions.

Voice over Internet protocol (VoIP) a technology that allows individuals to make telephone calls using a broadband Internet connection instead of a regular telephone line.

Volatile memory computer memory that becomes inoperative when it loses power.

Watchdog processor a fault-tolerant system that uses two processors. If something happens to the first processor, the second processor takes over the processing work.

Waterfall model is a description of the four phases are the system development life cycle (SDLC) of a business information system. Logically, the activities in these phases flow from stage to stage in only one direction, like water flowing in a stream.

Web browser such as Microsoft's Internet Explorer allows for the view of graphics.

What-if analysis performed by project leaders when using project management software; for example, to experiment with different systems implementation work schedules or determine how delays in specific activities are likely to affect other project tasks.

Wide area network (WAN) computer networks spanning regional, national, or global geographic areas.

Wi-Fi (wireless fidelity) refers to transmitting voice-grade signals or digital data over wireless communication channels. Wi-Fi creates a wireless Ethernet network using access hubs and receiver cards in PCs, cell phones, and PDAs, thereby turning cell phones and similar wireless devices into cordless, multifunction "web appliances."

Wireless application protocol (WAP) a data communication protocol mostly used by mobile phones and PDAs to connect to the Internet.

Wireless communications means transmitting voice-grade signals or digital data over wireless communication channels.

Worm (write-once, read-many) media are secondary storage media such as "CD-R" CD-ROMs that can be recorded only once but which cannot be updated (because new information cannot be written on them once they have been encoded).

Worm program a program that disrupts normal data processing and is usually able to replicate itself onto other files, computer systems, or networks. Examples of these viruses are boot-sector viruses, worm programs, trojan horse programs, and logic bomb programs.

XBRL instance document an XML document that was created using XBRL standards.

XBRL International Consortium has about 450 members and is in charge of developing XBRL standards.

Index